MRS BEETON'S
FAMILY COOKBOOK

WARD LOCK

First published in Great Britain in 1983
by Ward Lock Limited, Villiers House, 41–47 Strand,
London WC2N 5JE, a Cassell company.

Reprinted 1988, 1989, 1991

Edited by Susan Dixon
Line drawings by Sue Sharples
Jacket photograph by Tim Hill

Text filmset in Photina by
MS Filmsetting Limited, Frome, Somerset
Printed and bound in Great Britain by
HarperCollins Book Manufacturing, Glasgow

British Library Cataloguing in Publication Data

Beeton, Mrs
  Mrs Beeton's family cookbook.
  I. Cookery
  I. Title   II. Dixon, Susan
  641.5   TX717
  ISBN 0-7063-6211-X

CONTENTS

The publishers would like to thank the following people and organisations for their help in preparing this book.

Nic Barlow; Maggie Black; British Poultry Federation; British Turkey Federation; Clive Coates MW, Maître Jean Conil-Principal, Academy of Gastronomy; Mrs Carolyn Cheek Deynal MA—American Womens Club, London; Jill Eggleton; J. Audrey Ellison BSc, FSFST, FAHE, FRSH—food consultant and writer; Flour Advisory Bureau; EMC plc; Linda Fraser; Shirley Hislop; Jan Hopcraft—cookery writer; Mrs Joyce Hughes BSc, MAHE—consultant home economist; Patricia Jacobs; Bob Komar; Peter Lackington—Youngs Seafoods Ltd; Margaret Leach MBE—home economist; Barbara Logan MHEA—consultant home economist; Moya Maynard; Meat and Livestock Commission; David Mellor; Shirley Melville; Barbara Morrison FAHE—consultant home economist; Mary Norwak—cookery writer; Gabor Oliver—managing director, Cheeses from Switzerland Ltd; Ann Page-Wood; Miss Joan Peters—consultant home economist; Jennie Reekie; Christopher G Smith BA MCHIMA; Grant Symon; Roger Tuff.

WEIGHTS, MEASURES, TEMPERATURES AND OTHER BASIC INFORMATION

Metric quantities are easy to weigh and measure; all you need are weighing scales giving metric quantities, a metric measuring jug, and a set of metric measuring spoons for small quantities.

Metric Units used in Cookery

Weight	gram	(g)		*Length*	millimetre	(mm)
	kilogram = 1000g	(kg)			centimetre	(cm)
Capacity	millilitre	(ml)			metre = 1000mm	(m)
	centilitre	(cl)			100cm	
	decilitre	(dl)		*Temperature*	degree Celsius	(°C)
	litre = 1000ml	(litre)			(Centigrade)	
	100cl					
	10dl					

Measuring by Weight

Spring balance and loose weight metric scales are available in various sizes and designs. Those calibrated in 10g divisions for small amounts and 25g or 50g for larger amounts are the most useful.

Measuring by Capacity

Using a metric jug

Measuring jugs are available in 500ml, 1 litre and 2 litre sizes calibrated in divisions of 50ml, 100ml and 200ml, and sometimes, in decimals or fractions of a litre.

Using metric measuring spoons

These spoons are used for measuring small quantities of both dry and liquid ingredients, and are available in sets containing the following sizes:

*1.25ml
2.5ml
5ml
10ml
15ml
*20ml

* These two spoons are not as widely available as the others and are not used in the recipes in this book

Metric spoons are described by capacity rather than as teaspoons, dessertspoons or tablespoons; this avoids confusion with domestic spoons which vary considerably.

Guide to spoon measures

This table gives 10g, 15g, 25g and 40g quantities of many common ingredients which you may find easy to measure using standard spoons. Results are, however, only approximate as measuring is not as accurate as weighing. The quantities for dry ingredients refer to full spoons levelled with a knife edge.

	Spoons equivalent to			
Ingredient	**10g approx**	**15g approx**	**25g approx**	**40g approx**
almonds, ground	2 × 10ml	3 × 10ml	5 × 10ml	5 × 15ml
butter, margarine, lard	1 × 15ml	2 × 10ml	2 × 15ml	3 × 15ml
chocolate, grated	3 × 15ml	4 × 15ml	6 × 15ml	9 × 15ml
cocoa	2 × 10ml	2 × 15ml	4 × 15ml	6 × 15ml
cornflour, custard powder	2 × 10ml	3 × 10ml	3 × 15ml	7 × 10ml
desiccated coconut	2 × 15ml	3 × 15ml	5 × 15ml	8 × 15ml
drinking chocolate	3 × 5ml	4 × 5ml	4 × 10ml	7 × 10ml
flour, unsifted	2 × 10ml	3 × 10ml	3 × 15ml	5 × 15ml
gelatine	2 × 10ml	5 × 5ml	3 × 15ml	6 × 10ml
golden syrup, clear honey, black treacle, molasses, corn syrup, maple syrup, etc	1 × 10ml	1 × 15ml	1 × 15ml	2 × 15ml
ground rice	1 × 15ml	2 × 10ml	4 × 10ml	4 × 15ml
jam (eg raspberry)*	1 × 10ml	1 × 15ml	2 × 10ml	2 × 15ml
mixed peel	1 × 15ml	2 × 10ml	2 × 15ml	4 × 15ml
oats, rolled	2 × 15ml	3 × 15ml	5 × 15ml	7 × 15ml
rice	1 × 15ml	2 × 10ml	2 × 15ml	5 × 10ml
salt	1 × 10ml	3 × 5ml	2 × 10ml	7 × 5ml
sugar – granulated, caster	5 × 2.5ml	2 × 10ml	2 × 15ml	3 × 15ml
sugar – Demerara	5 × 2.5ml	2 × 10ml	2 × 15ml	3 × 15ml
sugar – soft brown	1 × 15ml	2 × 10ml	2 × 15ml	5 × 10ml
sugar – icing	1 × 15ml	3 × 10ml	3 × 15ml	7 × 10ml
Crumbs				
breadcrumbs, fresh white	3 × 15ml	7 × 10ml	7 × 15ml	12 × 15ml
bread raspings, dried white breadcrumbs	2 × 10ml	3 × 10ml	3 × 15ml	7 × 10ml
plain sponge cake crumbs	2 × 15ml	3 × 15ml	5 × 15ml	8 × 15ml
crispbread, oatcake, digestive biscuits, cornflake crumbs	2 × 15ml	3 × 15ml	4 × 15ml	7 × 15ml
dried yeast	5 × 2.5ml	2 × 10ml	2 × 15ml	3 × 15ml
Cheese				
Cheddar, coarsely grated	2 × 10ml	2 × 15ml	3 × 15ml	5 × 15ml
finely grated	1 × 10ml	1 × 15ml	4 × 15ml	5 × 15ml
Parmesan, grated	3 × 10ml	4 × 10ml	4 × 15ml	6 × 15ml
soft paste or soft (without rind)	1 × 10ml	1 × 15ml	5 × 5ml	4 × 10ml

* *varies according to how much whole fruit jam contains*

Cookware

The size of cookware varies from manufacturer to manufacturer, so sizes given in recipes should be treated as approximations only. The following range of measurements will help you select the appropriate-sized piece of cookware:

Dimension

Metric	imperial equivalent	Metric	imperial equivalent
2cm	¾ inch	25cm	10 inches
5cm	2 inches	30cm	12 inches
7cm	2¾ inches	35cm	14 inches
10cm	4 inches	40cm	16 inches
15cm	6 inches	45cm	18 inches
20cm	8 inches	50cm	20 inches

Capacity

Metric	imperial equivalent	Metric	imperial equivalent
125–150ml	¼ pint	750–900ml	1½ pints
250–300ml	½ pint	1 litre–1.25 litres	1¾–2 pints
375–450ml	¾ pint	1.4–1.75 litres	3 pints
500 (0.5 litre)–600ml	1 pint	1.8–2 litres	4 pints
625–700ml	1¼ pints	3 litres	6 pints

Dimension is used most frequently to describe the length of straight edge tins or the diameter of round cookware. Height and depth are used where they are particularly important.

Capacity measurements apply largely to pans, ovenproof dishes, bowls, moulds, and basins, and soufflé or pie dishes. The exact equivalent depends on the other ingredients in the recipe.

Note Some cookware, such as loaf tins, can also be described by the average weight of the contents, the most common weights being 1kg (2lb) and 500g (1lb).

Temperatures

Oven temperatures

°C	°F	Gas mark	Oven heat
70	150		
80	175		
100	200		
110	225	¼	very cool
120	250	½	very cool
140	275	1	very cool
150	300	2	cool
160	325	3	warm
180	350	4	moderate
190	375	5	fairly hot
200	400	6	fairly hot
220	425	7	hot
230	450	8	very hot
240	475	9	very hot
260	500		
270	525		
290	550		

Deep fat frying temperatures

These are basic guidelines only, since the temperature depends so much on the thickness of the food to be cooked, whether more is added during frying, whether it is frozen, etc.

Using a thermometer

Temperatures are given for the principal types of food to be deep fried, and should be used as a guide for all similar recipes.

VEGETABLES, PASTA AND CEREALS

	°C	Approx. frying time (minutes)		°C	Approx. frying time (minutes)
Potatoes			**Other vegetables**		
chips			**(raw)**		
cook from raw	185	4–6	sliced and coated	175–180	2–3
final browning	190	1–2	sliced uncoated	175–180	1–2
small cut			**Other vegetables**		
cook from raw	185	3	**(parboiled)**		
final browning	190	1	in batter	175–180	3–4
potato puffs			**Onion rings**		
cook from raw	175	soft	dipped in milk	180–185	2–3
second cooking	190	well puffed	and flour		
game chips, potato ribbons	190	3	**Parsley**	190	5–10 secs
			Crisp noodles	175–180	2–3
croquettes	190	4–5			
with choux pastry	190	golden-brown			

FISH AND SHELLFISH			**Fish, whole**		
Fish fillets, thin			sole 250–350g	170–175	5–6
in batter or breadcrumbed	175–180	3–5	smelts, sprats	180–185	1–2
			whitebait	190–195	½–1
goujons (eg plaice)	175	2–3	whiting 250–300g	170–175	6–8
Fish portions, thick			**Fish cakes,** croquettes, rissolettes	175–180	2–3
in batter or breadcrumbed	170–175	3–5	**Shellfish** (eg scampi, oysters)	175–180	2–3

MEAT AND POULTRY					
Cooked meat and poultry			**Poultry/Game** portions		
croquettes, etc	175–180	2–4	breadcrumbed		
cutlets	175–180	2–5	large	160–165	8–12
fritters, other batters	175–180	2–4	small	175–180	6–10
kromeskies, rissoles, pancakes, etc	180–185	3–4	cooked in batter	175–180	4–7

Note Sausages, hamburgers and similar raw meat items are better shallow fried as they exude animal fat which contaminates the frying medium.

DAIRY FOODS AND EGGS			SWEET ITEMS		
	°C	*Approx. frying time (minutes)*		°C	*Approx. frying time (minutes)*
Scotch Eggs	170–175	5–6	Fruit fritters		
egg croquettes	175–180	2–3	in batter		
choux fritters,	170–175	6–7	apple	175–180	3–4
meringues			other fruits	180–185	2–3
			Doughnuts	185–190	3–4

Bread Test

The other method of testing the temperature of deep fat or oil is by lowering a 2cm square of day-old thickly sliced bread into the hot fat as follows:

To reach temperature of	Bread turns brown in:
160°C	2 minutes
170°C	1½ minutes
180°C	1 minute
190°C	½ minute

Egg Grading Systems

The European Economic Community (EEC) has two grading systems.

The first is based on weight, and ranges between Grade 1 and Grade 7:

Grade 1 – 70g and over   Grade 5 – 50g–54g
Grade 2 – 65g–69g   Grade 6 – 45g–49g
Grade 3 – 60g–64g   Grade 7 – below 45g
Grade 4 – 55g–59g

Eggs of Grades 1 and 2 correspond approximately to the old-style large eggs, Grades 3 and 4 to standard eggs, Grades 5 and 6 to medium eggs, and Grade 7 to small and extra small eggs.

The second grading system, based on quality, ranges between Grade A and Grade C. Grade A eggs are fresh, with clean unstained shells, sound texture, and a good shape. The egg content should have no visible blemish or discoloration when tested. The yolk should be positioned centrally and defined clearly. The white should be translucent with the two parts visible. The air space should not exceed 5mm in depth.

Some packs containing Grade A eggs have a red band, with the word 'Extra' around them. This means superior quality with air cells of less than 4mm in depth at the time of packing, which itself has been less than 7 days. In addition, they will have come from a producer from whom the packer collects at least twice a week. (Once a week is sufficient for other eggs.) The shopkeeper is expected to remove this band if the eggs have not been sold within 7 days.

Grade B are second quality eggs which have been downgraded because they may have enlarged air cells, indicating age, or they may have been stored or refrigerated.

Grade C eggs are only suitable for manufacturers. They are neither graded by weight nor available in retail shops.

Convenience Foods – Chart of Storage Life

Food	Method of production/ packaging	Storage life (unopened)	Food	Method of production/ packaging	Storage life (unopened)
Baby food	Bottled	12–18 months	Ham, sterilized, below 900g	Canned	2–3 years
	Canned	1–2 years			
Bread	Dried mix	6 months, 1 month if opened	Jams and marmalades	Bottled	2 years
				Canned	2 years
	Pre-baked loaf	6 months	Jellies	Crystals	12–18 months
Cake decorations	Packeted	6 months		Tablets	1 year
Cakes	Dried mix	6 months, 1 month if opened	Meat products	Vacuum packed	Date stamped
			Meat products, processed	Bottled	2 years
Carbonated drinks	Canned	6–12 months	Meat products, solid packed	Canned	5 years
Casserole mixes	Dried mix	18 months	Milk products	Canned	1 year
Cheeses	Tube	1 year		Dried	6 months
	Vacuum packed	Date stamped	Pasta	Dried	2 years
Coatings	Dried mix	1 year	Pasta, cook-in sauces	Canned	2 years
Coffee, liquid	Bottled	1 year			
Coffee, instant	Jars	1 year	Pastes	Bottled	6 months
	Packeted	1 year		Canned	1 year
Desserts	Dried mix	18 months		Tube	1 year
Dessert toppings	Bottled	1 year	Pastry mixes	Dried mix	6 months, 1 month if opened
	Canned	1 year			
	Dried mix	18 months	Pâtés	Bottled	6 months
Fish in brine	Bottled	9–12 months		Canned	2 years
Fish in oil	Canned	5 years	Pickles	Bottled	2 years
Fish in sauce	Canned	2 years	Porridge oats	Packeted	1 year
Flavourings, alcohol base	Bottled	5 years	Raising agents	Dried	6 months
Flavourings, non-alcoholic	Bottled	18 months	Rice	Canned	2 years
				Dried	2 years
Flours	Packeted	6–9 months	Sauces	Bottled	6 months
Fruit juices	Bottled	1 year		Canned	2 years
	Canned	2 years		Dried mix	18 months
	Carton	Date stamped	Seasonings	Dried mix	6 months
	Concentrated, frozen	6 months	Soups	Canned	2 years
	Dried mix	18 months		Dried mix	6–12 months
Fruit pie fillings	Canned	1–2 years*	Stock cubes	Dried mix	1 year
Fruits	Bottled	1 year	Stuffings	Dried mix	1 year
	Canned	1–2 years	Sugars	Packeted	5 years
	Dried	2 years	Textured vegetable protein (TVP)	Dried	5 years
Gelatine	Leaf	6–12 months			
	Powdered	6–12 months	Vegetables	Canned	2 years***
Gravies	Canned	1–2 years		Dried	1–2 years
	Dried mix	1 year	Vegetables in brine or water	Bottled	2 years
Ham, pasteurized, above 900g	Canned	6 months, refrigerated**	Yeast extracts	Bottled	2 years
			Yeast granules	Dried	1 year

*Rhubarb and prunes should be kept for 1 year only, and gooseberries, plums, blackberries and blackcurrants for 18 months

**This is an exception to the general guide that cans should not be stored in the refrigerator

***New potatoes should only be kept for 18 months

Metric/Imperial Equivalents

25g=0.875oz	500g=1.1lbs	1kg=2.2lbs
25ml=0.875fl oz	500ml=0.88 pint	1 litre=1.76 pints

The figures above link metric and imperial quantities exactly. As these are very inconvenient to use, the following approximate conversions should be used to convert British imperial recipes to metric, if the following points are borne in mind:

1) The fundamental proportions in metric recipes are the same as imperial ones, so that a rich pastry will use half fat to flour in both metric and imperial versions.
2) *Always* convert all ingredients, solid and liquid.
3) *Never* use both metric and imperial in the same recipe.
4) Using the 25g/ounce equivalent you will decrease all quantities by approximately 10% when converting imperial quantities to metric. When using small quantities, the reduction will be insignificant, so existing cookware can still be used and the baking time will be the same. For large recipe quantities, smaller tins and shorter baking times will be needed.

Note If you wish to convert metric measures to imperial ones, remember that metric measures based on the 25g/ounce give 10% more of any goods weighed in oz/lb than the equivalent gram/kg.

WEIGHT		CAPACITY	
Metric	*Approx. imperial equivalent*	*Metric*	*Approx. imperial equivalent*
10–15g	½oz	25ml	1 fl oz
25g	1oz	50ml	2 fl oz
50g	2oz	125–150ml	¼ pint (5 fl oz/1 gill)
75g	3oz	250–300ml	½ pint
100–125g	4oz	375–450ml	¾ pint
150–175g	6oz	500–600ml	1pt (20 fl oz)
200–250g	8oz	750–900ml	1½ pints
300–375g	12oz	1–1.25 litres	1¾–2 pints
400–500g	1lb	1.4–1.75 litres	3 pints
600–750g	1¼lb		
800–1000g (1kg)	2lb		
1.5kg	3lb		

Where alternative metric figures are shown, the weight or capacity used depends on the type of recipe, and the proportion of other ingredients. For large-scale recipes such as those for breads or jams, the larger figure is more suitable. For ½oz, 10g or 15g may be selected according to the importance of the ingredient in the recipe.

FIRST-COURSE DISHES

Artichoke Salad
6 helpings

6 globe artichokes   vinaigrette sauce

Boil or steam the artichokes. Trim the bases so that they stand upright. When cold, trim off the tips of the leaves, if liked. Place the artichokes on individual dishes and serve the vinaigrette sauce separately.

Artichokes are generally served as a starter by themselves.

Dressed Artichoke Bases or Fonds
6 helpings

12 small cooked **or** canned artichoke   200g macédoine of cooked vegetables
  bases   (p58)
2–3 gherkins   125ml mayonnaise
1 × 15ml spoon capers

Garnish
strips of canned pimento   4–6 sliced stuffed olives

Trim the artichokes neatly. Chop the gherkins finely and mix with the capers, vegetables, and enough mayonnaise to moisten. Fill the hollow parts of the artichoke with the mixture. Arrange on a serving plate and spoon the remaining mayonnaise over the vegetables. Garnish with the pimento and olives.

Note Artichoke bases are the round fleshy parts of the artichoke found under the hairy choke.

VARIATION

The stuffing mixture is also good as a filling for avocado pears. Use the quantities above to fill 4 halved pears, to serve four.

Avocado Pears Vinaigrette
4 helpings

2 large, firm, ripe avocado pears   vinaigrette sauce
2 × 15ml spoons lemon juice

Make sure the pears are firm but ripe, and are not discoloured. If they show any signs of over-ripeness such as being soft or blackened, use them for a cooked dish.

Halve the pears lengthways and remove the stones. Brush the halved pears with lemon juice immediately to prevent discoloration. Serve 1 half pear per person, cut side uppermost on a small plate, with a special avocado spoon, stainless steel or silver teaspoon or a grapefruit spoon. Serve the vinaigrette sauce separately.

Avocado Pears with Prawns or Avocado Royale
4 helpings

2 × 15ml spoons olive oil
2 × 15ml spoons distilled vinegar
a pinch each of salt and pepper
a little mixed French mustard
   (not Dijon)
2 large avocado pears

a pinch of sugar (optional)
½ clove of garlic (optional)
100g peeled prawns, fresh, frozen **or**
   canned
crisp lettuce leaves

Garnish
lemon wedges

Blend the oil, vinegar, and seasonings together. Halve and stone the pears, and brush all over with a little of the dressing. Add the sugar and crush and add the garlic to the remaining dressing, if used. Toss the prawns in this; then spoon into the pear halves. Place on crisp lettuce leaves. Garnish with lemon wedges.
Note Frozen prawns should be squeezed gently before using to get rid of any excess moisture.

Celeriac in Mustard Dressing
4 helpings

450g **or** 1 medium-sized celeriac
3 × 2.5ml spoons salt
3 × 2.5ml spoons lemon juice
4 × 15ml spoons French mustard

3 × 15ml spoons boiling water
100ml olive oil **or** as needed
2 × 15ml spoons white vinegar
salt and pepper

Garnish
2 × 15ml spoons chopped mixed herbs
  or parsley

Peel the celeriac, and cut it into matchsticks. Toss the sticks in a bowl with the salt and lemon juice, and leave to stand for 30 minutes. Rinse in a strainer under cold running water, drain well, and pat dry. Put the mustard into a warmed bowl, and very gradually whisk in the boiling water. Then whisk in the oil drop by drop as when making mayonnaise (p262), using enough to make a thick sauce. Whisk in the vinegar in the same way. Season with salt and pepper. Fold in the celeriac matchsticks, cover loosely with a cloth, and leave in a cool place for several hours or overnight. Sprinkle the herbs over the dish before serving.

Crudités

These are small raw or blanched vegetables, cut up or grated, and served as a first course with an oil and vinegar dressing, French dressing or a dip. They are usually arranged in a decorative pattern on a large flat dish or tray, from which people help themselves. Suitable items to include are:

1) apples (cubed, dipped in lemon juice)
2) black or green olives
3) carrots (cut into matchsticks)
4) cauliflower florets (blanched)
5) celery (raw or blanched, sliced thinly)
6) courgettes (unpeeled, cut into matchsticks)
7) cucumber (cubed or sliced thickly)
8) fennel (raw or blanched, sliced thinly)
9) green or red pepper (cut in rings or strips)
10) radishes (small, whole)
11) spring onions
12) tomatoes (thin wedges, slices, or if small, halved)

Soured Cream Dip for Crudités

3–4 helpings

½ clove of garlic
1 × 15ml spoon chilli sauce
1 × 5ml spoon creamed horseradish
1 × 15ml spoon Worcestershire sauce

½ × 2.5ml spoon dry mustard
a pinch of Cayenne pepper
1 × 5ml spoon lemon juice
250ml soured cream

Crush the garlic. In a small basin, combine all the ingredients. Chill for 2–3 hours to allow the flavours to develop.

Serve with crudités or with cream crackers or potato crisps.

Cucumber in Soured Cream

4 helpings

3 cucumbers
salt
1 × 5cm piece fennel stem **or** 1 thick
    slice of the bulb
1 hard-boiled egg yolk

pepper
150ml soured cream
1 × 10ml spoon cider vinegar **or**
    white wine vinegar

Slice the cucumbers very thinly, sprinkle with the salt; then leave for 30 minutes. Drain and pat dry. Slice the fennel thinly. Crumble the egg yolk coarsely and mix it with the fennel. Just before serving, sprinkle the cucumber with pepper, mix the soured cream with salt and the vinegar, and pour it over the cucumbers. Sprinkle with the fennel and egg.

Note This can also be served with meat rissoles, fish cakes, grilled meat or fried fish.

Eggs Courtet
4 helpings

4 tomatoes (75g each approx)	salt and pepper
4 eggs	25g butter
4 × 15ml spoons milk	150ml aspic jelly

Garnish
chopped parsley

Cut the tomatoes in half and scoop out the centres. Leave upside-down to drain. Beat the eggs, milk, salt, and pepper together lightly. Melt the butter in a small pan, add the beaten egg, reduce the heat and cook gently, stirring all the time, until the eggs are just set and creamy. Fill the tomato cups with the eggs and leave until cold.

Melt the aspic jelly; then chill it until at setting point but still liquid. Coat each filled tomato half with jelly. Chill the remaining jelly until set; then chop it roughly. Serve the tomato cups surrounded by the chopped jelly on a platter of salad, and garnish with parsley.

Eggs Rémoulade
4 helpings

4 hard-boiled eggs	1 × 2.5ml spoon anchovy essence
4 × 15ml spoons thick mayonnaise	

Garnish

tomato	4 crisp lettuce leaves
gherkin	

Cut the eggs in half lengthways. Pat dry with kitchen paper. Mix together the mayonnaise and anchovy essence. Turn the eggs, cut side down and coat the white outside with the mayonnaise mixture. Arrange small pieces of tomato or gherkin on top. Place 2 egg halves, cut side down, on each lettuce leaf.

Stuffed Russian Eggs
6 helpings

6 hard-boiled eggs	oil
1 × 100g jar lumpfish roe	vinegar
3 × 15ml spoons mayonnaise	salt and pepper
2–3 even-sized tomatoes	chopped parsley

Garnish
chopped parsley

Cut the eggs in half lengthways, remove the yolks, and trim a small slice off the rounded side of each half white to make them stand firmly. Fill with lumpfish roe. Rub the yolks through a sieve, blend with the mayonnaise, and using a forcing bag with a star nozzle, pipe the mixture on to the stuffed egg whites. Cut the tomatoes into slices, and season with oil, vinegar, salt, and pepper. Sprinkle with chopped parsley. Serve the eggs on the slices of tomato and garnish with extra chopped parsley.

Grapefruit
4 helpings

2 large firm grapefuit
white **or** brown sugar

4 × 10ml spoons medium-dry sherry
  (optional)

Decoration
2 maraschino **or** glacé cherries

angelica (optional)

Choose sound, ripe fruit and wipe them. Cut them in half crossways, and remove the pips. Snip out the cores with scissors. With a stainless steel knife (preferably with a saw edge) or a grapefruit knife, cut round each half between the flesh and the pith, to loosen the flesh. Cut between the membranes which divide the segments, but leave the flesh in the halved skins as if uncut. Sweeten to taste with sugar, or, if preferred, pour 1 × 10ml spoon sherry over each half grapefruit, and serve sugar separately. Decorate the centre of each half fruit with a halved cherry and with angelica, if liked. Chill before serving. Serve 1 half fruit per person.

Spiced Grapefruit
4 helpings

2 large grapefruit
25g softened butter

25–50g brown sugar
½–1 × 5ml spoon ground mixed spice

Decoration
4 glacé or maraschino cherries

Cut the grapefruit in half crossways and prepare as in the recipe for Grapefruit. Spread the butter over the grapefruit and sprinkle with the sugar and spice. Put under a hot grill for 4 minutes, or in a fairly hot oven at 200°C, Gas 6, for 10 minutes. Decorate with the cherries and serve at once.

Herring Rolls
4 helpings

4 salted **or** rollmop herrings
2 hard-boiled eggs
8 anchovy fillets

25g butter
Cayenne pepper
lemon juice

Garnish
8 lemon slices
4–6 sliced gherkins

1 small diced beetroot
chopped parsley

If using salted herrings, soak them in cold water for several hours, then fillet, and remove all the bones. If using rollmop herrings, divide each into 2 fillets. Separate the egg yolks and whites. Chop the anchovy fillets and egg yolks finely, and mix them with the butter and pepper. Spread most of the anchovy mixture on the herring fillets and roll up firmly. Spread the remaining mixture thinly on the round ends of each roll. Chop the egg whites finely and use to coat the spread end of the rolls. Sprinkle with lemon juice and garnish with lemon slices, gherkins, beetroot, and parsley.

Kipper Mousse
4 helpings

600g kipper fillets
1 small onion
50g butter
50ml Velouté sauce (p249)
250ml mayonnaise
15g gelatine

75ml dry white wine
250ml double cream
salt and black pepper
lemon juice
butter for greasing

Garnish
lemon slices

parsley sprigs

Skin the kipper fillets and cut into 2–3cm pieces. Skin the onion and slice it finely. Fry the fish and onion gently in the butter for 7 minutes. Mix in the Velouté sauce and mayonnaise. Pound, or process in an electric blender to make a smooth purée. Soften the gelatine in the wine in a small heatproof container. Stand the container in hot water and stir until the gelatine dissolves. Add it to the purée and mix very thoroughly. Blend in the cream and season to taste. Add a squeeze of lemon juice. Spoon into a lightly buttered soufflé dish or oval pâté mould and chill for 2 hours. Serve from the dish, or turn out the mousse on to a serving dish and garnish with lemon slices and parsley sprigs.

Serve with hot toast and lemon slices.

Liver Pâté
Makes 700g (approx)

200g calf's **or** pig's liver
200g poultry livers
1 small onion
100g very lean ham **or** bacon
75g butter
a few gherkins (optional)

1–2 hard-boiled eggs
salt and pepper
1–2 × 5ml spoons dried mixed herbs
butter for greasing
melted clarified butter (p563)

Remove any skin and tubes from the livers. Skin the onion. Chop the liver, onion, and ham or bacon into small pieces. Melt the butter in a pan and cook the meats and onion for 5–6 minutes. Mince finely twice or process in an electric blender to make a smooth paste. Chop the gherkins, if used, and the hard-boiled eggs and add to the liver mixture together with the seasoning and herbs. Put into an ovenproof terrine or similar dish and cover with buttered greaseproof paper. Stand the dish in a pan of hot water which comes half-way up the sides. Bake in a moderate oven at 180°C, Gas 4, for about 30 minutes.

When cooked, either cover immediately with a layer of clarified butter and leave to cool, then chill before serving; or place under a light weight (p20) and cover with clarified butter as soon as cold. Serve the pâté in the dish in which it has been cooked, or cut into slices and place on a bed of crisp lettuce.

Serve with hot dry toast or brown bread rolled sandwiches.

Weighting and Cooling a Pâté

If a pâté needs to be weighted, first cut a piece of stout card to fit the top of the dish, inside the rim, and cover it with foil. Place over the dish and put a weight on top, eg a can of fruit, a large stone, flat iron or brick. Use a light weright first, especially if there is any melted fat round the sides which may well up and spill over if a heavy weight is used. As the dish cools, the pressure can be increased with a heavier weight. The heavier the weight, the more solid or condensed the pâté will be.

Cool the pâté by standing the dish in a pan of ice or very cold water which comes half-way up its sides, for between 12–24 hours, or as indicated in the recipe. Leave on a cold surface such as a stone slab or floor, or a metal table, in a cool place. Remove the weight, take out of the water, cover with clingfilm, and chill in a refrigerator or very cool place to allow the flavours to blend and mature. Pâtés should be eaten as soon as possible, so should not be stored for very long.
Note Remove any melted fat from the sides before serving.

Melon

Melon makes a refreshing starter throughout the year. The varieties most often used are the Cantaloup, honeydew, Ogen, Charentais, and watermelon. Always serve lightly chilled, but not too cold or the delicate flavour will be lost.

To serve a large Cantaloup or honeydew melon, cut it in half lengthways, then cut into segments and remove the seeds with a spoon. Serve 1 segment per person; a large melon should supply 8 segments.

Serve the melon with the flesh attached to the skin, or cut the flesh from the skin with a sharp knife but leave the skin underneath the melon segment. The melon flesh can then also be cut into small pieces which are easier to eat.

Smaller melons, such as Ogen and Charentais, should just be cut in half crossways, and the pips scooped out with a spoon. They serve 2 people as a rule, although they can be cut into quarters, to serve four.

Watermelon should be cut into suitably sized segments. Small spoons should be provided for removing the seeds, as well as knives and forks for cutting up the melon.

Ripe melons may not require any sugar, but sugar can be served separately, with chopped stem ginger or ground ginger, or with lemon or lime.

Melon with Parma Ham

This is a more elaborate dish using paper-thin slices of Parma or other smoked ham. For each person, serve 3 loosely rolled sices of ham arranged in a line alternately with 7 × 2cm sticks of firm, ripe, green-fleshed melon.

Marinated Melon

4 helpings

2 Ogen **or** Charentais melons   4 × 15ml spoons maraschino liqueur
                                                                    or port

Cut the melons in half crossways and scoop out the seeds. Spoon 1 × 15ml spoon of maraschino liqueur or port into the centre and chill for 1 hour before serving. Sugar can be served with the melons as well, if desired.

Mixed Hors d'Oeuvre Wheel

4–6 helpings

6–8 anchovy fillets
150g liver pâté
100–150g Cucumber in Soured Cream
  (p16)
2 medium-sized red-skinned dessert
  apples
lemon juice
75g black and stuffed green olives

200g Celeriac in Mustard Dressing
  (p15)
2 medium-sized carrots
oil
4 or 6 Stuffed Russian Eggs, using
  2 or 3 whole eggs (p17)
grated orange rind
salt and pepper

Garnish
parsley sprigs

Use a large, flat, round hors d'oeuvre wheel. Drain the anchovy fillets and wind them round the black olives using cocktail sticks, if necessary. Arrange with the stuffed olives in the centre. Cut the pâté in neat slices, 1 per person. Prepare the cucumber and soured cream but keep the fennel and egg garnish aside. Core and cube the apples and sprinkle with lemon juice. Prepare the celeriac for serving. Grate the carrots and mix with a little oil. Prepare the Russian Eggs.

Arrange all these ingredients in triangular sections on the wheel. Sprinkle the cucumbers with their fennel and egg garnish, and the carrots with grated orange rind and seasoning. Garnish with parsley sprigs.

Offer small spoons for people to help themselves. Serve slices of dark rye bread separately.
Note Instead of a wheel a 25–30cm platter with a small dish in the centre, can be used.

Mrs Beeton's Dressed Whitebait

3–4 helpings

50g flour
salt and pepper
100g whitebait

milk
fat for deep frying
Cayenne pepper

Garnish
parsley sprigs   lemon wedges

Season the flour with salt and pepper. Wash the whitebait, dip in the milk, and coat with flour, by shaking them together in a tea-towel or plastic bag. Make sure that the fish are separate. Heat the fat (p10), and fry the fish in small batches until crisp. Check that the fat is at the correct temperature before putting in each batch. When all the fish are fried, sprinkle with salt and Cayenne pepper. Serve immediately, garnished with parsley and lemon wedges, with thinly cut brown bread and butter.
Note Whitebait are eaten whole.

Oysters Rockefeller
2 helpings

24 oysters
100g shallots
100g spinach
2 stalks celery
1 sprig thyme
100ml water

1 × 15ml spoon Worcestershire sauce
100g butter
25ml pastis
50g soft white breadcrumbs

Open the oysters (p77) and leave on the half shell. Reserve the liquid. Place the oysters on an ovenproof dish.

Skin the shallots, clean the celery, and chop the shallots, spinach, celery, and thyme finely. Put in a saucepan, add the oyster liquid and water. Boil for 5–7 minutes. Add the Worcestershire sauce and butter. Beat until all the ingredients are well-blended. Add the pastis and mix in well. Pour the sauce over the oysters. Sprinkle with the breadcrumbs. Bake in a hot oven at 220°C, Gas 7, for 5–10 minutes.

Platter of Pork Meats
Choose 4–6 varieties of bought sausage and other pork meats, ready to eat, allowing 100–125g per person. Arrange them in a decorative pattern on a bed of lettuce leaves. Serve with small forks, and offer rolled sandwiches of dark rye bread or pumpernickel.

Some suitable meats to offer are, for instance:
1) salami
2) thin slices of Italian raw smoked ham, loosely rolled
3) cooked British sausages, thinly sliced diagonally
4) very small slices of cooked pork fillet
5) thin slices or 2cm cubes of pickled pork or pork luncheon meat

Potted Shrimps or Prawns
Makes 500g (approx)

200g unsalted butter
400g cooked, peeled shrimps or prawns
$\frac{1}{2}$ × 2.5ml spoon ground white pepper

$\frac{1}{2}$ × 2.5ml spoon ground mace
$\frac{1}{2}$ × 2.5ml spoon ground cloves
melted clarified butter (p563)

Melt the butter in a pan and heat the shellfish very gently, without boiling, with the pepper, mace and cloves. Turn into small pots with a little of the butter. Leave the remaining butter until the residue has settled, then pour the butter over the shellfish. Chill. When firm, cover with clarified butter. Store in a refrigerator for not more than 48 hours before use.

Prawn Cocktail
4 helpings

4 lettuce leaves
200g peeled prawns
5 × 15ml spoons mayonnaise
1 × 15ml spoon concentrated tomato
   purée **or** tomato ketchup

a pinch of Cayenne pepper **or** a few
   drops Tabasco sauce
salt (optional)
1 × 5ml spoon chilli vinegar **or**
   tarragon vinegar (optional)

Garnish
4 shell-on prawns

Shred the lettuce leaves. Place a little shredded lettuce at the bottom of 4 glass dishes. Put the prawns on top. Mix the mayonnaise with the tomato purée or ketchup and add a pinch of Cayenne pepper or a few drops of Tabasco sauce. Season with salt and vinegar if required. Pour the mayonnaise over the prawns and garnish each dish with an unshelled prawn.

Serve with rolled brown bread and butter.

Russian Salad
4 helpings

1 small cooked cauliflower
3 boiled potatoes
2 tomatoes
50g ham **or** tongue (optional)
3 gherkins
a few lettuce leaves
4 × 15ml spoons peas

2 × 15ml spoons diced cooked carrot
2 × 15ml spoons diced cooked turnip
50g peeled prawns **or** shrimps
   (optional)
salt and pepper
3 × 15ml spoons mayonnaise

Garnish
1 small diced cooked beetroot
50g smoked salmon, cut into strips
   (optional)

4 olives
1 × 15ml spoon capers
4 anchovy fillets (optional)

Break the cauliflower into small sprigs. Peel and dice the potatoes. Skin, de-seed, and dice the tomatoes. Cut the ham or tongue into small strips, if used. Chop the gherkins and shred the lettuce leaves. Put the vegetables, meat, and fish, if used, in layers in a salad bowl, sprinkling each layer with salt, pepper, and mayonnaise. Garnish with the remaining ingredients.
Note If using Russian Salad as part of a mixed hors d'oeuvre or for stuffing items such as eggs, omit the lettuce and garnish, and mix all the ingredients together lightly.

Salad Niçoise
4–6 helpings

250g French beans
2 hard-boiled eggs
3 tomatoes
1 large lettuce
1 clove of garlic

225g canned tuna
50g black olives
4 × 15ml spoons French dressing
salt and pepper

Garnish
50g canned anchovy fillets

Boil or steam the beans until just tender. Cut the eggs into quarters. Skin and quarter the tomatoes. Wash the lettuce and dry thoroughly. Skin and crush the garlic, and drain and flake the tuna. Line a large salad bowl with the lettuce leaves. Put the beans, eggs, tomatoes, garlic, tuna, most of the olives, and the dressing into a bowl and toss lightly. Season to taste. Pile into the centre of the salad bowl and garnish with the remaining olives and the anchovy fillets before serving.

Smoked Mackerel Pâté
Makes 450g (approx)

2 shallots
25g clarified butter (p563)
75g concentrated tomato purée
1 × 5ml spoon soft light brown sugar
juice of $\frac{1}{2}$ lemon
8 crushed peppercorns
1 × 5ml spoon chopped fresh basil

$\frac{1}{2}$ × 2.5ml spoon dried tarragon
a few drops Tabasco sauce
400g skinned smoked mackerel fillets
75ml double cream
additional melted clarified butter
   (p563) for sealing

Skin and chop the shallots very finely. Melt the clarified butter in a pan and cook the shallots gently until softened. Add the purée, sugar, lemon juice, peppercorns, and herbs, and cook gently for 4–5 minutes to make a sauce. Add the Tabasco sauce, remove from the heat and leave to cool. Process the sauce, mackerel, and cream in an electric blender or pound to a smooth paste. Turn into a suitable dish or mould and leave to cool. Cover with clarified butter. Leave until the butter is firm.

Serve with hot dry toast.

Taramasalata
4 helpings

100g smoked cod's roe
1 clove of garlic
2 × 15ml spoons lemon juice

4 × 15ml spoons olive oil
2 × 15ml spoons cold water
freshly ground black pepper

Skin the roe and garlic. Pound them in a mortar with the lemon juice until smooth. Add small amounts of oil and water alternately until the mixture is completely blended. Season to taste with black pepper, and serve with pita bread.

SOUPS

Stocks

Brown Stock (Beef stock)
Makes 1.5 litres (approx)

500g beef or veal marrow bones
500g lean shin of beef
1.5 litres cold water
1 × 5ml spoon salt
1 medium-sized onion (100g approx)

1 medium-sized carrot (50g approx)
1 stick of celery (50g approx)
bouquet garni (see Note)
1 × 2.5ml spoon black peppercorns

Ask the butcher to chop the bones into manageable pieces. Wipe them thoroughly. Trim off any fat and cut the meat into small pieces. Put the bones and meat in a roasting tin in a hot oven at 220°C, Gas 7, for 30–40 minutes to brown, turning them occasionally.

Put the browned bones and meat in a large saucepan with the water and salt. Prepare and slice the vegetables. Add them to the pan with the bouquet garni and peppercorns. Heat slowly to boiling point, skim well, and cover the pan with a tight-fitting lid. Reduce the heat and simmer very gently for 4 hours. Strain through a fine sieve and leave to cool. When cold, remove any fat from the surface.

Note To make a *bouquet garni*, tie together 3 parsley stalks, 1 sprig of thyme and 1 bay leaf, and tie in a square of muslin or cheesecloth. Alternatively tie 1 × 10ml spoon mixed dried herbs and 1 bay leaf in muslin. Vary the herbs and add spices as liked.

General Household Stock
Makes 1 litre (approx)

1kg cooked or raw bones of any meat
    or poultry, cooked or raw meat
    trimmings, giblets, and bacon rinds
500g onions, carrots, celery, and leeks

salt
1 bay leaf
4 black peppercorns

Break or chop the bones into manageable pieces. Wipe thoroughly. Prepare and slice the vegetables, retaining a piece of brown onion skin if a brown stock is required. Put the bones and meat trimmings into a saucepan. Cover with cold water and add 1 × 2.5ml spoon salt for each litre of water used. Heat slowly to simmering point. Add the other ingredients. Simmer, uncovered, for at least 3 hours. Strain and cool quickly by standing the pan in chilled water. When cold, skim off the fat. If the stock is not required at once, keep it cold. Use within 24 hours, or within 3 days if kept in a refrigerator. Reboil before use.

White Stock
Makes 2 litres (approx)

1kg knuckle of veal
1 medium-sized onion (100g approx)
1 stick of celery (50g approx)
2 litres cold water
1 × 10ml spoon salt

1 × 10ml spoon white vinegar **or**
  lemon juice
1 × 2.5ml spoon white peppercorns
a small strip of lemon rind
1 bay leaf

Chop the knuckle into manageable pieces. Scrape the bones, trim off any fat, and wipe the bones thoroughly. Prepare and slice the onion and celery. Put the bones in a large pan with the cold water, salt, and vinegar or lemon juice. Heat to boiling point and skim. Add the vegetables and the other ingredients. Bring back to the boil, cover, reduce the heat, and simmer gently for 4 hours. Strain the stock through a fine sieve and cool it quickly by standing the pan in chilled water. When cold, skim off the fat. Store as for General Household Stock (p25).

Chicken or Game Stock
Makes 1 litre (using 1 litre water)

1 medium-sized onion (100g approx)
1 stick of celery (50g approx)
carcass of 1 chicken **or** game bird,
  including the giblets

cleaned feet of bird (optional)
1 × 10ml spoon salt
4 white peppercorns
bouquet garni

Prepare and slice the vegetables. Break or chop the carcass into manageable pieces. Put the carcass, giblets, and feet, if used, in a large saucepan, cover with cold water, and add the salt. Heat to boiling point. Draw the pan off the heat and leave to stand for 2–3 minutes, then skim off any fat. Add the vegetables, peppercorns, and bouquet garni. Re-heat to boiling point, cover, reduce the heat, and simmer very gently for 3–4 hours. Strain the stock through a fine sieve and cool it quickly by standing the container in chilled water. When cold, skim off the fat. Store as for General Household Stock (p25).

Fish Stock
Makes 1 litre (using 1 litre water)

bones, skin, and heads from filleted fish
  or fish trimmings **or** cod's **or** other
  fish heads **or** any mixture of these
1 × 5ml spoon salt

1 small onion (50g approx)
1 stick of celery (50g approx)
4 white peppercorns
bouquet garni

Break up the bones and wash the fish trimmings, if used. Prepare and slice the vegetables. Put the bones, fish trimmings or heads in a saucepan and cover with cold water. Add the salt. Heat to boiling point. Add the vegetables, the peppercorns, and bouquet garni. Cover, and simmer gently for 40 minutes. Strain the stock through a fine sieve.

Note If cooked for longer than 40 minutes, fish stock tastes bitter. It does not keep unless frozen, and should be made only as required.

Vegetable Stock
Makes 2 litres (approx)

2 large carrots (200g approx)
2 medium-sized onions (200g approx)
3 sticks celery (150g approx)
2 tomatoes (100g approx)
25g butter **or** margarine
2 litres boiling water
1 × 2.5ml spoon yeast extract

bouquet garni
1 × 5ml spoon salt
6 black peppercorns
a blade of mace
outer leaves of 1 lettuce **or** ¼ small
    cabbage (100g approx)

Slice the carrots, onions, and celery thinly and chop the tomatoes. Melt the fat in a large saucepan and fry the carrots, onions, and celery for 5–10 minutes until the onions are golden-brown. Add the tomatoes and fry for a further minute. Add the water and the rest of the ingredients, except the lettuce or cabbage. Cover, and simmer for 1 hour. Shred the lettuce or cabbage, and add to the pan. Simmer for a further 20 minutes. Strain through a fine sieve. Use the same day, if possible, or cool quickly and store in a refrigerator for up to 2 days.

Thin Soups

Beef Broth
4–6 helpings

1 medium-sized carrot (50g approx)
1 small turnip (50g approx)
1 medium-sized onion (100g approx)
1 clove of garlic (optional)
25g butter **or** margarine
1 litre brown **or** general household
    stock (p25)

1 × 2.5ml spoon salt
½ small cabbage (250g approx)
a sprig of parsley
a few chives
salt and pepper
grated nutmeg
6 thin slices French bread

Prepare the carrot, turnip, and onion, and slice them thinly. Skin and crush the garlic, if used. Melt the fat in a large saucepan, add the vegetables, cover, and fry gently for 10 minutes. Heat the stock to boiling point and add to the vegetables in the pan with the salt. Cover and simmer for 30 minutes.

Meanwhile, shred the cabbage and chop the parsley and chives. Add the cabbage to the broth, cover, and simmer for a further 20 minutes. Season to taste with salt, pepper, and a little nutmeg. Add the parsley and chives. Keep over very low heat while toasting the bread slices until golden. Put one in each soup bowl or cup and pour the broth over them.

Serve with grated cheese, if liked.

Beef Tea

2 helpings

400g shin, flank **or** skirt of beef
500ml water

1 × 2.5ml spoon salt

Wipe the meat and trim off all visible fat; cut into 2cm cubes. Put the meat into an ovenproof casserole or basin, and add the water and salt. Cover the container with a saucer or lid, and cook in a very cool oven, 140°C, Gas 1, for 3 hours.

Strain the liquid through muslin or a fine sieve, and allow to cool. Skim any fat from the top. Re-heat, without boiling, and serve as a light soup or beverage, with toast or dry biscuits.

VARIATION

To the basic ingredients, add the following thinly sliced vegetables: 1 small carrot, $\frac{1}{3}$ small turnip, and 1 small onion. Add them to the meat and water, with a few sprigs of parsley and 2 bay leaves, and continue cooking as in the basic recipe.

Note Beef tea can be stored in a refrigerator for 2 days. If this is not possible, it must be freshly made each time it is wanted.

Chicken Broth

8 helpings

1 small boiling fowl (1.5kg approx) **or**
  1 chicken carcass with some flesh
  left on it
giblets of the bird
1.5–2 litres water
1 × 5ml spoon salt
1 medium-sized onion (100g approx)
2 medium-sized carrots (100g approx)

1 stick of celery (50g approx)
$\frac{1}{2}$ × 2.5ml spoon ground pepper
a blade of mace
bouquet garni
a strip of lemon rind
25g long-grain rice (optional)
1 × 15ml spoon chopped parsley

Joint the boiling fowl or break up the carcass bones, and wash the giblets. Put them into a large saucepan and cover with the cold water. Add the salt, and heat slowly to simmering point. Cut the onion in half, and dice the carrots and celery. Add the vegetables to the pan with the pepper, mace, bouquet garni, and lemon rind. Cover, and simmer gently for 3–3$\frac{1}{2}$ hours if using a raw boiling fowl, or for 1$\frac{1}{2}$ hours if using a chicken carcass. Strain the broth through a colander. Skim off the fat.

Return the broth to the pan and re-heat to simmering point. Wash the rice, if used, and sprinkle it into the broth. Cover, and simmer for a further 15–20 minutes until the rice is cooked.

Some of the meat can be chopped finely and added to the broth, the rest can be used in made-up dishes, eg a fricassée. Just before serving the broth, re-season if required, and add the chopped parsley.

Cock-a-leekie
8 helpings

100g prunes
1 small boiling fowl with giblets
  (1.5kg approx)
3 rashers streaky bacon, without
  rinds (optional)
1kg veal **or** beef marrow bones
  (optional)

500g leeks
1.5–2 litres cold water
2 × 5ml spoons salt
$\frac{1}{2}$ × 2.5ml spoon pepper
bouquet garni

Soak the prunes overnight in cold water; then stone them. Wipe the fowl and wash the giblets. Chop the bacon, if used. Chop the bones into manageable pieces, if used. Wash and trim the leeks and cut them into thin rings. Put the fowl, giblets, marrow bones, and bacon into a deep pan, cover with cold water, add the salt, and heat very slowly to simmering point. Reserve 4 × 15ml spoons of the leeks and add the remaining leeks, the pepper, and bouquet garni to the pan. Cover, and simmer gently for about 3 hours, or until the fowl is tender.

Remove the fowl, carve off the meat, and cut it into fairly large serving pieces. Strain the liquid. Return the pieces to the soup with the soaked and stoned prunes and the remaining sliced leeks. Simmer very gently for 30 minutes until the prunes are just tender but not broken. Re-season if required, and serve the soup with the prunes.

Scots or Scotch Broth
4–6 helpings

500g scrag end of neck of mutton
1 × 5ml spoon salt
1 litre cold water
50g pearl barley
2 medium carrots

2 leeks
1 small turnip
1 stick of celery
pepper
1 × 10ml spoon chopped parsley

Wipe and trim the meat, and cut into 2cm pieces. Put into a deep pan with the bones, salt, and cold water. Heat gently to simmering point. Blanch the barley. Add to the pan, cover, and simmer gently for 2 hours. Prepare the vegetables, setting aside one whole carrot and cutting the rest into 5mm dice. Add them to the broth, cover, and simmer for another hour. Grate the whole carrot and add it to the broth 20 minutes before serving. Skim the fat. Remove the bones. Season to taste with pepper and add the chopped parsley just before serving.

Veal Broth
4–5 helpings

1 knuckle of veal (600–750g approx)
1.5 litres water
1 × 10ml spoon lemon juice
3 × 2.5ml spoons salt
25g pearl barley **or** rice
2 medium-sized carrots (100g approx)
1 small turnip (50g approx)

1 leek **or** medium-sized onion
  (100g approx)
1 stick of celery (50g approx)
bouquet garni
a strip of lemon rind
4 white peppercorns
1 × 10ml spoon chopped parsley

Wipe the knuckle and put it into a pan with the water. Heat slowly to simmering point, and add the lemon juice and salt. Blanch the pearl barley or rice and add it to the pan. Cover, and simmer gently for 2 hours. Cut the vegetables into 5mm dice. After the broth has simmered for 2 hours, add the vegetables, bouquet garni, lemon rind, and peppercorns. Cover, and simmer for a further hour. Lift out the knuckle of veal. Remove all the meat from the bone and cut it into 5mm dice. Strain the broth through a colander and return it to the pan; keep hot. Remove the bouquet garni, lemon rind, and peppercorns from the vegetables. Return the meat and vegetables to the broth and add the parsley. Re-season if required. Re-heat before serving.
Note The bone can be used again for stock.

Calf's Foot Broth
4–6 helpings

1 calf's foot
1.5 litres water
2–3 strips lemon rind

salt and pepper
egg yolks
milk

Wash the foot thoroughly. Put it into a large saucepan with the water, heat to simmering point, cover, and simmer gently for 3 hours. Strain through a colander or a sieve into a basin and leave to cool. When cold, skim the fat. Re-heat the broth with the lemon rind until sufficiently flavoured. Remove the lemon rind. Season to taste. For each 250ml broth, allow 1 egg yolk and 4 × 15ml spoons milk. Beat together the egg yolks and milk with a fork until well blended. Beat into a little hot soup, and fold into the rest of the soup. Stir over low heat until thickened. Do not allow the broth to boil or it will curdle. Serve hot.

Consommé
Makes 1 litre (approx)

100g lean shin of beef
125ml water
1 small onion (50g approx)
1 small carrot (25g approx)
1 small stick of celery (25g approx)

1.25 litres cold brown stock (p25)
bouquet garni
$\frac{1}{2}$ × 2.5ml spoon salt
4 white peppercorns
white and crushed shell of 1 egg

Shred the beef finely, trimming off all the fat. Soak the meat in the water for 15 minutes. Prepare the vegetables. Put the meat, water, and the rest of the ingredients into a deep saucepan, adding the egg white and shell last. Heat slowly to simmering point, whisking all the time, until a froth rises to the surface. Remove the whisk, cover, and simmer the consommé very gently for 1½–2 hours. Do not allow to boil or the froth will break up and cloud the consommé. Strain slowly into a basin through muslin or a scalded jelly bag. If necessary, strain the consommé again. Re-heat, re-season if required, and serve plain or with a garnish (see below).

Consommé Brunoise
4–6 helpings

1 litre consommé
1 × 2.5ml spoon lemon juice

1 × 15ml spoon sherry (optional)

Garnish
1 × 15ml spoon finely diced carrot
1 × 15ml spoon finely diced turnip

1 × 15ml spoon finely diced green leek
1 × 15ml spoon finely diced celery

Cook the diced vegetables for the garnish very carefully in boiling salted water until just tender. Drain and rinse the vegetables; then put them into a warmed tureen.

Meanwhile, heat the consommé to boiling point and add the lemon juice and sherry, if used. Pour the hot consommé over the diced vegetables, and serve.

Consommé Julienne
4–6 helpings

1 litre consommé

Garnish
1 × 15ml spoon julienne carrot
1 × 15ml spoon julienne turnip

1 × 15ml spoon julienne leek

Cook the vegetables for the garnish separately in boiling salted water until just tender. Drain and rinse them, then put them into a warmed tureen.

Meanwhile, heat the consommé to boiling point. Pour the hot consommé over the vegetables, and serve.

Consommé with Rice
4–6 helpings

1 litre consommé (p31)

Garnish
25g Patna rice

Cook the rice in boiling salted water until just tender. Rinse and drain. Heat the consommé to boiling point, add the rice, and heat through.

Consommé Royale
4–6 helpings

1 litre consommé (p31)

Garnish (Royale Custard)
1 egg yolk   butter for greasing
salt and pepper
1 × 15ml spoon white stock (p26)
    or milk **or** cream

Mix the egg yolk, seasoning, and stock or milk or cream. Strain into a small greased basin and cover with buttered greaseproof paper or foil. Stand the basin in a pan of simmering water and steam the custard for about 8 minutes or until firm. Leave until cold and turn out. Cut into thin slices and then into tiny fancy shapes. Rinse the custard shapes in hot water, and drain.

Heat the consommé to boiling point and add the custard garnishes just before serving.

Iced Consommé (Consommé Frappé)
6 helpings

1 litre brown stock (p25) **or** chicken   1 × 15ml spoon (approx) dry sherry
    stock (p26) made with veal bones   ice (optional)

Garnish
chopped parsley, chives, and tarragon   finely chopped hard-boiled egg white
    or chervil   small squares of skinned tomato
finely diced raw cucumber

Make the stock with veal bones to give a firmer jelly when it is iced. Clear the stock as for Consommé (p31). Season it carefully before cooling the consommé. When cool, add the sherry. Chill in a refrigerator, or in a bowl surrounded by ice, for 1–2 hours. The chilled consommé should be a soft jelly. Just before serving, whip the jelly lightly with a fork so that it is not quite solid. Serve in chilled soup bowls with one of the above garnishes.

Note Canned consommé can also be served iced. Check that it will 'jelly' by chilling it. Heat the canned consommé until liquid. Add a little dissolved gelatine, if necessary. Check the seasoning, leave to cool, then add sherry to taste. Chill, and serve as above.

Thick Soups

Butter Bean Soup
6 helpings

150g butter beans
1 litre water **or** general household stock (p25)
a few bacon scraps **or** rinds **or** a bacon bone
1 medium-sized onion (100g approx)
2 sticks celery

½ small turnip (25g approx)
1 medium-sized potato (100g approx)
1 × 10ml spoon bacon fat
bouquet garni
a blade of mace
250ml milk
salt and pepper

Wash the beans. Heat the water or stock to boiling point, pour it over the beans, and leave to soak overnight. Chop the bacon, if used. Prepare and slice the vegetables. Heat the bacon fat in a deep saucepan, add the bacon or bone, and vegetables, and fry gently for 10 minutes. Add the soaked beans and the liquid, the bouquet garni, and mace. Heat to boiling point, cover, and simmer for 2 hours or until the beans are quite soft. Remove the bouquet garni and bone, if used, and rub the vegetables and cooking liquid through a sieve, or process in an electric blender. Return to a clean pan and add the milk. No starch thickener other than the potato should be needed. Re-heat and season to taste.

VARIATIONS

Dried Pea Soup
Substitute 150g dried, whole or split peas for the butter beans, and add a sprig of mint or a little dried mint.

Haricot Bean Soup
Substitute 150g haricot beans for the butter beans.

Lentil Soup
Substitute 150g red or brown lentils for the butter beans, and add 50g carrot to the flavouring vegetables.

Split Pea and Ham Soup
Substitute 150g split peas for the butter beans, and add a ham or bacon bone to the soup.

Basque Bean Soup
4 helpings

100g haricot beans
1 litre water
2 medium-sized onions (200g approx)
200g white cabbage

50g bacon **or** pork fat
1 clove of garlic
salt and pepper
a few drops white wine vinegar

Garnish
2 × 15ml spoons crumbled cooked
    bacon

Soak the beans in the water overnight. Skin and slice the onions and shred the cabbage. Heat the bacon or pork fat in a saucepan, add the onions, and fry gently for about 10 minutes until browned. Add the cabbage, and shake the pan over gentle heat for 2–3 minutes. Skin and crush the garlic and add to the pan with the soaked beans and water. Heat the soup to simmering point, cover, and simmer for 1½–2½ hours until the beans are quite soft. Season and add the vinegar to taste. Just before serving, sprinkle the bacon on top.

Cream of Chicken Soup
4–6 helpings

25g cornflour
125ml milk
1 litre chicken stock (p26)
50g cooked chicken
salt and pepper

1 × 5ml spoon lemon juice
a pinch of grated nutmeg
2 egg yolks
2 × 15ml spoons single cream

Blend the cornflour with a little of the milk. Heat the stock to boiling point and stir into the blended cornflour. Return the mixture to the pan and re-heat to boiling point, stirring all the time. Reduce the heat, cover, and simmer for 20 minutes. Cut the chicken into 5mm dice and heat these in the soup. Season to taste, and add the lemon juice and nutmeg. Beat the yolks with the rest of the milk and the cream; beat in a little hot soup, and fold into the rest of the soup. Heat until it thickens, but do not allow it to boil.

Fisherman's Hot Pot
4 helpings

50g white cabbage
100g leek
250g potatoes
100g onions
25g red pepper
2 slices white bread
50ml cooking oil
25g butter
250g cod **or** other white fish fillets
  (see **Note**)

150ml Muscadet **or** other dry white
  wine
1 litre water
50g concentrated tomato purée
1 chicken stock cube
bouquet garni
1 clove of garlic
salt and pepper

Garnish
1 × 15ml spoon chopped parsley

Shred the cabbage, slice the leek and potatoes, chop the onion and pepper. Remove the crusts from the bread, cut into 1cm cubes, and dry in the oven for 10 minutes.

Heat the oil and butter in a large saucepan, add the vegetables, cover, and cook gently for 7–8 minutes; do not let them colour. Skin the fish, cut them into 3cm cubes, and fry for 3 minutes with the vegetables, turning them over to firm the surface of the cubes. Pour in the wine, water, and tomato purée. Crumble in the stock cube. Skin and crush the garlic. Add the bouquet garni and garlic, and season to taste. Heat to simmering point and simmer for 20 minutes. Discard the bouquet garni. Pour into a soup tureen and sprinkle with the chopped parsley.

Serve with the sippets of bread.

Note Any white fish can be used for the hot pot, eg haddock, hake, whiting, ling, etc.

Giblet Soup
4 helpings

2–3 sets chicken giblets **or** 1 set of
  turkey **or** goose giblets
1 litre water
1 medium-sized onion (100g approx)
1 medium-sized carrot (50g approx)
1 stick of celery
bouquet garni

1 clove
a small blade of mace
6 black peppercorns
1 × 5ml spoon salt
25g butter **or** margarine
25g flour

Prepare the giblets if required (pp183–84). Put them in a saucepan and add the cold water. Heat gently to simmering point. Prepare the vegetables and either leave them whole or chop coarsely. Add them to the pan with the bouquet garni, spices, peppercorns, and salt. Cover, and simmer for 2½ hours. Strain the stock. Melt the fat in a saucepan, stir in the flour, and brown very slowly, stirring all the time. Gradually add the stock and stir until boiling. Boil for 5 minutes, stirring all the time. Dice the best pieces of giblets finely and add to the soup. Re-season if required. Re-heat and serve.

Game Soup

4 helpings

remains of 1 roast pheasant **or** 2–3
    smaller game birds
50g lean bacon, without rinds
25g butter **or** margarine
1 medium-sized onion (100g approx)
1 large carrot (100g approx)
1 litre general household stock (p25)
    or game stock (p26)

bouquet garni
a blade of mace
1 chicken's liver **or** 50g calf's liver
25g flour
4 × 10ml spoons port **or** sherry
    (optional)
salt and pepper

Cut any large pieces of meat from the carcass of the game birds and cut the bacon into small cubes. Melt the fat in a frying pan and fry the game pieces and bacon lightly. Put to one side. Prepare and slice the vegetables. Put the stock and game bones in a large stewpan and add the vegetables, bouquet garni, and mace. Heat to boiling point, cover, and simmer for 2–2½ hours.

Remove any skin and tubes from the liver; add the liver to the pan and simmer for another 15 minutes. Lift out the liver; then strain the soup through a colander into a clean pan. Discard the bones. Purée the liver and reserved meat and bacon with a little of the fat in the pan if a rich purée is wanted. Re-heat the rest of the fat in the pan, stir in the flour, and cook for 4–5 minutes, stirring all the time, until nut brown. Stir the roux gradually into the meat purée. Heat the soup to boiling point; then draw the pan off the heat. Stir in the purée mixture in small spoonfulls. Return to gentle heat and stir until the soup thickens to the preferred consistency. Add the port or sherry, if used, and season to taste.

Serve with fried bread croûtons or sprigs of watercress.

Hare Soup

6 helpings

1 hare
1.5 litres general household stock
    (p25) **or** water
1 medium-sized onion (100g approx)
1 large carrot (100g approx)
½ turnip (25g approx)
1 small parsnip (50g approx)

1 stick of celery
3 × 10ml spoons dripping **or** lard
bouquet garni
3 × 2.5ml spoons salt
8 black peppercorns
4 × 15ml spoons flour
4 × 10ml spoons port

Prepare and paunch the hare (pp211–12) or ask the butcher to do it for you. Fillet the meat from the back and legs, and use for another recipe. Only the head, flaps, bones, and blood of the hare are used for the soup.

Split the head, break the bones, and put them and the meat trimmings into a large saucepan. Cover with stock or water, and leave to stand for 1 hour. Prepare and slice the vegetables.

Heat the fat in a saucepan, add the vegetables, and fry until golden-grown. Lift out the vegetables and reserve the fat in the pan. Heat the bones and liquid very slowly to simmering point. Add the fried vegetables, bouquet garni, salt, and peppercorns. Cover, and simmer very gently for 3–4 hours.

Meanwhile, add the flour to the fat in the saucepan and fry gently, until golden-brown, stirring all the time. Strain the soup. Remove all pieces of meat from the bones and cut them into small dice. Whisk the fried flour into the soup and heat to boiling point, whisking all the time. Stir in the diced meat, blood, and port. Re-season if required. Re-heat gently without boiling.

Note Hare Soup can be served with Forcemeat Balls (p47).

Kidney Soup
4 helpings

200g ox kidney	1 stick of celery
25g plain flour	1 litre general household stock (p25)
25g dripping **or** lard	bouquet garni
1 medium-sized onion (100g approx)	6 black peppercorns
1 large carrot (100g approx)	salt
1 small turnip (50g approx)	a little extra stock **or** cold water

Skin, core, and cut the kidney into small pieces. Coat with flour. Keep any remaining flour to thicken the soup at the end. Heat the fat in a large saucepan. Fry the kidney lightly until just browned, then remove from the pan. Prepare and slice the vegetables. Fry them in the fat for about 5 minutes until they begin to brown. Drain off any excess fat. Add the stock, bouquet garni, and seasoning. Heat to boiling point, cover, reduce the heat, and simmer gently for 2 hours.

Remove the bouquet garni and strain the soup. Reserve a few kidney pieces for the garnish. Purée the rest and add to the soup. Blend any remaining flour with a little stock or water, add to the soup, and stir until boiling. Reduce the heat and simmer for 5 minutes. Chop the reserved kidney pieces and add to the soup. Re-season if required.

Note Kidney Soup can be served with Herb Dumplings (p53).

Liver Soup
4 helpings

1 medium-sized carrot (50g approx)	$\frac{1}{2}$ × 2.5ml spoon yeast **or** meat extract
1 medium-sized onion (100g approx)	salt and pepper
25g butter **or** margarine	2 tomatoes (100g approx)
25g flour	200g calf's, ox **or** lamb's liver
1 litre general household stock (p25)	1 × 5ml spoon lemon juice
a blade of mace	

Prepare and slice the carrot and onion. Melt the fat in a large saucepan, and fry the vegetables until they begin to brown. Add the flour, and fry gently until browned, stirring occasionally. Gradually add the stock and stir until boiling. Add the mace, yeast or meat extract, and seasoning. Cover, reduce the heat and simmer for 1 hour.

Meanwhile, skin and chop the tomatoes. Add to the soup, cover, and continue simmering for another 30 minutes. Rub the soup through a fine sieve. Remove the skin and tubes from the liver, and mince or chop it finely. Whisk it into the soup with the lemon juice. Re-heat the soup and simmer until the liver just loses its red colour. Re-season if required.

Minestrone
4–6 helpings

75g butter beans **or** haricot beans
2 rashers streaky bacon, without rinds
1 clove of garlic
1 leek
1 onion
2 carrots
50g French beans
3 sticks celery
2 potatoes

150g white cabbage
25g butter
1 bay leaf
1 × 10ml spoon concentrated tomato
   purée
1.25 litres white stock (p26)
salt and pepper
50g pasta rings

Garnish
grated Parmesan cheese

Soak the beans overnight in cold water. Drain thoroughly. Chop the bacon. Skin and crush the garlic. Slice the leek, onion, carrots, and French beans, chop the celery, dice the potatoes, and shred the cabbage. Fry the bacon in a saucepan for 2–3 minutes, add the garlic and butter, and fry for 2–3 minutes. Add all the vegetables and cook for 3–4 minutes. Add the bay leaf, tomato purée, stock, salt, and pepper. Heat to boiling point, cover, then simmer for 45–50 minutes. Add the pasta rings and cook for a further 6–8 minutes.

Serve hot, garnished with grated Parmesan cheese.

Mulligatawny Soup
4 helpings

400g lean mutton, rabbit, stewing veal
   or shin of beef
1 medium-sized onion (100g approx)
1 small cooking apple (100g approx)
25g butter **or** margarine
2–3 × 15ml spoons curry powder
25g plain flour
1 litre water

1 large carrot (100g approx)
$\frac{1}{2}$ small parsnip (50g approx)
bouquet garni
1 × 2.5ml spoon lemon juice
1 × 2.5ml spoon salt
$\frac{1}{2}$ × 2.5ml spoon black treacle **or**
   extra lemon juice

Trim off any fat and cut the meat into small pieces. Prepare the onion and apple and chop them finely. Melt the fat in a deep saucepan and fry the onion and apple quickly for 2–3 minutes. Add the curry powder, cook gently for 2 minutes, then stir in the flour. Gradually add the water and stir until boiling. Add the meat. Prepare and slice the carrot and parsnip, and add to the pan with the bouquet garni, lemon juice, and salt. Simmer until the meat is very tender. This will take 2 hours for rabbit, 3 hours for stewing veal and mutton, and 4 hours for shin of beef.

Taste the soup, and add black treacle or more lemon juice to obtain a flavour that is neither predominantly sweet nor acid. Strain the soup. Dice some of the meat finely, add to the soup and re-heat.

Serve with boiled long-grain rice.

Oxtail Soup
4–6 helpings

1 oxtail
25g beef dripping
1 medium-sized onion (100g approx)
1 large carrot (100g approx)
1 turnip (25g approx)
1 stick of celery

1 litre water **or** general household stock
  (p25)
1 × 5ml spoon salt
bouquet garni
6 black peppercorns
25g plain flour

Wash, trim off any fat, and joint the tail. Heat the dripping in a saucepan. Add half the jointed tail and fry until the meat is browned. Lift out the meat and reserve the fat in the pan. Prepare and slice the vegetables. Fry in the hot dripping until golden-brown, then remove. Put all the oxtail and the fried vegetables into a deep saucepan. Add the water or stock, and heat very slowly to·boiling point. Add the salt, bouquet garni, and peppercorns. Cover, and simmer very gently for 3–4 hours.

Meanwhile, stir the flour into the dripping in the saucepan and fry gently until golden-brown. Strain the soup. Remove all the meat from the bones. Return some of the smaller pieces of meat and any small slices of carrot to the soup. Whisk in the browned flour. Re-heat the soup to boiling point, whisking all the time. Re-season if required.

Prawn Bisque
4–6 helpings

100g butter
250g cooked shelled prawns
25g flour
750ml fish stock (p26) in which
  prawn shells have been cooked
125ml white wine
125ml court bouillon (p79)

1 egg yolk
125ml single cream **or** milk **or**
  half cream and half milk
salt and pepper
lemon juice
a pinch of grated nutmeg

Melt 25g of the butter in a saucepan. Add the prawns, and toss over gentle heat for 5 minutes. Pound the prawns, gradually working in another 50g of the butter. Rub the pounded prawn and butter mixture through a sieve, or process briefly in an electric blender. Melt the remaining 25g butter in a deep saucepan. Stir in the flour and cook gently for 1–2 minutes. Strain the fish stock and gradually stir it into the flour with the wine and court bouillon. Heat to boiling point. Mix the egg yolk with the cream or milk or both. Season the soup and add lemon juice and nutmeg to taste. Whisk the prawn butter into the soup, at just below boiling point, adding a small pat at a time. Add the egg yolk and cream mixture and stir over low heat, without boiling, to thicken the egg.

VARIATION
Shrimp Bisque
Substitute shrimps for the prawns.

White Fish Chowder
4 helpings

125ml dry white wine	75g leek
1 litre of water	75g carrot
bouquet garni	50g butter
salt and pepper	50g flour
400g skinned coley fillets **or** other coarse-fleshed white fish	1 × 5ml spoon turmeric
	3 × 15ml spoons chopped parsley

Put the wine, water, bouquet garni, and seasoning in a pan and poach the fish gently in the liquid until tender. Meanwhile, prepare and dice the leek and carrot. Strain the soup into a clean pan. Remove the bouquet garni and cut the fish into 1.5cm cubes. Return the pan to the heat and heat to simmering point. Cream the butter and flour to a smooth paste, then add it gradually to the soup, whisking in each addition. Stir in the turmeric. Add the diced vegetables and simmer gently for 7 minutes. Add the fish and the parsley. Simmer for a further 5 minutes. Serve hot with crusty bread.

Vegetable Soup *Basic recipe*
4 helpings

500g vegetables (approx)	salt and pepper
15–25g butter, margarine **or** other fat	125ml milk
500ml–1 litre white stock (p26) **or** general household stock (p25)	2 × 10ml spoons thickening (flour, cornflour, ground rice, tapioca, **or** potato) for each 500ml puréed soup
bouquet garni **or** flavouring herbs	cold stock, water **or** milk
lemon juice	

For Cream of Vegetable Soup
add
4–8 × 15ml spoons single cream
   and/or 1 egg yolk

Prepare and chop the vegetables. Melt the fat in a deep saucepan, add the vegetables, and fry gently for 5–10 minutes without browning them. Add the stock, bouquet garni or herbs, lemon juice, and seasoning to taste. Heat to boiling point, reduce the heat, and simmer gently until the vegetables are quite soft. Do not overcook.

Remove the bouquet garni. Purée the vegetables and liquid by either rubbing through a fine sieve, or by processing in an electric blender. Add the milk, measure the soup, and return it to a clean pan. Weigh the thickening in the correct proportion and blend it with a little cold stock, water or milk. Stir it into the soup. Bring to the boil, stirring all the time, and cook for 5 minutes. Re-season if required. Serve with croûtons (p51). Melba or fairy toast (p54).

Note To make a cream of vegetable soup, remove the pan from the heat after the soup has been thickened and leave to cool slightly. Add a little of the hot soup to the single cream (which can replace some of the milk in the main recipe) and egg yolk, if using, and beat well. Whisk the mixture into the rest of the soup. Return the soup to gentle heat and re-heat, without boiling, stirring all the time.

Green Pea Soup
4 helpings

600g green peas in the pod
1 medium-sized onion (100g approx)
a few spinach leaves
1 × 10ml spoon butter
500ml white stock (p26)
a sprig of mint
a few parsley stalks

2 × 10ml spoons cornflour for each
  500ml puréed soup
cold stock, water **or** milk
salt and pepper
sugar
a few drops green food colouring
  (optional)

For Cream of Green Pea Soup
add
4 × 15ml spoons single cream (see
  Method)

Garnish
a few shelled peas

4 × 15ml spoons chilled whipping
  cream

Shell the peas and wash half the pods. Trim off any hard parts. Skin and slice the onion. Wash the spinach leaves and chop them roughly. Melt the butter in a deep saucepan, add the washed pods and onion, and fry very gently for 10 minutes. Add the stock and heat to boiling point. Add the peas, spinach leaves, and herbs. Simmer for 10–20 minutes or until the peas are just cooked. Proceed as for Vegetable Soup (p40). Season to taste with salt, pepper, and sugar; add the colouring, if liked. Stir in the cream, if used, at boiling point, off the heat.

Meanwhile, cook the peas for the garnish in boiling salted water until just tender. Whip the cream until stiff. Add the cooked peas and blobs of whipped cream to the soup just before serving.

Hot Vichyssoise Cream Soup
4 helpings

250g leeks, white parts only
250g potatoes
25g butter
500ml white stock (p26)

salt and pepper
125ml milk
4–8 × 15ml spoons single cream

Make as for Vegetable Soup (p40). No thickening is required.

VARIATION
Iced Vichyssoise
Make as above but chill the soup well before serving it.

Italian Tomato Soup

4 helpings

600g fresh tomatoes
1 × 15ml spoon olive oil
500ml white stock (p26)
1 clove of garlic
a sprig of parsley
a pinch of dried basil

a pinch of dried marjoram
salt and pepper
2 × 10ml spoons ground rice
4 × 15ml spoons single cream
    (optional)
1 egg yolk (optional)

Chop the tomatoes finely to shorten their cooking time. Proceed as for Vegetable Soup (p40), but cook the tomatoes in the stock for 5 minutes only before sieving them.

Note This soup can be iced if it is not thickened. Sprinkle in 4 × 10ml spoons finely sieved brown breadcrumbs before chilling it.

Gazpacho Andaluz

4 helpings

3 large tomatoes
4 green peppers
½ cucumber
150g soft white breadcrumbs
8 × 10ml spoons olive oil

1 litre water
salt and pepper
2 cloves garlic
6 × 10ml spoons white wine vinegar

Skin and chop the tomatoes, de-seed the peppers, and chop finely with the cucumber. Put the breadcrumbs, tomatoes, peppers and cucumbers into a large bowl with the olive oil. Stir in the water and leave for 1 hour. Rub through a sieve or process in an electric blender. Add salt and pepper to taste. Crush the garlic, stir it into the vinegar, and add to the bowl. Cover with foil, and chill well before serving.

STUFFINGS, GARNISHES, AND ACCOMPANIMENTS

STUFFINGS OR FORCEMEATS

Breadcrumbs (to make)

Soft breadcrumbs: Remove the crusts from white or brown bread that is at least 1 day old. Either process in an electric blender, or grate coarsely. Alternatively, rub through a wire sieve, or between the palms of the hand until fine crumbs are obtained.
Note Soft crumbs can be stored in a clean polythene bag or sealed polythene container for 2 to 3 days in a refrigerator, or up to 3 months in a freezer. Frozen breadcrumbs remain separate and the required quantity can be removed from the container easily.

Dried breadcrumbs: Prepare soft breadcrumbs and dry them slowly without colouring in a very cool oven, or in a warm place, until thoroughly dry.
Note Dried breadcrumbs can be stored in an airtight jar or tin for 2–3 weeks in a cool place. However, they develop a strong stale taste if kept longer.

Browned breadcrumbs (raspings): Put crusts or any pieces of stale bread in a moderate oven, 180°C, Gas 4, and bake them until golden-brown and crisp. Crush with a rolling-pin or process in an electric blender. These crumbs are not used for stuffings, but for coating croquettes, fish cakes, rissoles, etc or for covering *au gratin* dishes.
Note They can be stored in an airtight jar or tin for 2–3 weeks in a cool place. Like dried breadcrumbs, they develop a strong stale taste if kept longer.

Buttered breadcrumbs: Lightly fork 125g soft breadcrumbs with 25g melted butter. When the crumbs have absorbed the fat, spread them on a baking sheet and dry them without browning, in a very cool oven, 110°C, Gas ¼. Buttered crumbs can be used as they are for coating meat, fish or croquettes, or for covering *au gratin* dishes.

To use in place of soft crumbs, soak buttered crumbs in a little hot water (100g buttered crumbs to 5 × 15ml spoons water) for 5 minutes. Soaked buttered crumbs can be used for bread sauce and stuffings.
Note Buttered crumbs keep better and longer than either soft crumbs or raspings (unless these are frozen). They can be stored in an airtight container in a cool place for up to 2 months.

Apricot Stuffing

*Enough for 1 boned joint of pork or a 2.5kg duck; double the quantity will stuff a
4–5kg goose*

75g dried apricots
75g boiled long-grain rice **or** soft
  white breadcrumbs
25g butter
1 × 2.5ml spoon salt
1 × 2.5ml spoon ground pepper

a pinch each of dried thyme, ground
  mace and grated nutmeg
1 stick celery **or** 50g green pepper
white stock (p26) **or** water from
  soaked apricots

Soak the apricots overnight in cold water. Drain and reserve the liquid. Chop the
apricots and mix with the rice or breadcrumbs. Melt the butter and stir it into the
stuffing with the seasoning, herbs, and spices. Prepare the celery or green pepper,
chop finely, and add to the mixture. Moisten the stuffing with a little stock or water
reserved from the soaked apricots.

Use as above, or for roast chicken, turkey, guineafowl, and lamb.

Basic Herb Stuffing or Forcemeat

*Enough for a 1.5–2kg chicken, a boned joint of veal or eight 75g thin fish fillets;
use double the quantity for the neck end of a 5–6kg turkey*

50g shredded suet **or** margarine
100g soft breadcrumbs
a pinch of grated nutmeg
1 × 15ml spoon chopped parsley
1 × 5ml spoon chopped fresh mixed
  herbs

grated rind of $\frac{1}{2}$ lemon
salt and pepper
1 egg

Melt the margarine, if using. Mix the breadcrumbs with the suet or margarine. Add
the nutmeg, herbs, and lemon rind. Season, beat the egg until liquid, and stir into the
mixture to bind it.

Use as above, or for vegetables. Alternatively, form the mixture into 12 or 16 balls,
and bake in a moderate oven at 180°C, Gas 4, for 15–20 minutes, or fry in deep or
shallow fat until golden.

VARIATIONS

Thyme and Parsley Stuffing

Substitute 1 × 5ml spoon thyme for the mixed herbs and omit the grated nutmeg.

Ham Stuffing

Mince or shred 100g lean ham or bacon, and add to the breadcrumbs before mixing
with the fat. Use a little milk or chicken stock with the egg to bind the mixture if
necessary.

Use for veal, poultry or rabbit. When made with suet, the stuffing can also be used
for hare.

Prawn or Shrimp Stuffing
Enough for four 450g whole fish, 6 fish cutlets or eight 75g thin fish fillets
Add 100g prawns or shrimps to the breadcrumbs before mixing with the fat. Chop large prawns roughly, leave small fish whole. Add a little milk with the egg, if necessary, to bind.

Glazed Forcemeat Balls
Brush the balls with egg wash before baking them.

Crumbed Forcemeat Balls
Coat the balls with beaten egg yolk; then roll in dried or browned breadcrumbs before baking or frying them.

Nut Forcemeat Balls
Coat the balls with beaten egg yolk; then roll in finely chopped or ground nuts before baking them.

Chestnut Stuffing
Enough for the neck end of a 5–6kg turkey; half the quantity will stuff a 1.5kg chicken

800g chestnuts **or** 500g shelled **or**
   canned chestnuts (approx)
125–250ml stock
50g butter

salt and pepper
a pinch of ground cinnamon
1 × 2.5ml spoon sugar

Make a slit in the rounded side of chestnuts in their shells and bake or boil them for 20 minutes. Remove the shells and skins while hot. Put the chestnuts in a pan with just enough stock to cover them. Heat to boiling point, reduce the heat, cover, and stew until the chestnuts are tender. Drain and reserve the stock. Rub the chestnuts through a fine wire sieve into a bowl. Add the butter, seasoning, cinnamon, and the sugar. Stir in enough stock to make a soft stuffing.

Calf or Chicken Liver Stuffing
Enough for a 2kg chicken

200g calf **or** chicken liver
4 thick bacon rashers, without rinds
   or 100g pork sausage-meat
1 small onion
25g butter

2 × 15ml spoons beaten egg
1 × 2.5ml spoon chopped fresh herbs
1 × 5ml spoon chopped parsley
salt and pepper

Remove the skin and tubes, and cut the liver into 5mm dice together with the bacon rashers, if used. Skin the onion and chop it finely. Melt the butter in a frying pan and stir in the liver, bacon or sausage-meat, and the onion. Fry gently for 10 minutes, stirring the mixture and turning it over often. Leave to cool; then chop the liver mixture more finely. Mix in the beaten egg, herbs, and seasoning.
    Use as above, or for game.

Chicken Giblet Stuffing

Enough for a 2kg chicken or the neck end of a 5–6kg turkey

1 set of chicken giblets
1 medium-sized onion
100g soft white breadcrumbs
50g butter or margarine
1 × 15ml spoon chopped parsley

1 × 2.5ml spoon dried mixed herbs
grated rind of ½ lemon
salt and pepper
1 egg

Prepare the giblets if required (pp183–84). Skin the onion and slice it thickly. Put into a saucepan with the giblets, cover with water, heat to boiling point, reduce the heat, and simmer for 45 minutes or until the giblets are cooked. Strain, and reserve 125ml of the cooking liquid; use the rest to make a gravy, soup or sauce.

Pick all the meat off the neck bones, and cut out the lining of the gizzard; chop or mince the flesh of all the giblets. Soak the crumbs in the reserved stock to moisten them. Melt the butter or margarine, and mix together with the giblets, breadcrumbs, herbs, and lemon rind. Season to taste. Beat the egg until liquid and stir into the stuffing mixture.

Use as above, or for pasta (eg cannelloni) or vegetables such as peppers.

VARIATION

Turkey Giblet Stuffing

Substitute turkey giblets for chicken giblets, and use double the quantity of bread-crumbs, stock, and butter or margarine.

Flour Panada *Basic recipe*

125ml water, stock or milk
25g butter

25g plain flour
salt and pepper

Put the liquid and butter in a small pan, and heat to boiling point. Sift the flour and add to the pan, stirring briskly with a wooden spoon. Continue to stir over heat until the panada forms a stiff ball and leaves the sides of the pan clean. Season to taste. Spread the panada on a plate, and when cool, use to bind savoury pancake fillings and croquette mixtures.

Fish Forcemeat

Enough for twelve 75g thin fish fillets, 8 fish cutlets or 4 whole fish weighing 350–450g

1 egg
100g panada, using fish stock (p26)
    or milk
salt and pepper

200g raw white fish, without skin or
    bone
grated rind and juice of ½ lemon

Beat the egg until liquid. Add it gradually to the cooled panada, beating well after each addition. Season to taste. Flake the fish and beat it into the panada. Add the grated lemon rind and juice to taste.

Use as above, or for vegetables.

Mrs Beeton's Forcemeat or Forcemeat Balls for Hare
Enough for a large hare

50g ham **or** bacon, without rinds
100g shredded suet
grated rind of 1 lemon
1 × 5ml spoon chopped parsley
1 × 5ml spoon chopped fresh mixed
   herbs

salt
a few grains Cayenne pepper
a pinch of ground mace
150g soft white breadcrumbs
3 eggs
lard for frying (optional)

Shred the ham or bacon. Put it in a bowl with the suet, lemon rind, herbs, and seasonings. Mix well with a fork, then mix in the breadcrumbs. Beat the eggs lightly until liquid and stir gradually into the dry ingredients, adding enough egg to make a smooth firm mixture. Use as above, or for veal or poultry.

VARIATION

Roll the mixture into small balls. Fry in hot lard until browned on all sides, or place in the roasting tin with the hare for the last 30 minutes of the cooking time.

Oyster Stuffing
Enough to fill the neck end of a 4kg turkey or the body cavity of a 2–2.5kg boiling fowl

6 fresh **or** canned oysters
100g soft white breadcrumbs
50g shredded suet **or** or butter
1 × 5ml spoon chopped fresh mixed
   herbs

a pinch of grated nutmeg
salt and pepper
1 egg

Open fresh oysters (p77) and simmer very gently in their own liquor for 10 minutes. Canned oysters need no cooking. Drain, and reserve a little of the liquor. Cut the oysters into small pieces. Mix the breadcrumbs with the suet or with melted butter. Add the oysters, herbs, and nutmeg, and season to taste. Beat the egg until liquid and stir into the oyster mixture, adding a little oyster liquor if necessary to bind it.

Prune and Apple Stuffing
Enough for 1 boned joint of pork or a 2.5kg duck; double the quantity will stuff a 4–5kg goose

100g prunes
4 × 10ml spoons long-grain rice **or**
   125g cooked rice
1 large cooking apple
50g shredded almonds

50g shredded suet **or** butter
salt and pepper
grated rind and juice of ½ lemon
1 egg

Soak the prunes overnight in cold water. Drain off the liquid. Cook the rice in boiling salted water until tender; then drain. Stone and chop the prunes. Peel, core, and chop the apple roughly, and mix together with the prunes, rice, apple, almonds, and suet or butter. Season to taste and add the lemon rind and juice. Beat the egg until liquid and mix into the stuffing to bind it.

Rice Stuffing
Enough for a 2kg chicken

50g long-grain rice **or** 150g cooked rice
1 chicken liver
1 small onion
50g seedless raisins
50g ground almonds

25g butter
2 × 15ml spoons chopped parsley
a sprig of thyme
salt and pepper
1 egg

Cook the rice in boiling salted water until just tender; then drain. Remove the skin and tubes, and chop the liver. Skin the onion and chop it finely. Mix together with the rice, liver, raisins, and almonds. Mash in the butter with a fork. Add the herbs, and season to taste. Mix well. Beat the egg until liquid and mix into the stuffing to bind it. Use for roast chicken, other meats, fish or vegetables.

Wild Rice Stuffing
Enough for a brace of pheasants or 1 large guinea-fowl

giblets of the bird to be stuffed
750ml water
1 × 5ml spoon salt
150g wild rice
2 shallots
15g green pepper

1 small stick of celery
100g mushrooms
50g butter
4 × 15ml spoons concentrated tomato
    purée

Prepare the giblets if required (pp183–84), and cut into small pieces. Put into a pan with the water and salt. Heat to boiling point, reduce the heat, cover, and simmer for 15 minutes. Remove the giblets. Re-heat the liquid to boiling point and stir in the rice. Reduce the heat, cover, and simmer for about 30 minutes until nearly tender; then drain. Prepare and chop the vegetables. Melt the butter in a pan, add the vegetables, and fry gently for 3 minutes. Remove from the heat, add the rice and tomato purée, and mix well. Use as above, or for other roast game birds.

Brown Rice and Fruit Stuffing
Enough for 2.5kg chicken or 1 large marrow

50g dried apricots
50g prunes
40g brown rice
1 large **or** 2 small cooking pears
juice and grated rind of ½ lemon

25g pine kernels
25g butter
salt and pepper
1 egg

Put the apricots and prunes into a large bowl and cover with boiling water. Soak for about 4 hours until tender and swollen. Put the rice into a saucepan, drain the liquid from the dried fruit into it, add extra water if required, and bring slowly to the boil. Reduce the heat, cover, and simmer for about 40 minutes until tender.

Meanwhile, chop the fruit finely and discard any stones. Peel, core, and chop the pears, and mix with the lemon rind and juice. Chop the nuts coarsely. Drain the rice and add the fruit and nuts. Melt the butter and add to the rice, mixing it in well. Beat the egg until liquid and mix into the stuffing to bind it.

Sage and Onion Stuffing

Enough for a 2.5kg duck; double the quantity will stuff a 4–5kg goose

2 small onions
4 young sage leaves **or**
  1 × 2.5ml spoon dried sage
100g soft white breadcrumbs

50g butter **or** margarine
salt and pepper
1 egg (optional)

Skin the onions and slice them thickly. Put them in a pan with a little water and parboil. Drain and chop the onions finely. Scald the fresh sage leaves, if used, and chop them finely. Mix together with the onions and breadcrumbs. Melt the butter or margarine, add to the stuffing, and season to taste. Mix together thoroughly. If the stuffing is to be shaped into balls, beat the egg until liquid and add enough to the stuffing to bind it.

Use as above, or for pork.

Sausage-meat Stuffing

Enough for a 1.5–2kg chicken; triple the quantity will stuff a 5–6kg turkey

liver of the bird to be stuffed
500g pork sausage-meat
50g soft white breadcrumbs
1 × 15ml spoon chopped parsley

1 × 5ml spoon dried mixed herbs
1 egg
salt and pepper

Remove the skin and tubes, and chop the liver finely. Mix together with the sausage-meat and breadcrumbs, Add the herbs. Beat the egg until liquid and mix into the stuffing to bind it. Season to taste.

Tomato Stuffing

Enough for 1 wild duck, 2 pigeons or 1.5kg coarse white fish

2 large ripe tomatoes
1 sweet red pepper **or** 2 canned
  pimentos

1 clove of garlic
50g soft brown breadcrumbs (approx)
salt and pepper

Skin, de-seed, and chop the tomatoes. Remove the membranes and seeds from the pepper and chop the flesh of the pepper or pimentos finely. Skin and crush the garlic. Mix the ingredients together, using enough breadcrumbs to absorb the juice of the tomatoes. Season to taste.

Use as above, or for other small game birds.

GARNISHES AND ACCOMPANIMENTS

Anchovy Fillets
Well-drained anchovy fillets are used to garnish pizzas and some salads.

Apple Slices (fried)
4 helpings

2 large cooking apples
sugar (optional)
flour for coating

salt and ground black pepper
fat for shallow frying

Peel and core the apples and cut each apple into 4 round slices. Discard the rounded ends. Sprinkle the slices with a little sugar if very sour. Season the flour with salt and pepper and coat the slices quickly before they discolour. Heat a little fat in a frying pan and fry the slices gently, turning once, until golden and just tender but not yet soft.

Use as a garnish for any fried or grilled pork dish.

Aspic Jelly
Makes 1 litre (approx)

1 litre brown stock (p25) **or**
  white stock (p26)
125ml white wine **or** 4 × 15ml spoons
  white wine and 4 × 15ml spoons
  dry sherry (for use with red meats
  or game)

2 × 15ml spoons white wine vinegar
40–50g gelatine
bouquet garni
whites and crushed shells of 2 eggs

Leave the stock to cool completely, if necessary. Skim off the fat. Put into a scalded enamel or tin-lined (not aluminium) pan with the rest of the ingredients. Stir with a scalded whisk until the gelatine softens; then bring almost to boiling point whisking all the time. Remove the whisk and leave for a few minutes. Let the liquid rise to the top of the pan, and remove from the heat.

Strain the crust and liquid very gently into a basin through muslin or a scalded jelly bag; do not break the crust as it acts as an extra filter. If it is cloudy, strain again to obtain a sparklingly clear jelly.

Note It is possible, but seldom economic or practical today, to make the jellied stock with 2 calf's feet or 500g cracked veal knuckles and 100g pork rind, instead of using the gelatine. The long, slow boiling of the large quantity of stock needed to make 1 litre of jellied stock is costly and time consuming.

Bacon Rashers

These can be fried or grilled and served as they are. The rinds can be removed before cooking if a plain garnish is required, but the rashers curl and look more decorative if the rinds are left on. The bacon should be cooked until crisp.

Uncooked rashers are used to line a terrine to form a 'jacket' for certain pâtés. They can also be wrapped round prunes, then cooked and served as a garnish for hot savoury dishes. Long, narrow strips of bacon can be wrapped in spirals round food such as sausages, and cooked with them. Small, narrow strips of bacon can be used to bard the surface of a piece of meat for a decorative effect.

Bacon Rolls (fried or grilled)

Cut the rinds off the rashers of streaky bacon, if required. Roll up each rasher. If frying, secure the outer end with a wooden toothpick inserted along each roll. If grilling, thread the rolls on short skewers. Put in a dry frying pan or under moderate grilling heat, and fry or grill for 3–5 minutes, turning frequently, until crisp.

Crumbled Cooked Bacon

Crisp bacon makes an excellent garnish if it is crumbled finely and evenly. It can then be scattered over any meat or vegetable dish, or combined with grated cheese, browned breadcrumbs or hard-boiled egg yolk.

Bread Croûtons

Cut bread slices into 5mm–1cm dice and fry in deep or shallow fat until golden-brown. Alternatively, butter a 5mm thick slice of crustless bread, cut into dice, and place, buttered side up, in a shallow tin. Bake in a moderate oven at 180°C, Gas 4, until golden-brown and crisp. Serve hot in a separate dish or sprinkle over any kind of soup.

Crescents of Fried Bread

Remove the crusts, and cut each slice of bread into crescents. Fry in shallow fat until golden-brown. Use to garnish blanquettes or fricassées and various fish dishes.

Fried Breadcrumbs

Heat a little butter in a frying pan or baking tin, add some soft white breadcrumbs, season to taste with salt and pepper, and either fry or bake until well browned. Drain well on soft kitchen paper. Serve hot with roast game.

Sippets or Toasted Croûtons

Toast thin slices of bread until crisp and golden. Cut into triangles, 'fingers' or small dice. Serve hot, separately, with thick soups.

Celery Curls

Wash a young tender stick of celery and cut it into 5cm lengths. Slice lengthways into very fine strips, or shred by drawing the pieces lengthways over a coarse grater or mandoline. Put the shreds into very cold water (iced if possible) and leave for 30 minutes. Drain the curls thoroughly, first in a colander and then on soft kitchen paper. Use chiefly for garnishing plates of cocktail snacks or for mixed hors d'oeuvres and salads. Can also garnish hot dishes containing celery.

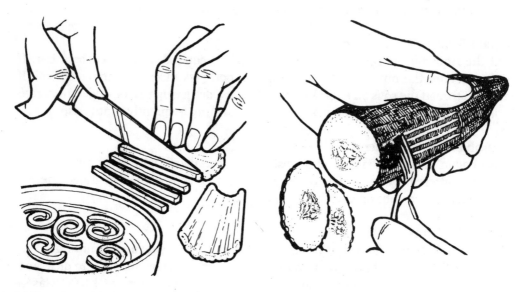

Making celery curls   *Scoring cucumber with a fork*

Cucumber (sliced)

Peel or score lengthways with the prongs of a fork or with a canelling knife. Slice thinly on to a plate. Sprinkle with salt and leave for 30 minutes with the plate slightly tilted. Drain off the liquid.

Thinly sliced cucumber, laid in overlapping lines, is used to garnish a great many cold dishes and salads. It is the classic garnish or accompaniment for cold poached salmon.

Cold Horseradish Cream

Makes 150ml (approx)

125ml double cream
2 × 15ml spoons fresh grated
  horseradish
1 × 15ml spoon white wine vinegar **or**
  lemon juice

1 × 10ml spoon caster sugar
½ × 2.5ml spoon made English mustard
salt and pepper

Whip the cream lightly until semi-stiff. Carefully fold in the other ingredients. Chill until ready to use.

Serve with beef.

Accompaniments for Curries

bombay duck
chapatti (small, flat cake of unleavened bread)
chilli sauce or paste
chopped salted nuts, usually almonds or peanuts
desiccated coconut
diced fresh pineapple
fresh or dried dates or other dried fruits (often mixed with chopped apple or other tart
    fruit dipped in lemon juice)
hard-boiled eggs cut in sections
lemon wedges
mango or other fruit chutney (a sharp-flavoured and a sweet chutney can be offered
    as alternatives)
okra
poppadoms (thin, crisp pancakes)
sliced banana dipped in lemon juice
sliced cucumber
sliced cucumber in soured cream
sliced tomato sprinkled with oil, vinegar, and chopped chives or mint
small strips of red and green sweet peppers
thick natural yoghurt or curd cheese
thin rings of finely sliced raw onion

Apart from rice, certain accompaniments for curries have become traditional and a selection of those listed here is usually served with curries in Europe, even though they may not form part of Eastern cuisines.

Serve them in small dishes or bowls, placed on the table so that diners can help themselves.

Most of these accompaniments are also served with Indonesian, Malaysian and other South East Asian curries and similar dishes such as *satés*; also with grain-based dishes such as the Indonesian *ryjsttavel* (rice table).

Dumplings *Basic recipe*
Makes 16 (approx)

100g self-raising flour   salt and pepper
50g shredded suet

Mix together the flour, suet, and seasoning to taste. Bind with enough cold water to make a soft smooth dough. With floured hands, divide the dough into 16 portions and roll into balls. Drop into simmering salted water, stock, soup or into a stew, and simmer for 15–20 minutes.

Serve with the liquid or with boiled meat, stew or vegetables.

VARIATIONS

Herb Dumplings

Add 25g finely grated onion and 1 × 2.5ml spoon chopped fresh herbs to the flour and suet.

Variations continue over

Meat Dumplings

Add 2 × 15ml spoons finely minced or puréed meat to the flour and fat, and bind the dumplings with the meat stock instead of water.

Soya Dumplings

Substitute 1 × 15ml spoon soya flour for 1 × 15ml flour, and add 1 × 2.5ml spoon dried mixed herbs.

Liver Dumplings

Makes 30–36

2 slices white bread
a little milk **or** water
500g calf **or** chicken liver
1 small onion
grated rind of ½ lemon
1 × 5ml spoon chopped parsley
salt and pepper

a pinch of grated nutmeg
2 × 15ml spoons plain flour
2 eggs
1.5 litres general hoousehold stock
   (p25) **or** water
50g butter (optional)

Cut the crusts off the bread and soak the bread in milk or water. Remove the skin and tubes from the liver and chop or mince the liver finely. Squeeze the bread as dry as possible and add it to the liver. Skin the onion and chop it finely. Add to the liver and bread with the lemon rind, parsley, seasoning, nutmeg, and flour. Mix together well. Beat the eggs until liquid, and mix with the other ingredients.
Form the mixture into quenelles as follows:

Dip 2 dessertspoons in hot water, and form oval shapes by filling each with the mixture. Cover the first spoonful with the second and scrape the loose mixture from the side.

Meanwhile, heat the stock or water to boiling point in a large pan and gently lower the quenelles into the liquid. Simmer for 15 minutes.

Serve in meat purées and other thick soups. Alternatively, drain, and serve with melted butter poured over them or with sautéed onions.

Note It is advisable to test the first dumpling before forming the others. If it crumbles, add a little more egg to the rest of the mixture. It is important not to have the mixture too stiff. It should be of a dropping consistency and not possible to form the dumplings with the hands.

Fairy Toast

Bake very thin slices of bread in a cool oven at 150°C, Gas 2, until golden and very crisp. Serve hot, separately, with most soups.

Melba Toast

Toast thin slices of white bread, then split carefully through the middle and toast the untoasted surfaces under a hot grill, or bake in a cool oven until crisp and golden. Serve with any hot soup.

Pulled Bread

Break apart a fresh French loaf, pull out the inside, and dry in a very cool oven until pale golden and crisp. Serve with soup or pâté.

Fleurons of Puff Pastry

Roll out the pastry, 5cm thick, and cut out circles with a 6cm cutter. Move the cutter half-way across the circle and cut it again, making a half moon and an almond shape. Lay the half moon shapes on a baking sheet, brush the tops with egg wash, and bake in a fairly hot oven at 200°C, Gas 6, for 8–10 minutes. Roll out and re-cut the almond shapes, or bake and serve them as small biscuits.

Use to garnish dishes in a white or creamy sauce.

Fried Onion Rings

Skin an onion and slice thinly. Dip the rings in egg white, or milk and flour, and fry in a little fat, until golden-brown and crisp. Add to a thick soup just before it is served or serve with grilled or fried meat dishes.

Raw Onion Rings

Thin rings of sliced, raw onion, sometimes lightly blanched, can garnish a number of salads and spicy savoury dishes.

Grated Hard Cheese

Serve separately with Minestrone (p38) and other mixed vegetable soups. Can also be sprinkled over the soup just before it is served. Finely grated Parmesan cheese is usually served with these soups.

Devilling Mustard for Cold Meats

Devilling Pepper

1 × 2.5ml spoon Cayenne pepper   1 × 5ml spoon ground black pepper
1 × 5ml spoon salt

Mustard
dry English mustard   water
Worcestershire sauce

Make up the devilling pepper by mixing all 3 ingredients thoroughly. Store in an airtight jar for use when required.

Make the mustard, using equal quantities of Worcestershire sauce and water. Season to taste with the devilling pepper.

Score cuts in any cooked cold joint of dark meat. Rub the mustard well into the cuts. Dot the meat with butter, then grill or bake, turning as required, until very hot and aromatic.

Serve at once with savoury or plain rice.

Note The devilling mustard is very good with marrow bones.

Making gherkin fans

Gherkin Fans
Make about 6 cuts from the top almost to the base of each gherkin, taking care not to cut right through the base. Spread the gherkins out carefully into fan shapes, with the base as a hinge.

Use to garnish cocktail snacks and salads.

Hard-boiled Egg
Crumbled or sieved hard-boiled egg yolk makes an attractive, colourful garnish sprinkled over hot or cold dishes. When sprinkled over a vegetable salad, it is known as a Mimosa salad.

It can be mixed with about half its quantity of fried breadcrumbs, crumbled, crisply fried bacon, grated hard cheese or finely chopped fresh parsley.

Whole hard-boiled eggs, sliced or cut into wedges, make an attractive garnish for many salads. Run cold water over the eggs as soon as their cooking time is up, and before shelling them, to prevent a dark line developing round the yolk.

Herbs
Fresh herbs, chopped and sprinkled over a dish, are one of the simplest yet most attractive garnishes. They should be chopped and put on the dish just before it is served, so that their aroma and flavour are at their strongest. No addition is needed except perhaps a few grains of salt or 1–2 drops of lemon juice. Chives are particularly good for their fresh sharp flavour. Use chopped basil, marjoram, mint, parsley or thyme. The feathery sprays of dill and fennel make a delicately attractive garnish.

Dried herbs have little appeal as a garnish and should not be substituted for fresh herbs.

Julienne Vegetables
Finely shred vegetables into strips about 2–3cm in length. Use as required.

Lemon, Orange or Grapefruit Baskets

Take a clean lemon, orange or grapefruit and, with a sharp knife, cut out almost a whole quarter segment. Leave a strip of rind wide enough for the handle (about 5mm) and then cut out the corresponding segment on the other side. Carefully cut out the pulp from the handle and then remove the pulp from the lower half.

Alternatively, proceed as for Tomato Lilies (p63); then cut out the flesh from each half. Fill with any cold savoury or sweet mixture which has lemon, orange or grapefruit in its flavouring.

Note For melon and pineapple baskets and containers, see p347.

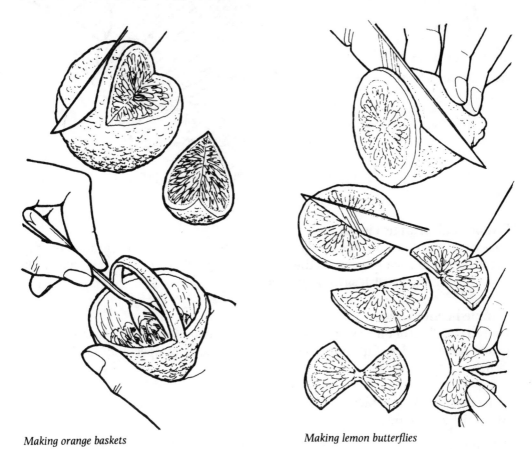

Making orange baskets *Making lemon butterflies*

Lemon Butterflies

Take a clean lemon and, with a sharp knife, cut it into thin slices, discarding the end pieces. Depending on the size of 'wings' required and the size of the lemon, cut the slices either into halves or quarters. Cut through the rind in the middle of each piece and gently pull into 2 wings without breaking into 2 pieces. A piece of parsley may be placed in the centre to represent the 'butterfly's' body.

Lemon 'butterflies' can garnish both savoury and sweet dishes. They are served on breadcrumbed, fried or grilled meats, such as veal escalopes, and on several fish dishes.

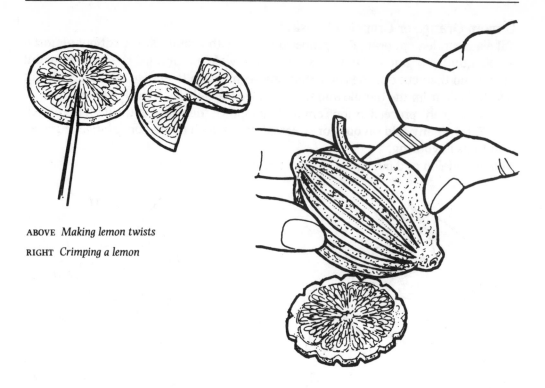

ABOVE *Making lemon twists*

RIGHT *Crimping a lemon*

Lemon and Orange Twists

Take a clean lemon, and slice thinly, discarding the end pieces. Cut through the rind in the middle of each piece up to the centre, then gently twist each half in opposite directions. Use to garnish savoury dishes.

Crimped Lemon Slices

Using a canelling or other knife, score from the top to the bottom of a whole lemon to give a serrated edge. Cut into slices. Use to garnish escalopes and other savoury dishes.

Macédoine of Vegetables

Makes 500g (approx)

1 turnip	200g shelled peas
100g carrot	750ml water
200g potatoes	1 × 5ml spoon salt
a few runner beans	3–4 × 15ml spoons butter
a few cauliflower florets	pepper

Prepare all the vegetables. Cut the turnip, carrot, and potatoes into 1cm dice. Cut the beans into 1cm diamond shapes. Bring the water to the boil, and add the salt. Put in the turnip and carrots, and boil for 3 minutes. Add the beans, and boil for another 3 minutes; then add the remaining vegetables. Boil for 5–10 minutes until the vegetables are tender but not broken. Drain thoroughly and toss in the butter. Season to taste, and use as a border or in small piles round a dish of meat. Serve hot.

Meat Glaze

This can be made from any strong, dark, meat stock made with lean meat and bones. It is strained, then boiled steadily until syrupy. When cooled, it should set like a rich, shiny, brown jelly. If the stock has been made without bones, gelatine is sometimes added to make it set, but it lacks the clarity of flavour of reduced bone stock and it does not keep as well.

Meat glaze is used to augment and improve the flavour of gravy and sauces, and it is sometimes added to vegetables for the same purpose. It can also be brushed over meats, such as roast beef or tongue, or over a galantine or pâté to improve its appearance, although it will not give it an aspic coating.

Meat Glaze (made with gelatine)
Makes 150ml (approx)

4 × 15ml spoons gelatine
125ml cold water
1 × 5ml spoon beef extract **or** yeast
  extract

a few grains onion salt (optional)
a few drops dry sherry (optional)
1–2 drops gravy browning (optional)

Using a metal spoon, stir the gelatine into the cold water in a heatproof container. Stand the container in a pan of hot water and stir until dissolved; then stir in the extract and chosen flavouring. Add gravy browning if a darker colour is wanted. Brush the glaze at once, while still hot, over cold meats, galantines or pâtés. If it starts to set in ridges or lumps while brushing, replace the bowl in hot water to keep it warm.

Note Do not store the glaze for more than 48 hours. Keep covered in a refrigerator.

Other Glazes

1) *Hot meat and poultry:* Brush very lightly with butter or oil just before serving.
2a) *Crackling on roast pork:* Brush with apricot glaze (p440) or smooth apricot jam 7–10 minutes before the end of the cooking time. Return to the oven to finish cooking and to set the glaze.
  b) Melted, cooled redcurrant jelly can be used in the same way; so can clear honey flavoured with lemon juice or mixed English mustard.
  c) Sieved fine-cut marmalade is sometimes used as a glaze and can be flavoured with whisky.
  d) A fruit syrup glaze, eg from canned fruit, has less colour than a jam glaze, but gives a clear crisp coating.
  e) If a non-sweet glaze is wanted for the crackling, brush with lightly salted butter or oil, with a little extra salt added. Raise the oven heat for a short time so that the crackling is, in effect, 'fried'.
3) *Frothing:* Dredge meat or poultry with flour and baste thoroughly with its cooking juices or with fat, shortly before the end of the cooking time. Return to the oven at a high heat to give a well-browned glazed appearance.
4) *Glazes for Pastry:* See p453.

Mint Sauce
Makes 125ml (approx)

4 × 15ml spoons chopped fresh mint
1 × 10ml spoon sugar

1 × 15ml spoon boiling water
2 × 15ml spoons vinegar

Put the mint into a sauce-boat. Sprinkle with the sugar. Add the boiling water, and stir until the sugar dissolves; then add the vinegar. Leave the sauce for 1–2 hours for the flavours to infuse.

Serve with roast lamb.

Mushroom Slices
Slice mushrooms thinly and fry gently in a little butter for a few minutes, until softened. Add to thick soups.

Parsley (fried)
Unless the parsley is very dirty, do not wash it before frying as parsley is difficult to dry and the moisture causes the fat to bubble and spit, which can be dangerous. Allow 4 good sprigs of parsley for each person and cut off the main stalks. Heat a pan of deep oil or fat (p10), place the parsley sprigs in the frying basket and put it into the pan. Remove from the pan immediately the hissing noise stops. Drain and serve.

Use to garnish grilled or fried fish and steaks.

Pasta
Pasta, such as macaroni and tagliatelli, can be added, in short lengths, to thin soups. Cook the pasta separately so that the soup is not clouded. Add the hot, drained pasta to the soup just before it is served.

Potatoes
Whole boiled potatoes are so often used to garnish fish dishes that they are called 'fish potatoes'. Boiled new potatoes topped with butter and chopped parsley are a common garnish for fish, white meats, poultry, and rabbit.

Potatoes Parisienne
4–6 helpings

1kg potatoes
25g butter
1 × 15ml spoon oil
½ × 2.5ml spoon salt
3 × 15ml spoons softened butter

3 × 15ml spoons finely chopped fresh
   mixed herbs (parsley, chives,
   tarragon)
pepper

Peel the potatoes and cut into small, round balls, using a potato ball scoop. Dry in a clean cloth. Heat the butter and oil in a frying pan large enough to hold all the potatoes in 1 layer. Put in the potatoes and coat evenly in the fat. Fry them gently until the potatoes are a light golden colour all over. Reduce the heat, sprinkle with the salt and cover the pan. Continue frying very gently for 12–15 minutes, shaking the pan frequently, until the potatoes are tender. Drain off the fat. Raise the heat and shake the potatoes in the pan until sizzling. Remove from the heat, add the softened butter and herbs, season well with pepper, and roll the potatoes round the pan until coated with herbs. Arrange round a meat dish or serve separately in a warmed dish. **Note** Carrots, turnips, and similar vegetables can be cooked in the same way as the potatoes.

Duchesse Potatoes
Makes 500g (approx)

500g old potatoes
25g butter **or** margarine
1 egg **or** 2 egg yolks
salt and pepper

a little grated nutmeg (optional)
butter **or** margarine for greasing
a little beaten egg for brushing
   (optional)

Prepare the potatoes, and boil or steam them. Drain thoroughly, and sieve. Beat in the fat and egg or egg yolks. Season to taste with salt and pepper and add the nutmeg, if used. Spoon the mixture into a piping bag fitted with a large rose nozzle and pipe rounds of potato on to a greased baking tray or round the edge of a heatproof serving dish. Brush with a little beaten egg, or leave plain for a white border. Bake in a fairly hot oven at 200°C, Gas 6, for about 15 minutes or until the potatoes are a good golden-brown. Transfer to a serving dish if necessary.

Alternatively, form the potato into a long, narrow roll with your hands and, using as little flour as possible, arrange the roll on a serving dish or baking sheet in the shape you want. Glaze it with beaten egg, if liked, and bake as above.

Use to garnish fish and meat dishes in sauces. A border of creamed potato is often used to garnish fish dishes in scallop shells and *au gratin* dishes.

Prawns
Cooked shelled prawns are often scattered over a hot fish dish or cold fish salad. Unshelled prawns may be arranged round the edge of a hot dish, eg, Sweet and Sour Prawns (p93). Use 1 unshelled prawn to garnish an individual dish such as fish cooked *au gratin* and presented in a scallop shell. Unshelled prawns also make an attractive garnish for a cold fish dish such as a prawn cocktail or a salad.

Many dishes for sole are garnished with prawns.

Rice
Dry boiled rice can be added to soup just before it is served, or it can be cooked in the soup. In this case, it should be added about 15 minutes before the end of the cooking time.

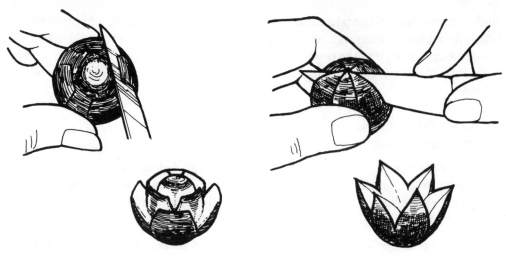

Making radish roses   *Making radish water lilies*

Radish Roses

Wash the radishes, cut off the stalks and a very thin slice of the root end. Cut thin petals from the root to the stem, taking care not to cut right through; then place the radishes in cold water (preferably iced) until they open out like roses.

Radish Water Lilies

Wash the radishes and cut off the stalks and the roots. Make 4–6 cuts from the root to the stem, taking care not to cut right through. Place in cold water (preferably iced) and leave until the radishes open out like lilies.

Sharp Sauce (hot or cold)

Makes 200ml (approx)

1 shallot
2 hard-boiled egg yolks
4 anchovies
1 × 2.5ml spoon made English mustard

1 × 10ml spoon vinegar
1 × 5ml spoon chopped capers
salt and pepper
caster sugar

For a Cold Sauce
125ml single cream

For a Hot Sauce
125ml thin gravy (p269)

Skin and chop the shallot finely. Rub the egg yolks through a sieve. Pound the shallot, egg yolks, and anchovies together to form a paste. Add the mustard, vinegar, and capers, and blend together.

For a cold sauce, whip the cream until it forms soft peaks, and fold it carefully into the other ingredients.

For a hot sauce, heat the gravy to boiling point and add to the other ingredients. Return to the pan and heat to just below boiling point.

Serve with roast or grilled meats, or grilled or baked fish.

Spiced Pears, Peaches or Apricots
4 helpings

2 (fresh or canned) pears **or** peaches
   or 8 apricots
25g butter

1 × 15ml spoon soft light brown sugar
½ × 2.5ml spoon ground cinnamon
¼ × 2.5ml spoon grated nutmeg

Peel the pears, if using fresh ones, cut in half and remove the cores. Halve fresh peaches or apricots and remove the stones. If using canned fruit, drain off the syrup. Arrange the fruit, cut side up, in a shallow tin. Place a small nut of butter in each hollow and sprinkle lightly with the brown sugar, cinnamon, and nutmeg. Bake in the oven for 5–10 minutes with the joint.

Serve with baked ham or with roast pork.

Tomatoes
Small, whole baked tomatoes, halved, baked or grilled tomatoes, or sliced, grilled or fried tomatoes are often used as a garnish for grilled and fried meat dishes, especially a mixed grill, kebabs or chops. They are also used to garnish grilled chicken or game birds.

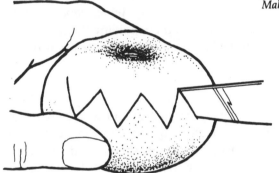

Making tomato lilies

Tomato Lilies
Take a clean, firm tomato and, using a sharp knife, halve it by making a series of zigzag cuts. When you have gone right round the tomato, gently pull the halves apart. Alternatively, use a potato peeler to make the zigzag cuts.

Besides being a decorative way of presenting tomatoes as part of a large salad, small cherry tomatoes made into 'lilies' can also garnish hot or cold sliced meats.

Watercress
Wash, dry, and break into small sprigs. Keep in a polythene bag in a refrigerator until needed. Add to thick soups, especially chicken or vegetable purée soups, just before serving. Use also to garnish cold poultry.

MAIN COURSES

FISH AND SHELLFISH

Preparing Fish

Except for small round fish, most fish caught by commercial fishermen are gutted at sea. Only fish such as herrings, mackerel, and red mullet have to be gutted by the fishmonger or in the kitchen.

Scaling Fish

If the scales are thick and coarse and need to be taken off, eg from sea bream, herring, or red mullet, this job must be done first. Lay the fish on soft kitchen paper to make cleaning up easier. With sharp scissors, cut off the fins; then, holding the tail, scrape both sides of the fish towards the head with the back of the knife. Rinse occasionally to remove the loose scales.

Cleaning Fish

Some small fish, like fresh sardines and whitebait, are cooked and served complete, but most have to be gutted. This simply means making a cut in the right place, removing the intestines and cleaning the cavity of blood, membrane, and black skin. At some seasons, the roe takes up a lot of the cavity space, and both hard and soft roes should be kept as they make good eating. After cleaning, lightly rinse the cut area with cold water and pat dry.

Flat fish: Place the fish, dark skin up, on soft kitchen paper and locate the gill cover, positioned just behind the head. Make a deep cut from the centre line of the fish out to the fin just at the rear of the gill opening. Remove the intestines, but if the fish is to be cooked whole, leave the roe in place. To complete the cleaning, trim the 'frill' fins and tail back to the body. You can cut off the heads of plaice and lemon sole, but the head of a Dover sole is normally left on.

Large round fish: Cut the belly lengthways, from the gills to a point about two-thirds the length of the fish from the head. Remove the entrails, saving the roe if required, rinse thoroughly, and pat dry.

Small round fish: Clean most white fish and trout as described above. It is usual to remove mackerel heads before preparing, which makes cleaning easier. Herring are different because the entrails to be disposed of are minimal. So just make a downward cut behind the gills and pull the head back; then clean the area before rinsing. Leave the roe in place if grilling or cooking whole.

Avocado Pears with Prawns (p.15)

Soured Cream Dip for Crudités (p.16)

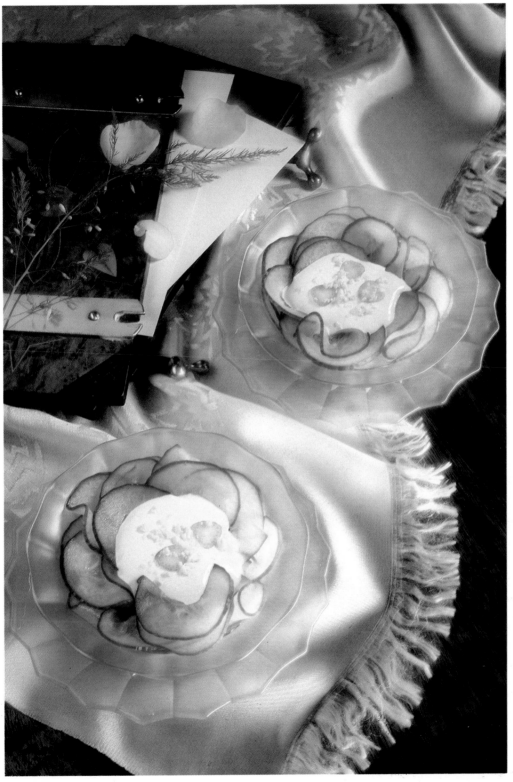

Cucumber in Soured Cream (p.16)

Brown Stock (p.25)

Chicken Broth (p.28)

Cock-a-Leekie (p.29)

Marinated Melon (p.20)

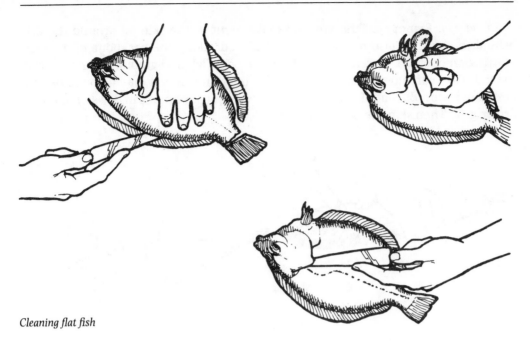

Cleaning flat fish

Skinning Fish

Removing the skin from a slippery fish can be tricky and it may be simpler to cook the fish first. Dover soles should have at least the dark skin removed because it is coarser than that of lemon sole or plaice.

Flat fish: Lay the fish on a wooden board, white side down. With a sharp knife or scissors cut the 'frill' fin and tail back to the fish, if not already done, and scrape the tail end until the skin starts to lift. It is then easy to free a piece of skin; now slip the thumb or the end of a round-bladed knife under it and loosen the skin from the flesh, working towards the head. When enough has been loosened like this, pull it off from the tail to head end. Repeat the process on the white side if required.

Work cautiously on soft-skinned fish, so as not to tear the flesh.

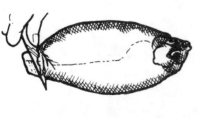

Skinning flat fish

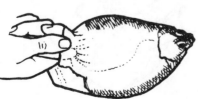

Round fish: Remove all the fins and make a cut in the skin all around the fish behind the head. It also helps to make a thin cut along the backbone of the fish. Starting on one side, loosen the skin from the belly flap and gradually pull towards the tail. Take care not to remove the flesh at the same time. It may help to hold the flesh down with the flat of a knife blade, and to dip your fingers in dry salt to give a firmer grip. Then skin the other side of the fish.

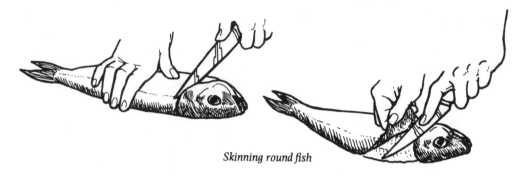

Skinning round fish

Filleting Fish

Filleting means removing the flesh in two or four whole slices from the head and central bone structure. The head, bones, and skin of white fish are the basis for natural fish stock and should not be thrown away. If the fishmonger is filleting the fish, always ask him for the bones and trimmings. You have paid for them, and are entitled to them.

Flat fish: Lay the fish on a flat surface with its tail towards you. With a sharp, pointed knife, make a cut down the centre of the back right down to the backbone, from just behind the head to the tail. Then, turning the knife so that it lies flat against the bones, cut the flesh free from the bone, using the bone structure as a guide. Cut and loosen the fillet all the way to the edge of the fish and lift free.

Repeat the process with the other top fillet; then turn the fish over, and remove the two fillets from the other side in the same way.

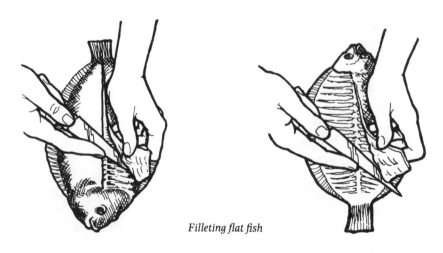

Filleting flat fish

Round fish: Lay the gutted fish on its side and cut round behind the head. Then insert the point of the knife into the back of the fish, just behind the head, and cut right down the backbone all the way to the tail. Keeping the knife flat, and pressed against the rib bones, slice the fillet free along the length of the fish. Turn the fish over and remove the second fillet in the same fashion. Rinse, check for bones, and cut off the fins.

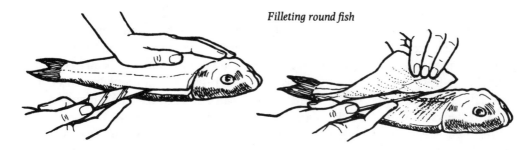

Filleting round fish

Boning Fish

Herring, mackerel or trout: Remove the head and cut the belly right to the tail. Open the fish flat, and set aside the roe; then place the fish, skin side up, on a board and press both sides of the backbone all the way down the fish. Turn over and pull the backbone clear, cut off end of bone and tail. Rinse and check for any remaining bones. For boning sprats, see p73.

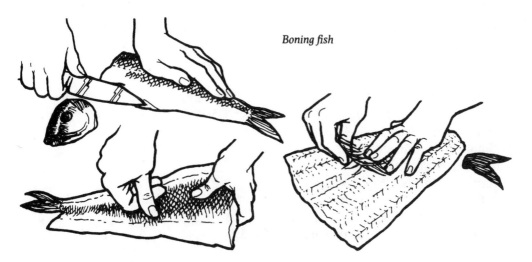

Boning fish

Other Specialized Preparations

Skate: Fish other than the two main types may require a more specialized filleting technique. For instance, when preparing skate or any of the other rays, only the 'wings' are used for cooking. The skate wings are cut from either side of the backbone and cooked whole or cut into portions, depending on size; skate bones are large and pliable, so there is no need to fillet the wings. However, the dark skin is a problem and the sharp hooks embedded in the skin should be carefully cut out after skinning. Skate carry a good deal of natural slime and this should be scrubbed off first; then nick out the flesh along the thick side, just under the skin, to provide a purchase point. Use a strong pair of pliers to grip the skin and pull it off in one piece.

Dogfish or tope: These members of the shark family present the same sort of problem. The fish has a soft boned (cartilaginous) structure so there is no need to fillet it. The skin, however, is very tough and needs to be removed before cooking. Gut the fish as for round fish and remove the fins and tail. To skin, follow the method described for eel (below).

Monkfish: Of the remaining soft-boned fish, the monkfish is the most common. Although an unattractive fish, the flesh is white, close-textured, and has much flavour. The large head should be removed where the definite shape of the tail commences. The meaty tail portion is easy to skin and cut into portions before cooking.

Eels: Both fresh-water and conger eels pose a slightly different problem in preparation. The larger sea-water species are difficult to skin, and are best cooked gutted and cut into steaks or fillets. The skin can then be removed after cooking.

Fresh-water eels, unlike other fish, live for a long time out of water. They are sold live, killed at the point of sale, and then skinned if necessary. If large, hang the eel up by a string round the 'neck', and make a cut through the skin all round the eel, just behind the head. Loosen the skin with a knife and pull the skin downwards over the tail. If small, just secure the head, and proceed in the same way. Clean the eel after skinning and cut into sections across the body before cooking. The very small young eels called elvers can, however, be cooked whole.

Cooking Times for Fish

Cooking times for fish depend largely on the thickness of whole fish or fillets and on whether they are frozen or stuffed, or on the size of small pieces or cubes. The following times should therefore be taken as a general guide only.

Baking White and Oily Fish

1) Whole large fish and cuts   *25–35 minutes per 500g*
   If frozen or stuffed   *35–45 minutes per 500g*
2) Small whole fish, steaks, and thick fillets   *15–20 minutes*
   If frozen or stuffed   *20–30 minutes*
3) Small thin fillets   *8–12 minutes*
   If frozen or stuffed   *15–20 minutes*
   If stuffed and rolled   *20–30 minutes*

Treat fish *wrapped in foil* like frozen or stuffed fish.

Frying and Grilling White and Oily Fish

1) Thin fillets and pieces, and kebab cubes
   Coated and deep fried   *5–10 minutes*
   Coated and shallow fried   *10–15 minutes*
   Uncoated and shallow fried   *5–10 minutes*
   Grilled   *7–8 minutes*
2) Steaks and thick whole fish or pieces
   Grilled   *10–15 minutes*

Poaching White and Oily Fish
1) Small thin fillets and portions   *3–5 minutes*
2) Medium and thick fillets   *6–10 minutes*
3) Steaks and thick portions and small whole fish *8–15 minutes*
4) 700g–1kg whole fish or cut   *8–15 minutes*
5) 1.8–2.6kg   *15–18 minutes*
6) Larger fish   *5–12 minutes per 500g*

These times are also suitable for smoked fish. Allow 5–8 minutes extra if the fish is frozen, stuffed or rolled. Allow 5–10 minutes extra for *steaming* fish.

Stewing White and Oily Fish
1) Cubes and thick small pieces of coarse fish *8–10 minutes*
2) Cubes and thick small pieces of soft fish   *4–7 minutes*

Casseroling White and Oily Fish
1) Thick whole fish, thick cuts and steaks   *20–30 minutes*
2) Thin whole fish, fillets   *15 minutes (approx)*

Allow 5–8 minutes extra if the fish is frozen.

Types of Fish
The supply of fish varies with weather conditions and the seasons. However, many white fish, and some others, are interchangeable in cooking; so if the particular fish you want is scarce or expensive, you can easily substitute another.

Bream (Red Fish, Ocean Perch)
This delicately flavoured white fish gives a deep fillet when large, or can be cooked whole when small. Cook like other white sea fish.

Fresh-water bream are deep-bodied, with a reddish tinge to the scales. Soak in salt water for 30–45 minutes; then cook as for other river fish.

Brill
In season all the year, but reaches its best condition from April to July. Good flavour, but not as firm as turbot. Soak well in salted water; then cook like carp, but handle the soft flesh carefully.

Carp
A fresh-water fish, at its best from November to January. There are several types, but the common carp (scales all over), and mirror carp (olive colour and isolated large scales) are most valued for the table. The fish should be cleaned, soaked in salt water, and rinsed in vinegar and water before cooking. Cook as for other river fish.

Catfish (Wolf-fish, Rock-fish)
The wolf-fish, a variety of catfish, commonly sold in the UK under the name of rock-fish, has a large head, with strong jaws and striped body. The flesh is pinkish white with a small amount of bone. Bake or grill with a sprinkling of lemon juice.

Cod

Cod is available everywhere, wet or frozen. Smoked fillets and roe are also popular. Cod has firm, flaky white flesh, and can be cooked in all the accepted ways for white fish. Take care not to overcook.

Coley (Saithe)

A close relation of cod but has darker coloured skin and flesh. In cooking, the fish turns white and can be used as an alternative to cod and haddock. Available everywhere, wet or frozen.

Dab

A smaller member of the plaice family, in season all year round. Gut, trim fins, and fry or grill whole. Larger dabs can be cooked like plaice.

Dogfish (Huss, Flake, Tope)

Available all the year. It is most popular in batter and deep fried but is even better grilled, baked or in kebabs, soups, and fish stock, because of its firm flesh.

Eel

Fresh-water eels are olive in colour, with very rich, oily flesh. Though always in season, they are less good in summer. Available live from specialist fishmongers, also cooked and jellied. Because of their fat content, eels are excellent smoked for eating raw. Unsmoked eels are poached and sauced, baked or grilled, and are an essential ingredient in continental fish hot-pots, chowders, and cotriades.

Conger, a sea-water fish, can grow up to 3 metres in length. Dark grey in colour, the medium-sized ones are best for eating. Can be used in recipes for monkfish or dogfish, or instead of freshwater eels in most recipes.

Grey Mullet

Best from July to February. Clean and soak in several changes of salt water before cooking. Cook like mackerel or red mullet.

Gudgeon

Gut the fish and remove gills, dip in egg and breadcrumbs and deepfry. Serve whole, 3–4 per person depending on size.

Gurnet (Gurnard)

These colourful fish can be grey, red or yellow, depending on the type. They are easily identified by their large angular bony heads. The red-coloured fish is the best for eating, and is available at good fishmongers. Most seasonable from July to April. Cook whole or filleted. Try poaching in court bouillon and serving cold with mayonnaise.

Haddock

In season all year round, but best from November to February. Available everywhere, wet or frozen. Cook wet fish gently to appreciate its sweet, fresh flavour.

Finnan haddock are either split or left on the bone; they are lightly cold smoked. They have a delicious, mild flavour. *Smoked haddock cutlets* (boned), unlike finnan haddock, have been dyed and quite heavily smoked. *Arbroath smokies* are headless and hot smoked, so can be eaten cold or heated in the oven.

Poach smoked fish in half milk and half water, and serve with a generous pat of plain or savoury butter.

Hake

This fish belongs to the same family as haddock and cod, but it has a longer, slimmer shape. In best condition from June to January when it is quite widely available from fishmongers, especially those in the west and south western areas of the country.

Frozen hake usually comes from South Atlantic fishing grounds, and has a drier, more fibrous texture than the silver hake from more northerly waters.

Halibut

A very large flat fish, rich in vitamins A and D. Widely available from fishmongers as whole fish (up to 1.5kg, it is called chicken halibut) or in steaks from larger fish. The pre-sawn frozen steaks of Pacific halibut make a good alternative to the Atlantic ones. Both types are available fresh and frozen.

Greenland halibut is grey-brown with rather more watery flesh than the Atlantic or Pacific fish. This has led to it being called 'mock' halibut.

Herring

This excellent fish is found in many guises, and it also provides both hard and soft roes. It can be split, boned, and cold smoked to produce a *kipper* Most kippers are now in fact, salted and dyed to give a pleasant traditional taste and tint. (Uncoloured kippers are also available though.) Kippers are also sold as cutlets, with the head and backbone removed, or as fillets.

Bloaters are ungutted herrings lightly smoked. They must be cooked as soon as they are purchased. *Buckling* are the same fish hot smoked, and can be used as an alternative to smoked trout without further cooking.

Red herrings are heavily smoked and salted, but are rarely seen in Britain, most of them being exported. They need long soaking before cooking.

Herrings are also available in various sauces and continental styles. *Matjes herrings* are preserved in a light brine, *Bismarck herrings* in a marinade of white wine and vinegar with onions and juniper berries, and the most popular preserved herrings, *rollmops*, are packed with gherkins and onions in a vinegar marinade.

Herrings are oily fish and a little mustard or horseradish sauce helps to offset the richness. They can be grilled, baked or fried without adding fat.

Ling

This is another member of the cod family, with a distinctive elongated body and an underchin barbel. Fairly widely available, and in best condition from September to May. Cook as for other white fish.

Mackerel

Available everywhere wet or frozen; at its best in the winter and spring. Grill, souse, or stuff and bake *en papillote*.

Smoked mackerel is also widely available either as whole fish or fillets; it is popular in salads and as a pâté. It is available hot smoked and therefore cooked and ready to eat, or cold smoked and vacuum packed.

Kippered mackerel is cold smoked and needs cooking, like kippers. Like herring, the flesh is savoury and rich, so horseradish, mustard or some other piquant condiment or side dish should be served with the fish.

Megrim

Closely related to brill and turbot. Cook in the same ways.

Monkfish

As a rule only the tail of this strange-looking fish is seen on the fishmonger's slab. The firm white meat is delicious and can be cooked in all the ways suggested for halibut or turbot; it is excellent eaten either hot or cold.

Perch

A fresh-water fish, olive-green with vertical black stripes. Has a large spiny dorsal fin with a sting. Good eating quality although bony. Fillet and poach in court bouillon; then remove skin and scales. Alternatively, fillet, skin, and cook *à la meunière*.

Pike

A large, fierce fresh-water fish. Medium-sized fish of up to 3kg are best for cooking. Gut and remove the head, tail, and fins; then soak for 5–6 hours in salt water. Rinse in vinegar before poaching in court bouillon or fish stock. The flesh breaks easily, making it good for quenelles (p87). Alternatively, grill long fillets with bacon.

Plaice

Easily recognized flat fish with dark coloured upperside dotted with orange spots. Widely available as whole fish or fillets, wet or frozen; when frozen, plaice are often sold ready-prepared in breadcrumbs or sauced. In best condition from May to January. The flesh is white and distinctive in flavour; it should not be overcooked. Frozen prepared fish or fillets are suitable for deep or shallow frying, steaming or poaching, and for baked dishes with a sauce.

Salmon

For appearance and flavour, the salmon is the king of all fish. Its deep red flesh turns pink when cooked. Frozen Pacific salmon is less expensive than European fresh salmon, and with careful defrosting and cooking makes an attractive, more economical alternative. Poach salmon whole in court bouillon, cook *en papillote*; poach, grill or fry steaks or cutlets cut across the fish.

Smoked salmon is the cold smoked fillet or flank of the fish, either Atlantic or Pacific, the latter being cheaper. Slice very thinly and serve with lemon wedges, Cayenne pepper, and brown bread and butter. Alternatively, form thicker slices into cornets and secure with cocktail sticks, if necessary. Smoked salmon can also be served on canapés.

Canned salmon, containing Pacific fish, is a useful standby, but because the fish is already cooked, its culinary uses are restricted.

Salmon Trout (Sea Trout)

Since it has the colour of salmon and the texture of trout, the salmon trout has the attributes of both fish, and can truly be called the finest fresh-water fish. At its best in spring and summer, and available from most good fishmongers. When *rainbow trout* (see trout) are sea-farmed and fed on shellfish, the flesh turns pink, making an acceptable, cheaper alternative to true salmon trout.

Sardines

Fresh sardines make a stylish first course when grilled or floured and shallow fried. There is no need to gut or head the fish. Cook through and serve 4–5 fish per person with lemon wedges.

Canned small sardines in oil from Spain, Portugal or France are a delicacy in their own right. The best quality packs use good olive oil, and the sardines are allowed to mature in the can. Serve with lemon and a crisp green salad or as part of a mixed hors d'oeuvre platter.

Skate

Only the wings are eaten, the best part being the fleshier centre cut. The flesh is firm and delicate with a simple, soft bone formation. It is available everywhere from fishmongers. Portions of the wing can be deep or shallow fried, or used in the classic Skate in Black Butter (p89).

Sole (Dover)

The finest flat fish of all. The 'tear drop' shape of this fish differentiates it from distant relations like *lemon sole.* Available everywhere, wet or frozen, but always relatively expensive. Has firm white flesh, with a succulent flavour, easy to separate from bones. Remove the dark skin; then grill, cook *à la meunière*, or use in any of the recipes on pp90–91.

Sole (Lemon)

Widely available wet and frozen, comes between Dover sole and plaice in flesh, texture, and flavour, and is a pleasant alternative to either. Fry or poach fillets, or cook whole to retain the natural juices.

Sprats

Bright little silvery fish widely available during the winter months. Can be grilled, deep-fried or home-smoked. Allow 500g for 3 portions. Cut off the head and split the fish by running the thumbnail down the belly to the tail. Open out and pull the backbone out starting at the head end.

Commercially smoked sprats are also available and make a good first course.

Brisling are small sprats canned and ready to serve in the same way as sardines.

Trout (Rainbow)

With the advance of modern fish farming, trout is now as popular as some of the better-known sea fish. It can be cooked plainly *à la meunière*, yet also lends itself well to more elaborate cooking and to various sauces. Gut and remove the gills before cooking. Grilled, baked (especially *en papillote*), poached, or fried *à la meunière*, the fish is easy to bone, and with good presentation adds style to any meal.

Turbot

A large flat fish, available most of the year. Rated next to Dover sole for quality of flesh. Large fish must be sliced into cutlets, but the smaller (chicken turbot) fish can be foil-wrapped and cooked whole with butter and seasoning. Serve with a savoury herb butter or a shrimp sauce, or serve grilled cutlets with Maître d'Hôtel butter (p564) or Béarnaise sauce (p252).

Whitebait

These are the fry (young fish) of herring and sprats. Certainly the smallest fish eaten, but with a long gastronomic history and always a fashionable dish. Caught in several large estuaries round British coasts, the bulk of the catch is now frozen because the little fish deteriorate quickly. They should be floured and deep fried whole.

Whiting

Another member of the great cod family. The flesh is white, flaky, very soft, and tender. Available everywhere, the gutted and headed fish can be egg and bread-crumbed before frying. Opened and with the backbone removed, the whiting can be grilled or poached in milk with seasoning and is an easily digested dish suitable for invalids.

Blue whiting are slimmer and less well fleshed than the true whiting; these fish are caught in deep water. The flesh is darker though quite pleasant when cooked. Cut off the head, gut, and skin; then fry. As the fish are small, allow 2–3 per portion.

Types of Shellfish

Cockle

Rarely sold uncooked. However, if supplies are available, keep alive for 24 hours in sea water to clear sand from the intestine, and wash in several changes of water; then boil in salt water for 5–6 minutes until the shells open. Cool, and discard the shells; eat with salad or in a mixed fish dish.

Shelled cockle meat is quite widely available loose or in frozen packs, and canned or bottled. Fresh or frozen cockles are better than canned or bottled ones for cooked dishes because they are vinegar-free. Wash well before cooking to remove any particles of grit.

Crab

Available live, cooked or as frozen crabmeat, crabs are plentiful. Choose a crab by weight rather than size, and if bought ready-cooked make sure that the shell is fresh and dry, and the legs and claws tight against the body.

British crabs produce white meat from the claws and legs and spicy brown meat from inside the main shell. Frozen or canned crab packs usually contain foreign *Pacific King* crab or the smaller *Atlantic Queen* crab. Both are closer to spider crabs which have large legs containing good white meat, but have very little meat in the body.

Crabmeat has many uses from conventional salad dishes to seafood flans, stuffings, and soups. The brown meat (the liver and roe) of the female is particularly good as a flavouring for sauces or savoury butters.

To cook a live crab: Choose a good-sized heavy crab and kill it either by piercing it through the shell above the mouth, or by drowning it in tepid fresh water for 2 hours. It is wise to kill the crab before boiling it to prevent water entering the body.

Place in a large pan of boiling water containing 2 × 15ml spoons of salt per litre. Boil for 3 minutes, then lower the heat and simmer for a further 25 minutes; remove and leave to cool.

To pick and dress a cooked crab: Turn the crab on its back. Male crabs have a slim flap on the underside, the females have a broader one. Twist off the legs and claws. Press firmly on the 'crown' where the legs join the body, and remove in one piece. Discard the grey finger-like gills and pick out the meat. Remove the meat from the main shell, keeping dark meat and pink coral separate from the white meat. Crack the claws and legs with nutcrackers or a clean hammer, and pick out the white meat. The crab should give 25–30% of its total cooked weight in meat; males usually give more white meat.

Scrub and dry the main shell inside and out, and break off the undershell to the dark line around the perimeter. Flake the white meat from the legs and claws. Cream together the darker meat, liver and coral, and add 2 × 15ml spoons of fresh brown breadcrumbs and a little seasoning. Mix thoroughly and fill both ends of the shell. Place the white meat in the centre.

Lobster

Available all year round, the most popular sizes range between 500g and 1.5kg in weight. When live they should feel heavy for their size and be lively when picked up. The dark shells turn bright red on being cooked; if buying a ready-cooked lobster look for a dry, firm shell and tightly curled tail. Lobsters are often dressed and eaten cold with mayonnaise, but there are also many superb hot lobster dishes; many of them call for the meat to be prepared, then returned to the shell for presentation.

To boil a lobster: There are several methods of cooking a live lobster. The simplest is to half-fill a suitably sized pan with salt water (2 × 15ml spoons salt per litre), bring the water to the boil and drop the lobster in quickly. Place a lid on the pan and weight it down; then lower the heat to keep the water just under boiling point. Cook for 15–20 minutes, depending on the lobster's size.

An alternative method is to put the live lobster into cool, salted water or court bouillon, and bring to the boil, then to cook as described. Perhaps a less harrowing method is to drown the lobster by leaving it in tepid fresh water for 2–3 hours before cooking.

After cooking, allow the lobster to cool, then place on a cutting board with the tail spread behind. Take a large, sharp, broad-bladed knife and insert the point in the

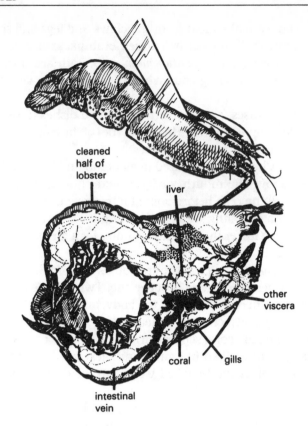

cleaned
half of
lobster

liver

other
viscera

coral   gills

intestinal
vein

middle of the head. Lower the blade of the knife and cut through the shell, along the centre line, splitting the shellfish into 2 equal parts. Pull out the intestinal tract that runs from the head to the tail and clear out the head cavity. Remove the sponge-like gills also. The dark, mustard-coloured meat is the liver and is good for flavouring sauces. The pink coral sometimes found in the female is also valuable for lobster butter, a luxurious accompaniment for grilled fish.

To dress a lobster to eat cold: Place the half lobster, cut side up, on a suitable plate. Crack the claws and arrange them round the half-shell. (Offer a suitable thin fork or lobster pick to get all the meat out of them.) Garnish the half lobster by filling the head cavity with Russian salad (p23) and serve chilled with mayonnaise and salad. A half lobster is generally thought enough for a single portion as a first course.

Mussels

These under-valued, black bivalve molluscs are abundant around northern European coastlines. If you collect them personally, make sure that it is in a pure water area. They are of better quality when there is an 'R' in the month. Mussels are farmed commercially in carefully selected sea-water areas. Buy from a reliable dealer, and make sure that the mussels have tightly closed shells. This shows that they are alive. Mussel meat can also be bought frozen, bottled or canned; the frozen ones are better for cooked and mixed seafood dishes since they have not been preserved in salt or vinegar. When adding any cooked shellfish, but particularly mussels, to a recipe, cook for as short a time as possible, to avoid making them tough.

To prepare mussels: Wash in several changes of clean water; then scrape off the byssus threads (the beard), found near the hinge of the two shells, using a sharp knife; these are the anchors which hold the shellfish to the rocks. Check again that each mussel is tightly shut before cooking. For the basic cooking, follow the Moules Marinière recipe (p93) as it produces a bonus of delicious mussel liquor.

Oysters

Among several types available, the native oyster is the most highly prized. An oyster is enclosed by one concave and one flat shell, roughly circular and greyish-brown. Portuguese and Pacific oysters are cheaper, and easily distinguished by their deeper, longer, and more irregular shaped shells.

All oysters are farmed. This ensures that the shellfish are pure, a vital point since they are most often eaten raw. Native oysters can be bought fresh from specialist fishmongers when there is an 'R' in the month; like any shellfish they must be inspected to ensure that the shells are tightly closed.

To open, use a proper oyster knife; work the blade between the shells and cut the ligament hinge which keeps the shells shut. Pass the knife under the oyster to free it from the shell. Serve on the deep half shell (6–12 per portion) on a bed of crushed ice, with lemon wedges and brown bread and butter.

To keep oysters alive for up to 24 hours before opening, put them in a wet sack and keep in a cool, dark place.

Prawns

For cocktails, salads, and cold dishes, shell-on or peeled cold-water prawns are best. Warm-water prawns are more suited to cooked dishes and curries.

Nearly all prawns sold in Britain, whether shell-on or peeled, are imported ready-cooked; they are sold widely, fresh or in frozen packs. Always allow a reasonable defrosting time; never defrost quickly in water. The best method is to sprinkle the prawns lightly with salt and then to defrost them on a plate overnight in a refrigerator.

King Prawns: These larger prawns come from various warm water fishing areas round the world. All supplies in Britain are frozen raw, headless, but with the shells. Packs of 1kg contain 16–20 prawns, depending on size. King prawns should be marinated before cooking, and their size and texture then make them well suited to grilling or barbecuing. If the prawns are wanted for a cold dish, poach in fish stock and allow to cool in the liquid. Chill well before serving.

Crystal Prawns: These come from Middle East or Far East fishing grounds. The large whole prawns are sold ready-cooked, and are pink to orange in colour. Defrost overnight in a refrigerator.

Scallops

When buying scallps on the half shell, always ask for the deep shells to hold the many 'scalloped' cooked fish dishes, eg Coquilles St Jacques (p94).

Large scallops can be bought frozen all year round, but fresh only from November to March. The scallop is very tender, with a high natural liquid content, and great care should be taken when cooking. Just let the shellfish turn from translucent to solid white over a low heat in a little white wine or seasoned milk; if they must be heated in a sauce, add them at the last possible moment to prevent toughening and shrinkage.

Queen Scallops: These smaller versions are usually sold shelled and frozen. Cook in the same way as larger scallops, using minimal heat. Queen scallops are excellent dipped in batter or egg and breadcrumbs, and briefly deep fried.

Scampi

These are often referred to as Dublin Bay Prawns. They are closely related to lobster and crawfish, but do not change colour when cooked. Widely distributed from Iceland to the Mediterranean, they are popular everywhere.

Scampi (from Italian *scampo*) is, properly, the term for the tail meat from shellfish de-headed at sea, and is most often fried. However, the whole shellfish can be poached, and then served cold or grilled.

Scampi flesh is sweet and tender, but deteriorates quickly, so most supplies are frozen. Like scallops, scampi should be cooked briefly. In dishes using a sauce, the defrosted shellfish should be added at the last moment to prevent overcooking.

Shrimps

Smaller and rounder-bodied than prawns, shrimps are caught in shallow sandy water and turn from grey to pinkish-brown when cooked in salted water. They must be boiled alive to have the characteristic springy curled shape.

Peeled shrimps have a particularly good and sweet shellfish flavour, and are used in mixed sea-food dishes, as stuffings or fillings, in sauces, and as a garnish.

Fresh shell-on shrimps are widely available and so are frozen and potted shrimps.

Pink Shrimps: These are smaller relatives of a certain type of prawn. Slim in body like cold-water prawns but the size of brown shrimps, they are caught in the same areas, and turn pink when boiled. Very colourful for display. Use like brown shrimps.

Squid (Ink Fish, Calamares)

Before cooking, cut off the heads (eyes) and tentacles, remove the transparent central 'bone' and pull out the dark coloured ink sac at the same time. Wash and pull off any visible outer skin.

Squid can be stuffed or thinly sliced (body and tentacles), coated, and deep fried. Alternatively, slice and poach in a little white wine or seasoned milk, chill and mix with peeled prawns, cockles, mussels, and white crabmeat as a seafood salad.

Whelks and Winkles

Whelks are boiled in salt water and shelled before sale. The firm, cream-coloured flesh can be eaten with vinegar or in a mixed seafood hors d'oeuvre. It can also be minced or diced for adding to stuffings, sauces, and soups.

The whelk and winkle are the only shellfish which need steady boiling in salted water for 5–10 minutes. Wash in several changes of fresh water beforehand, and allow the shellfish to cool in the boiling liquid.

The winkle has a flat black cover to the shell opening and this should be discarded before removing the shellfish entire with a pin or needle. They can make an interesting contribution to a mixed shellfish platter.

Basic Recipes for Cooking Fish

In the following recipes the fish are assumed to be gutted and filleted where required.

Court Bouillon (for salmon, salmon trout, and other whole fish)

water
500ml dry white wine **or** dry cider to
   each litre water
2 × 15ml spoons white wine vinegar to
   each litre water
2 large carrots

2 large onions
2–3 sticks celery
parsley stalks
1 bouquet garni to each litre water
a few peppercorns
salt and pepper

Put the liquids in a large pan. Slice the carrots and onions, chop the celery, and crush the parsley stalks. Add to the liquid with the remaining ingredients. Simmer for 30 minutes, leave to cool, then strain and use as required.

Basic Recipe for Grilling Fish

fish fillets
salt and pepper
1 × 5ml spoon chopped gherkins
   (optional)
1 × 5ml spoon chopped capers
   (optional)

2 × 10ml spoons salad oil
1 × 10ml spoon white wine vinegar **or**
   lemon juice

Garnish
chopped parsley

Remove the rack of the grill pan. Wipe the fish and season it with salt and pepper. Mix the gherkins and capers, if used, with the oil and vinegar. Heat the grill to give a medium cooking heat. Snip or slash the skin of the fish to prevent curling, if necessary. Lay it in the bottom of the grill pan, skin side up. Pour most of the liquid mixture over it. Grill, basting frequently. Turn the fish over and pour the remaining liquid over it. Grill for about another 5 minutes. Calculate the total grilling time from the table on p68. Sprinkle with chopped parsley and serve immediately.

Note Use gherkins and capers for fairly large thick fillets and for most river fish. Thin, delicately flavoured fillets can be grilled with just a sprinkling of lemon juice instead of vinegar.

Basic Recipe for Poaching Fish

1 small whole fish **or** fillets   court bouillon (p79)
juice of ½ lemon

Garnish
lemon wedges   parsley sprigs

Allow 100–150g fish for each helping. Clean a whole fish inside, rinse the cavity and wipe both inside and outside dry. Cut off the fins. Wipe fillets, if used. Sprinkle the fish or fillets with a little lemon juice.

Put the fish into a large, deep frying pan, and add enough court bouillon to cover 1–2cm of the pan depth when the fish is in it. Cover with a spatterproof lid or a plate, and poach gently, with the liquid barely shivering. Calculate the cooking time from the table on p69. Lift out the cooked fish gently with a broad slice, drain, and slide it on to a warmed serving dish. Garnish with lemon wedges and parsley sprigs.

Steaming Fish

This is a good way to cook fish without fat, yet without making it too moist. It also avoids any risk of overcooking small thin fillets. It is useful for those on a light diet, or for precooking fish which will be finished in a sauce or served cold.

Take a plate which fits neatly on top of a saucepan, half fill the pan with water and heat until it boils; then reduce the heat so that the water only simmers. Place the plate on the saucepan and, if wished, warm a knob of butter on the plate until it melts, and add just a little water, wine, milk or lemon juice. Add any seasoning required; then put the prepared fish fillet on the plate and cover with another plate. See the table on p69 for cooking times. Serve with a little of the liquid.

Basic Recipe for Baking Fish

1 whole fish   water **or** fish stock (p26) (optional)
salt and pepper   50g butter
butter for greasing

Wash the cleaned fish inside and out and pat dry. Season with salt and pepper and place in a well-greased baking dish. Add enough water or stock to cover 5mm of the dish, if desired. Dot with small pieces of butter. Cover loosely with greased paper and bake in a fairly hot oven at 190°C, Gas 5. Calculate the cooking time from the table on p68.

Basic Recipe for Deep Frying Fish in Batter

fish fillets
flour for coating

salt and pepper
oil **or** fat for deep frying

Batter
100g plain flour
$\frac{1}{2} \times 2.5$ml spoon salt

1 egg
125ml milk

Make the batter first. Sift the flour and salt into a bowl. Make a well in the centre of the flour and add the egg and a little of the milk. Gradually work in the flour from the sides, then beat until smooth. Stir in the rest of the milk.

Cut the fish into serving portions, if required; the pieces should all be of a similar size. Season the flour with salt and pepper. Dry the pieces of fish well and coat in the flour. Stir the batter well and dip the pieces of fish into it. Heat the oil or fat (p10) and fry until golden-brown. Drain on soft kitchen paper and serve immediately.
Note Do not use a basket when frying fish in batter as it will stick. Use a perforated spoon or broad slice to lift it out.

For Fish and Chips use the basic recipe above with any suitable fish, eg cod, haddock or plaice, and the recipe for potato chips on p299.

Basic Recipe for Shallow Frying Fish

small whole fish **or** fish fillets
flour for coating
salt and pepper

1 egg
dry white breadcrumbs for coating
fat for shallow frying

Garnish
lemon wedges

Cut the fish into serving portions, if required. Season the flour with salt and pepper and beat the egg lightly. Coat the fish with flour, then dip in the egg, and coat with breadcrumbs. Heat the fat in a frying pan and fry the fish, turning once, for the time given in the table on p68, until the coating is golden-brown. Serve immediately with lemon wedges.
Note Fry the flesh side of fillets first, and the skin side afterwards.

Basic Recipe for Frying Fish (à la meunière)

small whole fish **or** fish fillets
flour for coating
salt and pepper

50g butter
1×10ml spoon chopped parsley
juice of $\frac{1}{2}$ lemon

Trim off the fins if necessary, rinse the fish, and dry well with soft kitchen paper. Season the flour with salt and pepper and coat the fish with the flour. Heat the butter in a frying pan. When foaming, place the fish in the pan. Cook gently for the time given in the table on p68, turning once. When the fish is golden-brown and cooked through, arrange on a serving dish and keep hot. Season the butter left in the pan and heat until it is nut-brown. Add the parsley and lemon juice, pour over the fish, and serve at once.

Recipes for Sea and River Fish

Brill and Potato Mornay
6 helpings

800g potatoes
75g butter
600g brill fillets
salt and pepper

juice of 1 lemon
500ml cheese sauce (p237)
50g Cheddar cheese

Boil the potatoes in their skins and keep them hot. Use a little of the butter to grease a shallow oven-to-table baking dish and a sheet of greaseproof paper. Lay the fish in the buttered dish, season with salt and pepper, dot with butter, and sprinkle with lemon juice. Cover the dish with the sheet of buttered greaseproof paper and bake in a moderate oven at 180°C, Gas 4, for 15 minutes. Meanwhile, make the cheese sauce. Peel the potatoes, cut into rounds, and cover the fish with them in a neat pattern. Pour the cheese sauce over the fish, then grate the cheese, and sprinkle it evenly on top. Brown under the grill.

Golden Grilled Cod
4 helpings

4 cod cutlets **or** steaks (2cm thick
 approx)

margarine for greasing

Topping
50g mild Cheddar **or** Gruyère cheese
25g soft margarine

2×15ml spoons milk (optional)
salt and pepper

Garnish
grilled tomatoes

watercress sprigs

Trim and rinse the fish and pat dry. Place the fish in a greased shallow flameproof dish and grill under moderate heat for 2–3 minutes on one side only. Meanwhile, grate the cheese and cream the margarine with it. Work in the milk, a few drops at a time, if used, and season to taste.

Turn the fish over, spread the topping on the uncooked side, and return to the grill. Reduce the heat slightly and cook for 10–12 minutes until the fish is cooked through and the topping is golden-brown. Serve garnished with grilled halved tomatoes and watercress sprigs.

Cod à la Maître d'Hôtel
5–6 helpings

800g cod fillets (cold leftovers can be used)
100g butter
2 × 15ml spoons chopped onion

1 × 15ml spoon chopped parsley
juice of ½ lemon
salt and pepper

Poach the cod if required, and remove the skin when cool. Separate the flesh into large flakes. Melt the butter in a saucepan, add the onion, and fry for 2–3 minutes without browning. Add the fish and sprinkle it with the chopped parsley, lemon juice, and a good pinch of salt and pepper. Cook over low heat for 5 minutes, stirring gently all the time.

Serve with boiled potatoes.

Fish Mousse
4 helpings

50g onion
1 celery stick
250ml milk
1 bay leaf
3–4 peppercorns
500g haddock **or** cod fillets
25g butter

25g flour
grated rind and juice of ½ lemon
1 × 15ml spoon chopped parsley
salt and pepper
1 × 10ml spoon gelatine
2 × 15ml spoons water
125ml double cream

Garnish
125ml aspic jelly
watercress leaves

thin strips of lemon rind

Slice the onion and celery thickly. Put into a pan with the milk, bay leaf, peppercorns and fish. Bring to the boil slowly, cover, and draw off the heat for 10 minutes. Lift out the fish, remove any skin or bones, and flake the flesh. Strain the milk.

Melt the butter, stir in the flour, and cook for 1–2 minutes. Add the flavoured milk gradually. Bring to the boil and cook for 1–2 minutes, stirring all the time. Remove from the heat and stir in the flaked fish, lemon rind and juice, chopped parsley, and a generous amount of salt and pepper.

Soften the gelatine in the water in a small heatproof basin. Stand the basin in a pan of hot water and stir until it has dissolved. Add a little of the fish mixture, stir, then mix into the rest. Stir in well. Put in a cool place.

When it is on the point of setting, whip the cream until it forms soft peaks and fold in until evenly distributed. Put into an 800ml dish, level the top, and chill until set.

Spoon sufficient liquid aspic jelly on to the mousse to cover it by 2mm. When the aspic has set, arrange the watercress and lemon rind cut into shapes on top, and spoon over enough liquid jelly to cover the garnish. Leave to set.

Note Fish mousses can be made more piquant by substituting 100ml home-made mayonnaise (p262) for the double cream and adding 2 × 15ml spoons double cream, lightly whipped.

Fish Cakes
4 helpings

300g cooked white fish (cod, haddock, coley, etc)
500g cold boiled potatoes
25g butter
2 × 15ml spoons cream

1 × 15ml spoon finely chopped parsley
salt and pepper
flour for coating
fat for shallow frying

Flake the fish and remove all the bones. Mash the potatoes until smooth, and mix in the butter and cream. Add the flaked fish and parsley, and season to taste. Divide the mixture into 8 portions, and shape into flat, round cakes. Season the flour, and dip each cake in it. Shallow fry in butter or oil for 6–8 minutes, turning once.

VARIATION
Instead of coating with flour, dip each cake in beaten egg, coat in breadcrumbs, and deep fry (p10) until crisp and golden-brown.

Kedgeree
4 helpings

150g long-grain rice
400g smoked haddock
100ml milk
100ml water
50g butter

1 × 15ml spoon curry powder
salt and pepper
Cayenne pepper
2 hard-boiled eggs

Garnish
1 × 15ml spoon chopped parsley   butter

Boil the rice for 12 minutes and drain thoroughly. Keep warm. Poach the haddock in equal quantities of milk and water in a covered pan for 4 minutes. Remove from the pan and drain. Remove the skin and tail, and break up the fish into fairly large flakes. Melt half the butter in a saucepan. Blend in the curry powder and add the flaked fish. Warm the mixture through. Warm the rice in the rest of the butter. Season both the fish mixture and the rice with salt, pepper, and a few grains of Cayenne pepper. Chop the hard-boiled eggs coarsely. Add them to the fish and combine the mixture with the rice. Pile on a heated dish and sprinkle with chopped parsley. Dot with butter and serve immediately.

Cooking time 25 minutes (approx)

Hake with Sweet and Sour Sauce
3–4 helpings

400g hake fillets
1 green pepper

cornflour for coating
oil for deep frying

Marinade
2 spring onions
1 × 15ml spoon medium-dry sherry

2 × 15ml spoons soy sauce
1 × 15ml spoon chopped ginger root

Sauce
6 × 15ml spoons pineapple juice
2 × 5ml spoons cornflour
2 × 15ml spoons soy sauce
1 × 15ml spoon medium-dry sherry

1 × 5ml spoon white wine **or** malt
   vinegar
1 × 5ml spoon cooking oil
1 × 227g can pineapple pieces

Skin the fillets if necessary. Cut the fish into 2cm cubes. Chop the spring onions. Mix together the sherry, soy sauce, ginger, and spring onions; marinate the fish in this mixture for 1–2 hours. De-seed and chop the green pepper finely.

Make the sauce. Mix the pineapple juice with the cornflour. When blended, add all the other sauce ingredients except the pineapple pieces. Bring to the boil, stirring all the time, reduce the heat, and simmer for 3 minutes.

Drain the fish and roll in cornflour. Heat the oil (p10) and fry the fish until well and evenly browned. Dry the fish with soft kitchen paper. Place in a warmed serving dish and sprinkle with the chopped green pepper. Add the pineapple pieces to the sauce, heat through, and pour the sauce over the fish.

Scalloped Halibut
4 helpings

butter for greasing
100g Gruyère cheese
250ml Mornay sauce (p246)
100g mushrooms
400g halibut

500ml court bouillon (p79)
400g soft white breadcrumbs
400g creamed potato
25g butter

Grease lightly 4 deep scallop shells or other suitable oven-to-table individual dishes. Grate the cheese and add half to the Mornay sauce. Clean and slice the mushrooms. Poach the fish in the court bouillon for 10 minutes, add the mushrooms for the last 5 minutes. Leave to cool; then remove the bones from the fish and flake the flesh. Divide the fish and mushrooms between the shells or dishes and cover with the sauce. Mix together the remaining cheese and breadcrumbs and sprinkle over the dishes. Pipe the creamed potato around the rims. Dot with the butter and bake in a fairly hot oven at 190°C, Gas 5, for 15–20 minutes.

Herrings with Mustard Sauce
4 helpings

4 herrings
2 × 5ml spoons lemon juice
salt and pepper
1 × 10ml spoon dry mustard
2 egg yolks

50g butter
2 × 15ml spoons double cream
1 × 15ml spoon chopped capers
1 × 15ml spoon chopped gherkin

Scale the herrings, cut off the heads, and bone the fish. Sprinkle the flesh with lemon juice and season well. Grill, using moderate heat, for 3–5 minutes on each side. Keep hot. Put the dry mustard and egg yolks in a basin and whisk over a pan of hot water until creamy. Divide the butter into small pieces, and whisk into the sauce one by one. When the sauce thickens, remove from the heat and stir in the cream. Add the finely chopped capers and gherkin. Season well. Serve the sauce hot with the herrings.

Jugged or Poached Kippers
4 helpings

4 kippers

Garnish (optional)
4 pats chilled Maître d'Hôtel butter
(p564)

Put the kippers, tail end up, in a tall, heatproof jug. Pour boiling water over the whole fish except the tails. Cover the jug with a cloth, and leave to stand for 5 minutes. Tilt the jug gently over a sink, and drain off the water. Do not try to pull the kippers out by their tails. Serve them on warmed plates, topped with pats of Maître d'Hôtel butter, if liked.

Grilled Kippers
4 helpings

4 kippers   4 × 5ml spoons butter **or** margarine

Garnish
4 pats chilled butter   chopped parsley

Lay the kippers flat, skin side up, on the grill pan base (not on the rack). Grill under medium heat for 3 minutes. Turn, dot each kipper with 1 × 5ml spoon butter or margarine, and grill for another 3 minutes. Serve on warmed plates, topped with pats of chilled butter and sprinkled with parsley.

Mackerel with Gooseberry Sauce
4 helpings

flour for coating	50g butter
salt and pepper	25g parsley (approx)
8 mackerel fillets	juice of 1 lemon

Sauce

400g gooseberries	25g butter
50ml dry still cider	1 × 15ml spoon caster sugar

Make the sauce first. Wash and prepare the gooseberries, and poach in the cider and butter until tender. Sieve to make a smooth purée. Add the sugar. Put into a saucepan and put to one side.

Meanwhile, season the flour with salt and pepper. Dip the fish fillets in the flour. Heat the butter in a frying pan and fry the fillets gently for 5–7 minutes, turning once. Remove them, arrange on a serving plate and keep hot. Reserve the butter in the pan. Chop the parsley.

Heat the gooseberry sauce and keep hot. Add the remaining butter to the pan, and heat until light brown. Add the lemon juice and chopped parsley, and pour this over the fish.

Serve the gooseberry sauce separately.

Pike Quenelles (Quenelles de Brochet)
4–6 helpings

400g pike fillets	salt and pepper
4–5 egg whites	a pinch of grated nutmeg
500ml double cream	1 litre court bouillon (p79)

Skin the fillets if necessary. Dice the fish finely, add the egg whites, and process in an electric blender to a smooth purée. Rub the mixture through a sieve. Whip the cream to the same consistency as the fish purée. Fold it in lightly but thoroughly. Season the mixture with salt, pepper and nutmeg, and chill in the refrigerator for several hours.

Heat the court bouillon until just simmering. Shape the chilled fish mixture into quenelles with warmed rounded dessertspoons, and gently lower into the liquid. Simmer for 8–10 minutes. Drain with a perforated spoon.

Serve immediately with 500ml of either hot Aurora (p246) or Mushroom (p238) Sauce.

Plaice Portugaise
4 helpings

2 shallots	butter for greasing
300g tomatoes	8 plaice fillets (75g each approx)
25g butter	100ml medium-dry white wine
100g button mushrooms	salt and pepper

Skin and slice the shallots. Skin, de-seed, and chop the tomatoes and fry in the butter with the shallots. Add the mushrooms and heat gently for 4–5 minutes. Pour into a buttered oven-to-table baking dish. Fold each fillet into three, skin side in, and lay on the tomato mixture. Pour over the wine, season, and cover loosely. Bake in a fairly hot oven at 190°C, Gas 5, for 25 minutes. Bast the fish with the mixture before serving.

Goujons of Plaice
6 helpings

12 plaice fillets (100g each approx)	100ml milk
flour for coating	oil **or** fat for deep frying
salt and pepper	

Garnish

fried parsley (p60)	lemon wedges

Cut the fillets lengthways into short strips 3–4cms wide. Season the flour with salt and pepper. Dip the fish in the milk and coat with the flour, shaking off any excess. Heat the oil (p10) and fry the strips until golden-brown. Serve hot on a dish, garnish with fried parsley and lemon wedges, and serve with Tartare Sauce (p264).

Stuffed Whole Plaice
4 helpings

4 small plaice (300g each approx)	25g butter

Stuffing

100g mild Cheddar cheese	1 × 10ml spoon mixed dried herbs
50g soft white breadcrumbs	juice of ½ lemon
1 × 5ml spoon dry mustard	2 × 15ml spoons beaten egg
salt and pepper	

Garnish

lemon wedges	parsley sprigs

Make a cut down the centre of the entire length of the fish as for filleting. Loosen the flesh from the bone on each side of the cut, but do not detach it. Make the stuffing. Grate the cheese and mix with the crumbs, together with the mustard, seasoning, herbs, lemon juice, and beaten egg. Raise the 2 loose flaps of the fish and fill the pockets with the stuffing. Place the fish in a buttered oven-to-table baking dish, dot with the rest of the butter, and cover loosely with foil. Bake in a fairly hot oven at 190°C, Gas 5, for 20–30 minutes. Garnish with lemon wedges and parsley sprigs.

Grilled Salmon Steaks

clarified butter (p563) for brushing
1 salmon steak per person (150–200g
   each approx)

salt and pepper

Garnish
Maître d'Hôtel butter (p564)

Melt the butter. Season each salmon steak well with salt and pepper. Brush liberally
with melted butter. Grill, using moderate heat, for 4–5 minutes on each side, turning
once. Serve garnished with Maître d'Hôtel butter.

Poached Salmon

1 salmon (1.6–3.2kg)

3–4 litres (approx) court bouillon
   (p79)

Weigh the fish to determine the cooking time (see p69), if it is to be served hot. Put
the fish into a fish kettle and pour over the court bouillon. Bring gently to the boil. If
the salmon is to be served cold, simmer for 5 minutes, then leave to cool in the
cooking liquid before draining. If the fish is to be served hot, bring the liquid to
boiling point, reduce the heat and simmer for the required time. Drain and skin.
   Hot salmon can be served with Hollandaise Sauce (p257).
   Cold salmon is served glazed with fish fumet or aspic jelly, and garnished with a
line of cucumber slices along each side of the fish.
   Allow about 150g salmon per helping.

Skate in Black Butter
3–4 helpings

1–2 skate wings (800g approx)
1 litre court bouillon (p79)
25g butter
salt and pepper

2 × 15ml spoons capers
2 × 10ml spoons chopped parsley
75ml wine vinegar

Rinse and dry the skate and cut it into serving portions. Put the fish in a deep frying
pan and cover with the court bouillon. Bring to the boil, reduce the heat, cover, and
simmer for 15–20 minutes. Lift out the fish, drain on soft kitchen paper, and gently
scrape away the skin. Place in an ovenproof dish and keep hot.
   To make the black butter, pour off the stock, put in the butter and heat until it is a
rich golden-brown colour. Spoon it quickly over the fish, season with salt and pepper, and scatter the capers and chopped parsley over the fish. Add the vinegar to the
pan, heat quickly, and pour over the dish. Serve immediately.

Fillets of Sole Bonne Femme
4 helpings

8 lemon sole fillets	salt and pepper
butter for greasing	125ml dry white wine
150g mushrooms	125ml Velouté sauce (p249)
1 shallot	25g butter
1 × 10ml spoon chopped parsley	

Put the fish in a greased oven-to-table baking dish. Clean and slice the mushrooms. Skin and slice the shallot. Sprinkle them over the fish, add the parsley, and season well. Add the wine and cover the dish loosely with greased paper or foil. Bake in a moderate oven at 180°C, Gas 4, for 20 minutes.

Remove the fish and keep hot. Strain the liquid into a clean saucepan and boil it rapidly until reduced by half. Stir in the hot Velouté sauce and the butter. As soon as the butter has melted, pour the sauce over the fillets, and place under a hot grill until lightly browned. Serve at once.

Sole Colbert
6 helpings

6 Dover soles	fat for deep frying
2 eggs	200g Maître d'Hôtel butter (p564)
100g flour	2 × 5ml spoons finely chopped
salt and pepper	tarragon
soft white breadcrumbs	2 × 15ml spoons meat glaze (p59)

Garnish

fried parsley (p60)	lemon wedges

Remove the dark skin of the fish. Cut down the backbone on the skinned side and slice under the flesh, following the bones to make a pocket on each side. Cut the backbone in 3 places with sharp scissors, to allow removal after cooking.

Beat the eggs until liquid. Season the flour with salt and pepper. Coat the fish with flour, then with egg and breadcrumbs. Heat the fat and deep fry the fish (p10) until golden-brown. Drain, then remove the bone where cut and arrange on a serving dish. Keep hot. Mix together the Maître d'Hôtel butter, tarragon, and meat glaze to make Colbert butter. Fill the pockets of the fish with the Colbert butter. Serve immediately, garnished with fried parsley and lemon wedges.

Sole Véronique
4 helpings

4 large lemon sole fillets	125ml water
2 shallots	100g small white grapes
50g button mushrooms	25g butter
parsley sprigs	2 × 15ml spoons flour
1 bay leaf	125ml milk
salt and pepper	juice of ½ lemon
125ml dry white wine	2 × 15ml spoons single cream

Garnish

fleurons of puff pastry (p55)   chopped parsley

Lay the fillets in a shallow ovenproof dish. Skin and chop the shallots and clean and chop the mushrooms. Sprinkle them over the fish. Add the herbs, season well, and pour the wine and water over the dish. Cover and bake in a fairly hot oven at 190°C, Gas 5, for 15 minutes.

Meanwhile, peel and de-pip the grapes. Drain the fish, and keep it hot. Reserve the cooking liquid, and reduce it to half by boiling uncovered. Melt the butter and stir in the flour. Cook for 2–3 minutes without colouring. Add the cooking liquid and milk gradually, stirring all the time, and heat the sauce until it thickens. Stir in the grapes, saving a few to garnish the dish. Add the lemon juice and cream. Pour over the fish, garnish with the reserved grapes, the fleurons and parsley, and serve immediately.

Trout with Almonds
4 helpings

4 trout	50g flaked blanched almonds
100g butter	125ml double cream
salt and pepper	3 egg yolks
juice of ½ lemon	

Garnish
parsley sprigs

Clean the trout and remove the fins. Melt the butter in a grill pan under medium heat. Lay the trout in the pan, season, and sprinkle with lemon juice. Grill for 5 minutes, and then turn the fish. Sprinkle the trout with most of the almonds, spread the rest at the side of the pan, and continue grilling for a further 3–5 minutes until the trout are tender and the almonds are browned. Drain the trout and almonds on soft kitchen paper. Put the almonds to one side.

Mix the cream with the egg yolks and put into a small pan with any juices from the grill pan. Heat gently, stirring well, until thickened; do not let the mixture boil. Lay the trout on a serving dish, and spoon the cream sauce over them. Garnish with the reserved almonds and with parsley.

Recipes for Shellfish

Crab Au Gratin
4 helpings

400g white crabmeat	250ml milk
100g Gruyère cheese	salt and pepper
25g butter	50g soft white breadcrumbs
25g plain flour	grated Parmesan cheese

Garnish

2 sliced tomatoes	parsley sprigs

Flake the crabmeat. Grate the cheese. Make a roux with the butter and flour, add the milk gradually, and stir until the sauce thickens. Season well. Add the crabmeat and the Gruyère cheese and stir into the sauce. Re-season if required. Put the mixture into empty crab shells or an ovenproof dish, and sprinkle with the breadcrumbs and Parmesan cheese. Brown under the grill for 2–3 minutes. Garnish with slices of tomato and parsley sprigs.

Lobster Thermidor
4 helpings

2 shallots	125ml double cream
3 × 15ml spoons butter	2 × 15ml spoons French mustard
150ml dry white wine (approx)	2 × 15ml spoons grated Parmesan
1 × 5ml spoon chopped tarragon	cheese
1 × 5ml spoon chopped chervil	salt and pepper
200ml Béchamel sauce (p245)	2 cooked lobsters (pp75–76)

Garnish
watercress sprigs

Skin and finely chop the shallots. Melt the butter and fry them gently until soft. Add the wine and herbs and boil, uncovered, until the liquid is reduced by half; then add the Béchamel sauce. Remove from the heat. Stir well, and mix in the cream, mustard, and half the cheese. Season well and put to one side.

Split the lobsters in half lengthways. Remove the meat from the claws and body and chop coarsely. Mix with most of the sauce, keeping a little sauce separate to complete the dish; return the sauced lobster meat to the shells. Place the shells on a flat dish, cut side up, and coat the surface of the shellfish with the remaining sauce. Sprinkle with the rest of the cheese and brown in a fairly hot oven at 200°C, Gas 6, for 10–15 minutes. Garnish with watercress sprigs and serve very hot.

Moules Marinière
4–6 helpings

1.6kg live mussels
1 onion
1 carrot
1 stick of celery
bouquet garni

125ml water
125ml white wine
25g butter
1 × 15ml spoon flour
pepper

Garnish
chopped parsley

Scrub and beard the mussels, making sure that all are tightly closed, and put them into a large pan. Peel and slice the vegetables and tuck them among the mussels with the bouquet garni. Pour the water and wine over the mussels and place over moderate heat. Leave until the liquid boils up over them. Shake the pan 2 or 3 times and draw to one side.

Blend the butter and flour together into a smooth beurre manié and put to one side. Strain the liquid from the pan of mussels, through muslin, into a smaller pan. Keep the mussels warm. Add the butter and flour mixture to the liquid in small pieces, whisking well. Heat until boiling, then season well with pepper. Put the mussels into a deep dish and pour the cooking liquid over them. Sprinkle with chopped parsley.

Serve with pieces of crusty bread.
Cooking time 10-15 minutes

Sweet and Sour Prawns
4 helpings

200g peeled prawns
1 × 15ml spoon medium-dry sherry
salt and pepper
2 onions
2 green peppers
2 × 15ml spoons oil

125ml chicken stock
1 × 227g can pineapple pieces
1 × 15ml spoon cornflour
2 × 15ml spoons soy sauce
125ml white wine vinegar
75g sugar

Garnish
unpeeled prawns

Marinate the prawns in the sherry for 30 minutes and season well. Skin the onions and de-seed the green peppers. Slice them into rings. Heat the oil in a saucepan and fry the onions and peppers gently until tender. Add the stock, and drain; then add the pineapple. Cover and cook for 3–5 minutes. Blend the cornflour, soy sauce, vinegar, and sugar together, and add to the mixture. Stir until thickened. Add the prawns, and cook for 1 minute.

Serve hot on boiled rice garnished with prawns.

Coquilles St Jacques Mornay
4 helpings

1 small onion
400g scallops
salt and pepper
1 bay leaf
50ml dry white wine
75ml water
juice of ½ lemon
25g butter
25g flour

125ml milk
75ml single cream
butter for greasing
200g mashed potatoes
3 × 15ml spoons dry white
    breadcrumbs
4 × 15ml spoons grated Parmesan
    cheese

Skin and slice the onion. Wash the scallops and place in a pan with the sliced onion, seasoning, and bay leaf. Pour the wine, water, and lemon juice over them. Poach gently for 5 minutes. Strain off the liquid and put to one side with the scallops.

Melt the butter in a pan, then stir in the flour. Blend in the liquid strained from the scallops, and stir over gentle heat until the sauce starts to thicken. Add the milk and simmer for 2–3 minutes. Stir in the cream. Slice the scallops and divide between 4 lightly greased scallop shells or suitable small flameproof dishes. Coat with the sauce. Pipe the mashed potato around the edge of each shell. Sprinkle lightly with the breadcrumbs and Parmesan cheese. Bake in a fairly hot oven at 200°C, Gas 6, for 10–15 minutes.

Fried Scampi
2 helpings

flour for coating
salt and pepper

225g peeled scampi
oil **or** fat for deep frying

Batter
1 egg
100g plain flour
salt

1 × 15ml spoon cooking oil
2–3 × 15ml spoons milk

Garnish
lemon wedges

Season the flour with salt and pepper in a plastic bag and toss the scampi in the flour. Separate the egg. Mix the flour, salt, oil, egg yolk, and milk to a stiff batter. Just before cooking, whisk the egg white until stiff and fold it into the batter. Heat the oil (p10). Dip the scampi in the batter and fry, a few at a time, until golden-brown. Drain, and serve garnished with lemon wedges.

Offer Tartare Sauce (p264) separately.

MEAT

Methods of Cooking Meat

Roasting

Method 1 – Quick roasting: The meat is cooked in a very hot oven, 230°C, Gas 8, for about 10 minutes to sear or brown the outside of the meat and seal in the juices. The temperature is then reduced to fairly hot, 190°C, Gas 5, to finish the cooking. (See Meat Roasting Chart on page 96.) This method preserves the full flavour of prime joints. However, it is not very suitable for a small joint because it will shrink.

Method 2 – Slow roasting: The meat is cooked in a warm or moderate oven, 160°–180°C, Gas 3–4, for a longer time. (See Meat Roasting Chart on page 96.) This method is best suited to the poorer quality roasting joints and small joints, since it causes less shrinkage and provides a more tender joint.

Whichever roasting method is used, any joint must be weighed in order to calculate its cooking time. Both its size and shape influence this also. The larger the joint, the shorter the time per kg; joints on the bone cook faster than boned ones because the bone conducts heat more quickly than muscle fibres. Roasting in foil also affects the cooking time (see below).

The cooking times given in the Meat Roasting Chart are, therefore, only approximate. If you roast varied types of joints, it is worth investing in a meat thermometer which registers the internal temperature of the meat and takes a great deal of the guesswork out of roasting times. The meat thermometer should be inserted into the thickest part of the meat before it is cooked, taking care that it does not touch bone or fat as they will affect the reading. When the right temperature is reached, the joint is cooked. A meat thermometer is particularly useful for calculating the cooking time for beef according to whether you want the meat to be lightly cooked, still pink inside (known as 'rare'), or fully cooked ('well-done').

Where a meat thermometer is not available, a good indication of readiness is the colour of the juice which seeps out of the meat when a skewer is pushed into the centre and withdrawn. The juice from a well-done joint or piece of meat will be colourless, juice from a rare joint will be pinkish-red, and there will be various shades of pink in between.

Joints for roasting should be placed, fat side up, on a wire rack in a shallow roasting tin. If the outside covering of fat varies in thickness, then the thickest part should be uppermost. A rib, cooked on the bone, should be prepared by the butcher so that it will stand upright. A rolled piece of beef should be slightly flattened on one side so that it will stand level. It is advisable to rub a lean joint with dripping or lard before putting it in the oven. Place the roasting tin in the centre of the oven so that air circulates round it freely. During roasting, enough fat should come from the meat to baste it naturally. However, basting the joint from time to time will give an improved flavour and moistness.

Roasting in foil or clear plastic roasting bags is popular, mainly because it keeps the oven cleaner. It is also particularly beneficial when roasting slightly tough joints because the moist heat tenderizes the meat; when roasting small joints of 1.5kg or less, it reduces the shrinkage and any drying out. When using foil, the joint should be wrapped loosely in it and the edges sealed; this does away with the need to baste the joint during cooking. However, it is advisable to remove the foil for the last 15–30 minutes of cooking time to brown the surface of the joint. Foil deflects the heat, and so the oven temperature should be raised by 10°–20°C or by one Gas mark; alternatively the cooking time should be increased.

Follow the manufacturer's instructions when using clear plastic roasting bags. The bag need only be removed when the joint has finished cooking since the meat browns whilst in the bag.

Meat Roasting Chart

Meat	Method 1 – Quick Roasting 230°C, Gas 8, reducing to 190°C, Gas 5, after 10 mins	Method 2 – Slow Roasting at 160°–180°C, Gas 3–4	Meat thermometer temperatures
Beef (with bone)	15 minutes per 0.5kg plus 15 minutes extra	25 minutes per 0.5kg plus 25 minutes extra	rare – 60°C
Beef (without bone – rolled)	20 minutes per 0.5kg plus 20 minutes extra	30 minutes per 0.5kg plus 30 minutes extra	medium – 68°–70°C well-done – 75°–77°C
Lamb (with bone)	20 minutes per 0.5kg plus 20 minutes extra	25 minutes per 0.5kg plus 25 minutes extra	80°–82°C
Lamb and Mutton- (without bone – rolled)	25 minutes per 0.5kg plus 25 minutes extra	30 minutes per 0.5kg plus 30 minutes extra	
Mutton (with bone)	20–25 minutes per 0.5kg plus 25 minutes extra	30–35 minutes per 0.5kg plus 35 minutes extra	
Veal (with bone)	25 minutes per 0.5kg plus 25 minutes extra	30 minutes per 0.5kg plus 30 minutes extra	80°–82°C
Veal (without bone – rolled)	30 minutes per 0.5kg plus 30 minutes extra	40 minutes per 0.5kg plus 30 minutes extra	
Pork (with bone)	25–30 minutes per 0.5kg plus 25–30 minutes extra	35 minutes per 0.5kg plus 35 minutes extra	85°–88°C
Pork (without bone – rolled)	35 minutes per 0.5kg plus 35 minutes extra		

Note The above cooking times are approximate. The exact time will depend on the form and thickness of the joint, its age and condition, and its preparation.

Grilling

Grilled meat is cooked by radiant heat under a hot grill, usually preheated. It is an ideal cooking method for small, tender cuts, and other items: prime steak, chops, sausages, liver, kidney, bacon and gammon rashers or steaks, if you do not want to use much fat. The meat is only lightly brushed with oil or fat before placing it under the grill; this prevents the high heat from drying the meat out. The grill bars or grid must also be greased to prevent the meat sticking to them. The meat is cooked on one side until it is lightly browned. It is then turned over (using a palette knife and spoon to avoid piercing the meat and letting its juices run out) to brown the other side quickly. The heat is reduced, if necessary, after browning, to allow the meat time to cook through. Beef is usually cooked using high heat throughout, while other meats are cooked more slowly.

Frying

Frying is used for the same cuts of meat as grilling. Frying times are the same as grilling times. In addition, some meats, notably mutton, lamb and veal, are often coated with egg and breadcrumbs before frying.

Meat is almost always shallow fried. Use just enough fat and/or oil to cover the base of the pan. Dripping can be used for beef, or lard for pork; butter gives the best flavour to other meats. Add the meat to the hot (but not smoking) fat or oil. Fry it over high heat, turning once only, again taking care not to puncture the surface. For thick cuts, the heat should be reduced considerably after the outside has been seared and the cooking continued until the meat is well-done.

For cooking times, see the Chart below and the Steak Grilling and Frying Chart on p111.

Grilling and Frying Chart

Cuts	Approx cooking time	Cuts	Approx cooking time
Beef		**Bacon and Gammon**	
Steaks	see Chart. p111	*Bacon chops*	10–15 minutes
		Bacon rashers (thin)	5 minutes
Lamb and Mutton		*Gammon steaks*	10–15 minutes
Chops (loin and chump)	8–15 minutes		
Cutlets	7–10 minutes	**Offal**	
		Kidney	5–10 minutes
Veal		*Liver (1cm thick)*	8–10 minutes
Cutlets	12–15 minutes		
Escalopes (beaten and crumbed)	7–10 minutes	**Sausages**	
		Large	10–15 minutes
Pork		*Chipolata*	7–10 minutes
Chops (loin, chump and spare rib)	15–20 minutes		

Pot-roasting

This is best for smaller and less tender joints of meat. The meat is browned all over in hot fat in a deep, heavy-based pan. It is then put on a wire rack or a bed of root vegetables in the pan, covered with a tight-fitting lid and cooked slowly over low heat or in a warm oven, 160°C, Gas 3, for 45 minutes per 0.5kg or until tender.

Braising

This method combines pot-roasting and stewing. The meat is browned all over in hot fat. It is then placed on a bed of fried vegetables called a mirepoix (see p307), in a casserole or heavy-based pan. Stock or water is added to cover the vegetables. The casserole or pan is covered with a tight-fitting lid and the meat cooked slowly over low heat or in a warm oven, 160°C, Gas 3, for 2–3 hours or until tender.

Casseroling and Stewing

These are long, slow, moist methods of cooking suitable for tougher cuts of meat. Solid cuts or small pieces of meat are browned quickly in hot fat and then cooked in liquid, with vegetables, in a pan covered with a tight-fitting lid or in a heatproof casserole over gentle heat; or they are cooked in a warm oven, 160°C, Gas 3, for 1½–4 hours until tender.

Boiling
This is a moist method of cooking whole joints, but a rather more tender cut is used for boiling than for stewing. The meat is totally or almost covered with stock or water. Herbs, spices, seasonings, and onions may be added for extra flavour. The liquid is heated to boiling point, skimmed well, then reduced to simmering point until the meat is tender. A little of the liquid may be served with the meat, and the rest used as a basis for a sauce, to make broth or, where suitable, as a general stock.

Using Dripping and Other Meat-flavoured Fat
This makes an appetizing spread on hot toast. It can also be used for flavouring vegetables, for making plain cakes (p407) and in various other ways, especially if it is cleared, or clarified. Hard fat or suet cut off raw meat can also be used if all skin and gristle are removed. This can be done by melting (rendering) the fat.

To Clarify Fat
To clean fat which has been used for cooking meat, eg for frying, put the fat into a large saucepan and add about the same volume of cold water. Heat very gently until the water begins to boil, removing the scum as it rises. Allow to simmer for about 5 minutes, then strain into a bowl and leave the fat to cool and solidify. Remove the fat in one piece, dry it on soft kitchen paper and scrape away the sediment from underneath. Heat the fat very gently until all bubbling ceases, to drive off any water.

To Render Fat or Suet
Cut the fat into small pieces, and heat very gently in a frying pan or in a cool oven, 150°C, Gas 2, until the fat has melted and the pieces of tissue or skin are quite crisp. While hot, strain the fat through a fine metal strainer into a clean basin, pressing the pieces of tissue and skin against the strainer to extract all the fat. The crispy bits left are called by different names in different parts of the UK, eg mammocks, scraps, scratchings or scruggins, and are used sometimes in old recipes. When crushed, they make a good topping for baked meat or vegetable dishes.

Carving
Carving is an acquired skill requiring practice and a really sharp knife. A sharp knife is essential since it can be used lightly and is always under control. Carving knives should be sharpened before use either with a hone, steel, patent sharpener or an oilstone. When a knife fails to produce a good edge with a domestic sharpener, take it to an ironmonger or send it to the manufacturer for regrinding.
Note Some modern, stainless steel knives have a hollowed-out grooved blade; these seldom require sharpening.

Sharpening a Carving Knife
Hold the steel in your left hand (if you are right-handed), with your thumb on top of the handle. Hold the carving knife in your right hand. Angle both the steel and the knife upwards. Place the heel of the blade on the handle end of the steel, almost flat against it, and draw the blade sharply along the steel with a stroking movement.

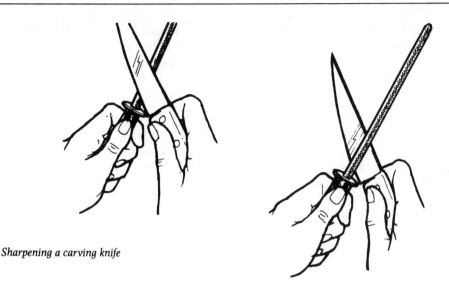

Sharpening a carving knife

Repeat, but start with the blade *under* the steel, and sharpen the other side of the knife. Go on doing this, alternately holding the knife on top of the steel and under it, until the knife has a sharp, tapered, cutting edge. About 6 strokes on each side should be enough to sharpen any good quality knife.

Carving knives can also be sharpened on a fine oil-stone or carborundum stone. First dip the stone in water, then sharpen the knife as above.

Another method of using an oil-stone, which may be easier, is to lay the knife almost flat on the stone, with the cutting edge towards you. Draw the knife along the stone, away from you; then turn the knife over, lay it on the far end of the stone and draw it towards you. Repeat several times.

How to Carve

A knife should be used in the same way as a saw, ie drawn back and forth through the meat. Never try to push even a sharp knife through meat without using a sawing movement. If the knife is sharp, keep the backward and forward movements long and light, and the knife will cut through the meat quickly and smoothly. Try to hold the knife slanted at the same angle all the way through the joint, and to make each slice equally thick when cutting slices of meat from a partly carved joint.

When cutting slices from the top of a rolled joint which is standing on end, always try to cut from right to left (if you are right-handed), not towards you, so that there is no danger of the knife slipping and cutting you. Protect the left hand by using a proper carving fork with a thumb guard. A modern carving dish studded with small, sharp prongs which hold the joint steady can be a great help.

Boned and rolled joints rarely present carving problems since the bones have already been removed, so a beginner learning to carve should start on them. When carving rolled joints, leave some strings and skewers in place until you have carved down to them and then only remove the one which impedes further carving. Any-one who carves meat on the bone should, however, know how the bones lie in the meat, and where the knuckle ends are.

Meat is usually carved across the grain or run of muscle in the UK, because this makes it more tender to cut and eat. The thickness of the slices varies with each type of meat. In general, carve thin slices of beef from a boneless joint and thicker slices from fillet or sirloin. Carve moderately thick slices of pork and veal, and still thicker slices of lamb and mutton.

Beef

Joints on the bone are carved from the outside fat towards the bone after making a vertical cut at the edge of the chine bone. At the base bone, the knife is turned parallel with it and the slices are gently eased off the bone. When dealing with a sirloin or ribs, try to carve the outside rib muscles first as these are better eaten really hot. Save the least cooked meat in the centre for eating cold.

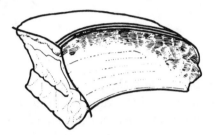

Carving a joint on the bone

Brisket of beef on the bone: The joint should be cut in even slices across the whole width of the joint, across the bones.

Ribs of beef: Loosen the meat from the ribs by inserting the knife between the meat and bones. Cut thin slices off the sides, starting at the thick end and carving through to the thin end.

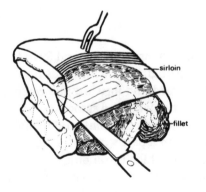

LEFT *Carving rib of beef*

BELOW *Carving the fillet*

Sirloin of beef: A sirloin is carved on the bone. First cut out the fillet or undercut. Carve it into a suitable number of slices. It is best eaten hot. Then turn the sirloin over, so that it rests on the bone, and carve the meat across the width of the joint and straight down towards the blade of the bone. These slices are cut thicker than slices from a boneless joint.

Round of beef: Use a thin-bladed and very sharp knife. Cut a thick slice first from the outside of the joint, at its top, leaving the surface smooth; then carve thin, even slices to leave a level-topped joint.

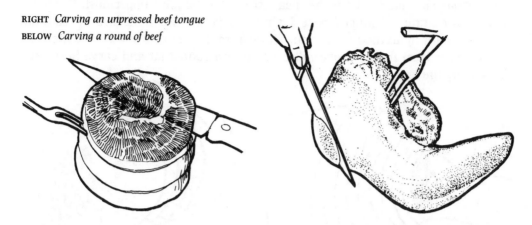

Beef tongue (pressed): Carve thinly across the top, parallel to the round base.

Beef tongue (unpressed): Cut across the tongue at the thickest part, all the way through it. Cut out and serve a fairly thick slice. Continue carving in this way towards the tip of the tongue until all the best meat on the upper side has been served. The fat which lies around the root of the tongue can be turned over, sliced, and served.

Lamb and Mutton

Mutton and, to a lesser extent, lamb, should always be served as quickly as possible and on very hot plates. This is because the flavour of mutton is soon lost, and because lamb and mutton fat have a higher melting point than other animal fats. On a cold plate, they solidify, leaving semi-solid fat which coats the palate, producing a 'furry' or diminished sense of taste.

Forequarter of lamb: When carving a forequarter of lamb, first separate the shoulder from the breast. To do this, raise the shoulder, into which the fork should be firmly

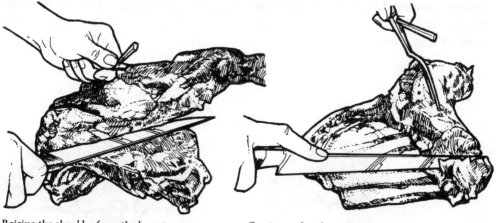

Raising the shoulder from the breast   *Carving cutlets from the ribs*

fixed. It will then come away easily by cutting round the outline of the shoulder and slipping the knife beneath it. The main part of the joint is then turned over and served as cutlets carved from the ribs. The shoulder can be served cold later.

Leg of lamb or mutton: Turn the meatiest side of the joint uppermost. Begin the carving by cutting a V-shaped piece down to the bone close to the knuckle end. Cut slices at a slant up to the thicker end. Those from the knuckle end will be the most fully cooked. Turn the joint over, discard any unwanted fat and carve horizontal slices along the leg.

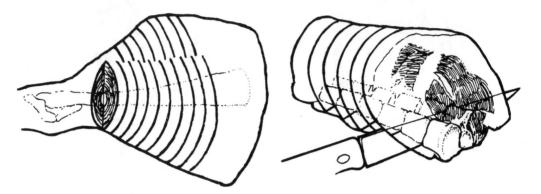

Carving a leg of lamb or mutton   *Carving a loin of lamb or mutton*

Loin of lamb or mutton: Loin, and other similar pieces, should be well-jointed before cooking. Ask the butcher to chine or saw it across the blade parts of the bone or to chop it through the joints for serving in cutlets. If this has not been done, use an old knife and knock the blade through between the joints where they are separated by white discs of gristle, before trying to carve. Carve the loin downwards, in thick slices or in chops, following the natural division of the bones. If boned and rolled, the loin can be carved in thinner slices, like any other boned and rolled joint.

Saddle of lamb or mutton: There are two ways of carving a saddle, either by carving the slices at right angles to the backbone (spine), or by cutting the slices parallel to it.

For the first method, cut down one side of the spine, and then slip the knife under the meat and cut slices at right angles to the spine, separating the meat from them. Repeat this on the other side of the spine.

Cutting down one side of the spine   *Cutting slices at right angles to the spine*

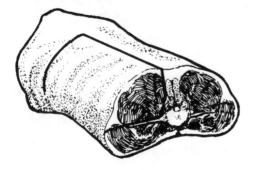
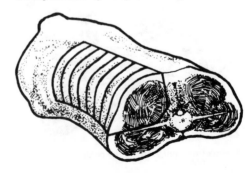

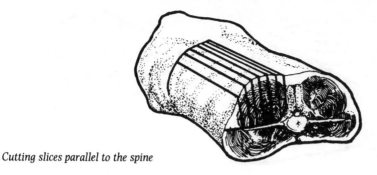

Cutting slices parallel to the spine

For the second method, cut down each side of the spine and separate the meat from the rib bones as in the first method. Make a cut, parallel to the spine a few centimetres up from the lower edge of the meat, then cut slices off downwards parallel to the spine and the cut line. This can be done in the kitchen; the slices can then be put back in place for serving at the table.

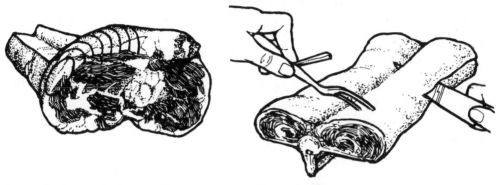

Carving the chops at the chump end   *Slicing the fillet*

To finish both methods, carve the chops at the chump end from each side in turn, slanting the knife towards the centre of the joint.

Turn the joint over and slice the fillet along the length of the joint.

Shoulder of lamb or mutton: Before cooking, insert a sharp knife and ease the meat away from the whole surface of the bladebone, to make carving easier. Turn the joint over, if necessary, so that the thickest part is on top. When cooked, carve a vertical slice at the narrow end of this bladebone right down to the bone. Then carve thick

Carving thick slices along the length of the bladebone

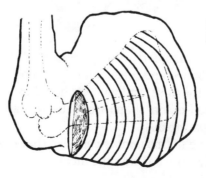

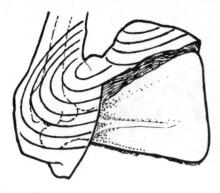

Carving the shank in horizontal slices along the shank bone

Carving the remaining meat

slices along the length of the bladebone until all the shoulder meat on top has been carved, leaving only the shank of the foreleg. Carve this in horizontal slices along the shank bone until all the meat has been cut from the top of the joint. Turn the joint over, and carve the remaining meat in horizontal slices.

Veal

Breast of veal: A breast of veal consists of two parts – the rib bones and the gristly brisket. Separate these first by passing the knife sharply through the centre of the joint. Then cut off each rib bone and serve it. The brisket can be served by cutting pieces from the centre part of the joint. If the veal is boned and stuffed, carve it by cutting downwards across the end of the rolled joint.

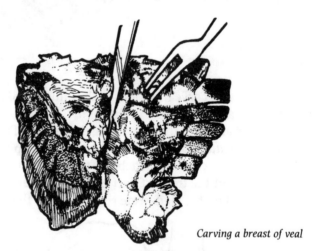

Carving a breast of veal

Calf's head: A calf's head is nearly always boned before serving, and is then cut into slices like any other boned and rolled joint. If the bones have not been removed, cut strips from the ear to the nose, and with each of these serve a piece of the throat sweetbreads, cut in a half-moon shape from the throat. The tongue and brains should be served on a separate dish.

Fillet of veal: The carving of this joint is very like that of a round or roll of beef. A stuffing is inserted between the flap and the meat.

Loin of veal: As in the case of a loin of lamb, the careful jointing of a loin of veal greatly lessens the difficulty in carving it. Ask the butcher to do this. When properly jointed, there should be little difficulty in separating the chops from each other. Each helping should include a piece of the kidney and kidney fat.

Pork and Cured Pig Meat

When carving a joint with crackling, first take off a small section of crackling, but only enough to serve one or two people. Cut it into serving portions.

Leg of pork: This joint, a favourite with many people, is easy to carve. Having removed some of the crackling, begin to carve by cutting a V-shaped piece down to the bone close to the knuckle end. Cut slices at a slant up to the thicker end, as when carving a leg of lamb.

Loin of pork: Like a loin of lamb, a loin of pork must be properly chined before roasting, and the crackling must be scored. Ask the butcher to do both. Cut through the cooked meat between the bones into neat, even chops. A boned and rolled loin of pork can be carved in thinner slices, but remove more of the crackling first to make carving easier.

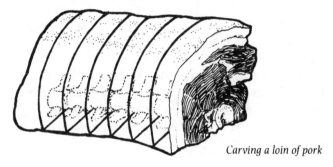

Carving a loin of pork

Hand and spring of pork: Using a sharp, thin-bladed knife, remove the rib bones from the underside and the crackling from the top.

Carve the meat from each side of the bone in downward slices until the bone is reached. Turn the joint over and carve the rest of the meat across the grain.

Removing the rib bones   *Carving the meat from each side of the bone*

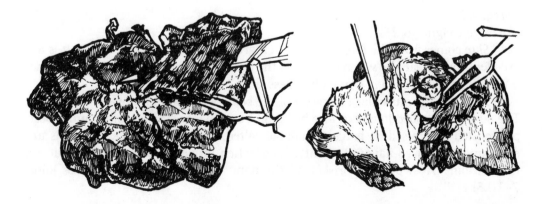

Suckling-pig: A suckling-pig seems, at first sight, an elaborate dish to carve. Like poultry, it is mainly jointed rather than sliced. It is usually prepared by splitting it in half lengthways; the head is then separated from the body. Detach the shoulders from the carcass in the same way as a shoulder is separated from a forequarter of lamb. Then take off the hind legs; the ribs are then ready to be cut up and may be served as 2 or 3 helpings.

Whole gammon or ham: Turn the meatiest side of the joint uppermost. Using a very sharp and thin knife, begin carving at the knuckle end. Make a V-shaped cut into one side of the joint, down to the bone. Take out the slice of meat. Then take thin slices down the side of the joint. Repeat this on the other side of the joint until all the gammon or ham has been carved.

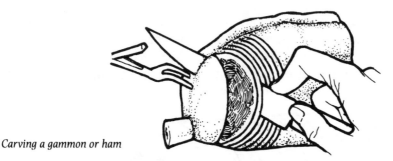

Carving a gammon or ham

Middle gammon: Using a sharp, thin knife, cut thin slices through to the bone. Because this joint narrows towards the bone end, make the cuts into the joint opposite the bone thicker at the outside, then taper them towards the bone.

Note All pot-roasted and braised whole joints are carved in the same way as the roasted joints above.

Beef

Beef Cuts

Cuts of beef vary considerably in different parts of Great Britain. Those described are the most widely used British cuts, but they are by no means standard and reference is made to some of the other terms used. The cuts will be better understood from the diagram opposite.

Forequarter

(Average weight 66.25kg)

1) *Shin* comes from the foreleg, has much gristle, and is relatively cheap. It is an excellent soup meat and when cooked on the bone provides a good, jellied stock and is ideal for making brawn. (Av wt boneless shin 2–2.5kg)

2) *Brisket* is the muscular extension of the belly of the animal towards the chest. The boned and rolled joint can also be bought cut up into smaller joints and is best pot-roasted or braised. It is also available salted, ready for boiling. Brisket is an economical, yet well-flavoured joint which, when properly cooked, is little fattier than sirloin. (Av wt whole brisket on the bone 9–13.5kg; Av wt boneless joint 7–10.5kg)

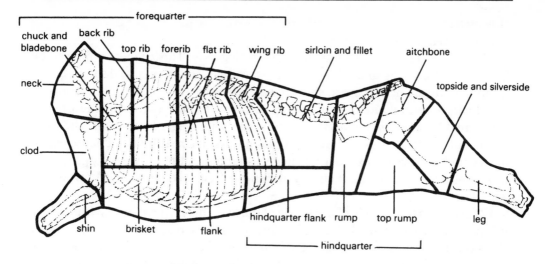

forequarter

chuck and bladebone | back rib | top rib | forerib | flat rib | wing rib | sirloin and fillet | aitchbone

neck

topside and silverside

clod

shin | brisket | flank | hindquarter flank | rump | top rump | leg

hindquarter

3) *Flank* is also from the belly of the animal. It is a cheaper cut which deserves wider recognition. It provides a more fatty joint than brisket and is ideal for pot-roasting, braising or boiling. It is sometimes salted or pickled before being boiled for pressed beef. (Av wt 1–2.25kg)

4) *Flat rib* comes from between the flank and foreribs. Like the forerib, this joint should be slowly roasted. (Av wt 5kg)

5) *Wing rib* is a rib joint cut from between the forerib and sirloin. It is one of the most expensive cuts and is particularly good when roasted. (Av wt 2–6kg)

6) *Forerib* is merely an extension of the sirloin, but it requires slower cooking at a lower temperature than the sirloin because the muscles of the live animal were more fully exercised. The forerib can be bought either on the bone, or boned and rolled. (Av wt on the bone 1.4–2.6kg; Av wt boneless 1–2kg)

7) *Top rib* along with the *back rib* is also known as middle rib or thick ribs or leg-of-mutton cut, and comes from the ribs between the foreribs and shoulders. In other words, it is an extension of the foreribs. The joint is often divided into two (top and back ribs) and partly boned and rolled which makes it easier to carve. There is less bone in these joints than in forerib joints and they are very good when slow roasted or pot-roasted. (Av wt 7–11.5kg)

8) *Chuck* and *bladebone* are similar types of beef; the meat is removed from the bone and sold as chuck steak for braising, stewing, and as fillings for puddings and pies. Though sold for stewing, chuck steak needs a shorter cooking time than any other cut of stewing meat. Many butchers cut blade of beef into dice and mix it with chopped kidney, ready for filling puddings and pies. Chuck is known in the north of England as a chine, and in Scotland the chuck and blade together is known as a shoulder. (Av wt boneless chuck – 4.5kg; Av wt boneless bladebone – 3kg)

9) *Clod* or *front chest* and

10) *Sticking* or *neck* of the animal provide meat suitable for casseroling or stewing. These cuts contain less connective tissue than the shin or leg and less marbling fat than chuck steak and bladebone. Both clod and sticking are usually cheap. There is, however, a little wastage due to gristle. (Av wt clod (de-fatted) – 4.5kg; Av wt sticking – 3.5kg)

Hindquarter
(Average weight 71.5–72kg)

11) *Leg of beef* is the name used for the hind leg only. The leg meat is only suitable for long, slow cooking and is best used for stews, casseroles, pies, and soups. It can be cut in two ways. Cut in strips, it shows clearly the structure of the working muscle as it is sheathed with white or transparent connective tissue gathered together at the ends into thick pieces of white gristle. Cut in slices, it reveals 'lines' where the various sheaths of connective tissue have been cut across. There is little to choose between the leg and the foreleg, except that the leg is larger and so provides bigger pieces of meat for stewing. In Scotland, the leg and shin are called the hough. (Av wt boneless leg – 4kg)

12) *Topside* is the muscle of the inside of the leg. This is a lean joint without bones. It can be slow roasted but a piece of barding fat must be tied round the joint to keep it moist during cooking. It is really better pot-roasted or braised. (Av wt 8.5–8.75kg)

13) *Silverside* is the muscle of the outside of the thigh and buttock. It is common for this joint to be roasted but it is best suited to salting and boiling, as in the past (Av wt boneless silverside – 5.5kg)

14) *Top rump* or *thick flank* is the muscle of the front of the thigh, which is usually cut into 2 joints and barded with fat. This makes an acceptable joint for slow roasting or, better still, for moist cooking such as pot-roasting. It may also be sold sliced, ready for frying or braising. (Av wt boned and trimmed 5.25–5.5kg)

15) *Aitchbone* is the cut lying over the rump bone. It is a large joint on the bone which can be roasted or braised. Can be boned and cut into smaller joints. Not cut very often nowadays. (Av wt on the bone – 5.4kg)

16) *Rump* is the joint next to the sirloin and is one of the commonest cuts for frying and grilling. In Scotland rump steak is sometimes called 'pope's eye'. Although not as tender as fillet, it is preferred by many people for its fuller flavour. The meat should be close-grained and should have about 5mm fat on the outside edge and no gristle. (Av wt boned and trimmed rump 8.25–8.5kg)

17) *Sirloin* (which properly includes the fillet) is the traditional joint for roast beef. It is tender and full of flavour, but is also the most expensive joint. It is often sold without the fillet which makes it slightly cheaper. Sirloin is also sold sliced as steaks for grilling or frying. (Av wt sirloin with bone and fillet – 12.25kg)

18) *Fillet* is found on the inside of the sirloin bone, and fillet and sirloin may be boned and rolled together to provide a luxury roast. If the sirloin is bought on the bone, the fillet can be removed for roasting by itself in the piece, or for slicing into fillet steaks, which are the most tender steaks for grilling or frying. (Av wt fillet 1.5–2.25kg)

19) *Hindquarter flank* is the belly of the animal, which provides a cheap and delicious joint for pot-roasting, braising or boiling. It is, however, rather fatty. It is not suitable for dry heat cooking methods. (Av wt with bone – 6.25kg)

Steaks
Several terms are used for various types of beef steaks. They are not new terms and some have already been mentioned.

Fillet (undercut) is a lean and boneless piece lying below the ribs of the sirloin. It is the most expensive steak meat and is usually sliced for grilling or frying. The tiny flecks of fat running through the meat are evidence that the steak will grill or fry well. Fillet steak can be served in several ways and under several names.

Tournedos is a slice from the fillet, weighing about 125–150g, usually 2cm thick and a neat round shape. It is sometimes tied to preserve its shape.

Châteaubriand is a piece of fillet enough for 2 people, ideally about 4cm thick and cut from the centre of the fillet. A popular and delicious steak. Its average weight is 250g.

Rump is the best flavoured steak, particularly good for grilling and frying. It is not as tender as fillet steak but has a good texture. This steak should have about 5mm fat on the outside edge.

Sirloin (contre-fillet) provides tender steaks with a good flavour. However, the texture is not as good as fillet or rump. Sirloin, like fillet, is cut in several ways and served under several names.

Porterhouse is a thick steak about 2–2.5cm thick, cut from the wing end (thick end) of the sirloin. Excellent for grilling.

T-bone is a steak cut through the sirloin so that it contains, on one side at least, the T-shaped loin bone. It has 2 'eyes', that of the loin meat and that of the fillet.

Entrecôte is a sirloin steak without the undercut (fillet) and without the bone. In other words, it is the eye meat of the loin cut into steaks. Each steak is usually cut 2–3cm thick.

Minute steak is a very thin steak from the upper part of the sirloin or occasionally from the fillet, weighing 125–150g without any trimmings or fat.

Roasted and Baked Dishes
Roast Beef *Basic recipe*

a joint of beef suitable for roasting	beef dripping (25g per 0.5kg meat
salt and pepper	approx)

Select the method of roasting, ie quick or slow roasting (p95). Weigh the meat to calculate the cooking time (p96). Wipe, trim, and tie the meat into a neat shape. Place the joint, fat side up, on a wire rack if available, in a shallow roasting tin. Season the meat, and rub or spread it with the dripping. Place the roasting tin in the oven and cook for the required time.

Transfer the cooked meat to a warmed serving dish, remove any string and secure with a metal skewer if necessary. Keep hot. Drain off the fat from the roasting tin and make a gravy from the sediment in the tin, if liked.

Serve with Yorkshire Pudding (p225) and Cold Horseradish Cream (p25) if using traditional accompaniments.

Mrs Beeton's Roast Ribs of Beef
6–8 helpings

2.5kg forerib of beef   50–75g clarified dripping (p98)
flour for dredging   salt and pepper

Garnish
shredded horseradish

Ask the butcher to trim the thin ends of the rib bones so that the joint will stand upright. Wipe the meat but do not salt it. Dredge it lightly with flour. Melt 50g dripping in a roasting tin and brush some of it over the meat. Put the meat in the tin and roast in a very hot oven, 230°C, Gas 8, for 10 minutes. Baste well, reduce the heat to moderate, 180°C, Gas 4, and continue to roast for 1¾ hours for rare meat, or 2¼ hours for well-done meat. Baste frequently during cooking, using extra dripping if required.

When cooked, salt the meat lightly. Transfer the joint to a warmed serving dish and keep hot. Pour off almost all the fat in the roasting tin, leaving the sediment. Pour in enough water to make a thin gravy, then heat to boiling point, stirring all the time. Taste, and season with salt and pepper. Strain the gravy into a warmed gravy-boat. Garnish the dish with 1 or 2 small heaps of shredded horseradish.

Serve with Yorkshire Pudding (p225) and Cold Horseradish Cream (p52).

Fillet of Beef en Croûte
6 helpings

750g–1kg fillet of beef   1 × 5ml spoon chopped parsley
ground pepper   450g prepared puff pastry (p458)
25g butter   flour for rolling out
1 × 15ml spoon oil   beaten egg for glazing
100g button mushrooms
1 × 5ml spoon fresh mixed herbs,
    chopped

Wipe, trim, and tie the meat into a neat shape. Season with pepper. Heat the butter and oil in a large pan, add the fillet and brown it quickly all over. Reserve the fat in the pan and draw it off the heat. Transfer the fillet to a roasting tin and roast it in a very hot oven, 230°C, Gas 8, for 10 minutes. Remove the fillet, and leave it to get cold.

Meanwhile, clean and slice the mushrooms. Sauté them in the remaining oil and butter in the pan for 2–3 minutes. Remove from the heat, add the herbs, and leave to cool.

Roll out the puff pastry on a lightly floured surface to make a rectangle large enough to enclose the fillet. Put the mushroom mixture on one half of the pastry. Lay the beef on top of the mushroom mixture. Wrap the pastry round the beef to form a neat parcel, sealing the edges well. Place the parcel on a baking tray with the cut edges underneath. Decorate with leaves cut from the pastry trimmings and brush the pastry with the beaten egg. Bake in a hot oven, 220°C, Gas 7, for 20–30 minutes, or until the pastry is well-browned. Serve hot or cold.

Steaks
Steak Grilling and Frying Chart

	Fillet	Tournedos	Châteaubriand	Rump	Sirloin	Porterhouse	T-bone	Entrecôte	Minute
Thickness of meat	2cm	2–3cm	4cm	2cm	2–2.5cm	4–5cm	4–5cm	2–3cm	1cm
Helpings	1	1	2	4	1	2	2–3	1	1
Cooking times (in minutes):									
Rare	6	6–7	15–17	6–7	5	7–8	7–8	5	1–1.5
Medium rare	7	8	18–20	8–10	6–7	9–12	9–12	6–7	2–3
Well-done	8	9–10	21–24	12–14	9–10	14–16	14–16	9–10	4–5

Grilled Steak *Basic recipe*

150–200g steak per person
oil **or** melted butter

freshly ground pepper

Garnish
Maître d'Hôtel butter (p564)

Wipe the steaks and trim off any excess fat. Beat each steak lightly on both sides with a cutlet bat or rolling-pin. Brush with oil or melted butter and, if possible, leave for 1 hour before cooking.

Season with pepper. (Do not salt steaks before grilling because it makes the juices run.) Heat the grill to a high heat and oil the grid, or brush with melted butter. Place the meat on the grid and cook under the grill until the steak has browned lightly on one side. Turn the meat over, using a palette knife or spoons. Grill quickly to brown the other side. If the steaks are required medium rare or well-done, lower the grid or the grill heat and continue cooking as required (see Steak Grilling Chart above). Serve at once with a pat of Maître d'Hôtel butter on the top of each helping.

Serve with chipped potatoes, grilled mushrooms, and/or grilled tomatoes, and a sprig of watercress.

Fried Steaks *Basic recipe*

150–200g steak, 2cm thick, per
  person
freshly ground pepper
1 × 15ml spoon oil, dripping **or** butter
  (approx)

a pinch of onion salt (optional)
1–2 × 5ml spoons flour for gravy
  (optional)
100ml boiling water (optional)

Garnish
Maître d'Hôtel **or** other savoury butter
  (pp563–66)

Wipe the steaks and trim off any excess fat. Beat each steak lightly on both sides with a cutlet bat or rolling-pin. Season with pepper. (Do not salt steaks before frying because it makes the juices run.) Heat a thick, heavy frying pan on full heat until hot. Add enough oil, dripping or butter just to cover the bottom of the frying pan and, when hot, put in the prepared steaks. Keep on full heat until they are well-browned on one side; then turn them over with a palette knife or spoons, and brown the other side. Reduce the heat if necessary to complete the cooking time (see Chart on p111). Serve at once garnished with a pat of Maître d'Hôtel or other butter.

If serving gravy with the steak, drain any fat from the frying pan, keeping back the sediment. Add a pinch of ground black pepper and onion salt, and stir in the flour. Gradually add the water, and stir until boiling. Skim and strain the gravy.

Serve with chipped potatoes, grilled mushrooms and/or grilled tomatoes, and a sprig of watercress.

Steak au Poivre
4 helpings

4 steaks (fillet **or** sirloin **or** entrecôte,
  150–200g each)
2 × 10ml spoons whole black and
  white peppercorns, mixed

1 clove of garlic
4 × 15ml spoons olive oil
50g unsalted butter

Garnish
50g herb butter (p564)

Wipe the steaks and trim off any excess fat. Crush the peppercorns coarsely in a mortar or in a paper or polythene bag using a rolling-pin. Skin and cut the garlic in half and rub the steaks on both sides with the garlic. Brush each steak on both sides with 1 × 15ml spoon of olive oil. With the heel of your hand, press the crushed peppercorns into the surface of the meat on each side.

Heat the butter in a frying pan and fry the steaks over high heat for 1 minute on both sides until sealed and browned. Reduce the heat and fry the steaks for 4–5 minutes for rare, 7 minutes for medium-rare, and 9 minutes for well-done steaks, turning them 2 or 3 times. Remove with a palette knife or spoons, and place on a warmed serving dish. Garnish with pats of herb butter and serve at once.

Tournedos Rossini
4 helpings

4 tournedos steaks (175g each approx)
4 slices white bread
50g butter
1 × 15ml spoon cooking oil
50g unsalted butter

50ml Madeira **or** dry Marsala
75ml brown stock (p25)
100ml Espagnole sauce (p248)
salt and freshly ground black pepper

Garnish

4 rounds good quality liver pâté
  (5mm thick)
4 small flat mushrooms

4 × 5ml spoons chilled butter
sprigs of watercress

Wipe, trim, and tie the tournedos into a neat shape. Cut 4 rounds from the bread slices, a little wider than the tournedos' bases. Heat the butter and oil in a large, deep frying pan, and fry the bread rounds over moderate heat until light gold and crisp on both sides. Transfer them to a warmed serving dish and keep warm under buttered paper.

Put half the unsalted butter into the pan. Pat the tournedos dry, add them to the pan, raise the heat, and fry the steaks quickly, turning as required, until they are well seared and browned all over but rare inside. Remove them with a palette knife or spoons. Place them on the fried bread rounds and keep warm.

Lower the heat and stir the wine and stock quickly into the pan, scraping up all the drippings. Simmer for 3 minutes, then stir in the sauce and simmer until reduced to the desired consistency.

Meanwhile, heat the remaining 25g unsalted butter in a small frying pan, and turn the pâté slices and mushrooms in it for 2–3 minutes over high heat, until the mushrooms are soft and the pâté is lightly browned but not melted.

Place a slice of pâté on each tournedos and cap it with a mushroom, gill side down. Garnish the top of each mushroom with 1 × 5ml spoon chilled butter. Serve at once, with the sauce in a warmed sauceboat. Garnish the dish with watercress and offer a peppermill of black pepper with the steaks.

Châteaubriand Steak

2 helpings

a double fillet steak, not less than 4cm
   thick
olive oil **or** or melted butter

freshly ground pepper
fat for greasing

Garnish
Maitre d'Hôtel butter (p564)

Wipe, trim the fillet and, if necessary, flatten it slightly with a cutlet bat or rolling-pin. Brush both sides with oil or melted butter, and season with pepper. Place the steak on a greased grid and cook under a very hot grill until browned and sealed. Turn the steak over, using a palette knife or spoons, and grill until browned. Reduce the heat slightly and continue grilling for 4–5 minutes, turning it once or twice, until the steak is well-browned on the outside but slightly underdone on the inside. Garnish with pats of Maître d'Hôtel butter and serve at once.

Serve with Potato Straws (p299) and Demi-glace Sauce (p249), Fresh Tomato Sauce (p255) or Béchamel Sauce (p245).

Note To serve, slice downwards at a slight angle, into 4–6 even slices.

Steak Tartare

4 helpings

400–600g lean fillet **or** rump steak **or**
   topside
salt and freshly ground black pepper
4 small onions **or** 6 shallots
2 cloves garlic (optional)

1 red **or** green pepper (optional)
4 × 15ml spoon capers
3 × 15ml spoons chopped parsley
4 egg yolks (in half shells)

Garnish
8 anchovy fillets (optional)

paprika

Mince the meat finely and season very well. Skin the onions or shallots and the garlic, if used, and chop together. De-seed and chop the pepper, if used. Chop the capers.

Form the meat into 4 thick patties and put each on a separate plate. Arrange small mounds of the onion or shallot mixture, the pepper, capers, and parsley around the meat. Make a hollow in the centre of each patty, and put in it the egg yolk, still in the half shell. Alternatively, cross 2 anchovy fillets over each yolk if not using the shells. Sprinkle with paprika. Hand oil and vinegar separately, if used.

At the table, the ingredients are mixed together with a fork.

Braised, Casseroled, Stewed and Boiled Dishes
Mrs Beeton's Beef à la Mode
4 helpings

2 rashers back bacon (100g approx)
1kg thick flank of beef (see **Note**)
100ml red wine vinegar

75ml port
salt and pepper

Seasoning
1 clove
4 black peppercorns
3 allspice berries
3 sprigs parsley

1 sprig of fresh thyme **or** a good pinch
   of dried thyme
1 bay leaf

Mirepoix
1 medium-sized onion (100g approx)
2 sticks celery
1 medium-sized carrot (50g approx)

½ turnip (50g approx)
50g clarified dripping (p98)
250ml water

Cut the bacon into strips 2cm wide crossways, including lean and fat in each strip. Wipe the meat and make deep slits in the flesh with a sharp-pointed knife. Make the same number of slits as strips of bacon.

Make the seasoning mixture. Pound the clove, peppercorns, and allspice berries in a mortar. Chop the parsley and thyme finely and crumble the bay leaf finely. Mix the ingredients together to make 1 × 5ml spoon seasoning.

Dip the bacon strips in the vinegar, then coat them with about one-third of the seasoning mixture. Insert 1 bacon strip into each slit in the meat. Rub the meat all over with the remaining seasoning and tie the meat into a neat shape.

Prepare the vegetables for the mirepoix. Slice the onion and celery, and chop the carrot and turnip. Melt the dripping in a flameproof casserole or stewpan. Add the onion and fry gently until softened and golden-brown. Add the celery, carrot, and turnip. Place the meat on the vegetables. Pour the vinegar and water gently over the vegetables, then cover the pan closely. Heat to boiling point, reduce the heat, and simmer very gently for 1 hour 40 minutes. Turn the meat over after 40 minutes cooking time, and again after a further 30 minutes.

When cooked, transfer the meat to a warmed serving dish and keep hot. Strain the cooking liquid into a pan, skim off the fat, and add the port. Heat gently to boiling point. Taste, and season if required. Remove the strings from the meat and pour a little of the sauce over the meat. Serve the rest separately in a warmed sauce-boat.
Note Thick flank or top rump, as it is often called, is usually sold with extra fat tied round it. In this recipe the weight of the meat is without the added fat.

Beef Olives
4 helpings

500g rump **or** chuck steak
100g basic herb stuffing (p44)
3 × 15ml spoons dripping
1 large onion (200g approx)
3 × 15ml spoons plain flour

625ml general household **or** brown
  stock (p25)
1 tomato
1 medium-sized carrot (50g approx)
1 × 15ml spoon Worcestershire sauce
salt and pepper

Wipe, trim, and flatten the slices of meat with a cutlet bat or rolling-pin. Cut the meat into 4 slices. Divide the stuffing into 4 portions. Spread 1 portion on each slice of meat, roll up tightly and tie securely with fine string or cotton.

Heat the dripping in a large saucepan and fry the beef olives, turning them frequently until browned. Transfer to a warmed dish and keep hot. Skin and slice the onion, and fry in the fat until golden-brown. Remove with a perforated spoon and keep hot with the beef olives. Add the flour to the fat, stir, and cook until golden-brown. Draw the pan off the heat and gradually stir in the stock. Return to the heat and stir until boiling, then reduce the heat and simmer for 5 minutes. Skin the tomato, scrape the carrot, and slice them. Return the beef olives and onion to the pan. Add the tomato, carrot, Worcestershire sauce, and seasoning to taste. Cover the pan with a tight-fitting lid and simmer for 1½–2 hours; or cook in a moderate oven, 180°C, Gas 4, for 1½ hours.

Remove the strings from the beef olives, and serve the meat arranged in a row on a bed of mashed potatoes. Strain the sauce and pour it over the beef olives.

Carbonnade of Beef *Basic recipe*
6 helpings

700g stewing steak (chuck, blade, skirt
  or thin flank)
50g dripping
2 large onions (400g approx)
1 clove of garlic
1 × 15ml spoon plain flour
250ml beef stock **or** water
375ml brown ale
salt and pepper

bouquet garni
a pinch of grated nutmeg
a pinch of light soft brown sugar
1 × 5ml spoon red wine vinegar
6 thin slices from a French bâton loaf
1 × 15ml spoon French mustard **or**
  1 × 15ml spoon English mustard
  mixed with vinegar to taste

Wipe the meat and trim off any excess fat. Cut the meat into 3–4cm cubes. Heat the dripping in a large pan. Fry the meat quickly until browned on all sides. Transfer to a casserole and keep warm. Skin and slice the onions and fry them in the fat in the pan until lightly browned. Skin and crush the garlic, add it to the onions and fry gently for 1 minute. Pour off any excess fat. Sprinkle the flour over the onion and garlic and cook, stirring until just beginning to brown. Gradually stir in the stock or water, and the ale. Add the salt and pepper, bouquet garni, nutmeg, sugar, and vinegar. Heat to boiling point and pour the liquid over the meat in the casserole. Cover, and cook in a warm oven, 160°C, Gas 3, for 1½–2 hours.

When cooked, remove the bouquet garni, spread the slices of bread with mustard, and press them well down into the gravy. Return the casserole, uncovered, to the oven, for about 15 minutes to allow the bread to brown slightly. Serve from the casserole.

Boeuf Bourguignonne
4–6 helpings

600g chuck steak	2 rashers bacon, without rinds
250ml red wine	3 × 15ml spoons oil
½ × 2.5ml spoon black pepper	12 small onions **or** shallots
1 × 2.5ml spoon salt	12 button mushrooms
bouquet garni	25g flour
1 small onion	salt and pepper
1 small carrot	250ml beef stock (approx)
2 cloves garlic	

Garnish

sippets of fried bread	chopped parsley

Wipe the steak and cut it into 2cm cubes. Put it in a basin, pour the wine over it, and add the pepper, salt, and bouquet garni. Prepare and finely slice the onion and carrot. Skin and crush the garlic. Add these to the meat and wine, cover, and leave to marinate for about 6 hours.

Cut the bacon into small pieces. Heat most of the oil in a frying pan, add the bacon, and fry lightly, then remove and put to one side. Fry the onions or shallots and the mushrooms in the oil for 3–4 minutes, then remove and put to one side. Drain the meat, reserving the marinade, and pat dry on soft kitchen paper. Season the flour with salt and pepper and coat the meat in the flour. Add a little more oil to the frying pan and fry the meat until sealed all over. Put into a 1.5 litre ovenproof casserole. Stir in the bacon, onions, and mushrooms. Strain the marinade over the meat and add about 250ml stock. Cover, and cook in a warm oven, 160°C, Gas 3, for about 2 hours. Season to taste. Serve garnished with the sippets and chopped parsley.

Beef Stroganoff (1)

4 helpings

500g fillet of beef
1 onion
3 × 10ml spoons vegetable oil
salt and pepper

1 × 10ml spoon flour
250ml soured cream
1 × 10ml spoon Piquant sauce (p243)

Garnish
chopped fennel **or** parsley

Wipe and trim the meat, cut into small slices, and beat well with a cutlet bat or rolling-pin. Cut into fine slivers. Skin and slice the onion finely. Heat the oil, and fry the onion until softened. Add the sliced meat, season to taste, and fry for 5–6 minutes, stirring slowly with a fork. Sprinkle the meat with the flour, stir, and cook for 2–3 minutes. Add the soured cream, stir, and cook for a further 2–3 minutes. Add the Piquant sauce and salt to taste. Sprinkle with chopped fennel or parsley.

Serve with fried potatoes.

Brown Stew

6 helpings

700g stewing steak (chuck, blade **or**
   neck)
1 large onion (200g approx)
2 large carrots (200g approx)
1 large turnip (100g approx)
25g dripping

3 × 15ml spoons plain flour
750ml general household **or** brown
   stock (p25) **or** water
salt and pepper
bouquet garni

Wipe the meat and trim off any excess fat. Cut the meat into neat pieces 2–3cm thick. Prepare the vegetables; then slice the onion and carrots, and dice the turnip.

Heat the dripping in a stewpan. Put in the meat, and fry quickly until browned on all sides. Take the meat out of the pan, and put in the onion. Reduce the heat, and fry the onion gently until lightly browned. Stir in the flour and cook slowly until it turns a rich brown colour. Gradually add the stock or water, and heat to boiling point, stirring all the time. Add the seasoning and bouquet garni. Return the meat to the pan, cover with a tight-fitting lid, and simmer for $1\frac{1}{2}$ hours. Skim off any fat on the surface. Add the carrot and turnip, replace the lid and simmer for another hour or until the meat and vegetables are tender. Again skim off any fat. Re-season if required, and remove the bouquet garni before serving.

Note If preferred, the stew can be cooked in a warm oven, 160°C, Gas 3, for $1\frac{1}{2}$–2 hours. Add the carrot and turnip for the last hour of cooking.

Exeter Stew
6 helpings

700g chuck steak **or** blade **or** neck
   of beef
3 × 10ml spoons dripping
3 medium-sized onions (300g approx)

3 × 15ml spoons plain flour
625ml water
1 × 5ml spoon vinegar
salt and pepper

Savoury Parsley Balls
100g plain flour
½ × 2.5ml spoon baking powder
4½ × 15ml spoons shredded suet
1 × 15ml spoon finely chopped parsley

1 × 2.5ml spoon dried mixed herbs
1 × 5ml spoon salt
1 × 2.5ml spoon ground pepper
1 egg **or** 3 × 15ml spoons milk

Wipe the meat and trim off any excess fat. Cut the meat into 5cm cubes. Heat the dripping in a stewpan and fry the meat in it until browned on all sides. Remove the meat and put to one side. Skin and slice the onions. Put them in the pan, and fry gently until light brown. Add the flour, and cook, stirring until browned. Mix in the water and stir until boiling. Reduce the heat to simmering point. Add the vinegar and seasoning to taste. Return the meat, cover and simmer gently for 1½ hours.

To make the parsley balls, sift the flour and baking powder into a bowl. Add the suet, herbs, salt and pepper, and mix together. Beat the egg, if used, until liquid and bind the dry ingredients together with the beaten egg or milk to form a stiff dough. Divide the dough into 12 equal pieces and roll each into a ball.

Heat the stew to boiling point and drop in the balls. Reduce the heat and simmer for a further 30 minutes with the pan half-covered. Pile the meat in the centre of a warmed serving dish, pour the gravy over it and arrange the balls round the base.

Beef Creole
6–8 helpings

1kg topside **or** rump **or** brisket of beef
1 × 5ml spoon salt
1 × 5ml spoon ground pepper
75g streaky bacon, without rinds

500g onions
500g tomatoes
1 green pepper (125g approx)
a little beef stock **or** water (optional)

Wipe, trim, and tie the meat into a neat shape, if necessary. Season with salt and pepper. Lay the rashers in the bottom of an ovenproof casserole. Place the meat on the bacon. Skin and slice the onions and tomatoes. De-seed and slice the pepper. Cover the meat with the vegetables. Cover the casserole with a tight-fitting lid and cook in a warm oven, 160°C, Gas 3, for about 2½ hours, until the meat is tender. Lift out the meat, remove the string, and cut the meat into slices. Arrange the slices on a warmed serving dish and keep hot.

Rub the onions, tomatoes, and pepper through a sieve into a saucepan and re-heat to form a sauce, thinning with a little stock or water, if necessary. Pour the sauce round the beef slices.

Boiled Beef with Vegetables and Dumplings *Basic recipe*
8–10 helpings

1–1.25kg brisket **or** silverside **or** aitchbone of beef
1 × 5ml spoon salt
3 cloves
10 peppercorns

bouquet garni
3 medium-sized onions (300g approx)
4 large carrots (400g approx)
2 small turnips (100g approx)

Suet Dumplings
200g self-raising flour
100g suet

½ × 2.5ml spoon salt

Weigh the meat and calculate the cooking time, allowing 25 minutes per 0.5kg plus 20 minutes over. Wipe, trim, and tie the meat into a neat shape with string, if necessary. Put the meat into a large stewpan, cover with boiling water, and add the salt. Bring to the boil again and boil for 5 minutes to seal the surface of the meat. Reduce the heat to simmering point, and skim. Add the cloves, peppercorns, and bouquet garni. Cover the pan and simmer for the rest of the calculated cooking time.

Meanwhile, prepare the vegetables and cut them into serving-sized pieces. About 45 minutes before the end of the cooking time, add the vegetables to the meat and re-heat to simmering point.

Prepare the dumplings. Mix the flour, suet, and salt in a bowl. Add enough cold water to make a fairly stiff dough. Divide this mixture into walnut-sized pieces and roll them into balls. Drop them into the pan with the beef, so that they simmer for the final 20–30 minutes of the cooking time. Keep the pan covered and turn the dumplings over once during this time.

To serve, remove the bouquet garni. Take out the dumplings and vegetables with a perforated spoon, and arrange them as a border on a large warmed serving dish. Remove any strings from the meat, skewer if necessary, and set it in the centre of the dish. Serve some of the liquid separately in a sauce-boat.

Note When adding the dumplings, make sure they have plenty of room to swell. If the pan is very full, it is better to cook them separately in stock.

Pastry and Minced Dishes
Mrs Beeton's Steak Pie
6 helpings

600g lean stewing steak (chuck, blade or neck)
3 × 15ml spoons plain flour
1 × 5ml spoon salt
½ × 2.5ml spoon ground pepper
2 medium-sized onions (200g approx)

250ml beef stock or water (approx)
flaky (p458) or rough puff (p457) pastry using 100g flour or shortcrust pastry (p453) using 200g flour
flour for rolling out
beaten egg or milk for glazing

Wipe the meat and trim off any excess fat. Cut the meat into 1–2cm cubes. Mix the flour with the salt and pepper in a bag or deep bowl. Toss the cubes of meat in the seasoned flour and put them in a 1 litre pie dish, piling them higher in the centre. Skin and chop the onions, and sprinkle them between the pieces of meat. Pour in stock or water to quarter-fill the dish.

Roll out the pastry on a lightly floured surface and use to cover the dish. Trim the edge, knock up with the back of a knife and flute the edge. Make a small hole in the centre of the lid, and decorate round with leaves of pastry. Make a pastry tassel or rose to cover the hole after baking, if liked. Brush the pastry with the beaten egg or milk.

Bake the pie in a very hot oven, 230°C, Gas 8, until the pastry is risen and light brown. Bake the tassel or rose blind, if made. Reduce the oven heat to moderate, 180°C, Gas 4, and, if necessary, place the pie on a lower shelf. Cover with greaseproof paper to prevent the pastry over-browning, and continue cooking for about 2 hours until the meat is quite tender when tested with a skewer. Heat the remaining stock and pour in enough to fill the dish by funnelling it through the hole in the pastry. Insert the pastry tassel or rose, if made, and serve.

VARIATIONS
Steak and Kidney Pie
Follow the recipe for Steak Pie, but add 2 sheep's or 150g ox kidneys. Skin, core, and cut the kidneys into slices before mixing with the steak and onions.

Steak and Mushroom Pie
Follow the recipe for Steak Pie, but add 100g mushrooms, cleaned and sliced, to the meat in the pie dish.

Steak and Potato Pie
Follow the recipe for Steak Pie, but add about 300g potatoes. Slice the meat and dip in seasoned flour. Prepare and slice the potatoes thinly. Place a layer of sliced potatoes on the bottom of the pie dish, season, and cover with a layer of meat. Add a little of the chopped onion. Repeat the layers of potato, meat, onion, and seasoning until the dish is full. Add enough stock or water to fill one-third of the dish. Proceed as for Steak Pie.

Steak Pudding
6 helpings

600g stewing steak (chuck, blade **or** neck)	suet crust pastry (p454) using 200g flour
3 × 15ml spoons plain flour	flour for rolling out
1 × 5ml spoon salt	fat for greasing
½ × 2.5ml spoon ground pepper	3 × 15ml spoons beef stock **or** water

Wipe the meat and trim off any excess fat. Cut the meat into 1cm cubes. Mix the flour with the salt and pepper in a bag or deep bowl. Toss the cubes of meat in the seasoned flour.

Reserve one-quarter of the pastry for the lid. Roll out the rest on a lightly floured surface so that it is 1cm larger than the top of a greased 750ml basin, and 5mm thick. Press well into the basin to remove any creases. Half fill the basin with the prepared meat and add the stock or water; then add the rest of the meat. Roll out the pastry reserved for the lid to fit the top of the basin. Dampen the edges, place the lid in position, and seal. Cover with greased greaseproof paper or foil.

Place the basin in a steamer, or on a saucer in a pan with water coming half-way up the basin's sides. Steam, or half-steam, for 3–3½ hours, topping up the steamer or pan with boiling water when it is reduced by a third. Serve from the basin or turn out on to a warmed serving dish. Serve with a thin beef gravy.

VARIATION
Steak and Kidney Pudding
Follow the recipe for Steak Pudding, but add 2 sheep's kidneys or 150g ox kidney. Cut the meat into thin slices about 8 × 5cm. Dip them in the seasoned flour. Skin, core, and cut the kidneys into thin slices a little smaller than the meat. Dip them in the seasoned flour. Place a slice of kidney on each slice of meat, roll up tightly, and place the rolls on end in the pastry-lined basin. Proceed as for Steak Pudding.

Cornish Pasties
Makes 6

300g chuck steak **or** blade of beef	shortcrust pastry (p453) using 200g flour
1 large potato (150g approx)	flour for rolling out
1 small onion (50g approx)	beaten egg **or** milk for glazing
salt and pepper	(optional)
2 × 15ml spoons water **or** beef stock	

Wipe the meat and trim off any excess fat. Cut the meat into 5mm dice. Prepare and dice the potato; skin and chop the onion finely. Mix together the meat, potato, onion, and add seasoning to taste. Add the water or stock to moisten.

Divide the pastry into 6 portions. Roll each portion on a lightly floured surface into a circle 12–14cm in diameter (approx). Trim the edges neatly. (A saucer or small plate can be used to cut the rounds.) Divide the meat filling into 6 portions and pile one portion on one half of each circle of pastry. Dampen the edges of the pastry and fold over to cover the mixture. Press the edges of the pastry together. Turn the pasties so that the sealed edges are on the top. Flute the sealed edges with the fingers. Brush with beaten egg or milk, if liked. Place the pasties on a baking tray. Bake in a hot oven, 220°C, Gas 7, for about 10 minutes, then reduce the heat to moderate, 180°C, Gas 4, and cook for 30–40 minutes.

Sea Pie
6 helpings

600g stewing steak (chuck, blade **or** neck)
3 × 15ml spoons plain flour
2 × 5ml spoons salt
½ × 2.5ml spoon ground pepper
1 medium-sized onion (100g approx)

1 large carrot (100g approx)
2 small turnips (100g approx)
brown stock (p25) **or** water to cover
suet crust pastry (p454) using
    200g flour
flour for rolling out

Wipe the meat and trim off any excess fat. Cut the meat into thin slices about 5cm square. Mix the flour with the salt and pepper in a bag or deep bowl. Toss the pieces of meat in the seasoned flour. Skin and slice the onion and dice the carrot and turnips. Put the meat and vegetables into a pan. Heat to boiling point just enough stock or water to cover the meat and vegetables and pour into the pan. Re-heat, cover with a tight-fitting lid, and simmer very gently for about 1½ hours.

Roll out the pastry on a lightly floured surface to a round a little smaller than the top of the stewpan. Place the pastry on top of the meat and vegetables. Cover with the pan lid and continue cooking for 1 hour. Cut the pastry into portions and serve with the meat.

Minced Beef *Basic recipe*
4–5 helpings

1 large onion (200g approx)
1 clove of garlic
2 × 15ml spoons oil
500g raw minced beef
salt and pepper

250g canned tomatoes
1 × 15ml spoon chopped parsley **or**
    1 × 5ml spoon dried parsley
a pinch of dried mixed herbs
1 bay leaf

Skin and chop the onion and garlic. Heat the oil in a stewpan. Add the onion and garlic, and fry gently until softened. Add the minced meat and fry until browned, stirring all the time. Season, and add the tomatoes and herbs. Stir well, and heat to boiling point. Reduce the heat and simmer, uncovered, for about 30 minutes, stirring from time to time.

Serve with vegetables, pasta or rice, or use as a filling for green peppers, baked potatoes, etc.

Note Minced beef from the butcher may be prepared from coarse cuts and trimmings or from good quality braising or stewing steak. The price is often the only indication of the quality. If you want to be certain of the type of meat, buy the cut first, then ask the butcher to mince it, or mince it yourself.

Hamburgers *Basic recipe*
4 helpings

500g raw blade **or** chuck steak, minced
2 × 5ml spoons grated onion (optional)
freshly ground black pepper
coarse salt

4 × 5ml spoons butter
Tabasco sauce
Worcestershire sauce
lemon juice

Garnish
chopped parsley

chopped chives

Mix together the minced beef and onion, if used, and season with pepper. Shape the meat lightly into 4 flat round cakes about 1cm thick. Sprinkle a thin layer of salt in a cold frying pan. Place the frying pan over high heat and put in the patties. Cook for about 5 minutes until well browned underneath. Turn the patties over and cook to the degree of rareness wanted. For a rare hamburger, cook for 1–2 minutes only, lowering the heat to medium after 30 seconds. When cooked, top each patty with 1 × 5ml spoon butter, and sprinkle with Tabasco and Worcestershire sauce and lemon juice. Transfer to a warmed serving dish, pour any pan juices over them, and serve garnished with parsley and chives.

VARIATIONS

1) Add 1 × 2.5ml spoon salt, a pinch of paprika and 2 × 15ml spoons double cream to the meat mixture. Brush the pan lightly with melted bacon fat instead of using salt. Brown the patties on both sides over high heat, then reduce the heat and cook slowly as required.

2) Prepare the patties as for variation 1. Wrap each in a rasher of bacon secured with a toothpick before cooking.

3) After cooking the patties as for the basic recipe, transfer them to a warmed serving dish but omit the sauces and lemon juice. Instead, add to the pan 50ml red wine or soured cream or 2 × 15ml spoons sherry or brandy; swill round, scraping up the pan juices, and pour the sauce over the patties.

4) Prepare the patties as for the basic recipe. Brush them lightly with melted butter, then grill under high heat for 5 minutes. Lower the heat and cook the second side for 1–2 minutes, or longer for well-done patties. Season and garnish as for the basic recipe.

5) Prepare and cook the patties and serve on buttered toast seasoned with the pan juices.

6) Garnish each cooked hamburger with a fried onion ring and 1 × 5ml spoon tomato ketchup or chutney instead of parsley and chives.

7) Split 4 round soft dinner rolls in half horizontally. Prepare the patties as for the basic recipe, brush lightly with butter, then grill them on one side only. Place them on the bottom halves of the rolls, cooked side down, then grill the second side. Top each with a fried onion ring and 1 × 5ml spoon tomato ketchup or chutney and replace the top halves of the rolls.

Beef Galantine
6–8 helpings

200g lean bacon, without rinds
500g chuck steak **or** blade of beef, minced
150g soft white **or** brown breadcrumbs
salt and pepper

1 egg
125ml brown stock (p25)
margarine **or** lard for greasing
2 × 15ml spoons raspings (p43) **or** 1 × 15ml spoon meat glaze (p59)

Garnish
125ml chopped aspic jelly

Mince the bacon. Put into a bowl with the meat, breadcrumbs and seasoning to taste, and mix together well. Beat the egg until liquid, add the stock, and stir into the meat mixture to bind. Shape the mixture into a short, thick roll, wrap it in greased greaseproof paper, wrap in a scalded pudding cloth, and secure the ends. Steam for $2\frac{1}{2}$–3 hours or, if preferred, boil gently in stock for about 2 hours.

When cooked, remove the meat, unwrap it, and then roll it up tightly in a clean dry cloth. Press the roll between 2 plates until cold. When cold, remove the cloth and roll the meat in the raspings, or brush all over with melted meat glaze. Garnish with aspic jelly.

Spaghetti Bolognese
4 helpings

75g unsmoked streaky bacon, without rinds
1 medium-sized onion
1 medium-sized carrot
$\frac{1}{2}$ stick celery
200g lean beef mince
100g chicken livers
15g butter
1 × 15ml spoon olive oil

1 × 15ml spoon concentrated tomato purée
125ml dry white wine
salt and pepper
a pinch of grated nutmeg
200ml beef stock
300g spaghetti
a knob of butter

Chop the bacon into small pieces. Prepare and chop finely the onion, carrot, and celery. Break down any lumps in the mince with a fork. Cut the chicken livers into small shreds. Heat the butter and oil in a saucepan, and cook the bacon gently until brown. Add the vegetables and fry until tender and browned. Stir in the mince, and turn it until browned all over. Add the chicken livers and continue cooking for 3 minutes, turning the livers over to brown them. Mix in gradually the tomato purée and then the wine. Season with salt, pepper, and nutmeg. Lower the heat so that the sauce just simmers. Stir in the stock, cover the pan, and simmer for 30–40 minutes or until the sauce is the desired consistency. Meanwhile, boil the spaghetti as directed. Drain it and pile on a warmed serving dish. Pour the sauce over the spaghetti. Top with a knob of butter and serve Parmesan cheese separately.

Chilli con Carne
6 helpings

400g dried red kidney beans **or**
   1 × 430g can red kidney beans
1 large onion (200g approx)
1 clove of garlic
2 × 15ml spoons vegetable oil

750g raw minced beef
1 × 396g can tomatoes
1 × 10ml spoon chilli powder
salt and pepper

Soak the dried kidney beans, if used, overnight, then boil for at least 10 minutes. Drain, then cook them gently in boiling salted water until tender. Drain and leave to cool. Drain the canned beans, if used. Skin the onion and chop it coarsely; skin the garlic and slice it thinly. Heat the oil in a large saucepan, add the onion and garlic, and cook until softened. Add the meat, break up any lumps with a fork, and stir until browned all over. Add the tomatoes, kidney beans, and chilli powder. Cover the pan with a lid, heat to simmering point and simmer for 2 hours. Season with salt and pepper to taste. For a spicier Chilli con Carne, add extra chilli powder. The mixture should be very thick. If possible, keep it for 24 hours before use to let the flavours blend and mellow; then re-heat.

Baked Green Lasagne with Meat Sauce
4 helpings

50g onion
1 clove of garlic
50g celery
50g carrot
250g green lasagne
50g lean lamb
500g lean beef
50g lard **or** 4 × 15ml spoons oil
300ml beef stock

50g concentrated tomato purée
pepper
250g tomatoes
50g red pepper
75g walnut pieces
75g butter and bacon fat, mixed
50g sultanas
150ml cold Béchamel sauce (p245)
150g grated Parmesan cheese

Prepare and chop the onion, garlic, celery, and carrot. Cook the lasagne in boiling salted water for 15 minutes. Drain, rinse under hot water, and place on a slightly dampened tea-towel, side by side but not touching. Leave to dry.

Mince the lamb and beef. Heat the lard or oil in a frying pan, and sauté the chopped onion, garlic, celery and carrot together for 5 minutes. Add the minced meat and brown it lightly all over. Add the stock, tomato purée, and seasoning. Bring to the boil, reduce the heat, and simmer for 30 minutes. Skin, de-seed, and chop the tomatoes and pepper. Chop the nuts finely.

Grease a shallow ovenproof dish with the bacon fat and butter. Line the bottom with half the pasta and cover with the meat mixture, then sprinkle with nuts, sultanas, tomatoes, and pepper. Cover with the remaining pasta. Coat with thick, cold Béchamel sauce, and sprinkle with the Parmesan cheese. Bake in a moderate oven, 180°C, Gas 4, for 20 minutes.

Shepherd's Pie (Cottage Pie)
4–6 helpings

600g lean beef mince
2 medium-sized onions
25g dripping
1 × 15ml spoon flour
150ml strong beef stock
salt and freshly ground black pepper

700g potatoes
a pinch of grated nutmeg
milk
1–2 × 15ml spoons butter (optional)
butter for greasing

Break up any lumps in the meat with a fork. Skin and slice the onions. Melt the dripping in a saucepan, and fry the onions until softened but not coloured. Stir in the flour, and cook gently for 1–2 minutes, stirring all the time. Gradually add the stock, without letting lumps form, and stir until boiling. Reduce the heat, and simmer for 2–3 minutes until the sauce thickens. Stir in the mince, cover the pan, and simmer for 20 minutes. Season well, replace the lid, and simmer for 10 minutes longer or until the mince is cooked through and tender.

Meanwhile, prepare the potatoes and boil them in salted water until tender. Mash them until smooth with a seasoning of salt, pepper, nutmeg, enough milk to make them creamy, and butter if liked. Put the meat and sauce into a greased pie dish or shallow oven-to-table baking dish. Cover with the potato, smooth the top, then flick it up into small peaks or score a pattern on the surface with a fork. Bake for 10–15 minutes in a hot oven, 220°C, Gas 7, until browned on top. Serve hot.

Beef Croquettes
4 helpings

250g cooked beef
25g cooking fat
25g finely chopped onion
25g flour
150ml beef stock
salt and pepper
1 × 5ml spoon chopped parsley

1 × 5ml spoon any bottled savoury
    sauce
flour for dusting
2 eggs
50g dry white breadcrumbs
oil **or** fat for deep frying

Remove any fat, skin or gristle, and mince the meat. Melt the fat in a large frying pan and fry the onion for 2–3 minutes. Stir in the stock and bring to the boil, stirring all the time. Cook for 2 minutes until the sauce thickens. Add the meat, seasoning, parsley, and sauce. Stir over the heat for a moment. Turn the mixture on to a plate, level the surface, cover with a second plate, and leave to cool completely.

When cold, divide into 8 equal-sized portions. On a floured surface, form into neat cork or roll-shaped pieces. Beat the eggs until liquid. Scatter the crumbs on a sheet of greaseproof paper. Dip each croquette into the egg, brushing it all over to make sure it is evenly covered, then roll it in the crumbs until it is completely covered. Press the crumbs on lightly. Heat the fat (p10). Coat each croquette a second time. Fry in the hot fat, a few at a time, until crisp and browned all over. Drain well. Keep the first batches hot while cooking the rest.

Note The filling should have a soft creamy texture, contrasting with the crisp coating.

Offal Dishes
Baked Stuffed Ox Heart
6 helpings

1 ox heart
1.50g sage and onion stuffing (p49)
    or basic herb or ham stuffing (p44)
50–75g dripping

25g flour
500ml strong general household or
    brown stock (p25)

Wash the heart thoroughly under running water or in several changes of cold water. Cut off the flaps and lobes, and remove any gristle. Cut away the membranes which separate the cavities inside the heart and see that it is quite free from blood inside. Soak in cold water for 30 minutes. Drain and dry the heart thoroughly and fill it with the stuffing. Sew up the top with fine string or cotton, or skewer securely.

Heat the dripping in a roasting tin, and put in the heart. Baste well and bake in a warm oven, 160°C, Gas 3, for 3 hours. Baste frequently and turn it occasionally. When tender, remove the string, cotton or skewer, place the heart on a warmed serving dish and keep hot. Pour off most of the fat from the baking tin, retaining about 1 × 15ml spoon of the sediment. Stir in the flour and cook until browned. Gradually add the stock and stir until boiling. Boil for 3 minutes. Pour a little round the heart and serve the rest separately.

Serve redcurrant jelly with the heart if stuffed with basic herb stuffing; serve Cranberry Sauce (p254) if it is stuffed with ham or sage and onion stuffing.

Liver Hot Pot
6 helpings

650g ox liver
25g flour
salt and pepper
100g streaky bacon, without rinds
3 large onions

900g–1kg potatoes
3 × 2.5ml spoons dried sage
beef stock or water to cover
dripping

Garnish
chopped parsley

Remove the skin and tubes, and cut the liver into 5mm slices. Season the flour with salt and pepper in a bag or bowl, and toss the liver slices in it. Cut the bacon into small squares. Skin the onions and slice them thinly. Prepare and slice the potatoes.

Place alternate layers of liver, bacon, onion and potatoes in a pie dish or casserole, sprinkling each layer with a little sage and seasoning. End with a thick layer of potatoes. Pour in just enough stock or water to cover the contents of the dish, cover with a lid, and cook in a moderate oven, 180°C, Gas 4, for about 2 hours. Remove the lid 30 minutes before serving, dot the top of the dish with dripping, and leave to cook, uncovered, to brown the potatoes. Sprinkle with parsley, and serve from the dish.

SOUPS.

CHAPTER V.

GENERAL DIRECTIONS FOR MAKING SOUPS,

Oxtail Soup (p.39)

Grapefruit Baskets (p.57)

Prawns (p.61)

Smoked Salmon (p.72)

Fresh Herring (p.71), Forcemeat (p.46) and Kedgeree (p.84)

Braised Oxtail
4–6 helpings

1.5kg oxtail	salt and pepper
50g beef dripping	bouquet garni
2 medium-sized onions (200g approx)	2 cloves
25g plain flour	1 blade of mace
500ml water **or** beef stock	juice of ½ lemon

Garnish

fried bread croûtons

diced **or** julienne strips of cooked carrot and turnip

Wash the oxtail, dry it thoroughly, and trim off any excess fat. Cut into joints, if not already jointed by the butcher, and divide the thick parts in half.

Heat the dripping in a stewpan. Fry the pieces of oxtail until browned all over, then remove them from the pan and put to one side. Skin and slice the onions. Fry them slowly in the fat until browned. Stir in the flour and cook for 1–2 minutes. Gradually add the water or stock, then add the seasoning, bouquet garni and spices, and stir until boiling. Return the pieces of oxtail to the pan, cover with a tight-fitting lid, reduce the heat, and simmer gently for 2½–3 hours. Remove the meat and arrange it on a warmed serving dish. Add the lemon juice to the sauce and re-season if required. Strain the sauce and pour it over the oxtail. Garnish with the bread croûtons, carrot and turnip.

Mrs Beeton's Boiled Marrow Bones
2 pieces of marrow bone per helping

marrow bones (150g approx each)   flour

Choose marrow bones from the leg or shin. Ask your butcher to saw them across into pieces 7cm long or do it yourself. Shape the thick ends by chopping them so that the bones will stand upright. Mix some flour to a stiff paste with water, and plaster this paste over the open end of each bone to seal in the marrow. Tie each bone in a floured cloth.

Stand the bones upright in a deep saucepan containing enough boiling water to come half-way up the bones. Cover the pan with a tight-fitting lid, reduce the heat, and simmer gently for about 1½ hours. Refill the pan with boiling water, if necessary. When cooked, remove the bones from the cloths and scrape off the paste. Fasten a paper napkin round each one and serve with a pointed teaspoon to extract the marrow.

Serve with Melba or hot dry toast and a seasoning of pepper.

Kidney in Italian Sauce
4 helpings

500g ox kidney
3 × 15ml spoons plain flour
1 × 2.5ml spoon salt
pepper
1 small onion (50g approx)
3 × 10ml spoons beef dripping

25g butter **or** margarine
375ml general household **or** brown
    stock (p25)
100g mushrooms
1–2 × 15ml spoons sherry (optional)

Garnish
100g cooked green peas

Skin, core, and cut the kidney into slices about 1cm thick. Season the flour with the salt and a generous pinch of pepper in a bag or bowl and toss the kidney in it until well-coated. Skin and chop the onion. Heat the dripping in a sauté pan and fry the kidney quickly on both sides. Add the onion, reduce the heat, cover, and fry gently for 20 minutes.

Meanwhile, melt the butter or margarine in a saucepan. Stir in the flour left after coating the kidney and cook until a nut-brown colour. Gradually add the stock and stir until boiling. Reduce the heat and simmer for 5 minutes. Drain the kidney and onion from the fat, add them to the sauce, half cover the pan and simmer for about 45 minutes. Clean and slice the mushrooms and add them to the pan with the sherry, if used, and extra seasoning, if liked. Simmer for a further 15 minutes. Serve hot, garnished with green peas.

Mrs Beeton's Stewed Ox Cheek
6 helpings

1 boned ox cheek
2 medium-sized onions (200g approx)
2 large carrots (200g approx)
1 turnip (50g approx)
12 peppercorns
2 cloves
bouquet garni

2 × 5ml spoons salt
2 × 10ml spoons butter **or** margarine
4 × 10ml spoons plain flour
2–3 × 15ml spoons sherry (optional)
2 × 5ml spoons lemon juice
salt and pepper

Garnish
diced **or** julienne strips of cooked carrot
    and turnip

Wash the ox cheek well in cold water. Soak for at least 12 hours in salted water, changing the water 2 or 3 times; then wash it well in warm water. Cut the cheek into convenient-sized pieces. Put them into a stewpan and cover with cold water. Heat to boiling point and skim well. Prepare the vegetables and slice them thickly. Add to the pan with the peppercorns, cloves, bouquet garni, and salt. Re-heat to boiling point, reduce the heat, cover with a tight-fitting lid, and simmer very gently for 1½–2 hours, or until the meat is tender, keeping it just covered with liquid the whole time.

When cooked, strain the liquid from the meat into a measuring jug. Put the meat to one side. Melt the butter or margarine in a saucepan, stir in the flour and cook over gentle heat until lightly browned. Gradually add 625ml of the reserved liquid and stir until boiling; reduce the heat and simmer for 10 minutes. Add the sherry, if used, the lemon juice, and seasoning to taste. Add the pieces of meat to the sauce, and re-heat briefly. Serve on a warmed dish, and garnish with the carrot and turnip. **Note** The rest of the cooking liquid will make an excellent soup stock.

Boiled Ox Tongue
9–12 helpings

1 fresh ox tongue (2kg approx)	1 turnip
1 medium-sized onion	bouquet garni
1 medium-sized carrot	6 black peppercorns

Hot Garnish
boiled sprigs of cauliflower **or**
   Brussels sprouts

Cold Garnish
chopped parsley   savoury butter (optional) (pp563–66)

Weigh the tongue, then wash it thoroughly. Soak for 2 hours. Drain and put in a large pan. Cover with cold water, heat to boiling point, then drain thoroughly.

Return to the pan and cover a second time with fresh cold water. Prepare and dice the vegetables. Add to the pan with the bouquet garni and peppercorns. Heat to boiling point, cover with a tight-fitting lid, reduce the heat and simmer gently, allowing 30 minutes per 0.5kg plus 30 minutes over. When cooked, lift out the tongue and plunge it into cold water. Drain. Remove the skin carefully, and the small bones at the root of the tongue, together with any excess fat, glands, and gristle.

To serve hot: Garnish the tongue with sprigs of cauliflower or Brussels sprouts.

To serve cold: (1) Place the tongue on a board and stick a fork through the root and another through the top to straighten it. Leave to cool completely, then trim. Glaze with meat glaze (p59) or aspic jelly and garnish with parsley. Decorate with rosettes of a smooth savoury butter, if liked.

(2) Bend and roll the tongue into a round shape and press it into a deep round cake tin, just big enough to hold it (18cm in diameter approx). Spoon over a little of the strained stock in which the tongue was cooked to fill up the crevices. Put a flat plate on the tongue and then a heavy weight. Leave to set, then turn out and serve in slices.

VARIATION
Pickled, Rolled Ox Tongue
Follow the recipe for Boiled Ox Tongue but use a pickled (salted) ox tongue. Soak overnight in cold water before proceeding with the recipe. Finish by the method given under *To serve cold* (2).

Boiled Cow-Heel

6 helpings

2 cow-heels	25g butter **or** dripping
water **or** general household stock (p25) to cover	25g flour
	1 × 10ml spoon chopped parsley
fat for greasing	salt and pepper

Wash the heels and blanch them for 6–8 minutes in boiling water. Drain, and put them in a large saucepan. Cover with fresh cold water or stock. Heat to boiling point, reduce the heat, cover the pan with a tight-fitting lid, and simmer very gently for about 3 hours.

Just before the end of the cooking time, melt the butter or dripping in a saucepan, add the flour, and cook without colouring for 2–3 minutes, stirring all the time. Pour off 500ml of the liquid in which the cow-heels have cooked and gradually stir it into the roux. Put the pan containing the cow-heels to one side. Heat the stock in the saucepan to boiling point, stirring all the time, then reduce the heat and simmer for 5 minutes. Add the parsley and seasoning to taste. Leave the pan over the lowest possible heat.

Drain the cow-heels, then remove the bones, holding each heel in a cloth. Arrange the pieces of meat on a warmed serving dish. Pour the hot sauce over them and serve at once.

VARIATION

Boiled Calf's Feet

Cook as for Boiled Cow-Heel, but reduce the simmering time to 1½ hours.

Tripe Lyonnaise

4 helpings

500g dressed tripe	6 black peppercorns
bouquet garni	1 × 5ml spoon salt
2 medium-sized onions (200g approx)	50g butter **or** margarine
1 large carrot (100g approx)	1 × 10ml spoon chopped parsley
1 leek	1 × 10ml spoon vinegar
1 stick of celery (50g approx)	salt and pepper

Wash the tripe. Put in a stewpan, cover with water, and add the bouquet garni. Heat slowly to boiling point. Meanwhile, prepare one of the onions and the rest of the vegetables, and slice them thinly. Add to the pan with the peppercorns and salt. Cover with a tight-fitting lid, reduce the heat and simmer gently until the tripe is tender (the length of time should be suggested by the butcher). Drain thoroughly (the stock can be used in a soup or casserole). Leave to cool slightly, then cut the tripe into pieces 5cm square (approx).

Skin and slice the second onion. Melt the butter or margarine in a frying pan and fry the onion until soft and golden-brown. Add the tripe, parsley, vinegar, and seasoning. Toss in the pan for a few minutes until heated through. Serve at once.

Tripe and Onion
4 helpings

500g dressed tripe
500ml milk
salt and pepper

3 medium-sized onions (300g approx)
25g butter **or** margarine
25g flour

Garnish
1 × 15ml spoon chopped parsley

toasted croûtons

Wash the tripe and cut it into pieces 5cm square (approx). Put into a stewpan, pour over the milk and, if necessary, add some water to cover. Add salt and pepper to taste. Skin and chop the onions. Add them to the pan. Heat to boiling point, cover with a tight-fitting lid, reduce the heat and simmer gently until the tripe is tender (the length of time should be suggested by the butcher).

Knead the butter or margarine and flour together until evenly blended, and add it in small pieces to the contents of the pan. Stir until smooth, then continue cooking for another 30 minutes. Serve the tripe on a warmed dish and garnish with chopped parsley and toasted croûtons.

Lamb and Mutton

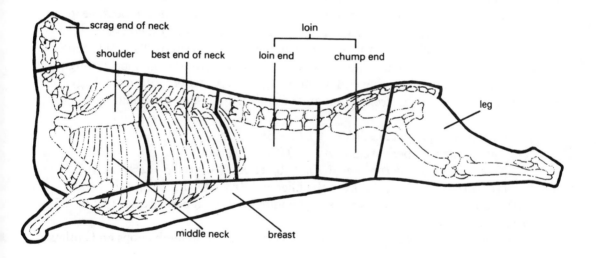

Lamb and Mutton Cuts
English lamb and mutton and most imported, chilled and frozen lamb and mutton are usually cut in a similar way to beef, ie into sides and quarters before jointing. As with beef, cuts vary in different parts of Great Britain. The diagram above shows the most usual ones.

1) *Leg* or hind limb, also known as gigot in Scotland, is an excellent roasting joint on the bone or boned, stuffed and rolled. The leg is often divided into fillet and shank end. Leg is leaner (tougher and slightly drier) than the shoulder (forelimb) and is also more expensive. (Av wt leg of lamb – 2kg; Av wt leg of mutton – 2.5kg)

2) *Loin* can be roasted whole on the bone or boned, stuffed, and rolled. However, it is usually divided into loin end and chump end, and is cut into loin chops and chump chops (see below). (Av wt loin of lamb – 1.5kg; Av wt loin of mutton – 2kg)

3) *Saddle* is the whole loin from both sides of the animal, left in one piece. (Av wt saddle of lamb – 3.5kg; Av wt saddle of mutton – 4.5kg)

4) *Best end of neck* can be roasted on the bone or boned, stuffed, and rolled. It is often sold as chops or cutlets for grilling and frying. These chops or cutlets are sometimes served as noisettes which are prepared by removing the backbone (chine bone) and trimming away some of the meat at the rib end. Two best ends of neck are used to make a Crown Roast (pp136–37) or Guard of Honour (pp 137–38). (Av wt best end of neck of lamb – 1 kg; Av wt best end of neck of mutton – 2.5 kg)

5) *Breast* is the most economical cut for roasting or braising and for tasty stews. Because of its high fat content it is best roasted with a stuffing to which no fat has been added so that much of the lamb fat is absorbed, making it a more palatable dish. (Av wt breast of lamb – 675g; Av wt breast of mutton – 1kg)

6) *Shoulder* is an economical roast on the bone or boned, stuffed, and rolled. It is fattier than the leg and is more moist after roasting. It is often divided into two smaller cuts: the blade or best end and the knuckle end. Both are ideal for roasting, braising, and casseroling. In Scotland, shoulder is not cut as a separate joint. The entire forequarter is usually divided in half, boned and rolled, then cut into smaller rolled joints. (Av wt shoulder of lamb – 1.75kg; Av wt shoulder of mutton – 2.5kg)

7) *Middle neck* is usually cut into chops for casseroles and stews. It is possible to cut 2 or 3 chops for grilling or frying from the meat closest to the best end of neck.

8) *Scrag end of neck* is a very economical cut for stews and soups. To avoid splinters of bone, look for scrag which has been cut into neat rings and not chopped roughly. (Av wt middle neck and scrag end of lamb – 0.75kg; Av wt of mutton – 1.5kg)

9) *Lamb chops* are cut from the loin or from the leg. Good for grilling, frying or braising.

    Chump: 4–6 per carcass. (Av wt 125–150g each)
    Loin: 6 (approx) per carcass. (Av wt 100–150g each)
    Neck (cutlet with rib bone removed): 4–6 per cut. (Av wt 75–125g each)
    Leg (chops or cutlets): Cut from the fillet end. (Av wt 100–150g each)

10) *Lamb cutlets* are cut from the best end of neck. 4–6 per carcass. (Av wt 75–150g each)

Mutton chops and cutlets are thicker and weigh more than lamb chops and cutlets.

Roasted and Baked Dishes
Roast Leg of Lamb or Mutton *Basic recipe*

a leg of lamb **or** mutton   oil **or** fat for basting
salt and pepper

Select the method of roasting, ie quick or slow roasting (p95). Weigh the joint to calculate the cooking time (p96). Wipe the meat. Place on a wire rack, if available, in a shallow roasting tin. Season the meat, and either pour over it a little oil or rub it with a little fat. Place the roasting tin in the oven, and cook for the required time.

Transfer the cooked meat from the oven to a warmed meat dish, and keep hot. Prepare a gravy, if liked, from the sediment in the roasting tin.

Serve roast leg of lamb with Mint Sauce (p60), and roast leg of mutton with Onion Sauce (p239) and redcurrant jelly.

Stuffed Roast Shoulder of Lamb or Mutton
6–10 helpings

a shoulder of lamb **or** mutton
salt and pepper

150–200g basic herb (p44) **or**
  sage and onion (p49) stuffing
dripping

Remove all the bones from the meat. Wipe the meat and trim off any skin and excess fat. Flatten the meat with a cutlet bat or rolling-pin. Season the inner surface of the meat well with salt and pepper and spread on the stuffing. Roll it up and tie securely with fine string.

Weigh the meat to calculate the cooking time, allowing 30 minutes per 0.5kg plus either 30 minutes over for lamb, or 35 minutes over for mutton. Heat the dripping in a roasting tin, put in the meat, and baste with the dripping. Cover the roasting tin and roast in a moderate oven, 180°C, Gas 4, until tender. Baste occasionally during the cooking time.

Serve on a warmed dish with lamb gravy (p269) or Foundation Brown Sauce (p241).

Lamb Cutlets en Papillotes
6 helpings

6 lamb cutlets
4–6 slices cooked ham
1 medium-sized onion (100g approx)
25g flat **or** button mushrooms
1 × 10ml spoon oil **or** butter

1 × 10ml spoon chopped parsley
salt and pepper
grated rind of $\frac{1}{2}$ lemon
oil **or** butter for greasing

Wipe and trim the cutlets neatly. Cut 12 small rounds of ham just large enough to cover the round part of the cutlet. Prepare the onion and mushrooms and chop finely. Heat the oil or butter in a small pan, and fry the onion until tender and lightly browned. Remove from the heat and stir in the mushrooms, parsley, salt and pepper to taste, and the grated lemon rind. Leave to cool.

Cut out 6 heart-shaped pieces of strong white paper or double thickness grease-proof paper or foil large enough to hold the cutlets. Grease them well with oil or butter. Place a slice of ham on half of each paper or foil, and spread on top a little of the cooled onion mixture. Then arrange the cutlet, a little more of the onion mixture, and a round of ham in layers on top. Fold over the paper or foil and twist the edges well together. Lay the cutlets in a greased baking tin and cook in a fairly hot oven, 190°C, Gas 5, for 30 minutes. Arrange the cutlets in the paper or foil on a warmed serving dish.

Foundation Brown Sauce (p241) or gravy can be served separately.

Crown Roast of Lamb with Saffron Rice
6 helpings

2 best ends of neck of lamb (6 cutlets each)

oil for brushing
salt and pepper

Saffron Rice
1 stick of celery (50g approx)
1 medium-sized onion (100g approx)
500ml chicken stock
$\frac{1}{2} \times 2.5$ml spoon powdered saffron
50g butter

150g long-grain white rice
4×15ml spoons dry white wine
25g blanched almonds
2 dessert apples (250g approx)
50g frozen green peas

Ask the butcher to prepare the crown roast or prepare it as follows. Wipe the meat. Remove the fat and meat from the top 4–5cm of the thin ends of the bones and scrape the bone ends clean. Slice the lower half of each best end of neck between each bone, about two-thirds up from the base. Trim off any excess fat. Turn the joints so that bones are on the outside and the meat is on the inside, and sew the pieces together with a trussing needle and fine string. The thick ends of the meat will be the base of the crown, so make sure they stand level.

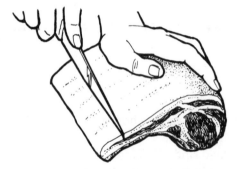

Removing the fat and meat from the bone ends

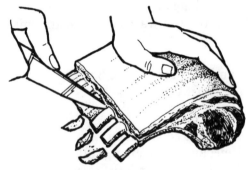

Scraping the bone ends clean

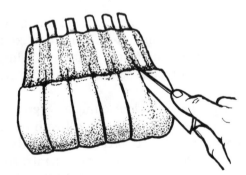

Slicing between each bone

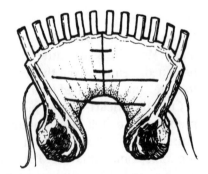

Sewing pieces to form a crown roast

Place the prepared crown roast in a roasting tin. Brush it with oil and season well with salt and pepper. Wrap a piece of foil round the top of each cutlet bone to prevent it from scorching. Cook in a fairly hot oven, 190°C, Gas 5, for $1\frac{1}{4}$–$1\frac{1}{2}$ hours.

About 30 minutes before the end of the cooking time, make the saffron rice. Prepare and chop the celery and onion. Heat the chicken stock in a saucepan with the powdered saffron. Heat 25g of the butter in a saucepan and fry the celery and onion gently until softened but not browned. Wash the rice, stir it into the vegetables and cook for 1–2 minutes. Pour on the wine and cook gently until the rice has absorbed it. Add 250ml of the hot stock and cook, uncovered, stirring occasionally, until almost all the liquid is absorbed. Pour the remaining stock into the rice and cook gently until it has been completely absorbed and the rice is just tender. Chop the almonds and peel, core, and dice the apples. Remove the rice from the heat and add the almonds, diced apple, peas, and butter. Cover the pan with a tight-fitting lid, and leave to cook in its own steam until the peas are thawed and heated through, and the roast is ready.

When cooked, place the crown roast on a warmed serving dish. Remove the foil from the cutlet bones. Fill the hollow centre of the roast with the hot saffron rice. Top each cutlet with a cutlet frill and serve. Any extra rice can be served separately.

Guard of Honour
6 helpings

2 best ends of neck of lamb (6–7 cutlets
    each)

2 × 15ml spoons oil

Stuffing

1 small onion (50g approx)
50g mushrooms
25g butter **or** margarine
100g soft white breadcrumbs
1 × 15ml spoon chopped parsley

grated rind of 1 lemon
salt and pepper
1 egg
a little milk

Gravy

1 × 15ml spoon plain flour
250ml vegetable stock (p27)

salt and pepper
gravy browning (optional)

Garnish
sprigs of parsley

Ask the butcher to chine the joints. Remove the fat and meat from the top 5cm of the thin end of the bones and scrape the bone ends clean. Wipe the meat and score the fat with a sharp knife in a lattice pattern. Place the joints together to form an arch.

Make the stuffing. Prepare the onion and mushrooms. Melt the butter or margarine in a frying pan and fry the onion gently for 5 minutes until softened but not browned. Mix together the fried onion, mushrooms, breadcrumbs, parsley, lemon rind, and seasoning to taste. Beat the egg until liquid and add it to the stuffing with enough milk to bind it together. Stuff the cavity of the Guard of Honour.

Close the joints together at the top, by criss-crossing the bones. Cover the bones with foil to prevent them from scorching. Heat the oil in a baking tin and put in the Guard of Honour. Bake in a fairly hot oven, 190°C, Gas 5, for $1\frac{1}{4}$–$1\frac{1}{2}$ hours or until the lamb is tender. When cooked, transfer the lamb to a warmed serving dish, and allow to rest in the turned-off oven.

Best ends of neck placed together to form an arch

Meanwhile, make the gravy. Pour off most of the fat from the roasting tin. Stir in the flour, and cook gently for a few minutes. Gradually add the stock and stir until boiling. Reduce the heat and simmer for 2 minutes. Season to taste and add gravy browning if liked. Pour into a warmed gravy-boat.

Remove the foil from the bones of the Guard of Honour and replace with cutlet frills. Garnish with sprigs of parsley.

Grilled and Fried Dishes
Grilled Lamb or Mutton Cutlets or Chops *Basic recipe*
6–8 helpings

6–8 lamb **or** mutton cutlets **or** chops   oil for brushing
salt and pepper

Garnish (optional)
pats of any savoury butter (pp563–66)

Choose plump cutlets or chops with the nut of meat 2–2.5cm thick so that they will not curl up when grilled. Wipe and trim the cutlets or chops into a neat shape. Season with salt and pepper and brush them all over with oil. Cook on the grid or base of the grilling pan, turning once or twice; keep well-brushed with oil. Cutlets require 7–10 minutes in all, and chops require 8–15 minutes, according to their thickness. When cooked, the cutlets or chops should be well-browned with crisp fat on the outside, and slightly pink on the inside when cut. Garnish with pats of any savoury butter, if liked. The ends of the cutlet bones can be covered with cutlet frills before serving.

Suitable accompaniments are green peas, baby carrots, new, creamed or chipped potatoes, and lamb gravy (p269) or Demi-glace Sauce (p249).

Lamb Shish Kebab
6 helpings

1kg boned lean lamb, preferably
   from the leg

6 firm tomatoes
3 small green peppers

Marinade
1 large onion (200g approx)
$1\frac{1}{2} \times 15$ml spoons olive oil
3×15ml spoons lemon juice

5×5ml spoons salt
1×2.5ml spoon ground black pepper

Wipe the meat and trim off any excess fat. Cut the meat into 2cm cubes.

Make the marinade. Skin the onion and slice it thinly. Put it in a deep bowl. Sprinkle the olive oil, lemon juice, salt and pepper over the onion slices. Add the meat and stir well to coat the pieces of meat thoroughly. Marinate the meat at room temperature for several hours, turning it occasionally.

Remove the lamb from the marinade and drain thoroughly. Cut the tomatoes crossways into slices. Cut the green pepper into chunks and remove the membranes and seeds. Thread tomato slices, meat, and chunks of pepper on each skewer. Grill the skewers of meat and vegetables under high heat, or over a charcoal fire, turning the skewers occasionally, until the vegetables are well-browned and the lamb is done to taste. For pink lamb, allow about 10 minutes; for well-done lamb, allow about 15 minutes. Slide the lamb and vegetables off the skewers on to warmed individual plates.

Serve with boiled rice.

Fried Lamb or Mutton Cutlets or Chops *Basic recipe*
6–8 helpings

6–8 lamb **or** mutton cutlets **or** chops
salt and pepper
1×15ml spoon plain flour
1 egg
6×15ml spoons dried white
   breadcrumbs

2×15ml spoons oil
25g butter
250ml Fresh Tomato sauce (p255)

Garnish
200g cooked green peas

Wipe and trim the cutlets and scrape clean about 2cm of the thin end of the bones, or wipe and trim the chops neatly. Season well on both sides. Dust lightly with the flour. Beat the egg until liquid and brush the cutlets or chops all over with the beaten egg; then coat them lightly with the crumbs.

Heat the oil and butter together in a frying pan and fry the meat until golden-brown on both sides and cooked through; this takes 7–10 minutes for cutlets and 8–15 minutes for chops, depending on their thickness. Drain thoroughly. Arrange the fried cutlets or chops on a warmed serving dish, and garnish with the peas. Pour some of the tomato sauce round and serve the rest separately.

Note The cutlets or chops can be fried without the egg and breadcrumb coating.

Noisettes of Lamb Jardinière
6 helpings

1kg boned best end of neck of lamb
salt and pepper
2 × 15ml spoons oil for grilling **or**
   frying

500g creamed potatoes
250ml lamb gravy (p269) **or**
   Demi-glace sauce (p249)

Garnish

2 × 15ml spoons diced green beans
2 × 15ml spoons diced carrot

2 × 15ml spoons diced turnip
2 × 15ml spoons diced celery

Wipe the meat. Roll it up and tie it with fine string at 2–3cm intervals. Cut through the roll between the string to make noisettes. Season the noisettes on both sides. Either brush them with oil and grill for 6–7 minutes, turning once or twice, or heat the oil in a frying pan and fry them, turning once or twice, until cooked through and browned on both sides.

At the same time, cook each vegetable for the garnish separately in boiling salted water until tender. Drain and mix together.

Spoon or pipe the hot creamed potatoes in a border on a warmed serving dish and arrange the noisettes on top. Garnish with the vegetables, pour a little of the hot gravy or Demi-glace sauce round the noisettes, and serve the rest in a warmed sauce-boat.

Casseroled, Braised and Boiled Dishes
Lancashire Hot Pot
6 helpings

1kg middle neck of lamb **or** mutton
3 sheep's kidneys
1kg potatoes
1 large onion (200g approx)

fat for greasing
salt and pepper
250ml general household stock (p25)
25g lard **or** dripping

Wipe the meat, cut it into neat cutlets, and trim off any excess fat. Skin, core, and slice the kidneys. Prepare the potatoes, slice half of them, and cut the rest into chunks or in half, if small, for the top of the casserole. Skin and slice the onion.

Put a layer of potatoes in the bottom of a greased, large, deep casserole. Arrange the cutlets on top, slightly overlapping each other, and cover with the kidneys and onion. Season well. Arrange the remainder of the potatoes (halves or chunks) neatly on top. Pour in the hot stock. Melt the lard or dripping and brush it over the top layer of potatoes. Cover the casserole with a tight-fitting lid and bake in a moderate oven, 180°C, Gas 4, for about 2 hours or until the meat and potatoes are tender. Remove the lid, increase the oven temperature to hot, 220°C, Gas 7, and cook for another 20 minutes or until the top layer of potatoes is brown and crisp. Serve from the casserole.

Irish Stew

4–6 helpings

1kg middle neck **or** scrag end of neck
   of lamb **or** mutton
2 large onions (400g approx)
1kg potatoes

salt and pepper
water **or** general household stock
   (p25) as required

Garnish
2 × 15ml spoons chopped parsley

Wipe the meat, cut it into neat cutlets or pieces, and trim off any excess fat. Skin the onions and slice them thinly; prepare and slice the potatoes. In a stewpan, place layers of meat, onions, and potatoes, adding seasoning between each layer, and finishing with a layer of potatoes. Add enough water or stock to come half-way up the meat and vegetables. Cover the pan with a lid, heat to simmering point, and simmer gently for 2½ hours. Alternatively, cook the stew in a casserole, covered with a lid, in a fairly hot oven, 190°C, Gas 5, for 2–2½ hours. Serve garnished with chopped parsley.

Curried Lamb

6 helpings

650–700g lean leg **or** loin of lamb
50g dripping
2 medium-sized onions (200g approx)
1 clove of garlic (optional)
2–3 × 5ml spoons curry powder
25g ground rice
1 cooking apple (150g approx)
25g tamarind **or** mango chutney
1 × 10ml spoon plum jam

1 × 10ml spoon desiccated coconut
6 black peppercorns
4 allspice berries
Cayenne pepper
salt
50g concentrated tomato purée
675ml white **or** chicken stock (p26)
lemon juice (optional)

Wipe the meat and cut it into 2cm cubes. Heat the dripping in a stewpan and fry the meat lightly, then put the meat to one side. Skin and slice the onions thinly, and skin and crush the garlic, if used. Fry the onion and garlic in the fat until pale golden. Add the curry powder and ground rice, and fry for 6 minutes. Peel, core, and chop the apple. Add the apple and the rest of the ingredients, except the lemon juice, to the pan. Heat to boiling point, stirring all the time. Return the meat to the pan, cover with a tight-fitting lid, and simmer gently for about 1½ hours, stirring frequently. Lift the meat out on to a warmed serving dish. Add the lemon juice, if used, to the sauce and re-season if required. Strain the sauce over the meat.

Serve in a border of plain boiled rice and serve extra rice separately.

Biriani
(Spiced Lamb with Saffron Rice)

4–5 helpings

1 × 2.5ml spoon saffron strands	300g natural yoghurt
4 × 10ml spoons boiling water	300ml vegetable oil
100g fresh **or** frozen peas	4 × 5ml spoons salt
700g leg of lamb	1 × 2.5ml spoon chilli powder
900g onions	3 small green chillies
200g Basmati rice	1 × 5ml spoon ground garam masala
6 cloves garlic	400ml boiling salted water
1 × 5cm piece ginger root	juice of 2 lemons **or** limes
2 × 15ml spoons fresh coriander leaves	150ml milk

Whole Garam Masala

1 × 5ml spoon cumin seeds	8 whole cardamoms
2 × 10cm pieces cinnamon stick	8 black peppercorns
8 cloves	12 bay leaves

Make the whole garam masala first. Add all the spices and herbs together and put to one side in a small bowl. Steep two-thirds of the saffron strands with the 4 × 10ml spoons boiling water in a small cup. Cook the peas, and put to one side. Bone the lamb and cut it into 2cm cubes. Skin the onions, and slice as thinly as possible. Wash and drain the rice thoroughly. Skin and crush the garlic, grate the ginger root, and chop the coriander leaves finely. Beat the yoghurt with a fork until smooth.

Heat the oil in a saucepan, and fry the onions until golden-brown. Drain off any excess oil, with about 200g of the onions, and reserve them. Add the meat to the saucepan with the remaining saffron strands, garlic, ginger, coriander leaves, yoghurt, 2 × 5ml spoons salt, the chilli powder, whole chillies, and the ground garam masala. Add the prepared whole garam masala. Stir the ingredients together, and fry over moderate heat until the meat cubes are browned. Reduce the heat, and simmer for about 40–45 minutes until the meat is three-quarters cooked. The sauce should be thick and well reduced.

Meanwhile, boil the rice for 2 minutes in the 400ml boiling salted water, reduce the heat and simmer, uncovered, for 10 minutes or until the rice is almost cooked. Drain into a warmed dish or bowl. Transfer one-third of the rice to a second bowl, and mix in the soaked saffron and its water.

Put a layer of boiled white rice in a large, oven-to-table flameproof casserole. Cover with a layer of saffron-coloured rice. Sprinkle with the reserved peas and fried onions. Cover with a layer of the spiced lamb mixture. Repeat these layers until all the ingredients are used, ending with a layer of saffron rice. Pour the lemon or lime juice and milk over the dish, and cover with a tight-fitting lid. Cook over high heat for 2 minutes, reduce the heat to simmering point, and cook very gently for 25 minutes or until the rice and meat are cooked through.

Serve hot from the casserole as a main dish, with an onion salad.

Braised Lamb or Mutton Provençale
8–12 helpings

a leg **or** shoulder **or** loin of lamb
   or mutton

fat for greasing
meat glaze (p59)

Stuffing
50g lean ham
50g pork **or** veal
6 button mushrooms
1 shallot
1 egg

50g soft white breadcrumbs
1 × 5ml spoon chopped parsley
1 × 2.5ml spoon dried mixed herbs
1 × 2.5ml spoon grated lemon rind
salt and pepper

Mirepoix
2 medium-sized onions (200g approx)
2 medium-sized carrots (100g approx)
1 turnip (75g approx)
2 sticks celery (100g approx)

75g dripping
bouquet garni
10 black peppercorns
1 litre beef stock (approx)

Provençale Sauce
500ml foundation brown sauce (p241)
1 tomato (50g approx)
1 small onion (50g approx)
2 large mushrooms (25g approx)

25g butter **or** margarine
1 × 2.5ml spoon chopped parsley
1 × 2.5ml spoon lemon juice

Garnish
baked tomatoes

baked mushrooms

Wipe the meat. Bone it, or ask the butcher to do it for you.

Make the stuffing. Mince the meat. Prepare the mushrooms and shallot and chop them. Beat the egg until liquid. Mix together all the stuffing ingredients. Press the mixture lightly into the cavity left by the bone and sew up the opening.

Prepare the vegetables for the mirepoix and slice them thickly. Heat the dripping in a large stewpan and fry the vegetables gently for 3–5 minutes. Add the bouquet garni and peppercorns. Pour in enough stock to come three-quarters of the way up the vegetables. Place the meat on top. Lay a piece of greased greaseproof paper on top of the pan, greased side down, and cover with a tight-fitting lid. Cook over low heat for 2 hours for lamb or 2½ hours for mutton, basting frequently and making up the volume of stock as it reduces.

Transfer the meat to a baking tin and cook in a fairly hot oven, 200°C, Gas 6, for another 30 minutes, basting with a little stock as needed.

Meanwhile, strain the braising liquid from the stewpan and use it to make the brown sauce if not already made. Prepare and slice the tomato, onion, and mushrooms. Melt the butter or margarine in a saucepan. Add the vegetables and chopped parsley, half cover and cook gently for 15–20 minutes. Add the brown sauce to this mixture and simmer for another 10 minutes. Season carefully and strain through a sieve. Re-heat without boiling, add the lemon juice, and keep hot.

When cooked, transfer the meat to a warmed serving dish. Brush with warm meat glaze. Garnish with baked tomatoes and mushrooms. Serve the sauce separately.

Boiled Leg of Lamb or Mutton with Caper Sauce
8–10 helpings

a leg of lamb (2kg approx) **or** a small
   leg of mutton (2.5kg approx)
1 × 5ml spoon salt
10 black peppercorns
2 medium-sized onions (200g approx)

4 medium-sized carrots (200g approx)
2 turnips **or** 1 large parsnip
   (100g approx)
1–2 leeks
375–500ml Caper sauce (p238)

Wipe the meat and trim off any excess fat. Put the meat in a large stewpan with the salt, peppercorns, and enough cold water to cover. Heat to boiling point. Skim, reduce the heat, cover the pan with a tight-fitting lid, and simmer over gentle heat for 2½–3 hours or until the meat is tender.

Meanwhile, prepare the vegetables and leave whole if small, or cut into large neat pieces. Add the vegetables 45 minutes before the end of the cooking time. When cooked, drain the meat and vegetables from the cooking liquid. Place the meat on a warmed serving dish, coat with the Caper sauce, and arrange with the vegetables.

Pastry and Minced Dishes
Lamb Pie
4–6 helpings

1kg best end **or** middle neck **or** breast
   of lamb
salt and pepper
1–2 sheep's kidneys
stock **or** water

shortcrust pastry (p453) using
   150g flour **or** puff pastry (p458)
   using 100g flour
flour for rolling out

Wipe the meat and remove the fat and bones. Boil the bones to make stock for the gravy. Cut the meat into 2cm cubes and put them in a 750ml pie dish. Sprinkle each layer with salt and pepper. Skin, core, and slice the kidneys thinly. Add them to the meat in the pie dish. Half fill the dish with stock or water. Roll out the pastry on a lightly floured surface and use to cover the dish. Make a hole in the centre of the lid for the steam to escape. Bake in a moderate oven, 180°C, Gas 4, for 1½–2 hours, until the meat is tender (test with a skewer).

Strain the liquid off the bones. Season it to taste. Just before serving, pour enough of this gravy stock through the hole in the centre of the pie to fill the dish.

Lamb or Mutton Pudding
5–6 helpings

500g lean lamb **or** mutton
3 × 15ml spoons plain flour
salt and pepper
1–2 sheep's kidneys
suet crust pastry (p454) using
   250g flour

flour for rolling out
fat for greasing
3 × 15ml spoons general household
   stock (p25) **or** water

Follow the directions for Steak and Kidney Pudding (p122).

Cumberland Mutton Pies
6 helpings

300g lean mutton
1 medium-sized onion (100g approx)
1 × 10ml spoon dripping
100g mushrooms
1 × 10ml spoon chopped parsley
a pinch of dried thyme
salt and pepper

shortcrust pastry (p453) using
    300g flour
flour for rolling out
6 × 10ml spoons general household
    stock (p25)
beaten egg or milk for glazing

Wipe and mince the meat. Skin and chop the onion. Heat the dripping in a pan and fry the onion lightly. Remove the onion and mix it with the mutton. Clean and chop the mushrooms, and add them to the meat with the parsley, thyme, and seasoning to taste.

Roll out half the pastry on a lightly floured surface, and cut out 6 circles to line 6 small round tins or saucers. Divide the mixture between the tins. Add to each 1 × 10ml spoon stock to moisten. Roll out the rest of the pastry and cut out 6 lids for the pies. Dampen the edges of the pies, put on the lids and seal well. Brush with beaten egg or milk. Make a hole in the lid of each pie to allow steam to escape. Bake in a moderate oven, 180°C, Gas 4, for 40–45 minutes.

Lamb or Mutton Roll
6 helpings

650g lean lamb or mutton
200g ham or bacon
1 × 2.5ml spoon finely chopped onion
3 × 15ml spoons soft white
    breadcrumbs
1 × 5ml spoon chopped parsley
½ × 2.5ml spoon dried mixed herbs
a pinch of grated nutmeg
1 × 2.5ml spoon grated lemon rind

salt and pepper
1 egg
2 × 15ml spoons chicken stock (p26)
    or lamb gravy (p269)
1 × 15ml spoon plain flour or
    beaten egg and 2 × 15ml spoons
    breadcrumbs
2 × 15ml spoons dripping

Wipe the lamb or mutton. Finely chop or mince all the meat. Put in a bowl and mix it well with the onion, breadcrumbs, herbs, nutmeg, and grated lemon rind. Season to taste. Beat the egg until liquid, and add it with the stock or gravy to moisten the mixture. Shape it into a short thick roll. Wrap the roll in foil or several thicknesses of greaseproof paper to keep it in shape and to protect the meat. Bake in a moderate oven, 180°C, Gas 4, for 1½ hours.

Remove the foil or paper and lightly dredge the roll with the flour, or brush it with the beaten egg and coat it with breadcrumbs. Heat the dripping in a baking tin and place the roll in the tin. Baste well and return it to the oven for a further 30 minutes until browned.

Serve with gravy.

Note Under-cooked cold lamb or mutton can be used. The roll should then be cooked for only 1 hour before browning it.

Moussaka

4 helpings

1 medium-sized aubergine	1 × 10ml spoon chopped parsley
salt	150ml dry white wine
1 large onion	300ml milk
1 clove of garlic	1 egg
2 medium-sized tomatoes	2 egg yolks
2 × 15ml spoons olive oil	a pinch of grated nutmeg
500g raw lamb **or** beef, minced	75g Kefalotiri **or** Parmesan cheese
pepper	fat for greasing

Cut the aubergine into 1cm slices, sprinkle them with salt and put to one side on a large platter to drain. Chop the onion, grate the garlic, and skin, de-seed, and chop the tomatoes. Heat the olive oil, add the onion and garlic, and sauté gently until the onion is soft. Add the minced meat and continue cooking, stirring with a fork to break up any lumps in the meat. When the meat is thoroughly browned, add salt, pepper, parsley, and the tomatoes. Mix well, and add the white wine. Simmer the mixture for a few minutes to blend the flavours, then remove from the heat.

In a basin, beat together the milk, egg, egg yolks, salt, and a good pinch of grated nutmeg. Grate the cheese, add about half to the egg mixture, and beat again briefly.

Grease a 20 × 10 × 10cm oven-to-table baking dish. Drain the aubergine slices and pat dry with soft kitchen paper. Place half in the bottom of the casserole and cover with the meat mixture. Lay the remaining aubergine slices on the meat and pour the milk and egg mixture over them. Sprinkle the remaining cheese on top. Bake in a moderate oven, 180°C, Gas 4, for 30–40 minutes, until the custard is set and the top is light golden-brown. Serve from the dish.

Offal Dishes
Lamb's Liver and Bacon

4–6 helpings

500g sheep's **or** lamb's liver	250g back bacon rashers, without
50g flour	rinds
salt and pepper	400ml brown stock (p25)

Garnish
sprigs of parsley

Remove the skin and tubes, and cut the liver into 1cm thick slices. Season the flour with salt and pepper. Dip each slice of liver in the seasoned flour. Cook the bacon rashers in a frying pan. Transfer the bacon to a warmed dish and keep hot. Fry the slices of liver lightly and quickly in the fat from the bacon until browned on both sides, without hardening or over-cooking them. Transfer the liver to a warmed serving dish, arrange the bacon around it and keep hot.

Drain off all but about 1 × 10ml spoon of fat, stir in the remaining seasoned flour and cook until browned. Gradually add the stock and stir until boiling. Re-season if required. Garnish the liver and bacon with sprigs of parsley and serve the sauce separately.

Sautéed Kidneys(1)
4 helpings

4 sheep's **or** lamb's kidneys
1 small onion
50g butter
1 × 5ml spoon chopped parsley

125ml foundation brown sauce (p241)
salt and pepper
4 slices fried bread

Garnish
chopped parsley

Skin and core the kidneys, and slice them very thinly. Skin the onion, and chop it finely. Melt the butter in a frying pan, and fry the onion until just golden-brown. Add the kidney slices and parsley. Stir, and turn over in the fat for 2–3 minutes until very lightly fried. Add the brown sauce, and season to taste. Bring the sauce just to the boil. Pour the mixture on to a warmed serving dish. Cut the slices of fried bread into triangles, and arrange around the edge of the dish. Garnish with chopped parsley, and serve at once.

Lamb's Fry
6 helpings

650–700g lamb's fry (liver, heart,
   lights, melts, sweetbreads)
1 small onion (50g approx)
1 small carrot (25g approx)
bouquet garni
salt and pepper
1 × 15ml spoon lemon juice

1 egg
4–6 × 15ml spoons soft white
   breadcrumbs
75g dripping **or** lard
25g plain flour
1 × 5ml spoon finely chopped parsley

Garnish
6 grilled bacon rolls (p51)

Prepare the fry as for Fried Pig's Fry (p168). Prepare the onion and carrot, and slice them thinly. Put the fry, onion, carrot, and bouquet garni into a stewpan and cover with cold water. Heat to boiling point, reduce the heat, cover the pan, and simmer gently for about 30 minutes. Allow the meat to cool in the stock. When cold, strain and reserve the stock, and divide the meat into 2 portions.

Cut 1 portion of the meat into thin slices. Season with salt and pepper. Sprinkle with the lemon juice. Beat the egg until liquid and coat the slices with beaten egg and then with the breadcrumbs, and put to one side. Dice the rest of the meat.

Melt 25g of the dripping or lard in a saucepan. Stir in the flour and cook for 3 minutes. Gradually add 250ml of the strained stock and stir until boiling. Season to taste. Add the diced meat and parsley. Cover the pan and keep hot without boiling. Heat the remaining 50g dripping or lard in a frying pan. Fry the breadcrumbed slices of fry quickly on both sides until browned. Drain thoroughly.

Pile the diced meat and sauce from the saucepan into the centre of a warmed serving dish. Arrange the slices of fried meat round the outside and garnish with the bacon rolls.

Brains on Toast
6 helpings

3 sheep's **or** lamb's brains	25g butter
salt and pepper	1 × 5ml spoon chopped parsley
1 hard-boiled egg	

Soak the brains in lightly salted cold water for 30 minutes to remove all traces of blood; then cut off any membranes. Wash thoroughly but very gently. Tie the brains in muslin. Heat a pan of water to boiling point, add 1 × 2.5ml spoon of salt and the brains, and cook gently for 15 minutes.

Drain the brains and remove them from the muslin. Chop the brains and the egg roughly. Melt the butter in a pan, add the brains and egg, and heat through. Season to taste and add the parsley.

Serve hot on buttered toast.

Note This recipe can also be used for calf's or pig's brains.

Sweetbreads Bourgeoise
6 helpings

3 pairs lamb's sweetbreads (650–675g approx)	2 × 15ml spoons peas
	2 × 15ml spoons diced turnip
25g butter **or** margarine	2 × 15ml spoons diced carrot
white **or** chicken stock (p26) to cover	250ml foundation brown (p241) **or** Espagnole (p248) sauce
salt and pepper	

Soak the sweetbreads in cold water for 1–2 hours to remove all the blood. Drain, and put them in a pan with cold water to cover. Heat to boiling point and pour off the liquid. Rinse the sweetbreads under cold water. Remove the black veins and as much as possible of the membranes which cover them.

Heat the butter or margarine in a saucepan and toss the sweetbreads in it. Then barely cover them with the stock. Season to taste with salt and pepper. Heat to simmering point, cover the pan, and cook gently for 45 minutes–1 hour, until tender. Transfer to a warmed dish and keep hot.

Prepare the vegetables and cook them separately in boiling salted water until just tender. Drain, and add them to the hot brown or Espagnole Sauce. Divide the sweetbreads between 6 soup bowls and pour the sauce over them. Serve very hot.

Boiled Sheep's Head *Basic recipe*
3–5 helpings

a sheep's head
salt
2 medium-sized onions (200g approx)

2 medium-sized carrots (100g approx)
10 black peppercorns
bouquet garni

Garnish
1 × 10ml spoon chopped parsley

Ask the butcher to split the head if not already done. Remove the brains and put to one side. Snip off any remaining hairy bits of skin, scrub the teeth and jaw bones with salt and scrape the bones from the nostrils. Rinse the head and soak it in cold water. Add 1 × 15ml spoon salt to each litre of water. Put the brains in the water with the head and soak them for 30 minutes to remove all traces of blood; then cut off any membranes. Wash thoroughly but very gently. The brains can be used separately or tied in muslin, cooked for part of the time with the head, and used with the meat of the head.

Cover the head with cold water, heat to boiling point, and pour the water away. Cover the head with fresh cold water. Prepare the onions and carrots and add them to the pan with 2 × 5ml spoons salt, the peppercorns, and bouquet garni. Heat to boiling point, reduce the heat, cover the pan with a tight-fitting lid, and simmer gently for 2 hours until the meat is tender.

If the brains are not to be used separately, tie them in muslin and add them to the pan for the last 10–15 minutes of the cooking time. Remove the head and brains, if cooked, from the pan and put to one side until they are cool enough to handle. Strain the liquid into a clean pan. Reserve a little for serving with the meat. Alternatively, reserve 375ml to make brain sauce (p237) to serve with the meat.

Put the head on a board. Remove and slice the meat from the bones. Strip the skin from the tongue, remove the small bones at the root, together with the excess fat and gristle. Remove the brains from the muslin. Slice the tongue and the brains, if they are to be served with the meat. Re-heat the meats in the strained stock in the pan. Season to taste.

Serve garnished with chopped parsley and with either the reserved stock or brain sauce.

Note A calf's head can be prepared in the same way.

Boiled Sheep's or Lamb's Tongues

4 helpings

2 sheep's **or** 4 lamb's tongues	1 × 15ml spoon plain flour
500ml general household stock (p25)	1 × 15ml spoon capers (optional)
salt and pepper	1 × 15ml spoon dry sherry (optional)
25g butter	

Soak the tongues in cold salted water for 1 hour, then drain them. Place them in a pan, cover with cold water and heat to boiling point. Pour off the water, and dry the tongues.

Put them in the pan, cover with stock, and season with salt and pepper. Heat to boiling point, reduce the heat, cover the pan with a tight-fitting lid and simmer for about 2 hours until tender. Drain, and reserve 250ml stock. Strip the skin and remove the small bones at the root of the tongue, together with the excess fat and gristle. Divide the sheep's tongues lengthways into three, and the lamb's tongues lengthways in half. Transfer to a warmed dish and keep hot.

Melt the butter in a saucepan. Stir in the flour and cook for 3 minutes. Gradually add the seasoned stock and stir until boiling, then reduce the heat and simmer for 2 minutes. Season to taste. Chop and add the capers, and the sherry, if used; then add the sliced tongues and re-heat.

Serve hot in a border of cooked spaghetti, creamed potatoes or chopped spinach.

Veal

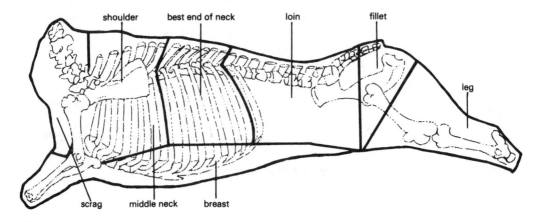

Veal Cuts

Veal is cut in the same way as lamb and the cuts are usually described by the same names. See diagram above.

Taking an average carcass weight of 22kg, the approximate weights of the cuts are as follows:

1) *Leg* is a large and expensive joint. The hind knuckle or shin is removed at the knee joint or boned and used for pie veal. The rest of the leg can be roasted on the bone. Because of the continental method of cutting a leg of veal lengthways along the muscles, escalopes are usually taken from the topside (cushion) of veal or *noix*.

This cut (escalope) gives solid slices of meat cut across the grain, which do not curl in cooking. British butchers do not usually cut a leg in this way, so escalopes are often cut from the fleshy part of the leg, and must be snipped at the edges to prevent curling. They should be cut 1cm thick, and beaten out to 5mm thick, then left to regain resilience before cooking. (Av wt boneless leg – 3.5kg)

2) *Fillet* is the most expensive of the veal cuts. Usually cut into fillet steaks or escalopes but can be larded and roasted whole. (Av wt bobby calves 225–300g; Av wt veal calves – 900g)

3) *Loin* is suitable for roasting as a joint on the bone or as a boned, stuffed and rolled joint. It can also be cut into loin chops, suitable for grilling and frying. The end of the loin closest to the leg is often called the chump end. (Av wt 1.5–1.75kg)

4) *Best end of neck* is suitable for roasting or braising. Also available cut into cutlets for grilling, frying or baking. (Av wt – 1kg)

5) *Breast* when boned, stuffed and roasted is a most tasty and economical cut of veal. (Av wt – 675g)

6) *Shoulder* (also called Oyster of Veal after the fore knuckle has been removed) is suitable for roasting on the bone or boned and rolled. (Av wt – 2.5kg)

7) *Middle neck* and

8) *Scrag* are economical cuts, but there is a high proportion of bone. Middle neck is usually sold in cutlets for braising or stewing or is boned for pie veal. Scrag is mainly sold for boiling, stewing or casseroles. (Av wt both joints – 1.5kg)

9) *Cutlets* are obtained from the best end of neck. 6 per carcass. (Av wt – 175g each)

10) *Chops* from the loin (with or without kidney) can be cut to any size, so the number varies. (Av wt – 225g each)

Roasted, Grilled and Fried Dishes
Roast Veal *Basic recipe*

a joint of veal suitable for roasting
salt and pepper

grated lemon rind
strips of bacon **or** pork fat

Choose the method of roasting, ie quick or slow roasting (p95). Weigh the joint to calculate the cooking time (p96). Wipe the meat. Place the joint on a wire rack, if available, in a shallow roasting tin. Season the meat well with salt, pepper, and a light sprinkling of grated lemon rind. Cover the top of the joint with strips of bacon or pork fat, and cook for the required time.

Transfer the cooked meat from the oven to a warmed serving dish and keep hot. Prepare gravy from the sediment in the roasting tin.

Serve roast veal with basic herb stuffing or forcemeat balls (p44) and with bacon rolls (p51) and lemon wedges.

Grilled Veal Cutlets

6 helpings

600–700g best end **or** middle neck
   of veal, cut into cutlets
1 egg
salt and pepper
dried white breadcrumbs for coating

a little melted butter **or** oil
375ml Italian (p246) **or** Fresh
   Tomato (p255) **or** Demi-glace (p249)
   sauce

Garnish

sprigs of parsley

slices of lemon

Wipe and trim the cutlets. Beat the egg lightly until liquid and season to taste. Brush the cutlets with the beaten egg and coat with breadcrumbs, pressing them on well; then brush the cutlets carefully with a little melted butter or oil. Place them on the rack of a grill pan and cook under a hot grill for about 10–15 minutes, basting occasionally with more melted butter or oil to prevent the breadcrumbs burning, until the cutlets are golden-brown on both sides and cooked through. Arrange them on a warmed serving dish and garnish with parsley and slices of lemon. Pour some of the chosen sauce round the cutlets and serve the rest separately.

Fried Veal Cutlets

6 helpings

600–700g best end **or** middle neck
   of veal, cut into cutlets
1 egg
2 × 15ml spoons milk
1 × 5ml spoon chopped parsley
½ × 2.5ml spoon dried thyme
1 × 2.5ml spoon grated lemon rind

salt and pepper
1 × 10ml spoon melted butter
dried white breadcrumbs for coating
butter **or** oil and butter for frying
375ml Fresh Tomato (p255),
   Demi-glace (p249) **or** Piquant (p243)
   sauce

Garnish

sprigs of parsley

slices of lemon

Wipe and trim the cutlets. Beat the egg and milk together and mix with the parsley, thyme, lemon rind, seasoning, and melted butter. Brush the cutlets with the egg mixture and coat with breadcrumbs, pressing them on well.

Heat the butter or oil and butter mixture in a frying pan, and fry the cutlets over moderate heat, turning once, until golden-brown on both sides; then reduce the heat and cook more slowly for 10–15 minutes in all. Remove the cutlets from the pan and drain thoroughly. Arrange on a warmed serving dish. Garnish with sprigs of parsley and lemon slices.

Serve with Fresh Tomato Sauce, Demi-glace Sauce or Piquant Sauce.

Escalopes of Veal (Wiener Schnitzel)
6 helpings

6 thin escalopes of veal (13 × 8cm approx)	1 egg
plain flour	2–3 drops oil
salt and pepper	dried white breadcrumbs for coating
	butter **or** oil and butter for frying

Garnish

6 crimped lemon slices (p58)   1 × 15ml spoon chopped parsley

Wipe the meat. Season the flour with salt and pepper. Dip the escalopes in the seasoned flour. Beat the egg until liquid with the oil. Brush the escalopes with the egg mixture and coat with breadcrumbs, pressing them on well. Heat the butter or mixture of oil and butter in a large frying pan. Put in the escalopes and fry over moderate to gentle heat for 7–10 minutes, turning them once only.

Remove the escalopes and place them, overlapping slightly, on a warmed, flat serving dish. Garnish the middle of each escalope with a crimped slice of lemon sprinkled with parsley.

VARIATION

Holstein Schnitzel
Cook as for Wiener Schnitzel, but serve with a fried, poached or chopped hard-boiled egg. Garnish with small heaps of chopped gherkin and beetroot, whole capers, whole green olives, and drained anchovy fillets. Place a crimped slice of lemon or 'lemon butterfly' (p57) on the schnitzel, and pour a little Beurre Noisette (p252) over the schnitzel before serving.

Parisian Veal
3–4 helpings

300g fillet of veal	1 × 10ml spoon finely chopped onion
salt and pepper	200ml Madeira sauce (p249)
1 × 15ml spoon olive oil	1 × 5ml spoon chopped parsley

Garnish

potatoes Parisienne (p60)   fried bread croûtons

Wipe, trim, and cut the meat into 3 or 4 slices 1cm thick (approx). Season each slice well. Heat the oil in a frying pan and fry the fillets gently, turning once until lightly browned on both sides. Add the onion and continue frying gently until the onion is transparent. Add the sauce, cover the pan loosely, and cook gently for about 30 minutes until the meat is tender. Add the chopped parsley and arrange on a warmed serving dish. Garnish with potatoes Parisienne and bread croûtons.

Braised, Stewed and Steamed Dishes
Stuffed Breast of Veal
6 helpings

a thick end of breast of veal
(1kg approx)
salt and pepper
300g pork **or** beef sausage-meat
1 large onion (200g approx)
1 large carrot (100g approx)
½ turnip (25g approx)

bouquet garni
6 black peppercorns
white stock (p26) **or** water to cover
butter for greasing
225g short-grain rice
50g grated Parmesan cheese
meat glaze (p59) (optional)

Garnish
slices of lemon

Remove all bones and tendons from the meat. Wipe, and tie into a neat shape. Season well. Spread the sausage-meat evenly over the inner surface of the meat, roll up and tie securely with fine string. Prepare and slice the vegetables. Put them with the bones and trimmings in a large pan. Add the bouquet garni, peppercorns, salt and pepper, and enough stock or water to cover the vegetables. Place the meat on top, cover with buttered greaseproof paper and a tight-fitting lid. Heat to boiling point, reduce the heat and simmer gently for about 2½ hours. Baste occasionally and add more stock or water if necessary. Transfer to a warmed dish and keep hot.

Strain off the liquid and make it up to 750ml with stock or water. Put the stock in a pan and bring to the boil. Wash the rice and cook it in the stock until the stock is absorbed. Season to taste and stir in the cheese. Place the rice in a layer on a warmed serving dish and put the meat on top. Brush the meat with glaze, if used, and garnish with slices of lemon.

Stewed Rolled Breast of Veal
6 helpings

1.25–1.5kg breast of veal
salt and pepper
200g basic herb stuffing (p44)

3 × 15ml spoons oil
1.5–2 litres white **or** chicken stock
(p26)
250ml slightly thickened gravy (p270)

Garnish
6 fried bacon rolls (p51)

slices of lemon

Wipe and bone the meat, and flatten it with a cutlet bat or rolling-pin. Season, and spread with a thin layer of stuffing. Roll up the meat and skewer or tie it securely. Heat the oil in a pan and brown the meat lightly. Form the rest of the stuffing into balls for frying. Heat enough stock in a large saucepan to cover the rolled meat. When boiling, place the meat in it, re-heat to boiling point, and skim. Cover the pan with a tight-fitting lid, reduce the heat, and simmer gently for about 3 hours.

Place the veal on a warmed serving dish, remove the skewers or string, and pour a little gravy over it if liked. Garnish with the bacon rolls, forcemeat balls, and lemon slices. Serve the rest of the gravy separately.

Ossi Buchi (Braised Veal Knuckles in Wine)
4 helpings

50g flour
salt and pepper
4 veal knuckles **or** shanks sawn
   across the bone (175g each approx)
4 × 15ml spoons cooking oil
2 medium-sized carrots (50g each
   approx)
1–2 sticks celery (75g approx)
1 medium-sized onion (100g approx)

2 cloves garlic
150g tomatoes
25g concentrated tomato purée
200ml beef stock
juice of 1 lemon
150ml dry white wine
Saffron rice (p136)
1 × 15ml spoon cornflour
3 × 15ml spoons water

Garnish
1–2 × 15ml spoons finely chopped
   fresh herbs (oregano, basil, chervil,
   mint, parsley, or as available)

grated rind of 1 lemon

Season the flour with salt and pepper and toss the knuckles or shanks in it. Shake off any surplus flour. Heat the oil in a large frying pan and fry the meat for 8 minutes, turning as required, until browned all over. Put the meat into a shallow ovenproof baking dish.

Prepare and chop the carrots, celery and onion finely, and put into the frying pan. Fry for 5 minutes, turning them over. Skin and crush the garlic, and add to the pan. Fry for 2 minutes. Put to one side.

Prepare and chop the tomatoes, and mix with the tomato purée, stock, and salt and pepper to taste. Stir the mixture into the frying pan and cook over moderate heat until boiling, scraping in any sediment in the pan. Remove from the heat. Add the lemon juice and wine. Pour the sauce over the veal, cover tightly with foil, and bake in a moderate oven, 180°C, Gas 4, for 1½–2 hours, or until the meat is very tender.

When cooked, place the meat on a bed of Saffron rice on a warmed serving dish and keep hot. Strain the sauce into a small saucepan. Blend the cornflour with the water, and stir it into the sauce. Heat the sauce to boiling point and cook until it thickens, stirring all the time. Pour it over the veal. Sprinkle with the garnish of chopped fresh herbs and grated lemon rind.

Steamed Veal
6 helpings

600–800g topside leg of veal
salt and pepper
3 sticks celery (150g approx)
25g butter

25g plain flour
250ml milk
1–2 egg yolks
1–2 × 5ml spoons lemon juice

Garnish (optional)
6 grilled bacon rolls (p51)

sprigs of cooked cauliflower

Wipe, trim, and tie the veal into a neat shape. Season well. Wash the celery and cut it into 2cm lengths. Put the meat and celery in the top of a steamer. Steam for $1\frac{1}{2}$–2 hours or until tender.

When the veal is nearly ready, melt the butter in a small saucepan. Stir in the flour and cook for 2–3 minutes over low heat, stirring well. Do not allow to brown. Gradually add the milk and any liquid in the steamer and stir until boiling. Reduce the heat and simmer for 5 minutes. Remove the pan from the heat. Beat the egg yolks in a bowl and stir into them a little of the hot sauce. Return the egg yolk mixture to the rest of the sauce in the pan, stirring well. Add the lemon juice and season to taste. Place the veal on a warmed serving dish, remove the string, and pour the sauce over the meat. Garnish, if liked, with bacon rolls and sprigs of cooked cauliflower.

Pastry and Minced Dishes
Veal and Ham Pie
6–8 helpings

puff **or** flaky pastry (p458)
    using 100g flour
500g fillet, breast or neck of veal
250g ham
salt
1 × 2.5ml spoon pepper
1 × 2.5ml spoon mixed herbs

1 × 2.5ml spoon ground mace
grated rind of 1 lemon
well-flavoured, cooled and jellied stock
    (pp25–27), as required
2 hard-boiled eggs
flour for rolling out
beaten egg for glazing

Prepare the pastry and leave to stand in a cool place. Cut the veal and ham into 1cm cubes, and add the seasoning and flavourings. Heat the stock until melted and mix a small amount in with the meat. Slice the hard-boiled eggs. Put half the meat mixture into a 500ml pie dish, cover with the sliced eggs and add the remaining meat. Moisten with the stock, but do not overfill the dish with liquid.

Roll out the pastry on a lightly floured surface, and cut it to fit the top of the pie dish. Dampen the edges of the dish with water. Use some of the trimmings to line the rim of the dish. Dampen the pastry rim, lift the top crust into position, and seal the edge. Make a hole in the centre of the pie, decorate with pastry leaves, and brush with beaten egg. Bake in a hot oven, 220°C, Gas 7, for 15 minutes, then reduce the heat to moderate, 180°C, Gas 4, and bake for $1\frac{1}{2}$ hours. Remove the pie from the oven, make a second hole in the crust and pour in a little more stock. Leave to cool thoroughly, preferably overnight, in a refrigerator.

Serve cold with salads.

Pot Pie of Veal
6 helpings

500g lean pie veal
200g salt (pickled) pork
salt and pepper
white (p26) **or** general household (p25)
   stock to cover

500g potatoes
puff (p458) **or** rough puff (p457) pastry
   using 150g flour
flour for rolling out
beaten egg **or** milk for glazing

Wipe the veal and cut it into 3–5cm cubes, and the pork into thin strips. Place the veal and pork in layers in a 1.5 litre pie dish, seasoning each layer well with salt and pepper. Fill the dish three-quarters full with stock. Cover with a lid and cook in a moderate oven, 180°C, Gas 4, for $1\frac{1}{2}$ hours.

Meanwhile, prepare and parboil the potatoes in salted water. Drain, and slice thickly. Remove the meat from the oven and cool slightly. Add extra stock to the dish to bring it back to its original level, if necessary. Arrange the potatoes evenly on top of the meat. Roll out the pastry on a lightly floured surface to cover the top of the pie dish. Brush with the beaten egg or milk. Make a hole in the centre to let the steam escape. Bake in a very hot oven, 230°C, Gas 8, for 10–15 minutes until the pastry is set, then reduce the heat to fairly hot, 190°C, Gas 5, and cook for 25–30 minutes. Add more hot stock through the hole in the top to fill the pie.

Raised Veal, Pork, and Egg Pie
6 helpings

hot water crust pastry (p456) using
   400g flour
400g pie veal
400g lean pork
25g plain flour
$1\frac{1}{2} \times$ 5ml spoons salt
$\frac{1}{2} \times$ 2.5ml spoon ground pepper

3 hard-boiled eggs
2 × 15ml spoons water
beaten egg for glazing
125ml (approx) well-flavoured, cooled
   and jellied stock **or** canned
   consommé

Line a 20cm round pie mould with three-quarters of the pastry, or use a round cake tin to mould the pie as described on pp456–57. Use the remaining quarter for the lid.

Cut the meat into small pieces, removing any gristle or fat. Season the flour with salt and pepper, and toss the meat in it. Put half into the pastry case and put in the whole eggs. Add the rest of the meat and the water. Put on the lid, brush with beaten egg, and make a hole in the centre to let steam escape. Bake in a very hot oven, 230°C, Gas 8, for 15 minutes. Reduce the heat to very cool, 140°C, Gas 1, and continue cooking for $2\frac{1}{2}$ hours. Remove the greaseproof paper or mould for the last 30 minutes of the cooking time and brush the top and sides of the pastry with beaten egg.

Heat the stock or consommé until melted and, when the pie is cooked, funnel it through the hole in the lid until the pie is full. Cool completely before serving.

Note If preferred, the ingredients can be made into 6 individual pies. Slice the eggs.

Veal and Ham Pudding
6 helpings

600–800g lean pie veal
150g ham **or** bacon **or** salt (pickled)
   pork
suet crust pastry (p454) using
   200g flour
flour for rolling out

fat for greasing
salt and pepper
4×15ml spoons general household
   stock (p25)
375ml thickened gravy (p270)

Garnish
chopped parsley

Wipe the veal and cut it into small neat pieces. Cut the ham, bacon or pork into narrow strips. Reserve one-quarter of the pastry for the lid. Roll out the rest on a lightly floured surface so that it is 1cm larger than the top of a greased 1 litre basin, and 5mm thick. Press well into the basin to remove any creases. Fill with alternate layers of veal and ham, bacon or pork, seasoning each layer well. Add the stock when the basin is half full. Roll out the reserved pastry to fit the top of the basin. Dampen the edges, place the lid in position, and seal. Cover with a round of greased greaseproof paper, then cover tightly with foil.

Place the basin in a steamer, or on a saucer in a pan with water coming half-way up the basin's sides. Steam, or half steam the pudding for 3 hours, topping up the steamer or pan with boiling water when it is reduced by a third.

Remove the foil and paper from the pudding when ready. Serve in the basin, garnished with chopped parsley. Serve the gravy separately.

Fricadelles of Veal
4–6 helpings

500g boned lean veal (see **Note**)
75g white bread
50ml milk
200g shredded suet
1×5ml spoon grated lemon rind
a pinch of grated nutmeg
salt and pepper

3 eggs
750ml white stock (p26) **or** salted
   water
soft white breadcrumbs for coating
oil for deep frying
375ml foundation brown sauce (p241)

Garnish
slices of lemon   chopped parsley

Wipe and trim the meat. Cut the crusts off the bread. Soak the bread in the milk for 5 minutes, and then squeeze it as dry as possible and rub out any lumps. Mince the veal. Mix it with the bread, suet, lemon rind, nutmeg, and salt and pepper. Beat two of the eggs until liquid, and stir into the veal mixture. Shape into balls about the size of a large walnut. Bring the stock or salted water to the boil in a pan. Drop the balls into it and cook for 6 minutes. Drain, and dry thoroughly.

Beat the remaining egg until liquid. Coat the balls with beaten egg, then with breadcrumbs. Heat the oil (p10) and fry the fricadelles until golden-brown. Drain, and add them to the brown sauce in a saucepan. Heat to simmering point and simmer very gently for 30 minutes. Serve in the sauce, garnished with lemon and chopped parsley.

Note If the meat is boned by the butcher, make sure he gives you the bones. These, together with the meat trimmings, can be used to make the white stock and the brown sauce.

Offal Dishes
Brains in Black Butter (Cervelles au Beurre Noir)
4 helpings

2 sets calf's brains	bouquet garni
salt	flour for dusting
1 × 5ml spoon lemon juice	ground pepper
1 small onion	2 × 15ml spoons butter
1 litre water	butter for greasing
2 × 15ml spoons white wine vinegar	

Black Butter

4 × 15ml spoons butter	
1 × 15ml spoon white wine vinegar	2 × 15ml spoons capers (optional)

Garnish
sprig of parsley

Soak the brains for 30 minutes in lightly salted cold water sharpened with the lemon juice to remove all traces of blood. Meanwhile, skin and halve the onion, and put it in a saucepan with the water, vinegar, and bouquet garni. Heat to simmering point and simmer for 30 minutes. Leave the stock to cool.

Drain the brains, and cut off any membranes. Wash thoroughly but very gently. Put the brains into the stock, heat slowly to simmering point, and poach for 20 minutes. Drain thoroughly, and put into very cold water to cool. Drain again and pat dry. Season the flour with salt and pepper, and dust the brains with it. Heat the 2 × 15ml spoons butter in a frying pan, and fry the brains lightly, turning them over, until just browned on all sides. Put them in a shallow serving dish, and keep them warm under buttered paper.

Take any bits of brain out of the frying pan, add the butter for the Black Butter and heat until golden-brown. Add the vinegar, and let it boil up. As soon as it foams, pour the mixture over the brains, adding the capers, if used. Serve at once, garnished with a sprig of parsley.

Calf's Liver with Savoury Rice
6 helpings

500g calf's liver
1 medium-sized onion (100g approx)
2 cloves garlic (optional)
40g butter **or** margarine
150g Patna rice
375ml well-flavoured white stock
   (p26)

salt and pepper
½–1 × 2.5ml spoon powdered saffron
plain flour
butter **or** oil for frying
250ml foundation brown sauce (p241)
juice of ½ lemon
butter for greasing

Garnish
baked **or** fried bacon rolls (p51)   paprika

Remove the skin and tubes, and cut the liver into thin slices. Skin the onion and garlic cloves, if used, and chop them finely. Heat 25g of the butter or margarine in a pan and sauté the onion and garlic without colouring for 2–3 minutes. Wash the rice and add it to the pan. Mix well and cook for about 3 minutes. Add the stock, salt and pepper to taste, and the saffron. Cover the pan, and cook for 30–45 minutes over gentle heat, or in a moderate oven, 180°C, Gas 4, until the rice is tender and has absorbed all the stock. Add the remaining butter or margarine, mix well, and press into a border mould. Put to one side until set.

Season some flour with salt and pepper and dip the slices of liver in it. Heat a little butter or oil in a frying pan and fry the liver, turning once, until browned and cooked through. Drain thoroughly. Heat the brown sauce in a saucepan to boiling point, add the lemon juice and the liver, and heat through. Turn the rice on to a warmed dish, cover with buttered greaseproof paper, and heat in a warm oven, 160°C, Gas 3, for 10–12 minutes. Place the liver and sauce in the centre of the mould, and garnish with the bacon rolls and paprika.

Braised Veal Sweetbreads
6 helpings

3 pairs veal sweetbreads
1 small onion (50g approx)
1 small carrot (25g approx)
½ small turnip (25g approx)
25g butter **or** margarine
bouquet garni
6 black peppercorns

salt
white (p26) **or** general household (p25)
   stock to cover
butter for greasing
1 slice of white bread 5cm thick
fat **or** oil for frying

Prepare the sweetbreads (p148). Press between 2 plates until quite cold.

Prepare and slice the vegetables. Melt the fat in a flameproof casserole, and fry the vegetables for about 10 minutes. Add the bouquet garni, peppercorns, salt to taste, and enough stock almost to cover the vegetables. Place the sweetbreads on top of the vegetables, cover with buttered greaseproof paper, and heat to boiling point. Baste the sweetbreads well, cover the casserole and cook in a moderate oven, 180°C, Gas 4, for about 1 hour. Add more stock, if necessary, and baste occasionally.

Meanwhile, cut a croûte from the slice of bread and fry it in shallow fat or oil, turning once, until golden-brown on both sides. Drain thoroughly. Place the croûte on a warmed serving dish and serve the sweetbreads on top.

Note Use the stock and vegetables for soup.

Calf's Foot Jelly
3–4 helpings

1 calf's foot	1 egg white and shell
1 litre water	a pinch of ground cinnamon
salt and pepper	2 cloves
pared rind and juice of 1 large lemon	25ml dry sherry (optional)

Cut the foot into convenient-sized pieces to fit into a stewpan. Wash and blanch them by putting them in the stewpan, covering with cold water and heating to boiling point, then skimming and draining.

Put the pieces back in the pan with 1 litre water, and add salt and pepper to taste. Heat to boiling point, cover with a tight-fitting lid, reduce the heat, and simmer gently for 3–4 hours, removing any scum which rises. Strain, and measure the stock. If more than 500ml, return to the pan and boil until reduced to 500ml. Leave to cool completely, then remove any fat.

Return the stock to the pan with the lemon rind and juice, egg white and shell, cinnamon, and cloves. Heat to simmering point and simmer for 10 minutes, then allow to stand for 10 minutes. Strain through a fine sieve or jelly bag. Stir in the sherry, if used. Store in a refrigerator or very cool place.

Pork

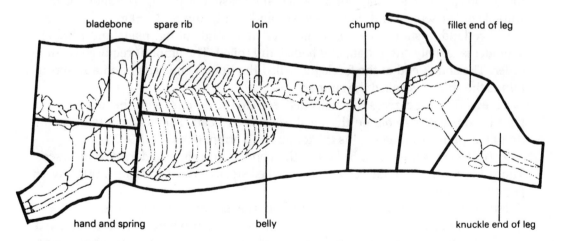

Pork cuts

English and Scottish cuts of pork vary considerably. Those noted below are the most widely used English cuts. See also the diagram above.

1) *Leg* is a succulent and popular roasting joint. In Scotland a leg is known as a gigot. Often divided into fillet end and knuckle end, and used as follows (p162):

Fillet end: The top of the leg which is ideal for roasting or for slicing into steaks for grilling and frying. (Av wt – 2.5kg)

Knuckle end: The lower half of the leg which can be roasted whole or boned and stuffed. (Av wt – 2.5kg)

2) *Loin* is a popular roast on the bone or boned, stuffed and rolled. It is often divided into loin and chump chops. (Av wt – 4–5.5kg)

Tenderloin is the lean cut found on the inside of the loin bone. It is sometimes called 'pork fillet' but it must not be confused with 'fillet end' from the leg. Ideal for roasting, braising, grilling, and frying. (Av wt 0.5–2.5kg)

3) *Belly* (also called draft or flank pork) is suitable (fresh or pickled) for braising, stewing or boiling. Sliced belly is a very economical cut for grilling and frying. Thick end of belly can make an economical and tasty roast, particularly when stuffed. (Av wt 1.5–2.25kg)

4) *Bladebone* is a roasting joint, tasty when boned and stuffed. It is also ideal for boiling, either fresh or pickled. (Av wt 1.75–2kg)

5) *Spare rib* is almost a parallel cut to the middle neck of lamb. It is a lean and economical roasting joint with little top fat. Meat from this cut makes the best filling for home-made pork pies. It can also be cut into spare rib chops. (Av wt 2.75–3.25kg)

6) *Spare ribs* (American-style) are cut from the belly and are removed in 1 sheath or slab, leaving the meat between the sections of rib bones. (They may also be sold under the name of pork rib bones.) They are usually barbecued. Chinese-style spare ribs are cut from the rib cage and have little meat on them. They are served roasted or braised in a sweet-sour sauce. (Av wt 2.7–3.2kg; Av wt Chinese – 2.3kg)

7) *Hand* and *spring* is cut from the foreleg of the pig and, in bone structure, is similar to knuckle half shoulder of lamb. It is a large economical roasting joint. However, it is often too large for a small family, so it is sometimes sold divided into hand and shank. The hand can be boned and roasted or boiled. The shank is most suitable for casseroles and stews. (Av wt hand and spring 3–3.25kg)

In Scotland, a shoulder of pork includes hand and spring, blade and ribs. The shoulder is usually cut in half, and boned and rolled. The amount required is cut to order. The shank end of the foreleg is called the hough end. The hand and spring, minus the shank, is called the runner.

8) *Head:* The pig carcass is usually delivered to the butcher with the head on, so a pig's head is easier to obtain than a sheep's or ox head. The head contains a considerable quantity of meat, plus the tongue and brain. (Av wt 1.75–2kg)

9) *Trotters* or *pettitoes* can be boiled, then boned, crumbed, and fried or fricasséed. The stock is used to make aspic jelly or jellied stock. (Av wt trotter – 200g; Av wt pettitoe – 150g)

10) *Chops* are thick slices of meat cut from the loin or spare rib joints.

Chump: First 2–3 chops cut from the end of loin where the leg is removed. Chump chops are large and meaty and are good for grilling, frying or baking. (Av wt 200–300g each)

Middle loin: Sometimes sold with the kidney and, occasionally, with the tenderloin (fillet). All cut from the loin. (Av wt 125–300g each)

Fore loin: Similar to neck of lamb chops. (Av wt 125–175g)

Spare rib: Cut from spare rib; grill, fry or braise. (Av wt 125–175g)

Roasted, Fried and Grilled Dishes
Roast Pork *Basic recipe*

a joint of pork on the bone suitable for   salt and pepper
   roasting   oil **or** fat for basting

Ask the butcher to score the rind in narrow lines, or do it yourself with a sharp knife. Select the method of roasting, ie quick or slow roasting (p95). Weigh the joint to calculate the cooking time (p96). Wipe the meat. Place the joint on a rack in a shallow roasting tin. Season the meat with salt and pepper and pour over a little oil or rub it with a little fat. Rub some salt into the scored rind to produce crisp crackling. Place the roasting tin in the oven, and cook for the required time.

If liked, brush the joint with apricot jam or glaze or with syrup from canned peaches, 10 minutes before the end of the cooking time. Alternatively, sprinkle the rind with brown sugar mixed with a little dry mustard. These mixtures give a sweeter crisp crackling.

Transfer the cooked meat to a warmed meat dish and keep hot. Prepare the gravy from the sediment in the roasting tin.

Serve roast pork with sage and onion stuffing (p49) and apple sauce.

Roast Savoury Loin of Pork
6–7 helpings

1.5kg loin of pork on the bone   a pinch of dry mustard
1 × 15ml spoon finely chopped onion   glaze (p59) (optional)
1 × 2.5ml spoon dried sage   125ml apple sauce
1 × 2.5ml spoon salt   250ml thickened gravy (p270)
½ × 2.5ml spoon freshly ground pepper

Ask the butcher to chine the pork and score the rind in narrow lines, or do it yourself with a sharp knife. Wipe the meat. Mix the onion with sage, salt, pepper, and mustard. Rub the mixture well into the surface of the meat. Roast the pork in a hot oven, 220°C, Gas 7, for 10 minutes, then reduce the heat to moderate, 180°C, Gas 4, for the rest of the calculated cooking time, allowing 30 minutes per 0.5kg plus 30 minutes over. About 30 minutes before serving, cover with glaze, if liked, and continue cooking to crisp the crackling. Serve hot apple sauce and gravy separately.

Fried Pork Chops *Basic recipe*
6 helpings

6 chump **or** middle loin **or** fore loin **or**   1 × 15ml spoon oil **or** butter **or** lard
    spare rib pork chops   salt
ground pepper   1 × 15ml spoon plain flour
dried sage   250ml general household stock (p25)

Wipe the chops and trim off any excess fat. Sprinkle each chop with pepper and sage. Heat the fat in a frying pan. Add the chops and fry until sealed and browned on the underside. Turn with a palette knife and continue to fry until the other side is browned. Reduce the heat and continue to fry, turning once or twice, until the meat is cooked through. The total frying time is 15–20 minutes, or longer for thick chops. Transfer the chops to a warmed serving dish, sprinkle with salt, and keep hot.

Pour the fat from the pan, reserving the sediment. Stir in the flour, and cook. Gradually add the stock and stir until boiling. Season to taste. Serve the gravy separately in a sauce-boat.

VARIATION
Fried Pork Chops with Peaches
Follow the recipe for Fried Pork Chops until the chops are cooked through. Arrange the fried chops on a warmed serving dish and keep hot. Pour off the fat and sediment from the frying pan and reserve for making gravy, if liked. Melt 25g butter and add 6 drained, canned peach halves. Fry gently until golden on both sides. Top each chop with a peach half, cut side down. Garnish with mustard and cress. If serving gravy, make it as for Fried Pork Chops.

Grilled Pork Chops *Basic recipe*
6 helpings

6 chump **or** middle loin **or** fore loin   caster sugar
    or spare rib pork chops   salt
2 × 15ml spoons oil **or** melted butter   1 × 15ml spoon plain flour
ground pepper   250ml general household stock (p25)
dried sage   125ml apple sauce
dried marjoram

Wipe the chops and trim off any excess fat. Brush the grill rack with oil or melted butter and place the chops on it. Brush the upper surface of the chops with oil or melted butter and sprinkle with pepper, sage, marjoram, and sugar. Cook under a hot grill until one side is lightly browned. Draw off the heat and turn the chops over with a palette knife and spoon. Brush the second side with oil or melted butter and sprinkle with pepper, herbs, and sugar. Return to the heat and brown quickly. Reduce the heat and grill until the chops are cooked through. The total grilling time is 15–20 minutes for loin and spare rib chops, a little longer for the larger chump chops. Arrange the chops on a warmed serving dish, sprinkle with salt and keep hot.

Pour the fat from the grill pan and scrape the sediment into a small pan. Stir in the flour, then gradually add the stock and stir until boiling. Season to taste. Serve the gravy and hot apple sauce separately.

VARIATION
Grilled Pork Chops with Apple Slices
Follow the recipe for Grilled Pork Chops. When cooked, transfer the chops to a warmed serving dish and keep hot. Peel, core, and cut 6 slices (1cm thick) of a sharp apple. Put on to the grill rack, brush with the fat in the pan, and brown lightly on both sides. Place 1 apple slice on each chop and garnish with sprigs of parsley.

Braised and Casseroled Dishes
Braised Pork *Basic recipe*
8–10 helpings

a bladebone **or** a spare rib joint of pork (2kg approx)	1 clove of garlic
50g lard **or** 3 × 15ml spoons cooking oil	125ml dry cider
1 large onion (200g approx)	125ml general household stock (p25)
2 large carrots (200g approx)	bouquet garni
	salt and pepper

Wipe and trim the meat. Weigh it to calculate the cooking time. Heat the lard or oil in a large, deep frying pan and fry the joint, turning often, until browned all over. Remove the meat and put to one side. Prepare and slice the onion and carrots. Skin and crush the garlic. Add the vegetables and garlic to the pan and fry gently for 5 minutes. Pour in the cider and stock and add the bouquet garni. Return the meat to the pan and season well with salt and pepper. Heat to boiling point, cover the pan, reduce the heat, and simmer gently, allowing 35 minutes per 0.5kg meat. Turn the meat occasionally. When cooked, transfer to a warmed serving dish.

Strain the liquid from the pan, skim off the fat, re-heat, and serve in a sauce-boat.

Pork Fillets Stuffed with Prunes
6 helpings

100g prunes	100ml boiling water
800g fillet of pork	200ml single cream
2 small cooking apples (200g approx)	salt and pepper
50g butter **or** margarine	2 × 10ml spoons butter

Garnish
chopped parsley

Soak the prunes in cold water overnight, or cover them with boiling water and soak for 2 hours. Wipe the fillets and trim off any skin and fat, then slice them down the middle almost but not quite right through. Drain and stone the prunes; peel, core and slice the apples. Put the prunes and apple slices into the slits in the fillets, press the fillets back into shape, and tie them with thin string.

Heat the butter or margarine in a large pan, put in the fillets and brown them all over. Add the boiling water, 100ml of the cream, and salt and pepper to taste. Cover the pan, and cook gently for 30 minutes. Transfer the fillets to a warmed serving dish, remove the string, and keep hot. Add the rest of the cream to the pan, whisk well, then add a little cold butter. Pour the sauce over the fillets and serve hot. Garnish with chopped parsley.

Pork and Apple Hot Pot
4 helpings

4 loin **or** spare rib chops	100g mushrooms
1 medium-sized cooking apple	fat for greasing
(200g approx)	1 × 2.5ml spoon dried sage **or** savory
1 medium-sized onion (100g approx)	500g potatoes
50g lard **or** oil	salt and pepper

Garnish
chopped parsley

Wipe the chops and trim off any excess fat. Prepare the apple and onion and slice them thinly. Heat the lard or oil in a pan and fry the apple and onion until golden-brown. Clean and slice the mushrooms.

Grease a casserole and put the mushrooms in the bottom. Lay the chops on the mushrooms and cover with the apple and onion. Sprinkle the herb over the top. Prepare the potatoes and cut them into 1.5cm cubes. Top the casserole with the potatoes and brush them with the fat remaining in the pan. Season with salt and pepper. Pour in enough water to come half-way up the meat and vegetables. Cover the pan with a tight-fitting lid and cook in a moderate oven, 180°C, Gas 4, for $1\frac{1}{2}$ hours. Remove the lid 30 minutes before the end of the cooking time to allow the potatoes to brown. Garnish with chopped parsley and serve from the casserole.

Pastry Dishes and Offal
Raised Pork Pie
6 helpings

400g pork bones (approx)	hot water crust pastry (p456) using
1 small onion	250g flour
salt and pepper	500g lean pork
150ml cold water **or** stock	$\frac{1}{2}$ × 2.5ml spoon dried sage
	beaten egg **or** milk for glazing

Put the pork bones in a saucepan. Skin and chop the onion finely. Add it to the pan with salt, pepper, and the water or stock. Cover the pan, heat to simmering point, and simmer for 2 hours. Leave to cool until jellied.

Line a 1kg pie mould with three-quarters of the pastry, or use a round cake tin to mould the pie as described on pp456–57, keeping it about 5mm thick. Use the remaining quarter for the lid. Wipe and dice the pork. Season with salt, pepper, and sage. Put into the prepared pie crust and add 2 × 15ml spoons of the jellied stock. Put on the lid, brush with beaten egg or milk, and make a hole in the centre to allow steam to escape. Bake in a hot oven, 220°C, Gas 7, for 15 minutes. Reduce the heat to moderate, 180°C, Gas 4, and cook the pie for a further $1\frac{1}{2}$ hours. Remove the greaseproof paper or mould for the last 30 minutes of the cooking time and brush the top and sides of the pastry with egg or milk.

When cooked, remove from the oven and cool. Warm the remaining jellied stock and funnel it through the hole in the lid until the pie is full. Cool for 2 hours until the stock sets.

Pork Sausage-meat *Basic recipe*
Makes 650–700g

450g lean pork
1 slice of dry white bread
200g hard pork fat
1 × 2.5ml spoon ground mace **or**
  allspice

freshly ground black pepper
a pinch of dried thyme
25g dry white breadcrumbs
1 × 5ml spoon salt (see **Note**)

Wipe the meat. Remove the crusts from the bread. Mince the pork very finely together with the fat and bread. Season thoroughly with the spice, pepper, and thyme. Mix in the breadcrumbs, and add salt as needed. Use as required.

Braised Pig's Liver
6–8 helpings

1kg pig's liver in 1 piece
200g streaky bacon, without rinds
8 small carrots (200g approx)
1 medium-sized onion (100g approx)
1 clove

bouquet garni
1 × 5ml spoon salt
freshly ground pepper
100ml dry white wine **or** dry cider
chicken stock to cover

Remove the skin and tubes, but leave the liver whole. Put 100g of the bacon rashers in the bottom of a casserole and place the liver on top. Prepare the vegetables and press the clove into the skinned onion. Add the carrots, onion, and bouquet garni to the casserole, and season with salt and pepper. Pour the wine or cider over them. Add enough stock to come to the top of the liver. Put the rest of the bacon on top of the liver. Cover the casserole with a lid and bake in a moderate oven, 180°C, Gas 4, for about 45 minutes or until the liver is cooked through. Transfer the liver and bacon to a warmed serving dish and keep hot.
  Strain the sauce into a clean pan. Bring to the boil over high heat until the sauce is reduced by half. Pour the sauce over the liver, and serve hot.
Note Lamb's or calf's liver can be cooked in the same way.

Fried Pig's Kidneys
4 helpings

4 pig's kidneys
2 small onions (100g approx)
50g butter **or** oil
salt and pepper
2 × 15ml spoons mushroom ketchup

1 × 10ml spoon chopped parsley
1 × 10ml spoon plain flour
125ml general household (p25) **or**
  chicken (p26) stock

Skin, core, and cut the kidneys into thin slices. Skin and chop the onions finely. Heat the butter or oil in a frying pan and fry the onions until lightly browned. Add the kidney slices, seasoning, and mushroom ketchup. Toss gently over heat for 3–4 minutes. Add the parsley and lift out on to a warmed serving dish. Sprinkle the flour into the pan and cook until browned. Gradually add the stock and stir until boiling. Re-season if required. Pour the sauce round the kidney slices and serve hot.

Fried Pig's Fry

6 helpings

800–900g pig's fry (sweetbreads, heart, liver, lights, melts)	flour for coating
	ground pepper
salt	1 × 5ml spoon dried sage
1 small onion (50g approx)	fat for shallow frying

Prepare the sweetbreads (p148) and the heart (p128). Remove the skin and tubes of the liver. Lights need no preparation. Trim excess fat and skin off the melts.

Put the fry in a saucepan with just enough water to cover it. Salt lightly. Skin and add the onion. Heat to boiling point, skim, reduce the heat, and simmer for 30 minutes. Drain, dry thoroughly, and cut all the meats into thin slices. Season the flour with salt, pepper and sage, and use it to coat the slices lightly. Heat the fat in a frying pan, put in the slices, and fry gently, turning once, until browned on both sides.

Serve with a well-flavoured thickened gravy or with fried apple slices (p50) and crab-apple jelly.

Faggots or Savoury Ducks

4–6 helpings

800g pig's liver **or** fry (sweetbreads, heart, liver, lights, melts)	salt and pepper
	a pinch of grated nutmeg
100g fat belly of pork	1 egg
2 medium-sized onions (200g approx)	100g soft white breadcrumbs
a pinch of dried thyme	caul fat **or** flour, as preferred
1 × 2.5ml spoon dried sage	fat for greasing
a pinch of dried basil (optional)	

Prepare the liver or fry as for Fried Pig's Fry. Slice the liver or fry and pork belly. Skin and slice the onions. Put the meat and onions in a saucepan with just enough water to cover them. Heat to boiling point, cover the pan, reduce the heat, and simmer for 30 minutes. Strain off the liquid and reserve it for the gravy.

Mince the meat and onions finely. Add the herbs, salt, pepper, and nutmeg. Beat the egg until liquid and stir it in. Mix in enough breadcrumbs to make a mixture which can be moulded. Divide it into 8 equal portions and shape them into round balls. Cut squares of caul fat, if used, large enough to encase the balls and wrap each ball in a piece of fat. Alternatively, roll each ball in flour. Lay the faggots side by side in a greased baking tin. Cover the tin loosely with foil. Bake in a moderate oven, 180°C, Gas 4, for 25 minutes. Remove the foil and bake for 10 minutes to brown the tops of the faggots.

Serve hot, with a thickened gravy made from the cooking liquid or with Fresh Tomato Sauce (p255).

Pork Brawn
10–12 helpings

½ pig's head
400g shin of beef on the bone
1 × 5ml spoon salt
2 medium-sized onions (200g approx)
4 cloves

2 small carrots (50g approx)
½ × 2.5ml spoon ground mace
6 black peppercorns
bouquet garni
salt and pepper

Ask the butcher to remove the hair, eye and snout, and to chop the half head into 2 or 3 manageable pieces and the shin beef bone in half crossways. Remove the brains and tongue from the head and use these for another dish. Scald and clean the ear and wash the head well in cold water. Soak the head meat in salted water for 2 hours, changing the water 3 or 4 times. Drain thoroughly.

Put all the meat and the salt in a large pan. Skin the onions, and press 2 cloves in each. Scrape the carrots. Add the onions and carrots to the pan with the mace, peppercorns, and bouquet garni. Cover with cold water. Heat to boiling point, skim carefully, cover with a lid, reduce the heat, and simmer gently for 2–3 hours until the meat is tender.

Lift the meat out of the stock and drain thoroughly. Reserve the stock in the pan. Remove all the meat from the bones, trimming off the skin and fat, and dice the meat finely. Put the meat in a wetted mould, basin or cake tin.

Return the bones to the pan of stock. Bring the stock to the boil and boil rapidly, uncovered, to reduce it by about half. Strain the stock and season to taste. Pour just enough stock over the meat to cover it. Stir gently to distribute the meat evenly. Allow to cool. Cover, and leave in a refrigerator or cold place until set. Turn out to serve.

VARIATION

A pickled head can be bought from a butcher which gives additional flavour to brawn. Treat in the same way as the unpickled head, but reduce the cooking time to 1½–1¾ hours.

Pig's Trotters in Jelly
3–4 helpings

4 pig's trotters
2 pig's ears
1 × 10ml spoon chopped parsley

1 × 2.5ml spoon chopped fresh sage
salt and pepper

Singe off the hairs. Wash the trotters and ears thoroughly in salted water. Scald the ears. Put the trotters and ears in a large pan with just enough cold water to cover them. Heat to boiling point, cover the pan with a tight-fitting lid, reduce the heat and simmer gently for about 3 hours until the bones can be removed easily. Lift out the trotters and ears, reserving the liquid in the pan. Cut the meat into neat dice and replace it in the liquid. Add the herbs, and season to taste. Simmer gently for 15 minutes. Turn into a mould or basin and leave until cold and set.

Fricasséed Pig's Trotters or Pettitoes
4–6 helpings

4 pig's trotters **or** 8 pettitoes (see **Note**)
100g pig's liver
100g pig's heart (1 small **or**
    ½ large heart)
white stock (p26) to cover
½ small onion (25g approx)
1 blade of mace

6 white peppercorns
salt and pepper
a thin strip of lemon rind
25g butter **or** margarine
1 × 15ml spoon flour
1 × 15ml spoon single cream **or** milk

Wash the trotters or pettitoes thoroughly in salted water. Remove the skin and tubes from the liver and prepare the heart (p128). Put the trotters or pettitoes, liver and heart in a large pan and cover with stock. Skin the onion and add it with the mace, peppercorns, salt and pepper to taste, and lemon rind. Heat to boiling point, cover the pan with a tight-fitting lid, reduce the heat, and simmer for 1 hour. Remove the liver and heart, chop them finely, and put to one side. Allow the trotters or pettitoes to continue cooking for another 1–2 hours until the meat can be easily removed from the bones. (Pettitoes may take less time to cook than trotters.) Lift out the trotters or pettitoes, split them open, remove the bones and cut the meat into neat pieces. Put to one side with the liver and heart. Strain the stock and measure 250ml.

Melt the butter or margarine in a saucepan. Stir in the flour and cook for 2–3 minutes. Gradually add the 250ml stock, stir until boiling, and cook for 2–3 minutes. Season to taste. Add the meat. Heat through and stir in the cream or milk. Turn at once into a warmed dish and serve very hot.

Note Pig's trotters are the feet and leg up to the knuckle of a pig. Pettitoes are the same as trotters but taken from a suckling-pig and, therefore, smaller.

Bacon, Gammon and Ham

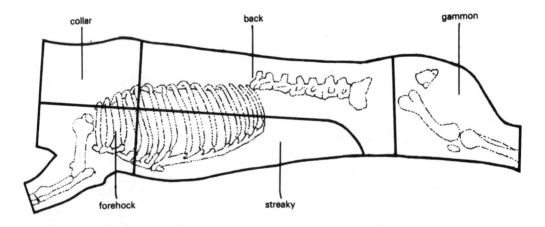

Bacon Pig Cuts
Cuts vary in different parts of Great Britain. The following are the most usual ones. See also the diagram above.

1) *Forehock* can be cooked whole. It bakes well or can be boiled (Av wt – 3.5kg) It can be cut into three smaller joints.

Butt: The leanest end of the forehock, usually boiled. (Av wt – 1.7kg)

Small hock: Not recommended as a joint. Remove the bone, and casserole or mince the meat. (Av wt – 1.3kg)

Fore slipper: Fat but good taste, usually boiled. Forehock joints are cheaper than gammon because their muscle structure is less regular. (Av wt – 0.5kg)

2) *Streaky* is usually divided into smaller cuts (Av wt – 3.7kg)

Top streaky can be boned and boiled or cut into thin rashers for frying or grilling (Av wt – 2.5kg)

Prime streaky can be boiled in a piece or cut into rashers for frying or grilling. (Av wt – 2.5kg)

Thin streaky is sliced to make crisp small rashers or bacon rolls. (Av wt – 0.7kg)

3) *Back* is usually divided into smaller cuts (Av wt – 8.7kg)

Flank is sliced and can be served with liver and kidneys. Economical. (Av wt – 1.2kg)

Long back and *oyster* are sliced for grilling or frying. (Av wt – 1.2kg)

Short back is cut into prime rashers for grilling or frying. (Av wt – 2.3kg)

Back and ribs can be boiled in a piece or cut into lean, economical rashers. (Av wt – 3kg)

Top back can be boiled or braised or cut into bacon chops. (Av wt – 1kg)

4) *Collar* can be bought whole and is most suitable for boiling. (Av wt – 3.6kg) It is often divided into smaller cuts.

Prime collar is a good boiling joint whole or cut into smaller joints. (Av wt – 2.7kg)

End collar is economical. Skin and press after boiling or baking. (Av wt – 0.9kg)

5) *Head* can be boiled for brawn or cooked whole for an occasion. (Av wt half head – 3kg)

6) *Chap* is the lower jaw and cheek of a pig. Boiled for Bath Chap. (Av wt 350–450g)

7) *Gammon* can be divided into four cuts. (Av wt 6.5–8kg)

Gammon slipper is a small, lean joint for boiling. (Av wt – 0.7kg)

Gammon hock is boiled or parboiled and then baked. Very good cold. High proportion of bone. (Av wt – 2kg)

Middle gammon is the best joint for boiling. Can be sliced into rashers for grilled gammon with eggs, etc. (Av wt – 2.3kg)

Corner gammon is a lean joint for boiling or for cutting into rashers for grilling. (Av wt – 1.8kg)

Cooking Bacon, Gammon and Ham

Cured pig meat which has been dried or smoked must generally be boiled before it can be used. After boiling, it can be used hot, but it is often reboiled or baked before it is served. Home-cured bacon, if very salty, can be soaked for 30 minutes in cold water or covered in boiling water and allowed to stand for 1 minute.

The small, family-sized bacon, gammon and ham joints in the shops have either been precooked before being cut, or they have been cut with special instruments which do not tear or spoil the meat.

A whole raw gammon or ham weighs at least 6.5kg and may weigh as much as 10kg. It is possible to cook a whole, bought or home-cured raw gammon or ham at home, but only given certain conditions. These are:

1) The whole gammon or ham can be boiled, par-boiled or baked, in 1 piece and in a very large container in both cases. An average joint measures about $56 \times 30 \times 13$cm and so a boiling pan and an oven of at least this size, is needed if the joint is to be baked.

2) There are several hours available in which to cook the gammon or ham. A solid fuel cooker cuts the fuel costs.

3) There is a hook or similar appliance, hanging above the cooker, to suspend the joint in its cooking pot. During the initial boiling, the knuckle end of the gammon or ham should be out of the water for the first part of the cooking time, otherwise it will cook before the bulkier part of the meat, and will be sodden and partly wasted through shrinkage.

An economic factor to be considered before boiling a bought or home-cured raw gammon or ham is the wastage. An average-sized joint will lose up to 1kg during its first boiling. In a joint smaller than 6.5kg, the ratio of bone to meat is too high to make it economic to cure the joint. These smaller joints are, therefore, normally used as fresh meat.

Because a gammon or ham can vary so much in size, in the ratio of bone to meat, in the uses to which the meat is put, and on the thickness of the slices cut, it is impossible to give an average number of helpings per joint. As a rule, cold meat can be cut more thinly than hot meat.

Fried Bacon

rashers of back, streaky **or** long cut
    bacon **or** thin slices from any
    suitable bacon joint

Cut the rinds off the bacon rashers to prevent the bacon curling. Heat a frying pan for 1–2 minutes, then lay the rashers or slices in the pan in 1 layer. Cook until the fat is becoming transparent and the underside of the bacon is lightly browned. Turn the rashers or slices over with tongs or a palette knife, and fry the second side to the preferred degree of crispness. The total frying time is 3–4 minutes. Drain thoroughly. Serve quickly before the fat congeals.

Grilled Bacon

rashers of back, streaky **or** long cut
    bacon **or** thin slices from any
    suitable bacon joint **or** thick slices
    or steaks from a joint **or** gammon
    steaks

Cut the rinds off the bacon rashers or snip them at intervals to prevent the bacon curling. Heat the grill for 1–2 minutes. Lay the rashers, slices or steaks on the grill rack or pan in 1 layer. Place under the grill, and cook for 2–3 minutes until the fat is bubbling and the meat is beginning to brown. Turn the bacon or gammon over with tongs or a palette knife, reduce the heat and continue cooking to the degree of crispness preferred (for rashers and slices) or until thoroughly heated and cooked through (for steaks). The total grilling time is 4–8 minutes. Drain thoroughly. Serve quickly before the fat congeals.

Boiled Bacon *Basic recipe*

any bacon joint suitable for boiling
cider (optional)
sugar (optional)
ginger root (optional)
4 cloves (optional)

1 onion (optional)
6–8 black peppercorns (optional)
1 bay leaf (optional)
2–3 juniper berries (optional)

Garnish (optional)
raspings (p43)   Demerara sugar

A bought or home-cured bacon joint will probably need soaking for 1–12 hours before cooking, depending on the saltiness of the meat. Packaged and similar joints do not need soaking as a rule. They can be put into a pan, covered with boiling water, then drained.

Weigh the joint and measure its thickness. Calculate the cooking time according to the thickness of the joint. As a guide, allow 30 minutes per 0.5kg meat plus 30 minutes over for any joint more than 10cm thick, eg cook a 1kg joint for 1½ hours. Do not undercook the meat, but on no account cook it fast or it will shrink and be tough.

Scrape the underside and rind before boiling any bacon joint. Choose a pan large enough to hold the meat comfortably with a little space to spare, especially if boiling more than 1 joint at a time. Add enough cold, fresh water to cover the meat, or use a mixture of cider and water, if preferred. Add sugar, ginger root or other spices, if liked (see **Note**). Cloves can be pressed into a whole onion, or tied in a square of muslin with the peppercorns, bay leaf and juniper berries, if preferred. Heat to simmering point, then simmer steadily for the calculated time. Test for tenderness by piercing the meat, near the bone if it has one, with a skewer.

Alternatively, shorten the cooking time by 15 minutes, and let the meat lie in the hot cooking liquid, off the heat, for 30 minutes. This gives an easier, firmer joint to carve.

Lift out the joint, pat dry, place it on a board and remove the rind. It should come off easily, in one piece. Coat the skinned area thoroughly with raspings, mixed with a little Demerara sugar, if liked. Serve hot or cold.

As a rule, the cooking liquid is too salty to use for stock.

Note Optional spices include coriander seeds, cumin seeds, allspice berries, a blade of mace, small pieces of nutmeg, or a whole, small, red chilli pepper.

Boiled Ham

a raw ham **or** gammon

Garnish

raspings (p43)   Demerara sugar

To ensure that the ham is sweet before cooking, insert a sharp knife close to the bone; when withdrawn, it should not give off any unpleasant odour or be slimy.

If the ham or gammon has been hung for a long time, and is very dry and salty, soak it for 24 hours at least, changing the water every 6–8 hours. For most hams, about 12 hours soaking or less is enough.

Drain; then weigh the ham and calculate the cooking time after soaking the ham (see Boiled Bacon p173). Clean and trim off any 'rusty' parts. Put the ham into a boiling pot big enough to hold it, but keep the knuckle end out of the water. Add enough cold water to cover the joint when laid flat, and cover the pan with a cloth to prevent undue evaporation. Heat to simmering point and simmer gently until tender or until parboiled, if to be baked after boiling. Do not let the water level sink below the surface of the ham when it is laid flat. Top up the pot with boiling water when required. Calculate the cooking time for the knuckle end on the thickness of the meat, and lay the ham flat in the pot to cook it (usually for about three-quarters of the total cooking time).

When cooked, lift out the ham and remove the rind. If to be eaten hot, immediately cover the skinned side with equal quantities of raspings and Demerara sugar. If to be eaten cold, put it back in its cooking liquid until cold, then drain, and cover the ham with the raspings and sugar mixture. If the ham is to be reboiled or baked, leave the coating until ready to serve.

Honey-glazed Ham with Pineapple
8–10 helpings

1.5–2kg parboiled York **or**   4 × 5ml spoons softened butter
   Virginia ham   1 × 15ml spoon double cream
500ml dry cider

Garnish

1 × 5ml spoon mixed English mustard   1 × 226g can pineapple chunks
3 × 15ml spoons stiff honey   or rings
a good pinch of ground cloves   maraschino cherries
                                        sprigs of watercress

Put the ham in a baking tin with the cider. Cover the tin tightly with foil. Bake the ham in a moderate oven, 180°C, Gas 4, for 30 minutes.

Meanwhile, mix together the mustard, honey, and cloves for the glaze. Drain the pineapple, reserving the juice. Cut pineapple rings into cubes, if used. Halve the cherries.

When the ham is baked, remove the foil and pour off the cider into a measuring jug. Remove the rind. Score the fat in a pattern of 4–5cm squares, then brush it all over with the mustard and honey glaze. Place pineapple pieces and halved cherries, cut side down, in alternate squares on the ham. Brush over with a little more glaze. Bake, loosely covered with the foil, in the oven for 20–30 minutes until the glaze is set.

Meanwhile, measure the cider and make it up to 500ml with the reserved pineapple juice, if required. Heat to simmering point in a saucepan. Stir in the butter, in small pieces, and melt. Simmer until well reduced and flavoured. Remove from the heat, and stir in the cream. Pour the sauce into a warmed sauce-boat and keep warm.

Place the ham on a carving dish and garnish with watercress. Serve the sauce separately.

Ham Slices with Fruit
3 main-course or 6 light first-course or supper helpings

6 ham **or** gammon slices **or** steaks
  (1cm thick approx)
150g soft light brown sugar

75g soft white breadcrumbs
200ml pineapple juice

Garnish
3 apples

75g margarine

Remove the rind from the ham or gammon and snip the fat at intervals to prevent curling. Put the slices or steaks in a frying pan with a very little water, heat to simmering point, and simmer for 10 minutes, turning them once. Drain. Lay the slices or steaks in an overlapping layer in a large, shallow, ovenproof baking dish. Mix together the sugar and breadcrumbs, and spread it over the slices or steaks, then trickle the pineapple juice over them. Bake, uncovered, in a moderate oven, 180°C, Gas 4, for 25 minutes.

Meanwhile, peel, core, and cut the apples into rings, 2cm thick (approx). Melt the margarine in a frying pan, and fry the rings until tender but not soft. Decorate the cooked dish with the apple rings, and serve at once.

VARIATIONS

1) *Apricots:* Soak 100g dried apricots in hot water for 20 minutes, then spread them over the prepared ham, and bake. Use the apricot water with the juice of an orange instead of the pineapple juice.

2) *Pineapple:* Spread 6 pineapple slices (canned or fresh) over the ham and breadcrumbs, add the pineapple juice, and bake for 20 minutes. Add the sugar, dot with butter, and continue baking for 15 minutes until the pineapple is glazed.

3) *Bacon chops:* Substitute chops for slices to make a more substantial meal. Fry the chops until browned on both sides, then continue as above.

Gammon Steaks with Marmalade
4 helpings

4 medium-sized gammon steaks
ground pepper
1 small onion
1 × 5ml spoon butter **or** margarine

4 × 15ml spoons medium-cut orange
  marmalade
2 × 5ml spoons vinegar

Garnish
chopped parsley

Remove the rind from the gammon steaks and snip the fat at intervals to prevent curling. Place on a grill rack and season with pepper to taste. Cook under a moderate grill, turning once, for 10–15 minutes depending on the thickness of the steaks. When cooked, transfer the steaks to a warmed serving dish and keep hot.

Skin the onion and chop it finely. Melt the fat in a pan and cook the onion gently for 5 minutes without browning it. Draw the pan off the heat and stir in the marmalade and vinegar, with any fat and juices left in the grill pan. Return to the heat and heat to boiling point, to reduce slightly.

Spoon the sauce over the gammon steaks. Garnish with chopped parsley and serve at once.

POULTRY

Preparing Poultry for Cooking

With the exception of some very small birds (see p203), the following instructions for preparing poultry apply to game birds as well.

Plucking
Plucking of any poultry should be done as soon as possible after the bird has been killed, preferably while it is still warm. If you have a strong hook in the wall, tie the two feet together and hang them over it. Otherwise, put the bird breast downwards on a large sheet of paper or clean cloth. Whichever method is used, first draw out one wing and pull out the under-feathers, taking a few at a time. Work towards the breast and then down to the tail. Repeat on the other side. Only pluck the lower half of the neck; the rest is cut off. The flight feathers (large quilled feathers at the ends of the wings) are best snapped, away from the direction of growth. Small hairs can be singed off with a taper; burnt feathers, however, will give the bird an unpleasant flavour. Scoop the feathers and down into a plastic bag as you pluck. If left lying about, they can irritate the nasal membranes, and they become difficult to clear up.

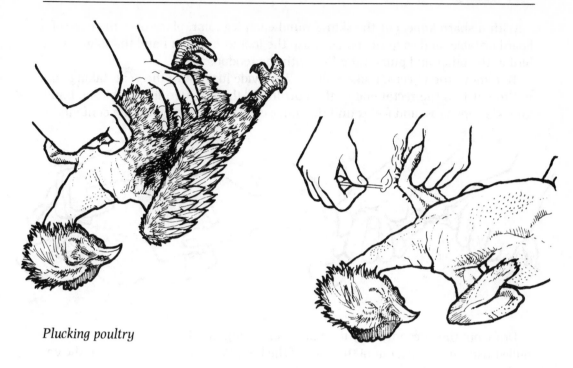

Plucking poultry

Drawing

Half-way along the neck cut a ring round the outer skin, and pull or cut off the head. Slip the knife under the skin and cut it loose from the neck all round, without puncturing it.

Holding the neck in a dry cloth, pull the skin back from it, leaving it bare. At the base of the neck, cut through the meat only.

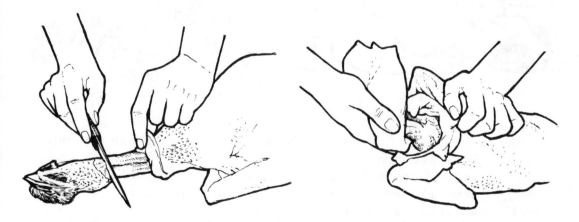

Then, still holding the neck in a dry cloth, twist it around, to break the bone. Cut through the broken bone; then withdraw the neck from the skin, and keep it for stock. Push one finger into the crop cavity to loosen the crop and gizzard.

With a sharp knife, cut the skin around each leg joint, place over the edge of a board or table, and snap the bone. Grasp the foot in one hand and the thigh of the bird in the other and pull off the foot with the tendons.

To remove the viscera, make a slit 5–7cm wide just above the vent, taking care not to cut into the rectal end of the gut. Insert the first two fingers of one hand, knuckles upwards, and feel round the inner cavity wall, loosening the contents.

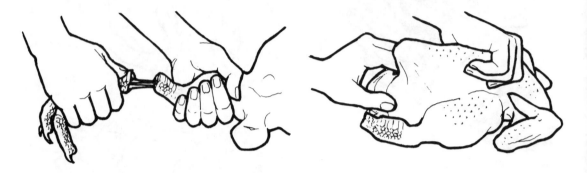

Draw out the intestines. Try to remove all the organs at once. The crop has to be pulled with the gizzard out of the back of the bird. When they are free, trim the end of the intestines and the vent.

The liver can now be separated from the gall bladder; take care not to break the latter.

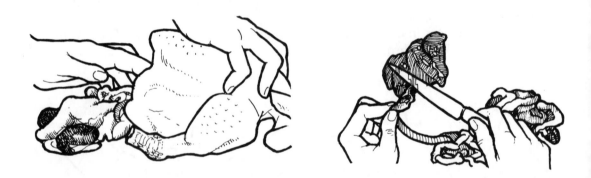

The meaty outside of the crop can be skinned or cut away from the gritty contents, for use as stock meat.

The lungs, which are bright red, lie close to the ribs. They are best removed by wrapping your index finger in a dry cloth and pushing in turn down from the backbone and out along each rib.

Destroy the inedible waste (head and feet usually, intestines, lungs, crop, container of grit from gizzard, etc) immediately. Keep the giblets (neck, gizzard, liver and heart) away from the bird so that its flesh will not be discoloured. Wipe the inside of the bird, but do not wash it unless it is to be cooked immediately.

Trussing

The object of trussing a bird is to make it look attractive and to secure the stuffing.

The easiest way to truss is with a large needle and stout thread. Needles designed specifically for trussing can be bought at most shops selling kitchen equipment.

Put the uncooked bird on its back, and hold the legs together to form a V-shape pointing towards the neck end. Insert the threaded needle into one leg, just above the thigh bone; pass it through the body and out at the same point the other side. Leave a good length of thread on either side.

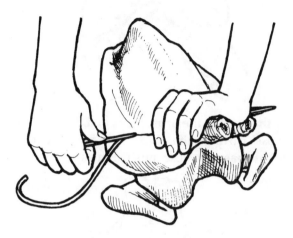

Turn the bird breast downwards and carry the thread through the elbow joint of the wing on each side.

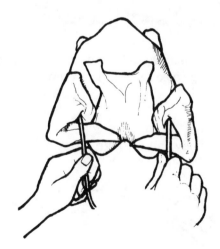

Twist the end of the wing under the neck to hold the flap of skin in place; tie the ends of the thread together, not too tightly.

Loop the thread over the ends of the drumsticks and draw them together, tying off round the 'parson's nose'. To make this easier, a slit may be cut in the flesh above the original vent cut and the 'parson's nose' pushed through.

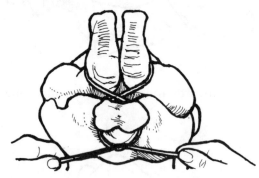

When the bird is trussed, the skin should still be complete if possible, to prevent any loss of fat from the bird during cooking, as this can result in over-dry and unpalatable meat.

Jointing
Pull the leg away from the body; cut through the skin; break leg from body at joint; cut through the joint.

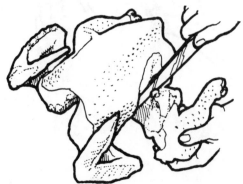

Cut the thigh from the drumstick at the joint.

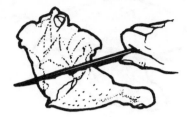

Cut the breast meat straight down to the wing joint; break the joint and cut so that the piece of breast meat and the wing are all in one piece.

With a heavy knife, cut down the back of the carcass, from vent to neck end.

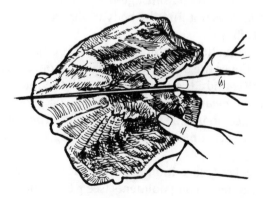

Cut the breast into two or four pieces, according to size.

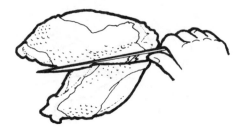

Cut off the pinions (extreme tips) of the wings (these can be cooked with the giblets); remove all small bones.

Boning
See Stuffed Boned Duck (p202).

Skinning
Loosen skin at the neck end exposing the wishbone. Using the fingertips and working under the skin, gradually loosen the skin from both sides of the breastbone. Slit the skin carefully along the length of the breastbone.

With a tugging movement and a firm grip, pull the skin off thigh and wing joints. Use a sharp knife if necessary to separate skin where it adheres to the bone. Chop away the last two sections of the wing joints and the last leg joint on the drumstick. Pull off the last remaining skin.

General Instructions for Roasting Whole Birds
Chickens, capons, and small turkeys: Traditionally, chicken is stuffed at the neck end with forcemeat or other stuffing, or just with fresh herbs; turkey with basic forcemeat, or chestnut stuffing in the crop and sausage-meat in the body. Nowadays however, the stuffing is almost always put into the body cavity; and only a large turkey for a festive dinner has 2 stuffings.

Put the bird in a roasting tin, preferably on a trivet or upturned saucer, and brush with melted fat or oil. Cover the breast with streaky bacon, if liked, or with foil. Cook for 20 minutes per 500g and 20 minutes over, until the thickest parts of the thigh, when pricked, give out a clear liquid without any blood.

The bird can be roasted on its side to start with and turned over half-way through the cooking to keep the breast moist. The final cooking should be breast side upper-most.

When the bird is cooked, place it on a warmed serving dish and keep hot. Serve with the traditional or other accompaniments (see p184) and gravy made with giblet stock if possible.

Large turkeys: Stuff the neck end and body cavity with the chosen stuffings. Place in a roasting tin and prepare as for smaller birds. (The bird can also be started on its side if liked.) Cover the breast with foil to prevent excess browning. This should be removed for the last 30 minutes – 1 hour.

For birds which are fully stuffed, cook for 15–20 minutes in a fairly hot oven, 200°C, Gas 6, then reduce to moderate, 180°C, Gas 4, and cook until tender. For unstuffed birds or ones with only the neck stuffed, cook in a warm oven, 160°C, Gas 3, until tender.

Approximate cooking times:

weight	unstuffed or with neck end only stuffed, at 160°C, Gas 3	fully stuffed, at 180°C, Gas 4 (after 20 mins at 200°C, Gas 6)
2.5 kg	$2\frac{1}{2}$–3 hrs	$2\frac{1}{2}$–3 hrs
2.75–3.5 kg	3 –$3\frac{1}{4}$ hrs	3 –$3\frac{3}{4}$ hrs
3.5–4.5 kg	$3\frac{1}{2}$–4 hrs	$3\frac{3}{4}$–$4\frac{1}{2}$ hrs
4.5–5.5 kg	4 –$4\frac{1}{2}$ hrs	$4\frac{1}{2}$–5 hrs
5.5–13.5 kg	20 mins per 500g + 20 mins	20 mins per 500g + 20 mins

Ducks: These are usually, although not always, stuffed before roasting. They are normally roasted in a fairly hot oven, 190°–200°C, Gas 5–6, allowing 15–20 minutes per 500g for a young bird, 20–25 minutes per 500g for an older one, a few minutes longer if fully stuffed. Allow about 300g stuffing for an average-sized bird.

The skin of a duck is sometimes pricked all over with a fork before roasting to encourage the fat to run, and some cooks pour boiling water over the bird to encourage this further. The bird is roasted on a trivet with buttered paper over the breast. An average-sized bird takes 1–$1\frac{1}{2}$ hours.

Geese: These are generally stuffed, and are usually roasted in a moderate oven, 180°C, Gas 4, for 20–25 minutes per 500g, although this may vary slightly with the age and size of the bird. A buttered paper is put over the breast instead of bacon; apart from this, it is roasted like turkey. An average-sized bird, when stuffed, takes 2–$2\frac{1}{2}$ hours to roast. Allow 1.3–1.5kg stuffing for a 4–4.5kg goose.

Guinea-fowl can be treated either like chicken or like pheasant.

Roasting in Foil

This is a more convenient and cleaner method of roasting poultry than open roasting, since the bird is completely enclosed in foil and no basting is required; the juices are kept within the parcel and can be poured off and used for gravy, leaving the roasting tin clean. Use a piece of foil large enough to enclose the bird. Put the foil in the roasting tin, place the bird on top, and fold up the foil to enclose the bird, making a loose parcel. Open the foil for the last 15–20 minutes of the cooking time, to brown the bird.

Cook in a hot oven, 220°C, Gas 7, for approximately the following times:

Chicken up to 1.75kg	30–35 mins per 500g
1.75–3.5kg	25 mins per 500g
Turkey over 3.75kg	23 mins per 500g

For ducks, allow 10 minutes per 500g more than the times shown on p172, and for geese, 20 minutes extra per 500g when roasting in foil.

Preparing Giblets for Cooking

The giblets usually kept and used are the liver, heart, neck, and gizzard. If bought from a poulterer or obtained with a frozen bird they are ready prepared for cooking. If using giblets from a bird bought before eviscerating, cut the small greenish gall-bladder away from the liver without breaking it; it will give the giblets a very bitter flavour. Cut any small sinews from the liver, and cut excess fat off the heart and gizzard. Break the neck into 2 or 3 pieces (a turkey neck into 4 or 5 pieces). Rinse the giblets in cold water briefly if necessary, then use them as the recipe directs.

Note Once the bones and meat have been removed, the skin of the neck of larger birds is sometimes used to contain a stuffing mixture in the same way as sausage skins.

What to Serve with Roasted Poultry

Any stuffing, sauce, garnish, and vegetable can be served with a plainly cooked bird, but the trimmings which are traditional because they have proved particularly good. Duck and goose, which are fatty and strongly flavoured, need a drier stuffing than chicken, and a thickened, less sharp gravy.

Roast Chicken
1) Thin gravy (p269)
2) Basic herb stuffing (p44)
3) Bacon rolls (p51)
4) Bread sauce (p253)
5) Watercress to garnish

Roast Turkey
1) Thickened gravy (p270)
2) For the crop: chestnut stuffing (p45) or basic herb stuffing (p44)
3) For the body: sausage-meat stuffing (p49)
4) Bacon rolls (p51)
5) Grilled chipolata sausages
6) Bread sauce (p253) or cranberry sauce (p254)

Roast Duck
1) Thickened gravy (p270)
2) Sage and onion stuffing (p49)
3) Apple sauce (p251) or cranberry sauce (p254) or Cumberland sauce (p255)
4) Watercress to garnish

Roast Goose
1) Thickened gravy (p270)
2) Sage and onion stuffing (p49)
3) Apple sauce (p251)

Carving

Good carving, skilfully done, can make a bird much more economical.

Chicken, Small Turkey, Capon and Guinea-fowl

Insert a carving fork firmly in the breast of the bird. On each side, make a downward cut with a sharp knife between the thigh and the body, then turn the blade outward so that the joint is exposed. Cut it through with either poultry shears or a sharp carving knife. Put the legs to one side.

With the fork still inserted in the breast, remove the wings by cutting widely, but not too deeply, over the adjacent part of the breast, to give the wing enough meat without depriving the breast of too much flesh.

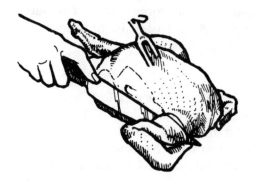

The breast of a large fowl can be sliced from the carcass as a whole.

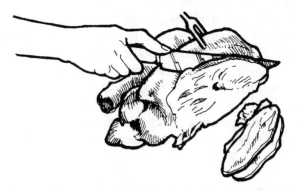

Alternatively, it can be separated from the back by cutting through the rib bones with poultry shears or a sharp knife. The breast of a small bird is detached from the carcass whole, thus providing two portions.

Carve the brown meat off the legs, if liked, working downwards in thin slices, following the direction of the bone. Serve some breast and some dark meat to each person.

To complete the carving of a large bird whose breast and back have been separated, place the back on the dish with the rib bones facing downwards; press the knife firmly across the centre of it, and raise the neck end at the same time with the fork to divide the back into two pieces.

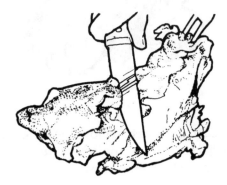

Remove the two 'oysters' (choice morsels of dark-coloured flesh) from the shallow hollows beside the thigh sockets. To do this, the tail part of the back must be stood on end and held firmly with the fork.

Large Turkey

Holding the bird steady with one carving fork, use a second one to bend each leg outward and downward, exposing the joint. Cut it through with poultry shears or a sharp carving knife. Put the legs to one side. Remove the wings in the same way. Do not take off any breast meat with the wing joints.

Carve the breast meat on the carcass, cutting downwards, parallel with the breast-bone.

The legs (thighs and drumsticks) should be carved downwards in thin slices, following the direction of the bone. Alternatively, the drumsticks can be reserved for another meal. Serve both white and dark meat to each person, together with a portion of each of the stuffings. To obtain these, slit the skin vertically down the centre of the vent and neck ends, open out the slits and serve the stuffings with a spoon.

When the breast meat has been cleared, remove any remaining stuffing to a warmed plate. Detach the wishbone. With the knife or shears, cut horizontally all round the bird through the thinnest part of the rib bones, and lift off the top part of the carcass. Turn the back part of the bird over, and carve any remaining meat off the back and sides parallel with the bone. Serve with the remaining stuffings.

Duck

Cut off the legs, and then the wings with a little breast meat attached to each. The breast is carved in quite thick, wedge-shaped slices: make the first cut down along the breastbone, and, with the blade of the knife slanted slightly towards the centre, make a series of cuts down the breast, parallel to the first cut. Remove the slices by cutting upwards towards the breastbone.

Duckling

To split the bird in half, cut down along the breastbone. Use poultry shears to cut through the bone. To divide each half into leg and wing portions, cut between the ribs so that some breast meat is attached to each joint.

Goose

Goose can be carved in the same way as duck. The breast is the best part. If the bird is large, carve only the breast and save the legs and wings for cold or re-heated dishes.

Chickens

Roast Chicken

4–6 helpings

1 roasting chicken	1 × 15ml spoon plain flour
oil **or** fat for basting	275ml chicken stock
salt and pepper	gravy browning
2–3 rashers streaky bacon (optional)	

Truss the chicken if liked. Put the oil or fat in a roasting tin and place for a few minutes in a fairly hot oven, 190°C–200°C, Gas 5–6. Remove from the oven. Place the chicken in the roasting tin, on **a trivet** if liked. Baste, sprinkle with salt **and** pepper, and place the bacon, if used, over the breast. Cover the breast with a piece of foil or buttered greaseproof paper, if liked. Return to the oven and cook the bird for the recommended time (p183), until tender. (Prick the thigh to test for tenderness; if there is any trace of blood, the chicken is not cooked.) Remove the bacon and foil or greaseproof paper 10–15 minutes before serving, to allow the breast to brown.

When cooked, place the chicken on a hot carving dish, remove trussing strings or skewers, and keep hot. Pour out and discard the excess fat from the tin, keeping back the sediment for gravy. Sprinkle in the flour, stir well, and add the stock gradually. Bring to the boil and boil for 2–3 minutes. Season to taste, add a little gravy browning, and strain into a hot sauce-boat. Serve with chicken accompaniments (p184).

Roast Chicken with Honey and Almonds

4–6 helpings

1 roasting chicken	50g blanched almonds
½ lemon	a pinch of powdered saffron (optional)
salt and pepper	2 × 15ml spoons oil
3 × 15ml spoons honey	

Truss the chicken. Rub all over with the lemon, then sprinkle with salt and pepper. Line a roasting tin with a piece of foil large enough to cover the bird and to meet over the top. Put the bird on the boil, and rub all over with honey. Slice the almonds and sprinkle them and the saffron, if used, over the bird. Pour the oil over the bird very gently. Wrap it completely in the foil, keeping it clear of the skin. Seal by folding over the edges. Roast in a moderate – fairly hot oven, 180°–190°C, Gas 4–5, for about 1½ hours until tender. Unwrap for the last 10 minutes to allow the breast to brown.

Grilled Chicken Joints
1 helping

1 breast and wing **or** leg of chicken   1 × 15ml spoon butter
salt and pepper

Garnish
Maître d'Hôtel butter (p564) **or**
    sauce (p238)

Remove the pinion from the wing, if used, and any excess skin. Trim away the bone end while still keeping the joint in a neat shape. Season it lightly with salt and pepper. Melt the butter and brush it over the chicken. Grill under high heat, turning 2 or 3 times during grilling to ensure even cooking. It should take 10–15 minutes to cook, depending on size.
    Serve with a little Maître d'Hôtel butter or sauce.
Note Pheasant or grouse can be cooked in the same way.

Devilled Chicken
1 helping

1 poussin **or** chicken joint   1 × 5ml spoon chopped parsley
salt and pepper   1 × 5ml spoon chopped shallot
a pinch of ground ginger   1 × 10ml spoon cooking oil
a pinch of mustard powder

Split the poussin, if used, along the back, open it out, and skewer it into a neat flattish shape. Season to taste with salt, pepper, ginger and mustard, and sprinkle the parsley and shallot over it. Allow to stand for about 1 hour, turning occasionally so that the meat absorbs the various flavours. Brush with oil. Grill for 20–30 minutes or until tender, turning 2 or 3 times while cooking so that the outside is lightly browned. Serve very hot.

Viennese Chicken in Breadcrumbs
4–6 helpings

1 chicken   2 × 15ml spoons flour
salt   100g dry white breadcrumbs
2 eggs   200g lard

Garnish
lemon wedges

Cut the chicken into 4–6 joints. Sprinkle each joint with salt and leave for 30 minutes. Beat the eggs until liquid. Dip each joint first into flour, then into beaten egg, and finally into the breadcrumbs. Leave to firm up for 30 minutes.
    Heat the lard in a pan for deep frying (p10). Fry the chicken joints until tender inside and crisp outside. Drain on soft kitchen paper. Garnish with lemon wedges, and serve with a green salad.

Spatchcocked Chicken
2 helpings

1 spring chicken	salt and pepper
25g butter	

Garnish

bacon rolls (p51)	parsley sprigs

Split the bird in half, cutting through the back only. Flatten out the bird, removing the breastbone if necessary. Break the joints and remove the pinions from the wings, to make flattening easier. Use skewers to keep it in shape while cooking.

Melt the butter and brush it on both sides of the chicken; season lightly. Grill for 20 minutes, or until cooked. Brush the chicken with more butter and turn while grilling to ensure even cooking. Remove the skewers when done.

Serve garnished with bacon rolls and parsley sprigs, and accompanied by Tartare Sauce (p257) or Piquant Sauce (p243).

Chicken Kiev
4 helpings

4 chicken breast and wing joints	1 egg
salt and pepper	100g soft white breadcrumbs (approx)
flour for coating	fat **or** oil for deep frying

Butter Filling

finely grated rind of ½ lemon	salt and freshly ground black pepper
1 × 15ml spoon chopped parsley	2 small cloves garlic
100g softened butter	

Garnish

lemon wedges	parsley sprigs

Make the butter filling first. Work the lemon rind and parsley thoroughly into the butter, and season to taste. Crush and work in the garlic. Form the butter into a roll, wrap in clingfilm and chill.

To prepare the chicken, cut off the wing pinions. Turn the joints, flesh side up, and cut out all bones except the wing bone which is left in place. Do not cut right through the flesh. Flatten out the boned meat, cover with greaseproof paper, and beat lightly with a cutlet bat or heavy knife. Cut the seasoned butter into 4 long pieces and place one on each piece of chicken. Fold the flesh over the butter to enclose it completely, and secure with wooden cocktail sticks. The wing bone should protrude at one end of each cutlet. Season the flour with salt and pepper and roll each piece of chicken in it. Beat the egg lightly on a plate. Roll or dip the chicken in the egg, coating each cutlet completely; then roll each in the breadcrumbs. Heat the fat or oil (p10) and deep fry 2 cutlets at a time until they are golden-brown and cooked through. Drain thoroughly and keep hot while frying the remaining two. Place the cutlets on a warmed serving dish with the bones overlapping in the centre. Remove the cocktail sticks and garnish with lemon wedges and parsley before serving.

Braised Chicken with Chestnuts and Sausages
4–6 helpings

1 chicken
salt and pepper
flour for coating
3 × 15ml spoons oil
1 onion

3 rashers streaky bacon, without rinds
150ml chicken stock **or** water
25g flour
25g butter

Stuffing

450g chestnuts
250ml chicken stock (approx)
50g ham
100g fine soft white breadcrumbs
grated rind of 1 lemon

salt and pepper
a few sprigs parsley
25g butter
1 egg

Garnish

450g fried chipolata sausages

lemon slices

Make the stuffing first. Remove the shells and skins of the chestnuts. Place the cleaned nuts in a saucepan, just cover with stock, and bring to the boil. Cover, reduce the heat until the liquid is only just boiling, and cook for about 1 hour or until the nuts are tender. Drain and mash them or put them through a fine sieve. Chop the ham finely. Mix the nuts, ham, breadcrumbs, and lemon rind together, and season with salt and pepper. Chop the parsley finely. Melt the butter slowly, and add the chopped parsley. Beat the egg until liquid. Mix all the ingredients for the stuffing together well. Stuff the bird with the mixture, and truss it.

Season the flour and roll the bird in it. Heat the oil in a large, heavy-bottomed flameproof casserole or pan with a lid. Fry the bird on all sides until lightly browned, then remove it. Skin and slice the onion, and cut the bacon into strips. Fry the onion and bacon lightly in the pan. Place a trivet or inverted saucer in the pan and place the chicken on it. Pour in the stock or water. Cover the pan, bring to the boil, then lower the heat until the liquid is just simmering. Cook for about 1½ hours, or until the chicken is tender. Add a little more stock if necessary before the end of the cooking time.

Remove the chicken. Sieve the pan juices or process in an electric blender. Knead the flour and butter into a beurre manié for the sauce. Heat the juices, then remove from the heat and add the beurre manié in small balls, stirring all the time. Return to the heat and stir until the mixture boils. Cook for a few minutes, then season to taste.

Garnish with fried sausages and lemon slices. Offer the sauce separately.

Chicken Casserole
6 helpings

1 chicken **or** 6 small chicken joints	50g mushrooms
salt and pepper	25g shallots
25g flour	50g butter **or** fat
125g streaky bacon, without rinds	500ml chicken stock

Joint the chicken. Season the flour, and dip the joints in it. Cut the bacon into strips 1cm wide, slice the mushrooms, and skin and chop the shallots. Heat the fat in a flameproof casserole and fry the bacon, mushrooms, and shallots gently. Add the chicken joints and fry them until golden on all sides, turning them as required.

Add enough hot stock just to cover the chicken pieces. Simmer for 1–1½ hours or until tender. Re-season if required. Serve from the casserole.

Chicken Chasseur
4–6 helpings

1 roasting chicken	25g onion **or** shallot
salt and pepper	175g button mushrooms
25g flour	150ml dry white wine
1 × 15ml spoon cooking oil	275ml chicken stock
50g butter	1 sprig each of fresh tarragon, chervil,
3 tomatoes **or** 1 × 15ml spoon concentrated tomato purée	and parsley

Divide the chicken into 8 serving portions. Season the flour with salt and pepper, and use to dust the portions. Heat the oil and butter in a frying pan, and fry the chicken pieces until tender and browned all over, allowing 15–20 minutes for dark meat (drumsticks and thighs), 10–12 minutes for light meat (breast and wings). When tender, remove from the pan, drain on soft kitchen paper, and transfer to a warmed serving dish. Cover loosely with buttered paper and keep hot.

Skin and chop the tomatoes if used, and the onion or shallot. Put the onion or shallot into the pan, in the fat in which the chicken was cooked, and fry gently without colouring. Meanwhile, slice the mushrooms, add them to the pan, and continue frying until they are tender. Pour in the wine, and add the chopped tomatoes or the tomato purée and the stock. Stir until well blended, then simmer gently for 10 minutes. Chop the herbs and add most of them to the sauce. Season to taste.

Pour the sauce over the chicken, sprinkle with the remaining herbs, and serve very hot.

Coq au Vin
4–6 helpings

1 chicken with giblets	50g unsalted butter
bouquet garni	1 × 15ml spoon oil
salt and pepper	2 × 15ml spoons brandy
125g belly of pickled pork **or**	575ml Burgundy **or** other red wine
green bacon rashers	2 × 5ml spoons concentrated
175g button mushrooms	tomato purée
125g button onions	25g butter
1 clove of garlic	25g plain flour

Garnish

croûtes of fried bread   chopped parsley

Joint the chicken. Place the giblets in a saucepan, cover with water, and add the bouquet garni, salt, and pepper. Cook gently for 1 hour to make 275ml stock.

Remove the rind from the belly of pork or bacon rashers, and chop the pork or bacon. Clean the mushrooms if necessary, skin the onions, and skin and crush the garlic. Heat the 50g butter and the oil in a flameproof casserole, add the pork or bacon, and the onions, and cook slowly until the fat runs and the onions are lightly coloured. Remove them to a plate.

Brown the chicken lightly all over in the same fat, then pour off any surplus fat. Warm the brandy, set alight, and pour it over the chicken. When the flame dies down, add the wine, stock, pork or bacon, onions, mushrooms, garlic, and tomato purée. Cover with a lid and cook over low heat, or in a cool oven, 150°C, Gas 2, for 1 hour or until the chicken is tender.

Remove the chicken to a serving dish and keep hot. Using a perforated spoon, remove the onions, bacon, and mushrooms, and arrange over the chicken. Simmer the liquid until reduced by about one-third. Meanwhile, make a beurre manié by kneading together the 25g butter and flour. Lower the heat of the liquid to below boiling point and gradually whisk in the beurre manié in small pieces. Continue to whisk until the sauce thickens. Pour it over the chicken. Arrange croûtes of fried bread round the dish and sprinkle with chopped parsley.

Hindle Wakes
6 helpings

1 x 1.5kg chicken
350ml chicken stock

grated rind and juice of ½ lemon
a blade of mace (optional)

Stuffing

175g prunes
50g onion
125g soft white breadcrumbs
1 x 5ml dried mixed herbs

50g shredded suet
1 x 15ml spoon Demerara sugar
salt and pepper
1 x 15ml spoon malt vinegar

Garnish

6 soaked prunes (see Method)
lemon slices

parsley (optional)

Make the stuffing first. Put the prunes in a basin, cover with cold water, and leave to soak overnight. Reserving 6 for the garnish, stone and chop the rest. Skin the onion and chop it finely. Mix it with the prunes, breadcrumbs, mixed herbs, suet, sugar, salt, and pepper. Sprinkle the mixture with the vinegar and mix together. Use the stuffing to fill the body cavity of the chicken.

Truss the chicken and place it in a large saucepan or flameproof casserole. Bring the stock to the boil, add the lemon rind and juice, and a blade of mace. Pour the stock over the chicken. Bring to the boil, reduce the heat, cover, and simmer for 1½ hours until tender. Drain, and garnish with the reserved prunes and lemon slices. Arrange in lines along the back of the chicken, using cocktail sticks to secure the garnish. Parsley sprigs can also be used. Serve with the stuffing and hot lemon stock.

Chicken with Macaroni
4–6 helpings

1 chicken
1 litre (approx) chicken (p26) **or**
   vegetable stock (p27)
150ml Fresh Tomato sauce (p255)

150ml Espagnole sauce (p248)
lemon juice **or** tarragon vinegar
salt and pepper
100g quick-cooking macaroni

Truss the chicken, put it in the stock, and poach or boil it for about 45 minutes until half cooked. Drain well, and cut it into convenient pieces for serving. Heat the sauce together in a heavy pan, put in the chicken pieces, and add lemon juice or tarragon vinegar and seasoning to taste. Simmer very gently for 30–45 minutes until the chicken is fully cooked. Meanwhile, add the macaroni to fast-boiling salted water, and cook for 8–10 minutes. Drain well. Put the macaroni in a heated serving dish, pile the chicken on top, pour the sauce over it, and serve hot.

Poultry Hot Pot
4−6 helpings

1 boiling fowl with giblets
3 rashers streaky bacon, without rinds
salt and pepper
nutmeg

2 onions
2 carrots
275ml chicken stock
3 × 10ml spoons flour

Garnish
2 × 15ml spoons chopped parsley

Joint the fowl and remove the skin. Place the joints, with the liver and heart, in a casserole or saucepan with a tight-fitting lid. Cut the bacon into strips, and add with the salt, pepper, and nutmeg. Prepare and slice the onions and carrots, and add with the stock. Cover, then either cook in a fairly hot oven, 190−200°C, Gas 5−6, or simmer for about 2−2½ hours until tender. Blend the flour with a little water, add some of the chicken stock, and return to the pan. Stir it in, and cook until thickened. Serve sprinkled with parsley.

   Boiled rice makes a good accompaniment.

Mrs Beeton's Chicken or Fowl Pie
6−8 helpings

1 chicken or boiling fowl with giblets
250ml water
1 onion
salt and pepper
bouquet garni
1 blade of whole mace
chicken fat or margarine for greasing
1 × 2.5ml spoon grated nutmeg
1 × 2.5ml spoon ground macé

6 slices lean cooked ham
150g basic herb forcemeat (p44) or
   250−300g sausage-meat
3 hard-boiled eggs
150−200ml water
flour for dredging
puff pastry (p458) using 150g flour
beaten egg for glazing

Skin the chicken or fowl and cut it into small serving joints. Put the leftover bones, neck, and gizzard into a small pan with the water. Split the onion in half and add it to the pan with the seasoning, bouquet garni, and mace. Half cover and simmer gently for about 45 minutes until the liquid is well reduced and strongly flavoured. Put to one side.

   Grease lightly a 1.5 litre pie dish or oven-to-table baking dish. Put a layer of chicken joints in the bottom. Season lightly with salt, pepper, nutmeg, and ground mace. Cover with a layer of ham, then with forcemeat or sausage-meat; re-season. Slice the eggs, place a layer over the forcemeat, and season again. Repeat the layers until the dish is full and all the ingredients are used, ending with a layer of chicken joints. Pour 150−200ml water into the dish and dredge lightly with flour.

   Roll out the pastry on a lightly floured surface to the same shape as the dish but 3cm larger all round. Cut off the outside 2cm of the pastry. Lay the pastry strip on the rim of the dish. Dampen the strip and lay the lid on top. Knock up the edge, trim, and use any trimmings to decorate the crust with pastry leaves. Make a pastry rose and put to one side. Brush the pastry with the beaten egg. Make a small hole in the centre of the pie. Bake in a hot oven, 220°C, Gas 7, for 15 minutes to set the pastry, then reduce the temperature to moderate, 180°C, Gas 4, and cover the pastry loosely with greaseproof paper. Bake for 1–1¼ hours if using forcemeat, for 1½–2 hours if using sausage-meat. Bake the pastry rose with the pie for the final 20 minutes but bake it blind. Test whether the joints are cooked through by running a small heated skewer into the pie through the central hole. It should come out clean with no trace of blood or smell of raw meat on it.

Just before the pie is cooked, re-heat the stock and strain it. When the pie is cooked, pour the stock in through the central hole, and cover with the pastry rose. Serve hot or cold.

Note For serving cold the joints can be boned. In this case sausage-meat should be used. Add the bones to the saucepan when making stock, and use a smaller dish. The cooking time will be the same.

Stuffed Chicken Legs
4 helpings

4 cooked drumsticks
salt and Cayenne pepper
1 × 15ml spoon vegetable oil
2 × 15ml spoons soft white
   breadcrumbs
1 × 2.5ml spoon mixed herbs

1 × 5ml spoon chopped parsley
1 small onion
1 × 2.5ml spoon grated lemon rind
1 egg
4 gammon rashers
fat for greasing

Garnish
parsley sprigs

Season each drumstick with salt and Cayenne pepper and moisten with oil. Mix the breadcrumbs, herbs, and finely chopped parsley in a basin. Skin, blanch, and chop the onion finely and add it to the basin together with the lemon rind. Moisten the mixture with the egg. Spread each gammon rasher with this stuffing, and wrap one rasher around each drumstick. Tie or skewer the rasher securely in place. Put the drumsticks on a greased baking tray and cook in a moderate oven, 180°C, Gas 4, for 20 minutes; then cover them with foil, and cook for a further 20 minutes. Garnish with parsley sprigs.

Serve at once on trimmed slices of hot buttered toast.

Paella Valenciana
6–8 helpings

2 spring **or** grilling chickens **or** 1
    roasting chicken (1–1.5kg aprox)
flour for coating
olive oil for frying
1kg live mussels

2 cloves garlic
75g short-grain Spanish **or** Italian
    rice per person
a pinch of saffron strands
salt

Garnish

50g cooked shellfish per person
    (prawns, crayfish, lobster **or** crab)

strips of canned pimento
green **or** black olives

Joint the chicken and coat lightly with flour. Heat 4 × 10ml spoons olive oil, and brown the pieces all over. Put to one side. Wash, scrape, and beard the mussels (p77). Put into a large saucepan with very little water. Cover, and heat gently for 5–10 minutes, shaking occasionally until they open. Discard any that do *not* open. Remove the open mussels with a perforated spoon and leave to cool. Reserve the liquid in the pan. Remove the mussels from their shells, retaining the best half-shells. Strain the mussel liquor through muslin, and add it to the liquid in the pan.

Slice half a clove of garlic thinly. Heat some olive oil in a deep frying pan or shallow flameproof oven-to-table casserole. Fry the slices of garlic until golden-brown, then discard them. Add 75g rice per person to the flavoured oil, and fry very gently. Crush the remaining garlic with the saffron and a little water. Scatter the mixture over the rice, and season with salt. Measure 150ml of the mussel liquid per person (made up with water if necessary), and add to the rice. Heat to simmering point, stirring well. Cook for 5 minutes, still stirring. Add the chicken pieces, and cook them with the rice for a further 15 minutes, until they are tender and the rice is cooked through.

Garnish with the shellfish, pimento, and olives. Replace the mussels in the half-shells, and use as an additional garnish. Remove the pan from the heat, and cover with a cloth for 10 minutes before serving. Serve from the pan.

Note Success depends upon correct cooking of the proper type of Spanish or Italian rice; the grains should be separate and not soggy. There is no need to use expensive shellfish. A well-made paella with chicken and mussels, or even chicken alone, is delicious. Traditionally, very young chicken is used.

Chicken Rissoles
4 helpings

100g cooked chicken
50g cooked ham **or** tongue
25g button mushrooms
25g butter
25g flour
150ml chicken stock
1 × 15ml spoon double cream

salt and pepper
shortcrust (p453) **or** rough puff (p457)
    pastry using 200g flour
flour for rolling out
oil **or** fat for deep frying
1 egg
fine dry white breadcrumbs for coating

Chop the chicken and ham finely. Chop the mushrooms. Melt the butter gently in a fairly large pan, add the mushrooms and cook for 1–2 minutes. Stir in the flour, add the stock gradually, and bring to the boil, stirring all the time. Cook for 1–2 minutes. Add the meat, cream, and seasoning. Leave to cool completely between 2 plates.

Roll out the pastry very thinly on a lightly floured surface, and cut into eight 12cm rounds. Divide the filling between the rounds, dampen the edges, and fold over to form half circles. Press the edges together and seal firmly. Heat the fat (p10). Beat the egg until liquid. Coat the rissoles with the beaten egg and breadcrumbs. Fry in the fat until golden-brown on both sides. Drain well.

Chaudfroid of Chicken
6 helpings

6 cooked chicken joints
125ml aspic jelly
375ml mayonnaise

lettuce leaves
3 sticks celery
2 hard-boiled eggs

Garnish
stoned olives **or** gherkins

tomato wedges **or** slices

Remove the skin, excess fat, and bones from the chicken joints, keeping the pieces in neat shapes. Melt the aspic jelly, and leave to cool. Just before it reaches setting point, while still tepid, add half the mayonnaise, and whisk in. Blend to a smooth consistency. Place the chicken joints on a wire cooling tray and coat with the mayonnaise sauce as soon as it reaches a good coating consistency. Arrange the lettuce leaves on a serving dish and place the chicken joints on top. Prepare and chop the celery, slice the eggs, and arrange these round the chicken. Spoon the remaining mayonnaise over the celery and egg. Garnish with the olives or gherkins and the tomatoes.

Chicken Mayonnaise
6 helpings

1 cold cooked chicken **or** 6 cooked
   chicken joints

275ml aspic jelly
425ml mayonnaise

Garnish
pickled walnuts

pieces of red and green pepper

Joint the whole chicken, if used; remove the skin, excess fat, and as much bone as possible, and trim the joints to a neat shape. Melt the aspic jelly. When almost cool, blend 150ml of it carefully into the mayonnaise. Beat well to blend thoroughly. Place the pieces of chicken on a wire cooling rack, and when the sauce is a good coating consistency, coat the pieces, using a large spoon. Cut the pickled nuts and the pieces of red and green pepper into attractive shapes for garnishing, dry well on soft kitchen paper, and stick on the chicken with dabs of half-set mayonnaise. Melt the remaining aspic jelly again if necessary; cool until it is on the point of setting, and use to coat the chicken thinly.

Galantine of Chicken
8–10 helpings

1 cooked boiling fowl
salt and pepper
100g ham **or** tongue
2 hard-boiled eggs
6 mushrooms
10–15g pistachio nuts **or** almonds

450g sausage-meat
750ml chicken stock (approx)
1 chicken stock cube
500ml White Chaudfroid sauce (p258)
125ml aspic jelly

Garnish
chopped pimento
strips of lemon rind

sliced hard-boiled egg

Cut down the back of the fowl, then remove all the bones neatly. Spread out the boned bird like a spatchcocked chicken (p189), distributing any loose pieces of meat evenly over the surface. Season well. Cut the ham or tongue into 1 × 3cm strips, slice the eggs, and chop the mushrooms. Blanch, skin, and chop the nuts. Spread 225g of the sausage-meat on the bird. Arrange the ham or tongue, egg slices, mushrooms, and nuts on top. Season well, then cover with the remaining sausage-meat.

    Lift the 2 halves of the bird, and bring them together so that it is as near its original shape as possible. Wrap the bird in foil. Heat the chicken stock and add the cube. Put in the chicken in foil, and simmer gently for $2\frac{1}{2}$ hours. Allow to cool slightly in the stock. Remove and drain. Tighten the foil to allow for any shrinkage while cooking. Press the 'parcel' between 2 large plates or boards and leave until quite cold.

    Unwrap, remove the skin, and wipe away any excess grease. Spoon the Chaudfroid sauce over the chicken. Chop the aspic coarsely and place round the chicken. Garnish in a decorative pattern with the pimento, lemon rind, and egg.

Turkey

Mrs Beeton's Roast Turkey

1 turkey	2–3 rashers fat bacon
450g basic herb forcemeat (p44)	fat for basting
500g–1.5kg seasoned sausage-meat	

Stuff the neck of the bird with basic forcemeat and put the sausage-meat inside the body. Truss, and lay the bacon rashers over the breast. Roast in a hot oven, 220°C, Gas 7, for 15–20 minutes, then reduce the heat to moderate, 180°C, Gas 4. (For the overall cooking time see p183.) Baste frequently. About 20 minutes before serving, remove the bacon to allow the breast to brown. Remove the trussing string. Serve on a hot dish.

Serve with the traditional accompaniments (p184) and with roast potatoes and Brussels sprouts.

Note A 6kg bird will just fit comfortably into an oven with an interior capacity of 0.07 cubic metres (42 × 40 × 40cm). If the oven is smaller than this, or if one wishes to cook a larger bird, it can sometimes be done by removing the legs and cooking them separately. In any recipe for a whole roast turkey, the quantity of stuffing and the accompaniments should be adapted to fit the size of the bird.

The breast meat of a large turkey may become dry before the legs are cooked. To avoid this problem, remove the legs either before roasting the bird or when the breast is cooked, and use them for another meal.

The quantity of stuffing required will vary to some extent with the type of stuffing. One uses less of a light fluffy stuffing which needs room to swell than of a dense stuffing such as sausage-meat. As a very general guide, 700g sausage-meat and 450g basic forcemeat will stuff an average-sized (6kg) turkey.

Turkey Loaf
6–8 helpings

50g long-grain rice	25g (approx) thyme and parsley
225g cooked turkey meat	stuffing mix
4 rashers streaky bacon, without rinds	grated rind of $\frac{1}{2}$ lemon
salt and pepper	1 × 5ml spoon paprika
1 egg	fat for greasing

Cook the rice in boiling salted water for 10 minutes. Mince the turkey and the bacon rashers, and mix with the salt, pepper, and egg. Drain the rice and add to the turkey mixture. Mix thoroughly.

Make up the stuffing according to the directions on the packet. Add the lemon rind and paprika. Mix well. Place half the turkey mixture in a greased tin, and spread with stuffing; cover with the remaining turkey mixture. Cook in a fairly hot oven, 190°C, Gas 5, for 35 minutes. Serve hot or cold.

Goose, Duck and Guinea-fowl

Roast Goose with Fruit Stuffing and Red Cabbage
6−8 helpings

350g prunes	salt and pepper
1 goose with giblets	450g cooking apples
1.5 litres water	1 × 15ml spoon redcurrant jelly
½ lemon	

Red Cabbage

1.5kg red cabbage	75ml water
50g butter	75ml malt **or** cider vinegar
50g Demerara sugar	salt and pepper

Soak the prunes overnight. Remove the giblets from the goose and simmer them in 1.5 litres water until the liquid is reduced by half. Weigh the goose and calculate the cooking time at 20 minutes for every 500g. Remove the excess fat usually found around the vent. Rinse the inside of the bird, then rub the skin with lemon. Season with salt and pepper. Remove the stones from the prunes and chop the flesh. Peel and core the apples and chop them roughly. Mix with the prunes and season to taste. Stuff into the body of the bird. Place in a very hot oven, 230°C, Gas 8, reduce the temperature immediately to moderate, 180°C, Gas 4, and cook for the calculated time.

Meanwhile, prepare the red cabbage, shred finely. Melt the butter in a large flame-proof casserole. Add the sugar and cabbage and stir well. Add the water, vinegar, and seasoning, cover and cook in the bottom of the oven for about 2 hours, stirring occasionally.

When the goose is cooked, drain off the excess fat, retaining the juices in the pan. Add the redcurrant jelly and stir until it melts.

Serve the gravy and red cabbage separately.

English Roast Duck
4−5 helpings

1 duck	3 × 10ml spoons flour
sage and onion stuffing (p49)	275ml stock
fat for basting	salt and pepper

Fill the duck with sage and onion stuffing, and truss for roasting. Heat the fat and baste the duck well. Roast in a fairly hot oven, 190−200°C, Gas 5−6, covered with buttered paper, for 1−1½ hours or until tender, basting frequently. Uncover for the last 30 minutes. Keep the duck hot. Pour off the fat from the roasting tin, sprinkle in the flour, and brown it. Stir in the stock, simmer for 3−4 minutes, season, and strain. Remove the trussing string from the duck.

Serve hot with traditional accompaniments (p184).

Roast Duck with Orange
4–5 helpings

1 duck	3 × 10ml spoons flour
basic herb forcemeat (p44)	275ml stock
fat for basting	salt and pepper

Garnish

1 large orange	1 × 15ml spoon brandy

Truss and roast the duck as for English Roast Duck (p200), but use basic forcemeat instead of sage and onion stuffing. Meanwhile, pare the rind of the orange and remove all the pith. Cut the orange into segments, discard the membranes, and soak the segments in the brandy. Cut the rind into thin strips, boil in a little water for 5 minutes, then drain. Heat the orange segments gently in the brandy. Serve the cooked duck with the strips of rind and hot orange segments as a garnish.

Roast Guinea-fowl
4–5 helpings

1 guinea-fowl	2 rashers fat bacon
50g butter	flour for dredging
salt and pepper	

Garnish

watercress sprigs	French dressing

Wipe the bird, mix the butter and seasoning, place it in the body of the bird and on the thighs. Lay rashers of bacon over the breast, and roast in a moderate oven, 180°C, Gas 4, for 1–1½ hours, basting frequently. When the bird is almost cooked, dredge the breast with flour, baste, and finish cooking.

Wash and dry the watercress, and toss it lightly in the French dressing. Remove any trussing strings from the bird, and garnish with the watercress.

Serve with browned breadcrumbs (p43), Bread Sauce (p253), and Espagnole Sauce (p248).

Stuffed Boned Duck
6—8 helpings

100g onion	1 egg
25g butter **or** margarine	50g peanuts
100g long-grain rice	225g ham
275ml chicken stock	50g seedless raisins
1 bay leaf	1 duck
salt and pepper	2 × 15ml spoons corn oil
1 small red pepper	

Skin and chop the onion finely. Melt the butter or margarine, and fry the onion without browning. Stir in the rice and cook until it is translucent. Pour on the stock, add the bay leaf, salt and pepper, and cook for 12–15 minutes or until the rice is tender and the stock has been absorbed. Drain if necessary, and remove the bay leaf.

Wash the pepper, remove the membranes and seeds. Place in cold water, bring to the boil, and cook for 5 minutes. Drain well and cool under cold water. Beat the egg until liquid. Chop the peanuts coarsely. Mince the ham, raisins, pepper, peanuts, and rice together, add the egg, and stir in. Add salt and pepper.

Remove any trussing string from the duck. Use a small pointed knife to loosen and remove the wishbone. Slit the skin right along the backbone. Ease the flesh away from the bones either side of the backbone and down as far as the leg joints. Place the breast meat flat, skin side down, on a board. At the leg joints, cut the sinew joining them to the body; then, holding the leg firmly, gradually scrape and push the flesh away from the bones. Remove the bones. Repeat the process on the other leg. Cut away the first 2 joints of the wing, scrape the flesh down so that the bones can be pulled out. Repeat the process on the other wing. Continue carefully cutting away the flesh from the breastbone, being careful not to puncture the skin. Carefully remove the breastbone. If serving the duck hot, cover the bones with water, cook, and make stock for the gravy.

Put the stuffing in the body of the bird, make it a good shape, and sew the skin together. Heat the oil in a roasting tin in a fairly hot oven, 190–200°C, Gas 5–6. Place the duck in the tin, breast side up, and baste with the hot oil. Cook for 1–1½ hours. Serve hot or cold.

Note The above directions for boning can be followed for any poultry or game bird.

GAME

Game Birds

Hanging Game Birds

All water birds should be eaten as fresh as possible. Most other game birds of any size should be hung before being eaten to tenderize the meat, and to give it the characteristic gamey flavour. The birds should hang in a cool place where air can circulate freely. The time for which it should be hung depends on the type of bird, the weather, and on individual taste. A pheasant may mature in 3–4 days in warm weather but only after 10 days in cold weather. Small birds such as woodcock need only 2–3 days hanging, if any.

Most game birds should be hung by the neck, unplucked, and undrawn. They are ready for cooking when the tail feathers come out easily. If there is a distinct bluish or greenish tinge to the skin, they have probably been hung too long for most tastes. In this case, they should be washed with salted water containing a little vinegar, then rinsed. Fresh powdered charcoal tied in muslin and left in the crop during cooking will also help to remove any over-strong flavour.

Plucking, Drawing, Trussing, and Jointing Game Birds

For most birds, follow the general procedures for poultry (pp176–82).

Very small birds, such as snipe and woodcock, are cooked without being drawn. They are traditionally dressed with their heads left on, and skewered with the bird's own long beak. If the head is removed, the bird is just skewered into a neat shape for cooking.

Traditionally, pheasant is roasted with its head left on, but the modern style is to truss as for chicken.

Cooking Game Birds

Unless they are old or badly damaged by shot, most game birds are plainly roasted. The basic recipe for roast grouse on p204 can be used for any other tender, unblemished, and unstuffed bird, by adjusting the cooking time to the appropriate one in the chart below.

Roasting Time Chart

These roasting times are for unstuffed birds. Allow up to 10 minutes extra for a small stuffed bird up to 375g, 15–18 minutes extra for a bigger bird.

Blackcock   *40–50 minutes*
Grouse   *25–36 minutes*
Pheasant   *45–60 minutes*
Partridge   *20–30 minutes*
Teal   *15–20 minutes*
Widgeon   *25–35 minutes*

Pintail   *20–30 minutes*
Mallard   *30–45 minutes*
Tame pigeon   *30–40 minutes*
Squab (young pigeon)   *15–25 minutes*
Woodpigeon   *35–45 minutes*
Other small birds   *10–15 minutes*

Note If you joint or cut up a game bird before cooking, eg for a pie, always cut off and discard the vent end of the body, since it may give the dish a bitter flavour.

What to Serve with Game Birds

Since most game birds are plainly roasted, the same traditional accompaniments are served with all of them. These are:

1) A croûte of fried or toasted bread to fit under medium-sized and small birds or fried breadcrumbs (p51) for larger birds
2) Thin gravy or giblet gravy (p269)
3) Game chips or potato straws (p299)
4) Bread Sauce (p253) for grouse, pheasant, and partridge; Cumberland Sauce (p255) for wild duck; Piquant Sauce (p243) for woodpigeon
5) Redcurrant or other sharp fruit jelly
6) Watercress sprigs as garnish
7) A green vegetable such as Brussels sprouts or a green salad is usually the only other accompaniment.

In all the following recipes, the birds are assumed to be ready for marinating or other cooking preparations.

Roast Grouse
2 helpings

a brace of grouse
red wine marinade (p271) (see
    Method)
50g butter
salt and pepper

2 rashers fat bacon, without rinds
fat for basting
2 croûtes fried bread, each big enough
    to put under 1 bird
flour for dredging

Garnish
watercress sprigs

Marinate the birds if home-shot or at all tough (birds sold as oven-ready need not be marinated as a rule).

Cream the butter with enough salt and pepper to give a good flavour, and put half into the body of each bird. Truss for roasting. Cover the breast of each bird with a bacon rasher. Place on a trivet or rack in a roasting tin, and roast in a fairly hot oven, 190°C, Gas 5, for about 30 minutes, until tender. Baste with fat several times while cooking.

Half-way through the cooking time, put the croûtes in the tin, under the birds. Remove the bacon 7–8 minutes before the end of the cooking time, dredge the birds lightly with flour, baste well, and return to the oven to finish cooking and to brown. Serve the birds on the croûtes, and garnish with watercress sprigs.

Serve thin gravy (p269), Bread Sauce (p253), and fried breadcrumbs (p51) separately.

Note A grouse can be cut in half lengthways through the breast-bone and spine, to make 2 helpings. Each half is served cut side down. If necessary, a third helping can be carved by removing the legs and thighs with a small portion of extra meat such as the 'oyster' on the back, before splitting the bird.

Young Blackcock or Grouse Fillets Financière
5–6 helpings

2 young blackcock **or** grouse
1 medium-sized onion
1 small carrot
½ turnip
3 rashers streaky bacon, without
   rinds
100ml game stock (p26)

250ml foundation brown sauce
   (p241)
butter for frying
12 button mushrooms
75ml (approx) sherry **or** Madeira
   (optional)
salt and pepper

Joint the birds and cut the meat into fillets. Prepare and slice the vegetables and place them in a sauté or frying pan with the bacon; put the fillets on top. Add the stock, cover with a buttered paper and a tight-fitting lid, and simmer gently for 30 minutes.

Meanwhile, heat the brown sauce. Melt the butter, fry the mushrooms, and keep them hot. Add the wine to the sauce, if used. Season to taste and keep the sauce hot.

When the fillets are cooked, arrange them on a hot dish, strain the sauce over them, and use the mushrooms and bacon as a garnish.

Grouse Pie
6–8 helpings

2 grouse
350g rump steak
2 hard-boiled eggs
2–3 rashers bacon, without rinds
salt and pepper

250ml game stock (p26) **or** general
   household stock (p25)
flour for rolling out
100g prepared puff pastry (p458)
beaten egg **or** milk for glazing

Joint the birds. Slice the steak thinly and slice the eggs. Cut the bacon rashers into strips. Season the steak and eggs to taste. Line the bottom of a 1 litre pie dish with some of the pieces of seasoned steak, cover with a layer of grouse, and pack round them some bacon, egg, and seasoning. Repeat the layers until the dish is full. Add enough stock to fill three-quarters of the pie dish. Roll out the pastry on a lightly floured surface to make a lid. Moisten the rim of the dish and fit on the lid. Trim, crimp the edge, and make a small hole in the centre to allow steam to escape. Decorate with the trimmings. Bake the pie in the hot oven, 220°C, Gas 7 for 20 minutes, then lower the heat to moderate, 180°C, Gas 4, and cook for another 1¼–1½ hours. Glaze the pastry with the egg or milk 30 minutes before the cooking is complete.

Meanwhile, simmer the necks and trimmings of the birds in the remaining stock; strain and season. Pour the hot stock into the pie through the hole just before serving.

Note Finely chopped mushrooms, parsley, and shallots can be added to the pie, if liked.

Roast Stuffed Pheasant
6 helpings

2 pheasants	50g butter
½ onion	

Stuffing

100g onion	75g soft white breadcrumbs
25g butter **or** margarine	salt and pepper
100g mushrooms	1 × 15ml spoon game stock (p26)
50g ham	(optional)

Garnish

watercress sprigs	French dressing

Wash the pheasant giblets, cover with cold water, add the half onion, and simmer gently for 40 minutes to make stock for the gravy.

Make the stuffing. Skin the onion and chop it finely. Melt the butter or margarine and cook the onion until soft. Chop the mushrooms and add them to the onion; cook for a few minutes. Chop the ham, and add with the breadcrumbs. Stir, add salt and pepper, and the stock if the stuffing is too crumbly.

Divide the stuffing between the birds, filling the body cavities only. Truss neatly and put in a roasting tin; spread with the 50g butter. Roast in a fairly hot oven, 190°C, Gas 5, for 45 minutes–1 hour, depending on the size of the birds; baste occasionally while roasting. Transfer to a heated serving dish, and remove the trussing strings. Garnish with watercress tossed very lightly in French dressing.

Serve with gravy (p270), Bread Sauce (p253), and fried breadcrumbs (p51).

Note A pheasant trussed in modern style should be carved like chicken; if trussed in traditional style with its head on, cut it off before carving.

Pheasant with Oysters
4–5 helpings

1 pheasant	1 carrot
oyster stuffing (p47)	½ small turnip
550ml chicken stock	bouquet garni
1 onion	400ml oyster sauce (p239)

Fill the cavity of the bird with oyster stuffing. Truss the bird for roasting. Bring the stock to boiling point. Skin and slice the onion. Peel and slice the carrot and turnip. Wrap the bird securely in well greased foil, then put the bird into the boiling stock. Bring back to boiling point, add the sliced vegetables and bouquet garni to the pan, reduce the heat, and simmer gently for about 1 hour. Remove the trussing strings and serve the bird on a hot dish with a little oyster sauce poured round. Serve the rest of the sauce in a sauce-boat.

VARIATIONS

Chestnut stuffing (p45) can be substituted for oyster stuffing. Alternatively, the bird can be cooked with chopped vegetables in the body cavity instead of stuffing, and served with Celery (p254) or Oyster (p239) Sauce.

Jugged Pigeons
6 helpings

3 woodpigeons
75g butter
1 small onion
500ml beef stock

salt and pepper
25g flour
100ml (approx) port **or** claret
    (optional)

Garnish

fried balls of basic herb forcemeat
    (p44)

croûtons of fried bread
parsley sprigs

Truss the pigeons for roasting. Heat 50g of the butter, and fry them in it until well browned. Remove the birds to a casserole, preferably earthenware. Skin and chop the onion and brown it in the same butter as the pigeons. Add the onion to the pigeons, together with the stock and seasoning to taste. Cover, and cook in a warm oven, 160°C, Gas 3, for 1¾ hours.

Knead together the flour and remaining 25g butter to make a beurre manié and drop small pieces into the stock, stirring all the time. Continue cooking for a further 15 minutes. Add the wine, if used, and cook for another 15 minutes. Serve the pigeons with the sauce poured over them, and garnish with forcemeat balls, croûtons, and parsley.

Pigeon Pie
4 helpings

3 small woodpigeons
salt and pepper
200g grilling steak
100g ham **or** bacon
2 hard-boiled eggs

350ml general household stock (p25)
puff pastry (p458) using 175g flour
flour for rolling out
beaten egg **or** milk for glazing

Remove the feet from the pigeons and cut each bird into quarters. Season well. Cut the steak in small thin slices, the ham or bacon in strips, and slice the eggs. Layer all the ingredients in a 1 litre pie dish, seasoning the layers well. Three-quarters fill the dish with stock. Roll out the pastry on a lightly floured surface to fit the dish. Moisten the rim of the pie dish and cover the pie with the pastry leaving a small hole in the centre. Brush with the egg or milk to glaze it. Cook in a hot oven, 220°C, Gas 7, for 20 minutes, until the pastry is risen and set; then lower the heat to moderate, 180°C, Gas 4 and bake for 1 hour longer. Heat the remaining stock. Before serving the pie, fill it with the remaining hot stock poured through the central hole.

VARIATION

Make the pie with 1 jointed pheasant or 2 partridges.

Compôte of Pigeons
6 helpings

3 woodpigeons **or** large tame pigeons	40g butter
100g ham **or** bacon	500ml general household stock (p25)
3 shallots **or** 1 large onion	bouquet garni
1 carrot	25g flour
½ turnip	salt and pepper

Truss the pigeons for roasting. Cut the ham or bacon into small pieces. Skin the shallots, or skin and slice the onion. Slice the carrot and turnip. Heat the butter in a large pan and fry the pigeons, ham or bacon, and onions until well browned. Add the stock and bring to boiling point. Add the bouquet garni, carrot, and turnip. Cover, reduce the heat, and simmer steadily for 1–1½ hours, or until the pigeons are tender.

Blend the flour with a little cold water and add a little of the hot cooking liquid; blend well and add to the pan. Bring to boiling point, stirring all the time; re-cover, and simmer for 10 minutes. Skim off any excess fat and season to taste. Remove the pigeons, cut off the trussing strings, and split the birds in half. Serve them on a hot dish with the sauce poured over them.

Mrs Beeton's Hashed Partridges
3–4 helpings

3 cooked partridges **or** 1 cooked grouse **or** pheasant	25g button mushrooms
1 × 25g slice ham	375ml game stock (p26)
75g carrots	bouquet garni
50g mild onion **or** shallots	4 whole cloves
25g butter	4 black peppercorns
oil for frying	100ml medium-dry sherry **or** Madeira
	1 lump of sugar (if using sherry)

Garnish
fried bread croûtons

Joint the bird or birds. Skin the wings, legs, and breasts; keep the skin and carcasses. Dice the ham. Prepare the carrot and onion or shallots, and slice them thinly. Heat the butter and a little oil in a large, heavy-bottomed stewpan, and fry the ham and vegetables gently for 6–8 minutes until softened but not browned. Add the stock and bouquet garni. Tie the spices in muslin and add them, with the skin and carcasses. Simmer for 15 minutes. Strain the sauce and chill it.

When cold, take off all the fat. Add the wine and sugar, if used. Return to the pan with the joints. Heat thoroughly to boiling point, then turn into a heated serving dish. Scatter the croûtons over the dish and serve very hot.

Roast Partridges Stuffed with Juniper
4 helpings

4 young partridges
juice of 1 lemon
a thin sheet of pork fat for barding
50g butter
50ml dry white wine
150ml game stock (p26)

flour for dredging and for making
  gravy
4 large slices white bread from tin loaf
butter for shallow frying
extra game stock (p26) for gravy

Stuffing
12 juniper berries
100g ham
2 medium-sized onions
grated rind of 1 lemon
100g butter

2 eggs
a pinch of dried marjoram
75g soft white breadcrumbs
salt and pepper

Garnish
watercress sprigs
potato straws (p299) **or** fried
  breadcrumbs (p51)

lemon wedges

Make the stuffing first. Crush the juniper berries, shred the ham, and skin and chop the onions. Mix with the lemon rind in a bowl. Melt the butter and add it to the bowl. Beat the eggs lightly, and mix them in with the marjoram and breadcrumbs. Season well with salt and pepper. Use the mixture to stuff the birds.

Truss the birds for roasting, sprinkle with a little of the lemon juice, and bard them with the pork fat. Put into a roasting tin. Melt the butter and brush it over the birds. Add the wine and game stock to the tin, and roast in a fairly hot oven, 190°C, Gas 5, for 45 minutes, basting often with the pan juices. About 15 minutes before the end of the cooking time, remove the pork barding fat. Dredge the birds lightly with a little flour, and return them to the oven to finish cooking, and to brown. Fry the bread slices in butter until golden and lightly crisped, cut off the crusts, and keep aside.

When the birds are cooked, place each on a croûte of fried bread, and arrange them on a serving dish with their drumsticks in the centre. Keep warm under buttered paper while making the gravy. Skim the fat off the pan juices, sprinkle in a little flour, and place over moderate heat. Stir for 2 minutes, scraping in any sediment. Stir in enough stock to make a thin, well-flavoured gravy.

Garnish the birds with watercress sprigs in the centre of the dish. Place small piles of potato straws or fried crumbs between them, and lemon wedges on top.

Serve the gravy separately in a warmed sauce-boat, with Bread Sauce (p253) and redcurrant jelly or Cumberland Sauce (p255).
Note A partridge may be cut in half lengthways through the breast-bone and spine. Although a partridge is seldom large enough to serve more than 2 people, a third portion can be carved, if necessary, in the same way as grouse (p204). As the wings of the partridge and other small birds are often dry and bony, they are usually cut off before serving.

Roast Wild Duck (Mallard, Pintail or Widgeon)
3 helpings

1 wild duck	1 large slice of white bread to fit
butter for basting	under the bird
flour for dredging	

Garnish
watercress sprigs

Cut off the toes of the bird, and scald and scrape the feet. Truss the bird with the feet twisted underneath the body. Warm the butter until melted, and brush the bird all over with melted butter. Dredge lightly with flour. Place on a trivet in a roasting tin, baste with any remaining butter, and roast in a fairly hot oven, 190°C, Gas 5, for 20–30 minutes. Baste often during cooking.

As soon as the bird is in the oven, cut the crusts off the bread, and toast it lightly on both sides. Place it while still warm in the roasting tin, under the bird.

Remove the bird and the bread croûte from the oven as soon as it is tender. Serve it slightly underdone, or the flavour will be lost. Place on a heated serving dish, and garnish with watercress sprigs just before serving.

Serve game chips (p299), Cumberland Sauce (p255) and redcurrant jelly with the bird. Bread Sauce (p253) can also be served, if liked.

Note Carve the breast like that of farmed duck. Remove the wings without any extra meat above the joint, and discard them. Remove the legs in the same way as a chicken's, and cut in half at the joint. Serve only the thighs.

To prevent water birds tasting fishy, pour boiling water over them before roasting; drain and pat dry with kitchen paper.

Game Animals

Hare
A hare is usually bought ready hung, but if freshly killed should be hung for 7–10 days, depending on the weather. It should hang by the hind legs unskinned and unpaunched in a cool, dry, well-ventilated place, with the head in a tin mug to catch the blood. If buying a pre-hung hare from a butcher, make sure that you also get its blood. Add 1–2 drops of vinegar to the blood to prevent it clotting and keep it in a refrigerator for use in casseroled and jugged dishes.

The best parts of the meat are the back or saddle, as it is also called, and the hind legs, which can be sautéed or roasted. The shoulders and forelegs are usually divided into 3 or 4 pieces and braised or jugged. If the hare is not young, and fairly small, it can be jugged whole.

Rabbit
A newly killed rabbit is treated much like a hare, but it should be paunched immediately it is killed. There is no need to hang rabbit as the flavour will not improve by so doing. It can, however, hang for about a day. Some experts say that if a rabbit is skinned as soon as it is killed, the meat will not have the musty flavour often associated with it.

A rabbit is best for eating between 3 and 4 months old, when it has thick foot joints, smooth claws, a flexible jaw, and ears which tear easily. The eyes should be bright, the fat whitish, and the liver bright red. Tame rabbits, especially, vary widely in weight according to type; a big Ostend rabbit can weigh as much as 4kg, although an average tame rabbit weighs 2–2.25kg.

Preparing Hares and Rabbits

Paunching: Make a slit the length of the stomach. Slide out all the entrails except the kidneys. Leave them in their fat attached to the back. Carefully detach and discard the greenish gall-bladder from the liver. Throw away all but the liver and heart. Reserve these for cooking.

Skinning: Cut off the feet at the foot joint with a small thin-bladed knife.

Cut the skin of a hare straight down the belly without penetrating the gut. (A rabbit will already have been paunched.)

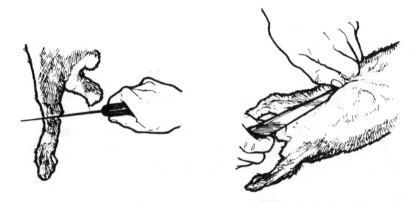

Loosen the skin from the meat on each side of the slit, then ease it away from the flesh, up towards the spine on both sides, until the centre of the body is completely free from its skin. Now push forward one hind leg and work the skin free. Repeat the process on the other leg, then pull the skin up and over to free the tail.

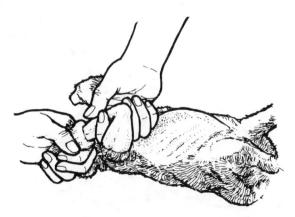

Holding the skinned hindquarters in the left hand, gently pull the skin up the back and over the shoulders, working each foreleg through in turn. The skin must now be eased with a knife from the neck and head so that the skin can be rolled back and pulled off like a jumper.

If the ears are being left on, as in a traditional roast, cut round the base of each before skinning the head. (Skinning the head is a difficult process, usually best done by the butcher. For this reason, the head is often left with its skin on and covered with foil to be roasted.) A hare is now ready to be paunched, as described above.

Cleaning and Marinating: A hare should only be wiped clean, but a rabbit can be washed in salted water. The meat will be lighter-coloured if it is left to soak in salted water with a few drops of lemon juice for 20–30 minutes. If its flavour is strong, it can be blanched; put it into cold water, bring to the boil, and simmer for 2 minutes. Drain and wipe dry.

A young hare can be marinated in a little oil and brandy with chopped fresh herbs; it needs only a few hours soaking. Older hares can be marinated for 1–2 days in a red wine marinade; if a venison marinade is used, dilute it with a little water.

An older or wild rabbit, in particular, will taste more delicate and be more digestible if steeped for 12 hours in water containing 1 × 5ml spoon white wine vinegar per 500ml water. Change the water at least once. Frozen whole rabbit can be steeped for up to 24 hours, but joints and boneless pieces for 30–60 minutes at most. For extra flavour, marinate a tame rabbit in white wine sharpened with a little lemon juice. Wild rabbits benefits from a herbal marinade, especially if it includes herbs the animal has fed on. See the red wine marinades on p271.

Trussing: The simplest method of trussing is to cut off the head and neck of the hare or rabbit, leaving a flap of skin which can be skewered over the cut surface like the skin over the neck end of a chicken. The limbs are tied or skewered as below. Roast the hare or rabbit on its belly; or cook it for half its cooking time on one side, and then turn it over to complete the cooking.

A hare for roasting is traditionally trussed with the head raised, and is balanced to lie on its belly as if alive and just alerted. (Any barding fat or stuffing should be put in place and secured before trussing.) To truss, hold the animal in this position. Crook the forelegs with the lower part lying on the plate level with the breast-bone, evenly balanced to hold the rib cage steady. Tie or skewer. Crook and skewer the hind legs in the same way. Remove the eyes. If the head has been left unskinned, cover with foil while cooking. In any case, the ears must be covered with foil.

Jointing: Remove the head, cutting straight down at the base of the neck. Cut off each foreleg in one piece. Cut off the hind legs at the pelvic joint. A rabbit's hind legs are usually left whole, except for a pie; but when jointing a hare, separate the thigh from the lower leg. Separate the rib cage from the saddle by cutting through the spine (about a third of the way down the back). Split the forepart of a hare along the spine to give two joints. Separate the saddle from the rump. The saddle can be split into two parts, if liked.

Venison

The best parts of the meat in an animal of any age are the haunch, saddle, loin, and shoulder. These can be roasted or cut into chops and cutlets for grilling or frying. The rest of the meat is best made into stews.

Hanging Venison

Unless bought ready for cooking, venison must always be hung; it has little flavour otherwise. When buying fresh venison, always ask the supplier whether it needs further hanging; venison frozen commercially can be assumed to be fully hung.

Whole venison should be hung from 10–14 days, depending on the weather and on the strength of gamey flavour wanted. Pieces need only be hung from 5–7 days. The meat must hang in a cool, dry, well-ventilated place.

Before hanging, the meat should be inspected thoroughly. If there is any musty smell, it should be washed in lukewarm water and dried thoroughly. It should then, in any case, be rubbed with a mixture of ground ginger and black pepper. While hanging, it should be inspected daily and any moisture seeping from it should be wiped off.

To test whether the meat is ready for cooking, run a small sharp knife into the flesh near the bone. If it smells over-strong, cook the meat at once or wash it with warm milk and water, dry thoroughly, and cover with more of the preserving mixture. Wash this off before cooking.

Preparing Venison

Marinades for venison and other game meat are given on p271. Marinate the meat for as long as required; this will depend on its age and quality. The older and tougher it is, the longer it needs. The marinating time also depends on the strength of gamey flavour wanted. Meat marinated for 24 hours will be tenderized but will have more or less its natural flavour; after 48 hours it will have a distinct gamey flavour which will get progressively stronger thereafter.

Although it is a dry meat, the fat should be cut off as it is unpleasant and makes the venison taste like goat's meat. Barding fat should be used instead. Sinews and gristle must also be removed; the meat tends to be sinewy in any case, and they add to the risk of toughness.

Cooking Game Animals

Game animals lend themselves to more varied cooking methods than birds. Venison can be cooked in any of the ways suggested for mutton or lamb, depending on its age, condition, and the cut of meat available. The rich, strongly flavoured meat of hare can be compared with that of goose or duck. Wild rabbits can be treated like grouse or pigeons, whereas farmed (tame) rabbits can be cooked in any of the ways given for chicken.

To counteract dryness and toughness in venison, always bard well. Pork fat or fat bacon wrapped round it in well-greased foil before cooking is an alternative.

Roasted, grilled, and fried venison, especially, must be served immediately after cooking, while still really hot; the meat cools quickly and any fat then has a tallowy taste.

What to Serve with Hare, Rabbit and Venison

Plainly roasted game meat is served with:
1) Basic herb stuffing (p44) or forcemeat balls (p45 and p47)
2) Thickened gravy (p270)
3) Roast potatoes for venison; potato straws (p299) for hare, rabbit; sautéed potatoes for rabbit
4) Bacon rolls (p51)
5) Redcurrant, cranberry or other sharp jelly.
Grilled or fried game meat is served with:
1) Game chips (p299) or potato crisps
2) Any grilled or fried garnish such as mushrooms or halved tomatoes, and watercress sprigs
3) Redcurrant or rowan-berry jelly or cranberry sauce (p254)
Note Cumberland (p255), Boar's Head (p253) or a similar sauce can be served with roasted, grilled or fried game instead of gravy and jelly, if preferred.

Carving Game Animals

Hare

If serving roasted hare, which has been trussed in the traditional way (p212), place it on its belly on a carving dish, remove the foil from the head and ears, and snip through the spine in 2 or 3 places with game shears, to make carving at table easier. At table, cut along the spine from the centre of the back to the buttock end.

Cut across through the middle, and remove one hind quarter. This releases any stuffing.

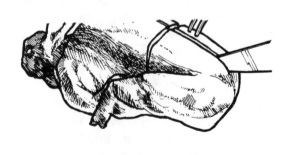

Divide the thigh and lower leg from the body meat, to make 2 portions; do the same using the second hind quarter. Traditionally, hare meat is served sliced off the bones, but this takes time, and hare meat is best served really hot.

Now cut through the spine just behind the shoulders, and divide the saddle (the centre back) into 2 or more joints.

If the drier forequarter meat is being served, remove any skewer through the neck, cut off the head, and divide the forequarter into 2 portions along the spine. Cut off the lower forelegs before serving.

If the hare has been trussed headless in modern style, 'seat' it, joint and carve it as above; alternatively, lay it on its side, and carve as above.

Rabbit (roasted or boiled)

Treat a large tame whole rabbit like hare. If serving a small wild rabbit whole, carve it in the same way, but serve the whole saddle as 1 portion or divided into 2 portions by cutting along the backbone instead of across it.

Venison

Haunch: Place the joint with the thick end facing you. Carve fairly thick slices parallel to the dish on which the joint rests.

Saddle: Carve as for saddle of mutton or lamb (pp102–3).

Roast Baron of Hare

3 helpings

1 hare	400ml foundation brown sauce
basic herb forcemeat (p44)	(p241)
6 rashers streaky bacon	100ml port (approx) (optional)
butter **or** game dripping	

Cut off the head, neck, and limbs of the hare. Use only the body. The legs, neck, and head can be used for soup or pâté.

Prepare the hare's liver and parboil it; chop it finely, and add it to the forcemeat. Stuff the hare with the mixture and sew up securely. Lard the hare with the bacon, then wrap it in well-greased foil or greaseproof paper. Roast in a fairly hot oven, 200°C, Gas 6, for 40–50 minutes, basting frequently with hot butter or dripping. Remove the foil or paper about 15 minutes before the end of the cooking time. Meanwhile, heat the brown sauce and add the wine, if used. When the meat is ready, remove the sewing thread, and place the hare on a heated platter for serving. Serve the sauce separately with redcurrant jelly.

Jugged Hare
6 helpings

1 hare
liver of the hare (optional)
blood of the hare (if obtainable)
1 × 5ml spoon vinegar (if required)
salt and pepper
2 × 15ml spoons flour
100g butter **or** margarine
100g onion (approx)
3 whole cloves

bouquet garni
a good pinch of ground mace
a good pinch of grated nutmeg
beef stock to moisten
125ml port **or** claret
50g redcurrant jelly
1 × 15ml spoon butter (optional)
1 × 15ml spoon flour (optional)
lemon juice (optional)

Garnish
heart-shaped **or** triangular sippets

forcemeat balls (p47)

Joint the hare. Reserve the liver and the blood. Mix the blood with the vinegar to prevent it coagulating. Season the flour with salt and pepper, and dust the hare joints with it. Heat the butter or margarine in a frying pan and brown the hare joints all over. Put to one side. Skin the onion, and press the cloves into it. Put the hare joints into a deep ovenproof pot or cooking jar, preferably earthenware. Add the onion, bouquet garni, spices, and just enough stock to cover about a quarter of the joints. Cover the dish very securely with foil, and stand it in a pan of very hot water. Cook in a moderate oven, 180°C, Gas 4, for about 3 hours, depending on the age and toughness of the hare.

Meanwhile, prepare the liver. When the hare is cooked, remove the meat to a serving dish, and keep hot. Pour off the juices into a smaller pan. Mash the hare's liver into the hot liquid, if using it. Add the port or claret, and redcurrant jelly. If using the hare's blood to thicken the sauce, add it to the liquids in the pan and re-heat, stirring all the time; do not allow it to boil. If not using the blood, mix the butter and flour to make a beurre manié, heat the liquids in the pan to simmering point, remove from the heat, and stir in the beurre manié in small spoonfuls. Return the pan to the heat and stir gently until the beurre manié is dissolved and the mixture boils and thickens. Sharpen with a few drops of lemon juice, if liked.

Pour the thickened sauce over the hare joints and serve garnished with the sippets and forcemeat balls.

Hare in Soured Cream
6 helpings

saddle and hindquarters of 1 large
  hare
200ml vinegar
1 large onion
1 bay leaf
a few peppercorns

25g lard
4 rashers streaky bacon, without
  rinds
250ml milk
250ml soured cream
salt and pepper

Garnish
forcemeat balls (p47) **or** small liver
  dumplings (p54)

chopped parsley

Put the hare in a bowl with the vinegar and enough water to cover. Skin the onion, add it with the bay leaf and peppercorns, and leave for several hours or overnight.

When ready to use the hare, remove it from the marinade, and dry it. Melt the lard and brush the hare with it. Chop the onion and put it with the bay leaf into a roasting tin; chop and add the bacon. Put in the hare and roast in a fairly hot oven, 200°C, Gas 6, for 1½–2 hours until tender. After the first 10 minutes, baste the hare with the milk; then baste it every 20 minutes.

When the meat is tender, remove the hare and cut it up. Place it on a hot dish. Strain the sauce into a pan and add the soured cream, salt, and pepper. Bring almost to the boil, and pour it over the hare.

Serve with cranberry or apple jelly, and garnish with forcemeat balls or small liver dumplings, and with chopped parsley.

Haricot of Hare
5–6 helpings

1 hare
3 × 15ml spoons butter
100g onions
100g turnips
200g carrots

salt and pepper
1 × 15ml spoon chopped parsley
1 × 2.5ml spoon dried thyme
1 litre general household stock (p25)

Joint the hare. Melt the butter in a saucepan and fry the joints until well browned on all sides. Prepare and dice the vegetables and add them to the hare with the seasoning, herbs, and stock. Cover tightly and stew gently for 2½–3 hours. Re-season if required.

Serve with apple or blackcurrant jelly.

Hashed Hare

remains of cold roast hare
400ml foundation brown sauce
   (p241)

100ml (approx) port, claret **or** cider
   (optional)
salt and pepper

Trim the hare meat into neat pieces. Make a stock with the bones and trimmings to use for the sauce or for another game dish. Heat the brown sauce, add the wine if used, put in the pieces of hare, and heat thoroughly for 15–20 minutes. Re-season if required.

Serve with a chestnut purée or mashed potatoes, and offer redcurrant jelly separately.

Note The forelegs and ribs of 1 hare will serve 4 people.

Roast Rabbit with Espagnole Sauce
4 helpings

1 tame rabbit
basic herb forcemeat (p44)
4 rashers streaky bacon

fat for basting
400ml Espagnole sauce (p248)

Garnish
cubed roasted potatoes (see Method)
4–8 bacon rolls (p51)

watercress sprigs

Prepare the garnish first. Cut 4 medium-sized potatoes into 2cm cubes and put in salted water to prevent them discolouring.

Stuff the rabbit with the forcemeat, skewer up the cavity opening, and truss using the simpler method (p212). Cover the back with the bacon rashers. Heat the oven to fairly hot, 200°C, Gas 6. Heat the fat in the oven, in the roasting tin to be used for the rabbit. Baste the rabbit with the hot fat, and put the rabbit into the tin. Roast it for 1–1½ hours, depending on its size. Baste it often while cooking.

About 30 minutes before the end of the cooking time, drain and dry the potatoes, and put into the roasting tin with the meat. Baste them well, and cook with the meat until tender and browned, turning them over often while cooking. Ten minutes before the rabbit is ready, remove the bacon rashers from the back, to let the meat brown. At the same time, put the bacon rolls in a small baking tin, and place in the oven on the rack below the rabbit to bake-fry in their own fat. While they cook, heat the sauce.

When the rabbit is cooked, remove the skewers. Place it on a heated dish, and pour a little of the sauce round it. Garnish with small piles of the potato and with the bacon rolls and watercress sprigs. Serve the sauce separately.

Note To make carving easier, the rabbit can be garnished only with watercress, and the potatoes and bacon rolls served on a separate dish.

Foundation Brown (p241) or Robert (p244) Sauce can be served instead of Espagnole sauce, if preferred.

Sandringham Rabbit
3–4 helpings

1 tame rabbit
salt and pepper
2 large tomatoes
1 small shallot
1 × 5ml spoon grated lemon rind
50g soft white breadcrumbs
1 × 5ml spoon chopped parsley

1 × 2.5ml spoon thyme
50g shredded suet
1 egg
1 rasher of bacon
2 × 15ml spoons cooking oil for
  basting

Garnish
bacon rolls (p51)

Season the rabbit well. Skin the tomatoes and chop them finely. Skin and chop the shallot. Mix the tomatoes with the shallot, lemon rind, breadcrumbs, parsley, thyme, and suet. Bind the mixture with the egg. Stuff the rabbit with the mixture and truss it using the simpler method (p212). Lay the bacon rasher on top of the rabbit. Brush with some of the oil. Roast the rabbit in a fairly hot oven, 200°C, Gas 6, for 50–60 minutes, basting with the oil from time to time. Remove the bacon about 10 minutes before serving to let the meat brown. At the same time, put the bacon rolls in the oven in a small baking tin to cook until crisp. When the meat is cooked, remove the trussing strings or skewers. Garnish with the bacon rolls.

Serve Fresh Tomato Sauce (p255) or Foundation Brown Sauce (p241) separately.

Rabbit Casserole
4 helpings

1 wild rabbit
salt and pepper
4 × 14ml spoons plain flour
65g butter

1 onion
225g cooking apples
1 × 213g can prunes
1 chicken stock cube

Garnish
chopped parsley   crescents of fried bread

Joint the rabbit, and discard the lower forelegs and rib-cage, or keep for stock. Season half the flour lightly with salt and pepper and coat the rabbit lightly. Melt 50g butter in a flameproof casserole or frying pan, add the rabbit, and brown lightly on all sides. Remove the joints to a plate. Skin and slice the onion and fry in the butter until soft but not brown. Peel, core, and slice the apples, and add them to the onion. Drain the prunes and make the juice up to 250ml with water. Add the stock cube. Return the rabbit to the casserole with the prunes and stock. Cover and cook in a moderate oven, 180°C, Gas 4, for 1½ hours or until tender.

When the rabbit is cooked, arrange the joints on a warmed serving dish with the apples and prunes; keep hot. Blend the remaining butter and flour to make a beurre manié and add in small pieces to the liquid in the casserole. Bring to the boil and stir until the sauce thickens. Re-season if required and pour over the rabbit. Sprinkle with chopped parsley. Surround with the fried bread, and serve at once.

Curried Rabbit

3–4 helpings

1 tame **or** wild rabbit
50g butter
1 small onion
1 × 10ml spoon flour
1 × 15ml spoon curry powder
1 × 10ml spoon curry paste
1 × 10ml spoon desiccated coconut
1 apple

400ml white stock (p26)
1 × 10ml spoon mango chutney
1 × 15ml spoon lemon juice
salt and pepper
25g sultanas
25g blanched almonds
2 × 15ml spoons single cream **or** top
    of milk (optional)

Garnish
paprika
lemon wedges

gherkin fans (p56) (optional)

Joint the rabbit. Heat the butter in a saucepan and fry the joints lightly. Remove the meat and drain it. Skin, chop, and fry the onion lightly in the same fat. Add the flour, curry powder and paste, and continue frying, stirring occasionally for 3–4 minutes. Tie the coconut in a piece of muslin. Peel, core, and chop the apple. Stir the stock into the pan and bring to the boil. Put in all the other ingredients except the cream or milk, and lay the rabbit joints on top. Simmer for 15 minutes, then remove the coconut. Simmer gently for a further 1½ hours, adding a little extra stock if necessary. Stir in the cream or milk, if used. Transfer to a heated serving dish, and pour over the sauce. Sprinkle with paprika and garnish with lemon wedges and gherkin fans, if used. Serve with some of the accompaniments on p214.

Rabbit Pie

4–5 helpings

450g boneless rabbit
1 small onion
salt and pepper
150ml water
2 × 15ml spoons cornflour
3 × 15ml spoons milk

2 × 15ml spoons chopped parsley
shortcrust pastry (p453) using
    250g flour
flour for rolling out
2 hard-boiled eggs
milk for glazing

Cut the rabbit into large pieces and put in a saucepan. Skin and chop the onion, and add to the pan with salt, pepper, and the water. Cover and simmer for 1¼ hours or until the rabbit is tender. Remove the rabbit meat. Blend the cornflour with the milk, and stir into the rabbit stock. Bring slowly to the boil, stirring all the time, and cook until the sauce thickens and clears. Stir in the parsley and rabbit meat. Cool.

Roll out the pastry on a lightly floured surface, and use half of it to line a 23cm shallow pie plate. Arrange the rabbit mixture in the centre. Slice the hard-boiled eggs and place on top. Dampen the edges of the base pastry lightly with milk, cover with the remaining pastry, seal, and crimp the edges. Glaze the top crust with milk, and make a small hole in the centre. Cook the pie in a hot oven, 220°C, Gas 7, for 15 minutes, then reduce the heat to fairly hot, 190°C, Gas 5, and bake for a further 25–30 minutes. Serve hot or cold.

Roast Haunch of Venison

a haunch of venison

clarified butter (p563) **or** dripping

flour for dredging

Saw off the knuckle-bone (or wrap the foot, if left on, in several layers of foil). Melt the clarified butter or dripping and brush the joint well all over; then wrap in well-greased aluminium foil or a sheet of greaseproof paper. If using paper, make a stiff paste of flour and water and cover the joint with it; then cover with another well-greased sheet of paper, and tie securely with string.

Roast the joint on a rack in a moderate oven, 180°C, Gas 4 (see below). 20–30 minutes before the cooking time is completed, remove the foil or paste and papers, dredge lightly with flour, and baste well with hot butter. Continue cooking until the joint is tender and a good brown colour.

Have the traditional or other accompaniments ready before removing the venison from the oven. Transfer to a heated carving dish, and serve at once. **Cooking time 15 minutes per 500g for large joints, 20 minutes per 500g for smaller joints weighing 1.5kg or less.**

Note The haunch can be replaced by a shoulder of venison.

Grilled Fillets of Venison

4 helpings

4 slices fillet of venison, 1cm thick

2 × 15ml spoons olive oil

freshly ground pepper

2 × 15ml spoons chopped fresh mixed herbs

Flatten the fillets a little, brush well with the olive oil, and sprinkle with pepper and fresh herbs. Leave to stand for about 1 hour. Grill under medium heat for 3–5 minutes on each side.

Serve Cumberland Sauce (p255) separately.

Fried Venison Cutlets

8 helpings

8 cutlets of venison from leg **or** loin

75ml olive oil

salt and pepper

4 × 15ml spoons flour

1 egg

75g fine dry breadcrumbs

75g butter

8 large mushrooms

100g redcurrant jelly

2 × 5ml spoons red wine vinegar

1 × 5ml spoon Demerara sugar

Soak the cutlets in the oil for about 1 hour. Drain well. Season the flour with salt and pepper and use to coat each cutlet. Beat the egg until liquid and coat each cutlet first in the egg and then in the crumbs, pressing them on well. Heat 40g of the butter and fry the cutlets for about 10–12 minutes, adding more butter if necessary, and turning once or twice. Drain and keep hot. Heat the remaining butter and fry the mushrooms; place a mushroom on each cutlet. Mix the jelly, vinegar, and sugar with the pan juices. Heat the jelly to melt it, and reduce it a little. Serve with the cutlets.

Civet of Venison

4–6 helpings

750g pieces **or** trimmings of venison for stewing
cooked red wine marinade (p271)
2 × 15ml spoons oil
125g streaky bacon rashers, without rinds
125g button mushrooms

1 × 15ml spoon concentrated tomato purée
25g butter
25g plain flour
salt and pepper
1 × 5ml spoon sugar

Garnish
croûtons of fried bread

Place the venison in a bowl, cover with the marinade, and leave for 24 hours. Drain the meat and reserve the marinade. Dry the meat well on soft kitchen paper.

Place 1 × 15ml spoon of the oil in a saucepan. Cut the bacon rashers into small pieces. Add to the saucepan with the mushrooms and cook for a few minutes until the bacon is lightly browned. Remove the bacon and mushrooms with a perforated spoon; put to one side. Add the remaining oil to the pan and heat it. Add the meat, and cook fairly quickly to brown it all over. Return the bacon and mushrooms to the saucepan. Add the marinade, stir in the tomato purée, cover with a lid, and simmer gently for 2–2½ hours until the meat is tender.

Meanwhile, soften the butter, and blend together with the flour to make a beurre manié. Off the heat, add this to the stew in small pieces. Return to the heat and stir until the beurre manié melts and the stew thickens. Add salt, pepper, and sugar to taste. Garnish with croûtons of fried bread.

Serve with boiled rice.

Hashed Venison

3–4 helpings

300g cold roast venison
400ml general household stock (p25)
40g butter
3 × 15ml spoons flour

50ml port (approx) (optional)
4 × 15ml spoons redcurrant jelly
salt and pepper

Garnish
croûtons of fried bread

Slice the meat neatly. Break up any bones and put them with any meat trimmings into the stock. Simmer the stock gently for 45 minutes, then strain it. Melt the butter and stir in the flour. Brown together slowly. Stir in the strained stock, and continue stirring until the sauce comes to the boil. Put in the meat, port, if used, and the jelly. Bring quickly to the boil and re-heat thoroughly. Season to taste. Garnish with the croûtons.

Serve at once, very hot, and offer extra redcurrant jelly separately.

MISCELLANEOUS

Beer Batter
Makes 375ml (approx)

100g plain flour
a pinch of salt
1 egg

1 × 15ml spoon oil **or** cool
    melted butter
250ml light beer

Sift the flour and salt into a bowl. Make a well in the centre of the flour, and add the egg and oil or butter. Stir in half the beer, gradually working the flour down from the sides. Beat vigorously until the mixture is smooth and bubbly. Stir in the rest of the beer. Let the batter rest for about 30 minutes to allow the beer froth to settle.

Use for savoury dishes such as Toad-in-the-hole.

Toad-in-the-hole
4 helpings

500g skinless sausages
25g cooking fat **or** dripping

375ml beer batter

Heat the oven to hot, 220°C, Gas 7. Cut each sausage into 3 pieces. Put the sausages and fat into a 17 × 27cm baking tin and heat in the oven for 5 minutes. Pour the batter round the sausages quickly, and bake for 30–35 minutes until brown and well-risen.

Serve cut into 4 pieces, with gravy.

Note 500g sausage-meat can be used instead, rolled into 8 sausage shapes on a floured board.

Coating Batter (1)
Makes 250ml (approx)

100g plain flour
½ × 2.5ml spoon salt
1 × 15ml spoon cooking oil **or**
    melted butter

125ml water **or** milk and water
2 egg whites

Sift the flour and salt into a bowl. Make a well in the centre of the flour and add the oil or butter and some of the liquid. Gradually work in the flour from the sides, then beat well until smooth. Stir in the rest of the liquid. Just before using, whisk the egg whites until stiff. Give the batter a final beat and fold in the egg whites lightly.

Alternatively, use an electric blender. Put the water and oil into the goblet. Add the flour and salt and blend until smooth. Just before using, whisk the egg whites until stiff in a separate bowl. Give the batter a quick mix, then pour it down the sides of the bowl containing the egg whites. Fold the egg whites into the mixture lightly.

This makes a crisp, light batter suitable for fruit fritters, small fish fillets, and kromeskies.

Note The egg yolks can be added to the flour but then only 100ml liquid should be added. This makes a thicker, richer batter.

Coating Batter (2)
Makes 175ml (approx)

100g plain flour   1 egg
½ × 2.5ml spoon salt   125ml milk

Sift the flour and salt into a bowl. Make a well in the centre of the flour, and add the egg and a little of the milk. Gradually work in the flour from the sides, then beat until smooth. Stir in the rest of the milk. Just before using, stir well.

Alternatively, use an electric blender. Put the milk and egg into the goblet. Add the flour and salt and blend until smooth.

This makes a firmer batter suitable for fish fillets, fish and meat cakes, and meat.

Coating Batter (3)
Makes 175ml (approx)

100g plain flour   125ml warm water
½ × 2.5ml spoon salt   1 × 5ml spoon baking powder
1 × 15ml spoon oil **or** melted butter

Sift the flour and salt into a bowl. Make a well in the centre of the flour, and add the oil or butter and a little of the water. Gradually work in the flour from the sides, then beat until smooth. Stir in the rest of the water. Alternatively, use a blender. Make in the same way as Batter (2). Just before using, sprinkle on the baking powder and give the batter a final beat. Use as for Batter (2).

Coating Batter (4)
Makes 400ml (approx)

125ml milk   ½ × 2.5ml spoon caster sugar
25g butter   100g plain flour
1 × 5ml spoon dried yeast **or** 10g fresh   a pinch of salt
  yeast

Warm the milk and butter until the butter melts. Do not let it get hot. Mix the yeast and sugar into the milk. Leave for 15 minutes in a warm place until frothy.

Put the flour and salt into a bowl, make a well in the centre, and pour in the yeast and milk. Gradually work in the flour from the sides to form a thick batter, the consistency of double cream. Cover and leave to stand in a warm place for 30–35 minutes, until the mixture doubles in size.

This makes a crisp, well-flavoured batter suitable for meat and fish.

Basic Thin Batter (for puddings and pancakes)
Makes 375ml (approx)

100g plain flour
$\frac{1}{2}$ × 2.5ml spoon salt

1 egg
250ml milk

Sift the flour and salt into a bowl, make a well in the centre and add the egg. Stir in half the milk, gradually working the flour down from the sides. Beat vigorously until the mixture is smooth and bubbly. Stir in the rest of the milk. Use as below, and for pancakes (pp226–27).

Note Half milk and half water can be used. Some cooks claim this gives a lighter batter.

VARIATIONS

Baked Batter Pudding

Heat the oven to hot, 220°C, Gas 7. Put 25g cooking fat or 25ml oil into a 17 × 27cm baking tin. Heat in the oven for 15 minutes. Pour in the batter quickly and bake for 30–35 minutes, until brown and well risen.

Serve immediately, cut into squares, either with a savoury sauce or gravy, or as an accompaniment to roast beef, sausages or braised vegetables. The batter can also be served as a sweet pudding; sprinkle with sugar and serve with jam.

Yorkshire Pudding

Plain baked batter is eaten most often as Yorkshire Pudding. It is the traditional British accompaniment to roast beef. In the north of England, the meat is roasted on a grid placed in the meat tin. Thirty minutes before the meat is cooked, the joint is basted for the last time, and then the batter is poured into the meat tin below the grid, where it cooks in the meat dripping. The pudding is served either with the meat or, more traditionally, as a first course with gravy.

Very often Yorkshire Pudding is cooked in a separate tin, using beef dripping for the flavour; the tin is placed on the shelf above the meat, and cooked as in the basic Baked Batter Pudding.

Individual Yorkshire Puddings

These should be baked in deep individual patty tins. Put a small knob of lard (about 1 × 5ml spoon) in each tin. Place in a preheated oven, 220°C, Gas 7, until the fat is smoking hot. Half fill the tins with basic thin batter and bake for at least 20–25 minutes, depending on the depth of the tins. The puddings will rise high above the tins, and will be almost hollow shells. Do not underbake or they will collapse when taken out of the oven.

Steamed Batter Pudding

Grease a 750ml pudding basin or 4 small basins. Pour in the basic thin batter. Cover securely with greased foil or doubled greaseproof paper. Steam a 750ml pudding for 2 hours, individual puddings for 30 minutes.

Plain Pancakes *Basic recipe*

Makes 8 pancakes

Prepare a basic thin batter (p225). Pour it into a jug. Heat a little cooking fat or oil in a clean 18cm frying pan or omelet pan. Pour off any excess fat or oil, as the pan should only be coated with a thin film of grease. Stir the batter and pour in 2–3 × 15ml spoons batter, just enough to cover the base of the pan thinly. Tilt and rotate the pan to make sure that the batter runs over the whole surface evenly. Cook over moderate heat for about 1 minute until the pancake is set and golden-brown underneath. Make sure the pancake is loose by shaking the pan, then either toss it or turn over with a palette knife or fish slice. Cook the second side for about 30 seconds until golden. Slide out on to a warmed plate so that the first side fried will be on the outside when the pancake is rolled up or folded.

Repeat until all the batter has been used, greasing the pan when necessary.

VARIATIONS

Rich Pancake Batter

Add 15g butter, melted and cooled, or 1 × 15ml spoon oil, and an egg yolk to the batter. Alternatively, add 1 whole extra egg.

Cream Pancake Batter

Use 150ml milk and 50ml single cream instead of 250ml milk. Add 2 eggs and 25g cooled butter. The mixture should only just coat the back of a spoon as the pancakes should be very thin. For sweet pancakes, 1 × 15ml spoon brandy can be added and 2 × 15ml spoons caster sugar.

Savoury Pancakes *Basic recipe*

Add salt and pepper to a basic thin batter (p225). Make the consistency a little thicker by using slightly less liquid than for sweet pancakes.

Savoury pancakes are usually rolled round a thick filling and arranged in an oven-proof dish. They are then heated in a moderate oven at 180°C, Gas 4, for 30 minutes if they have a cold filling and for 20 minutes if the filling is hot. Alternatively, pancakes with hot fillings can be browned lightly under the grill.

VARIATIONS

Beef Pancakes

Brown 500g minced beef in 2 × 15ml spoons oil. Add 2 × 5ml spoons chopped parsley, 4 × 15ml spoons cooked rice, 1 × 15ml spoon grated onion, salt and pepper, a pinch of herbs, and 125ml beef stock. Simmer for 5 minutes until the stock is absorbed. Fill the pancakes, sprinkle with 25g grated cheese and re-heat. (Cheddar, Cheshire, Lancashire or a mixture of Gruyère and Parmesan can be used.)

Cheese Pancakes

Add 50g grated strong cheese to 375ml thick white sauce (p236). Fill the pancakes, sprinkle with 25g grated hard cheese and 1 × 15ml spoon chopped parsley. Dot with butter and re-heat.

Chicken Pancakes

Mix 100g minced cooked chicken, 50g finely chopped red or green pepper, 50g grated onion, salt and pepper. Fill the pancakes and arrange in a dish. Mix 1 × 15ml spoon concentrated tomato purée with 125ml soured cream, pour over the pancakes, sprinkle with 1 × 15ml spoon grated cheese and re-heat.

Curried Turkey Pancakes

Fry 50g chopped onion in 50g fat for 5 minutes, until tender. Add 1 × 5ml spoon curry powder and cook for 1 minute. Stir in 25g flour and 250ml chicken stock to make a sauce. Add 300g chopped cooked turkey and 1 × 15ml spoon cream. Fill the pancakes, sprinkle with 25g grated cheese and re-heat.

Smoked Haddock Pancakes

Poach 300g smoked haddock fillets in a little water for 10–15 minutes. Drain and flake the fish. Make 250ml white sauce (p236). Add the fish and 2 chopped hard-boiled eggs, 1 × 5ml spoon chopped capers, 1 × 15ml spoon chopped parsley, 2 × 15ml spoons lemon juice, salt and pepper. Fill the pancakes, sprinkle with 25g grated cheese and re-heat.

Spinach Pancakes

Cook 300g frozen spinach and drain well. Add 200g cottage cheese, 3 lightly beaten eggs, 50g grated strong cheese, 100ml double cream, a pinch of ground nutmeg, salt and pepper. Fill the pancakes. Sprinkle with 25g grated cheese and re-heat.

Mrs Beeton's Macaroni with Cheese

4–6 helpings

200g thick pipe macaroni	100g butter (approx)
500ml milk	50g red **or** white Cheshire cheese
1 litre water	salt and pepper
1 × 10ml spoon salt	25g dry white breadcrumbs

Break the macaroni into 15cm lengths. Put the milk and water in a large pan with the salt. Bring to the boil, put in the macaroni and stir round once. Reduce the heat to just above simmering point, and cook the macaroni for 14 minutes or until tender.

Meanwhile, use some of the butter to grease a 1 litre pie dish or flameproof oven-to-table dish; reserve the rest. Grate the cheese coarsely. When the macaroni is ready, drain it in a colander or sieve. Place a layer of hot macaroni in the dish, and sprinkle it with some of the cheese. Dot with some of the remaining butter and sprinkle lightly with a little salt and pepper. Repeat the layers until the ingredients are used, apart from 25g cheese, and ending with a layer of macaroni. Sprinkle with the remaining 25g cheese and the breadcrumbs. Melt the reserved butter and sprinkle it over the dish. Place under a moderate grill heat for a few minutes, until the cheese melts and begins to brown. Serve at once.

Note If the dish is not served immediately, it can be placed in a *bain marie* of simmering water. This method of re-heating melts the cheese more gently and gives the dish a better flavour than heating in the oven.

Pizza con Mozzarella
Makes two 25cm pizze

Dough

15g fresh yeast	1 × 2.5ml spoon salt
125ml warm water	3 × 2.5ml spoons olive oil (approx)
a few grains caster sugar	polenta (cornmeal) for dusting
175g strong white flour	oil for greasing

Filling

150ml Salsa Pomodoro (p256)	4 × 15ml spoons olive oil
200g Mozzarella cheese	3 × 15ml spoons grated Parmesan
4 black olives	cheese
4 anchovy fillets	

Make the dough. Blend the yeast into a little of the warm water with the sugar, then stir in the remaining water. Leave in a warm place until frothy. Sift the flour and salt into a bowl. Pour in the yeast mixture and oil. Work into a dough and knead well until smooth and elastic. Dust lightly with flour and place in a lightly oiled polythene bag. Leave in a warm place for 1½ hours or until doubled in size. Knock back the dough and divide into two equal portions. Knead lightly. Roll out each portion on a board dusted with polenta into a circle 25cm in diameter and about 5mm thick. Heat the oven to very hot, 230°C, Gas 8.

Pinch up the edge of each dough circle to make a low rim. Pour half the Salsa Pomodoro into each pizza. Crumble half the Mozzarella cheese over the sauce. Halve and stone the olives. Place 2 anchovy fillets in the form of a cross on each pizza, and place the halved olives, cut side down, in the spaces between them. Trickle half the oil over each pizza, and sprinkle the Parmesan cheese on top. Bake on a lightly greased baking sheet for 5 minutes. Reduce the temperature to fairly hot, 200°C, Gas 6, and bake for a further 5 minutes until the dough is lightly browned and the cheese has melted. Serve at once.

Plain Omelet *Basic recipe*
1 helping

2 eggs	1 × 15ml spoon unsalted butter **or**
salt and pepper	margarine
1 × 15ml spoon water	

Break the eggs into a basin, season with salt and pepper, add the water, and beat lightly with a fork. Place the pan over gentle heat and when it is hot, add the butter or margarine. Tilt the pan so that the whole surface is greased lightly. Do not over-heat or let the butter brown. Without drawing the pan off the heat, pour the beaten eggs on to the hot fat. Leave to stand for 10 seconds; then with the back of the prongs of a fork, or with a spatula, draw the mixture gently from the sides to the centre as it sets and let the liquid egg from the centre run to the sides. Repeat this once or twice more, as necessary. Do not stir round, or it will become scrambled eggs. In about 1 minute, the egg will have set softly. Leave it to cook for a further 4–5 seconds until it is golden underneath. Remove the pan from the heat. Loosen the edges by shaking the pan or using a round-bladed knife. Tilt the pan slightly towards you, and as the omelet slides up the side of the pan towards the handle, use a palette knife or spatula to fold this third of the omelet towards the centre. Raise the handle of the pan, slide the omelet up the side furthest from the handle, and fold over the opposite third, also towards the centre.

Change your grip on the pan so that your hand is underneath the handle and it runs across the palm between the thumb and forefinger. Hold the plate in the other hand, and with a quick movement, tip the omelet on to it, folded sides underneath.

Filled Omelets

Any plain omelet can be filled. Some flavourings are added to the beaten eggs and some are added to the omelet just before it is folded.
Add to the beaten eggs one of the following:

Cheese Omelet

Grate 50g cheese and mix 40g with the eggs; sprinkle the rest over the omelet just before serving it.

Omelette Fines Herbes

Add 1 × 2.5ml spoon chopped tarragon, 1 × 2.5ml spoon chopped chervil, 1 × 5ml spoon chopped parsley, and a few chopped chives or 1 × 5ml spoon mixed dried herbs.

Fish Omelet

Add 50g flaked cooked fish.

Ham or Tongue Omelet

Add 50g chopped meat and 1 × 5ml spoon chopped parsley.

Onion Omelet

Chop 25g onion and sauté in butter in a saucepan until tender, ie about 5 minutes.

Put one or more of the following into the centre of the omelet before folding. Fold in half, rather than in thirds.

Bacon Omelet

Chop 2 rashers of rindless bacon; fry in a saucepan until crisp.

Mushroom Omelet

Clean and slice 50g mushrooms and cook in butter, in a saucepan, until soft.

Omelette Provençale

Mix together 1 skinned and chopped tomato, a little garlic, 50g finely chopped onion, 1 × 15ml spoon chopped parsley, a little chopped fresh tarragon, salt and pepper. Sauté in a little butter for 5 minutes, until the onion is tender.

Tomato Omelet

Peel and chop 1–2 tomatoes and fry in a little butter for 5 minutes, until soft and pulpy. Add $\frac{1}{2} \times 15$ml spoon chopped parsley.

If a 3-egg omelet is filled with a substantial filling it will make 2 helpings. Omelets of this type are:

Chicken Omelet

Chop 50g cooked chicken and heat gently in a little white sauce.

Prawn and Mushroom Omelet

Melt 25g butter, and sauté 25g chopped mushrooms; remove from the butter, and keep hot. Make a sauce using the butter, 3×10ml spoons flour, and 125ml milk. Add the mushrooms and 50g coarsely chopped prawns. Re-heat and season before filling the omelet.

Stacked Omelets

These serve four or more people. Make up three or four types of filling, such as shrimps mixed with a little cream, chopped mushrooms fried with onions, and grated cheese. Make a plain omelet and slide it on to a plate standing over hot water. Top with a filling. Make a second omelet and lay it over the first. Top with another type of filling. Repeat, allowing at least 1 omelet per person. To serve, cut the stack into wedge-shaped pieces.

Tortilla Espagnola

4 helpings

750g potatoes	salt
250g onions	6 eggs
olive oil for shallow frying	

Peel and dice the potatoes. Skin and slice the onions, and mix them together. Put enough oil into a large frying pan to cover the bottom by 5mm. Heat the oil until very hot, then add the potatoes and onions, and sprinkle with salt. Fry gently for about 20 minutes until soft but not crisp. Turn over or stir gently from time to time. Remove the vegetables from the pan with a perforated spoon.

Beat the eggs lightly with a pinch of salt, and stir into the fried vegetable mixture. Drain off any oil, clean the pan, and heat 1×5ml spoon of oil in it until very hot. Pour in the egg and vegetable mixture, and cook briefly, shaking the pan vigorously to prevent the mixture sticking. Slide the half-cooked omelet on to a large plate, turn it over on to a second plate, then slide it back into the pan, uncooked side down. Cook for another 2–3 minutes to brown the second side, shaking as before.

The finished tortilla should be about 2cm thick, crisp on the outside, and juicy in the middle.

Serve with a green salad.

Gnocchi alla Romana

4 helpings

600ml water
125g medium semolina
salt and pepper
a pinch of grated nutmeg
1 clove of garlic
50ml double cream

2 egg yolks
butter for greasing
250g tomatoes
butter and oil for shallow frying
50g grated Parmesan cheese

Bring the water to the boil, and sprinkle in the semolina, stirring all the time. Simmer for 10 minutes. Season well with salt, pepper, and nutmeg. Grate in the garlic. Draw the pan off the heat. Blend the cream and egg yolks, and stir them into the semolina. Return the pan to the heat, bring the mixture to simmering point, and cook for 2 minutes, stirring all the time. Remove from the heat. Grease a shallow baking tray thickly with butter. Turn in the hot semolina mixture, smooth the top, and leave to cool and firm up. Meanwhile, skin, de-seed, and chop the tomatoes.

When the gnocchi mixture is cold, cut it into 2cm squares, rectangles or rounds. Heat the butter and oil in a frying pan, and fry the gnocchi gently until light gold on both sides. Place them in a lightly greased, shallow flameproof dish. Cover with chopped tomatoes, then sprinkle with grated cheese. Brown quickly under a hot grill.

Risotto alla Milanese

4 helpings

50g onion
25g butter
25ml oil
350g Italian rice
900ml chicken stock

salt and pepper
a good pinch of turmeric
50g salted butter
150g grated Parmesan cheese

Skin the onion and chop it finely. Heat the butter and oil in a large pan, add the onion and fry gently until soft but not brown. Stir in the rice, and cook, stirring, for 2 minutes. Heat the stock to simmering point. Reserve 1 × 15ml spoon stock, and pour the rest into the pan with the rice. Season to taste. Bring to the boil, cover, and cook gently for 20 minutes. Shake the pan from time to time to prevent the rice sticking to the bottom, and add a little extra stock or hot water, if required.

Shortly before the end of the cooking time, when the liquid is almost all absorbed, blend the turmeric into the reserved 1 × 15ml spoon stock, and stir it into the rice. Blend together the butter and grated cheese, and stir into the rice when it is just cooked. Serve as soon as the cheese has melted.

Savoury Soufflé *Basic recipe*
4–6 helpings

50g butter	salt and pepper
5 × 15ml spoons flour	4 eggs
250ml milk	1 egg white

Heat the oven to fairly hot, 190°C. Gas 5, or put a steamer on to heat. Prepare the soufflé dish (see below). Melt the butter in a pan, stir in the flour, and cook slowly for 2–3 minutes, stirring all the time. Add the milk gradually and beat until smooth. Cook for another 1–2 minutes, still stirring all the time. Remove the pan from the heat and heat beat until the sauce comes away from the sides of the pan cleanly. Put into a bowl, season well, and add any flavouring (see variations). Separate the eggs and beat the yolks into the mixture one by one. Whisk all the egg whites until stiff. Using a metal spoon, stir 1 spoonful into the mixture and then fold in the rest until evenly distributed. Put into 1 prepared 800ml or 6 × 200ml dishes. Bake in the centre of the oven for 30–35 minutes, until well risen and browned; or cover with greaseproof paper and steam for 1 hour until just firm to the touch.

Serve immediately with hot buttered toast.

To Prepare a Soufflé Dish or Tin
Cut a strip from two thicknesses of greaseproof paper or vegetable parchment 8cm taller than the dish and long enough to go right round the dish with an overlap. Tie the paper round the dish with string. If the dish has sloping sides or a projecting rim, secure the paper above and below the rim with gummed tape or pins. Make sure that the paper is uncreased and forms a neat round shape. Grease the inside of the dish and paper collar for a hot soufflé with clarified butter or oil. Oil the inside of the collar for a cold soufflé. When the soufflé is ready for the table, ease the paper away from its sides with the blade of a knife.

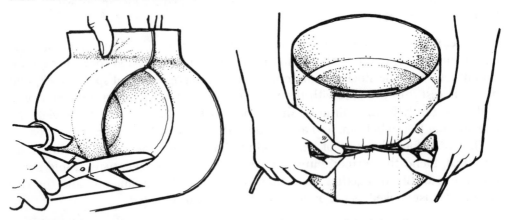

Cutting a strip to go round a soufflé dish with an overlap

Tying the paper round the dish with string

Preparing a soufflé dish can be tricky, and it is not essential to use a paper collar. A soufflé can be baked without one, although it will not rise as much as when a collar is used. A cold soufflé can be set in a dish big enough to hold all the mixture.

If a paper collar is used, put any of the following hot soufflés into an 800ml dish; otherwise use a 1 litre dish. Use a paper collar if the recipe tells you to prepare a soufflé dish before making the soufflé.

VARIATIONS

Asparagus Soufflé

Cook 200g frozen asparagus according to the directions on the packet or drain 200g canned asparagus. Chop it, and fold into the savoury soufflé mixture.

Cheese Soufflé

Reduce the flour to 25g and add 100–150g grated Cheddar cheese or 75–100g grated Parmesan and Gruyère cheese, and $\frac{1}{2} \times 2.5$ml spoon dry mustard or a pinch of Cayenne pepper.

Chicken Soufflé

Add 200g cooked minced chicken, 25g chopped sautéed onion, 2×15ml spoons lemon juice, and 1×5ml spoon chopped parsley.

Crab Soufflé

Add 200g flaked crabmeat, a few drops of Tabasco sauce, and 2×15ml spoons dry white wine.

Ham or Ham and Tongue Soufflé

Make a sauce using 125ml stock and 125ml tomato juice. Add 150g minced meat, 1×10ml spoon chopped parsley, grated nutmeg, and Cayenne pepper.

Smoked Haddock Soufflé

Cook 200g smoked haddock in the milk. Use the milk to make the sauce and then add the flaked fish, 50g grated mild cheese such as Gruyère, and a pinch of ground nutmeg. (Do not add too much salt.)

Smoked Salmon Soufflé

Add 100g chopped smoked salmon trimmings, 100g full-fat soft cheese, and 1×15ml spoon lemon juice.

Soufflé Panache

Divide the sauce into 2 portions. Flavour 1 portion with 50g cheese and the other portion with 2×15ml spoons spinach purée. Add 2 egg yolks and half the whisked white to each part. Spoon the mixtures alternately into the prepared dish.

Tomato Soufflé

Use tomato juice or fresh tomato pulp in place of the milk.

Scotch Eggs
4 helpings

250g sausage-meat
1 × 15ml spoon flour
1 egg
2 × 5ml spoons water

salt and pepper
4 hard-boiled eggs
50g soft white breadcrumbs
oil for deep frying

Garnish
parsley sprigs

Divide the sausage-meat into 4 equal pieces. On a lightly floured surface, roll each piece into a circle 12cm in diameter. Beat the egg with the water. Season the remaining flour with salt and pepper and toss the hard-boiled eggs in it. Place an egg in the centre of each circle of sausage-meat and mould evenly round the egg, making sure it fits closely. Seal the joins with the beaten egg and pinch well together. Mould each Scotch egg into a good shape, brush it all over with beaten egg, and then toss it in the breadcrumbs, covering the surface evenly. Press the crumbs well in. Put enough oil to cover the Scotch eggs into a deep pan and heat it (p11). Fry the eggs until golden-brown. Drain them on soft kitchen paper. Cut in half lengthways and garnish each half with a small piece of parsley.

Serve hot with Fresh Tomato Sauce (p255) or cold with salad.

Note As the sausage-meat is raw, it is important that the frying should not be hurried.

Pipérade Basque
4 helpings

2 onions
2 red **or** green peppers **or** 1 × 175g
    can pimentos
400g tomatoes
1 clove of garlic (optional)

50g butter
salt and pepper
6 eggs
3 × 15ml spoons milk

Skin the onion and slice it thinly. Cut the peppers into quarters and remove the seeds and membranes. Slice the flesh thinly. Drain canned pimentos and dice them. Skin the tomatoes, cut them into quarters, de-seed and chop the flesh roughly. Crush or chop the garlic, if used. Melt the butter and fry the peppers (if used) for about 5 minutes. Add the onions and garlic, and continue cooking gently for 5 minutes until softened. Add the tomatoes and pimentos (if used) and cook for a further 2–3 minutes. Season generously. Beat the eggs lightly together with the milk, and when the vegetables are mushy, pour in the eggs. Reduce the heat and cook gently, stirring all the time, until just set and creamy. Serve at once with chunks of bread.

Note Pipérade, a famous dish from the Basque country, is often served topped with fried rashers of bacon.

Welsh Rarebit
4 helpings

100–150g Cheddar cheese
25g butter **or** margarine
1 × 15ml spoon flour
75ml milk **or** 3 × 15ml spoons milk
   and 2 × 15ml spoons ale **or** beer

1 × 5ml spoon French mustard
a few drops Worcestershire sauce
salt and pepper
4 slices bread
butter for spreading

Grate the cheese. Melt the fat in a pan, and stir in the flour. Cook together for 2–3 minutes, stirring all the time; do not let the flour colour. Stir in the milk and blend to a smooth, thick mixture; then stir in the ale or beer, if used, the mustard and Worcestershire sauce. Add the cheese little by little, stir in, and season to taste. Remove from the heat as soon as well blended. Remove the crusts from the bread and toast lightly on both sides. Butter one side well and spread the cheese mixture on the buttered sides. Grill briefly, if liked, using high heat, to brown the surface of the cheese mixture. Serve immediately.

Note The term *rarebit* is generally considered as synonymous with *rabbit*.

VARIATIONS
Buck Rarebit
Make as for Welsh Rarebit, but top each slice with a poached egg. Serve at once.

Yorkshire Rarebit
Make as for Welsh Rarebit, but add 4 rashers of cooked bacon, without rinds.

Croque Monsieur
4 helpings

8 slices white bread
butter for greasing and spreading

4 thin slices cooked ham **or** bacon,
   without rinds
4 slices Gruyère cheese

Remove the crusts from the bread, and butter one side of each slice. Trim the ham or bacon and the cheese to fit the bread, and make 4 sandwiches with a filling of one thin layer of meat and one of cheese. Spread one side of each sandwich with butter. Grease a shallow baking dish or tin, large enough to hold the sandwiches in one layer. Place the tin in the oven, and heat to moderate, 180°C, Gas 4. Place the sandwiches in the hot tin, buttered side up, and return to the oven. Bake for 10 minutes, until golden and crisp on top.

VARIATION
Fry the sandwiches in butter on one side, turn over and coat the second side with fat, then toast the coated side, using moderate grill heat. Serve fried side uppermost.

SAUCES, GRAVIES AND MARINADES

SAUCES

English Foundation Sauces

Foundation White Sauce *Basic recipe*
Makes 500ml coating or pouring sauce

Coating Sauce
50g butter **or** margarine
50g plain flour

500ml milk **or** fish stock (p26) **or**
    white stock (p26) **or** a mixture of
    stock and milk
salt and pepper

Pouring Sauce
35g butter **or** margarine
35g plain flour

500ml liquid as for coating sauce
salt and pepper

1) *Roux Method*
Melt the fat in a saucepan, add the flour and stir over low heat for 2–3 minutes, without allowing the mixture (roux) to colour. Draw the pan off the heat and gradually add the liquid, stirring all the time. Return to moderate heat, and stir until the sauce boils and has thickened. Reduce the heat, and simmer for 1–2 minutes, beating briskly. (This helps to give the sauce a gloss.) Season to taste.

2) *Beurre Manié Method*
Knead the fat and flour, or work them together with a fork or spoon until they are blended smoothly. Heat the liquid in a saucepan and, when at just below boiling point, gradually whisk in the kneaded butter and flour in small pieces. Continue to whisk the sauce until it boils, by which time all the beurre manié must be smoothly blended in. Season to taste.

3) *All-in-one Method*
Put the fat, flour, and liquid in a saucepan. Whisk over moderate heat until the sauce comes to the boil. Reduce the heat and cook for 3–4 minutes, whisking all the time, until the sauce has thickened, and is smooth and glossy. Season to taste.

Note A coating sauce should coat the back of the spoon used for stirring. A pouring sauce should barely mask the spoon and should flow freely.

Sauces based on Foundation White Sauce

A foundation white sauce made by any of the three methods above can be used as the basis of many other savoury sauces. The quantities of the ingredients in the following recipes are for adding to 250ml Foundation White Sauce of either coating or pouring consistency. In most cases, this will give about 250ml completed sauce, the extra ingredients making up the small quantity lost by evaporation.

Anchovy Sauce

250ml foundation white sauce (p236) made with fish stock (p26) **or** half milk and half fish stock

1–2 × 5ml spoons anchovy essence
½ × 2.5ml spoon lemon juice
1–2 drops red colouring

Heat the sauce, if necessary; then stir in the anchovy essence to taste. Add the lemon juice and stir in enough red colouring to tint the sauce a dull pink.

Serve with fish.

Brain Sauce

1 set of sheep's brains
1 large onion (200g approx)
250ml white stock (p26)
250ml foundation white sauce (p236) made with white stock

1 × 2.5ml spoon lemon juice
1 × 10ml spoon chopped parsley
salt and pepper (optional)

Prepare the brains (p148). Skin and slice the onion. Put in a saucepan with the brains. Add the stock. Heat to boiling point, cover, reduce the heat and simmer gently for 30 minutes. Strain off the stock. Heat the sauce, if necessary. Chop the onion and brains. Add them to the white sauce with the lemon juice and parsley. Stir well, and re-season if required.

Serve with steamed or boiled meats.

Cheese Sauce

75g Cheddar cheese **or** other hard cheese
250ml foundation white sauce (p236) made with milk **or** half milk and half white stock

a pinch of dry English mustard
a pinch of Cayenne pepper
salt and pepper

Grate the cheese finely. Heat the sauce to boiling point, then remove the pan from the heat. Add the grated cheese, mustard, Cayenne pepper, and seasoning to taste. Stir well. Do not reboil the sauce; use at once.

Serve with vegetables, fish, ham, poultry, eggs or pasta.

Caper Sauce (1) (white)

250ml foundation white sauce (p236)
   made with white stock (p26) **or**
   half milk and half white stock

1 × 15ml spoon chopped capers
1 × 5ml spoon vinegar in which the
   capers were pickled

Heat the sauce, if necessary. Add the capers and vinegar, and stir well.
   Serve with boiled mutton or fish.

Herb Sauce

250ml foundation white sauce (p236)
   made with milk

1–2 × 15ml spoons chopped fresh
   mixed herbs (parsley, chives,
   tarragon, sorrel, thyme, marjoram,
   and savory)

Heat the sauce, if necessary. Add the herbs and simmer for 5 minutes.
   Serve with fish, poultry, veal or eggs.

Hot Horseradish Sauce

250ml foundation white sauce (p236)
   made with milk **or** half milk and
   half white stock

2 × 15ml spoons grated horseradish
1 × 5ml spoon vinegar
1 × 2.5ml spoon sugar

Heat the sauce, if necessary. Add the horseradish, vinegar, and sugar, and stir well.
   Serve with beef, trout, mackerel or herring.

Maître d'Hôtel Sauce

juice of ½ lemon
250ml foundation white sauce (p236)
   made with milk

2 × 15ml spoons finely chopped
   parsley
25g butter

Strain the lemon juice. Heat the sauce, if necessary, and add the lemon juice and parsley. When heated to just below boiling point, whisk the butter into the sauce, adding a small pat at a time.
   Serve with fish, poultry or vegetables.

Mushroom Sauce (white)

50–100g button mushrooms
15–25g butter

250ml foundation white sauce (p236)
   made with milk

Clean the mushrooms and slice them thinly. Melt the butter in a pan, add the mushrooms, and cook gently for 15–20 minutes. Heat the sauce, if necessary. Stir the mushrooms and their cooking juices into the sauce.
   Serve with most fish and meat entrées, poultry, ham, egg, and vegetable dishes.

Onion Sauce (1) (white)

2 medium-sized onions (200g approx)   a few drops lemon juice
250ml foundation white sauce (p236)
   made with half milk and half liquid
   in which onions were cooked

Skin and chop the onions. Put them in a saucepan and cover with salted water. Heat to boiling point, reduce the heat, and simmer for 10–15 minutes until softened. Drain thoroughly, and reserve the liquid to make the white sauce. Stir the onion into the sauce. Add the lemon juice.

   Serve with lamb or mutton, rabbit or tripe.

Oyster Sauce

8–10 large fresh oysters **or** 1 × 225g   250ml foundation white sauce (p236)
   can oysters (not smoked oysters)   made with fish stock after cooking
250–275ml fish stock (p26)   the oysters
milk **or** top of the milk,   salt and pepper
   if needed   a few drops lemon juice

Open the fresh oysters, if used (p77). Strain the liquor from the shells and add it to the fish stock. Reserve 6 oysters. Heat the stock gently to simmering point, add all except the 6 oysters, and simmer for 10 minutes. Strain the stock and make it up to 250ml with milk, if necessary. Use to make the white sauce. Cut the reserved oysters into 3–4 pieces. Add them to the hot sauce and simmer for 3–4 minutes until they just begin to stiffen. Season, and add lemon juice to taste.

   If using canned oysters, drain the liquid from the can and add it to the fish stock. Simmer the stock until reduced to 250ml. Strain, and use to make the white sauce. Cut 6–8 oysters into 3–4 pieces. Add them to the hot sauce and simmer for 2–3 minutes. Season, and add lemon juice to taste.

   Serve with fish or boiled chicken.

Parsley Sauce

250ml foundation white sauce (p236)   1–2 × 15ml spoons chopped parsley
   made with white **or** fish (p26) stock   25g butter
   or half milk and half stock

Heat the sauce, if necessary. Add the parsley and heat to just below boiling point. Whisk the butter into the sauce, adding a small pat at a time.

   Serve with fish, lamb or mutton, or light dishes such as quenelles or vegetables.

Savoury Lemon Sauce

juice and rind of 1 lemon
250ml foundation white sauce (p236)
   made with milk **or** half milk and
   half white stock (p26) **or** half milk
   and half fish stock (p26)

1–2 × 15ml spoons single cream
   (optional)
1 × 15ml spoon chopped parsley
   (optional)
1 × 2.5ml spoon sugar (optional)

Add the lemon rind to the milk or stock which is to be used to make the sauce, and simmer for 10 minutes. Strain the liquid and use it to make the white sauce. Carefully stir the lemon juice and the cream, if used, into the hot sauce. Do not reboil. Stir in the parsley and sugar, if used.

   Serve with fish, chicken or rabbit.

Sorrel Sauce (white)

100g sorrel leaves
15g butter
250ml foundation white sauce (p236)
   made with half milk and half
   vegetable stock (p27)

a small pinch grated nutmeg
2 × 15ml spoons single cream
   (optional)

Wash and chop the sorrel. Melt the butter in a saucepan, add the sorrel, and cook gently for 5 minutes. Rub through a fine nylon sieve. Heat the sauce, if necessary. Whisk the sorrel purée into the sauce at boiling point. Add the nutmeg, and stir in the cream, if used. Do not reboil.

   Serve with veal or poultry; without the cream, it can be served with goose.

White Wine Sauce

250ml foundation white sauce (p236)
   made with white **or** fish stock (p26)
4 × 15ml spoons white wine

1–2 egg yolks
juice of $\frac{1}{2}$ lemon
25g butter
salt and pepper

Heat the sauce, if necessary, add the wine and simmer for 10 minutes. Blend the egg yolks and lemon juice together. Whisk the butter into the sauce at just below boiling point, adding a small pat at a time. Draw the pan off the heat, and mix a little of the sauce with the egg yolk mixture. Beat this mixture into the rest of the sauce. Re-heat the sauce, stirring carefully, without allowing it to boil. Season to taste.

   Serve with fish or white meat.

Foundation Brown Sauce *Basic recipe*
Makes 300ml (approx)

1 small carrot	25g plain flour
1 medium-sized onion (100g approx)	500ml general household stock (p25)
25g dripping **or** lard	salt and pepper

Prepare and slice the carrot and onion. Melt the dripping or lard in a saucepan. Fry the carrot and onion slowly until the onion is golden-brown. Stir in the flour, reduce the heat, and cook the flour very gently until it is also golden-brown. Draw the pan off the heat and gradually add the stock, stirring all the time to prevent lumps forming. Return to moderate heat and stir the sauce until boiling. Reduce the heat, cover, and simmer for 30 minutes. Strain the sauce. Season to taste.

Note For extra flavour, add mushroom trimmings or a piece of celeriac to the carrot and onion. For extra colour add a piece of brown onion skin, a little gravy browning, meat or vegetable extract before the sauce is simmered.

Sauces based on Foundation Brown Sauce

The quantities of the ingredients in the following recipes are for adding to 300ml Foundation Brown Sauce. In most cases, this will give about 300ml completed sauce, the extra ingredients making up the small quantity lost by evaporation.

Bordelaise Sauce

1 medium-sized carrot (100g approx)	a few parsley stalks
2 small onions (100g approx) **or**	a sprig of tarragon
2 shallots (25g approx)	150ml red **or** white wine
1 clove of garlic	300ml foundation brown sauce
150ml general household stock (p25)	lemon juice
6 black peppercorns	Cayenne pepper
1 bay leaf	1 × 5ml spoon chopped fresh chervil
a sprig of thyme	1 × 5ml spoon chopped parsley

Prepare and chop the carrot and onions or shallots. Skin and crush the garlic. Put the stock, vegetables, garlic, peppercorns, bay leaf, thyme, parsley stalks, and the tarragon into a small saucepan. Heat slowly to simmering point and simmer until the liquid is reduced to a sticky consistency. Add the wine. Re-heat, and cook until the liquid is reduced slightly. Add the brown sauce and heat to boiling point. Strain the sauce. Add the lemon juice and Cayenne pepper to taste. Stir in the chervil and parsley just before serving.

Serve with beef, pork, ham or duck.

Caper Sauce (2) (brown)

1 small onion (50g approx) **or** 1 shallot
 (15g approx)
300ml foundation brown sauce (p241)
1 × 15ml spoon capers
1 × 5ml spoon vinegar in which
 capers were pickled

1 × 5ml spoon anchovy essence
Cayenne pepper
lemon juice

Skin and chop the onion or shallot. Add to the brown sauce and simmer for 10 minutes; then strain it. Halve the capers, and add to the sauce with the caper vinegar, essence, Cayenne pepper, and lemon juice to taste. Re-heat the sauce.
 Serve with steak, kidneys or fish.

Christopher North's Sauce

300ml foundation brown sauce
 (p241) in which mushroom
 trimmings have been cooked
75ml juices from roast game
2 × 10ml spoons mushroom ketchup

50–75ml port
caster sugar
Cayenne pepper
2 × 15ml spoons lemon juice
1 × 2.5ml spoon salt

Put the brown sauce, roast game juices, mushroom ketchup, and port in the top of a double boiler, or in a basin placed over a pan of simmering water. Add sugar and Cayenne pepper to taste, and the lemon juice and salt. Heat, but do not allow to boil.
 Serve with meat or game.

Italian Sauce (1) (brown)

a bunch of parsley stalks
a sprig of thyme
1 bay leaf
4 shallots (50g approx)
6 mushrooms (50g approx)
1 × 15ml spoon olive oil

4 × 15ml spoons general household
 stock (p25)
4 × 15ml spoons white wine (optional)
300ml foundation brown sauce (p241)
salt and pepper

Tie the herbs in a small square of cotton or muslin. Prepare and chop the shallots and mushrooms. Heat the olive oil in a small saucepan, and fry the chopped vegetables very gently for 10 minutes. Add the stock, wine, if used, and the herbs. Heat to boiling point, reduce the heat, and simmer gently until reduced by half. Add the brown sauce. Re-heat and simmer gently for 20 minutes. Remove the herbs. Season to taste.
 Serve with fish or meat.

Marsala Sauce

2 shallots
4 button mushrooms
50g raw ham
25g butter
125ml Marsala
125ml brown stock (p25)

1 clove
1 bay leaf
300ml foundation brown sauce
   (p241)
125ml fresh tomato sauce (p255)

Skin the shallots and clean the mushrooms. Chop the vegetables and ham finely. Melt the butter in a saucepan and fry the vegetables and ham gently for 10 minutes. Add the Marsala, stock, clove, and bay leaf. Bring to the boil and boil rapidly until the liquid is reduced by half. Stir in the brown and tomato sauces. Heat gently for 3–4 minutes; then strain and serve.

   Serve with pigeon, ham, or small game birds.

Onion Sauce (2) (brown)

300ml foundation brown sauce (p241)
   made with 2 medium-sized onions
   (200g approx) and omitting the
   carrot
a pinch of grated nutmeg

1 × 5ml spoon wine vinegar
1 × 2.5ml spoon made English or
   French mustard
salt and pepper

Prepare the sauce in the usual way, but do not strain it. Add a little grated nutmeg, the vinegar, and mustard. Season to taste.

   Serve with beef or offal.

Piquant Sauce

1 small onion (50g approx) or
   2 shallots (25g approx)
25g mushrooms
1 bay leaf
a blade of mace
2 × 15ml spoons vinegar

300ml foundation brown sauce (p241)
1 × 15ml spoon capers
1 × 15ml spoon gherkins
1 × 10ml spoon mushroom ketchup
1 × 2.5ml spoon sugar (optional)

Skin the onion or shallots and chop finely. Clean the mushrooms and chop coarsely. Put the onion or shallots, bay leaf, mace, and vinegar in a saucepan. Heat to boiling point, reduce the heat and simmer for 10 minutes. Heat the sauce, if necessary. Add the onion mixture and the mushrooms to the brown sauce, and simmer for about 15 minutes until the mushrooms are softened.

   Meanwhile, halve the capers and chop the gherkins. Remove the bay leaf and mace from the sauce, and add the capers, gherkins, mushroom ketchup, and sugar, if used. Re-heat if required.

   Serve with pork, mutton or vegetables.

Pepper Sauce (Poivrade Sauce)

2 shallots (25g approx)
a sprig of thyme
1 bay leaf
12 black peppercorns

4 × 15ml spoons red wine
2 × 15ml spoons wine vinegar
300ml foundation brown sauce (p241)
freshly ground pepper

Skin the shallots and chop them finely. Put into a saucepan with the herbs, pepper-corns, wine, and vinegar. Heat to boiling point, reduce the heat, and simmer until the liquid is reduced by half. Heat the sauce, if necessary. Strain the liquid into the brown sauce. Season to taste with pepper.

Serve with roast or grilled beef or game.

Reform Sauce

2 mushrooms (15g approx)
a little brown stock (p25)
6 cocktail gherkins
15g cooked tongue

white of 1 small hard-boiled egg
300ml Pepper sauce
2 × 15ml spoons port
1 × 15ml spoon redcurrant jelly

Clean the mushrooms, then poach in a little stock. Drain. Shred the mushrooms, gherkins, tongue, and egg white. Heat the sauce, if necessary. Add the port and redcurrant jelly to the sauce; then add the shredded ingredients. Re-heat the sauce.

Serve with lamb cutlets.

Robert Sauce

1 small onion (50g approx)
15g butter
½ × 2.5ml spoon made English mustard

1 × 2.5ml spoon sugar
4 × 15ml spoons white wine
300ml foundation brown sauce (p241)

Skin and chop the onion. Melt the butter in a saucepan, add the onion, and fry until golden-brown. Stir in the mustard, sugar, and wine, and simmer for 10 minutes. Add the brown sauce. Re-heat, and simmer for a further 10 minutes.

Serve with roast or grilled beef, lamb or mutton, pork or goose.

Venison Sauce

1 shallot (15g approx)
12 black peppercorns
a sprig of thyme
a few parsley stalks
1 bay leaf

2 × 15ml spoons port (optional)
2 × 15ml spoons vinegar
300ml foundation brown sauce
  (p241)
1 × 10ml spoon redcurrant jelly

Skin and chop the shallot. Crush the peppercorns. Put the shallot, peppercorns, and herbs into a saucepan with the port, if used, and the vinegar. Heat to simmering point and simmer very gently for 2 minutes. Add the brown sauce. Re-heat, half cover the pan, and simmer for 10 minutes. Strain the sauce. Add the redcurrant jelly, and re-heat.

Serve with venison or mutton.

Salmi Sauce

2 shallots (25g approx)
25g mushroom stalks
1 × 15ml spoon olive oil
125ml game **or** chicken stock (p26)
4 × 15ml spoons red wine (optional)

a sprig of thyme
1 bay leaf
300ml foundation brown sauce
  (p241)
1 × 10ml spoon redcurrant jelly

Prepare and chop the shallots and mushroom stalks. Heat the olive oil in a saucepan, add the vegetables, and fry them until golden-brown. Add the stock, wine, if used, and herbs. Heat to boiling point, reduce the heat, and simmer until reduced by half. Add the brown sauce, and simmer very gently for 10 minutes. Strain the sauce. Add the redcurrant jelly, and re-heat.

Serve with game or duck.

Note This sauce can also be made with Espagnole Sauce (p248).

French Foundation Sauces

Béchamel Sauce (French Foundation White Sauce) *Basic recipe*
Makes 500ml (approx)

1 small onion (50g approx)
1 small carrot (25g approx)
a piece of celery (15g approx)
500ml milk
1 bay leaf
a few parsley stalks
a sprig of thyme
salt

1 clove
6 white peppercorns
a blade of mace
50g butter
50g flour
4 × 15ml spoons single cream
  (optional)

Prepare the vegetables and heat gently to simmering point with the milk, herbs, salt, and spices. Cover with a lid, and stand the pan in a warm place on the cooker to infuse for 30 minutes. Do not allow to boil. Strain the milk.

Melt the butter in a saucepan, add the flour, and stir until smooth. Cook over gentle heat, without allowing it to colour, for 2–3 minutes, stirring until the mixture (roux) begins to bubble. Draw the pan off the heat, and gradually add the flavoured milk, stirring to prevent lumps forming. Return to moderate heat and bring the sauce to the boil, stirring all the time. When the sauce has thickened, simmer for 3–4 minutes, beating briskly. (This helps to give the sauce a gloss.) Re-season if required. If cream is used, add it to the sauce just at boiling point, and remove from the heat immediately. Do not let the sauce reboil.

Note This sauce can also be made with half white stock (p26) and half milk.

Sauces based on Béchamel Sauce

The quantities of the ingredients in the recipes which follow on pp246–47 are for adding to 125ml or 250ml Béchamel Sauce. In most cases, this will give about 125ml or 250ml completed sauce, the extra ingredients making up the small quantity lost by evaporation.

Aurora Sauce

250ml Béchamel sauce (p245) made
  from fish stock (p26)
2 × 15ml spoons concentrated
  tomato purée **or** 1 × 15ml spoon
  sieved, canned pimento

paprika
2 × 15ml spoons single cream
  (optional)

Heat the sauce, if necessary. Carefully stir the tomato purée or sieved pimento into the sauce. Add paprika to taste and the cream, if used. Re-heat the sauce without allowing it to boil.

    Serve with eggs, chicken or fish.

Note This sauce can also be made from Velouté Sauce based on fish stock (p26). Serve with fish.

Italian Sauce (2) (white)

2 shallots (25g approx)
50g button mushrooms
1 × 15ml spoon butter
50ml Béchamel sauce (p245)
50ml dry white wine (optional)

125ml chicken stock
salt and pepper
lemon juice
1 × 10ml spoon chopped parsley
2 × 15ml spoons single cream

Prepare the shallots and mushrooms and chop them finely. Melt the butter in a saucepan. Add the vegetables and cook very gently for 10 minutes. Stir in the sauce, wine, if used, and stock. Heat to simmering point, and simmer steadily until the mushrooms are softened and the sauce is reduced to a creamy consistency. Season with salt and pepper and add lemon juice to taste. Stir in the parsley. Just before serving, stir in the cream.

    Serve with chicken, veal or fish.

Mornay Sauce

250ml Béchamel sauce (p245)
1 egg yolk
40g grated Parmesan and Gruyère
  cheese, mixed

4 × 15ml spoons single cream
  (optional)
a few grains Cayenne pepper

Cool the sauce, if necessary. Stir a little into the yolk, and blend together. Add to the rest of the Béchamel Sauce. Heat the sauce gently, stirring carefully, to cook the egg yolk; do not let it boil. Stir the cheeses into the sauce. Add the cream, if used, and season with Cayenne pepper.

    Serve with fish, chicken, ham, eggs or vegetables.

Savoury Cream Sauce

250ml Béchamel sauce (p245)
Cayenne pepper
salt

lemon juice
4 × 15ml spoons single cream

Heat the sauce, if necessary. Add Cayenne pepper, salt, and lemon juice to taste. Heat to just below boiling point, then stir in the cream. Do not allow the sauce to boil. Use at once.

Serve with chicken, veal, fish or delicately flavoured vegetables.

Soubise Sauce

200g onions
40g butter
1–2 × 15ml spoons white stock (p26)
250ml Béchamel sauce (p245)

salt and pepper
sugar
grated nutmeg

Skin and slice the onions. Heat 15g of the butter in a saucepan. Add the onions and enough stock to moisten them. Cook gently until tender. Sieve the onions. Add the onion purée to the Béchamel sauce and re-heat. Season with salt and pepper, and add sugar and nutmeg to taste. When heated to boiling point, whisk the rest of the butter into the sauce, adding a small pat at a time. Do not allow the sauce to reboil. Use at once.

Serve with fish, poultry or vegetables.

Tartare Sauce (1) (hot)

250ml Béchamel sauce (p245)
1–2 egg yolks
1 × 15ml spoon single cream
1 × 5ml spoon chopped gherkins

1 × 15ml spoon chopped capers
1 × 10ml spoon chopped parsley
lemon juice **or** white wine vinegar

Cool the sauce, if necessary. Mix the egg yolks and cream, and stir in a little of the sauce. Add this to the rest of the sauce. Heat the sauce gently, without boiling, to cook the egg yolk. Stir the gherkins, capers, and parsley into the sauce. Add lemon juice or vinegar to taste. Use at once.

Serve with salmon or other fish.

Espagnole Sauce (French Foundation Brown Sauce) *Basic recipe*
Makes 350ml (when using tomato purée and omitting the sherry); makes 500ml (when using tomato pulp and sherry)

1 small onion (50g approx)
1 small carrot (25g approx)
50g mushrooms **or** mushroom
   trimmings
50g lean raw ham **or** bacon
50g butter
50g flour
500ml brown stock (p25)

bouquet garni
6 black peppercorns
1 bay leaf
125ml tomato pulp **or** 1 × 15ml spoon
   concentrated tomato purée
salt
4 × 15ml spoons sherry (optional)

Prepare and slice the vegetables. Chop the ham or bacon into small pieces. Melt the butter in a saucepan and fry the ham or bacon for 2–3 minutes. Add the vegetables, and fry very slowly for 8–10 minutes until golden-brown. Add the flour and stir until smooth. Cook over gentle heat, stirring frequently, for about 10 minutes or until the flour is a rich brown colour. Draw the pan off the heat and gradually add the stock, stirring all the time to prevent lumps forming. Add the bouquet garni, peppercorns, and bay leaf. Return to moderate heat and stir until boiling. Half cover the pan, reduce the heat and simmer the sauce gently for 30 minutes. Add the tomato pulp or concentrated tomato purée. Simmer the sauce for a further 30 minutes. Rub through a fine nylon sieve. Season to taste with salt. Add the sherry, if used. Re-heat the sauce before serving.

VARIATION
Substitute 1 large tomato for the mushrooms. Add the vegetables and flour to the ham or bacon in the saucepan and fry them together for 10 minutes. Add 1 × 10ml spoon mushroom ketchup with the stock instead of using tomato pulp or purée. Makes 425ml sauce.

Sauces based on Espagnole Sauce
The quantities of the ingredients in the following recipes are for adding to 250ml Espagnole Sauce. In most cases, this will give about 250ml completed sauce, the extra ingredients making up the small quantity lost by evaporation.

Bigarade Sauce

½ Seville orange
juice of ½ lemon
250ml Espagnole sauce
4 × 1·5ml spoons red wine (optional)

1 × 5ml spoon redcurrant jelly
salt
Cayenne pepper
sugar

Pare the orange rind and cut into neat, thin strips, Put them in a saucepan and cover with a little cold water. Heat to simmering point and cook until just tender. Drain. Squeeze the juice from the orange. Add to the Espagnole Sauce with the orange rind and lemon juice. Re-heat the sauce. Stir in the wine, if used, and the redcurrant jelly. Add salt, Cayenne pepper, and sugar to taste.
   Serve with roast duck, goose, wild duck, pork or ham.

Demi-Glace Sauce

125ml juices from roast meat **or**
  125ml bone stock (p25) and
  1 × 5ml spoon beef extract **or** meat
  glaze (p59)

250ml Espagnole sauce (p248)

Add the meat juices, stock or meat glaze to the sauce. Bring to the boil and boil until the sauce is well reduced. Skim off any fat.
  Serve with meat, poultry or game.

Madeira Sauce

250ml Demi-glace sauce
4 × 15ml spoons Madeira

salt and pepper
1 × 5ml spoon meat glaze (p59)

Heat the sauce, if necessary. Add the Madeira, and simmer together until well reduced. Season to taste. Add the meat glaze and stir until dissolved. Strain the sauce.
  Serve with meat, poultry or game.

Velouté Sauce (French Foundation Fawn Sauce) *Basic recipe*
Makes 500ml (when using 100ml cream)

50g butter
6 button mushrooms **or**
  25–50g mushroom trimmings
12 black peppercorns
a few parsley stalks
50g flour

500ml white stock (p26)
  (fish, vegetable or meat)
salt and pepper
lemon juice
4–8 × 15ml spoons single cream

Melt the butter in a saucepan, and add the mushrooms, peppercorns, and parsley stalks. Cook gently for 10 minutes. Add the flour, and stir over gentle heat for 2–3 minutes, without allowing it to colour. Draw the pan off the heat and add the stock gradually, stirring well to prevent lumps forming. Return to gentle heat and heat the sauce to simmering point, stirring all the time. Simmer for 3–4 minutes. Rub the sauce through a sieve. Season to taste with salt and pepper, and add lemon juice to taste. Re-heat the sauce to boiling point and stir in enough cream to give the desired flavour and consistency. Do not reboil. Use at once.
  Serve with meat, poultry, fish or vegetables.

Sauces based on Velouté Sauce
The quantities of the ingredients in the recipes which follow on p250 are for adding to 250ml Velouté Sauce. In most cases, this will give about 250ml completed sauce, the extra ingredients making up the small quantity lost by evaporation.

Bercy Sauce

2 shallots (25g approx)
4 × 15ml spoons white wine
250ml Velouté sauce (p249) made
    with fish stock (p26) **or** chicken
    stock (p26)

25g butter
1 × 10ml spoon chopped parsley

Skin and chop the shallots. Put into a small saucepan with the wine, and cook until the wine is reduced by half. Add the sauce, and re-heat without allowing it to boil. Whisk in the butter, adding a small pat at a time. Add the parsley to the sauce.
  Serve with fish or meat.

Ravigote Sauce (hot)

250ml Velouté sauce (p249)
1 × 15ml spoon wine vinegar
grated nutmeg

sugar
salt and pepper
25g Ravigote butter (p566)

Heat the sauce, if necessary. Add the vinegar, nutmeg, sugar, and seasoning to taste. When heated to just below boiling point, whisk in the Ravigote butter, adding a small pat at a time. Do not allow the sauce to boil. Use at once.
  Serve with meat, boiled fish or poultry.

Suprême Sauce

250ml Velouté sauce (p249)
2–4 × 15ml spoons single cream
1 egg yolk
15–25g butter

grated nutmeg
lemon juice
salt and pepper

Cool the sauce, if necessary. Mix the cream and egg yolk, using the larger quantity of cream for a rich sauce. Stir a little of the cooled sauce into the cream and yolk mixture. Add this to the rest of the Velouté sauce. Heat the sauce gently, stirring carefully to thicken the egg yolk; do not let it boil. Whisk in the butter, adding a small pat at a time. Add nutmeg, lemon juice, and seasoning to taste. Use at once.
  Serve with any meat, poultry, fish or vegetables.
Note Adjust the proportions of cream, butter, and seasoning in this classic sauce to give the flavour and richness you want.

Other Savoury Sauces

Agro-Dolce (Bitter-sweet Sauce)
Makes 250ml (approx)

1 onion
1 carrot
1 clove of garlic (optional)
1 bay leaf
6 black peppercorns
1 × 15ml spoon olive oil

125ml red wine
75ml wine vinegar
50g sugar
2 × 15ml spoons water
125ml good thin gravy (p269)

Sweetening
1 × 5ml spoon chopped mint
1 × 5ml spoon finely shredded candied
    orange peel

1 × 10ml spoon chopped nuts
1 × 10ml spoon sultanas
1 × 15ml spoon grated bitter chocolate

Prepare and chop the onion and carrot. Skin and crush the garlic, if used. Put them into a saucepan with the bay leaf, peppercorns, and oil, and cook very gently, half-covered, for 15–20 minutes. Drain off the oil, and add the wine and vinegar. Simmer gently for 30 minutes; remove the bay leaf and peppercorns.

Put the sugar and water into a separate pan. Heat gently until the sugar has dissolved, then boil rapidly, without stirring, until the sugar becomes a golden caramel. Remove from the heat immediately. Stir into the wine mixture with the gravy. Add any one, or a mixture, of the sweetening ingredients to taste.

Serve with braised meat or vegetables.

Apple Sauce
Makes 375ml (approx)

500g apples
2 × 15ml spoons water
15g butter **or** margarine

rind and juice of ½ lemon
sugar

Peel, core, and slice the apples. Put them into a saucepan with the water, fat, and lemon rind. Cover, and cook over low heat until the apple is reduced to a pulp. Beat until smooth, rub through a sieve, or process in an electric blender. Re-heat the sauce with the lemon juice and sugar to taste.

Serve hot or cold with roast pork, duck or goose.

Note Apple sauce is also excellent served as a sweet sauce with ginger pudding.

Béarnaise Sauce
Makes 200ml (approx)

1 shallot **or** 25g onion
1 × 15ml spoon chopped fresh tarragon
1 × 15ml spoon chopped fresh chervil
a small piece of bay leaf
4 peppercorns

4 × 15ml spoons wine **or** tarragon
  vinegar
2 egg yolks
100g softened butter
salt and pepper

Prepare and chop the shallot or onion finely. Put in a saucepan with the herbs. Crush the peppercorns and add with the vinegar. Bring to the boil, and boil gently until reduced by half. Leave to cool, then strain. Heat the sauce in a basin placed in a pan of hot water to avoid boiling the sauce. Whisk in the yolks, one at a time. Stir until thickened. Whisk in the butter, adding a small pat at a time. It should be as thick as mayonnaise. Season to taste.

Serve the sauce, lukewarm, as soon as possible. Keep warm, if necessary, over hot water and re-whisk before serving. This sauce is thicker and sharper in flavour than Hollandaise Sauce.

Serve with steaks, shellfish or grilled fish, poultry or eggs.

Black Butter (Beurre Noir)
Makes 200ml (approx)

150g butter
2 × 15ml spoons chopped parsley

1 × 15ml spoon chopped capers
1 × 10ml spoon vinegar (approx)

Heat the butter in a saucepan until nut-brown but not burned. Add the parsley and capers. Pour into a heated container. Heat the vinegar in the same pan and mix it with the butter.

Serve poured over brains, fish, and some vegetables.

Note Use also with eggs. Omit the parsley and capers.

VARIATION

Brown Butter (Beurre Noisette)
Heat the butter until a light hazelnut colour. Add lemon juice to taste.

Serve poured over eggs, brains, skate, soft roes, or various vegetables.

Meunière Butter

butter
chopped parsley

a few drops lemon juice
salt and pepper

Heat the butter to a light hazelnut colour. Add the parsley, lemon juice, and seasoning to taste. Use sizzling hot.

This butter is used mainly for cooking fish or other ingredients, but it can be made and served separately.

Boar's Head Sauce
Makes 250ml (approx)

2 large oranges
1 shallot
200g redcurrant jelly
2 × 15ml spoons port

25g sugar
½ × 2.5ml spoon made English
   mustard
Cayenne pepper

Grate the rind of the oranges. Squeeze the juice from 1 orange. Skin and chop the shallot. Put the rind, shallot, jelly and port into a small saucepan. Heat slowly to boiling point, cover, and infuse for 30 minutes over very gentle heat. Add the orange juice, sugar, mustard, and Cayenne pepper. Stir well, then strain and cool.
   Serve with game, venison or mutton.
Note This sauce can be bottled and stored for future use.

Bread Sauce
Makes 250ml (approx)

1 large onion (200g approx)
250ml milk
2 cloves
a blade of mace
4 peppercorns
1 allspice berry

1 bay leaf
50g dried white breadcrumbs
1 × 15ml spoon butter
salt and pepper
2 × 15ml spoons single cream
   (optional)

Skin the onion. Heat the milk very slowly to boiling point with the spices, bay leaf, and onion. Cover the pan and infuse over gentle heat for 30 minutes. Strain the liquid. Add the breadcrumbs and butter to the flavoured milk. Season to taste. Heat the mixture to just below simmering point and keep at this temperature for 20 minutes. Stir in the cream, if used.
   Serve with roast chicken or turkey.

Cherry Sauce
Makes 375ml (approx)

200g freshly stewed, bottled **or**
   canned cherries (preferably
   Morellos)
125ml juice in which cherries were
   cooked, bottled or canned
sugar

pepper
2 × 15ml spoons redcurrant jelly
1 × 5ml spoon vinegar
2 × 15ml spoons red wine
1 × 2.5ml spoon arrowroot (optional)
1 × 15ml spoon cold water (optional)

Stone the cherries, if necessary. Put all the ingredients, except the arrowroot and water, into a saucepan and simmer for about 20 minutes, or until the liquid is slightly syrupy.
   If preferred, put all the ingredients in a pan, except the arrowroot and water, and simmer for 5 minutes only; then blend the arrowroot with the cold water. Add to the pan and cook, stirring until the sauce thickens.
   Serve with roast or braised game or rabbit.

Celery Sauce
Makes 250ml (approx)

6 large sticks celery
250ml water
25g butter **or** margarine
25g plain flour

salt and pepper
1–2 drops lemon juice
1–2 × 15ml spoons single cream
(optional)

Wash the celery and cut into short lengths. Heat the water to boiling point, add the celery, reduce the heat, cover, and simmer for 20 minutes or until the celery is softened. Drain, and reserve the liquid. Rub the celery through a fine nylon sieve, or process in an electric blender and then sieve. Measure the purée and make it up to 250ml with the reserved liquid.

Melt the fat in a saucepan and add the flour. Stir over gentle heat, without allowing the flour to colour, for 2–3 minutes, or until the mixture begins to bubble. Draw the pan off the heat and gradually stir in the celery purée. Return to moderate heat and bring the sauce to the boil, stirring all the time to prevent lumps forming. When it has thickened, simmer for 3–4 minutes, beating vigorously. Season to taste. Remove from the heat, and stir in the lemon juice and the cream, if used.

Serve with lamb, mutton or rabbit.

Cranberry Sauce
Makes 300ml (approx)

125ml water
150g sugar

200g cranberries

Put the water and sugar in a saucepan and stir over gentle heat until the sugar dissolves. Add the cranberries, and cook gently for about 10 minutes until they have burst and are quite tender. Leave to cool.

Serve with roast turkey, chicken or game.

Currant Sauce
Makes 375ml (approx)

25g butter
25g flour
250ml water
75ml red wine
a pinch of grated nutmeg

juice of ½ lemon
a pinch of ground cloves
a pinch of ground ginger
50g currants
sugar

Melt the butter in a saucepan, add the flour, and cook until the flour is golden-brown. Draw the pan off the heat and gradually stir in the water and wine. Return to the heat and stir until boiling. Add the rest of the ingredients, reduce the heat, and simmer gently for 10 minutes.

Serve with roast pork, hare or venison.

VARIATION
Sultana Sauce
Substitute sultanas for the currants.

Chestnut Sauce
Makes 375ml (approx)

200g chestnuts
375ml chicken **or** white stock (p26)
a pinch of ground cinnamon
a small strip of lemon rind

25g butter
salt and pepper
75ml single cream (optional)

Make a slit in the rounded side of the shells of the chestnuts, and boil or bake them for 15–20 minutes. Remove the shells and skins while hot. Put the chestnuts in a saucepan with the stock, cinnamon, and lemon rind. Heat to simmering point, and simmer gently for 30 minutes or until the chestnuts are very tender. Remove the lemon rind. Rub the chestnuts and the liquid through a sieve, or process in an electric blender. Return the purée to the pan, add the butter, and season to taste. Heat gently for 2–3 minutes. Stir in the cream, if used, just before serving.
    Serve with roast chicken or turkey.

Cumberland Sauce
Makes 250ml (approx)

grated rind and juice of 1 orange
grated rind and juice of 1 lemon
75ml water
75ml port
2 × 15ml spoons vinegar

100g redcurrant jelly
$\frac{1}{2}$ × 2.5ml spoon made English mustard
salt
a pinch of Cayenne pepper

Put the orange and lemon rind into a small saucepan with the water and heat to simmering point. Simmer gently for 10 minutes. Add the port, vinegar, redcurrant jelly, and mustard, and heat gently until the jelly melts. Add the orange and lemon juice to the pan with the seasoning. Simmer for 3–4 minutes.
    Serve hot or cold with roast duck, mutton or ham.

Fresh Tomato Sauce
Makes 500ml (approx)

1 medium-sized onion
1 clove of garlic (optional)
1 rasher of streaky bacon, without
    rinds
750g tomatoes

2 × 15ml spoons olive oil
salt and pepper
a pinch of sugar
1 × 5ml spoon chopped fresh basil
    (optional)

Skin the onion and chop it finely. Skin and crush the garlic, if used. Chop the bacon rasher. Skin and chop the tomatoes. Heat the oil in a saucepan, and fry the onion, garlic, and bacon over gentle heat for 5 minutes. Add the rest of the ingredients, cover, and simmer gently for 30 minutes. Rub through a sieve or process in an electric blender until smooth. Re-heat and re-season if required.
    Serve with meat, some fish, and pasta.

Salsa Pomodoro (Tomato Sauce)
Makes 750ml (approx)

250g tomatoes
50g red pepper
50g lean bacon, without rinds
50g bacon fat
50g onion
1 clove of garlic
25g plain flour

50g concentrated tomato purée
300ml chicken stock
salt and pepper
1 × 10ml spoon thick honey
150ml sweet red vermouth (optional)
1 × 15ml spoon chopped herbs,
    eg oregano, basil, rosemary, mint

Skin and de-seed the tomatoes and chop them coarsely. De-seed the pepper. Mince the bacon. Heat the fat in a large pan and sauté the bacon for 2 minutes. Chop the onion, garlic, and pepper. Add them to the bacon, and cook gently for 5 minutes, turning with a spoon. Sprinkle in the flour; stir it in, and add the tomato purée. Cook for 3 minutes. Add the chopped tomatoes, and stir in the chicken stock. Bring to the boil, reduce the heat, and simmer gently for 30 minutes. Season well. Just before serving, stir in the honey, and the vermouth, if liked. Sprinkle with the herbs.

Quince Sauce
Makes 375ml (approx)

200g quinces
250ml water
a good pinch of grated nutmeg
a good pinch of ground cloves

1 × 15ml spoon lemon juice
75ml red wine (optional)
sugar

Peel, core, and slice the quinces. Put them into a saucepan with the water. Cover, and cook over low heat until reduced to a pulp. Beat, rub through a sieve, or process in an electric blender until smooth. Re-heat the sauce, and add the rest of the ingredients with sugar to taste.

Serve with roast pork or game.

Prune Sauce
Makes 375ml (approx)

200g prunes
250ml water
a strip of lemon rind
25g sugar

a pinch of ground cinnamon
1 × 15ml spoon rum **or** brandy
    (optional)
lemon juice

Soak the prunes in the water overnight. Put them into a saucepan with the lemon rind, and stew until tender. Remove the stones and lemon rind, and rub the prunes and liquid through a sieve, or process in an electric blender until smooth. Re-heat, and add the sugar, cinnamon, rum or brandy, if used, and lemon juice to taste.

Serve with roast pork, goose, venison or mutton.

Note This sauce can also be served with some hot milk and custard puddings or with Apple Pudding (steamed) (p331).

Roast Leg of Lamb (p.134)

Moussaka (p.146)

Stuffed Breast of Veal (p.154)

Gammon Steaks with Marmalade (p.176)

Pease Pudding (p.297)

Roast Savoury Loin of Pork (p.163), with Apple Sauce (p.251), and Sage and Onion Stuffing (p.49)

Hollandaise Sauce (1)

Makes 125ml (approx)

3 × 15ml spoons white wine vinegar
6 peppercorns
½ bay leaf
a blade of mace

3 egg yolks
100g softened butter
salt and pepper

Put the vinegar, peppercorns, bay leaf, and mace into a small saucepan and boil rapidly until the mixture is reduced to 1 × 15ml spoon. Strain, and leave to cool. Add the yolks and a nut of butter to the vinegar and beat well. Heat the sauce in a basin over a pan of hot water to avoid boiling the sauce. Beat the egg yolk mixture until thick. Add the rest of the butter, a small pat at a time, beating well between each addition. When all the butter has been added, the mixture should be thick and glossy. Season lightly with salt and pepper.

This is the classic sauce to serve with poached fish, asparagus or broccoli. Serve lukewarm.

Note If the sauce curdles, whisk in 1 × 10ml spoon cold water. If this fails to bind it, put an egg yolk in another basin and beat in the sauce gradually.

Hollandaise Sauce (2)

Makes 125ml (approx)

2 × 15ml spoons white wine vinegar
2 × 15ml spoons water
4 peppercorns
a small piece of bay leaf
2 egg yolks

100g softened butter
salt and pepper
Cayenne pepper
lemon juice (optional)

Put the vinegar and water into a small saucepan. Crush the peppercorns and add to the pan with the bay leaf. Bring to the boil, and continue boiling gently until the liquid is reduced by half. Leave to cool. Strain the liquid into a double boiler or a basin over a pan of hot water to avoid boiling the sauce. Whisk in the egg yolks, one at a time. Cook until the mixture is thick, whisking all the time. Whisk in the butter, adding a small pat at a time. The sauce should be just thick enough to hold its shape. Each addition must be thoroughly worked in before the next is added. Season lightly with salt, pepper, and Cayenne pepper. Add a little lemon juice, if liked, to give a slightly piquant flavour.

Note A Hollandaise Sauce with a more delicate flavour can be made by using 1 × 15ml spoon strained lemon juice and 1 × 15ml spoon water instead of the reduced vinegar.

VARIATION

Mousseline Hollandaise Sauce

Just before serving, fold in 2–3 × 15ml spoons lightly whipped double cream. Re-season if required.

Fruit Curry Sauce
Makes 500ml (approx)

½ small onion (25g approx)
½ cooking apple (100g approx)
1 banana (150g approx)
6 seedless raisins
1 tomato (50g approx)
25g butter **or** margarine

1 × 5ml spoon desiccated coconut
50g flour
1 × 10ml spoon curry powder
salt
500ml vegetable stock (p27)
lemon juice

Prepare the onion and apple, and chop them finely. Slice the banana. Chop the raisins. Skin and chop the tomato. Melt the fat in a saucepan, add the vegetables and fruit, and fry gently for 5 minutes. Add the coconut, flour, curry powder, and salt to taste, and stir well. Stir in the stock. Heat to simmering point, cover, and simmer gently for 20 minutes. Add lemon juice to taste.

Serve with vegetables or eggs.

Raisin Sauce
Makes 400ml (approx)

75g soft dark brown sugar
25g flour
1 × 15ml spoon dry English mustard
salt and pepper

350ml boiling water
50ml vinegar
50g seedless raisins
25g butter

Mix the dry ingredients in the top of a double saucepan or in a basin placed over simmering water. Stir in the boiling water and the vinegar gradually to prevent lumps forming. Cook slowly for 15–20 minutes. Add the raisins, and continue to cook for 5 minutes. Beat in the butter, a small pat at a time. Use at once.

Serve with hot ham dishes.

White Chaudfroid Sauce
Makes 375ml (approx)

250ml Béchamel sauce (p245)
125ml aspic jelly
1 × 10ml spoon gelatine
salt and pepper

1 × 5ml spoon white wine vinegar
 or lemon juice
1 × 15ml spoon double cream

Cool the Béchamel Sauce until tepid. Melt the aspic jelly in a basin placed over hot water. Add the gelatine to the melted aspic. Continue to stir over heat until the gelatine dissolves. Cool the aspic jelly until tepid, then fold it into the sauce. Season to taste. Add the vinegar or lemon juice. Rub the sauce through a fine sieve. Fold in the cream. Leave the sauce to cool completely but use while still liquid. Use the sauce to mask poultry, veal or fish served *en chaudfroid*.

VARIATIONS
Brown Chaudfroid Sauce
Make as for White Chaudfroid Sauce, substituting Espagnole Sauce (p248) for Béchamel Sauce
  Use for masking beef, mutton or game

Fawn Chaudfroid Sauce
Make as for White Chaudfroid Sauce, substituting Velouté Sauce (p249) for Béchamel Sauce.
  Use for masking lamb, veal or poultry.

Green Chaudfroid Sauce
Make as for White Chaudfroid Sauce, using 1 × 15ml spoon spinach purée (p302) or green colouring with the Béchamel Sauce.
  Use for masking veal or poultry.

Tomato Chaudfroid Sauce
Make as for White Chaudfroid Sauce, substituting Fresh Tomato Sauce (p255) for Béchamel Sauce.
  Use for masking fish, veal, poultry or lamb.

Salad Dressings and Sauces

Aïoli
Makes 200ml (approx)

4–6 cloves garlic **or** 4 shallots
1 egg yolk
a pinch of salt
125ml olive oil

1 × 15ml spoon lemon juice **or** wine
  vinegar
1 medium-sized potato
a pinch of Cayenne pepper

Crush the garlic or shallots and pound to a smooth pulp. Add the egg yolk and salt; then proceed as for mayonnaise (p262). Cook the potato for 20 minutes in enough boiling salted water to cover it. Drain, rub through a sieve, and leave to cool. Gradually work the sauce into the potato, beating thoroughly. Season to taste with Cayenne pepper.
  Serve with salads, vegetables, fish or meat.

Cold Mousseline Sauce
Makes 150ml (approx)

2 × 15ml spoons double cream   125ml mayonnaise (p262)

Whip the cream lightly until it holds its shape, then fold into the mayonnaise.
  Serve with fish.
VARIATION
Green Mousseline Sauce
Fold 1 × 15ml spoon of cooked spinach purée into the mayonnaise with the cream.

Cream Salad Dressing
Makes 100ml (approx)

1 × 2.5ml spoon made English mustard
½ × 2.5ml spoon salt
¼ × 2.5ml spoon caster sugar

4 × 15ml spoons double cream
1 × 15ml spoon malt **or** wine vinegar
1 × 5ml spoon tarragon vinegar

Mix the mustard, salt, and sugar together. Stir in the cream. Add the vinegars, drop by drop, beating the mixture all the time.

English Salad Dressing or Cream *Basic recipe*

Use the ingredients below in the proportions of:

1 hard-boiled egg yolk
½ × 2.5ml spoon mixed English
   mustard
1 × 5ml spoon Worcestershire sauce
   or to taste
salt and pepper
a pinch of caster sugar

1 × 10ml spoon cider **or**
   white wine vinegar
1 × 15ml spoon olive oil
2 × 15ml spoons double cream **or**
   evaporated milk prepared for
   whipping

Sieve the egg yolk. Work into it gradually the seasonings, vinegar, and oil. Whip the cream or evaporated milk lightly, and fold into the mixture. Use at once.

Epicurean Sauce
Makes 500ml (approx)

½ cucumber
salt
4 × 15ml spoons aspic jelly **or** good
   stock and 1 × 2.5ml spoon gelatine
1 × 15ml spoon tarragon vinegar
4 × 15ml spoons double cream

125ml mayonnaise (p262)
2 gherkins
1 × 10ml spoon chutney
1 × 5ml spoon anchovy essence
pepper
sugar

Peel and dice the cucumber. Cook in 5mm depth of salted water until tender, or steam. Sieve, or process in an electric blender to make a smooth purée. If using stock and gelatine, sprinkle the gelatine over the stock in a basin and leave for 5 minutes to soften. Stand the basin over a pan of hot water and leave until the gelatine dissolves. Allow to cool. Stir the cucumber purée and the vinegar into the stock or aspic jelly. Whip the cream until it holds its shape, then fold it into the mayonnaise. Finely chop the gherkins and any large pieces in the chutney. Fold into the mayonnaise with the anchovy essence, and finally fold in the aspic jelly and cucumber mixture. Season with salt and pepper and add sugar to taste.

   Serve with fish salads, asparagus or globe artichokes.

Evaporated Milk Dressing
Makes 100ml (approx)

4 × 15ml spoons unsweetened
   evaporated milk
1 × 15ml spoon malt **or** wine vinegar

½ × 2.5ml spoon made mustard
a good pinch of caster sugar
½ × 2.5ml spoon salt

Whisk the milk until it forms soft peaks. Beat in the vinegar, drop by drop, then the mustard, sugar, and salt.

French Dressing *Basic recipe*

Use the ingredients below in the proportions of:

2–3 × 15ml spoons olive oil
salt and freshly ground black pepper
a pinch of dry English mustard
   (optional)

a pinch of caster sugar (optional)
1 × 15ml spoon wine vinegar

Mix together the oil and seasonings. Add the vinegar gradually, stirring all the time with a wooden spoon so that an emulsion is formed. Alternatively, put all the ingredients into a small screw-topped jar, and shake vigorously until well blended.

   The standard basic French dressing is made with oil, salt and pepper and vinegar alone, but it can be varied in other ways, eg

1) Use ½ × 2.5ml spoon French or mixed English or German mustard instead of dry mustard.
2) Use white wine instead of some of the vinegar.
3) Use lemon juice instead of some or all of the vinegar.
4) In recipes which contain grapefruit or orange, use grapefruit or orange juice instead of the vinegar.
5) Add a little skinned garlic, crushed without salt, to the basic ingredients.

Note French dressing keeps well, so a large quantity can be made and stored in a screw-topped jar or bottle in a cool place. Shake well before use.

Vinaigrette Sauce
Makes 100ml (approx)

4 × 15ml spoons French dressing
1 × 5ml spoon finely chopped gherkin
1 × 2.5ml spoon finely chopped chives
   or shallot

1 × 2.5ml spoon finely chopped parsley
1 × 5ml spoon finely chopped capers
1 × 2.5ml spoon finely chopped
   tarragon **and/or** chervil

Mix all the ingredients together and leave for at least 1 hour before using for the flavours to blend.

Mayonnaise *Basic egg and oil sauce*
Makes 300ml (approx)

2 egg yolks
1 × 2.5ml spoon dry English mustard
1 × 2.5ml spoon salt
pepper

2 × 15ml spoons white wine vinegar,
    tarragon vinegar, **or** lemon juice
250ml oil, preferably either olive **or**
    corn oil

Blend the egg yolks with the mustard, salt, pepper, and 1 × 15ml spoon of the vinegar or lemon juice in a basin. Using either a balloon whisk, a wooden spoon, or an electric blender, beat in the oil very gradually, drop by drop, until about half of it has been added and the mixture looks thick and shiny. At this stage, the oil can be added in a slow thin stream. Add the remaining vinegar or lemon juice when all the oil has been incorporated.

If the mayonnaise curdles while making, beat a fresh egg yolk in another basin and beat the mixture into this gradually, 1 × 5ml spoonful at a time.

To store the mayonnaise, put it into a basin or jar, cover, and store in the least cold part of the refrigerator; if the mayonnaise becomes too cold, it will separate.

Note For the best results, all the ingredients should be at room temperature. If the eggs are used straight from the refrigerator, the mayonnaise is much more likely to curdle.

Cooked Mayonnaise
Makes 300ml (approx)

1 × 5ml spoon caster sugar
1 × 2.5ml spoon salt
1 × 2.5ml spoon dry mustard
a pinch of pepper
1 × 15ml spoon corn **or** vegetable oil

3 egg yolks
4 × 15ml spoons wine vinegar
1 × 5ml spoon tarragon vinegar
250ml milk **or** single cream

Mix the sugar, salt, mustard, and pepper. Stir in the oil, then the egg yolks. Beat well. Add the vinegars gradually and finally the milk or cream. Turn into the top of a double boiler, or into a basin placed over a pan of gently simmering water. Cook the sauce, stirring all the time until it thickens. Do not allow the sauce to boil or it will curdle. Remove from the heat and leave to cool, stirring frequently to prevent a skin forming. Re-season if required when cold.

Curry Mayonnaise
Makes 125ml (approx)

1 clove of garlic
125ml mayonnaise

1 × 2.5ml spoon curry powder

Crush the garlic and fold it into the mayonnaise with the curry powder.
    Serve with cold meat or fish; this sauce is particularly good with cold chicken.

Green Mayonnaise
Makes 150ml (approx)

25g mixed leaves of watercress,
   spinach, chervil, tarragon, parsley,
   and chives

salt
125ml mayonnaise (p262)

Cook the leaves in a very little boiling salted water until just tender. Drain thoroughly and sieve, or process in an electric blender to a smooth purée. Fold into the mayonnaise just before serving. Do not add the purée to the mayonnaise too early or it will lose its colour.
   Serve with fish and fish salads.

Tomato Mayonnaise
Makes 150ml (approx)

2 × 15ml spoons thick fresh tomato
   purée **or** 1 × 10ml spoon
   concentrated tomato purée **or**
   2 × 10ml spoons tomato ketchup

125ml mayonnaise (p262)

Fold the tomato purée or ketchup into the mayonnaise.
   Serve with meat or fish or shellfish salads.

VARIATION
Add a few drops of Worcestershire sauce.

Remoulade Sauce
Makes 125ml (approx)

1 × 5ml spoon French mustard
1 × 5ml spoon chopped capers
1 × 2.5ml spoon chopped parsley

1 × 2.5ml spoon chopped tarragon
1 × 2.5ml spoon chopped chervil
125ml mayonnaise (p262)

Fold the mustard, capers, and herbs into the mayonnaise. Leave the sauce to stand for at least 1 hour before serving for the flavours to blend.
   Serve with grilled meat or fish, or with salads.

Roquefort Salad Cream
Makes 375ml (approx)

200ml soured cream
100ml mayonnaise (p262)
2 × 15ml spoons grated onion

2 × 15ml spoons mild white vinegar
50g Roquefort cheese
1 clove of garlic

Combine the cream, mayonnaise, onion, and vinegar in a bowl or the goblet of an electric blender. Crumble the cheese, and add it to the mixture. Split the garlic clove and rub a salad bowl thoroughly with the cut sides. Discard the garlic. Whisk or blend the other ingredients until smooth. Use over a green salad placed in the bowl.
Note If to be stored, rub the garlic clove round the inside of the storage container before putting in the dressing. Store chilled.

Soured Cream Dressing
Makes 125ml (approx)

125ml soured cream
salt and pepper
1 × 5ml spoon French mustard **or**
   1 × 2.5ml spoon made English
   mustard

a pinch of caster sugar
milk **or** top of the milk
   (optional)

Stir the cream, then add the seasoning, mustard, and sugar. If liked, the dressing can be thinned down with a little milk or top of the milk.

VARIATION
Yoghurt Dressing
Use thick natural yoghurt instead of soured cream.

Soured Cream Cooked Dressing
Makes 250ml (approx)

1 × 10ml spoon flour
1 × 10ml spoon sugar
1 × 5ml spoon dry mustard
1 × 5ml spoon salt
a pinch of Cayenne pepper

1 egg yolk
3 × 15ml spoons white vinegar
1 × 15ml spoon melted butter
125ml soured cream

Put all the dry ingredients into the top of a double boiler or in a basin over a pan of hot water. Add the egg yolk and vinegar, and beat well. Cook gently for 7–8 minutes, stirring all the time. Add the butter. Remove from the heat and leave to cool. Fold into the soured cream before serving.

Tartare Sauce (2)
Makes 150ml (approx)

1 × 5ml spoon each of
   chopped gherkins
   chopped olives
   chopped capers
   chopped parsley
   chopped chives

125ml mayonnaise (p262)
½ × 2.5ml spoon French mustard
1 × 10ml spoon wine vinegar **or**
   lemon juice

Fold the chopped ingredients into the mayonnaise with the mustard, then add the vinegar or lemon juice. Leave the sauce to stand for at least 1 hour before serving for the flavours to blend.

Serve with grilled or fried fish and meat.

Thousand Islands Dressing
Makes 300ml (approx)

250ml mayonnaise (p262)
1 × 15ml spoon chopped parsley
1 × 15ml spoon finely chopped capers
1 × 15ml spoon finely chopped olives

1 × 15ml spoon finely chopped pickles
1 × 15ml spoon lemon juice
tomato juice

Put the mayonnaise into a basin, add the solid ingredients and lemon juice, and mix well. Stir in enough tomato juice to make a dressing of pouring consistency.

Sweet Sauces

Sweet Cornflour Sauce or Sweet White Sauce *Basic recipe*
Makes 250ml (approx)

2 × 10ml spoons cornflour
250ml milk

1–2 × 15ml spoons sugar
vanilla essence **or** other flavouring

1) *Blended Method*
Blend the cornflour to a smooth, thin paste with a little of the cold milk. Put the rest of the milk in a saucepan and heat to boiling point. Stir the boiling milk into the blended cornflour. Return to the pan and stir until boiling. Reduce the heat and cook for 3 minutes. Add the sugar and flavouring to taste.

2) *All-in-one Method*
Put the cornflour, milk, and sugar in a medium-sized saucepan. Whisk over moderate heat until the sauce comes to the boil. Reduce the heat, and cook for 2–3 minutes, whisking all the time, until the sauce is thickened and smooth.

Note If the sauce must be kept hot for a short time, cover with wet greaseproof paper and a lid. Just before serving, beat again to remove any lumps.
VARIATIONS
The following ingredients can be added to 250ml hot Sweet Cornflour Sauce:

Almond Sauce
Add 1–2 × 10ml spoon ground almonds to the cornflour when blending to a paste with the milk. Add 2–3 drops of almond essence, and vanilla essence to taste after the sauce has been cooked.

Brandy Sauce
Add 1–2 × 15ml spoons brandy.

Chocolate Sauce (1)
Add 1 × 15ml spoon cocoa powder and 1 × 15ml spoon sugar dissolved in 1 × 15ml spoon boiling water.

For further **variations,** see over

Coffee Sauce

Add 1×10ml spoon instant coffee dissolved in 1×10ml spoon boiling water **or** 1×15ml spoon coffee essence.

Ginger Sauce

Add 1×10ml spoon ground ginger and 50g finely chopped crystallized ginger (optional).

Lemon or Orange Sauce (1)

Add the grated rind of half an orange or lemon and a drop of orange or yellow colouring (optional).

Rich Sauce

Add 1 egg yolk and 2×15ml spoons cream. Re-heat the sauce but do not boil.

Rum Sauce

Add $1-2 \times 15$ml spoons rum.

Sweet Spice Sauce

Add 1×5ml spoon mixed spice **or** grated nutmeg.

Vanilla Sauce

Add $\frac{1}{2} \times 2.5$ml spoon vanilla essence and a drop of yellow colouring (optional).

Sweet Arrowroot Sauce *Basic recipe*
Makes 175ml (approx) using 125ml liquid

125–250ml water
thinly pared rind of lemon **or** other
   flavouring

100g sugar, golden syrup **or** honey
lemon juice
2×5ml spoons arrowroot

Put the water in a pan and add the lemon rind or other flavouring. Heat to boiling point, reduce the heat, and simmer gently for 15 minutes. Remove the lemon rind, if used. Add the sugar, syrup or honey. Re-heat to boiling point and boil for 5 minutes. Add lemon juice to taste. Blend the arrowroot with a little cold water until smooth and stir into the hot liquid. Heat gently for 1–2 minutes, stirring all the time until the arrowroot thickens.

VARIATIONS

Lemon Sauce (2)

Make as above, using 125ml water, the rind of half a lemon and the juice of 2 lemons.

Rich Lemon Sauce

Add a small glass of sherry and an egg yolk when the sauce is just below boiling point. The sauce must not be allowed to boil once the egg yolk has been added.

Orange Sauce (2)

Make as in the basic recipe, using 125ml water, the rind of half an orange and the juice of 1 orange instead of the lemon rind and juice.

Crème Anglaise (1) (Egg Custard Sauce)
Makes 300ml (approx)

250ml milk
a few drops vanilla essence **or** a strip
   of lemon rind

3 egg yolks
50g caster sugar

Put the milk and flavouring in a pan and warm gently but do not let it boil. Beat the egg yolks and sugar together until creamy. Remove the lemon rind, if used, and add the milk. Strain the custard into a double boiler or a basin placed over a pan of simmering water. Cook, stirring all the time with a wooden spoon, until the custard thickens and coats the back of the spoon. Take care not to let the custard curdle. Serve hot or cold.

VARIATIONS
Stir 125ml lightly whipped double cream and 2 × 15ml spoons Grand Marnier into the completed sauce.

Chocolate Custard Sauce

Grate 100g plain chocolate coarsely and add to the milk with vanilla essence instead of lemon rind. Warm until the chocolate melts, stir, and add to the egg yolks. Complete the recipe as above.

Caramel Custard Sauce

Put 25g sugar and 1 × 15ml spoon water in a small pan. Heat gently until the sugar dissolves; then boil the syrup until it is golden-brown. Remove from the heat, quickly add 2 × 15ml spoons cold water, and leave in a warm place to dissolve. Add enough caramel to the finished custard sauce to give a good flavour.

Chocolate Sauce (2)
Makes 150ml (approx)

100g plain chocolate
200g sugar
125ml water

salt
1 × 2.5ml spoon vanilla essence

Break up the chocolate and put into a saucepan with the other ingredients. Stir over gentle heat until the chocolate and sugar melt and blend together.

   Serve hot over ice cream, profiteroles or stewed pears.

Note Black coffee can be substituted for water.

Jam Sauce
Makes 300ml (approx)

4 × 15ml spoons seedless jam
250ml water
sugar

lemon juice
1 × 10ml spoon arrowroot
a few drops food colouring (optional)

Put the jam and the water in a saucepan and heat to boiling point. Add sugar and lemon juice to taste. Blend the arrowroot with a little cold water until smooth. Stir into the hot liquid and heat gently until the arrowroot thickens, stirring all the time. Colour if necessary.

Serve with steamed or baked puddings, ice cream or cold cornflour desserts.

Melba Sauce
Makes 100–125ml

200g fresh raspberries
3 × 15ml spoons icing sugar

white wine (optional)

Crush the raspberries in a sieve over a heatproof bowl. Add the sugar and rub through the sieve into the bowl. Place the bowl over a pan of simmering water and stir for 2–3 minutes to dissolve the sugar. Remove from the heat, and add a little white wine if a thinner consistency is preferred. The sauce should only just coat the back of a spoon. Chill before use.

Serve over Peach Melba (p379), meringues, or any hot or cold raspberry-flavoured dessert.

Thickened Fruit Sauce *Basic recipe*

fresh fruit (damsons, plums,
    raspberries, blueberries or
    blackberries)
sugar

lemon juice
1 × 5ml spoon arrowroot for every
    250ml fruit purée
1 × 5ml spoon water

Put the fruit into a pan with a very little water. Heat to simmering point and simmer until softened. Stone the fruit, then rub through a sieve, or process in an electric blender until smooth. Measure the fruit to calculate the quantity of arrowroot needed. Pour the fruit purée back into the saucepan and add sugar and lemon juice to taste. Blend the correct quantity of arrowroot with the water. Add to the fruit purée and bring to the boil, stirring all the time until the sauce thickens.

Note Canned or bottled fruit can be used, in which case it will be unnecessary to add extra sugar.

GRAVIES

Giblet Gravy (for roast poultry)
Makes 300ml (approx)

1 set of giblets
1 medium-sized onion (100g approx)
  (optional)
400ml water

pan juices
gravy browning (optional)
salt and pepper (optional)

Prepare the giblets (p183–84) and skin the onion, if used. Put the giblets and the onion in a pan and cover with cold water. Heat to boiling point, cover, reduce the heat, and simmer gently for 1 hour. Pour off the fat from the tin in which the bird has been roasted, leaving any sediment. Add the liquid from the giblets and stir until boiling. Boil for 2–3 minutes. If the gravy is pale, add a few drops of gravy browning. Season to taste, if required. Strain, and serve very hot.

Note The gravy can be thickened slightly, if liked, by adding 1 × 5ml spoon plain flour for each 250ml giblet stock. Blend the flour with the sediment before adding the stock. Boil for 3–4 minutes.

Thin Gravy (for roast beef)
Makes 250ml (approx)

pan juices
250ml hot water from cooking
  vegetables **or** beef stock

salt and pepper (optional)
gravy browning (optional)

After roasting a joint, carefully pour off the fat from the roasting tin, leaving all pan juices and sediment behind. Add the vegetable water or beef stock to the juices. Bring to the boil, stirring well until all the sediment dissolves, and boil for 2–3 minutes to reduce the liquid slightly. Season to taste. If the gravy is pale, add a few drops of gravy browning. Strain, and serve very hot.

Lamb Gravy (for roast lamb)
Makes 250ml (approx)

pan juices
1 × 5ml spoon plain flour
250ml hot water from vegetables **or**
  general household stock (p25)
  made with lamb meat trimmings
  and vegetables

salt and pepper (optional)
gravy browning (optional)

Make as for Thin Gravy but, after pouring off the fat, stir the flour into the pan juices. Add the hot vegetable water or stock gradually to prevent lumps forming, and stir until boiling. Season to taste, if required. If the gravy is pale, add a few drops of gravy browning. Strain, and serve very hot.

Thickened Gravy (for roast pork and roast veal)
Makes 250ml (approx)

pan juices
1 × 15ml spoon plain flour
250ml hot water from cooking
   vegetables **or** general household
   stock (p25) made with pork meat
   trimmings and vegetables

salt and pepper (optional)

After roasting a joint, pour off most of the fat from the roasting tin leaving 2 × 15ml spoons of fat and sediment in the tin. Sift the flour over the fat and blend thoroughly with the pan juices. Stir and cook until browned. Gradually add the hot liquid, and stir until boiling. Boil for 3–4 minutes. Season to taste. Strain, and serve very hot.

Vegetable Gravy (brown)
Makes 400ml (approx)

1 medium-sized onion (100g approx)
1 small carrot (25g approx)
½ small turnip (25g approx)
25g butter **or** margarine
1 × 15ml spoon plain flour
500ml water
bouquet garni

1 × 10ml spoon vinegar
1 × 2.5ml spoon sugar
2 cloves
½ blade of mace
salt and pepper
1 × 5ml spoon Worcestershire sauce

Prepare and chop the vegetables. Melt the fat in a saucepan, add the vegetables, and fry for about 10 minutes or until well browned. Stir in the flour. Gradually add the water and stir until boiling. Add the rest of the ingredients except the sauce. Reduce the heat, cover, and simmer gently for 1 hour. Strain. Add the Worcestershire sauce and re-season if required.

Gravy (for roast game)
Makes 400ml (approx)

200g bones, giblets, and game
   trimmings
500ml water
1 bay leaf
a sprig of thyme

1 clove
6 white peppercorns
50g onion for each 500ml water
pan juices
salt and pepper (optional)

Put the bones, giblets, and game trimmings in a saucepan and cover with the water. Heat to boiling point, add the herbs, clove, peppercorns, and onion. Reduce the heat, cover, and simmer gently for about 1 hour. Strain the stock. Pour off the fat from the tin in which the game has been roasted, leaving any sediment. Add the stock and stir until boiling. Boil for 2–3 minutes to reduce the gravy slightly. Skim off any fat. Serve very hot.

MARINADES

Uncooked White Wine Marinade (for fish or white meat)
Makes 325ml (approx)

1 onion	juice of 1 lemon
6–10 parsley stalks	50ml salad oil
1 × 5ml spoon fennel seeds (for fish)	250ml white wine **or** wine mixed with
1 × 5ml spoon dried thyme	water
1 bay leaf	salt and pepper

Skin and slice the onion and chop the parsley stalks. Tie very loosely in butter muslin with the fennel seeds, if used, and the herbs. Put the herb bag into a basin with the fish or meat and pour the liquids over them. Season to taste. Marinate for as long as required, turning over the contents of the dish occasionally.

Uncooked Red Wine Marinade (for red meat or game)
Makes 650ml (approx)

1 medium-sized onion	1 × 2.5ml spoon ground coriander
1 medium-sized carrot	(for game)
1 stick of celery	1 × 2.5ml spoon juniper berries
6–10 parsley stalks	(for game)
1 clove of garlic	salt and pepper
1 × 5ml spoon dried thyme	250ml brown stock (p25)
1 bay leaf	125ml red wine
6–8 black peppercorns	125ml water
1–2 cloves	125ml salad oil

Chop the vegetables and parsley stalks. Skin and crush the garlic. Mix the ingredients in a basin as for the uncooked white wine marinade above.

Cooked Red Wine Marinade (for red meat or game)
Makes 1.25 litres (approx)

1 carrot	1 × 15ml spoon salt
1 onion	250ml red wine
1 litre water	juice of 1 lemon
3 bay leaves	1 × 5ml spoon granulated sugar
12 black peppercorns	6 juniper berries (for game)

Prepare the carrot and onion and slice them thinly. Put in a saucepan with the water, bay leaves, peppercorns, and salt, and cook until the vegetables are tender.

When cooked, add the rest of the ingredients. Put the meat or game in a basin and pour the hot marinade over it. Marinate for as long as required, turning over the meat frequently. For a large piece of meat left to soak for 36 hours or longer, strain off the marinade on the second day, reboil it, and leave to cool completely; then pour it back over the meat. This can be done a second time over a 4–5 day period, if required. The marinade should not be reboiled more than twice.

VEGETABLES, PASTA AND RICE

VEGETABLES

Artichokes – *Globe*

Globe artichokes are available all year round, but are generally at their cheapest in the late summer. Although the artichoke bases, or *fonds* as they are also called, are served as a vegetable side dish, whole artichokes are generally served as a starter either hot or cold.

An artichoke base is the small fleshy part of the artichoke which is left after all the leaves and the furry 'choke' (the undeveloped flower) have been removed. It is sometimes served on its own with melted butter, Hollandaise sauce (p257) or a stuffing; or it can be deep fried. Artichoke hearts, which are the centres of very small, young artichokes, are also available frozen and in cans.

To buy: Allow 1 medium to large artichoke per person or 2 small ones. When fresh, the leaves of the artichoke should be stiff and have a slight bloom on them.

To store: Artichokes should be bought as fresh as possible, but they can be stored for several days in a cool vegetable rack or larder or in the bottom of a refrigerator.

To prepare: Wash the artichokes thoroughly in cold water. Cut the stalk level with the base and trim off any very coarse outer leaves. (The tops of the outer leaves are often also trimmed with scissors which gives a more attractive appearance.) Brush the cut surface of the artichokes with lemon juice to prevent discoloration.

To boil: Put the artichokes into a pan with just enough boiling salted water to cover them; if liked, a bouquet garni can be added to the pan. Cover and cook for 30–45 minutes, depending on the size of the artichokes; cooking is complete when one of the lower leaves can be easily pulled out. Remove from the pan and turn upside down for a minute to drain thoroughly. (The 'choke' in the centre of the artichoke can be removed before serving the artichoke if liked; it is best removed with a teaspoon.) Serve the artichokes either hot with melted butter or Hollandaise sauce (p257), or cold with vinaigrette sauce or mayonnaise.

To steam: Season with salt and cook in the top of a steamer over boiling water for 40–55 minutes. Serve as for boiled artichokes

To eat: Using your fingers, pull off each leaf, dip the soft fleshy end in the melted butter, sauce or mayonnaise and suck both together. When all the leaves have been pulled off in this way, the choke will be revealed if it has not previously been removed. Cut this off and eat the base (*fond*) beneath with a knife and fork.

To deep fry: Use only the artichoke bases. Cut 6–8 artichoke bases into 3–4 pieces according to size. Coat with batter and fry as for Jerusalem artichokes.

Artichokes – *Jerusalem*

These white tubers are not, in fact, artichokes at all; they belong to the sunflower family. They are a winter vegetable and are usually available from October to April. Jerusalem artichokes can be served in a variety of ways and in particular make an excellent soup.

To buy: Allow 150–200g per person. The tubers should be hard and firm. Prime tubers are fairly regular in shape and measure about 10 × 5cm. Try to avoid buying artichokes which are very mis-shapen because they are difficult to peel and consequently cause a lot of wastage.

To store: Artichokes will store for a few weeks in a cool vegetable rack or larder.

To prepare: Wash the artichokes thoroughly, then peel thinly or scrape, and put at once into acidulated water; this helps to keep the vegetables white. Cut into slices or pieces convenient for serving just before cooking.

To boil: Cook in just enough boiling, salted, acidulated water to cover for about 20 minutes or until tender. Drain thoroughly and serve either with melted butter and seasoned with freshly ground black pepper, or with a white, Béchamel or Hollandaise sauce.

To steam: Scrub the artichokes, but leave them whole and unpeeled. Season with salt and cook in the top of a steamer over a pan of boiling water for about 40 minutes. Peel and slice them and serve as for boiled artichokes.

To roast: Parboil the artichokes, as above, for 5 minutes. Drain thoroughly. Put into hot dripping in a roasting tin, or in the tin containing a roast joint. Roll in the fat and cook in a fairly hot oven, 190°C, Gas 5, for about 1 hour, turning 2–3 times during cooking. The colour of artichokes cooked in this way is not very good but the flavour is excellent.

To stew: Heat 50g butter for every 750g–1kg artichokes. Add the peeled and sliced artichokes and season to taste; cover tightly and cook for about 30 minutes, shaking the pan from time to time. Serve in the cooking liquor or add this to a white or Béchamel sauce.

To deep fry: (Method 1) Peel and slice the artichokes very thinly and soak in acidulated water for 10 minutes. Dry thoroughly and fry in deep fat or oil (p10) until golden-brown. Drain on soft kitchen paper and season with salt and pepper.

To deep fry: (Method 2) Peel the artichokes and cut into 1cm slices. Parboil for 5 minutes, drain, and dry thoroughly. For 750g artichokes, make up a double quantity of coating batter (1) (p223). Dip the artichoke slices into the batter and fry in deep fat or oil (p10) until golden-brown, turning once during cooking. Drain thoroughly and serve very hot with fried parsley (p60).

To purée: Mash, sieve or blend steamed or boiled artichokes, and to every 1kg artichokes (weight before cooking) add 2 × 15ml spoons milk and 25– 50g butter. Season to taste with salt and pepper and serve sprinkled with plenty of chopped parsley.

Asparagus

The season for home-grown asparagus is a short one, only May and June, but imported asparagus can be bought from March to July. It is also possible to buy asparagus at other times, but from only a few shops and usually at a premium price. Asparagus can also be bought frozen and canned. It can be served in many ways, but one of the best is to boil it, and then serve it with melted butter or Hollandaise sauce (p257) as a starter.

To buy: Fresh asparagus is generally sold in bundles and is graded according to the thickness of the stem and plumpness of the buds. The heads should be tight and well formed, and the stems should not be dry and woody. Allow 6–8 medium-sized heads per person, 150–200g approx.

To store: Asparagus is best bought on the day or the day before it is needed, although it will keep for a couple of days in the bottom of a refrigerator, if necessary.

To prepare: Cut the woody parts evenly from the base of the stems. Scrape the white part of each stalk with a knife. Tie into bundles and put into cold salted water until ready to cook.

To boil: The asparagus must stand upright in the saucepan because if it lies in the water, the heads will be overcooked and will drop off before the stems are tender. It is therefore important to use a deep saucepan (it is possible to buy special asparagus pans). The water in the saucepan should come to just below the heads of the asparagus. Salt the water and bring to the boil. Stand the asparagus in a jam jar or other heatproof pot if not using an asparagus pan. Put into the water, and cover the pan with a tight-fitting lid. Cook gently until the stems are tender; this will take 14–20 minutes depending on the thickness of the stems. Drain thoroughly and serve either with melted butter, seasoned and lightly flavoured with lemon juice, or with Hollandaise sauce (p257). Asparagus can also be served cold with vinaigrette sauce.

Asparagus Points or Tips

Sometimes, the thinner stalks of asparagus, or *sprue* as they are called, are sold loose. Cut the points and the tender green parts into short pieces. Cook in a small amount of gently boiling salted water for 5–10 minutes according to their size and age. Drain thoroughly, toss in butter, and season with salt and pepper. Serve as a garnish or as a main vegetable, or use as a filling for omelets.

Note It is a mistake to add anything which will impair the delicate flavour of asparagus, but a little chopped shallot and parsley may be fried in the butter before tossing with the asparagus.

Aubergines

Aubergines, also known as *eggplants*, are obtainable all year round, but are generally at their cheapest in late summer. They are used extensively in Mediterranean cooking and, in addition to being served as a vegetable on their own (often stuffed), are an important ingredient in such well-known dishes as Ratatouille (p308) and Moussaka (p146).

To buy: Allow 100–150g per person (an average aubergine weighs about 250g). Fresh aubergines are firm to the touch and have a firm, glossy skin, whereas those that have been in the shop for some time will be slightly soft and have a rather wrinkled skin.

To store: Aubergines can be kept for several days in a cool vegetable rack or larder or in the bottom of a refrigerator.

To prepare: Aubergines are used in a variety of ways, and preparation will vary according to the dish. They can be rather bitter, and in order to avoid this, cut them into 5mm–1cm slices, sprinkle salt over the cut surfaces, and leave in a sieve for 30 minutes to 1 hour, during which time a great deal of liquid will drain off. Rinse under cold water and dry thoroughly. If the aubergines are left whole for cooking, the skin should be scored with a knife in a few places and sprinkled with salt.

Deep-fried Aubergines
4–6 helpings

600g aubergines (approx)
salt
2 eggs

soft white **or** dried white breadcrumbs
fat **or** oil for deep frying

Cut the aubergines into slices about 8mm thick. Lay the slices flat on a large dish, sprinkle with salt, and leave for 30 minutes. Rinse and dry thoroughly. Beat the eggs until liquid. Dip the aubergine slices first in the egg and then in the breadcrumbs. Press the crumbs on firmly. Heat the fat or oil (p10) and fry the aubergine slices, a few at a time, until crisp and brown. Drain thoroughly on soft kitchen paper and serve very hot.

Beans – *Broad*
Broad beans are generally available from April to September, but can also be bought in cans; frozen beans are particularly good. Fresh beans are generally shelled before cooking although very small, young beans can be cooked in their pods.

To buy: Allow 300g per person. The pods should be full and a good green colour with no black markings; do not buy beans whose pods are shrivelled and yellow.

To store: Beans are best eaten on the day or day after they are bought, but they can be kept for a few days in a cool vegetable rack or larder or in the bottom of a refrigerator.

To prepare: Shell the beans unless using very young beans. These are cooked whole in the pod, in which case top and tail the pods and remove any strings as with runner beans. Shelled beans should be covered either with clingfilm or with some of the washed pods to prevent them drying out. If the beans are very mature, they may need to be skinned after cooking as the outer skin can be tough and unpalatable.

To boil: Add the beans to about 2cm boiling salted water, cover, and cook for 15–20 minutes for young beans in their pods or young shelled beans, or for about 30 minutes for more mature beans. If liked, a few leaves of summer savory or a sprig of parsley can also be added to the water. Drain the beans thoroughly and serve either tossed in butter with chopped parsley or savory, or with a white or Hollandaise sauce.

To steam: Season the beans with salt and cook in a steamer over a pan of boiling water for about 25–45 minutes, depending on the age of the beans. Serve as for boiled beans.

Beans – *French*
There are several varieties of French bean. The commonest is the straight bean, usually about 10–15cm long with no strings, which is also known by its French

name, *haricot vert.* Other beans include kidney beans, which are more heavily podded, with the kidney-shaped bean showing through; and pea beans, or bobby beans, which also have a heavier pod but round pea-like beans. Home-grown beans are available in the summer, but imported beans are available all year round. Frozen beans are also available, both whole and sliced.

To buy: Allow 100–150g per person. Choose beans which are a good colour, appear crisp and fresh, and are of an even size.

To store: French beans should be used as fresh as possible, but they can be stored for 2–3 days in a cool, dry place or in the bottom of a refrigerator.

To prepare: Top and tail the beans and remove any strings. Leave the beans whole.

To boil: Cook the beans in the minimum of boiling salted water for 5–10 minutes or until just tender. Drain thoroughly and toss in butter. Season with black pepper, preferably freshly ground, and top with chopped summer savory or tarragon, or a little crushed garlic, if liked.

To steam: Season the beans with salt and cook in a steamer over boiling water for 10–15 minutes or until just tender. Drain and serve as for boiled beans.

Beans – *Runner*

Runner beans are the type most often found in the UK, and are available from mid-July until the end of September. They are much larger than French beans and can vary in length from 15–30cm. Frozen runner beans are also easily obtainable, both whole and ready cut.

To buy: Allow 150g per person. The beans should be a bright green colour and it should be possible to snap them in half. The long beans are just as tender as the smaller ones but, especially early in the season, the pods should not be fat; if so, the bean inside has had time to develop, and the outside of the bean is likely to be tough. Avoid buying beans which are at all discoloured or are limp or misshapen.

To store: Runner beans can be kept for 2–3 days in a cool vegetable rack or larder or in the bottom of a refrigerator.

To prepare: Top and tail the beans and remove any strings, then cut into thin, oblique slices, about 3–5cm long.

To boil: Add the beans to about 2cm boiling salted water, cover, and cook for 5–10 minutes or until just tender. Drain thoroughly. Serve tossed with butter and a little chopped savory and well seasoned with black pepper.

To steam: Season the beans with salt and cook in a steamer over a pan of boiling water for about 10–15 minutes. Drain and serve as for boiled beans.

Beans – *Dried*

Dried beans, like other pulses, have a high protein content and can be used to make excellent, nourishing, and comparatively inexpensive meals. As well as being used as a hot vegetable, or in composite dishes, they are also very good when served cold in salads. There are many varieties of dried beans and a lot of them are known by different names according to the country of origin, but in most cases, these beans are interchangeable.

Aduki or azuki beans: Small round, red beans which are used extensively in Japanese cookery for both sweet and savoury dishes.

Black-eyed peas: Despite their name, these are in fact beans, small and white in colour and similar to a haricot bean, but, at the point of attachment to the pod, they have a small black 'eye'. They are used a great deal in South American cooking.

Borlotti beans: red or mottled pink beans used in salads and stews.

Brown beans: Medium-sized, kidney-shaped beans used extensively in Mediterranean cooking.

Butter beans: Large, white, kidney-shaped beans.

Haricot beans: There are several varieties of small white beans whose shape can vary from almost round to very long and thin, according to the variety and where it is grown.

Flageolet beans: Pale green haricot beans; a very choice variety.

Lima beans: A green American bean.

Pinto beans: These are similar to red kidney beans, but are a dappled pink in colour.

Red kidney beans: Kidney-shaped beans, traditionally used in Chilli Con Carne; deep purplish red and larger than haricot beans.

Soya beans: Creamy white and almost round. They have a very high protein content and are of particular value in a vegetarian diet.

To buy: Allow 40–50g dried beans per person.

To prepare: Soak the beans in cold water for 6–12 hours, preferably changing the water once during this time to prevent them fermenting.

Note Red kidney beans and soya beans must then be boiled for at least 10 minutes before adding them to oven-cooked dishes.

If cooking them in a slow cooker, they should be prepared in the same way before cooking them for at least 4 hours in the slow cooker.

To boil: Drain the beans and put them into a pan. Cover with fresh cold salted water and bring to the boil. Cover the pan and simmer gently for $1\frac{1}{2}$–$3\frac{1}{2}$ hours until tender.

The cooking time of beans varies with the type of bean and its age; freshly dried beans need a much shorter cooking time than older ones. If preferred, the beans can be cooked in stock to improve the flavour; alternatively or in addition, a chopped onion, a peeled clove of garlic, and sprigs of fresh herbs can be added to the water.

To serve: Drain off the excess liquid, toss in a little butter, season to taste, and sprinkle with chopped parsley.

To purée: Puréed beans, especially haricot and soya beans, are used in vegetarian cooking. Drain the beans, reserving the cooking liquor, then sieve or process in an electric blender with a little of the liquor to give a smooth purée. Season to taste and add a little butter and/or top of the milk.

Boston Roast

6 helpings

300g haricot beans
1 onion
1 × 15ml spoon oil
150g Cheddar cheese
2 × 15ml spoons meat or vegetable
   stock or water

1 egg
100g soft white breadcrumbs
salt and pepper
fat for greasing

Prepare and cook the beans. Drain and mash them finely. Skin and chop the onion. Heat the oil in a frying pan and fry the onion until golden-brown. Grate the cheese. Put all the ingredients into a bowl and mix well. Shape the mixture into a loaf, place in a greased baking tin, and cover with buttered greaseproof paper. Bake in a moderate oven, 180°C, Gas 4, for 45 minutes.

Serve with gravy and vegetables.

Cooking time 2½ hours (approx)

Bean Sprouts

Bean sprouts are available in many greengrocers' shops and supermarkets or can be grown at home. They are served both raw in salads and cooked. Excellent canned bean sprouts are also obtainable.

To buy: Allow 50g bean sprouts per person. Choose crisp fresh looking bean sprouts.

To sprout beans: Use young mung beans as old ones will not sprout. Discard any discoloured or decayed beans and soak the rest in plenty of cold water. Drain and place either on damp muslin stretched over a tray or in a jar with muslin or cheese-cloth stretched over it, and placed on its side.

Pour cold water over the beans to keep them moist and tilt the container to let the water run off. Repeat twice daily for 6–8 days until the beans have sprouted and the sprouts are 4–5cm long. Keep the beans well ventilated and at a fairly warm even temperature over 18°C and, if sprouting them in the dark, bring into the light for 24 hours before use.

To store: Bean sprouts do not keep well and should preferably be eaten on the day of purchase; if not, they can be kept for a day in the bottom of a refrigerator.

To prepare: Pick over the bean sprouts, remove any withered or brown stalks and wash in cold water.

To steam: Prepare as above and season with salt. Cook in the top of a steamer over a pan of boiling water for about 5–8 minutes or until just soft. Drain and serve as soon as possible.

To stir-fry (Chinese method): Heat 2 × 15ml spoons olive, corn or soya oil in a pan. Add the bean sprouts and cook, stirring all the time, for about 5 minutes or until they are just cooked, but are still slightly crisp. Serve as soon as possible after cooking.

Beetroot

Small, young beetroots make an excellent hot vegetable as well as being good in salads. Beetroot is available all year round, but the young ones are at their best in mid-summer. At this time of year, the leaves can be used as well as the roots and these should be cooked as for spinach (pp301–2). For salads, the beetroots should be baked, boiled or steamed, or they can be bought already cooked.

To buy: Allow 100–150g per person. Uncooked beetroots should be firm, the skins smooth and unbroken, and in the summer any leaves which have been left on should look fresh. If buying cooked beetroots, avoid buying any with a wrinkled skin which does not look moist because these tend to be hard and 'woody'.

To store: Young beetroots are best cooked and eaten as soon as possible after purchase, but older ones can be stored for several weeks in a cool airy place. Cooked beetroots can be wrapped in cling-film and stored in the bottom of a refrigerator for 2–3 days.

To prepare: Raw beetroot 'bleeds' so it is important that the skin is not damaged in any way. Cut off the leaves and trim the stalks to within 2cm of the top of the root. Wash thoroughly to remove any dirt.

To boil: Cook in a large pan of boiling salted water for 45 minutes–1 hour for small beetroots, or for up to 2 hours for large, older ones. Drain thoroughly if serving hot, or allow to cool in the cooking water. To serve beetroot hot, peel off the skin and either season with pepper and top with melted butter and chopped parsley or mint, or serve with a white, parsley or caper sauce.

To steam: Season the beetroots with salt. Cook in the top of a steamer over a pan of boiling water for $1\frac{1}{2}$ hours if small, or for up to $2\frac{1}{2}$ hours if large. Serve as for boiled beetroot.

To bake: If the skin of the beetroot has been damaged in any way, seal the damaged part with a little flour and water paste. Place each beetroot in a piece of buttered greaseproof paper and enclose it completely. Bake in a moderate oven, 180°C, Gas 4, for 1 hour (for young beetroots) or for up to 2 hours for older beetroots. Serve as for boiled beetroot.

Beetroot is also excellent cooked in a pressure cooker.

Broccoli

There are three different kinds of broccoli, and this often causes confusion.

1) Many of the winter cauliflowers available are, in fact, broccoli, because the broccoli plant is much hardier than the cauliflower; this broccoli should be cooked and treated exactly like cauliflower.

2) Heads of purple sprouting and white sprouting broccoli are found in the shops at the end of the winter and in early spring. After this central head has been removed, the plant gives out leafy side shoots with a small head which are available in the late spring.

3) The third and choicest type of broccoli is the green or Italian *Calabrese* variety. Home-grown *Calabrese* is in the shops from July to December, but if imported it is available at other times of the year. *Calabrese* also freezes well and is fairly widely obtainable in this form.

To buy: Allow 100–200g per person depending on the amount of leaf and consequent wastage. The heads of both *Calabrese* and purple sprouting broccoli should be a good colour. The leaves should appear fresh, and the stalks should be firm and not limp.

To store: Purple sprouting broccoli does not store well and should be kept for only 1–2 days in a cool, dry vegetable rack or larder or in a polythene bag in the bottom of a refrigerator. *Calabrese* will keep for 2–3 days in a polythene bag in a refrigerator, but should be eaten as fresh as possible.

To prepare: Calabrese does not generally require very much preparation since it is usually separated into small heads when bought. Simply trim the stalks to within 7–10cm of the head and wash thoroughly. The whole heads of purple sprouting broccoli should be trimmed and either left whole if they are small, or broken up into smaller heads if large. The leafy side shoots should be trimmed and any tough stalks discarded. It is often neater to tie the shoots in bundles before cooking.

To boil: Cook the broccoli in the minimum of boiling salted water for 10–15 minutes or until just tender. Drain thoroughly and turn into a serving dish. Season with pepper, preferably freshly ground, and either spoon melted butter over it or serve with Hollandaise (p257) or Béarnaise (p252) sauce.

To steam: Season the broccoli with salt. Cook in the top of a steamer over a pan of boiling water for 15–20 minutes. Drain thoroughly and serve as for boiled broccoli.

Brussels Sprouts

Brussels sprouts are in season from August to March, although the flavour is generally better after the first frosts. The best sprouts to buy are the small hard ones, also known as button sprouts, since these have the best flavour and texture and freeze well. Sprout tops, when available, should be cooked as for spinach.

To buy: Allow 150–200g sprouts per person. Choose sprouts which are small, firm, and green and which do not have a great many loose outside leaves. These should also be a good green colour and not yellow or wilted.

To store: Sprouts can be kept for 1–2 days in a cool, dry vegetable rack or larder, or for 2–3 days in a polythene bag in a refrigerator, but they are best eaten as fresh as possible.

To prepare: Cut a slice off the bottom of each sprout and remove the outer leaves. Soak the sprouts for 10 minutes in cold salted water and drain thoroughly. To cook large sprouts more quickly and evenly, cut a cross in the base.

To boil: Add the sprouts, a few at a time, to the minimum of boiling salted water so that the water does not leave the boil. Cook for 7–10 minutes according to size or until they are just tender. Do not overcook. Drain thoroughly and season with black pepper, preferably freshly ground. Toss in melted butter or soured cream or sprinkle with a little crumbled crisply fried or grilled bacon.

The sprouts can also be boiled in stock. Prepare 750g sprouts and cook in 500ml beef stock. Drain, reserving the cooking liquor, and keep warm. Boil the cooking liquor rapidly until it is reduced to a thin glaze. Pour over the sprouts and serve as soon as possible.

To steam: Season the sprouts with salt. Cook in the top of a steamer over a pan of boiling water for about 15 minutes or until the sprouts are just tender. Drain and serve as for boiled sprouts.

To braise: Parboil the sprouts in boiling salted water for 5 minutes. Fry a chopped onion in 25g butter until it is just soft. Pour 500ml stock over it, season, and simmer for 5 minutes. Add the sprouts and simmer for a further 10 minutes.

Cabbage

There are many varieties of cabbage, but the most common are:

1) the Savoy
2) the pale green, hard or 'white' (Dutch) cabbage
3) red cabbage
4) spring and summer cabbage.

To buy: Allow 200g per person. Always choose cabbages that are crisp and a good colour. They should never be limp with yellow edges; this indicates that they were picked some time ago and so probably lack both flavour and valuable vitamin C.

To store: Apart from red and white cabbage, which can be stored for some time, it is inadvisable to store cabbage for more than a few days. It should be kept in a cool, dry vegetable rack or larder. If only part of a cabbage is needed, wrap the rest and store in the bottom of a refrigerator.

To prepare: Remove the coarse outer leaves and trim off the stem. Cut the cabbage into half, cut out the hard part of the stalk, then cut into quarters. Spring and summer cabbage is usually left in quarters, but other varieties are generally finely shredded. This should not be done until shortly before the vegetable is to be cooked because mineral salts and vitamin C are rapidly lost. Wash the cabbage well in cold water; a little salt added to the water helps to draw out any small insects which may be between the leaves. Drain in a colander.

To boil: Add the cabbage, a little at a time, to boiling salted water so that the water does not leave the boil. Cover the pan and cook for 5–12 minutes or until the cabbage is just tender but not soggy; do not overcook. Drain thoroughly and season with a little pepper, preferably freshly ground, and any other flavouring desired; grated nutmeg or a few caraway seeds are popular. Toss in butter just before serving.

To steam: Season the cabbage with salt and cook in the top of a steamer over boiling water for 5–12 minutes or until just tender. Serve as for boiled cabbage.

To braise: Parboil wedges of cabbage for 10 minutes. Drain and dry thoroughly. Fry a chopped onion and carrot in a little lard or dripping. Add a bouquet garni and place the cabbage on top. Pour over just enough beef stock to cover the cabbage and cook for 1 hour. Remove from the pan with a perforated spoon and serve.

Stuffed Cabbage Leaves

4 helpings

8 large cabbage leaves

fat for greasing

Sauce

juice from the canned tomatoes

1 × 15ml spoon concentrated tomato purée

2 × 10ml spoons cornflour

a pinch of sugar

salt and pepper

Stuffing

1 medium-sized onion

1 × 15ml spoon oil

400g minced beef

1 × 400g can tomatoes

1 × 10ml spoon cornflour

1 × 15ml spoon Worcestershire sauce

½ × 2.5ml spoon dried mixed herbs

1 × 15ml spoon chopped parsley

salt and pepper

Remove the thick centre stems from the cabbage leaves, blanch in boiling water for 2 minutes, and drain thoroughly.

To make the stuffing, skin and chop the onion finely. Heat the oil in a pan and fry the onion gently for 5 minutes. Add the beef and cook, stirring until the beef has browned. Drain the tomatoes and reserve the juice. Add the tomatoes to the meat mixture. Blend the cornflour with the Worcestershire sauce and stir into the meat mixture with the herbs and seasoning. Cover and simmer for 20 minutes, stirring occasionally.

Divide the stuffing between the cabbage leaves and roll up, folding over the edges of the leaves to enclose the meat completely. Place in a greased, shallow, ovenproof dish, cover with foil, and bake in a fairly hot oven, 190°C, Gas 5, for 20 minutes.

Prepare the sauce while the cabbage leaves are cooking. Blend the reserved juice from the tomatoes with the tomato purée and make up to 250ml with water. Blend the cornflour with 1 × 15ml spoon of the sauce. Pour the rest of the sauce into a pan and bring to the boil. Pour in the blended cornflour and bring to the boil, stirring all the time, until the sauce has thickened. Add the sugar and season to taste. Pour the sauce over the cabbage leaves just before serving.

Cooking time 1 hour (approx)

Red Cabbage

Red cabbage can be cooked as for ordinary green cabbage but is more usually braised gently for about 1½ hours until very tender.

Carrots

Carrots are a most useful vegetable since they are used extensively as a flavouring for all kinds of soups, casseroles, and sauces. They are available throughout the year, although young carrots, which have the best flavour for serving as a vegetable, are usually only obtainable during the late spring and summer. Frozen young carrots are also available, and both young and old carrots can be bought in cans.

To buy: Allow 100–150g per person. The tops of young carrots should appear fresh and green, and the carrots should be of an even size. If the head of the carrot is green, however, the carrot is insufficiently mature. Older carrots should be firm and smooth and not broken or pitted. Care should be taken when buying prepacked carrots because they are sometimes not in prime condition and can be slimy.

To store: For the maximum flavour, young carrots should be eaten as fresh as possible, preferably on the day they are bought, although they can be stored for 1–2 days in a cool, dry vegetable rack or larder. Older carrots can be kept for several weeks, provided they are in a cool, dry place.

To prepare: Young carrots need only to be topped and tailed and scrubbed with a stiff brush. More mature carrots need to be either scraped with a knife or thinly peeled, depending on age. Young carrots should be left whole, but older carrots should be sliced and cut into strips or fancy shapes.

To boil (conservation method): Carrots should be cooked in the minimum of water to give the best flavour and to preserve all the vitamins. For 600g carrots, melt 25g butter or margarine in a heavy-based pan. Add the carrots and cook very gently for 10 minutes, shaking the pan frequently so that the carrots do not stick to the bottom. Pour over approximately 100ml boiling salted water, cover the pan, and cook the carrots gently for a further 10–15 minutes depending on their age. Serve the carrots with the cooking liquor and sprinkle them liberally with chopped parsley, mint, chervil or marjoram, and a little lemon juice, if liked. The carrots can also be served with a parsley sauce or 1–2 × 15ml spoons cream can be added to the carrots in the pan just before serving.

To steam: Young carrots are particularly good steamed. Season with salt and cook in the top of a steamer over boiling water for 10–30 minutes, depending on the age of the carrots. Serve as for boiled carrots.

To deep fry: This is suitable for old carrots. Parboil the carrots for 5 minutes, drain, and dry thoroughly. Coat with batter and fry as for Jerusalem artichokes.

To purée: Older carrots make a good purée and can be mixed with an equal quantity of puréed potatoes. Cook the carrots as above and sieve, mash or process in an electric blender together with the cooking liquor. Add 25g butter, season with salt and pepper, preferably freshly ground, and add a little cream or top of the milk, if liked, Sprinkle with chopped parsley before serving, or add a little grated orange rind for a more unusual flavour.

Cauliflower

Cauliflower is one of our most useful green vegetables because it is available throughout the year. Served with a cheese sauce, cauliflower is a popular and substantial supper dish, but it is also excellent as a side vegetable or when used for soup. Some supermarkets also sell prepacked cauliflower florets, and these can be a good buy because there is no waste. Frozen cauliflower florets are also available.

To buy: Allow 100g per person if buying florets, but 150g per person if buying a whole cauliflower. The head or curds of the cauliflower should be a good creamy white and should have no marks or blemishes. The leaves round the cauliflower should be a good green colour and should not appear yellow or wilted.

To store: Cauliflower will keep for 2–3 days in a cool, dry vegetable rack or larder, or in a refrigerator. To save space in a refrigerator it is usually easier to divide the head into florets first.

To prepare: Fresh florets should simply be washed in cold salted water. Whole cauliflower should be trimmed of most of the outside leaves and the stalk cut so that the cauliflower will stand upright. To ensure the stalk cooks quickly, either make a cross in the base, or cut out the first 2cm of the stalk with an apple corer. Soak the whole cauliflower for 10 minutes in salted water before cooking to draw out any insects.

To boil: Florets should be cooked in the minimum of boiling salted water for 8–10 minutes, or until just tender; they should then be drained. Put a whole cauliflower head, stalk down, in 2cm boiling salted water in a large pan, season with salt, and bring back to the boil. Cover, and cook over fairly high heat for about 15 minutes or until tender. Cauliflower should never be overcooked. Drain thoroughly and place on a serving dish with the head uppermost. Season with pepper, preferably freshly ground black pepper, and spoon over some melted butter and chopped chives or parsley; alternatively, sprinkle with crumbled, fried or grilled bacon or chopped and lightly fried almonds; or pour a white or light cream sauce over the cauliflower.

To steam: Steaming is particularly good for cauliflower florets. Season with salt and cook in the top of a steamer over boiling water for 15 minutes for florets, or for up to 40 minutes for a large, whole head. Do not overcook. Drain thoroughly and serve as for boiled cauliflower.

To deep fry: Divide the cauliflower into florets and parboil for about 8 minutes. Drain and dry thoroughly. For a medium-sized cauliflower or 600g florets, make up a double quantity of coating batter (1) (p223) and coat and fry as for Jerusalem artichokes. Serve deep-fried cauliflower with Tartare sauce (p247).

Cauliflower Cheese
4 helpings

1 medium-sized firm cauliflower	a pinch of dry mustard
2 × 15ml spoons butter **or** margarine	a pinch of Cayenne pepper
4 × 15ml spoons flour	salt and pepper
200ml milk	25g fine dry white breadcrumbs
125g grated Cheddar cheese	

Prepare the cauliflower. Put the head in a saucepan containing enough boiling salted water to half-cover it. Cover the pan, and cook gently for 20–30 minutes until tender. Drain well, reserving 175ml of the cooking water. Break the head carefully into sections, and place in a warmed ovenproof dish. Keep warm under greased greaseproof paper.

Melt the fat in a medium-sized pan, stir in the flour, and cook for 2–3 minutes, stirring all the time, without letting the flour colour. Mix together the milk and reserved cooking water, and gradually add to the pan, stirring all the time to prevent lumps forming. Bring the sauce to the boil, lower the heat, and simmer until thickened. Remove from the heat, and stir in 100g of the cheese, with the mustard and Cayenne pepper. Season to taste. Stir until the cheese is fully melted, then pour the sauce over the cauliflower. Mix the remaining cheese with the breadcrumbs, and sprinkle them on top. Place in a hot oven, 220°C, Gas 7, for 7–10 minutes, to brown the top. Serve at once.

Note A mixture of 2 × 15ml spoons grated Cheddar cheese and 1 × 15ml spoon grated Parmesan cheese can be used for sprinkling, if liked, or 1–2 crumbled, crisply fried rashers of streaky bacon.

Celeriac

This large swede-like root has a flavour very like that of celery and can be used in the same way for flavouring soups, stews, and casseroles. It can also be used raw, shredded, in salads. For a more delicate flavour it can be blanched in acidulated water for 2 minutes before shredding. Celeriac is available from October to April.

To buy: Allow 150g celeriac per person. The root should be firm to the touch and not caked in too much mud and earth.

To store: Celeriac, like other root vegetables, will keep well for several weeks in a cool, dry place.

To prepare: Celeriac can be cooked either whole or cut into slices 1cm thick. Unfortunately, celeriac is not easy to peel because it is rather knobbly. Wash it first in cold water to remove all the mud and earth. If it is to be cooked in slices, slice and then peel it; if it is to be cooked whole, peel thickly with a small sharp knife. As soon as the celeriac has been peeled, it should be put into acidulated water to preserve the colour.

To boil: Cook the whole or sliced celeriac in boiling, salted, acidulated water for 25–30 minutes for sliced celeriac, or for 45 minutes–1 hour for whole celeriac. Drain thoroughly, season with pepper, preferably freshly ground, and either spoon melted butter and/or a squeeze of lemon juice over it, or serve with a white, cheese or Hollandaise sauce.

To steam: Season the celeriac with salt and toss in lemon juice to preserve the colour. Cook in the top of a steamer over boiling water for 30–35 minutes if sliced or for 1–1½ hours if whole.

To bake: Cut the celeriac root in half lengthways without peeling it. Heat 5mm depth of bacon fat or dripping in a roasting tin. Put the celeriac into the fat, cut side down, and bake in a moderate oven, 180°C, Gas 4, for 1–1½ hours. The celeriac is cooked when a skewer pierces it easily. Turn it cut side up for serving, and cut in wedges as with melon.

To shallow fry: Cut the celeriac into slices and parboil for 10 minutes. Drain and dry thoroughly. Fry in some butter or margarine until they are golden-brown. Drain thoroughly, sprinkle with chopped parsley, and serve as soon as possible.

To deep fry: Cut the celeriac into slices and parboil for 10 minutes. Drain and dry thoroughly. Coat in batter and fry as for Jerusalem artichokes.

To purée: Boil or steam the celeriac, drain, and then sieve, mash or process in an electric blender. Because it has a very strong flavour, celeriac purée is best mixed with an equal quantity of potato purée. Season with salt and pepper and add a good knob of butter and a little cream or top of the milk.

Celery

Celery is generally served braised as a side vegetable, but is also used extensively as a flavouring in soups, stews, and casseroles (for which the tough outer stalks can be used), as well as raw in salads, or with cheese. Celery is available all year round, although the best home-grown celery comes in November after the first frosts. Celery hearts (the tender inner part of the vegetable), are also available in cans.

To buy: Allow 1 small head per person if braising or half a head if boiling, steaming or frying. The celery should be crisp and white, without too many thick outer stalks.

To store: Celery can be kept for 2–3 days in a cool, dry vegetable rack but is best separated into stalks and stood in a jug of cold water to keep it crisp and fresh. Outer celery stalks, which you may wish to reserve for flavouring, can be kept for several days in a polythene bag in a refrigerator until they are required.

To prepare: Remove the outer stalks of the celery and put on one side to use as flavouring. Either separate the celery into stalks or leave the head whole. Wash or wipe the celery if required. Leave the stalks whole, or cut in half lengthways if very wide. Cut the whole head or the stalks crossways into halves or quarters.

To boil: Cut the celery stalks into 2cm pieces and cook in the minimum of boiling salted water for 15–20 minutes or until just tender. Drain, season with pepper, preferably freshly ground, and spoon over some melted butter or a white or cheese sauce.

To steam: Cut the celery stalks into 2cm pieces and season with salt. Cook in the top of a steamer over boiling water for 20–30 minutes until tender. Drain and serve as for boiled celery.

To deep fry: Cut the celery into 2cm pieces and parboil for 5 minutes. Drain thoroughly. Coat in batter and fry as for Jerusalem artichokes.

To braise: Trim the celery, but leave it whole. For 4 small heads of celery make a mirepoix (p307) and add enough stock to half-cover the vegetables. Bring to the boil and place the celery on top. Baste some of the stock over the celery. Cover the pan with a piece of greaseproof paper or foil and then with the lid. Cook over gentle heat for 1½ hours or until the celery is very tender, basting with the stock from time to time. Remove the celery from the pan with a perforated spoon and place in a serving dish. Drain the cooking liquor into a small pan and add 1 × 5ml spoon meat glaze (p59), if available. Boil the liquor rapidly until it is reduced to a thin glaze, and then pour it over the celery. The mirepoix can be served as a separate vegetable dish, sprinkled with chopped parsley.

Chicory

People sometimes confuse chicory with endive because its French name is *endive* Chicory is, however, a clump of fleshy white leaves with yellow tips, widely used raw in salads. It is also served as a side vegetable and is available from September to May.

To buy: Allow 1 large or 2 small heads per person (75–100g approx). Buy chicory which looks fresh and has no withered stems. The ends should be yellow, not green; green ends tend to be very bitter.

To store: Chicory can be kept for 2–3 days in a cool, dry vegetable rack or larder, or for up to a week in a polythene bag in the bottom of a refrigerator.

To prepare: Cut a slice off the base and remove a few outer leaves. Wash thoroughly in cold water. To reduce the bitterness, first blanch the chicory for 5 minutes in boiling water, and then drain and cook as required. Do not leave chicory standing once it has been cut because it tends to discolour.

To boil: Blanch the chicory as above. Cook in a very little boiling salted water for

15–20 minutes or until just tender. Drain thoroughly and season with pepper. Spoon a little melted butter over it or serve with a white or cheese sauce.

To braise: Blanch the chicory as above. Cook as for braised celery.

Courgettes

Courgettes, or *zucchini* as they are also called, are small vegetable marrows, produced by using special strains of seed. They are available all year round, but are generally at their cheapest and best from June to September. Besides being served as a side vegetable, they are also excellent stuffed and served hot or cold as a main course or starter.

To buy: Allow 100–150g per person. Courgettes vary considerably in size from almost finger thickness and length, to 4–5cm in diameter and 25cm long. If they are too thick, however, the flavour will not be as good. The courgettes should be a good green colour, firm to the touch, and not limp.

To store: Courgettes can be kept for several days in a cool, dry vegetable rack or larder.

To prepare: Very small courgettes can be cooked whole. Simply trim off each end, and wash in cold water. Larger courgettes should be trimmed at either end and cut into 1–2cm slices; or they can be trimmed, and then sliced after cooking. To remove some of the excess liquid from slightly older courgettes, especially if frying, place them in a colander, sprinkle with salt, and leave for 30 minutes. Drain and dry thoroughly.

To boil: Cook the courgettes in the minimum of boiling salted water for about 10 minutes or until just tender. Drain thoroughly, season with pepper, and spoon melted butter and some chopped parsley, thyme or tarragon over them. Courgettes can also be served with a white, parsley, or cheese sauce or topped with crisply fried or grilled and roughly chopped or crumbled bacon.

To steam: Courgettes are generally best left whole for steaming. Season with salt and cook in the top of a steamer over a pan of boiling water for 10–20 minutes, depending on the size of the courgettes, until they are just tender. Drain and cut into slices, if large. Serve as for boiled courgettes.

To bake: Leave the courgettes whole and parboil for 5 minutes in boiling salted water. Drain thoroughly. For 500g courgettes, melt 50g butter in an ovenproof dish. Add the courgettes, roll in the butter and season with salt and pepper. Bake for 25 minutes in a fairly hot oven, 190°C, Gas 5.

To shallow fry: Cut the courgettes into slices. For 500g courgettes, melt 50g butter in a frying pan and fry a little chopped onion, if liked, until golden. Add the sliced courgettes and fry until golden-brown, turning frequently. Drain and serve topped with chopped tarragon, thyme or parsley.

To deep fry: Cut the courgettes into slices and parboil for 5 minutes. Drain and dry thoroughly. Coat in batter and fry as for Jerusalem artichokes.

To stew: Cut the courgettes into slices. For 500g courgettes, melt 50g butter in a pan, add the sliced courgettes, and season. Cover the pan and cook over gentle heat for 10–15 minutes, shaking the pan frequently to prevent the courgettes sticking to the bottom. Sprinkle with chopped herbs before serving in the cooking liquor.

Cucumber

Cucumbers are usually eaten raw in salads or pickled, but they are extremely useful as a side vegetable, and this is a particularly good way of using the outdoor or ridge cucumbers. Cucumbers should not be boiled because they contain a very high percentage of water; they should be either steamed or fried.

To buy: Allow 150–200g per person, or one-third of a large cucumber. Make sure the cucumbers are firm and the skin is not tough and wrinkled.

To store: Cucumbers keep for several days in a cool vegetable rack or larder or in a refrigerator.

To prepare: Hot-house cucumbers can be peeled or not, according to taste, but the skin contains much of the flavour and minute amounts of the substances which help the body to digest the cucumber flesh. Outdoor cucumbers generally have a rather tough skin, and these should be peeled. Slice the cucumber or leave whole.

To steam: Either cut the cucumber into slices 5cm thick or leave whole. Season and place in the top of a steamer over a pan of boiling water for 10 minutes, if sliced, or for up to 20 minutes, if whole. Drain thoroughly and cut into slices if the cucumber has been left whole. Season with pepper, preferably freshly ground, and serve topped with melted butter and chopped herbs (dill, tarragon, parsley, mint), with a plain white or cheese sauce with chopped tarragon, dill or celery seed added, or with Hollandaise sauce (p257).

To bake: Cut the cucumbers into 5cm pieces. Put in an ovenproof dish and cover. Dot the cucumber with butter and sprinkle with a few chopped herbs, if liked. Bake in a fairly hot oven, 190°C, Gas 5, for 30 minutes.

To fry: Cut the cucumbers into slices 2cm thick. Steam as above for 5 minutes, drain, and dry thoroughly. Dredge the cucumber slices lightly with flour and fry them in butter or margarine until golden-brown, turning frequently. Drain thoroughly, season with salt and pepper, and serve at once.

Endive

Endive, pronounced in the English way, should not be confused with chicory which is known in France as *endive*. Endive is a green vegetable, resembling a curly lettuce, which is generally used in winter salads. It is in season from November to March.

To buy: Allow 1 small or half a large endive per person. Choose endive with a good yellow heart and not too many discoloured, tough outer leaves.

To store: Endive is best stored for 2–3 days in a polythene bag in the bottom of a refrigerator.

To prepare: Cut off the stumps and discard any tough, discoloured outer leaves. The very centre of the endive can be removed and served as a salad. Wash the endive thoroughly in plenty of cold water to remove any dirt, grit, and sand. Because endive tends to be bitter, blanch it for 10 minutes in boiling water and drain thoroughly.

To braise: Blanch the endive as above. Cook as for braised celery.

Fennel

The bulbous Florence fennel can be used raw in salads or braised; it has a slight aniseed flavour. The part eaten is the swollen stem base, although the leaves can be used in soups and make an attractive feathery garnish for salads.

To buy: Allow 1 small bulb (about 150g) per person. Choose clean white fennel on which any leaf tips are still fresh and green.

To store: Fennel can be stored for 2–3 days in a cool, dry vegetable rack or larder or in the bottom of a refrigerator.

To prepare: Remove the coarse outer sheaths and trim the stalks.

To deep fry: Parboil the fennel for 10 minutes. Drain, dry thoroughly, and cut into slices. Dip the slices in batter and fry as for Jerusalem artichokes. Drain thoroughly and serve with lemon juice.

To braise: Parboil the fennel in boiling salted water for 5 minutes. Drain thoroughly and cook as for braised celery.

Kohlrabi

Kohlrabi, although a root, is really a swollen-stemmed cabbage. It has a flavour between that of a turnip and a swede, and is in season from July to April.

To buy: Allow 150g per person. Choose kohlrabi which is a good purple colour with a smooth skin. Avoid large kohlrabi because it has a coarse flavour, and reject any on which the skin is shrivelled or the leaves are withered.

To store: Kohlrabi does not store well and should be used as soon as possible after buying or picking.

To prepare: Kohlrabi can either be thinly peeled and sliced or diced before cooking, or it can simply be washed, trimmed, and cooked in the skin, which preserves the maximum flavour.

To boil: Cook in boiling salted water for 30 minutes–1 hour, depending on size. Drain and peel if cooked in the skin. Serve kohlrabi either seasoned with pepper, preferably freshly ground, and with melted butter, or with a cream or Hollandaise sauce.

To steam: Season with salt and cook in the top of a steamer over a pan of boiling water for 45 minutes–1½ hours depending on size. Drain and serve as for boiled kohlrabi.

To braise: Parboil the kohlrabi for 5 minutes. Drain, peel, and cut into quarters. Cook as for braised celery.

Leeks

Leeks are in season from August to May and as well as being served as a vegetable are also used extensively to flavour soups and casseroles. They can also be served cooked and cold, or blanched and raw in salads.

To buy: Allow 150–200g leeks per person. Choose leeks that are of an even size with fresh-looking green tips and a firm white stem.

To store: Leeks can be kept for 2–3 days in a cool, dry vegetable rack or larder.

To prepare: Leeks need to be cleaned thoroughly because dirt and grit gets between the leaves. First, trim off the leaves, leaving only about 5cm of the green stem. Trim the roots and remove the outer leaves. Push the point of the knife through each leek about 5cm from the top and cut through to the top. Do this a second time, then peel back the leaves and wash the leeks thoroughly under running cold water to remove every speck of dirt. Leeks can also be cut into slices, in which case the vertical cuts are omitted; after slicing, wash thoroughly under running cold water.

To boil: Boiled leeks are apt to be watery so they must be drained thoroughly. Leave the leeks whole or cut into 2cm slices. Cook in the very minimum of boiling salted water for 10 minutes if sliced, or 20 minutes if whole. Drain thoroughly, turn into a serving dish, and season with pepper. Serve with melted butter or with a cheese or white sauce.

To steam: Leave the leeks whole or cut into slices. Season with salt and place in a steamer over a pan of boiling water for 15 minutes if sliced, or for 30 minutes if whole. Drain and serve as for boiled leeks.

To deep fry: Cut the leeks into 2cm slices. Parboil for 5 minutes. Drain and dry thoroughly. Coat in batter and fry as for Jerusalem artichokes.

To stew: Cut the leeks into slices. For every 750g leeks, melt 50g butter in a pan. Add the leeks and 1 × 15ml spoon lemon juice, salt, and pepper. Cover the pan and cook the leeks very gently, shaking the pan from time to time, for about 30 minutes or until the leeks are very tender. Serve in the cooking liquor. If liked, 3–4 chopped rashers of bacon can also be cooked with the leeks.

To braise: Leave the leeks whole. Parboil for 5 minutes. Drain and cook as for braised celery.

Baked Leek Casserole
4 helpings

8 large leeks	a few drops Worcestershire sauce
1 small onion	a few drops lemon juice
75g butter **or** margarine	a pinch of sugar
tomato juice	salt and pepper

Prepare the leeks and keep them whole. Skin the onion and chop it finely. Melt 50g of the fat and fry the leeks and onion until the leeks are just gilded and the onion is transparent. Transfer to an ovenproof casserole which will hold the leeks in 2 layers. Pour enough tomato juice into the casserole to half-cover the leeks. Stir in the Worcestershire sauce, lemon juice, and sugar. Season well. Dot with the rest of the fat. Cover the casserole securely, and bake in a fairly hot oven, 190°C, Gas 5, for 1 hour. Serve with the cooking liquor.

Note This recipe can also be used for small heads of celery.

Lentils

There are several kinds of lentils; the most common are pink or red; these form a purée as soon as they are cooked. If whole lentils are required, the green or brown variety must be used. The best (and most expensive) lentils are the black *lentilles de Puy* which come from the Auvergne in France.

Lentils are excellent served cold in salads.

To buy: Allow 50g lentils per person.

To prepare: Lentils do not need long soaking like peas and beans, but they can profitably be soaked for 1–2 hours before cooking.

To boil: Put the lentils into a pan and cover with cold water or stock. A small skinned onion, a few parsley stalks or a bouquet garni, a ham bone or a few bacon rinds can be added to give extra flavour. Bring the water to the boil and simmer gently for about 1 hour or until the lentils are quite tender. Drain and remove any herbs and flavouring. Re-season if required, and serve hot. If using the pink lentils, drain and purée them before serving.

Spiced Lentils
4–6 helpings

50g red lentils
1 litre water
1 × 2.5ml spoon sea salt **or** 1 × 5ml spoon table salt
1 onion
1 × 5ml spoon turmeric
1 × 5ml spoon crushed ginger root **or** ground ginger

3 tomatoes
2 whole cardamoms
3 × 15ml spoons cooking oil
1 × 5ml spoon crushed garlic
1 × 5ml spoon ground coriander
a pinch of chilli powder

Garnish
chopped fresh coriander leaves

finely chopped **or** grated onion

Put the lentils into a large pan and cover with the water and salt. Bring to the boil, reduce the heat, and simmer for 30–45 minutes until tender. Drain and put to one side.

Meanwhile, skin and chop the onion, and mix with the turmeric and ginger. Chop the tomatoes, and crush the cardamoms in a pestle and mortar, or grind in a coffee or nut mill. Heat the oil in a large, deep frying pan, add the onion, ginger, and turmeric, and fry gently until soft and lightly browned. Add the tomatoes and all the remaining ingredients, and fry for 3–4 minutes, stirring all the time. Remove from the heat.

Add the lentils to the mixture in the pan, and mix thoroughly to coat them with oil. Replace over moderate heat, and cook until well heated through and quite mushy. Serve very hot, sprinkled with the coriander leaves and onion.

Note Although hot and spicy, this dish is not as hot as a curry. It can be served as an accompaniment to any pasta, pulse or plainly cooked root vegetable dish, or with a green vegetable salad as a main-course dish.

Lettuce

Although generally used raw as a salad ingredient, lettuces can also be served as a cooked vegetable, provided they are well-hearted or have crisp outer leaves. Cos lettuce is particularly good.

To buy: Choose fresh, green lettuces and allow 1 small lettuce per person. Alternatively, use the outside leaves of 2 lettuces and reserve the hearts for salads.

To store: Lettuces can be kept for 1–2 days in a cool, dry vegetable rack or larder or in a polythene bag in a refrigerator.

To prepare: Remove the very outside leaves of the lettuce. Trim off the root and wash the lettuce well in plenty of cold water to remove all the dirt and sand.

To stew: For 4 lettuces, melt 50g butter or margarine in a wide pan. Add the lettuces and season with salt. Cover the pan and stew for about 30 minutes or until the lettuces are very tender. Season to taste with salt and pepper before serving.

To braise: Make each lettuce into a neat bundle by tying the loose leaf tops together with fine string. Blanch the bundles for 5 minutes in boiling salted water and drain thoroughly. Cook as for braised celery.

Mushrooms

Cultivated mushrooms are available throughout the year. There are three main types which are all grown from the same spore, the only difference being their age. The youngest mushrooms are the small round button ones in which the underneath of the mushroom touches the stalks; cup mushrooms are slightly larger and flatter but still have a lip on the underside; the larger, flat mushrooms are the oldest and have the strongest flavour. For pale sauces, it is always best to use button or cup mushrooms because the black underside of flat mushrooms will discolour a sauce.

As for wild mushrooms, field mushrooms are similar to cultivated mushrooms. They can be cooked in all the same ways and are particularly good grilled or stuffed.

Although the whole of any mushroom can be used, the stalks are sometimes removed for appearance's sake or for easier cooking (eg stuffed mushrooms) and are used separately for flavouring sauces and casseroles.

Button mushrooms are also available in cans and make a very useful standby. Button and cup mushrooms can be bought frozen.

To buy: Allow 50–75g per person. Mushrooms should look fresh and moist, and the tops should be creamy white.

To store: Mushrooms should be eaten on the day of purchase, but they can be kept for a day in the bottom of a refrigerator.

To prepare: Cultivated mushrooms should not be peeled. Simply wipe with a damp cloth, or wash if they are very dirty, and trim a slice off the stalk ends. Either leave the mushrooms whole or cut them into slices, halves or quarters, depending on their size and how you wish to serve them.

To boil: Mushrooms are not generally boiled because their flavour is better when fried, grilled or baked, but this is a good method for slimmers. Cook the mushrooms in the minimum of boiling salted water, with a good squeeze of lemon juice, for about 5 minutes. Drain thoroughly and serve seasoned with black pepper, preferably freshly ground, and sprinkled with chopped parsley or chives.

To bake: Place the mushrooms in a greased ovenproof dish and dot with butter or margarine. Season with salt and pepper and a little powdered mace, grated nutmeg or chopped lemon thyme. Cover, and bake in a fairly hot oven, 190°C, Gas 5, for 25–30 minutes. Serve the mushrooms either in the dish in which they were cooked, or transfer them to a serving dish together with all the juices.

To grill: Grilling is suitable for flat or large cup mushrooms. Remove the stalks; these can be put into the grill pan under the rack and will cook in the juices from the caps. Brush both surfaces of the mushrooms with oil or dot with butter or margarine; season with salt and pepper. Place the mushrooms on the rack of the grill pan and cook under a moderate grill for about 5 minutes or until the mushrooms are very tender, turning once, and basting with fat several times to prevent them drying out. Serve with the juices collected in the grill pan.

To fry: For every 100g mushrooms, heat 25g butter, margarine or lard, or 2 × 15ml spoons oil in a frying pan. Fry the mushrooms for about 5 minutes or until they are very tender. Season with salt and black pepper, preferably freshly ground. Serve together with the cooking liquid, and sprinkle with chopped parsley, chives or lemon thyme. A squeeze of lemon juice added to the pan will also improve the flavour.

To deep fry: Whole button mushrooms are excellent deep-fried. Using 125g mushrooms, coat in batter, and fry as for Jerusalem artichokes.

Onions

Onions are used mostly as a flavouring for sauces, soups, stews, casseroles, and stuffings, although they make an excellent vegetable dish and can be cooked in various ways. Small pickling onions, or button onions as they are also called, are available from July to October, while main-crop onions grown in the UK are in season from September to March. Imported onions are available during the summer, and Spanish onions are generally available throughout the year. These are large onions with a mild flavour which originally came from Spain, although they are now grown in many other parts of the world. Spring onions, which are a mild small onion used mainly in salads, are also available throughout the year, although they are much scarcer in winter.

To buy: When serving as a side vegetable, allow 1 large or 2 medium-sized onions (150–200g) per person. Choose onions which are firm with a smooth skin. They should not have wrinkled skins or be at all soft since this generally indicates that they are bad inside. Avoid buying onions which have already begun to sprout.

To store: Onions keep well for several months in a cool, dry vegetable rack or larder, especially in winter. If you have sufficient storage space, it can be quite economical to buy a sack of onions in the autumn, when they are generally cheaper, so that some are always to hand.

To prepare: For certain methods of cooking, onions are cooked in their skins, but they are generally skinned and either left whole, chopped, or cut into rings.

To chop an onion, first cut it in half lengthways. Lay the flat surface on a chopping board and make 3 or 4 horizontal cuts, stopping about 1cm from the root. Holding the root end, make about 6 cuts at right angles to the root, but stopping 1cm short, then cut the onion across into small pieces. To prevent onions making you cry while preparing them, either skin the onions under running cold water or skin them under water, and then place them in cold water straight away.

To boil: Skin the onions but leave them whole. If you do not like a very strong flavour, blanch the onions first by putting them into a pan of cold water. Bring to the boil, boil for 1 minute, and then drain. Cook the onions in the minimum of boiling salted water for 20–25 minutes for button onions, for 45–50 minutes for medium-sized onions, and for up to $1\frac{1}{4}$ hours for large onions. Drain the onions thoroughly and serve topped with melted butter or with a white sauce made from half milk and half stock from cooking the onions. Onions can also be boiled in their skins, which colours the cooking water pale pink and helps to preserve the nutritional value of the onion.

To bake (Method 1): Skin medium-sized or large onions, but leave them whole. Parboil in boiling salted water for 20 minutes. Drain thoroughly. Place in a shallow, greased ovenproof dish. Season with salt and pepper and dot with butter. Pour in enough milk to come half-way up the onions. Cover and bake in a moderate oven,

180°C, Gas 4, for 45 minutes–1 hour or until the onions are very tender. Serve with the cooking liquor, which can be thickened with a little cornflour or arrowroot, if liked.

To bake (Method 2): Top and tail medium-sized or large onions, but leave the skins on. Parboil, if very large, for 20 minutes; drain and dry thoroughly. Wrap each onion in a piece of well-buttered greaseproof paper and place in an ovenproof dish. Bake in a moderate oven, 180°C, Gas 4, for 1–1¼ hours. Peel the onions before serving with butter and grated nutmeg.

To bake (Method 3): Place unpeeled medium-sized to large onions on a baking tray and bake in a fairly hot oven, 200°C, Gas 6, for 1½ hours or until tender. Remove from the oven and carefully skin. Place in a serving dish and dot with butter, salt, pepper, and a little grated nutmeg, if liked.

To shallow fry: Skin the onions and cut into rings. For every 400g onions, melt 25g butter, margarine or lard, or heat 2 × 15ml spoons oil in a pan. Fry the onions gently for about 30 minutes, turning them frequently until they are golden-brown. Season well, drain, and serve hot. A little chopped thyme or sage or a few caraway seeds can also be fried with the onions.

To deep fry: Skin the onions, slice into rings, and separate. Dip the onion rings in a little milk and then toss in seasoned flour. Fry the onion rings in deep oil or fat (p10) until they are golden-brown and crisp. Drain on soft kitchen paper and serve hot. Onion rings can also be dipped in batter and fried as for Jerusalem artichokes.

To stew: Skin and blanch the onions as above. Put into a pan just large enough to hold them all upright. For 6 large onions, pour over 500ml brown stock (p25) and add a bouquet garni. Cover and simmer gently for 1½ hours. Re-season if required, and serve the onions with the cooking liquor.

To braise: Skin the onions but leave them whole. Parboil for 5 minutes. Drain thoroughly. Cook as for braised celery.

Parsnips

Parsnips are in season from September to April, but are generally better when there has been a slight frost on the ground. They are an extremely useful winter vegetable and are excellent roasted with potatoes around a joint, or puréed and served on their own.

To buy: Allow 150g parsnips per person. Choose parsnips that are firm to the touch; the skins should not appear shrivelled and wrinkled.

To store: Parsnips can be stored for several days in a cool larder or vegetable rack, but are better eaten as soon as possible after purchase.

To prepare: Peel and trim the parsnips and either cut into slices, or cut into quarters lengthways according to the method of cooking. Remove any hard core from the quarters.

To boil: Like carrots, parsnips should be cooked in the minimum of water to give the best flavour and to preserve all the vitamins. For 600g parsnips, melt 25g butter or margarine in a heavy-based pan. Add the thinly sliced parsnips and cook very gently for 10 minutes, shaking the pan frequently so that they do not stick to the bottom. Pour approximately 100ml boiling salted water over them, cover the pan, and cook the parsnips for a further 15–20 minutes or until they are very tender.

Serve with the cooking liquor and sprinkle liberally with chopped parsley or chopped lemon thyme.

To steam: Steam only young parsnips. Cut into quarters, season with salt, and steam in the top of a double saucepan over a pan of boiling water for 35 minutes or until very tender. Drain and season with black pepper, preferably freshly ground, spoon melted butter over them, and sprinkle with chopped parsley.

To roast: Cut the parsnips into quarters lengthways. Parboil in boiling salted water for 10 minutes. Drain and dry thoroughly. Heat a little dripping in a roasting tin. Add the parsnips and roll in the hot dripping or put into the dripping in a pan around a roast joint. Roast in a fairly hot oven, 190°–200°C, Gas 5–6, for 45 minutes–1 hour or until tender and golden-brown.

To deep fry (Method 1): Cut the parsnips into thin slices. Parboil for 10 minutes and drain thoroughly. Coat in batter and fry as for Jerusalem artichokes.

To deep fry (Method 2): Cut the parsnips into paper-thin slices. Dry thoroughly and fry in deep fat as for game chips (p10).

To purée: Parsnips make an excellent purée, either on their own or mixed with carrots or mashed potato. Boil or steam the parsnips as above and sieve, mash, or process in an electric blender together with the cooking liquor. Add 25g butter, season with salt and pepper, preferably freshly ground, and add a little cream or top of the milk, if wished. Sprinkle with plenty of chopped parsley before serving.

Peas

Fresh peas are in season from May to September, although imported peas can be found at other times and mange-tout peas are available most of the year. Peas freeze extremely well, and both frozen and canned peas are easily obtainable.

To buy: When buying fresh peas, allow 300–400g per person, depending on the fullness of the pods. It is not always easy to buy good, fresh peas because the majority of the best crops are bought straight from the fields by large food companies for freezing. The peas should be a good green colour and the pods should appear moist. The peas should be starting to fill the pod and, if eaten raw, should taste sweet and juicy. Do not buy peas which have been allowed to grow too large because they will be dry and unpleasant.

To store: Peas should be eaten as fresh as possible, but can be kept for 1–2 days in a cool vegetable rack or larder or in the bottom of a refrigerator.

To prepare: Shell the peas and, if preparing them in advance, cover with the washed pods to keep them moist. The pods can be kept to make soup.

To boil: The peas should be cooked in the minimum of boiling salted water. Bring a pan of salted water to the boil and add a sprig of mint or chervil and a pinch of sugar, if liked. Add the peas and cook gently for about 10 minutes or until the peas are just tender. Do not overcook peas because this toughens them. Drain thoroughly and turn into a serving dish. Season with black pepper, preferably freshly ground, and dot with butter. Serve as soon as possible after cooking.

To steam: Shell the peas and season with salt. Cook in the top of a steamer over a pan of boiling water for 15–20 minutes or until tender. Drain and serve as for boiled peas.

Mange-tout Peas

These flat pea pods are widely available throughout most of the year. The word literally means 'eat all' which is what you do; mange-tout can therefore be extremely economical because there is no wastage.

To buy: Allow 50–75g per person. Choose mange-tout that are a good green colour and appear bright and fresh.

To store: They should be eaten as fresh as possible, but can be kept for 1–2 days in the bottom of a refrigerator.

To prepare: Remove the tops and tails of the mange-tout and any strings from the sides of older pods.

To boil: Cook the mange-tout in the very minimum of boiling salted water for about 2–3 minutes or until just tender. Drain thoroughly, turn into a serving dish, and season with pepper, preferably freshly ground. Spoon plenty of melted butter over them and serve as soon as possible.

To steam: Season the mange-tout with salt and cook in the top of a steamer over a pan of boiling water for 5 minutes. Drain and serve as for boiled mange-tout.

To stew: For every 200g mange-tout, heat 50g butter in a pan. Add the pea pods, season with salt and pepper, and cover. Cook for about 5 minutes or until they are quite tender, shaking the pan frequently to prevent the peas sticking to the bottom. Serve with the juices from the pan.

Peas – *Dried*

With the popularity of deep freezing, dried green peas are not used as widely as they used to be, although they can be a useful standby. Like other pulses, such as lentils and dried beans, they have a high protein content. The following are the main types of dried peas.

Green peas: These are dried garden peas which are used mainly for soups and purées.

Green and yellow split peas: Green split peas are traditionally used for Pease Pudding (see opposite), but are also used in soups, stews, and purées.

Chick-peas or *garbanzos:* These are large round peas which are used extensively in Spanish, Greek, Middle Eastern, and American cooking.

To buy: Allow 40–50g per person.

To prepare: Soak the peas for 6–12 hours in cold water, preferably changing the water once during this time to prevent the peas fermenting.

To boil: Drain and cover with fresh cold water. Season with salt and add a chopped onion, a few parsley stalks or a bouquet garni if liked. A few bacon rinds or bacon trimmings can also be added to the cooking liquor for extra flavour. Bring the water to the boil and cook for about 2–2½ hours or until the peas are very tender.

To purée: Cook the peas as above and drain thoroughly, reserving the cooking liquor. Sieve the peas or process in an electric blender, then add enough of the cooking liquor to give a thick purée, or add a little cream or top of the milk. Season to taste. Pea purée is excellent served with grilled or fried sausages, bacon, or bacon and eggs. If liked, the pea purée can be served garnished with crisply fried or grilled bacon or bacon rinds, which have been roughly chopped or crumbled.

Pease Pudding
6 helpings

600g split peas	salt and pepper
1 small onion	50g butter **or** margarine
bouquet garni	2 eggs

Soak the peas overnight. Drain, put into a pan, and cover with fresh cold water. Skin the onion and add to the pan with the bouquet garni and seasoning. Cover and simmer the peas slowly for about 2–2½ hours or until they are tender. Drain thoroughly and sieve or process in an electric blender. Cut the fat into small pieces, beat the eggs until liquid, and add both to the pea purée with the seasoning. Beat well together. Place the mixture in a floured cloth and tie tightly. Simmer gently in boiling salted water for 1 hour. Remove from the pan, take out of the cloth, and serve very hot.

Serve with sausages or pickled pork.

Peppers

Large, sweet or bell peppers, often called pimentos, are used raw in salads and form an important part of such dishes as Ratatouille (p308). Red peppers are the sweetest, followed by yellow and then green. Red and green peppers are available all year round, but yellow ones are less easy to obtain. The very small chilli peppers, which are extremely hot, are used as a seasoning in curries and for other highly spiced dishes. As some varieties are much hotter than others, they should always be used with caution.

To buy: Choose peppers with smooth firm skins and a good bright colour.

To store: Peppers will keep for 2–3 days in a cool vegetable rack or larder or, preferably, in the bottom of a refrigerator.

To prepare: Whether the pepper is to be used raw or cooked, the membranes and seeds must first be removed. Cut a slice off the top of the pepper, and discard the membranes and seeds. If liked, the skins of the peppers can also be removed. Heat the pepper over an open flame on a fork or skewer or under a grill until the skin blackens and splits, then skin as for a tomato. To reduce the slight bitterness of green peppers, it is sometimes preferable to blanch them before use. Plunge into boiling water for 2–3 minutes. Drain, rinse in cold water, and drain again.

To fry: Slice the peppers into rings. For 400g peppers, heat 4 × 15ml spoons olive oil in a frying pan. Add the peppers and fry gently over low heat for 30 minutes or until they are very tender. Season to taste with salt and pepper and serve with the cooking liquor. A few coriander seeds can also be added with a little chopped fennel, thyme or marjoram. A crushed clove of garlic can also be added, if liked.

Potatoes

Potatoes are a staple food in the UK, and they are certainly the most versatile of all vegetables. Different varieties of potato vary considerably, some being more suitable for boiling and mashing, and others better for frying or roasting. Home-grown new potatoes are available from May to August, and imported Jersey and other continental potatoes can be found a little earlier than this. These are generally best served boiled or steamed, although they can be sautéed or used for chips. Generally, the best potatoes to buy in the summer for chips or for roasting are Cyprus potatoes. Of the main-crop potatoes, King Edward, Redskin, Maris Piper, Pentland Hawk, and Pentland Ivory are some of the best varieties for boiling, mashing, and baking in their jackets, while Desirée and Majestic are better for roasting and frying.

To buy: Allow 150–200g per person for new potatoes and 200–250g per person for old potatoes because of the greater wastage. New potatoes should be bought as fresh as possible every few days. To test that they are fresh, make sure the skins rub off easily and the potatoes are damp to the touch. When buying main-crop potatoes from September onwards it is practical to buy in larger quantities, and, if suitable storage space is available, a large sack of potatoes can save a considerable amount of money, but the potatoes must be stored in a cool, dark place. Never buy potatoes which are green or which have been exposed to the light.

To prepare: New potatoes should, preferably, not be peeled because the maximum amount of flavour and vitamin C is found just under the skin and is lost when the potatoes are scraped or peeled. Simply wash thoroughly to remove all the dirt and mud. If the potatoes are scraped put into cold water immediately to prevent them browning. If the skin is not too thick on older potatoes, it can be left on for boiling or steaming and removed after cooking. Otherwise, older potatoes should be peeled using a small sharp knife or vegetable peeler. Small and medium-sized potatoes are generally left whole, and large potatoes are cut into halves or quarters.

To boil: Prepare the potatoes as above. Cook in the minimum of boiling salted water until just tender, about 15 minutes for small new potatoes or up to 30 minutes for larger old potatoes. Particularly when boiling larger old potatoes, do not allow the water to boil rapidly or the outsides will start to break up before the inside of the potatoes are cooked through. Drain the potatoes thoroughly, turn into a serving dish, and spoon plenty of melted butter over them. Sprinkle with chopped parsley or chives before serving.

To steam: Both new and old potatoes can be steamed, but this method is particularly good for small new potatoes. Prepare the potatoes as above, but do not peel them. Season with salt and cook in the top of a steamer over a pan of boiling water for 20 minutes for small new potatoes or up to 45 minutes to 1 hour for larger old potatoes. Peel, if liked, after cooking and serve as for boiled potatoes.

Mashed potatoes: Boil or steam old potatoes as above. Drain thoroughly and either mash with a potato masher, or sieve or beat with an electric hand mixer until smooth. To every 1kg potatoes (weight before cooking), beat in 25–50g butter or margarine, a little milk or single cream, and salt and pepper to taste. A little grated nutmeg can also be added, if liked. Turn into a serving dish and garnish with a sprig of parsley before serving.

For creamed potatoes, add more butter and cream to give a very smooth, creamy texture.

To bake: **Jacket potatoes** – Choose medium-sized to large old potatoes. Wash thoroughly, dry, and prick lightly with a fork. For a very crisp skin, brush the outside of the potatoes with oil and place on a baking tray. Bake in a fairly hot oven, 190°–200°C, Gas 5–6, for 1–1½ hours depending on the size of the potatoes. Test with a skewer to make sure the centre of the potato is cooked. Split the potatoes in half, or make a cross in the top and push with your fingers to open up the potato. Serve with plenty of butter and coarse salt, with soured cream and chopped chives or with cream cheese. Baked potatoes can also be stuffed in many ways. Baking is an excellent way of cooking potatoes if using an automatic oven.

To roast: (Method 1): Peel old potatoes and cut into even-sized pieces (halves or quarters). Parboil in boiling salted water for 5 minutes and drain thoroughly. Return the potatoes to the pan and stand over low heat for 1–2 minutes until the potatoes are quite dry. Heat a little lard or dripping in a roasting tin, add the potatoes, and turn in the fat so that they are evenly coated, or put the potatoes in the dripping around a joint of roast meat. Roast in a fairly hot to hot oven, 190°–220°C, Gas 5–7, for 40 minutes to 1 hour or until crisp and golden-brown. Baste the potatoes with some of the fat several times during cooking. The cooking time will vary according to the size of the potatoes and the oven temperature, which will depend on the type of joint being roasted. Parboiling helps to give a very crisp roast potato.

To roast (Method 2): Peel the potatoes and cut into even-sized pieces. Put into a roasting tin containing hot dripping or fat, coat evenly with fat, and roast as above for $1-1\frac{1}{4}$ hours depending on the size of the potatoes and the oven temperature.

To fry: **1) Chips** – Peel old potatoes and cut into sticks about 1cm thick and 8cm long. *For small French fried potatoes*, cut into small sticks about 5mm thick and 5cm long. *For potato straws*, cut into matchsticks. Leave the potatoes in cold water to remove some of the excess starch before frying; then drain and dry thoroughly. Heat the oil or deep fat in a chip pan (p10), put a layer of chips in the bottom of the wire basket and lower into the pan. Fry until the chips are pale golden. Remove from the pan and drain on soft kitchen paper. Repeat this with the remaining chips. Just before serving, re-heat the oil, and fry all the chips, French fried potatoes or potato straws until they are very crisp and golden.

2) Game chips – Peel old potatoes and cut into very thin slices, using either a very sharp knife or a mandoline. Rinse in cold water to remove the excess starch, then dry thoroughly. Heat the deep fat or oil (p10) and fry the chips until crisp and golden. Drain well on soft kitchen paper and sprinkle with salt before serving. Serve with roast game or poultry. These chips can also be served cold and will keep for several days in an airtight tin.

3) Potato puffs – Peel old potatoes and cut into slices 5mm thick. Trim into neat ovals and drop into cold water. Drain and dry them. Heat the oil or deep fat in a pan (p10), put the potato slices into the bottom of the basket and cook until they begin to rise to the surface. Drain on soft kitchen paper. Just before serving, re-heat the fat (p10) and fry the potato slices until they are well puffed. Drain again, and sprinkle with salt.

4) Potato ribbons – Peel old potatoes and cut across into slices 1cm thick. Trim the edges so that the potatoes have a smooth edge; then, with a sharp knife or potato peeler, cut round and round, making long ribbons. Fry as for Game Chips above.

To sauté: Boil or steam old potatoes as above, until they are just tender. Drain thoroughly and cut into 8mm slices. Heat some lard or dripping in a frying pan and fry the potato slices on both sides until crisp and golden. Drain thoroughly and serve garnished with chopped parsley.

Pumpkin

Pumpkins, which belong to the same family as marrows, can be used for both sweet and savoury dishes. They are in season from July to November and are generally sold in wedges, so that you can buy as much of the pumpkin as you wish. Pumpkin purée is available in cans.

To store: A whole pumpkin will keep for a couple of weeks in a cool larder, but a cut piece of pumpkin is best used as soon as possible. It can, however, be wrapped in clingfilm and stored for 1–2 days in the bottom of a refrigerator.

To prepare: Remove the seeds from the pumpkin, peel off the skin, and, unless roasting, cut into pieces about 5cm square.

To boil: Although pumpkin can be boiled, it is really better steamed because of the very high water content. Boil in the very minimum of boiling salted water for 20–30 minutes or until tender. If cooking the pumpkin for sweet dishes, use less salt in the cooking water. Drain the pumpkin thoroughly, turn into a serving dish, and season very well with salt and freshly ground black pepper. Dot liberally with butter and serve as soon as possible.

To steam: Season the pumpkin with salt, unless using for a sweet dish. Cook in the top of a steamer over a pan of boiling water for 35–40 minutes or until it is very tender. Drain and serve as for boiled pumpkin.

To roast: Remove the seeds from the pumpkin, peel, and cut into wedges. Roll the pumpkin in the dripping round a joint of meat and roast in a fairly hot oven, 200°C, Gas 6, for 45 minutes–1 hour.

To fry: Parboil or steam the pumpkin for 10 minutes. Drain and dry thoroughly. Coat in batter and fry as for Jerusalem artichokes.

To purée: Boil or steam the pumpkin as above. Drain thoroughly, then mash or sieve and to every 1kg pumpkin (weight before cooking) beat in 25g butter or margarine and 2 × 15ml spoons cream or milk. If serving as a savoury purée, season to taste with salt and plenty of freshly ground black pepper and serve garnished with chopped parsley.

Salsify and Scorzonera

These roots, which are in season from October to May, have a delicate and unusual flavour. Salsify is a white root, resembling a long thin parsnip, whereas scorzonera has a black skin and is generally considered to have a superior flavour. The young leaves can be used in salads or they can be cooked as for spinach.

To buy: Allow 150g per person. Choose roots that are of a good size and are not shrivelled. Any leaves which have been left on the roots should appear fresh.

To store: Salsify and scorzonera can be kept in a cool vegetable rack or larder for 3–4 days.

To prepare: If possible, scorzonera should not be scraped before cooking because much of the flavour lies just below the skin. Simply scrub and cut into 5cm lengths. Drop the scorzonera quickly into acidulated water to prevent it browning. Salsify can be scraped before cooking and cut into 5cm lengths, but it must be put immediately into acidulated water.

To boil: Cook in the minimum of boiling salted water for about 30 minutes or until just tender. If liked, a little lemon juice can also be added to the cooking water to preserve the colour. Drain the salsify or scorzonera and serve, seasoned with a little pepper and with melted butter spooned over it and/or lemon juice and chopped herbs, such as parsley, dill or tarragon. Boiled salsify can also be served in a white or cream sauce.

To shallow fry: Prepare the salsify or scorzonera but do not scrape. Boil in the skins until just tender. Drain thoroughly, peel, and cut into slices 1cm thick. Heat some butter or margarine in a pan and fry the slices until golden-brown, turning several times. Season with salt and pepper and serve hot.

To deep fry: Parboil the salsify or scorzonera for 15 minutes. Drain and dry thoroughly, coat in batter and fry as for Jerusalem artichokes.

Sorrel

Sorrel is used as both a vegetable and a herb. There are several different varieties, of which wild sorrel, which has the smallest leaves, is the most bitter. Sorrel is generally served as a purée and it should be prepared, cooked, and puréed in exactly the same way as spinach. To counteract the acidity of the sorrel, a little sugar can be added while it is cooking. Sorrel is excellent served with eggs, veal or white fish.

Spinach

Spinach is in season almost throughout the year because there are both winter and summer varieties. It is an extremely valuable source of iron and is generally a particularly good vegetable to serve to invalids and convalescents. Spinach can also be eaten raw in salads. It freezes well and can be bought frozen as either leaf spinach or chopped spinach; it is also available in cans.

To buy: When cooked, spinach reduces considerably because of its very high water content, so allow 250–300g per person. Choose spinach that is a good green colour and appears fresh without any withered yellow leaves.

To store: Once picked, spinach does not keep well and should preferably be eaten on the day of purchase, but it can be kept for 1–2 days in a cool vegetable rack or larder or in the bottom of a refrigerator.

To prepare: Remove any thick stalks from the spinach. (These can be kept and cooked as a separate vegetable. Wash them and tie together in a bundle; then boil or steam as for seakale until they are tender. Drain and serve with melted butter.) Spinach must be washed thoroughly because it can be gritty; wash in at least 3 changes of cold water.

To boil (Method 1): For 1kg spinach, melt 25g butter or margarine in a pan, then add the wet spinach leaves to the pan. Season with salt and stir for a few minutes until all the leaves are limp. Cover and cook slowly for about 10 minutes or until the spinach is tender. Drain thoroughly, pressing out the water. Heat 2 × 15ml spoons cream in the pan, replace the spinach, and cook for a minute. Season to taste with salt, pepper, and nutmeg. A small, crushed clove of garlic added to spinach helps to remove some of the iron tang, and the cream can be omitted, if preferred.

To boil (Method 2): Cook the spinach in 1cm depth of boiling salted water, adding the leaves a few at a time so that the water does not leave the boil. Cover, and cook for a further 10 minutes or until tender. Drain thoroughly, pressing all the water out and serve as for boiled spinach (1).

To purée: Cook the spinach as on p301. Drain thoroughly and either chop finely, sieve or process in an electric blender. For every 1.5kg spinach, melt 25g butter or margarine in a pan with 3 × 15ml spoons cream. Stir in the chopped or sieved spinach and heat gently. Season to taste with salt, pepper and nutmeg. Alternatively, thicken 125ml of the spinach liquor with 1 × 10ml spoon cornflour, and add the sieved or chopped spinach to this panada; or add 125ml thick foundation white (p236) or Béchamel (p245) sauce to the chopped or sieved spinach. The spinach purée can be served garnished with fleurons of puff pastry (p55), sieved hard-boiled egg yolk or crescents of fried bread.

Swedes

Swedes are generally an inexpensive root vegetable, yet very good, especially when puréed. They have a similar flavour to turnips but are milder; they are in season from September to May.

To buy: Allow 200g per person. Choose swedes of a good size, but not too large: the smaller roots have a better flavour. The skin should be firm and not wrinkled.

To store: Like other root vegetables, swedes will keep for several weeks in a cool, dark place.

To prepare: Peel the swedes thickly and cut into pieces about 8cm square or into wedges.

To boil: Cook swedes in the minimum of boiling salted water for about 30 minutes or until quite tender. Drain thoroughly, return to the pan, and put over gentle heat for 1–2 minutes to dry them out. Turn into a serving dish and season with pepper, preferably freshly ground black pepper, and a little nutmeg if liked. Spoon melted butter over the swedes and garnish with chopped parsley.

To steam: Season with salt and cook in the top of a steamer over a pan of boiling water for about 40 minutes or until tender. Drain thoroughly and serve as for boiled swedes.

To purée: Swedes can be served on their own in a purée, or mixed with potatoes, turnips or carrots. Cook the swedes as above, then mash or sieve. To every 1kg swede (weight before cooking), beat in 25g butter or margarine, 1–2 × 15ml spoons cream, if liked, seasoning, and nutmeg.

Sweetcorn (Corn)

Hot, boiled corn on the cob makes an excellent starter, or can be served as a vegetable main dish. Home-grown corn is available from July to November, but imported corn can be bought at other times of the year. Frozen and canned corn is obtainable, both on the cob and as kernels.

To buy: Allow one cob per person or 100g kernels. Once corn has been picked, the sugar in the kernels converts to starch, making the vegetable tough rather than sweet and juicy; corn should therefore be eaten as soon as possible after picking. Choose only cobs on which the kernels are a pale yellow; if they are a bright yellow they are likely to be over-ripe and hard. When pressed, the kernels should exude a milky liquid. Check also that the kernels go right to the tip of the cob and do not finish half-way up.

To store: Corn should not be stored and should be cooked as quickly as possible.

To prepare: Peel off the green husks of corn and reserve some of them if boiling the cobs. Take off the silks (threads), and trim the base end. To remove the kernels from the cob, use a sharp knife, and cut off the kernels in long strips from the centre to one end, then from the centre to the other end. Any flesh and juice which remains on the cob can also be scraped off.

To boil: **1) Cobs** – Place some of the husks in the bottom of a pan. Lay the cobs on top, cover with boiling water, and cook for 5–8 minutes, or until a kernel can easily be removed from the cob. Salt should not be added to the water because this tends to toughen the corn. Drain the cobs and serve hot with salt, freshly ground black pepper, and plenty of melted butter.

2) Kernels – Corn kernels should be cooked in boiling unsalted water for 3–5 minutes or until just tender. Drain, and serve like the cobs or with a white or parsley sauce.

To steam: Place the cobs or kernels in the top of a steamer over a pan of boiling water and steam for 10–15 minutes for cobs, or 5–10 minutes for kernels.

To bake: Put the cobs into a roasting tin and just cover with milk. Bake in a fairly hot oven, 190°C, Gas 5, for 35 minutes or until a kernel can easily be removed from the cob. Drain the cobs, toss in melted butter, and place under a hot grill for 2–3 minutes before serving, seasoned with salt and pepper.

To roast: For 6 cobs, melt 50g butter in a roasting tin. Roll the cobs in this so that they are lightly coated with butter. Roast in a fairly hot oven, 190°C, Gas 5, for about 20 minutes, turning them frequently, until a kernel can easily be removed from the cob. Season with salt and pepper and serve with the butter in which they have been cooked.

Tomatoes

Tomatoes are available throughout the year, although home-grown ones are in season only from March to November. In addition to the standard round tomatoes, large Mediterranean tomatoes and small Italian plum tomatoes can be bought, both of which have an excellent flavour.

To buy: When serving as a side vegetable allow 100g, ie 1 large or 2 medium-sized tomatoes, per person. For baking and stuffing, choose tomatoes of an even size and make sure that the skins are not cracked.

To store: Tomatoes keep well for several days in a cool, dry vegetable rack or larder.

To prepare: The preparation of tomatoes depends largely on the method of cooking. To skin tomatoes, either hold each tomato on a fork over a gas flame or under a grill until the skin blackens and splits, then skin; or place the tomatoes in a basin, cover with boiling water, leave for 1 minute, and then drain and skin.

To bake: Halve the tomatoes. Brush with oil or dot with butter or margarine and season with salt and pepper. If liked, the tomatoes can be sprinkled with a little finely chopped tarragon or basil. Place in a greased ovenproof dish, cover, and bake in a moderate oven, 180°C, Gas 4, for about 20 minutes or until soft.

To grill: Halve the tomatoes, or if very small, leave whole and mark a cross in the bottom with a sharp knife. Dot with a little butter or margarine or brush with oil and season with salt and pepper. Cook under a fairly hot grill, turning once. Serve hot.

To fry: Halve the tomatoes, season with salt and pepper, and fry in hot fat for about 5 minutes, turning once. Remove from the fat with a fish slice and serve hot.

Tomato and Onion Pie
4 helpings

400g onions, preferably Spanish	fat for greasing
50g butter	salt and pepper
800g tomatoes	50g soft white breadcrumbs
50g Cheddar cheese	

Skin the onions, put into a bowl, and cover with boiling water. Leave for 5 minutes, drain, dry thoroughly, and cut into slices. Melt half the butter in a pan and fry the onions until golden-brown. Skin and slice the tomatoes, and grate the cheese. Place the onions and tomatoes in alternate layers in a greased pie dish, sprinkle each layer lightly with salt and pepper and liberally with cheese and some of the breadcrumbs. Cover the whole with a layer of breadcrumbs and dot with the remaining butter. Bake in a fairly hot oven, 190°C, Gas 5, for 45 minutes.

Turnips

There are two varieties of turnip: the young summer or early turnip and the main-crop turnip. The former has a milder flavour than the main-crop vegetable. Early turnips are in season from April to July while main-crop turnips are found from August to March.

To buy: Allow 200g turnips per person. Early turnips should be a good white colour, with a hint of green and purple, and any remaining stalks should appear fresh. Older turnips should have a smooth, unwrinkled skin and be hard; do not buy turnips which appear spongy.

To store: Early turnips should be eaten as soon as possible after purchase, although they will keep for 1–2 days in a cool vegetable rack or larder. Main-crop turnips keep well for several weeks in a cool, dark place.

To prepare: Both early and main-crop turnips should be peeled thickly. Early turnips can be left whole or cut into halves or quarters; main-crop turnips should be cut into quarters or chunks about 8cm square.

To boil (Method 1): Cook the turnips in the minimum of boiling salted water for 20–30 minutes, depending on the size and age of the turnip. Drain thoroughly, turn into a serving dish, and season with pepper, preferably freshly ground, and spoon melted butter over them. Serve garnished with parsley or chopped chives. Turnips, particularly early turnips are excellent served in a cream or Béchamel sauce.

To boil (Method 2 – conservation method): For 800g turnips, heat 25g butter or margarine in a heavy-based pan. Add the turnips and cook very gently for 10 minutes, shaking the pan frequently so that the turnips do not stick to the bottom. Pour approximately 100ml boiling salted water over them, cover the pan, and cook the turnips gently for a further 15–20 minutes depending on their age. Serve the turnips with the cooking liquor and garnish with chopped parsley before serving, or serve in a sauce as in method (1). Stir 1 × 15ml spoon cream into the cooking liquor before serving.

To steam: Season the turnips with salt, and cook in the top of a steamer over a pan of boiling water for 30–40 minutes, depending on the size and age of the turnips. Drain and serve as for boiled turnips.

To purée: Boil or steam the turnips as above and drain if boiling by method (1) or steaming. If cooking by the conservation method, retain the cooking liquor. Mash or sieve the turnips and to every 1 kg turnips (weight before cooking) add 25g butter or margarine, 1–2 × 15ml spoons cream or top of the milk, and seasoning.

Turnip Greens

These, when young, are a most pleasant green vegetable, very rich in vitamin C. Turnip greens should be used as soon as they are picked. The stalks should be removed and the leaves shredded and cooked as for cabbage.

Vegetable Marrow

Together with pumpkins and courgettes, vegetable marrow forms part of the *gourd* family, known in the USA as *squash*. Other varieties are sometimes available in the UK markets; they can also be grown in gardens. They include *acorn squash* which is pale coloured and a similar, though smaller shape to marrow; *crookneck squash* which is yellow and the shape of an elongated pear; *custard marrow* which has deep ribbing and is the size of a small football; and *hubbard squash* which has a rough green skin and is melon shaped. They are all cooked in the same way as marrow, the length of cooking time depending on size.

Marrows have a very high water content and are best suited to steaming or stewing. They are in season from July to October. The biggest marrow may win the local horticultural show, but the flavour of smaller marrows is far superior.

To buy: Choose marrows not more than 30cm long. This serves 3–4 people.

To store: Marrows keep well for 1–2 weeks in a cool, dry vegetable rack or larder.

To prepare: For baking and stuffing, the marrow is often halved and the skin left on, but for steaming, stewing, and baking, cut the marrow into rings, peel thickly, and remove the seeds. Cut into halves or leave as rings.

To boil: Cook in the very minimum of boiling salted water for about 10 minutes or until just tender. Drain thoroughly. A slice of slightly stale bread put in the base of the serving dish will help to absorb excess water. Turn the marrow into a serving dish, season with pepper, preferably freshly ground, and spoon plenty of melted butter over it, or serve with a white or cheese sauce.

To steam: Season the marrow with salt and cook in the top of a steamer over a pan of boiling water for about 20 minutes, depending on the size of the marrow pieces. Serve as for boiled marrow.

To bake: Cut the marrow into rings. Place in a greased ovenproof dish, season with salt and pepper, and dot with 25g butter or margarine. Cover and bake in a fairly hot oven, 190°C, Gas 5, for 45 minutes. Serve with the cooking liquor.

To stew: Melt 25g butter or margarine in a pan. Add the pieces of marrow, and season with salt and pepper and a little chopped thyme and lemon juice, if wished. Coat the pieces of marrow with the fat, cover with a lid, and cook over gentle heat for about 30 minutes, shaking the pan from time to time. Serve the marrow together with the juices in the pan, or add these to a white or cheese sauce.

To purée: Marrow can also be served as a purée. Steam as above. Drain thoroughly, and mash; then beat in 25g butter or margarine, 1 × 15ml spoon beaten egg, and 1 × 15ml spoon cream (if liked). Season with salt, pepper, and nutmeg.

Mixed Vegetable Dishes and Salads

Bubble and Squeak

dripping or lard
thin slices of cold roast or braised or
  boiled meat as available
1 medium-sized onion
cold mashed potatoes as available

cold, cooked green vegetables of any
  kind, as available
salt and pepper
a dash of vinegar (optional)

Heat just enough dripping or lard in a frying pan to cover the bottom. Put in the meat, and fry quickly on both sides until lightly browned. Remove, and keep hot. Skin the onion, slice it thinly, and fry until lightly browned, adding a little more fat to the frying pan if necessary. Mix together the potatoes and green vegetables, season to taste, and add to the frying pan. Stir until thoroughly hot, then add a little vinegar, if liked. Allow to become slightly crusty on the bottom. Turn out on to a warmed dish. Place the meat on top and serve.

Note The name Bubble and Squeak is often given to a dish of re-heated vegetables without meat.

Mixed Vegetables
6 helpings

750g mixed vegetables:
  parsnips, turnips, carrots, leeks,
  cauliflower or broad beans, peas,
  spring onions, tomatoes, new
  carrots, new turnips

25g butter or margarine
100–150ml boiling water
salt and pepper

Garnish
1 × 15ml spoon chopped parsley

Prepare the vegetables; then thinly slice the parsnips, turnips, carrots, and leeks, if used, splitting the slices into halves or quarters if large. Break the cauliflower into florets. Leave most of the other vegetables whole, cutting the larger carrots into thick slices, trimming the spring onions rather short, and cutting the tomatoes into wedges. Melt the fat in a heavy-based saucepan. Add the vegetables at intervals, starting with those which take the longest time to cook. Put the lid on the pan after each addition and toss the vegetables in the fat. (Do not add the tomatoes until 5 minutes before serving.) Add the boiling water and salt; use very little water with the beans and new carrots, etc. Simmer gently until the vegetables are tender. Season with pepper and serve hot, garnished with the parsley.

Note These cooked vegetables can also be used to make a salad. Leave to cool and serve either tossed in French dressing or in mayonnaise.

Cooking time
Parsnips, etc 30–35 minutes
Broad beans, etc 20–25 minutes

VARIATIONS
Mixed Vegetables with Cheese
Cook the vegetables as above and drain off any cooking liquor. Make up 375ml cheese sauce (p237), using the cooking liquor. Coat the vegetables with the sauce in a heatproof dish and sprinkle with 1 × 15ml spoon grated Cheddar cheese. Put under a hot grill to brown or into a hot oven, 220°C, Gas 7, for 10 minutes or until golden-brown.

Note This mixture can also be used to stuff peppers or marrows for a vegetarian main course.

Curried Mixed Vegetables
Cook the vegetables as above and drain off any cooking liquor. Make up 375ml Fruit Curry sauce (p258), using the cooking liquor, and simmer the sauce for at least 2 hours. Add the cooked vegetables and re-heat gently.

Serve with boiled rice and the usual curry accompaniments.

Mirepoix of Vegetables
A mirepoix is used in the base of a pan when braising meat and vegetables to give flavour. It is generally discarded after cooking, although it can be kept and served as a vegetable, or puréed and used as a base for a soup. The ingredients can be varied according to the time of year and whatever is being braised. The proportions below give a well-flavoured mirepoix. Keeping these proportions, use larger or smaller quantities of the ingredients as the individual recipes require.

2 medium-sized onions (250g approx)	25g fat bacon
1 carrot (50g approx)	15g dripping
½ turnip (50g approx)	

Skin and chop the onions, carrot, and turnip. Chop the bacon. Melt the dripping in a pan, add the vegetables and bacon, cover, and fry gently for 10 minutes. Use as required.

Nut Mince
6 helpings

200g shelled nuts	1 × 15ml spoon mushroom ketchup **or** any similar sauce
1 medium-sized onion	
25g margarine	375ml (approx) vegetable stock
150g dried breadcrumbs	salt and pepper

Pass the nuts through a nut mill, process them in an electric blender, or chop very finely. Skin and grate the onion. Melt the margarine in a frying pan and fry the nuts, onion, and breadcrumbs until pale golden. Stir in the ketchup and stock, adding a little extra stock if the mixture is too dry. Season to taste and simmer gently for 20–30 minutes. Serve hot.

Ratatouille

4 helpings

250g onions (approx)
1 clove of garlic
100g green pepper (approx)
200g aubergine (approx)
200g courgettes

400g tomatoes
4 × 15ml spoons olive oil
salt and pepper
1 × 2.5ml spoon coriander seeds

Garnish
1 × 15ml spoon chopped parsley

Skin the onions and slice in rings. Skin and crush the garlic. Remove the membranes and seeds from the pepper and cut the flesh into thin strips. Cut the unpeeled aubergine and courgettes into 1cm slices. Skin and chop the tomatoes roughly.

Heat 2 × 15ml spoons of the oil in a pan and gently fry the onions, garlic, and pepper for about 10 minutes. Add the remaining oil, and aubergine, and the courgettes. Cover and simmer gently for 30 minutes, stirring occasionally to prevent the vegetables from sticking to the bottom. Add the tomatoes, seasoning and coriander seeds, and simmer for a further 15 minutes. Serve hot or cold, garnished with the parsley.

Green Salads

The simplest and most usual salad is a tossed green salad, but even this must be carefully prepared. The salad consists of green leaves of one type, or a mixture such as lettuce, watercress, chicory, and endive. The leaves must be fresh and crisp, and they must be dried thoroughly or the salad will be watery and tasteless. The vegetables should be tossed in a French dressing or vinaigrette sauce just before serving with chopped herbs, such as parsley, chervil, chives, savory, and marjoram, if liked. If you like garlic, a small crushed clove can be added to the dressing; or a *châpon* of bread can be put in the salad bowl, as is often done in France. To make a *châpon*, rub a crust of French or ordinary white bread all over with crushed garlic. Place the crust in the bottom of the salad bowl with the salad vegetables on top. Pour the dressing over it and toss the bread with the salad, so that the flavour of the garlic gently permeates the whole dish. Although the bread is only meant as a flavouring, garlic addicts will enjoy eating it afterwards!

Cooked Vegetable Salads

Not only raw vegetables are used in salads, although nutritionally this is the best way to eat them so that their full vitamin and mineral content is retained. Cooked vegetables of all kinds are also excellent served in a French dressing or in mayonnaise with other herbs and seasonings added. Ideally, most vegetables should be cooked especially for the salad and tossed in the dressing while they are still warm, but very good salads can be made from cooked, leftover vegetables, particularly root vegetables.

Salads with Pulses, Pasta, and Rice

Dried pulses – peas, beans, lentils etc, make appetising salads, especially in winter when good fresh vegetables are scarce. They should be tossed in their dressing while still warm, and left to cool and marinate for at least 2–3 hours. For maximum flavour, they can be cooked in stock rather than water; fresh herbs can be added with the dressing.

For more filling and economical salads, pasta and rice provide a good basis, to which can be added a wide variety of fruits and vegetables such as peppers, celery, chicory, carrots, cooked peas, apples, oranges, dried fruit, and nuts. While good for family meals, these salads are particularly useful for buffet parties, since they are easy to prepare in large quantities and are easy to eat with a fork.

Salads with Fruit

Adding fruit to mixed salads, or using it as a salad on its own, is an American custom which is now extremely popular in the UK. Fresh fruit is preferable, but frozen or canned can be used if it is not too sweet. Fruits which discolour quickly, such as apples, pears, bananas and peaches, must be quickly dipped in lemon juice or in the dressing in which they will be served – usually mayonnaise or French dressing, to preserve their colour. Apples can be peeled, but the bright green or red skins often give an attractive colour and texture contrast to other ingredients in the salad. Citrus fruit, such as oranges and grapefruit, should be stripped of every scrap of white pith; they are then generally cut into segments or slices and the thin skin between the segments is removed. Dried fruit, such as apricots, raisins and sultanas, and nuts (usually walnuts, hazelnuts and almonds) can also be added to rice and pasta salads, coleslaw, and other mixed vegetable salads.

Anchovy Chequerboard Salad
4 helpings

400g cod fillet	salt and pepper
2 × 15ml spoons water	1 large lettuce heart
2 × 15ml spoons lemon juice	1 hard-boiled egg
1 × 15ml spoon chopped parsley	1 × 100g can anchovy fillets
1 × 15ml spoon chopped chives	

Garnish

radish roses (p62)	parsley sprigs

Put the cod fillet in an ovenproof dish with the water. Cover and cook in a fairly hot oven, 190°C, Gas 5, for 20 minutes. Leave to cool. Remove any skin and bones, and flake the fish. Moisten it with the lemon juice, and stir in the parsley and chives with seasoning to taste. Shred the lettuce, and arrange in a flat layer on a platter. Arrange the fish neatly on the bed of shredded lettuce, and smooth the surface. Slice the egg. Drain the anchovy fillets and place in a grid pattern on top of the fish mixture. Fill the spaces with rings of hard-boiled egg. Garnish with radish roses and parsley sprigs.

Halibut, Orange, and Watercress Salad

4 helpings

4–6 halibut steaks
500ml court bouillon (p79)

1 lettuce
mayonnaise (p262)

Garnish
orange twists (p58)

watercress sprigs

Poach the fish steaks in the court bouillon for 7–10 minutes. Lift out, drain well and leave to cool. Remove the skin. Wash the lettuce, dry thoroughly and shred the outer leaves; arrange them on a salad dish. Coat the fish with mayonnaise, and arrange on the lettuce. Garnish with orange twists, the remaining lettuce, and watercress sprigs.

Mackerel Salad

4 helpings

8 mackerel fillets
500ml court bouillon
  (p79)

1 × 15ml spoon gelatine
50ml cider vinegar
50ml mayonnaise (p262)

Garnish
sprigs of tarragon, chervil
  or parsley

tomato wedges
watercress sprigs

Wash and dry the fillets, then poach them gently for 15 minutes in the court bouillon. Drain and leave to cool. Skin neatly.

While the fish is cooking, soften the gelatine in the vinegar, then stand the container in hot water, and stir until the gelatine dissolves. Mix with the mayonnaise, and chill until almost at setting point. Coat the skinned side of each fillet with the semi-set mayonnaise. Garnish each fillet with tarragon, chervil or parsley, and with tomato wedges and watercress sprigs.

Cooked Meat Salad

4 helpings

200g small potatoes
300g cold roast lamb, mutton, beef **or**
  veal
6 gherkins
25g canned mushrooms in brine
½ small onion
3 sprigs pickled cauliflower

1 hard-boiled egg
4 × 15ml spoons salad dressing
  (p260), soured cream **or** natural
  yoghurt
salt and pepper
1 lettuce
1 × 10ml spoon chopped parsley

Boil the potatoes in their skins and leave until cold before peeling them. Cut the meat into small neat pieces. Slice the gherkins and mushrooms, and chop the onion, cauliflower, and egg. Mix with the salad dressing, soured cream or yoghurt. Season to taste. Wash the lettuce, dry thoroughly and arrange a border of leaves in a salad bowl; spoon the salad into the centre. Sprinkle with the parsley.

Jellied Ham Salad
2–3 helpings

125g cooked ham
50g cooked macaroni
1 medium-sized tomato
salt and pepper
1 × 5ml spoon chopped parsley

150ml aspic jelly
2 hard-boiled eggs
2 × 10ml spoons gelatine
75ml white stock (p26)

Garnish
green salad (p308)

Chop or mince the ham, chop the macaroni, skin and chop the tomato. Mix together and add seasoning and a little of the chopped parsley. Line a small, flat roasting tin with half the aspic jelly. Slice the hard-boiled eggs and lay the slices on the jelly with the remaining chopped parsley. Leave to set. Dissolve the gelatine in the stock with the rest of the aspic jelly, and when cool, add to the mixed ingredients. Pour into the prepared tin when cold and leave until set. When set, unmould and cut into strips. Surround with the green salad.

Veal, Salami, and Olive Salad
4–6 helpings

200g cold roast veal
200g cold boiled potatoes
100g boiled beetroot
100g gherkins

1 × 15ml spoon capers
salt and pepper
100ml mayonnaise (p262)

Garnish
lettuce leaves
lemon slices

12 stoned green olives
12 slices salami

Dice the veal, potatoes, and beetroot. Slice the gherkins. Mix them together with the capers, and season to taste. Pile the mixture into a salad dish and pour the mayonnaise over it. Garnish with lettuce leaves, lemon slices, olives, and salami.

Curried Turkey or Chicken Salad
6–8 helpings

1 small cooked turkey or large
   chicken
150ml mayonnaise (p262)
25g curry powder

500g (approx) natural yoghurt
salt and pepper
paprika

Garnish
parsley sprigs

thin green pepper rings

Remove the cooked meat from the bones. Take off any skin or fat, and cut into small pieces. Mix the mayonnaise with the curry powder, stir in the yoghurt, and season to taste. Mix half the sauce with the turkey or chicken, arrange on a serving dish, and spoon the remaining sauce over. Sprinkle with a little paprika and garnish with the parsley and pepper rings.

Jellied Game Salad

4 helpings

4 hard-boiled eggs
350g lean cooked ham
¼ cucumber (approx)

500ml aspic jelly
450g cold cooked game meat (bird **or** animal)

Cut the eggs into round slices. Cut the ham into slices, then into rounds of the same size as the eggs. Peel the cucumber and cut into thin slices.

Rinse a plain 1 litre jelly mould with cold water, and line it with aspic jelly. Decorate the base of the mould with some of the ham and all the egg sandwiched together. Pour a little cold liquid aspic jelly over them and allow to set. Cut the game meat into neat small pieces. Sandwich together the remaining ham and cucumber slices. Arrange pieces of seasoned game and rounds of ham and cucumber on the set jelly, pour more jelly on top and allow this to set. Repeat the layers until the mould is full; chop and include any extra egg white from the ends of the eggs, if liked. Allow each layer of jelly to set firmly before adding the next layer of meat.

When the jelly has set firmly, unmould. Any remaining jelly can be chopped on a wet board and used for decoration.

Caesar Salad

6 helpings

3 cloves garlic
4 large thick slices bread
2 cos lettuces
150ml olive oil
1 egg

juice of 1 lemon
1 × 65g can anchovy fillets
50g grated Parmesan cheese
salt and freshly ground black pepper

Cut the garlic cloves in half. Cut the bread into 1cm cubes. Wash the lettuces, dry thoroughly, and tear into small pieces. Heat 4 × 15ml spoons olive oil in a frying pan with 2 cloves of garlic. Add the bread cubes and fry until crisp and golden on all sides. Remove from the pan and drain on soft kitchen paper. Discard the garlic and oil. Rub the remaining garlic clove all round the salad bowl. Add the lettuce and the rest of the olive oil, and toss until every leaf is coated. Cook the egg in boiling water for 1 minute, then remove from the pan and break over the lettuce. Add the lemon juice to the lettuce with the anchovies, cheese, and seasoning. Toss lightly, and re-season if required. Add the croûtons of fried bread, toss the salad again, and serve as soon as possible, while the croûtons are still crisp.

Harlequin Salad
4 helpings

75g Cheddar cheese
75g red Leicester cheese
75g blue Stilton cheese
75g white Wensleydale cheese
1 lettuce
4 medium-sized tomatoes

½ cucumber
1 small bunch of watercress
100ml soured cream
milk
1 × 15ml spoon chopped chives

Cut the cheeses into small cubes, and mix together without breaking them. Wash and dry the lettuce, slice the tomatoes and cucumber, and chop the watercress. Place the lettuce and watercress on a flat oval platter, in a flat layer. Pile the cheeses into the centre of the platter. Mix the cream with a little milk if required, to obtain a thick pouring consistency. Pour it round the cheeses, trickling a little over them. Arrange the tomato and cucumber in a decorative pattern round the cheeses, and sprinkle the dish with chives.

Note The cubes can be cut more easily if each cheese is bought in a block.

PASTA AND RICE

Cooking Pasta
All pasta can be cooked simply in fast-boiling, well-salted water. However, for some dishes such as lasagne, the pasta is removed after a few minutes only, when it will have just softened, and the dish is finished in the oven *(pasta al forno)*.

Basic method

1) Provide 50–75g pasta (uncooked weight) per person for a first-course dish, 75–100g for a main dish.
2) Use 1 litre water and 1 × 5ml spoon table salt or 1 × 2.5ml spoon household salt per 100g pasta. The addition of 2 × 15ml spoons of oil to the cooking water will help prevent the pasta sticking together.
3) Bring the water, salt, and oil, if used, to a fast boil. Break long pasta into 15–25cm lengths. Put them into the water and push them gently below the surface as they soften. Drop round pasta shapes into the water a few at a time, and stir once. Slide large pasta such as sheets of lasagne into the water individually to prevent them sticking together. Drop bundled (folded) pasta into the water, leave for 2 minutes, then stir with a fork to separate the strands. Do not allow the water to go off the boil.
4) Cook for the appropriate time (see table below), stirring once or twice with a fork to prevent the pasta sticking to the bottom of the pan. The pasta, when cooked, should have no floury taste, but should be *al dente*, firm to the bite, apart from dishes which are also to be baked in the oven.
5) Drain into a colander; then return to the dry pan, off the heat, if making a sauce. If the pasta must wait more than 4 minutes, place it on a damp cloth in a strainer or sieve, over simmering water.

Cooking Times for Pasta

The cooking time for dried pasta depends partly on the size of the shapes and partly on the flour used. Manufacturers usually state the cooking times for their pasta on each packet, and their directions should be followed. If none are given, use the following general guide:

String or tubular and flat ribbons, eg

cappellini, vermicelli, spaghettini	5 minutes
spaghetti, tagliatelle	7–12 minutes
macaroni	12–20 minutes

Fancy shapes and short lengths, eg

shells, bows, cocks-combs	8–10 minutes

Ridged, large, eg

cannelloni, rigatoni	16–20 minutes

Stuffed

ravioli	15–20 minutes

Soup

alphabets, stars, small wheels, small rings, small shells	4–8 minutes

Crisp Noodles
4–6 helpings

400g noodles   fat for deep frying

Cook the noodles in boiling salted water as directed; drain well. Leave to cool completely. Heat the fat (p10), put some noodles in a wire basket and cook in the fat until crisp and golden-brown. Drain on soft kitchen paper, and keep hot while cooking the rest of the noodles.

Cooking Rice
Everybody has their own way of cooking rice, especially boiled rice. But the differences are slight, and generally the results are the same if the preparation and cooking are done correctly.

Before cooking, wash the rice well under running cold water in a sieve or colander. This removes the loose surface starch which prevents rice drying out into separate grains when cooked. Remove also any dark or discoloured grains.

Do not overcook the rice. Something between 12–20 minutes is a basic guide, depending on the type of rice used. Test it after 10 minutes; it should be tender to the touch but still have a slight 'bite' for savoury dishes. Toss lightly with a fork before serving.

As rice almost trebles its bulk when boiled, 25–50g of dry rice is usually enough for one average helping.

Boiled Rice (white) *Basic recipe*

3–4 helpings

METHOD 1

Put 125g long-grain rice into a saucepan, pour in 375ml cold water and add 1 × 5ml spoon salt. Bring to the boil, stir once with a fork, reduce the heat, cover with a lid, and simmer for 12–15 minutes by which time the liquid should all be absorbed.

METHOD 2

Put 3 litres of water into a large saucepan, add 1 × 5ml spoon salt and bring to the boil. Sprinkle in 125g long-grain rice and stir two or three times with a fork until the water is at boiling point again. Reduce the heat so that the water is just boiling and cook for 15–18 minutes. Test for readiness after 10 minutes. Drain thoroughly before use.

Note The juice of half a lemon, added to the water, will help to keep the rice white.

Boiled Rice (brown) *Basic recipe*

4 helpings

Put 275g brown rice into a large saucepan, pour in 400ml water, and add 1 × 2.5ml spoon salt. Bring slowly to the boil. Reduce the heat, cover with a lid, and simmer gently for about 20 minutes. Do not stir. If the pan is dry, add a little more water. After 30 minutes, add a few drops more water if the rice is not yet cooked. When ready, the liquid should all be absorbed and the rice should just be beginning to stick to the bottom. Remove from the heat and let it stand, covered, for 10–15 minutes before use.

Note Brown rice keeps well for 4–5 days in a refrigerator, so it is worth cooking a fairly large quantity at one time.

Fried Rice

2–3 helpings

100g long-grain rice	salt and pepper
1 onion	2 eggs
50g ham	2 × 15ml spoons soy sauce
4 × 15ml spoons cooking oil	

Garnish
chopped parsley

Wash and drain the rice and cook it in boiling salted water for about 12 minutes. Drain well. Skin and chop the onion. Cut the ham into thin strips. Heat the oil in a frying pan, add the cooked rice and onion, and fry for about 5–6 minutes. Stir in the ham and seasoning. Beat the eggs until liquid, and pour them into the pan. Stir the mixture over low heat until the eggs are just beginning to set. Stir in the soy sauce quickly. Pile the rice on to a warmed serving dish and sprinkle with parsley.

PUDDINGS, DESSERTS AND ICES

HOT PUDDINGS AND DESSERTS

Milk and Custard Puddings

Large Grain Milk Puddings (eg whole or flaked rice, sago, flaked tapioca)
4–5 helpings

butter for greasing	50–75g caster sugar
100g grain	15g butter (optional)
1 litre milk	$\frac{1}{2} \times 2.5$ml spoon grated nutmeg **or**
a pinch of salt	similar flavouring (see **Note**)

Butter a 1.75 litre pie dish. Wash the grain in cold water, and put it into the dish with the milk. Leave to stand for 30 minutes. Add the salt and sugar, and sprinkle with flakes of butter and nutmeg, if used. Bake in a cool oven at 150°C, Gas 2, for $2-2\frac{1}{2}$ hours or until the pudding is thick and creamy, and brown on the top. The pudding is better if it cooks even more slowly, for 4–5 hours.

Note If using a flavouring essence, mix it into the milk before cooking. If using dried or canned milk, reduce the grain to 75g, use the quantity of milk product to make up 1 litre, and cook at 140°C, Gas 1, for at least $3\frac{1}{2}-4$ hours.

Large Grain Milk Puddings with Eggs
6 helpings

100g grain	50–75g caster sugar
1 litre milk	flavouring (eg grated lemon rind or
2–3 eggs	ground cinnamon)
a pinch of salt	butter for greasing

Wash the grain in cold water and put it into the top of a double boiler with the milk. Cook slowly for about 1 hour, or until the grain is tender. Remove from the heat and leave to cool slightly. Separate the eggs. Stir the egg yolks, salt, sugar and flavouring into the grain. Whisk the egg whites to the same consistency as the pudding, and fold into the mixture. Pour into a buttered 1.75 litre pie dish and bake in a warm oven at 160°C, Gas 3, for 40–45 minutes until the top is brown.

Medium and Small Grain Milk Puddings (eg coarsely ground rice, semolina or oatmeal, small sago, cornmeal)
6 helpings

1 litre milk	a pinch of salt
flavouring (eg grated lemon rind or	50–75g caster sugar
ground cinnamon)	butter for greasing (optional)
75g grain	

Warm the milk. Infuse any solid flavouring, if used, in the milk for about 10 minutes; then remove. Sprinkle the grain into the milk, stirring quickly to prevent lumps forming. Bring to simmering point, stirring all the time. Continue stirring, and simmer for 15–20 minutes or until the grain is transparent and cooked through. Add the salt, sugar, and any flavouring essence used.

The pudding can then be served as it is, hot or cold; alternatively, it can be poured into a well-buttered 1.75 litre pie dish, and baked in a moderate oven at 180°C, Gas 4, for 20–30 minutes until the top has browned.

Serve with stewed fruit, or with warmed jam or marmalade.

VARIATION
Medium and Small Grain Milk Puddings with Eggs
Cook the grain as above, but add the salt with the grain. Leave to cool slightly. Separate 2–3 eggs. Stir the yolks, 50–75g sugar, and any flavouring essence into the grain. Whisk the egg whites to the same consistency as the pudding, and fold into the mixture. Pour the mixture into a well-buttered 1.75 litre pie dish, and bake in a warm oven at 160°C, Gas 3, for 30–40 minutes until the top has browned.

Serve with stewed fruit, or with warmed jam or marmalade.

Powdered Grain Puddings (eg arrowroot, cornflour, custard powder, finely ground rice, fine oatmeal)
6 helpings

1 litre milk	a pinch of salt
flavouring (eg grated lemon rind or	50–75g caster sugar
ground cinnamon)	butter for greasing (optional)
65g grain	

Warm the milk. Infuse any solid flavouring, if used, in the milk for 30 minutes; then remove. Blend the grain with a little of the milk. Bring the rest of the milk to boiling point with the salt, and pour on to the blended paste, stirring briskly to prevent lumps forming. Return the mixture to the saucepan, heat until it thickens, and simmer for 2–3 minutes to cook the grain completely, stirring all the time. Add the sugar and any flavouring used.

The pudding can then be served as it is, hot or cold, or poured into a well-buttered 1.75 litre pie dish, and baked for 20–30 minutes in a moderate oven at 180°C, Gas 4, until the top has browned.

Serve with stewed fruit, or with warmed jam or marmalade.

For **variation**, see over

VARIATION
Powdered Grain Puddings with Eggs
Cook the grain as in the main recipe, but do not add the flavouring or the salt. Leave to cool slightly. Separate 2–4 eggs. Stir the egg yolks, salt, sugar, and any flavourings into the grain. Whisk the egg whites to the same consistency as the pudding, and fold into the mixture. Pour into a well-buttered 1.75 litre pie dish, and bake in a warm oven at 160°C, Gas 3, for about 30 minutes until the top has browned. Sprinkle with brown sugar and/or butter flakes before baking, if liked.

Serve with stewed fruit, or with warmed jam or marmalade.

Cup or 'Boiled' Custard (Coating custard)
4 helpings or 500ml (approx)

500ml milk	25g caster sugar
4 eggs **or** 3 eggs and 2 yolks	flavouring (see below)

Warm the milk to approximately 65°C. Mix the eggs and sugar together well, and stir in the milk. Strain the custard into a saucepan or into a heatproof bowl placed over a pan of simmering water. Alternatively, use a double boiler, but make sure the water does not touch the upper pan. Cook over very gentle heat for 15–25 minutes, stirring all the time with a wooden spoon, until the custard thickens to the consistency of single cream. Stir well round the sides as well as the base of the pan or basin to prevent lumps forming, especially if using a double boiler. Do *not* let the custard boil. If it shows the slightest sign of curdling, put the pan or bowl into a bowl of cold water, or turn the custard into a clean basin and whisk rapidly.

As soon as the custard thickens, pour it into a jug to stop further cooking. Keep it warm by standing the jug in a basin of hot water. If it is to be served cold, pour into a basin and cover with a piece of dampened greaseproof paper to prevent a skin forming. When cold, pour into a serving dish.

Note A mixture of whole eggs and yolks gives a richer, smoother custard.

Flavourings
Vanilla: Add a few drops of vanilla essence with the sugar.

Lemon: Infuse strips of lemon rind in the warm milk for 30 minutes, then remove before adding the milk to the eggs.

Bay: Infuse a piece of bay leaf in the warm milk for 30 minutes, then remove before adding to the eggs.

Nutmeg or cinnamon: Sprinkle the top of the cooked custard with grated nutmeg or ground cinnamon.

VARIATIONS
Pouring Custard
Make as above but use only 3 eggs or 2 eggs and 2 yolks. The custard will thicken only to the consistency of thin single cream or top of the milk.

Rich Custard
Stir 2 × 15ml spoons double cream into the custard when it is cooling.

Simple Custard
4 helpings or 500ml (approx)

1 × 10ml spoon cornflour
500ml milk
25g caster sugar

2 eggs
flavouring (p318)

This custard will not curdle as easily as a cup custard but still keeps the delicious creamy flavour of an egg custard.

Blend the cornflour to a smooth paste with a little of the cold milk. Heat the rest of the milk and when hot, pour it on to the blended cornflour, stirring well. Return to the saucepan, bring to the boil and boil for 1–2 minutes, stirring all the time, to cook the cornflour. Remove from the heat and add the sugar. Leave to cool. Beat the eggs together lightly. Add a little of the cooked cornflour mixture, stir well, then pour into the saucepan. Heat gently for a few minutes until the egg has thickened, stirring all the time. Do not boil.

Serve hot or cold as an accompaniment to a pudding or pie.

Baked Custard
4 helpings or 500ml (approx)

500ml milk
2 eggs (for a softly set custard) **or**
   3 eggs (for a firmer custard)
25g caster sugar

fat for greasing
grated nutmeg **or** other flavouring
   (see **Note**)

Warm the milk to approximately 65°C. Mix the eggs and sugar together and stir in the milk. Strain the custard into a greased 700ml ovenproof dish. Sprinkle nutmeg on top, if used. Stand the dish in a tin containing enough hot water to come half-way up the sides of the dish, and bake in a very cool oven at 140°–150°C, Gas 1–2, for 1 hour or until the custard is set in the centre.

Note If preferred, the nutmeg can be omitted and the custard flavoured by infusing a bay leaf or thinly cut strips of lemon rind in the milk for a few minutes; they must, however, be removed before adding the milk to the eggs.

Steamed Custard
4 helpings or 500ml (approx)

500ml milk
4 eggs **or** 3 eggs and 2 yolks
25g caster sugar

fat for greasing
flavouring (p318)

Warm the milk to approximately 65°C. Mix the eggs and sugar together and stir in the milk. Strain the custard into a greased 750ml heatproof dish, cover with greased foil or oiled greaseproof paper, and steam very gently for about 40 minutes until just firm in the centre.

Serve hot or cold with fruit or Jam Sauce (p268).

Note The custard can be turned out on to a warm plate for serving, but when it is removed from the steamer, leave it to stand for a few minutes before turning it out.

Crème Anglaise (2) (Thick custard)
4 helpings or 500ml (approx)

500ml milk

a few drops vanilla essence **or** other
flavouring (see below)

8 egg yolks

100g caster sugar

Warm the milk gently without letting it boil, and infuse any solid flavouring used; then remove. Beat the egg yolks and sugar together until creamy. Add the milk. Strain the custard into a double boiler or a basin placed over a pan of simmering water. Cook, stirring all the time with a wooden spoon, for 20–30 minutes or until the custard thickens and coats the back of the spoon. Take care not to let the custard curdle.

Use hot, or pour into a basin and cool, stirring from time to time to prevent a skin forming.

Flavourings

Lemon: Infuse a thin strip of lemon rind in the milk, then remove before adding the eggs.

Orange: Add orange rind in the same way as lemon rind.

Liqueur: Add 1 × 15ml spoon Kirsch, curaçao or rum at the end of the cooking time.

Praline: Top with crushed praline (p446).

VARIATION

A simpler Crème Anglaise can be made in an ordinary saucepan without curdling too easily. Use 6 egg yolks and blend them and the sugar with 2 × 5ml spoons cornflour or arrowroot. Continue as above.

Apple Snow (1)
6 helpings

1kg cooking apples

pared rind of 1 lemon

75ml water

175g caster sugar

2 eggs

250ml milk

butter for greasing

Peel, core, and slice the apples into a saucepan. Add the lemon rind and water. Cover and cook until the apples are pulped. Remove the lemon rind and beat the apple purée until smooth. Add 100g of the sugar. Separate the eggs and beat the yolks until liquid in a basin. Heat together the milk and 25g of the sugar and pour on to the egg yolks. Return the mixture to the saucepan and cook, stirring all the time, until the mixture coats the back of the spoon. Do not allow the mixture to boil. Put the apple purée into a buttered 1 litre pie dish, pour the custard over it, and bake in a warm oven at 160°C, Gas 3, for 30–40 minutes. Whisk the egg whites until stiff, fold in the remaining 50g sugar and pile on top of the custard. Return to the oven and bake for a further 10 minutes until the meringue is just set.

Serve with Simple Custard (p319) or cream.

Roast Chicken with Honey and Almonds (p.187)

Chicken Casserole (p.191)

Chicken Chasseur (p.191)

Chaudfroid of Chicken (p.197)

Roast Goose with Fruit Stuffing and Red Cabbage (p.200)

Tortilla Espagnola (p.230)

Boston Roast (p.278)

Spiced Lentils (p.291)

Banana Custard
4 helpings

500ml Coating Cup Custard (p318)   3 bananas (400g approx)

Decoration (optional)
4 × 5ml spoons crushed butterscotch
   or grated chocolate **or** browned
   flaked almonds

Make the custard. Peel and slice the bananas. Add to the custard and leave to stand for 5 minutes. Spoon into a serving dish or 4 glasses. Decorate before serving.

Bread and Butter Pudding
4 helpings

butter for greasing   a pinch of nutmeg **or** cinnamon
4 thin slices bread (100g approx)   400ml milk
25g butter   2 eggs
50g sultanas **or** currants   25g granulated sugar

Grease a 1 litre pie dish. Cut the crusts off the bread and spread the slices with the butter. Cut the bread into squares or triangles and arrange in alternate layers, buttered side up, with the sultanas or currants. Sprinkle each layer lightly with spices. Arrange the top layer of bread in an attractive pattern. Warm the milk to approximately 65°C; do not let it come near the boil. Beat together the eggs and most of the sugar with a fork and stir in the milk. Strain the custard over the bread, sprinkle some nutmeg and the remaining sugar on top, and leave to stand for 30 minutes. Bake in a moderate oven at 180°C, Gas 4, for 30–40 minutes until set and lightly browned.

Cabinet Pudding (plain)
4 helpings

fat for greasing   3 eggs
75g seedless raisins   25g caster sugar
3–4 slices white bread (100g approx)   1 × 5ml spoon grated lemon rind
400ml milk

Grease a 1 litre pudding basin and halve the raisins. Decorate the sides and base of the basin by pressing on some of the dried fruit. Chill. Remove the crusts from the bread and cut the slices into 5mm dice. Warm the milk to approximately 65°C; do not let it come near the boil. Beat the eggs and sugar together with a fork and stir in the milk. Add the lemon rind to the bread with the rest of the raisins. Strain the custard over the bread, stir, and leave to stand for 30 minutes. Pour into the prepared basin and cover with greased foil or greaseproof paper. Steam gently for 1 hour or until the pudding is firm in the centre. Remove the cooked pudding from the steamer, leave to stand for a few minutes, and turn out on to a warmed dish.
   Serve with Jam Sauce (p268).

Caramel Custard
4 helpings

100g lump or granulated sugar
150ml water
400ml milk or 300ml milk and
    100ml single cream

2 eggs and 2 yolks or 3 eggs
25g caster sugar
a few drops vanilla essence

Prepare a thickly folded band of newspaper long enough to encircle a 13cm round cake tin or charlotte mould. Heat the tin or mould in boiling water or in the oven and wrap the newspaper round it. Prepare the caramel by heating the sugar and water together, stirring occasionally, until the sugar dissolves completely. Bring to the boil gently, and boil, without stirring, for about 10 minutes until the syrup turns golden-brown. Do not let it turn dark brown as it will have a bitter taste. Pour a little of the caramel on to a metal plate and put to one side. Pour the remaining caramel into the warmed, dry tin, tilt and turn it, holding it by the paper, until the base and sides are evenly coated. Leave until cold and set.

Warm the milk and cream to approximately 65°C; do not let it come near the boil. Beat the eggs and sugar together with a fork and stir in the milk. Add a few drops of vanilla essence. Strain the custard into the tin and cover with greased foil or grease-proof paper. Steam very gently for about 40 minutes or until the custard is firm in the centre.

Alternatively, stand the custard in a shallow tin containing enough warm water to come half-way up the sides of the dish, and bake in a very cool oven at 140°–150°C, Gas 1–2, for 1 hour.

Remove the cooked custard and leave it to stand for a few minutes, then turn it out carefully on to a warmed dish. The caramel will run off and serve as a sauce. Break up the reserved caramel by tapping sharply with a metal spoon, and decorate the top of the custard with the pieces of broken caramel.

Note Individual caramel custards can be made in four 150ml ovenproof moulds. Steam for 20 minutes, or bake for 30 minutes.

Crème Brûlée
4 helpings

1 × 15ml spoon cornflour
250ml milk
250ml single cream
a few drops vanilla essence

3 eggs
50g caster sugar
fat for greasing
ground cinnamon (optional)

Blend the cornflour to a smooth paste with a little of the milk, and bring the rest of the milk to the boil. Pour the boiling milk on to the blended cornflour, stirring well. Return the mixture to the pan, bring to the boil, and boil for 1 minute, stirring all the time. Remove from the heat and leave to cool. Beat together the cream, vanilla essence, and eggs. Stir into the cooled mixture. Whisk over low heat for about 30 minutes or until the custard thickens; do not boil. Add 25g sugar and pour into a greased 600ml flameproof dish. Sprinkle the pudding with the rest of the sugar and a little cinnamon, if used. Place under a hot grill for 10 minutes or until the sugar has melted and turned brown. Keep the custard about 10cm from the heat. Serve hot or cold.

Alternatively, bake in a fairly hot oven at 200°C, Gas 6, for about 15 minutes until the pudding is browned.

Custard Tart
4 helpings

100g shortcrust pastry (p453) using 125g flour	2 eggs
flour for rolling out	50g caster sugar
250ml milk	a pinch of grated nutmeg

Put an 18cm flan ring on a heavy baking sheet or line an 18cm sandwich tin with foil. Roll out the pastry on a lightly floured surface and use it to line the flan ring or cake tin, taking care not to stretch the pastry. Warm the milk to approximately 65°C; do not let it come near the boil. Beat the eggs and sugar together with a fork and add the milk. Strain the mixture into the pastry case and sprinkle the top with grated nutmeg. Bake in a fairly hot oven at 190°C, Gas 5, for 10 minutes, reduce the temperature to cool, 150°C, Gas 2, and bake for a further 15–20 minutes or until the custard is just set. Serve hot or cold.

Queen of Puddings
4 helpings

75g soft white breadcrumbs	2 eggs
400ml milk	75g caster sugar
25g butter	fat for greasing
2 × 5ml spoons grated lemon rind	2 × 15ml spoons red jam

Dry the breadcrumbs slightly by placing in a cool oven for a few moments. Warm the milk with the butter and lemon rind, to approximately 65°C; do not let it come near the boil. Separate the eggs and stir 25g of the sugar into the yolks. Pour the warmed milk over the yolks, and stir in well. Add the crumbs and mix thoroughly. Pour the custard mixture into a greased 750ml pie dish and leave to stand for 30 minutes. Bake in a warm oven at 160°C, Gas 3, for 40–45 minutes until the pudding is lightly set.

Remove the pudding from the oven and reduce the temperature to 120°C, Gas $\frac{1}{2}$. Warm the jam and spread it over the pudding. Whisk the egg whites until stiff, add half the remaining sugar and whisk again. Fold in nearly all the remaining sugar. Spoon the meringue round the edge of the jam and sprinkle with the remainder of the caster sugar. (The piled-up meringue and the red jam centre then suggest a crown.) Return the pudding to the oven for 40–45 minutes or until the meringue is set.

Zabaglione
4 helpings

4 egg yolks
40g caster sugar

4 × 15ml spoons Marsala (Bual) **or**
Madeira **or** sweet sherry

Put the egg yolks into a deep heatproof basin and whisk lightly. Add the sugar and wine, and place the bowl over a pan of hot water. Whisk for about 10 minutes or until the mixture is very thick and creamy. When the whisk is lifted out of the bowl, a trail of the mixture from the whisk should lie on top for 2–3 seconds. Pour the custard into individual glasses and serve at once while still warm.

Serve with Mrs Beeton's Savoy Cakes (p419).

VARIATION

Cold Zabaglione
Dissolve 50g caster sugar in 4 × 15ml spoons water, and boil for 1–2 minutes until syrupy. Whisk with the egg yolks until pale and thick. Add 2 × 15ml spoons Marsala (Bual), Madeira or sweet sherry and 2 × 15ml spoons single cream while whisking. The finely grated rind of half a lemon can be added, if liked. Chill before serving.

Soufflés, Omelets, Pancakes and Waffles

Vanilla Soufflé *Basic recipe*
4 helpings

35g butter
35g plain flour
250ml milk
4 eggs

50g caster sugar
$\frac{1}{2}$ × 5ml spoon vanilla essence
1 egg white
caster **or** icing sugar for dredging

Heat the oven to moderate, 180°C, Gas 4, or put the steamer on to heat. Prepare a 1 litre soufflé dish (p232). Melt the butter in a saucepan, stir in the flour and cook slowly for 2–3 minutes, without colouring, stirring all the time. Add the milk gradually and beat until smooth. Cook for another 1–2 minutes, still stirring all the time. Remove from the heat and beat hard until the sauce comes away from the sides of the pan cleanly. Cool slightly and put into a bowl.

Separate the eggs and beat the yolks into the mixture one by one. Beat in the sugar and vanilla essence. Whisk all the egg whites until stiff. Using a metal spoon, stir 1 spoonful of the whites into the mixture, then fold in the rest until evenly distributed. Put into the dish and bake for 45 minutes until well risen and browned; alternatively, cover with greased greaseproof paper and steam slowly for 1 hour until just firm to the touch.

Dredge with caster or icing sugar and serve immediately from the dish, with Jam Sauce (p268).

VARIATIONS

A hot sweet soufflé can be flavoured in many different ways. Unless otherwise stated in the variations which follow, stir in the flavouring before adding the egg yolks. Omit the vanilla essence.

Almond Soufflé
Add 100g ground almonds, 1 × 15ml spoon lemon juice, and a few drops of ratafia essence. Reduce the sugar to 40g.

Apple Soufflé
Add 125ml thick sweet apple purée, 1 × 15ml spoon lemon juice, and a pinch of powdered cinnamon. Dust with cinnamon before serving.

Apricot Soufflé
Add 125ml thick apricot purée and 1 × 15ml spoon lemon juice, if using fresh apricots. If using canned apricots (1 × 400g can makes 125ml purée) use half milk and half syrup to make the sauce. A dried apricot purée is delicious.

Coffee Soufflé
Add 2 × 15ml spoons instant coffee dissolved in a little hot water, or use 125ml strong black coffee and only 125ml milk.

Lemon Soufflé
Add the thinly grated rind and juice of 1 lemon. Serve with Lemon Sauce (p266).

Orange Soufflé
Pare the rind of 2 oranges thinly. Put in a pan with the milk and bring slowly to the boil. Remove from the heat, cover, and leave to stand for 10 minutes, then remove the rind. Make up the sauce using the flavoured milk. Reduce the sugar to 40g. Add the strained juice of half an orange.

Pineapple Soufflé
Add 125ml crushed pineapple or 75g chopped pineapple, and make the sauce using half milk and half pineapple juice.

Praline Soufflé
Dissolve 2–3 × 15ml spoons almond praline (p446) in the milk before making the sauce, or crush and add just before the egg yolks.

Raspberry Soufflé
Add 125ml raspberry purée (1 × 400g can makes 125ml purée) and 1 × 10ml spoon lemon juice.

Soufflé Ambassadrice
Crumble 2 macaroons and soak them in 2 × 15ml spoons rum with 50g chopped blanched almonds. Stir into a vanilla soufflé mixture.

Soufflé Harlequin
Make up 2 half quantities of soufflé mixture in different flavours, eg chocolate and vanilla, or praline and coffee. Spoon alternately into the dish.

For another **variation**, see over

Strawberry Soufflé

Add 125ml strawberry purée, and make the sauce using half milk and half single cream. Add a little pink food colouring, if necessary.

Sweet Soufflé Omelet *Basic recipe*
1 helping

2 eggs
1 × 5ml spoon caster sugar
a few drops vanilla essence
2 × 15ml spoons water

1 × 15ml spoon unsalted butter **or**
   margarine
icing sugar for dredging

Separate the eggs. Whisk the yolks until creamy, add the sugar, vanilla essence and water, and whisk again. Whisk the egg whites until stiff and matt. Place an 18cm omelet pan over gentle heat and when it is hot add the butter or margarine. Tilt the pan so that the whole of the inside of the pan is greased. Pour out any excess. Fold the egg whites into the yolk mixture carefully until evenly distributed, using a metal spoon. Do not overmix, as it is most important not to break down the egg white foam. Pour the egg mixture into the pan, level the top very lightly, and cook for 1–2 minutes over a moderate heat until the omelet is golden-brown on the underside; the top should still be moist. (Use a palette knife to lift the edge of the omelet to look underneath.)

Put the pan under a moderate grill for 5–6 minutes until the omelet is risen and lightly browned on the top. The texture of the omelet should be firm yet spongy. Remove from the heat as soon as it is ready, as overcooking tends to make it tough. Run a palette knife gently round the edge and underneath to loosen it. Make a mark across the middle at right angles to the pan handle but do not cut the surface. Put any filling on one half, raise the handle of the pan and double the omelet over. Turn gently on to a warm plate, dredge with icing sugar and serve at once.

FILLINGS

Apricot Omelet

Add the grated rind of 1 orange to the egg yolks. Spread 2 × 15ml spoons warm, thick apricot purée over the omelet.

Jam Omelet

Spread the cooked omelet with 2 × 15ml spoons warmed jam.

Lemon Omelet

Add the grated rind of $\frac{1}{2}$ lemon to the egg yolks. Warm 3 × 15ml spoons lemon curd with 1 × 10ml spoon lemon juice, and spread over the omelet.

Rum Omelet

Add 1 × 15ml spoon rum to the egg yolks.

Strawberry Omelet

Hull 5 ripe strawberries, and soak in a little Kirsch. Mash slightly with icing sugar. Put in the centre of the omelet.

Branded Soufflé Omelets

Soufflé omelets are sometimes served 'branded' for a special occasion. A lattice decoration is marked on the top using hot skewers. Heat the pointed ends of 3 metal skewers until red-hot. When the omelet is on the plate, dredge with icing sugar, then quickly press the hot skewers, one at a time, on to the sugar, holding them there until the sugar caramelizes. Make a diagonal criss-cross design. Each skewer should make 2 marks if you work quickly.

Sweet Pancakes *Basic recipe*

Add 2 × 5ml spoons caster sugar to a basic thin batter (p225). Cook as for Plain Pancakes (p226). Slide on to sugared paper and roll or fold as preferred.

VARIATIONS

Apple Pancakes

Mix together 250ml sweetened, thick apple purée, 50g sultanas, and a pinch of powdered cinnamon. Spoon on to the pancakes when made, and roll up. If liked, sprinkle with caster sugar, and glaze in a very hot oven or under the grill.

Apricot Pancakes

Add 1 × 15ml spoon powdered cinnamon to the batter. Soak 50g dried apricots in 4 × 15ml spoons water, and then simmer with 50g sugar and a good squeeze of lemon juice, until soft and pulpy. Add 25g almonds, lightly browned and chopped. Fill the pancakes as for Apple Pancakes.

Banana Pancakes

Mash 4 bananas with 50g softened butter, 2 × 15ml spoons sugar, and the grated rind and juice of 1 lemon. Fill the pancakes as for Apple Pancakes.

Chocolate Pancakes

Sprinkle each pancake with grated plain chocolate and dredge with icing sugar when made. Stack the flat pancakes and dredge the top one with sugar. Serve cut in wedges, with cream.

Currant Pancakes

Scatter a few currants or sultanas on each pancake as it is cooking. Allow 50g in all. Do not add to the batter as they will sink to the bottom. Serve with lemon and sugar.

Jam Pancakes

Spread the pancakes with warmed jam before rolling up.

Lemon Pancakes

Sprinkle with lemon juice, roll up, and sprinkle with caster sugar. Serve with wedges of lemon. Serve on Shrove Tuesday.

Surprise Pancakes

Spoon some ice cream into the centre of each pancake and fold it in half like an omelet. Serve with Jam Sauce (p268).

Layered Pancakes

Stack the pancakes in layers, and fill each layer with the following: 100g curd cheese mixed with 1 egg yolk, 1 × 10ml spoon sugar and the grated rind of ½ lemon; warmed apricot jam; 50g finely chopped nuts mixed with 50g grated plain chocolate. Make a meringue from 2 egg whites and 100g caster sugar, and use to cover the pile of pancakes completely. Bake in a fairly hot oven at 190°C, Gas 5, for 15–20 minutes, until crisp and lightly browned. Serve cut in wedges.

Breakfast Pancakes

4 helpings

1 egg	100g plain flour
250ml milk	2 × 5ml spoons baking powder
2 × 15ml spoons melted butter **or** oil	1 × 2.5ml spoon salt
1 × 15ml spoon caster sugar	fat **or** oil for frying

Beat the egg until liquid, add the remaining ingredients and whisk until smooth. Heat a little fat or oil in a frying pan. Pour off any excess. Put 2 × 15ml spoons batter into the pan to make a pancake about 10cm in diameter. Bubbles will appear on the surface of the pancake. As soon as it is brown underneath but before the bubbles break, turn the pancake over and fry the other side until brown. Transfer to a clean tea-towel, fold the towel over it, and keep warm.

Cook the rest of the batter in the same way, greasing the pan when necessary.

Serve in piles of three with butter and maple syrup or marmalade, or with grilled sausages and bacon.

Waffles

Makes 8

75g butter	1 × 5ml spoon baking powder
250g self-raising flour	2 eggs
½ × 5ml spoon salt	375ml milk

Melt the butter and cool it. Sift the flour, salt, and baking powder into a bowl. Separate the eggs. Make a well in the centre of the flour. Add the egg yolks, cooled butter, and some of the milk. Gradually work in the flour from the sides and then beat well until smooth. Beat in the rest of the milk. Whisk the egg whites until stiff, and fold into the batter. It should be the consistency of thick cream.

Heat a waffle iron, pour in the batter, and cook for about 5 minutes until the steaming stops.

Serve hot with butter and golden or maple syrup.

Boiled, Steamed and Baked Puddings

Consistency of Mixture

A *dropping consistency* means the mixture should just drop from the spoon when shaken lightly.

A *soft dropping consistency* means that the mixture drops from the spoon easily.

A *slack consistency* means that it falls off the spoon almost of its own accord.

Preparing Containers

Always prepare the containers and a greased paper or foil cover before making the pudding. The inside of the container should be well greased with clarified butter or margarine, cooking fat or oil.

Note A charlotte mould, cake tin or foil container can be used instead of a pudding basin for a baked pudding. For individual puddings, small dariole moulds, ceramic cocottes or ramekins are useful.

To Line a Basin with Suet Crust

Cut off one-quarter of the pastry for the lid. Roll the remaining pastry 1cm larger than the top of the basin, and put the pastry into the greased basin. By pressing with the fingers, work evenly up the sides of the container to the top. Put in the required filling. Roll out the pastry for the lid to the same size as the top of the basin. Dampen the rim, and place it on top of the filling. Press the rim of the lid against the edge of the lining to seal the crust.

General Hints on Cooking

Steamed puddings: Only three-quarters fill the basin before putting on the pastry lid. Cover with greased paper or foil, to prevent steam getting in. Put the cover on greased side down. Either twist the edges under the rim of the basin, or tie them.

If you have a steamer, put the pudding in the perforated top part and have the water underneath boiling. If, however, a recipe calls for gentle steaming, only let the water simmer. Cover closely and steam for the time directed.

If you have no steamer, stand the pudding basin on an old saucer or plate in a saucepan, with water coming half-way up the basin's sides. Put a tight-fitting lid on the pan, and simmer gently. This method is called 'half-steaming'.

With either method, always top up the water with more boiling water when the water in the pan is reduced by a third.

After taking the pudding out of the steamer, let it stand for a few minutes to shrink and firm up before turning it out on to a dish. To turn out a steamed or boiled pudding, loosen the sides from the basin with a knife. Place the warmed serving dish upside-down over the basin and turn them over together. Do not use a plate for fruit puddings in case juice seeps out.

Boiled puddings: If you wish, you can boil a pudding in a basin covered with a floured cloth, or in a well-floured cloth only. Roly-poly puddings can be rolled in a scalded floured cloth, forming a sausage shape; tie loosely at each end, leaving room for the pudding to swell. If you use a basin, fill it completely and cover securely as for steamed puddings.

Have enough rapidly boiling water ready in a large saucepan to cover the pudding completely. Put the pudding into the fast-boiling water, and reduce the heat so that the water only simmers. Top up with boiling water when required, as above.

Let the pudding stand for a few moments after removing it from the water to let it shrink and firm up.

Baked puddings: Use a well-greased basin, pie dish, oven-to-table baking dish or a foil container with a really clean edge. Baked puddings are easier to handle if placed on a flat baking sheet in the oven.

Suet Pudding (unsweetened) *Basic recipe*
6−7 helpings

300g plain flour	150g shredded suet
$\frac{1}{2}$ × 2.5ml spoon salt	cold water
2 × 5ml spoons baking powder	flour for dusting

Sift the flour, salt, and baking powder together. Add the suet, and enough cold water to make a soft but not sticky dough. Shape into a roll. Lay the dough on a scalded, well-floured pudding cloth and roll up loosely. Tie up the ends of the cloth. Put into a saucepan of fast-boiling water, reduce the heat and simmer for 2−2$\frac{1}{2}$ hours. Drain well and unwrap.

Serve sliced, with meat or gravy or with any sweet sauce.

VARIATIONS

Roly-poly Pudding
Make the suet crust as in the basic recipe. Roll out the dough into a rectangle about 5mm thick. Spread with jam almost to the edge. Dampen the edges and roll up lightly. Seal the edges. Cook as in the basic recipe.

Fruit Roly-poly
Mix into the basic recipe 150g chopped dates, currants, sultanas, raisins or figs. Shape into a roll, and cook as in the basic recipe. Drain, unwrap, slice, and serve with any custard or sweet sauce, or with warmed golden syrup and cream.

Spotted Dick
Mix into the basic recipe 150g caster sugar and 150g currants. Use milk instead of water. Shape into a roll and cook as in the basic recipe. Drain, unwrap, slice, and serve with any custard or sweet sauce, or with warmed golden syrup and cream.

Boiled Apple Dumplings
6 helpings

6 cooking apples	75g Demerara sugar
300g prepared suet crust pastry (p454)	6 cloves
flour for dusting	

Core and peel the apples. Divide the pastry into 6 portions and, on a lightly floured surface, roll each into a round. Put an apple in the centre of each round of pastry and work the pastry round the apple until it almost meets at the top. Fill the core hole with sugar and stick a clove upright in the middle of each apple. Dampen the edges of the pastry, work it up to meet over the apple, and seal well, leaving the clove exposed. Tie each dumpling in a small well-floured pudding cloth. Put the dumplings into a saucepan of boiling water and boil gently for 40–50 minutes.

Drain well and serve with Apple Sauce (p251) and Pouring Cup Custard (p318).

Christmas Pudding (1) (rich boiled)
6 helpings per pudding

fat for greasing	250g currants
200g plain flour	200g seedless raisins
a pinch of salt	200g cut mixed peel
1 × 5ml spoon ground ginger	175g stale white breadcrumbs
1 × 5ml spoon mixed spice	6 eggs
1 × 5ml spoon grated nutmeg	75ml stout
50g chopped blanched almonds	juice of 1 orange
400g soft light **or** dark brown sugar	50ml brandy **or** to taste
250g shredded suet	125–250ml milk
250g sultanas	

Grease four 600ml basins. Sift together the flour, salt, ginger, mixed spice, and nutmeg into a mixing bowl. Add the nuts, sugar, suet, sultanas, currants, raisins, peel, and breadcrumbs. Beat together the eggs, stout, orange juice, brandy, and 125ml milk. Stir this into the dry ingredients, adding more milk if required, to give a soft dropping consistency. Put the mixture into the prepared basins, cover with greased paper or foil, and a floured cloth. Put into deep boiling water and boil steadily for 6–7 hours, or half steam for the same length of time.

To store, cover with a clean dry cloth, wrap in greaseproof paper and store in a cool place until required. To re-heat, boil or steam for $1\frac{1}{2}$–2 hours. Serve with Brandy Butter (p566) or Pouring Cup Custard (p318).

Apple Pudding (steamed)
5–6 helpings

150g cooking apples	a pinch of salt
100g shredded suet	2 eggs
100g stale white breadcrumbs	125ml milk (approx)
100g soft light brown sugar	fat for greasing
$\frac{1}{2}$ × 2.5ml spoon grated nutmeg	

Peel, core, and chop the apples coarsely. Mix together the apples, suet, breadcrumbs, sugar, nutmeg, and salt. Beat the eggs until liquid and stir into the dry ingredients with enough milk to make a soft dropping consistency. Leave to stand for 1 hour to allow the bread to soak. If very stiff, add a little more milk. Put the mixture into a greased 1 litre basin, cover with greased paper or foil and steam for $1\frac{3}{4}$–2 hours. Serve from the basin, or leave for 5–10 minutes at room temperature to firm up, then turn out. Serve with Pouring Cup Custard (p318).

VARIATIONS

Cumberland Pudding

Use 250g apples, and substitute 200g sifted plain flour with 2 × 5ml spoons baking powder for the breadcrumbs. Add 150g currants with the flour. Reduce the sugar to 75g and the milk to 75ml. Steam in a 750ml basin. Serve turned out, dredged with soft light brown sugar.

Other Fruit Puddings

Instead of apples, use the same quantity of prepared damsons, gooseberries, green-gages, plums or rhubarb.

Brown Bread Pudding

4–6 helpings

175g stale brown breadcrumbs	75g caster sugar
75g raisins	2 eggs
75g sultanas	milk
100g shredded suet	fat for greasing

Mix together all the ingredients, adding enough milk to make a dropping consistency. Leave to stand for 30 minutes. Add more milk if the pudding is too stiff, to give a dropping consistency. Put the mixture into a greased 750ml basin, cover with greased paper or foil and steam for 2½–3 hours. Serve from the basin, or leave for 5–10 minutes at room temperature to firm up, then turn out.

Serve with Pouring Cup Custard (p318) or Simple Custard (p319).

Christmas Pudding (2) (economical)

12 helpings

fat for greasing	200g shredded suet
1 cooking apple	150g mixed cut peel
100g plain flour	grated rind and juice of 1 lemon
25g self-raising flour	2 eggs
a pinch of salt	125ml milk (approx)
100g stale white breadcrumbs	1 × 5ml spoon almond essence
400g mixed dried fruit	1 × 5ml spoon gravy browning
100g soft light **or** dark brown sugar	

Grease two 600ml basins or one 1 litre basin. Peel, core, and chop the apple. Sift together the flours and salt into a bowl. Add the breadcrumbs, dried fruit, sugar, suet, peel, lemon rind, and juice. Beat together the eggs, milk, and almond essence and stir into the dry ingredients, adding more milk if required, to give a soft dropping consistency. Add the gravy browning to darken the mixture. Mix well, then put the mixture into the basins. Cover with greased paper or foil, and a floured cloth, and steam for 5 hours.

Store, re-heat and serve as for Christmas Pudding (rich boiled) (p331).

Golden Syrup Pudding
6–7 helpings

fat for greasing
3 × 15ml spoons golden syrup
150g plain flour
1 × 5ml spoon bicarbonate of soda
a pinch of salt
1 × 5ml spoon ground ginger

150g stale white breadcrumbs
100g shredded suet
50g caster sugar
1 egg
1 × 15ml spoon black treacle
75–100ml milk

Grease a 1 litre basin, and put 1 × 15ml spoon of golden syrup in the bottom. Sift together the flour, bicarbonate of soda, salt, and ginger. Add the breadcrumbs, suet, and sugar. Beat together the egg, remaining syrup, treacle, and 75ml of the milk. Stir this mixture into the dry ingredients, adding more milk if required, to make a soft dropping consistency. Put into the basin, cover with greased paper or foil and steam for 1½–2 hours. Leave for 5–10 minutes to firm up, then turn out.

Serve with warmed golden syrup and whipped cream.

Lemon Pudding
6–7 helpings

50g plain flour
a pinch of salt
1 × 5ml spoon baking powder
175g stale white breadcrumbs
100g caster sugar

100g shredded suet
grated rind and juice of 2 lemons
2 eggs
150–175ml milk
fat for greasing

Sift together the flour, salt, and baking powder. Stir in the breadcrumbs, sugar, suet, and lemon rind. Beat together the eggs, lemon juice, and about 50–75ml of the milk. Stir into the dry ingredients, adding more milk if required, to make a soft dropping consistency. Put into a greased 750ml basin, cover with greased paper or foil, and steam for 1½–2 hours. Leave for 5–10 minutes, then turn out.

Serve with Lemon Sauce (p266).

Steamed Sponge Pudding (Canary Pudding) *Basic recipe*
6 helpings

150g butter or margarine
150g caster sugar
3 eggs
grated rind of ½ lemon

150g plain flour
1 × 5ml spoon baking powder
fat for greasing

Work together the fat and sugar until light and creamy. Beat in the eggs gradually. Add the lemon rind. Sift together the flour and baking powder and fold lightly into the mixture. Put into a greased 750ml basin, cover with greased paper or foil and steam for 1¼–1½ hours. Leave in the basin at room temperature for 3–5 minutes, then turn out.

Serve with Pouring Cup Custard (p318) or Jam Sauce (p268).

For **variations,** see over

VARIATIONS

1) Add to the basic recipe one of the following: 50g desiccated coconut, 150g chopped stoned dates, 150g dried fruit, 75g glacé cherries, 25g cocoa, 50g chopped preserved ginger, grated rind of 1 orange or lemon.

    Serve with Simple Custard (p319).

2) Before putting the basic mixture into the basin, put in 2 × 15ml spoons golden syrup, jam, marmalade or lemon curd. Serve with the same preserve used in the recipe.

Mrs Beeton's Bachelor's Pudding
5–6 helpings

150g cooking apples	$\frac{1}{2}$ × 2.5ml spoon grated nutmeg
100g stale white breadcrumbs	2 eggs
grated rind of $\frac{1}{2}$ lemon	milk
100g currants	1 × 5ml spoon baking powder
75g caster sugar	fat for greasing
a pinch of salt	

Peel, core, and chop the apples coarsely. Mix together the breadcrumbs, apples, grated lemon rind, currants, sugar, salt and nutmeg. Beat the eggs until liquid and add to the dry ingredients with enough milk to form a soft dropping consistency. Leave to stand for 30 minutes. Stir in the baking powder. Put the mixture into a greased 1 litre basin, cover with greased paper or foil and steam for $2\frac{1}{2}$–3 hours. Leave in the basin for a few minutes, then turn out.

    Serve with Simple Custard (p319) or Vanilla Sauce (p266).

Chocolate Pudding
5–6 helpings

fat for greasing	40g caster sugar
50g plain chocolate	2 eggs
125ml milk	100g stale white breadcrumbs
40g butter or margarine	$\frac{1}{2}$ × 2.5ml spoon baking powder

Grease a 750ml basin or 6 dariole moulds. Grate the chocolate into a saucepan, add the milk and heat slowly to dissolve the chocolate. Cream together the fat and sugar. Separate the eggs and beat the yolks into the creamed mixture. Add the melted chocolate, breadcrumbs, and baking powder. Whisk the egg whites until fairly stiff and fold into the mixture. Put into the basin or moulds, cover with greased paper or foil, and steam for 1 hour for a large pudding, and 30 minutes for dariole moulds. Leave in the basin for a few minutes, then turn out.

    Serve with Chocolate Sauce (p267).

Baked Sponge Pudding *Basic recipe*
4–6 helpings

100g butter **or** margarine
100g caster sugar
2 eggs
150g plain flour

1 × 5ml spoon baking powder
½ × 2.5ml spoon vanilla essence
2 × 15ml spoons milk (approx)
fat for greasing

Cream the fat and sugar together until light and fluffy. Beat the eggs until liquid, then beat them gradually into the creamed mixture. Sift together the flour and baking powder, and fold them in. Add the essence and enough milk to form a soft dropping consistency. Put into a greased 1 litre pie dish and bake in a moderate oven at 180°C, Gas 4, for 30–35 minutes until well risen and golden-brown.

Serve from the dish with Pouring Cup Custard (p318) or any sweet sauce.

Note If using a pie dish it can be encircled with a pie frill before presenting at table.

VARIATIONS

Jam Sponge
Put 2 × 15ml spoons jam in the bottom of the dish before adding the sponge mixture.

Orange or Lemon Sponge
Add the grated rind of 1 orange or lemon to the creamed mixture.

Spicy Sponge
Sift 1 × 5ml spoon mixed spice, ground ginger, grated nutmeg or cinnamon with the flour.

Coconut Sponge
Substitute 25g desiccated coconut for 25g flour.

Chocolate Sponge
Substitute 50g cocoa for 50g flour.

Baked Jam Roll
6 helpings

300g plain flour
1 × 5ml spoon baking powder
a pinch of salt
150g shredded suet

flour for rolling out
200–300g jam
butter for greasing

Sift the flour, baking powder, and salt into a bowl. Add the suet and enough cold water to make a soft, but firm dough. On a lightly floured surface, roll into a rectangle about 5mm thick. Spread the jam almost to the edges, dampen the edges, and roll up lightly. Seal the edges at each end. Grease a baking sheet and place the roll on it, with the sealed edge underneath. Cover loosely with greased paper or foil. Bake in a fairly hot oven at 190°C, Gas 5, for 50–60 minutes until golden-brown.

Serve on a warm platter, sliced, with warmed jam.

Eve's Pudding
4 helpings

400g cooking apples	75g butter **or** margarine
grated rind and juice of 1 lemon	75g caster sugar
75g Demerara sugar	1 egg
1 × 15ml spoon water	100g self-raising flour
fat for greasing	

Peel, core, and slice the apples thinly. Mix together with the lemon rind and juice, Demerara sugar, and water, and put into a greased 1 litre pie dish. Cream the fat and caster sugar together until light and fluffy. Beat the egg until liquid and beat into the creamed mixture. Fold in the flour lightly and spread the mixture over the apples. Bake in a moderate oven at 180°C, Gas 4, for 40–45 minutes until the apples are soft and the sponge is firm.

Serve with Pouring Cup Custard (p318) or melted apple jelly and single cream.

Fruit Puddings and Desserts

Apple Amber (1)
4 helpings

3 eggs	500ml thick apple purée
1 × 15ml spoon lemon juice	250g caster sugar (approx)

Decoration

glacé cherries	angelica

Separate the eggs. Beat the lemon juice and yolks into the apple purée with about 75g of the sugar. Turn into a 750ml baking dish, cover, and bake in a moderate oven at 180°C, Gas 4, for 15 minutes. Whisk the egg whites until they form stiff peaks. Gradually whisk in 150g of the remaining sugar, adding 1 × 5ml spoonful at a time. Pile the meringue on top of the apple mixture and sprinkle with 1 × 15ml spoon sugar. Return to the oven and bake for a further 15 minutes or until the meringue is pale golden-brown.

Serve at once with Pouring Cup Custard (p318) or single cream.

Apple Batter Pudding
4 helpings

25g cooking fat **or** oil	50g sugar
500g cooking apples	grated rind of ½ lemon
basic thin batter (p225)	

Heat the oven to hot, 220°C, Gas 7. Put the fat or oil into a 17 × 27cm baking tin and heat in the oven for 5 minutes. Peel, core, and slice the apples thinly. Prepare the batter. Remove the tin from the oven, arrange the apple slices in an even layer on the bottom, and sprinkle with the sugar and lemon rind. Pour the batter over the apples and bake for 30–35 minutes until brown and well-risen.

Serve cut into 4 pieces, with golden syrup or a lemon sauce.

VARIATIONS

Apricot Batter Pudding

Just cover 100g dried apricots with water and soak until soft, preferably overnight. Put the apricots and water into a pan and simmer for 15 minutes. Drain. Heat the tin and put the apricots in an even layer on the bottom. Continue as for Apple Batter Pudding. Serve with an apricot jam sauce.

Dried Fruit Batter Pudding

Spread 50g mixed dried fruit over the bottom of the tin and sprinkle with $\frac{1}{2} \times 5$ml spoon mixed spice or ground cinnamon. Continue as for Apple Batter Pudding. Serve with a lemon sauce.

Black Cap Pudding

Grease 12 deep patty tins and divide 50g currants between them. Pour in enough batter to half-fill each tin and bake for 15–20 minutes. Turn out to serve.

Apple Charlotte

5–6 helpings

butter for greasing	50–75g butter
400g cooking apples	8–10 large slices white bread,
grated rind and juice of 1 lemon	5mm thick
100g soft light brown sugar	1 × 15ml spoon caster sugar
a pinch of ground cinnamon	

Grease a 1 litre charlotte mould or 16cm cake tin heavily with butter. Peel, core, and slice the apples. Simmer the apples, lemon rind and juice with the sugar and cinnamon until the apples soften to a thick purée. Leave to cool.

Melt the butter. Cut the crusts off the bread, and dip 1 slice in the butter. Cut it into a round to fit the bottom of the mould or tin. Fill any spaces if necessary. Dip the remaining bread slices in the butter. Line the inside of the mould with 6 slices, touching one another. Fill the bread case with the cooled purée. Complete the case by fitting the top with more bread slices. Cover loosely with greased paper or foil, and bake in a moderate oven at 180°C, Gas 4, for 40–45 minutes. For serving, turn out and dredge with caster sugar.

Serve with bramble jelly and cream.

VARIATIONS

1) Line the mould or tin with slices of bread and butter, placed buttered side out, instead of dipping bread in melted butter.

2) Instead of lining the sides of the mould or tin, arrange the purée and dipped bread in alternate layers in the mould or tin until all the ingredients are used, ending with a layer of bread.

Apple Crumble
6 helpings

600g cooking apples	75g butter or margarine
100g brown sugar	150g plain flour
50ml water	75g caster sugar
grated rind of 1 lemon	½ × 2.5ml spoon ground ginger
fat for greasing	

Peel, core, and slice the apples. Cook with the brown sugar, water, and lemon rind in a covered pan until soft. Fill a greased 1 litre pie dish with the apples. Rub the fat into the flour until it resembles fine breadcrumbs. Add the caster sugar and ginger and stir well, sprinkle the mixture over the apples, and press down lightly. Bake in a moderate oven at 180°C, Gas 4, for 30–40 minutes until the crumble is golden-brown.

VARIATION

Instead of apples, use 600g damsons, gooseberries, pears, plums, rhubarb, or raspberries.

Baked Apples
6 helpings

6 cooking apples	50g Demerara sugar
filling (see below)	75ml water

Wash and core the apples. Cut round the skin of each apple with the tip of a sharp knife two-thirds of the way up from the base. Put into an ovenproof dish, and fill the centres with the chosen filling. Sprinkle the Demerara sugar on top of the apples and pour the water round them. Bake in a moderate oven at 180°C, Gas 4, for 45–60 minutes, depending on the cooking quality and size of the apples.

Serve with Pouring Cup Custard (p318), ice cream or with whipped cream, sweetened and flavoured with brandy.

Fillings
1) Mix together 50g Barbados or other raw sugar and 50g butter.
2) Use blackcurrant, raspberry, strawberry or apricot jam, or marmalade.
3) Chop 75g stoned dates, sultanas, raisins or currants.
4) Mix together 50g soft light brown sugar and 1 × 5ml spoon ground cinnamon.

Brown Betty
6 helpings

1kg cooking apples
fat for greasing
150g stale wholemeal breadcrumbs
grated rind and juice of 1 lemon

4 × 15ml spoons golden syrup
100g Demerara sugar
2 × 15ml spoons water

Peel, core, and thinly slice the apples. Coat a greased 1 litre pie dish with a thin layer of breadcrumbs, then fill with alternate layers of apples, lemon rind, and breadcrumbs. Heat the syrup, sugar, water, and lemon juice in a saucepan and pour over the mixture. Bake in a warm oven at 160°C, Gas 3, for 1–1¼ hours until the pudding is brown and the apple cooked.

Serve with single cream or any pouring custard (p318).

Glazed Apple Dumplings
6 helpings

300g prepared shortcrust pastry
  (p453)
flour for rolling out
½ × 2.5ml spoon ground cinnamon
50g brown sugar

6 cooking apples
12 cloves (optional)
1 × 15ml spoon milk
25g caster sugar

Divide the pastry into 6 portions. On a lightly floured surface roll each out into a round. Mix together the cinnamon and brown sugar. Peel and core the apples and put each on a round of pastry. Fill the apple cavity with the sugar mixture, and press 2 cloves into the top of each apple, if liked. Work the pastry round the apple to enclose it, moisten the edges and press well together, leaving the cloves sticking out. Place the dumplings on a baking tray. Brush them with milk and dredge with caster sugar. Bake in a fairly hot oven at 200°C, Gas 6, for 30–35 minutes or until the apples are tender.

Serve with single cream.

Fruit Fritters
Prepare the fruit as below. Dry well on soft kitchen paper. Heat deep fat or oil (p11). Test the consistency of the batter to make sure that it coats the back of a spoon. Using a skewer or fork, dip the pieces of fruit, one by one, in coating batter (1) (p223). Put a few pieces into the fat and fry, turning once, until crisp and golden. Drain the fritters well on soft kitchen paper. Keep hot in a single layer on a baking sheet in a cool oven at about 150°C, Gas 2.

Serve while hot, sprinkled with caster sugar and with a suitable fruit sauce or cream.

Apples: Peel and core 500g apples, and cut into 5mm slices. Put into water containing a little lemon juice until needed. Drain well and dry with soft kitchen paper before coating. Coat, and fry. Serve with Lemon Sauce (p266).

Apricots: Sprinkle canned apricot halves with rum and leave for 15 minutes. Coat, and fry. Serve dredged with caster sugar and cinnamon, and with custard or cream.

Bananas: Peel 4 small bananas, cut in half lengthways, then in half across. Coat, and fry. Serve with Simple Custard (p319) flavoured with rum.

Oranges: Remove the peel and pith from 4 oranges. Divide them into pieces of 2 or 3 segments each. Carefully cut into the centre to remove any pips. Coat, and fry. Serve with custard or sweetened cream flavoured with an orange-flavoured liqueur.

Pears: Peel and core 4 pears. Cut into quarters, sprinkle with sugar and Kirsch, and leave to stand for 15 minutes. Crush 4 macaroons finely, and toss the pear pieces in the crumbs. Coat, and fry. Serve with Lemon Sauce (p266) or warmed apricot jam flavoured with Kirsch.

Pineapple: Drain 1 × 566g can pineapple slices, pat dry and sprinkle with 4 × 5ml spoons Kirsch; leave for 15 minutes before coating. Coat, and fry. Serve with the pineapple juice thickened with arrowroot or cornflour.

Gooseberry Fritters
4 helpings

400g gooseberries	caster sugar
oil **or** fat for deep frying	

Batter

50g plain flour	2 eggs
a pinch of salt	3 × 15ml spoons milk
1 × 15ml spoon caster sugar	

Prepare the batter first. Sift together the flour and salt. Add the sugar. Separate the eggs. Mix the yolks and milk into the flour and beat well to form a thick batter. Prepare and dry the gooseberries. Heat the fat (p11). Whisk the egg whites until stiff and fold into the batter. Add the gooseberries. Dip a metal tablespoon in the hot fat, and then lift 3 coated gooseberries on to it. Lower them into the hot fat, without separating them. As the batter cooks, the berries will fuse together. Fry until golden-brown, turning once. Drain well. Serve sprinkled with plenty of sugar.

VARIATIONS

Hulled strawberries, stoned cherries, red and blackcurrants can be cooked in the same way. Canned fruit can also be used but it must be drained very thoroughly. Alternatively, add 50g currants to the batter instead of the gooseberries. Serve sprinkled with sugar, and with Lemon Sauce (p266).

Pineapple Upside-Down Cake

1 × 227g can pineapple rings	1 × 5ml spoon ground cinnamon
100g butter	1 × 5ml spoon ground nutmeg
275g soft dark brown sugar	2 eggs
8 maraschino **or** glacé cherries	250ml milk
450g self-raising flour	

Drain the pineapple rings, reserving the syrup. Melt 50g of the butter in a 20cm square baking tin. Add 125g of the sugar and 1 × 15ml spoon of pineapple syrup;

mix well. Arrange the pineapple rings in an even pattern in the bottom of the tin, and place a cherry in the centre of each ring.

Sift together the flour, cinnamon, and nutmeg. Beat the eggs with the remaining brown sugar. Melt the remaining butter and add to the eggs and sugar with the milk; mix into the spiced flour. Pour this mixture carefully over the fruit in the baking tin without disturbing it. Bake in a moderate oven, 180°C, Gas 4, for 45–50 minutes. Remove the tin from the oven and at once turn upside-down on to a plate; allow the caramel to run over the cake before removing the baking tin.

Serve warm with cream as a dessert, or cold for afternoon tea.

Plums with Port
6 helpings

1kg plums   150ml port
100–150g soft light brown sugar

Cut the plums neatly in half and remove the stones. Put into a baking dish or casserole, sprinkle with the sugar (the amount required will depend on the sweetness of the plums) and pour the port on top. Cover securely with a lid or foil and bake in a cool oven at 150°C, Gas 2, for 45–60 minutes or until the plums are tender. Serve hot, or lightly chilled.

Stuffed Fresh Peaches
4–8 helpings

50g unsalted butter   125g plain **or** sponge cake crumbs
8 large peaches   2 egg whites
50g salted butter   2 drops almond essence **or** 1 × 15ml
125g caster sugar   spoon anisette liqueur
125g ground almonds

Grease a shallow ovenproof dish with the unsalted butter. With the point of a knife, make 2 slits in the skin of each peach. Scald the fruit for 40 seconds, drain and peel. Cut in half and remove the stones carefully without spoiling the shape. Place the peaches on the dish, hollows uppermost. Melt the salted butter. Mix the sugar, ground almonds, and crumbs with most of the melted butter. Add the egg whites and essence or liqueur and beat the mixture to a creamy consistency. Using a piping bag or spoon, fill the hollow of each peach with the mixture. Brush with the remaining melted butter and bake in a moderate oven at 180°C, Gas 4, for 20 minutes.

Serve hot with Crème Anglaise (p320), ice cream or Zabaglione (p324).

COLD PUDDINGS AND DESSERTS

Cereal Sweets

Large and Whole Grain Cereal Sweets (eg rice, tapioca, barley)
Makes 1 litre (approx)

150g grain	flavouring (p343)
1 litre milk	25g butter
75g sugar	

Wash the grain in cold water and put it into the top of a double boiler with the milk. Simmer gently with the lid on for 2–2½ hours until the grain is tender and the milk almost absorbed. Stir occasionally to prevent the grain from settling on the bottom of the pan. Stir in the sugar, flavouring, and butter. Pour into a wetted 1 litre mould or basin and leave for about 2 hours to set. Turn out and serve with stewed fruit or jam.

VARIATION

Creamed Rice (1)
Fold 125ml single cream into the cooked rice.

Small and Crushed Grain Cereal Sweets (eg flaked grains, semolina, sago)
Makes 450ml (approx)

500ml milk	2 × 15ml spoons cold water
50g grain	50g caster sugar
1 × 10ml spoon gelatine	flavouring (p343)

Heat the milk to boiling point, sprinkle in the grain and cook gently, stirring all the time, for 15–20 minutes until soft and smooth. Soften the gelatine in the cold water in a small heatproof container, stand the container in a pan of hot water and stir until the gelatine dissolves. Stir into the mixture. Add the sugar and flavourings. Leave to cool, stirring from time to time. When tepid, pour into a wetted 500ml mould and leave for about 2 hours to set. Turn out to serve.

VARIATIONS

Blend 40g cocoa with small or powdered grain, or add 50g grated plain chocolate when the mixture is almost cooked. Extra sugar can be added if required and also a few drops of vanilla, rum or coffee essence.

Creamed Rice (2)
Whip 125–250ml double cream until thick, and fold into the mixture just before moulding. Use a 650ml mould.

Powdered Grain Cereal Sweets (eg cornflour, custard powder, ground rice, arrowroot)
Makes 1 litre (approx)

75g grain   50g sugar
1 litre milk   flavouring (see below)

Blend the grain with a little of the cold milk. Bring the rest of the milk to the boil, and pour on to the blended mixture, stirring all the time. Return the mixture to the saucepan, and bring it to simmering point, stirring all the time. Simmer for 5–10 minutes. Add the sugar and flavouring. Pour into a wetted 1 litre mould and leave for about 2 hours to set. Turn out to serve.

Note When made with cornflour, ground rice or arrowroot, and without added colouring, this basic moulded mixture is a blancmange.

VARIATIONS

Ambrosia Mould

Stir 50g melted butter and 125ml sherry into the mixture after it has come to simmering point.

Pink Coconut Mould

Stir 50g desiccated coconut, 50g melted butter, and a few drops of cochineal into the mixture after it has come to simmering point. Use a 1.25 litre mould.

Flavourings for Cereal Sweets

Flavouring essences: Almond, lemon, vanilla or coffee essence can be added to the mixture with the sugar.

Lemon or orange: The grated rind can be stirred into the cooked mixture just before moulding (large grain sweets). Alternatively, thinly cut strips of rind from 1 orange or 1 lemon can be infused in the mixture while cooking (large grain sweets), or in the milk while heating (other cereal sweets). They should be removed before mixing the milk with the grain (small and powdered grain sweets).

Peach Condé
6 helpings

1 litre cold rice pudding (p342)   125ml peach syrup from can
1 × 410g can peach halves   2 drops pink food colouring
2 × 5ml spoons arrowroot   1–2 drops yellow food colouring

Decoration
whipped cream

Divide the rice pudding between 6 sundae glasses. Drain the peaches and arrange 1 half on top of each helping of rice, cut side down. Put the arrowroot into a small saucepan and stir in the syrup. Bring to the boil, stirring all the time, and boil for about 5 minutes until it thickens and clear. Add the colouring and pour over the peaches. Leave to set. Decorate with whipped cream.

Fruit Desserts

Stewed or Poached Fresh Fruit

Apples and pears: Peel, core, and leave whole if small, quarter if large. Make a syrup with 100g sugar and 250ml water (more if the fruit is very hard) per 500g fruit. Flavour with lemon rind, cloves or cinnamon stick. Colour the syrup with cochineal, if liked, or replace some of the water with white wine or cider. Put the prepared fruit into the liquid immediately to preserve its colour; it must be completely covered by the liquid. Stew either in a saucepan or in a casserole in a moderate oven. Cooking pears may take 4–5 hours in the oven.

Currants and other soft berry fruits: Clean and prepare the fruit; remove stalks from currants. Make a syrup with 100g sugar and 125ml water per 500g fruit. Either steep the fruit in the cooled syrup and then poach very gently; or, if it is to be served cold, reduce the syrup by boiling, put the fruit into the hot syrup, and leave it to cool.

Gooseberries: Top and tail, removing a little skin from the tail end to allow the syrup to penetrate; then wash. Make a syrup with 100g sugar and 125–375ml water (depending on the hardness of the fruit) per 500g fruit. Flavour with elder-flowers, if available. Poach very gently until the skins crack.

Peaches and apricots: Peel, stone, and halve or quarter the fruit, depending on its size. Make a syrup with 100g sugar and 250ml water per 500g fruit. Flavour with almond or vanilla essence or with a few kernels from the fruit stones. Replace some of the water with white wine if liked.

Plums, greengages, and damsons: Wash the fruit, remove the stalks, and the stones if liked. Make a syrup with 100g sugar and 250ml water per 500g fruit. Flavour with lemon rind, cloves, cinnamon stick, or with a few kernels from the fruit stones. Replace some of the water with red wine, for red plums, if liked. Stew either in a saucepan or in a casserole in a moderate oven.

Rhubarb: String older garden rhubarb, but just wipe young forced fruit. Cut into 2cm lengths, lay in a casserole, and cover with soft light brown sugar. Flavour with lemon rind, root ginger or cinnamon stick. Do not add water. Cover and bake very gently, overnight if possible, in a very cool oven at 110°C, Gas $\frac{1}{4}$.

Stewed Dried Fruit (eg prunes, apricots, peaches, figs, apple rings)

Wash the fruit thoroughly in tepid water. Put it in a large bowl, cover with fresh water or cold tea, allowing 750ml liquid per 500g dried fruit, and leave to soak for 12–24 hours.

Drain, and measure out 250ml liquid (use fresh water if the fruit was soaked in tea) for cooking each 500g soaked fruit. Add sugar as required: 50–100g per 500ml liquid for apricots, peaches, apple rings; 25g per 500ml for other fruit. Add either a strip of lemon rind or a piece of cinnamon stick (for prunes), and bring to the boil. Reduce the heat, simmer for 3–4 minutes, skim, and add the fruit. Simmer until tender, then drain the fruit with a perforated spoon, and transfer to a serving bowl. Discard any solid flavourings from the syrup and boil it until it is well reduced. Pour it over the fruit and serve either hot or cold.

Alternatively, the fruit can be cooked in the liquid without any added sugar. In this case, add the sugar when the syrup is being boiled down.

Fruit Purées

Fruit purées are used for a number of fruit desserts, such as mousses (see p355) and fools. Hard fruits are generally cooked, but soft fruits such as strawberries, raspberries, peaches, mangoes or melons are simply prepared (ie hulled, peeled, and stoned), then rubbed through a fine nylon sieve, or puréed in an electric blender, and sweetened to taste. Fruit such as raspberries, which contain pips, should be sieved, not blended, to remove all the pips.

Hard fruit should be cooked in as little water as possible, About 4–5 × 15ml spoons should be enough for every 500g fruit; allow slightly less for apples and rhubarb. Put the water in a heavy-bottomed pan, add the fruit, cover, and simmer gently until the fruit is tender. When cooked, remove any stones, then sieve or purée until smooth, and sweeten to taste. 500g fresh fruit will yield about 300ml fruit purée.
Note Apples can also be baked in a moderate oven at 180°C, Gas 4, for 45 minutes– 1 hour, then peeled, cored, and sieved or puréed.

Fruit Fool
6 helpings

750g fruit (approx), eg gooseberries, rhubarb, apricots, red, and black currants, raspberries, blackberries, etc	sugar 500ml thick pouring custard (p318) **or** 500ml double cream **or** 250ml double cream and 250ml custard

Decoration
ratafias **or** fresh fruit **or** whipped cream

Purée the fruit (see above), sweeten, and cool. If using cream, whip it until it holds its shape. Fold first the custard, if used, and then the cream into the purée. Turn into a serving bowl and chill. Decorate with ratafias, fresh fruit or whipped cream.
Note Some fruits especially soft berry fruits can be combined to make up the given weight, but as a rule the pure flavour of a single type is more attractive.

Stuffed Peaches in Brandy
6 helpings

250ml water	6 large ripe peaches
100g white sugar	25g blanched almonds
150ml medium-dry **or** slightly sweet white wine	125ml double cream
2 × 15ml spoons brandy	50g cut mixed peel

Put the water, sugar, wine, and brandy into a saucepan over low heat until the sugar dissolves. Peel the peaches (if difficult to peel, dip in boiling water for 1 minute first); then poach in the brandy syrup for 15 minutes. Cool completely.

Chop the blanched almonds, and whip the cream until it just holds its shape. Fold the mixed peel and almonds into the cream. Halve the peaches and remove the stones. Put a tablespoonful of the cream mixture in the hollow of 6 halves, then sandwich the peaches together again. Arrange in a shallow serving dish, and pour the syrup over the fruit. Chill until ready to serve.

Fruit Salad

Always try to include a good selection of fruit with different colours, textures and flavours. Fresh fruit has the most vital flavour, and a portion should always be included, but frozen, canned, and even a few cooked, dried fruits can be added for bulk or variety. Allow about 150g fruit per person and 100ml fruit syrup.

The recipe below is for a basic fruit syrup which can be varied by adding more lemon juice, or sherry, Kirsch, brandy, port, Cointreau, Grand Marnier, white rum etc, to taste.

Basic Fruit Syrup

pared rind and juice of 1 lemon   75g sugar
500ml water

Put the lemon rind and juice into a pan with the water and sugar. Heat gently until the sugar has dissolved, then bring to the boil, and continue boiling until the syrup has been reduced by about half. Remove from the heat, strain, and leave to cool.

Fresh fruit is prepared according to kind as follows:

Apples: Cut into quarters and remove the cores; peel if wished, but if the skins are not too thick they provide an attractive contrast of colour. Cut into thin slices and dip quickly in lemon juice to preserve the colour, or put straight into the fruit syrup if it contains plenty of lemon juice.

Apricots: Cut in half and remove the stones. Cut each half into 2 or 3 pieces and add to the syrup. The stones of the apricots can also be split in half, the kernel removed and added to the fruit salad.

Bananas: Peel the bananas and cut into slices. Dip quickly in lemon juice to preserve the colour, then add to the fruit syrup. Only a few bananas should be added to a fruit salad and they should not be added too long before serving; this is because, even if coated with lemon juice, they will tend to discolour; this also happens if they are chilled in a refrigerator.

Cherries: Stone, cut in halves or leave whole, then add to the syrup.

Chinese gooseberries (kiwi fruit): Peel and cut into slices, and add to the syrup.

Grapes: Cut in half and remove the pips; if wished, grapes can also be peeled, although they provide attractive colour if left unpeeled.

Loganberries: Hull, and add to the syrup shortly before serving. Like other soft fruit they may go soggy or disintegrate if left in the syrup for long, especially if frozen.

Lychees: Peel, halve, remove the stones, and add to the syrup.

Mangoes: Peel, cut into slices and discard the stone, and add to the syrup.

Melons: Cut ripe melons in half, remove the seeds, then cut into cubes or balls with a melon scoop; discard all the peel. Add to the syrup.

Nectarines: As for peaches; the skin may be left on.

Oranges: Using a sharp knife, peel the oranges, removing all the white pith. Carefully cut between the segment skins to remove the flesh alone; do this over a plate to catch any juice and squeeze out all the juice from the remaining pulp. Add to the fruit syrup, together with the juice.

It is easier to remove all the pith if the oranges are put into boiling water for 2 minutes, cooled for another 2 minutes, then peeled while still hot.

Peaches: As for apricots, but cut each half into smaller pieces, or slice thinly.

Pears: Peel and core, then cut into thin slices, or cubes. Dip quickly in lemon juice to preserve the colour, then add to the fruit syrup, or put quickly into the fruit syrup if it contains plenty of lemon juice.

Pineapple: Peel the pineapple, and remove all the eyes. Cut in half or quarters lengthways and cut out the hard core. Cut the fruit into small pieces. Add to the syrup.

Plums: Halve, remove the stones, and cut into quarters, if large. Add to the syrup.

Raspberries: Hull, and add to the syrup shortly before serving.

Strawberries: Hull, and add to the syrup shortly before serving.

Serve fruit salad either in a large serving bowl, preferably glass, to emphasize the varied colours of the fruits, or in a scooped-out pineapple or melon.

To scoop out the fruit, remove the top third crossways. Keeping the case intact, cut or scoop out the flesh from the rest of the fruit, leaving about a 1cm rim. Remove the core from the pineapple. Cut the fruit into small pieces, or into balls if using a melon, and add to the rest of the fruit salad. Fill the scooped-out fruit with the salad.

Alternatively, the fruit can be presented in the form of a basket. Prepare as follows:

If using a pineapple, cut off and discard the green leafy tuft from the top. Keeping the fruit upright, and leaving about a 2cm piece intact in the centre for the handle, cut 2 equal-sized wedges from either side of the top half. Carefully cut out the flesh from the handle, leaving a 1cm rim. Scoop out the flesh from the lower half and continue as above.

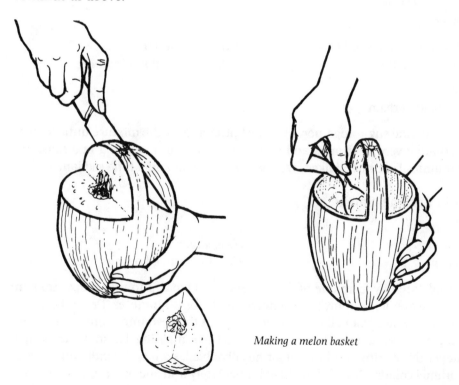

Making a melon basket

Note A pineapple container can also be prepared as for Sweet Pineapple Salad with Kirsch (p349).

Apple Snow (2)
6 helpings

4 large baking apples (750g approx)
juice and pared rind of 1 lemon
100g sugar (approx)
250ml milk

2–3 eggs
50g caster sugar
1 × 5ml spoon cornflour **or** arrowroot
4 individual sponge cakes

Decoration
glacé cherries

Bake and purée the apples (p345). Add the lemon juice to the purée, sweeten to taste, and leave to cool.

Put the lemon rind into a small pan with the milk and heat gently for 15 minutes, then strain. Separate the eggs and blend the yolks and sugar together with the cornflour or arrowroot. Add the lemon-infused milk. Cook, stirring all the time, in a saucepan for 20–30 minutes or until the custard coats the back of the spoon. Cool.

Split the sponge cakes in half and arrange them in the bottom of a glass dish. Pour the custard over them. Whisk the egg whites until they form stiff peaks, then fold into the apple purée. Pile the mixture on top of the custard and decorate with the glacé cherries.

Danish Apple Cake
4–6 helpings

150g dry white breadcrumbs
75g granulated sugar

100–125g butter
900g stewed apples (p344)

Decoration (optional)
300ml whipping cream   red jam

Mix the crumbs and sugar together. Melt the butter and fry the mixture until golden. Place alternate layers of crumbs and apples in a glass dish, starting and finishing with the crumbs. Decorate, if liked, with whipped cream and a little red jam.

Oranges in Caramel Sauce
4 helpings

6 oranges
250ml water

200g sugar
25–50ml chilled orange juice

Pare the rind carefully from one of the oranges, and cut it into thin strips. Soak in 125ml of the water for 1 hour, then simmer gently for 20 minutes. Drain. Peel and remove the white pith from all the oranges, and cut the flesh into 7mm thick slices. Place in a glass serving dish. Put the sugar and the remaining 125ml water into a pan. Heat gently, stirring until the sugar has dissolved, then boil rapidly until it is a golden caramel colour. Draw off the heat immediately and add enough orange juice to give the consistency of sauce required. Replace over the heat, stir until just blended, then add the orange rind. Pour the caramel sauce over the oranges and chill for at least 3 hours before serving.

Summer Pudding

6–8 helpings

1kg soft red fruit, eg black and red
    currants, blackberries, raspberries,
    and bilberries
100–150g caster sugar

1 strip lemon rind (optional)
8–10 slices day-old white bread
    (5mm thick)

Pick over and clean the fruit, put into a bowl with sugar to taste and the lemon rind, if used, and leave overnight. Turn the fruit and sugar into a pan, discarding the lemon rind, and simmer for 2–3 minutes until very lightly cooked. Remove from the heat. Cut the crusts off the bread, Cut a circle from 1 slice to fit the bottom of a 1.25 litre pudding basin. Line the base and sides of the basin with bread, leaving no spaces. Fill in any gaps with small pieces of bread. Fill with the fruit and any juice it has made while cooking. Cover with bread slices. Place a flat plate and a 1kg weight on top, and leave overnight, or longer if refrigerated.

Serve turned out, with chilled whipped cream, sweetened if liked.

Sweet Pineapple Salad with Kirsch

4 helpings

2 small pineapples
100g black grapes
1 banana
1 pear

1 × 15ml spoon lemon juice
2–3 × 15ml spoons Kirsch
sugar

Cut the pineapples in half lengthways. Cut out the core, then scoop out the flesh, using first a knife, then a spoon, but taking care to keep the pineapple cases intact. Discard the core, and chop the flesh. Put into a bowl, together with any pineapple juice. Halve and de-pip the grapes. Peel and slice the banana; peel, core, and slice the pear, and toss both fruits in the lemon juice, before adding to the other fruit in the bowl. Mix all the fruit together, pour the Kirsch over them, and sweeten to taste with the sugar. Pile the fruit back into the pineapple cases and chill until required.

Uncleared Jellies

1) Choose a large non-aluminium saucepan as the liquid jelly will rise during making. A thick enamel saucepan is ideal.
2) Use 2 × 10ml spoons powdered gelatine to 500ml water for general purposes, but when a slightly firmer 'set' is required use 3 × 10ml spoons gelatine to 500ml water. The larger amount of gelatine will be required:
   a) in hot weather
   b) if no refrigerator is available
   c) when pieces of fruit are to be set in the jelly and the mould turned out
   d) if the jelly is to be used for lining a mould or chopped for decoration.
3) Always make sure that gelatine is completely dissolved before adding it to other ingredients. Gelatine will dissolve easily if it is sprinkled on to cold water or liquid to soften first. Put the liquid into a small heatproof container, add the gelatine

and leave for 5 minutes. Place the container in a saucepan of hot water over low heat and stir, especially round the sides, until the gelatine has completely dissolved.

4) Do not use milk to dissolve gelatine as it will curdle.

5) Do not add a hot gelatine solution to a really cold mixture. It will not mix properly but will set in globules and 'string' as soon as it comes into contact with the cold mixture. The mixture should be at room temperature, tepid, or, ideally, at the same temperature as the gelatine. In any case, the dissolved gelatine should be blended in quickly and thoroughly to prevent it setting in blobs.

6) If the mixture has to be strained, strain through scalded, well-washed, damp butter muslin. The muslin may be held up in a sieve.

7) A jelly mould may be made of glass, china, metal or plastic. When gelatine is included in a recipe, a sharp clean outline to the turned-out shape will be obtained if a metal mould is used. Tin-lined copper moulds are costly but ensure a perfect finish to the jelly. All moulds must be scrupulously clean and rinsed out or wetted with cold water before use. They should be wet inside when the jelly is poured in, although there should be no free water in the bottom.

8) To turn out a jelly, run the tip of a knife or finger round the top of the mould. Dip the mould into hot water for a few seconds, remove, and dry it. Wet a serving plate and place upside-down on top of the mould. Hold the plate and mould together firmly and turn both over. Shake gently and carefully remove the mould.

9) If using fresh pineapple juice in making a jelly, it must first be boiled for 2–3 minutes. It contains an enzyme, which, if left untreated, destroys the setting power of gelatine.

Blackcurrant Jelly
2 helpings

125ml blackcurrant syrup
25g sugar

1 × 10ml spoon gelatine
125ml cold water

Heat together the syrup and sugar until the sugar has dissolved. Cool. Soften the gelatine in the water in a small heatproof container. Stand the container in a pan of hot water and stir until dissolved. Pour into the cooled syrup. Pour into wetted individual moulds and leave for about 1 hour to set.

Blackcurrant Whip
4 helpings

375ml blackcurrant juice
25–50g sugar

2 × 10ml spoons gelatine
3 × 15ml spoons cold water

Put the blackcurrant juice and sugar into a saucepan and heat until the sugar has dissolved. Leave to cool. Soften the gelatine in the water in a small heatproof container. Stand the container in a pan of hot water and stir until dissolved, then add to the saucepan. Pour into a basin and whisk well until thick and foamy. Pile quickly into individual serving dishes and leave for about 45 minutes to set.

Mrs Beeton's Dutch Flummery
4–6 helpings

25g gelatine
125ml cold water
juice and grated rind of 1 lemon

4 eggs
500ml dry sherry
50g caster sugar

Soften the gelatine in the water in a small heatproof container. Stand the container in a pan of hot water and stir until dissolved, then make up with cold water to 500ml. Strain the lemon juice into the gelatine and add the grated rind. Beat the eggs, sherry, and sugar together and add to the mixture. Pour into the top of a double boiler and cook slowly over low heat, stirring all the time, until the mixture coats the back of the spoon. Do not let the mixture boil. Strain the mixture into a wetted 1.5 litre mould and leave for 2–3 hours to set before turning out.

Note Make the day before using if possible.

Fresh Lemon Jelly
2 helpings

pared rind and juice of 2 lemons
175ml water

1 × 10ml spoon gelatine
2 × 10ml spoons caster sugar

Put the lemon rind into a saucepan with half the water and simmer for 5 minutes. Cool. Soften the gelatine in the remaining water in a small heatproof container. Stand the container in a pan of hot water and stir until the gelatine has dissolved. Add the lemon juice and sugar. Pour into individual wetted moulds and leave for about 1 hour to set.

VARIATION

Fresh Orange Jelly
Use 2 oranges instead of lemons and only 1 × 10ml spoon of sugar.

Milk Jelly
2 helpings

250ml milk
1 × 15ml spoon caster sugar
grated rind of 1 lemon

1 × 10ml spoon gelatine
4 × 15ml spoons cold water

Heat the milk, sugar, and lemon rind until the sugar has dissolved. Cool. Soften the gelatine in the cold water in a small heatproof container. Stand the container in a pan of hot water and stir until dissolved. Stir the gelatine into the cooled milk, then strain into a basin. Stir from time to time until it is the consistency of thick cream. Pour into a wetted mould and leave for about 1 hour to set.

VARIATIONS

The jelly can be flavoured with vanilla, coffee or other essence, if liked. If coffee essence is used, substitute orange rind for the lemon. Omit the rind if peppermint flavouring is used.

Cleared Jellies

Scald the saucepan, whisk, jelly bag, basins, and jelly mould before use, as the merest trace of grease may cause cloudiness in the finished jelly.

Whisk the egg whites lightly and crush the egg shells before adding to the mixture in the saucepan.

Heat the mixture and whisk constantly until a good head of foam is produced. It should be hot but not boiling. The correct temperature is about 70°C, when the foam begins to set or 'crust'. Care must be taken not to break up the 'crust' by whisking too long. Remove the whisk but continue to heat the liquid until the 'crust' has risen to the top of the saucepan; the gelatine must *not* boil.

Remove from the heat and let the contents of the saucepan settle in a warm place, covered, for 5–10 minutes.

Strain the settled, clear jelly through a jelly bag into a basin below, while the bag is still hot from scalding. Replace this basin of jelly with another basin and re-strain the jelly very carefully by pouring through the foam 'crust' which covers the bottom of the bag, acting as a filter.

If the jelly is not clear when a little is looked at in a spoon or glass, the filtering must be carried out again.

Filtering is most easily carried out using a jelly bag and stand, but if these are not available, the 4 corners of a clean cloth can be tied to the legs of an upturned stool.

Repeated filtering will cool the jelly, and, if done too often, can result in a poor yield of clear jelly as it will tend to solidify in the cloth.

Note Use lump sugar whenever possible for making clear jelly; it will give a more brilliant jelly than powdered sugar.

Lining and Decorating a Mould

Pour in just enough jelly to cover the base and sides of the mould, and leave to set completely. If canned fruit is being used, drain well before putting into the mould. Cut pieces of fruit to fit the shape of the mould, and place in a decorative pattern over the set jelly. Each piece of fruit can be dipped in a little liquid jelly, if liked, before being arranged in the mould. Carefully spoon a little liquid jelly over the decoration and allow to set before any other filling is added.

Filling the Mould

Moulds should be filled to the top; this prevents the shape of the mould being broken when it is shaken out. In the case of a cream mixture, liquid jelly may be used to fill the space if there is insufficient mixture.

Note If a jelly is to be set in layers, keep it in a warm place to avoid it setting.

Chopping Jelly for Decoration

Clear jelly should be quite firm. It should be coarsely chopped with a wet knife on wet greaseproof paper, so that the light is refracted from the cut surfaces as from the facets of a jewel.

Clear Lemon Jelly
6 helpings

4 lemons
750ml water
150g sugar
4 cloves

1 × 2cm piece cinnamon stick
40g gelatine
whites and shells of 2 eggs

Pare the rind from three of the lemons and squeeze the juice from all four. Make up the juice to 250ml with water, if necessary. Put the rind, juice, water, sugar, cloves, cinnamon stick, and gelatine into a large saucepan. Whisk the egg whites lightly, and crush the shells. Whisk over low heat until just below boiling point. Remove the whisk and allow the liquid to heat until it reaches the top of the pan. Simmer for 5 minutes. Remove from the heat and leave to stand for 5–10 minutes. Strain the liquid carefully through a jelly bag. Pour into a wetted mould and leave for 1–2 hours to set.

Note 2 × 15ml spoons of sherry may be added to the liquid just before filtering.

Fruit Jelly
6 helpings

fruit eg banana, grapes, cherries,
    tangerines, apricots, pineapple

750ml clear lemon jelly

Decoration
125ml chopped jelly (see **Note**)

Prepare enough fruit to decorate the sides of the mould and to make 3–4 layers of fruit in it.

Rinse a mould out with cold water. Pour in just enough jelly to cover the bottom of the mould and allow to set. Cut pieces of fruit to fit the shape of the mould; dip each piece in liquid jelly and place in the mould. Leave to set, then carefully cover the fruit with a little more liquid jelly. Leave to set again and repeat with layers of fruit and jelly, ensuring that each layer is set before the next layer is added, until the mould is full, finishing with a layer of jelly. Leave for about 2 hours to set, then turn out and decorate with chopped jelly.

Note For the decorative chopped jelly, choose a colour and flavour which suits the fruit, eg if using tangerines and grapes, use tangerine jelly.

Soufflés, Mousses and Creams

Lemon Soufflé (Milanaise Soufflé) *Basic recipe*
4 helpings

1 × 15ml spoon gelatine
3 × 15ml spoons water
3 eggs

grated rind and juice of 2 lemons
100g caster sugar
125ml double cream

Decoration
finely chopped nuts **or** cake crumbs
whipped double cream (optional)

crystallized lemon slices
angelica

Prepare a 500ml soufflé dish (p232). Soften the gelatine in the water in a small heatproof container. Stand the container in a pan of hot water and stir until dissolved. Cool slightly. Meanwhile, separate the eggs. Put the yolks, lemon rind and juice, and sugar into a heatproof basin and stand it over a pan half-full of hot water over low heat. Do not let the water boil or touch the basin. Whisk the mixture for 10–15 minutes until thick and pale. Remove from the heat and continue whisking until cool. Fold a little of the yolk mixture into the cooled gelatine, then whisk this into the yolk mixture. Put in a cool place until the mixture begins to set.

Whip the cream until it just holds its shape but is still soft. Using a large metal spoon, fold into the mixture until evenly mixed. Whisk the egg whites until stiff, and fold in until evenly blended. Tip the soufflé gently into the dish, and leave to set in a refrigerator for about 2 hours.

Remove the paper carefully, and decorate the sides of the soufflé with chopped nuts or cake crumbs. Pipe whipped cream on top, if liked, and decorate with crystallized lemon slices and small pieces of angelica.

VARIATIONS
In each of the variations below, omit the lemon rind and juice:

Chocolate Soufflé

Whisk the egg yolks with 2 × 15ml spoons water and 75g caster sugar. Melt 75g grated plain chocolate over a pan of hot water. Add to the yolk mixture with the dissolved gelatine and whisk well.

Coffee Soufflé

Dissolve 2 × 10ml spoons instant coffee in a little hot water, then add more water to make 100ml strong coffee. Whisk with the egg yolks. Decorate with grated chocolate, chopped walnuts, and cream.

Orange Soufflé

Whisk the egg yolks with the finely grated rind and juice of 2 oranges and use 75g caster sugar only. Add 2 × 15ml spoons Grand Marnier or orange curaçao, if liked. Dissolve the gelatine in 1 × 15ml spoon water and 2 × 15ml spoons lemon juice. When set, decorate the soufflé with crystallized orange slices, nuts, and cream.

Praline Soufflé
Prepare 75g praline (p446) and crush it. Dissolve 1 × 5ml spoon instant coffee in 2 × 15ml spoons hot water, and add 2 × 15ml spoons cold water. Whisk the liquid with the yolks. Add 50g crushed praline to the mixture with the whipped cream. Decorate with the remaining praline and cream.

Sherry Soufflé
Add 100ml sweet sherry, 1 × 15ml spoon lemon juice, and 75g caster sugar only to the egg yolks. Decorate with mimosa balls, angelica, coconut, and cream.

Blackcurrant Mousse *Basic recipe using purée*
4 helpings

250g fresh blackcurrants
50g caster sugar
1 × 10ml spoon lemon juice
1 × 10ml spoon gelatine

2 × 15ml spoons water
125ml double cream
2 egg whites

Decoration
whipped double cream

blackcurrant jam (optional)

Save a few whole blackcurrants for decorating the mousse, if liked; sieve the rest. Make the purée up to 150ml with a little water, if necessary. Put the purée, sugar, and lemon juice in a bowl. Soften the gelatine in the water in a small heatproof container. Stand the container in a pan of hot water and stir until completely dissolved. Cool. Mix in a little of the purée, then stir this mixture into the main purée. Leave in a cool place until beginning to set.

Whip the cream until it just holds its shape, and fold into the mixture using a metal spoon. Whisk the egg whites until fairly stiff and fold in. Make sure that the mixture is fully and evenly blended but do not overmix it. Pour gently into a 500ml dish or wetted mould, or into individual glasses. Leave to set in a refrigerator for 1–2 hours. Turn out, if liked. Decorate with whirls of whipped cream and with either the reserved fruit or jam.

Note Canned or bottled blackcurrants in syrup can also be used; in this case substitute 3 × 15ml spoons of the syrup for the sugar and water. Frozen fruit can also be used; it must be well thawed and drained, and any sugar added must depend on the type and strength of sweetening (if any) used when freezing the fruit.

VARIATIONS
1) Fresh, frozen or canned fruits can be used, eg strawberries, raspberries, blackberries, gooseberries, cherries, apricots or bananas. The amount of sugar will vary according to the sweetness of the purée.
2) Omit the gelatine; pour the mixture into ice trays and freeze it.

Chocolate Mousse (1)
4 helpings

150g plain chocolate	4 eggs
2 × 15ml spoons water	vanilla essence

Decoration

whipped double cream	chopped walnuts

Break up the chocolate or grate it. Put it into a large heatproof basin with the water and stand over a pan of hot water. Heat gently until the chocolate melts. Remove from the heat and stir until smooth. Separate the eggs. Beat the yolks and a few drops of vanilla essence into the chocolate. Whisk the egg whites until fairly stiff, and fold gently into the mixture until evenly blended. Pour into 4 individual dishes and leave for 1–2 hours to set.

   Serve decorated with cream and walnuts.

VARIATIONS

Mocha Mousse
Dissolve 1 × 5ml spoon instant coffee in 2 × 15ml spoons hot water and stir this liquid into the chocolate with the egg yolks and vanilla essence.

Choc-au-Rhum Mousse
Add 1 × 15ml spoon rum to the mixture, or use brandy, Grand Marnier or Tia Maria.

Chocolate Mousse (2)
4 helpings

100g plain chocolate	3 eggs
4 × 15ml spoons water	vanilla essence
1 × 10ml spoon gelatine	100ml double cream

Decoration

whipped double cream	coarsely grated chocolate

Break up the chocolate or grate it. Put it into a large heatproof basin with the water. Sprinkle in the gelatine and stand the basin over a pan of hot water. Heat gently until the chocolate has melted and the gelatine dissolved. Remove from the heat and stir until smooth. Separate the eggs. Beat the yolks and a few drops of vanilla essence into the chocolate. Whip the cream until it just holds its shape and fold it into the mixture. Whisk the egg whites until fairly stiff and fold in gently until evenly blended. Pour into a 750ml wetted mould or a deep serving bowl and chill for about 2 hours until set.

   If moulded, turn out on to a flat plate. In either case, decorate with the whipped double cream and coarsely grated chocolate.

Chocolate Roulade
6 helpings

oil for greasing
150g bitter-sweet dessert chocolate
4 eggs
125g caster sugar
3 × 15ml spoons hot water

butter for greasing
15g icing sugar
175ml double cream (approx)
a few drops vanilla essence

Brush a 30 × 42cm baking tray with oil. Line it with a piece of greaseproof paper letting the paper overlap the edge a little. Cut out an extra sheet of greaseproof paper the same size, to cover the roulade after it has been cooked, and have ready a damp cloth with which to cover the baking tray.

Break the chocolate into small pieces and place it in a bowl over a pan of water just taken off the boil. Leave to melt, stirring occasionally. Meanwhile, separate the eggs. Add the caster sugar to the yolks and beat briskly until the mixture is pale and creamy. Add the water to the melted chocolate and beat until well blended. Mix the chocolate into the yolk and sugar mixture, and whisk thoroughly. Whisk the egg whites until fairly stiff, then fold them carefully into the chocolate mixture using a metal spoon. Tip the roulade mixture gently into the prepared tin, and smooth it out evenly. Cook in a fairly hot oven at 190°C, Gas 5, for 20 minutes, until firm on the surface. When cooked, cover immediately with a sheet of buttered greaseproof paper and a damp cloth. Leave to stand overnight.

Next day, remove the cloth. Turn the paper buttered side up, sprinkle with icing sugar and replace sugared side down. Grip the paper and tin and invert both together so that the roulade is upside-down. Lay it down on the paper. Whip the cream until very stiff, stir in the vanilla essence and spread evenly over the surface of the roulade. Then, roll the roulade up as you would a Swiss roll, using the paper to help you. Dust with extra icing sugar and chill for several hours before serving. **Note** Successful rolling of the roulade depends to a certain extent upon its thickness. Cracks which appear while rolling can be filled with icing sugar.

French Chocolate Creams (rich)
6 helpings

150ml milk
6 × 10ml spoons caster sugar
a pinch of salt

100g plain chocolate
100g unsalted butter
8 egg yolks

Warm the milk, sugar, and salt in a small saucepan, and stir until the sugar dissolves. Put to one side. Grate the chocolate coarsely and chop the butter into small pieces. Put them into a large basin and stand it over a pan of hot water. Heat gently until melted, stirring all the time. When the mixture is quite smooth, add the milk and mix it in thoroughly. Using a balloon whisk if possible, beat in the egg yolks, one at a time; on no account let them curdle. Pour the cream into 6 small pots or ramekins and chill well before serving.

Velvet Cream *Basic recipe*

4 helpings

fresh lemon jelly (p351) (optional)	50g caster sugar
glacé cherries (optional)	2 × 15ml spoons sherry **or** a few drops
angelica (optional)	vanilla essence
3 × 15ml spoons water	250ml double cream
1 × 10ml spoon gelatine	250ml single cream

If the velvet cream is to be set in a mould, line a 750ml mould with some of the jelly. Cut the cherries into quarters and the angelica into leaf shapes and decorate the mould as described on p352. Chill the remaining jelly and use to decorate the mould.

To make the cream, put the water into a heatproof container, sprinkle in the gelatine and leave to soften. Stand the container in a pan of hot water and stir until the gelatine dissolves. Add the sugar and sherry or vanilla essence, and stir until the sugar dissolves completely. Put to one side.

Put the double and single cream into a bowl and whip lightly. Fold the flavoured gelatine into the cream and pour carefully into the prepared mould. Leave to set for about 2 hours.

Turn out on to a flat, wetted plate. Chop the chilled fresh lemon jelly (p352), and arrange on the plate around the cream.

Note Instead of being poured into a lined mould, the velvet cream can be poured into 4 individual glasses. A thin coating of lemon jelly can then be poured on top and decorated. Leave to set for about 1 hour.

VARIATIONS

In each of the variations below, omit the sherry or vanilla essence:

Almond Cream

Flavour with 1 × 2.5ml spoon almond essence.

Chocolate Cream

Flavour with 75g melted plain chocolate.

Coffee Cream

Flavour with 1 × 15ml spoon instant coffee dissolved in 1 × 15ml hot water. Add 1 × 15ml spoon rum, if liked.

Raspberry Cream

Use 375ml double cream and fold in 125ml sieved raspberry purée instead of the single cream.

Strawberry Cream

Make as for Raspberry Cream substituting strawberries.

Vanilla Bavarian Cream (Vanilla Bavarois) *Basic recipe*
4 helpings

200ml fresh lemon jelly (p351)	1 × 2.5ml spoon vanilla essence
angelica (optional)	4 × 15ml spoons water
250ml milk	1 × 10ml spoon gelatine
4 egg yolks **or** 1 whole egg and 2 yolks	125ml double cream
50g caster sugar	125ml single cream

Line a 750ml mould with lemon jelly, cut the angelica into leaf shapes, if used, and decorate the mould as described on p352. Chill the remaining jelly.

To make the cream, mix the eggs and sugar together until fluffy and pale. Warm the milk, but do not let it boil; slowly stir in the milk. Strain the custard back into the saucepan or into a double boiler or basin held over hot water. (Make sure the water does not touch the upper pan.) Cook over very low heat, unti it thickens. Do not let the custard boil.

Strain the thickened custard into a bowl, stir in the vanilla essence, and leave to cool.

Put the water into a heatproof container, sprinkle in the gelatine and leave to soften. Stand the container in a pan of hot water and stir until the gelatine dissolves. Cool until tepid and add to the custard. Leave in a cool place until it thickens at the edges, stirring from time to time to prevent a skin forming.

Put the double and single cream into a bowl and whip lightly. Fold into the custard mixture, and pour into the prepared mould. Leave to set for about 2 hours. Chop the chilled jelly (p352) and use to decorate the cream. Turn out on to a flat, wetted plate.
VARIATIONS
In each of the variations below, omit the vanilla essence:

Caramel Bavarois
Dissolve 100g granulated sugar in 1 × 15ml spoon water and heat until the syrup turns a rich brown colour. Add 4 × 15ml spoons hot water, remove from the heat, and stir until all the caramel dissolves. Stir into the custard.

Chocolate Bavarois
Grate 100g plain chocolate and add with the milk. It will melt in the warm custard. Add 1 × 5ml spoon vanilla essence.

Italian Bavarois
Infuse thin strips of rind from 1 lemon in the milk. Add the strained juice of the lemon to the custard with 1 × 15ml spoon brandy, if liked.

Neapolitan Cream
Line the whole mould with raspberry jelly. Divide the cream into 4 portions: flavour one with vanilla, the second with ratafia essence, colour it green, flavour the third with coffee, and the fourth with strawberry essence, colour it pink. Pour the vanilla cream into the mould and leave it to set, then add the others, allowing each layer to set first.

Apricot Custard Cream *Basic recipe*
4 helpings

oil for greasing
500g fresh apricots **or** 2 × 425g cans
   apricots
200ml milk
3 egg yolks **or** 1 whole egg and 1 yolk
50g sugar

lemon juice (optional)
4 × 15ml spoons water
1 × 10ml spoon gelatine
100ml double cream
100ml single cream

Oil a 750ml mould lightly. Poach fresh fruit in a little water and sugar if it needs cooking. Process any fruit in an electric blender when tender, or sieve it if it contains seeds (eg berries or currants). Make the purée up to 200ml, if necessary, with a little fruit juice, fruit syrup or water.

Warm the milk, but do not let it come near the boil. Mix together the eggs and 25g of the sugar until fluffy and pale, and slowly stir in the milk. Strain the custard back into the saucepan or into a double boiler or basin held over hot water. (Make sure the water does not touch the upper pan.) Cook over very low heat for 15–20 minutes, stirring all the time, until it thickens. Do not let it come near the boil. Strain the custard into a bowl and leave to cool. Blend together the fruit purée and the cooled custard. Taste, and add more sugar and a little lemon juice if required.

Put the water into a heatproof container, sprinkle in the gelatine and leave to soften. Stand the container in a pan of hot water and stir until the gelatine dissolves. Cool until tepid, and add to the custard. Leave in a cool place until it begins to set, stirring from time to time to prevent a skin forming.

Put all the cream into a bowl and whip lightly. Fold into the setting mixture, and pour gently into the mould. Leave to set for about 2 hours. Turn out on to a flat, wetted plate. Decorate as desired.

VARIATIONS
Blackcurrants, blackberries, damsons, gooseberries, peaches, raspberries, or straw-berries also make delicious fruit creams.

Quick Fruit Cream (using custard powder)
4 helpings

1 × 127g pkt orange jelly
100ml water
50ml orange juice

2 × 15ml spoons custard powder
250ml milk
125ml double cream

Chop the jelly tablet roughly. Heat the water, add the jelly, and stir until dissolved. Add the juice and leave to cool. Meanwhile, blend the custard powder with a little of the milk. Heat the rest of the milk until it boils. Pour it slowly on to the blended custard powder, stirring all the time. Return to the pan, bring to the boil and boil for 1–2 minutes, stirring all the time, until the custard thickens. Cool slightly and stir into the jelly. Cool until beginning to set. Whip the cream until it leaves a trail and fold into the setting mixture. Pour into individual glasses and chill for about 1 hour. Decorate as desired.

Trifles, Charlottes and Syllabubs

Mrs Beeton's Tipsy Cake or Brandy Trifle
4–6 helpings

1 × 15cm sponge cake (p419)	375ml milk
redcurrant jelly (optional)	125ml single cream
65–75ml brandy **or** white wine and	8 egg yolks
brandy	75g caster sugar
50g whole blanched almonds	

Put the cake in a glass bowl or dish 16cm in diameter and as deep as the cake. Spread the cake thinly with jelly, if used. Pour over as much brandy or brandy and wine as the cake can absorb. Cut the almonds into spikes lengthways and stick them into the top of the cake all over. Mix the milk and cream. Beat the yolks until liquid, and pour the milk and cream over them. Add the sugar. Cook gently in the top of a double boiler for about 10 minutes or until the custard thickens, stirring all the time. Let the custard cool slightly, then pour it over and around the cake. Cover and chill. When cold, decorate with small spoonfuls of redcurrant jelly.

Mrs Beeton's Traditional Trifle
6 helpings

4 individual sponge cakes	grated rind of ½ lemon
raspberry **or** strawberry jam	25ml thick hot custard (p320)
6 macaroons	125ml double cream
12 ratafias	1 egg white
125ml sherry	25g caster sugar
25g blanched shredded almonds	

Decoration

glacé cherries	angelica

Cut the sponge cakes in half and spread one half of each with jam. Sandwich together and arrange in a glass dish. Crush the macaroons and ratafias and put them into the dish. Pour the sherry over them. Sprinkle with the almonds and lemon rind. Cover with the custard and leave for about 30 minutes to cool. Cover with damp grease-proof paper to prevent a skin forming. Whip together the cream, egg white, and sugar until stiff and spread over the dish. Decorate with cherries and angelica.

Mrs Beeton's Charlotte Russe
6 helpings

24 sponge fingers (p419)
2 × 15ml spoons white glacé icing
  (p431)
3 × 5ml spoons gelatine
3 × 15ml spoons water

500ml single cream
3 × 15ml spoons any sweet liqueur
1 × 15ml spoon icing sugar or to taste
1 × 15cm round sponge cake (p419)
  or Genoese sponge (p420), 1cm thick

Cut 4 sponge fingers in half, and dip the rounded ends in icing. Line a 15cm soufflé dish with the halved fingers, placing them like a star, with the non-sugared sides uppermost and the iced ends in the centre. Dip one end of each of the remaining biscuits in icing. Line the sides of the dish with them, sugared sides outward, iced ends at the bottom. Trim the biscuits to fit the rim of the dish. Soften the gelatine in the water in a small heatproof container. Stand the container in a pan of hot water and stir until it dissolves. Remove from the heat and whisk together with the cream, liqueur, and sugar until frothy. Stand the mixture in a cool place until it begins to thicken. Fill the charlotte with the mixture, and cover it with the round of sponge cake. Leave in a cool place for 8–12 hours, until firm. Loosen the biscuits from the sides of the dish with a knife, carefully turn out the charlotte on to a plate, and serve.

Wine Syllabub
4 helpings

200ml double cream
2 egg whites
75g caster sugar

juice of ½ lemon
100ml sweet white wine or sherry

Decoration
crystallized lemon slices

Whip the cream until it just holds its shape. Whisk the egg whites until they form soft peaks. Fold the sugar into the egg whites, then gradually add the lemon juice and wine or sherry. Fold this mixture into the whipped cream. Pour into glasses and chill in a refrigerator for about 2 hours. Remove 20 minutes before serving. Serve decorated with the lemon slices.

Cider Syllabub
4 helpings

grated rind and juice of ½ lemon
50g caster sugar
125ml sweet cider

1 × 15ml spoon brandy (optional)
250ml double cream

Add the lemon rind and juice to the caster sugar with the cider, and the brandy, if used. Stir until the sugar is dissolved. Whip the cream until it stands in stiff peaks. Fold in the lemon and cider mixture gradually. Pour into stemmed glasses and chill in a refrigerator for about 2 hours. Remove 20 minutes before serving.

Serve with Mrs Beeton's Savoy Cakes (p419).

Gâteaux, Cheesecakes and Meringue Desserts

Black Forest Cherry Gâteau (Schwarzwälderkirschtorte)

10–12 helpings

1 × 20cm round chocolate sandwich
  cake (p418), using 3 eggs
250ml double cream
125ml single cream

1 × 540g can Morello cherries
Kirsch
25g plain chocolate

Cut the cake into 3 layers. Whip together the double and single cream until stiff. Drain and stone the cherries. Reserve the juice and 11 whole cherries. Halve the rest. Gently fold the halved cherries into half the cream. Put to one side. Strain the reserved cherry juice and mix it with Kirsch to taste. Prick the cake layers and sprinkle with the cherry juice and Kirsch until well saturated. Sandwich the layers together using the whipped cream and cherries. When assembled, cover with the remaining cream and use the whole cherries to decorate the top. Grate the chocolate and sprinkle it over the cream.

Chocolate Profiteroles

8 helpings

choux pastry (pp454–55) using 100g
  flour
250ml (approx) Chantilly cream,
  confectioners' custard **or** chocolate

butter cream (p442)
200g chocolate **or** coffee
  glacé icing (p432)

Use the choux pastry to pipe 24–30 small choux about 2cm in diameter (see p424). When cooked, open them at the bottom, remove any uncooked paste, and leave to dry out and cool completely. When cold, fill with the desired cream. Glaze the tops with glacé icing, reserving some for assembling the dish. Let the icing harden, then arrange the choux in a pyramid (if possible against the sides of a conical mould). Stick them together with small dabs of icing.

Serve 3 or 4 choux per person, with hot chocolate sauce (p267).

Mille-Feuille Gâteau

6–8 helpings

375g prepared puff pastry (p458)
flour for rolling out
250ml double cream **or** confectioners'
  custard (p442)

100g raspberry jam (optional)
glacé icing (p431) using 100g icing
  sugar

Roll out the pastry on a lightly floured surface 2mm thick and cut into six 15cm rounds. Place on baking trays, prick well, and bake in a very hot oven at 230°C, Gas 8, for 8–10 minutes until crisp and golden-brown. Lift the rounds off carefully and cool them on a wire rack. Whip the cream until thick, if used. Sandwich each layer of pastry together lightly with the jam and cream or confectioners' custard. (If using custard, the jam can be omitted.) Cover the top layer of pastry with the icing.

Gâteau St Honoré
10–12 helpings

Base

150g prepared shortcrust pastry
  (p453)
flour for rolling out

2 beaten eggs for glazing
choux pastry (pp454–55) using
  200g flour

Pastry Cream

3 eggs
50g caster sugar
35g plain flour
25g cornflour
a few drops vanilla essence

250ml milk
125ml double cream
50g granulated sugar
3 × 15ml spoons water

Decoration

glacé cherries

angelica

To make the base, roll out the shortcrust pastry on a lightly floured surface into a 20cm round and place on a baking tray. Prick the pastry well and brush with beaten egg. Using a 1cm nozzle, pipe a circle of choux paste round the edge of the pastry. Brush with beaten egg. Use the remaining choux to pipe 18–20 small choux buns separately (p470). Place the circle and buns on a greased baking tray, and brush with beaten egg. Bake in a fairly hot oven at 200°C, Gas 6, for 15 minutes, then reduce to fairly hot, 190°C, Gas 5, for a further 10–15 minutes, or until the choux ring is well risen and golden-brown. Cool on a wire rack.

To make the pastry cream, separate 2 of the eggs. Beat together the yolks, whole egg, and the caster sugar. Stir in the flour, cornflour, and vanilla esence. Heat the milk and gradually beat it into the egg mixture. Return the mixture to the pan, bring to the boil, stirring all the time. and boil for 2–3 minutes. Put the mixture into a clean basin, cover with buttered paper and leave until cold.

Whip the cream until stiff and pipe into the choux buns. Put the sugar and water into a small saucepan, heat until the sugar has dissolved, then boil until a light straw colour. Remove from the heat. Dip the bottom of each bun quickly in the syrup and arrange on the choux round. Spoon a little syrup over each choux bun. Whisk the 2 remaining egg whites until stiff and fold into the pastry cream, with any leftover whipped cream. Fill the centre of the gâteau with the pastry cream. Decorate the buns with glacé cherries and angelica.

Note This gâteau is the traditional birthday cake in France.

Savarin
6–8 helpings

Basic Mixture

75ml milk

15g fresh yeast **or** 1 × 10ml spoon
  dried yeast

150g strong white flour

¼ × 5ml spoon salt

1 × 10ml spoon sugar

75g butter

3 eggs

oil for greasing

Rum Syrup

75g lump sugar

125ml water

2 × 15ml spoons rum

1 × 15ml spoon lemon juice

Glaze

3 × 15ml spoons apricot jam

2 × 15ml spoons water

Warm the milk until tepid. Blend in the fresh yeast or sprinkle on the dried yeast. Stir in 25g of the flour and leave in a warm place for 20 minutes. Sift the rest of the flour, the salt, and the sugar into a bowl. Rub in the butter. Add the yeast to the mixture, then add the eggs and beat until well mixed. Oil a 20cm ring mould (a savarin mould). Pour the mixture into the tin, cover with a large, lightly oiled polythene bag, and leave in a warm place until the mixture has almost reached the top of the tin. Bake in a fairly hot oven at 200°C, Gas 6, for about 20 minutes or until golden-brown and springy to the touch.

To make the rum syrup, put the sugar and water in a pan and heat until the sugar has dissolved. Bring to the boil and boil steadily for 8 minutes. Add the rum and lemon juice. Turn the warm savarin on to a serving dish, prick all over with a fine skewer, and spoon the rum syrup over it.

To make the glaze, sieve the apricot jam into a saucepan, add the water and bring to the boil, stirring all the time. Brush the glaze all over the soaked savarin.

VARIATIONS

The basic savarin is used for a number of French desserts and cakes. Instead of soaking it in rum syrup it can be filled with various mixtures, such as flavoured whipped cream or fruit purée mixed with rum.

Rum Babas
Makes 12

Make the basic mixture as above but add 50g currants. Grease 12 baba tins. Half fill the tins with the mixture. Place in a large, lightly oiled polythene bag and leave in a warm place for about 20 minutes or until the tins are two-thirds full. Bake in a fairly hot oven at 200°C, Gas 6, for 10–15 minutes or until golden-brown and springy to the touch. While still warm, soak with rum syrup as above.

Sacher Torte
8–12 helpings

125g butter	125g self-raising flour
125g granulated sugar	fat for greasing
125g plain chocolate	flour for dredging
6 eggs	50g apricot jam (approx)

Filling

25g icing sugar	40g softened unsalted butter
50g plain chocolate	

Icing

175g plain chocolate	165ml water
165g lump sugar	25g unsalted butter

Cream the butter and sugar until light and fluffy. Break up or grate the chocolate, melt it in a basin over a pan of hot water, and cool slightly; then stir it into the creamed mixture. Separate the eggs. Beat in the yolks, one by one, until thoroughly blended. Sift the flour. Whisk the egg whites until they hold firm peaks, then fold them into the mixture alternately with the flour; use either a metal spoon or an electric blender on the lowest speed. Pour the mixture into an 18cm loose-bottomed greased and floured cake tin. Set on a baking tray. Make a slight hollow in the centre to ensure even rising.

Bake in a moderate–fairly hot oven, 180°–190°C, Gas 4–5, for about $1\frac{1}{2}$ hours. If the cake shows any signs of browning too much after 1 hour, lower the temperature to warm, 160°C, Gas 3, and continue baking until the cake is fully cooked. Test by inserting a skewer; it will come out clean when the cake is fully baked. Leave in the tin for a few minutes, then turn out on to a wire rack, and cool at room temperature.

Make the filling when the cake is cold. Sift the icing sugar. Break up or grate the chocolate, and melt it in a basin over a pan of hot water. Cream together the icing sugar, chocolate, and butter until very smooth and fully blended.

Split the cold cake in half and spread the filling over the cut surfaces. Sandwich the coated halves together. Warm the apricot jam until liquid, and spread it very thinly over the top and sides.

Make the icing. Break up or grate the chocolate, and melt it in a basin over a pan of hot water. Keep it soft over the hot water while preparing the syrup. Bring the sugar and water to the boil, and boil until they form a thread (103°C). Gradually stir this into the melted chocolate, and beat until the icing coats a wooden spoon thickly and can be drawn up to a point. Do not overbeat or the mixture will lose its gloss. Stir in the butter. Spread the icing quickly and smoothly over the cake, using a knife dipped in hot water.

Note If Sacher Torte is served as a dessert, it should be accompanied by sweetened whipped cream.

Coffee Cheesecake
10–12 helpings

Base

50g butter **or** margarine
50g caster sugar
1 egg

50g self-raising flour
1 × 2.5ml spoon baking powder

Filling

75g butter
100g caster sugar
2 × 15ml spoons instant coffee
1 × 15ml spoon boiling water
1 × 15ml spoon orange juice
2 × 15ml spoons brandy

1 egg
50g plain flour
75g sultanas
500g full-fat soft chesse
250ml double cream

Beat together all the ingredients for the base until smooth. Spread the mixture over the base of a deep loose-bottomed 20cm cake tin.

To make the filling, cream together the butter and sugar until light and fluffy. Dissolve the coffee in the boiling water and orange juice, and leave to cool. Beat it into the creamed mixture with the brandy and egg. Fold in the flour and sultanas. In a separate bowl, beat the cheese until smooth. Gradually beat in the cream. Fold the cheese mixture carefully into the butter mixture and pour into the prepared tin. Bake in a warm oven at 160°C, Gas 3, for $1\frac{1}{4}$–$1\frac{1}{2}$ hours or until firm. Cool. Remove from the tin and serve cold.

Curd Cheesecake
4 helpings

Base

shortcrust pastry (p453) using
    125g flour

flour for rolling out

Filling

curds from 500ml milk (75g approx)
    or 75g curd cheese
50g butter
1 egg
a pinch of salt

100g sugar
25g currants
grated nutmeg
1 × 5ml spoon baking powder

Roll out the pastry on a lightly floured surface and use it to line an 18cm flan ring. Break down the curds with a fork or, if very firm, rub them through a sieve. Melt the butter. Beat the egg until liquid. Mix the butter, egg, salt, sugar, currants, and a little grated nutmeg thoroughly into the curds. Add the baking powder last of all. Put the mixture into the flan case. Bake in a fairly hot oven at 190°C, Gas 5, for 25–30 minutes until the pastry is lightly browned and the filling set. Serve warm or cold.

Lemon Cheesecake
8 helpings

Base

100g digestive biscuits	25g caster sugar
50g butter	

Filling

200g full-fat soft cheese	15g gelatine
75g caster sugar	50ml water
2 eggs	grated rind and juice of 1 lemon
125ml soured cream	

Decoration

whipped cream	crystallized lemon slices

To make the base, crush the biscuits finely with a rolling-pin. Melt the butter and mix in the crumbs and sugar. Press the mixture on to the base of a 17cm loose-bottomed cake tin. Put in a cool place to set.

To make the filling, beat the cheese and sugar together. Separate the eggs, and beat the yolks into the cheese mixture. Stir in the soured cream. Soften the gelatine in the water in a small heatproof basin. Stand the basin in a pan of hot water and stir until the gelatine dissolves. Stir the lemon rind, juice, and gelatine into the cheese mixture. Whisk the egg whites until stiff and fold carefully into the mixture. Pour into the prepared tin and chill for 45 minutes–1 hour until firm. Remove from the tin and decorate with whipped cream and crystallized lemon slices.

Raspberry Yoghurt Cheesecake
8–10 helpings

Base

50g butter	25g walnuts
50g caster sugar	50g puffed rice cereal
1 × 15ml spoon golden syrup	fat for greasing

Filling

1 × 15ml spoon gelatine	3 eggs
50ml cold water	250g caster sugar
300g cottage cheese	250ml double cream
125ml raspberry flavoured yoghurt	1 × 175g can raspberries
1 × 15ml spoon lemon juice	

Glaze (optional)

syrup from canned raspberries	1 × 10ml spoon arrowroot
water	a few drops red food colouring

Melt the butter, sugar, and syrup together in a saucepan. Chop the walnuts, and add with the puffed rice cereal to the pan. Stir well and press the mixture on to the base of a greased 20cm loose-bottomed cake tin. Chill for 10 minutes.

Soften the gelatine in the water in a small heatproof basin. Stand the basin in a saucepan of hot water and stir until the gelatine dissolves. Sieve the cottage cheese, add the yoghurt and lemon juice and beat until smooth. Separate the eggs. Mix the yolks and 150g of the sugar in a pan, and cook over low heat, stirring all the time, until the mixture thickens. Remove from the heat, add the gelatine, mix well, and allow to cool until the mixture is beginning to thicken.

Stir the yoghurt and cheese mixture into the cooled gelatine. Whisk the egg whites until stiff, then gradually whisk in the remaining sugar. Whip the cream until it just holds its shape. Fold the whites and cream into the main mixture, and pour it carefully into the prepared tin. Chill for at least 4 hours. If leaving the cake unglazed, remove from the tin, drain the syrup from the can of raspberries and arrange the fruit on top. Chill before serving.

If glazing the cake, make up the syrup to 125ml with water and blend it into the arrowroot in a small saucepan. Bring to the boil, stirring all the time, and simmer for 2–3 minutes until the sauce thickens and clears. Add a few drops of red colouring. Arrange the fruit on top and coat with the glaze. Chill before serving.

Cooked Meringue (Meringue Cuite)
Makes 4 cases or baskets or 16–20 × 2cm cases for petits fours

4 egg whites   2–3 drops vanilla essence
250g icing sugar

Whisk the egg whites and sugar together in a basin over a pan of gently simmering water until the mixture is very thick and holds its shape. Flavour with vanilla essence. Bake in a very cool oven at 110°C, Gas ¼, for 1–1½ hours.

To make meringue baskets, line a baking tray as when making a meringue case and make up the meringue mixture. Spoon the meringue on to the tray into 4 portions. Keep them well apart. Hollow out the centres to make neat nest-like shapes.

Alternatively, use a small star vegetable nozzle to make 4 small basket shapes. Bake as for a meringue case.

Make very small meringue cases for use as petits fours in the same way. Make circles 2cm across and hollow out with the tip of a pointed spoon. Then proceed as for meringue baskets. The small cases will, however, dry in 45minutes–1 hour.

Italian Meringue

200g granulated sugar   4 egg whites
2 × 15ml spoons water

Put the sugar and water into a small, thick-based saucepan and heat slowly until the sugar has dissolved completely. Stir once or twice to make sure that every grain has dissolved. Increase the heat slightly and continue heating the syrup, without stirring, until it reaches 140°C. Keep the syrup warm. Whisk the egg whites until stiff. Pour the syrup on to the egg whites slowly and steadily, without a pause, while still whisking. (It is easier to get someone else to pour the syrup.) Continue whisking until the meringue is thick and cold. Bake in a very cool oven at 110°C, Gas ¼, for 1–1½ hours.

Use for a vacherin or to cover cold desserts.

Swiss or Chantilly Meringue (for shells, toppings, and cakes)

Makes 12–16 medium-sized shells, 24–30 small shells; covers 1 × 20–22cm flan or tart; makes 1 × 20cm case

4 egg whites
a pinch of salt
200g caster sugar

$\frac{1}{2}$ × 2.5ml spoon baking powder
(optional)

Cream filling (see Method)
125ml double cream
$\frac{1}{2}$ × 2.5ml spoon vanilla essence

1 × 5ml spoon caster sugar

Separate the whites from the yolks very carefully. No trace of yolk must be left, for the fat in them prevents the whites whisking properly. For the same reason the bowl and whisk must be absolutely clean and dry.

Put the whites into a large bowl with the salt. Whisk the whites until they are very stiff and standing up in points. They must be absolutely dry or the meringues will break down in baking. Gradually add half the caster sugar, 1 × 15ml spoonful at a time. Whisk very thoroughly after each addition until the mixture regains its stiffness. The sugar must be blended in very thoroughly or it forms droplets of syrup which brown, and may make the meringues sticky and difficult to remove from the paper. Sprinkle the remaining sugar all at once over the surface together with the baking powder (if used). Fold in very lightly using a metal spoon.

To make the cream filling, whip the cream with the essence and sugar until it just holds its shape.

For *meringue shells*, line a baking sheet with greaseproof paper and rub it lightly with cooking oil, or use vegetable parchment.

Put the meringue mixture into a forcing bag with a 1–2cm nozzle and pipe into rounds on the paper; or shape the mixture using 2 wet dessertspoons – take up a spoonful of the mixture and smooth it with a palette knife, bringing it up into a ridge in the centre. Slide it out with the other spoon on to the tray, with the ridge on top.

Dust the meringues with caster sugar and dry off in a very cool oven at 110°C, Gas $\frac{1}{4}$, for 3–4 hours until they are firm and crisp, but still white. If they begin to brown, prop the oven door open a little. When crisp on the outside, lift the meringues off the tray gently with a palette knife. Turn them on their sides and return them to the oven until their undersides are dry. If the meringues are large, press in the soft centres to dry them out completely.

Put the meringues on a cooling tray until absolutely cold. Sandwich them together with the sweetened flavoured cream not more than 1 hour before they are to be used, or they will go soft. Alternatively, use without the filling to decorate a cold dessert.

For *meringue topping*, use only 25–40g of sugar per egg white. Whisk the whites until stiff and fold the sugar in lightly. Pile the mixture on top of the pudding a few minutes before the end of the cooking time, and spread it out to cover the whole surface. It is more attractive if flicked up into small peaks.

By covering the pudding, the meringue seals it from the heat so that it does not dry out. Sprinkle the top of the meringue with caster sugar. Bake in a very cool oven at 140°C, Gas 1, for 30–40 minutes; or in a hot oven at 220°C, Gas 7, for about

10 minutes. In either case the meringue will be crisp and lightly coloured on the outside, but remain soft inside.

For *meringue cases* draw a 20cm circle on a sheet of greaseproof paper or vegetable parchment. Put the paper on a baking sheet. Oil the greaseproof paper very lightly.

Make up the meringue mixture as for shells. Spread some of the meringue all over the circle to form the base of the case. Put the rest of the mixture into a forcing bag and, using a large star vegetable nozzle, pipe it round the edge of the ring in a border 5–6cm high, or use a spoon to make the rim. Bake low down in a very cool oven at 110°C, Gas ¼, for 3–4 hours, or until quite dry. Leave to cool on a rack, remove the paper and fill the case with fruit and sweetened whipped cream.

Note If really dried out, meringue shells will keep for 1–2 weeks in an airtight tin.

Raspberry Vacherin *Basic recipe*
4 helpings

3 egg whites	250ml double cream
a pinch of salt	1 × 5ml spoon caster sugar
150g caster sugar	Kirsch
300g fresh raspberries	

Decoration
a few angelica leaves

Line 2 baking trays with greaseproof paper or vegetable parchment. Draw a 15cm circle on each one and very lightly oil the greaseproof paper, if used.

Make up a cooked or Italian meringue mixture (p369) from the egg whites, salt, and 150g caster sugar. Put the meringue into a forcing bag with a 1cm plain nozzle. Starting from the middle of one circle, pipe round and round to form a coiled, flat round 15cm in diameter. Pipe a similar round on the other tray. Use any remaining mixture to pipe small meringue shells. Bake in a very cool oven at 110°C, Gas ¼, for 1–1½ hours. Leave to cool.

Pick over the raspberries, and leave on a plate for 30 minutes. Clean and pat dry. Reserve a few choice berries for decoration. Whip the double cream until it is thick and stands in firm peaks, then stir in the 1 × 5ml spoon caster sugar and Kirsch to taste.

Place one of the meringue rounds on a serving plate, spread with some of the cream, and arrange half the raspberries on it in a flat layer. (Do not make the cream layer too thick or the vacherin will be difficult and messy to eat and serve.) Put the second meringue on top of the raspberries, arrange the rest of the raspberries in the centre, and pipe rosettes or a decorative edge of cream round the berries. Decorate the sides of the vacherin with the small meringues and angelica leaves.

Serve cut in wedges like a cake, using a flat cake slice to lift the meringue on to the plates.

Pavlova
4 helpings

3 egg whites
150g caster sugar
1 × 2.5ml spoon vinegar

1 × 2.5ml spoon vanilla essence
2 × 5ml spoons cornflour
filling (see below)

Line a baking sheet with greaseproof paper or vegetable parchment. Draw a 20cm circle on it and very lightly oil the greaseproof paper, if used.

Whisk the egg whites until very stiff. Continue whisking, gradually adding the sugar until the mixture is very stiff again and stands up in peaks. Beat in the vinegar, vanilla essence, and cornflour. Spread the meringue over the circle, piling it up at the edges to form a rim, or pipe the circle and rim from a forcing bag, using a 2cm star nozzle. Bake low down in a cool oven at 150°C, Gas 2, for about 1 hour. The Pavlova should be crisp and tinged a pale coffee colour on the outside and have a texture like marshmallow inside. Leave to cool. Remove the paper very gently and put the Pavlova on a large serving plate.

Note This Pavlova case will not store so it must be made on the day it is to be eaten and filled only just before it is served.

FILLINGS
1) Whip 250ml double cream until fairly stiff. Skin and slice 400g peaches. Combine the fruit and cream and fill the Pavlova case with the mixture just before serving. Decorate with glacé cherries and angelica.
2) Slice 4 bananas thinly and put into a basin. Add 2 × 15ml spoons brandy, and chill for 1 hour, turning the fruit from time to time. Whip 250ml double cream lightly and fold in the bananas and 100g halved, stoned fresh or maraschino cherries. Pile into the Pavlova case and sprinkle generously with grated chocolate and a few chopped nuts.

ICES AND FROZEN DESSERTS

Ices can be frozen in either a freezer or the ice-making compartment of a refrigerator. Whichever method is used, all equipment should be chilled before use.

Freezer
The dial should be set to 'fast freeze' about 1 hour before freezing. Except for *granités*, which are not beaten during freezing, any mixture should, if possible, be packed in a container in which it can be beaten. The mixture is beaten once or twice during freezing to break down the ice crystals and incorporate air. After beating, the mixture is put into its mould, if used, and frozen firm for immediate use, or storage at the freezer's normal temperature. Ices for storage must be sealed, or overwrapped and labelled. For details of storage life for ices, see p583.

Ice-making Compartment
The dial should be set at the coldest setting at least 1 hour before putting in the ice mixture. If there is room, the mixture should be frozen in a container, as in a home

freezer, and beaten in the same way. If there is no room in the compartment, the mixture can be frozen in ice trays with the dividers removed or in similar containers, and either put into another container for beating, or whisked in the trays with a fork. After beating, the ice is returned, covered, to the ice-making compartment until frozen firm, and the dial is then returned to its normal setting.

Electric Ice Cream Maker or Sorbetière

This appliance is placed in the ice-making compartment of a refrigerator, or a home freezer, and beats the mixture steadily until it is frozen, when it ceases automatically; it gives a very smooth texture and more bulk than when the mixture is hand beaten. A spare electric point near the refrigerator or freezer is needed to plug in the sorbetière. Electric churns for use outside the refrigerator are also available; they operate on the same principle as the hand churns described below, and need extra ice and salt.

Churn Freezer

A churn freezer consists of a metal container for the ice cream mixture, placed in an outer churn packed with crushed ice and salt. A 1 litre capacity freezing container needs 3.25kg crushed ice and 1kg common salt or freezing salt (obtainable from most large department stores and fishmongers), for the churn.

Containers

The governing factors in choosing containers are the size of the freezing space available, and the freezing time you can allow. A deep bowl or box, for example, may not fit into the ice-making compartment of the refrigerator, and a solid block of ice cream takes much longer to freeze than a shallow layer in an ice tray. The larger the quantity of ice mixture the more slowly it freezes, and since quick freezing is generally desirable to prevent the foremation of large ice crystals, it is wise to freeze ices in single quantities of 1 litre or less. If it is necessary to freeze more than this amount, use two containers. Rigic plastic, stainless steel, or any similar containers can be used, provided they have lids or can be covered securely with foil. If space allows, it is easier to use rigid plastic bowls with lids to freeze ice mixtures before beating; they can then be beaten in the bowl and transferred to the serving container.

Moulds

Large ice cream moulds are exactly like decorative jelly moulds, but have lids. Individual ice creams can be frozen in small fluted jelly moulds which hold about 100ml. Moulds without lids should be covered with foil while the mixture is freezing.

Bombes should be frozen in bell-shaped moulds, or in pudding basins. Use refrigerator ice trays or oblong foil trays for making a *biscuit glacé* or Neapolitan ice cream. Round, flat layers of ice cream for gâteaux can be frozen in deep cake tins, or in sandwich tins or foil dishes.

Other Equipment

An electric or rotary beater makes beating ice mixtures much easier both before and during freezing. A nylon (not metal) sieve for puréeing fruit is also necessary. Fruit can be processed in an electric blender, but fruits such as raspberries or grapes, with pips and skin, have to be sieved to make a really smooth purée. An ice cream scoop for serving individual portions of ice cream or water ices, or for shaping ice cream into small balls for a *plombière* is a useful, though not essential, piece of equipment.

Water Ices, Granités and Sorbets

1) After pouring the mixture into a suitable container, chill if a hot syrup has been used, cover closely, and half freeze unless otherwise directed.
2) Beat the half-frozen mixture thoroughly, scraping off any crystals. Re-cover and freeze completely; label and store.

Note The recipes in the Water Ice section below can be served as *granités*;they should be frozen completely and the beating omitted.

Syrup (1)
Makes 1 litre (approx)

1kg caster sugar
750ml water

3 × 2.5ml spoons liquid glucose
(optional)

Put the sugar and water in a strong saucepan and dissolve the sugar over gentle heat, without stirring. Bring the mixture to the boil and boil slowly for about 10 minutes or to a temperature of 110°C. Remove the scum as it rises. Strain, cool with a lid on the pan, add the liquid glucose, if used, and store in a glass bottle for use as required. If the syrup is to be used hot, re-heat in a covered pan, and keep covered during any waiting period.

Syrup (2)
Makes 500ml (approx)

200g lump sugar

500ml water

Make as for Syrup (1).

Lemon Water Ice
6 helpings

6 lemons
2 oranges

375ml hot syrup (1)

Pare the rind very thinly from the fruit, and put into a basin. Add the hot syrup, cover, and leave to cool. Add the juice of the lemons and oranges to the syrup mixture. Strain through a nylon sieve into a container, chill, and freeze as described above.

VARIATION
Orange Water Ice
Use 6 oranges and 2 lemons, and reduce the syrup quantity to 250ml.

Raspberry or Strawberry Water Ice
6 helpings

450g ripe strawberries, raspberries
  or loganberries

250ml cold syrup (1) (p374)
juice of 2 lemons

Rub the fruit through a nylon sieve, or process in an electric blender and sieve to make a smooth purée. Add the cold syrup and lemon juice, and mix well. Pour into a suitable container and freeze as described on p374.

Lemon Sorbet
6–8 helpings

2 × 5ml spoons gelatine
250ml water
150g caster sugar

1 × 2.5ml spoon grated lemon rind
250ml lemon juice
2 egg whites

Soften the gelatine in a little of the water over a pan of hot water. Boil the remaining water and sugar together for 10 minutes. Stir the dissolved gelatine into the syrup, add the lemon rind and juice, and leave to cool. Pour into a suitable container, cover, and freeze for 1 hour. Whisk the egg whites until they hold stiff peaks, beat the half-frozen ice mixture thoroughly, and fold the egg whites into it. Re-cover, and continue freezing for a further 2 hours.
Note This ice will not freeze hard.

Ice Creams, Puddings and Drinks

1) Cool hot custard unless required hot.
2) After turning the mixture into a container, chill until thoroughly cold, cover closely and half freeze unless otherwise directed.
3) Beat the mixture well and add any cream, if it has not been added before. Re-freeze until firm; label and store.

Note Ice creams made with an electric ice cream maker are prepared somewhat differently, and the manufacturer's directions should be followed.

Plain Custard (1)
Makes 500ml (approx)

2 × 15ml spoons custard powder
500ml milk

100g caster sugar

Blend the custard powder with a little of the milk. Heat the remaining milk to boiling point and pour on io the blended mixture. Return to the pan and simmer, stirring all the time, until the mixture thickens. Add the sugar, cover, and use hot or cold as required.

Plain Egg Custard (2)
Makes 500ml (approx)

500ml milk
3 eggs

100g caster sugar

Heat the milk until almost boiling. Beat the eggs and sugar together and add the hot milk, stirring well. Return the mixture to the pan and cook, without boiling, until the custard coats the back of a wooden spoon. Stir all the time. Strain, cover, and use as required.

Standard Custard (3)
Makes 500ml (approx)

500ml milk
8 egg yolks

2 eggs
100g caster sugar

Heat the milk until almost boiling. Beat the yolks, eggs, and sugar together until thick and white, and add the hot milk, stirring well. Return the mixture to the pan and cook, without boiling, until the custard thickens, stirring all the time. Strain, cover, and use as required.

Rich Custard (4)
Makes 500ml (approx)

8 egg yolks
100g caster sugar
500ml single cream

vanilla essence, ground spice, liqueur
or other flavouring

Beat the yolks and sugar together until very thick. Put the cream in a saucepan and bring slowly to the boil. Pour the cream over the yolks and sugar, stirring well. Return the mixture to the pan and cook, without boiling, until the custard thickens. Stir all the time. Strain, add a few drops of vanilla essence or other flavouring, cover, and use as required.

Vanilla Ice Cream
6 helpings

125ml double cream
500ml cold custard (1) (p375)

1 × 5ml spoon vanilla essence

Whip the cream until semi-stiff. Add the cold custard and vanilla essence. Turn into a suitable container, chill, and freeze as described on p375, beating once while freezing.

Rich Vanilla Ice Cream
6 helpings

250ml double cream
250ml cold custard (2) (p376)

1 × 5ml spoon vanilla essence
50g caster sugar

Whip the cream until semi-stiff. Add the cold custard, vanilla essence, and sugar. Turn into a suitable container, chill, and freeze as described on p375, beating once while freezing.

Rich Chocolate Ice Cream
6–8 helpings

100g plain chocolate
65ml water
250ml hot custard (3) **or** (4) (p376)

125ml double cream
1 × 5ml spoon vanilla essence

Break up the chocolate roughly and melt it in the water, either in a double saucepan or in a basin over hot water. Add the melted chocolate to the hot custard, and leave to cool. Whip the cream until semi-stiff and fold it into the custard mixture with the vanilla essence. Turn into a container, chill, and freeze as described on p375, beating once while freezing.

Lemon Ice Cream
6 helpings

8 egg yolks
200g caster sugar

juice of 2 lemons
250ml double cream

Beat the egg yolks until very thick, add the sugar, and beat again. Stir in the lemon juice. Whip the cream until semi-stiff, and add carefully to the egg and sugar mixture. Turn into a suitable container, chill, and freeze for 30 minutes. Beat thoroughly, and finish freezing as described on p375.

Strawberry or Raspberry Ice Cream
6 helpings

125ml milk
250ml double cream
2 egg yolks
150g caster sugar

400g strawberries **or** raspberries
1 × 15ml spoon granulated sugar
1 × 5ml spoon lemon juice
red food colouring

Put the milk and cream in a saucepan and bring almost to boiling point. Beat together the yolks and caster sugar, add to the milk and cream, and return to low heat, stirring all the time, until the mixture thickens. Rub the strawberries or raspberries through a nylon sieve. Fold the granulated sugar into the purée. Mix with the custard, and add lemon juice and a few drops of red food colouring. Turn into a suitable container, chill, and freeze as described on p375, beating once while freezing.

Baked Alaska
6–8 helpings

3 egg whites
150g caster sugar
1 × 20cm round Genoese or other
sponge cake

500ml vanilla ice cream (p376)

Heat the oven to very hot, 230°C, Gas 8. Whisk the egg whites until very stiff, gradually whisk in half the sugar and fold in the rest. Alternatively, use the whites and sugar to make an Italian meringue (see p369).

Place the sponge cake round on an ovenproof plate and pile the ice cream on to it, leaving 1cm sponge uncovered all round. Cover quickly with the meringue, making sure that both the ice cream and the sponge are completely covered. Put in the oven for 3–4 minutes until the meringue is just beginning to brown. Serve immediately.
Note The ice cream must be as hard as possible.

Banana Split
6 helpings

6 bananas
500ml vanilla ice cream (p376)

250ml Melba sauce (p268)
50g chopped walnuts

Decoration
125ml double cream
sugar

6 maraschino cherries

Split the bananas in half lengthways and place in small oval dishes. Place 2 small scoops or slices of ice cream between the banana halves. Coat the ice cream with Melba sauce, and sprinkle with the chopped nuts. Whip the cream until stiff and sweeten to taste. Decorate with the cream and cherries.

Coupe Jacques
6 helpings

50g grapes
1 banana
1 peach
50g raspberries

2 × 15ml spoons Kirsch
250ml lemon water ice (p374) or
vanilla ice cream (p376)
250ml strawberry ice cream (p377)

Decoration
125ml double cream

sugar

Chop and mix the fruit; soak in the Kirsch for 4 hours. Place one portion of each ice in each of 6 sundae glasses. Cover with the soaked fruit. Whip the cream until soft and sweeten to taste. Decorate each portion with the cream.

Knickerbocker Glory
6 helpings

1 × 500ml pkt yellow jelly
1 × 500ml pkt red jelly
200g canned peaches
200g canned pineapple chunks
150ml double cream

1 × 5ml spoon caster sugar
1 litre vanilla ice cream (p376)
500ml Melba sauce (p268)
50g chopped mixed nuts

Decoration
6 maraschino cherries

Make the jellies according to the directions on the packet. Leave until set. Drain the peaches and pineapple chunks, chop them, and mix the fruit together. Whip the cream until stiff, and sweeten with the caster sugar. Chop the set jellies with a fork until well broken up.

Put 1 × 15ml spoon of fruit in each of 6 sundae glasses. Cover with 1 × 15ml spoon of yellow jelly, add a scoop of ice cream, and coat with the Melba sauce. Repeat the process using the red jelly. Sprinkle with the chopped nuts, and pipe a rose of whipped cream on top. Decorate each portion with a maraschino cherry.
Note Tall wine glasses can be used instead of sundae glasses.

Neapolitan Ice
6 helpings

250ml double cream
250ml cold custard (3) (p376)
125ml strawberry **or** raspberry purée
75g caster sugar
red food colouring (optional)

$\frac{1}{2}$ × 2.5ml spoon almond **or** ratafia
   essence
green food colouring
2 × 5ml spoons vanilla essence

Whip the cream until semi-stiff and fold into the cold custard. Divide this mixture into 3 equal portions. Mix the fruit purée with one-third of the mixture, and add 25g sugar and a few drops of red food colouring, if necessary. Add the almond or ratafia essence to another third of the mixture with a further 25g sugar and enough food colouring to tint it a bright but not vivid green. Add the vanilla essence and the last 25g sugar to the remaining third of the mixture. Cover, and freeze in separate trays until almost firm; then pack in layers in a suitable square or oblong mould. Cover and freeze until required. Serve cut in slices.

Peach Melba
6 helpings

500ml vanilla ice cream (p376)
6 canned peaches

250ml Melba sauce (p268)
125ml double cream

Place a scoop or slice of ice cream in each of 6 sundae glasses. Cover each portion with a peach half. Coat with the Melba sauce. Whip the cream until stiff, and pipe a large rose on top of each portion.

Poire Belle Hélène
4 helpings

4 firm ripe pears
250ml vanilla ice cream (p376)

250ml chocolate sauce (p267)
125ml double cream

Decoration
25g crystallized violets

Peel the pears, cut them in half, and remove the cores. Place a scoop or slice of ice cream in each of 4 dishes. Top with the pear halves and mask with chocolate sauce. Whip the cream until stiff, and pipe a large rose on top of each portion. Decorate with the crystallized violets.

Strawberry Ice Cream Layer Gâteau
8–10 helpings

1 litre strawberry ice cream (p377)
1 litre lemon ice cream (p377)
125g digestive biscuits
50g chopped mixed nuts
75g butter

25g soft light brown sugar
250g strawberry jam
4 × 15ml spoons Kirsch
200ml double cream
icing sugar

Decoration
whole strawberries

Line an 18cm loose-bottomed, deep cake tin with vegetable parchment. Soften both ice creams. Crush the digestive biscuits with a rolling-pin. Put 25g crumbs aside with 25g of the nuts. Melt the butter, and mix in the rest of the crumbs and nuts, and the brown sugar. Press the mixture into the lined cake tin, and chill until firm.

Sieve the jam, and mix with 1 × 15ml spoon of the Kirsch. Mix the strawberries for the decoration with 1 × 15ml spoon Kirsch and a little icing sugar, if liked. Chill for at least 1 hour.

Cover the chilled biscuit crumb base with half the strawberry ice cream, and spread the top with a third of the jam. Sprinkle with one-third of the remaining crumbs and chopped nuts. Freeze until the ice cream is firm. Repeat the process with half the lemon ice cream, then with the rest of the ingredients until alternate layers of ice cream and jam, crumbs, and nuts have been formed. Freeze until each layer of ice cream is firm before adding the next.

Whip the cream until stiff with the remaining Kirsch, and icing sugar to taste. Remove the gâteau from the cake tin, and peel off the vegetable parchment. Put on to a suitable plate, and cover the top layer of lemon ice cream with the whipped cream. Decorate with the strawberries, chill again, and serve.

Note It is easier not to try and detach the crumb base from the bottom of the cake tin; simply put the gâteau on the plate with the bottom of the tin still in place.

Ice Cream Soda *Basic recipe*
4–6 helpings

200ml fresh fruit purée (p345)
150ml milk
50g caster sugar **or** to taste (depending on the sweetness of the fruit)

150g ice cream, suited to the fruit flavour used
250ml soda water

Process the fruit purée, milk, and sugar in an electric blender at medium speed until smooth. Add the ice cream and blend for a further 30 seconds. Pour into 4–6 glasses, and top up with the soda water.
Note Use a well-flavoured fruit purée.

Milk Shake *Basic recipe*
2 helpings

500ml milk
2 × 10ml spoons concentrated fruit juice **or** fruit syrup

2 scoops ice cream, suited to the fruit flavour used

Either simply stir the fruit flavouring into the milk, chill, and add the ice cream just before serving; or, mix all the ingredients together and chill well. Then just before serving, whisk thoroughly, or process briefly in an electric blender. Serve while still frothy.

VARIATIONS

Coffee Milk Shake
Substitute 1 × 10ml spoon coffee essence for the fruit flavouring. Use vanilla, chocolate or coffee ice cream.

Ginger Milk Shake
Use ginger syrup from a jar of stem ginger instead of fruit juice. Add 1 × 5ml spoon finely chopped stem ginger to the other ingredients when mixing.

Banana Milk Shake
1 helping

1 banana
250ml milk
4 ice cubes

1 × 5ml spoon honey
a pinch of grated nutmeg

Chop the banana roughly. Process in an electric blender for 1 minute with the milk, ice cubes, and honey. Pour into a glass, and sprinkle with the nutmeg before serving.

BREADS, CAKES, BISCUITS, ICINGS, FILLINGS AND DECORATIONS

BREADS

Yeast Breads

The fermentation method of raising dough involves the use of yeast, which is a living organism. Whenever it is used, twice as much fresh yeast is needed as dried yeast; in other words, 50g fresh yeast = 25g dried yeast.

Fresh Yeast is quick and easy to use but is not always easily obtainable, especially in urban areas. It should be creamy in colour, have a slightly beery smell, be cool to the touch and easy to break. It will store in a polythene bag in a refrigerator for up to a week and will freeze, if well wrapped, for up to 1 month. Fresh yeast should always be blended into a warm liquid rather than creamed with sugar, which tends to give yeasty 'off' flavours in the finished bread.

Dried Yeast, available in packets and tins, has a shelf-life, unopened, of up to 1 year. Once opened, however, it keeps for only 2–3 months, and must be stored in an airtight container.

Before use, dried yeast must be reconstituted. 1 × 5ml spoon of sugar is dissolved in a warm liquid (usually water and/or milk at a temperature of 38°C, ie hand-hot). The dried yeast is sprinkled on the liquid and left in a warm place for 10–15 minutes, or until the yeast has fully dissolved and the mixture is frothy. (This may take longer when using all milk.) If after 30 minutes the mixture has not frothed, the yeast is stale and should be thrown away.

Kneading

Most doughs must be worked after mixing in order to strengthen and develop them and to make them rise well. Very soft doughs are beaten; all others are kneaded.

To hand knead: On a floured surface, fold the dough towards you, then push down and away from you with the heel of your hand. Give the dough a quarter turn and repeat the folding and pushing action, developing a rocking rhythm. Continue until the dough feels firm and elastic and is no longer sticky.

To knead in an electric mixer: Follow the manufacturer's directions for using a dough hook. Place the yeast liquid in the mixer bowl first, then add the dry ingredients. Turn the machine to minimum speed and mix for 1 minute to form the dough. Increase the speed slightly and mix for a further 2 minutes. It may be necessary to hand knead the dough into one piece when it is removed from the mixer bowl.

Rising

All yeast doughs must rise at least once before baking. Generally, a dough gives a better flavour and texture if it rises twice, but raising it once makes quite acceptable bread if time is limited. (The second rising is generally called *proving*.)

Rising times vary according to the type of dough and the temperature of the rising place; the warmer the place, the quicker the rise. The rising place must not, however, be too warm or the finished loaf will be dry and will quickly become stale. The dough may also be over-stretched by the yeast working too actively. The bread may collapse in the oven, and the loaf may smell yeasty or sour. As a rough guide, the dough should have risen enough when it has doubled in bulk.

The dough can be left to rise overnight in a refrigerator. In this case, return it to room temperature before shaping. Do not, however, leave rolls to rise in this way. All doughs should be covered during rising to prevent the surface drying out and a skin forming. The most convenient, efficient, and hygienic form of covering is a large polythene bag which has been lightly oiled inside to prevent it sticking to the dough and spoiling the surface of the shaped bread. The dough should only be covered loosely when it is put in the bag; ie some air space should be left above it so that it can rise unimpeded.

Unrisen dough can also be frozen (see p586).

Basic White Bread
Makes two 800g loaves

800g strong white flour
1 × 10ml spoon salt
1 × 10ml spoon sugar
25g lard
25g fresh yeast **or** 1 × 15ml spoon
  dried yeast

500ml warm water
flour for kneading
fat for greasing
beaten egg **or** milk for glazing

Sift together the flour, salt, and sugar into a large bowl. Rub in the lard. Blend the fresh yeast into the warm water or reconstitute the dried yeast. Add the yeast liquid to the flour mixture and mix to a soft dough. Turn on to a floured surface and knead for about 8 minutes or until the dough is smooth, elastic, and no longer sticky. Place the dough in a large, lightly oiled polythene bag and leave in a warm place for about 1 hour or until the dough has doubled in size. Knead the dough again until firm. Cut into 2 equal portions and form each into a loaf shape. Place the dough in 2 greased 23 × 13 × 7cm loaf tins and brush the surface with beaten egg or milk. Place the tins in the polythene bag and leave in a warm place for about 45 minutes or until the dough has doubled in size. Bake in a very hot oven, 230°C, Gas 8, for 35–40 minutes until the loaves are crisp and golden-brown and sound hollow when tapped on the bottom.

VARIATIONS
Fancy Roll Shapes
Makes 26
Divide the risen Basic White Bread dough into 50g pieces and shape as over (p384).

Small Plaits

Divide each piece of dough into 3 equal portions; then shape each of these into a long strand. Plait the 3 strands together, pinching the ends securely.

Small Twists

Divide each piece of dough into 2 equal portions, and shape into strands about 12cm in length. Twist the 2 strands together, pinching the ends securely.

'S' Rolls

Shape each piece of dough into a roll about 15cm in length, and form it into an 'S' shape.

Cottage Rolls

Cut two-thirds off each piece of dough and shape into a ball. Shape the remaining third in the same way. Place the small ball on top of the larger one and push a hole through the centre of both with one finger, dusted with flour, so joining the 2 pieces firmly together.

Huffkins

Shape each piece of dough into an oval about 12mm thick, then make a hole in the centre with one finger, dusted with flour.

Single Knots

Shape each piece of dough into a roll about 15cm in length and tie it into a knot. Place the shaped rolls, spaced well apart, on to greased baking sheets. Brush the surface of each with beaten egg or milk. Place the sheets in a large, lightly oiled polythene bag and leave in a warm place for about 25 minutes or until the rolls have almost doubled in size. Bake as for Basic White Bread (p383) but reduce the cooking time to 10–15 minutes.

Lardy Cake

Makes 18–20 slices

$\frac{1}{4}$ recipe of risen Basic White Bread dough (p383) (350g approx)	100g caster sugar
	100g sultanas **or** currants
flour for rolling out	1 × 5ml spoon mixed spice
125g lard	

Glaze

1 × 10ml spoon caster sugar	1 × 15ml spoon water

On a floured surface, roll out the dough to a strip 2cm thick. Place a third of the lard in small pats over the surface of the dough. Sprinkle one-third of the sugar, dried fruit, and spice over it. Fold the dough into three. Repeat the rolling and folding twice more, using the remaining ingredients. Roll out to fit a 20cm square slab cake or baking tin. Score diamond shapes in the surface of the dough with a sharp knife. Place the tin in a large, lightly oiled polythene bag and leave in a warm place for about 45 minutes or until the dough has risen by half. Bake in a fairly hot oven, 200°C, Gas 6, for 40 minutes until crisp and golden-brown.

To make the glaze, boil together the sugar and water until syrupy, and brush over the surface of the warm cake.

Enriched Bread
Makes two 800g loaves

800g strong white flour
1 × 10ml spoon sugar
400ml milk
25g fresh yeast **or** 1 × 15ml spoon
   dried yeast
1 × 10ml spoon salt

100g butter **or** margarine
2 eggs
flour for kneading
fat for greasing
milk for glazing

Sift about 75g of the flour and all the sugar into a large bowl. Warm the milk until hand-hot, then blend in the fresh yeast or stir in the dried yeast. Pour the yeast liquid into the flour and sugar and beat well. Leave the bowl in a warm place for 20 minutes. Sift the remaining flour and salt into a bowl. Rub in the fat. Beat the eggs into the yeast mixture and stir in the flour and fat. Mix to a soft dough. Turn on to a lightly floured surface and knead for about 6 minutes or until the dough is smooth and no longer sticky. Place the dough in a large, lightly oiled polythene bag and leave in a warm place for about 1 hour or until it has doubled in size. Knead again until firm. Cut it into 2 equal portions and form each into a loaf shape. Place in 2 greased 23 × 13 × 7cm loaf tins and cover with the polythene bag. Leave in a warm place for about 30 minutes or until the dough has doubled in size. Brush the surface with milk and bake in a hot oven, 220°C, Gas 7, for 35–40 minutes until the loaves are golden-brown and sound hollow when tapped on the bottom.

VARIATIONS
Bread Plait
Make as for Enriched Bread. Cut the risen dough into 2 equal portions. Cut one of these into 3 equal pieces. Roll each piece into a strand 25–30cm long and plait the strands together. Repeat, using the second portion. Place the plaits on a greased baking tray, cover, rise, and bake as for Enriched Bread.

Fruit Bread
Make as for Enriched Bread but add 200g sultanas, currants or raisins to the dough when kneading for the second time.

Nut Bread
Make as for Enriched Bread but add 200g chopped nuts (walnuts, peanuts, etc) to the dough when kneading for the second time.

Poppy Seed Bread
Make as for Enriched Bread but sprinkle poppy seeds thickly over the dough before baking.

For further **variations**, see over

Bridge Rolls

Makes 34–38

Make as for Enriched Bread (p385) but cut the risen dough into 50g pieces. Roll each piece into a finger shape about 10cm long. Place on a greased baking tray so that the rolls almost touch each other. Dust the surface of the rolls with flour, cover, and leave to rise for about 20 minutes or until the rolls have joined together. Bake as for Enriched Bread but reduce the cooking time to 12–15 minutes.

Dinner Rolls

Makes 34–38

Make as for Enriched Bread (p385) but cut the risen dough into 50g pieces. Shape each piece into a ball. Place on a greased baking tray 5–8cm apart. Brush with beaten egg, cover, and leave to rise for about 20 minutes or until the rolls have doubled in size. Bake as for Enriched Bread but reduce the cooking time to 12–15 minutes.

French Bread

Makes 2 French sticks

350g plain white flour (see **Note**)
50g cornflour
1 × 5ml spoon salt
15g fresh yeast **or** 1 × 10ml spoon
    dried yeast

250ml warm water
flour
beaten egg for glazing

Sift the flours and salt into a large bowl. Blend the fresh yeast into the warm water or reconstitute the dried yeast. Stir the yeast liquid into the flours and mix to a firm dough. Turn the dough on to a floured surface and knead for about 4 minutes or until it is smooth and no longer sticky. Place the dough in a large, lightly oiled polythene bag and leave in a warm place for about 1 hour or until it has doubled in size. Cut it into 2 equal portions. On a floured surface, roll out 1 piece to an oval 40cm in length. Roll it up like a Swiss roll and place on a well-floured baking sheet. With a sharp knife, slash the top surface at intervals. Brush the surface with beaten egg. Repeat with the other piece of dough. Leave both, *uncovered*, in a warm place for about 30 minutes or until doubled in size.

Meanwhile, place a pan of hot water in the bottom of the oven and heat the oven to hot, 220°C, Gas 7. This is to provide steam to make the French bread expand fully before using dry heat to form the typical crisp crust. Bake the loaves for 15 minutes, remove the pan of water, and continue baking until they are very crisp and well browned.

Note The dough is left uncovered to rise for the second time, so that the surface dries out and a very crisp crust is obtained after the loaf has been 'blown up' by steam heat in the oven. This can be done only when the volume of dough is as small as it is here, otherwise the bread splits open on baking.

Strong flour is not suitable for this bread.

Cooking time 30–35 minutes

Wholemeal Bread
Makes two 800g loaves

800g wholemeal flour
1 × 10ml spoon sugar
1 × 15ml spoon salt
25g lard
25g fresh yeast **or** 1 × 15ml spoon
    dried yeast

500ml warm water
flour for kneading
fat for greasing
salted water

Mix together the flour, sugar, and salt in a large bowl. Rub in the lard. Blend the fresh yeast into the warm water or reconstitute the dried yeast. Add the yeast liquid to the flour mixture and mix to a soft dough. Turn on to a lightly floured surface and knead for about 4 minutes or until the dough is smooth and elastic and no longer sticky. Place in a large, lightly oiled polythene bag and leave in a warm place for about 1 hour or until the dough has doubled in size. Knead again until firm. Cut it into 2 equal portions and form each into a loaf shape. Place the dough in 2 lightly greased 23 × 13 × 7cm loaf tins and brush the surface with salted water. Place the tins in the polythene bag and leave in a warm place for about 45 minutes or until the dough has doubled in size. Bake in a very hot oven, 230°C, Gas 8, for 30–40 minutes until the loaves are golden-brown and crisp and sound hollow when tapped on the bottom.

VARIATION
Wholemeal Rolls
Make as for Wholemeal Bread but shape into balls or fancy roll shapes as described on pp383–84. Bake for 10–15 minutes only.

Wheatmeal Bread
Makes two 800g loaves

400g wholemeal flour
400g strong white flour
1 × 10ml spoon salt
1 × 10ml spoon sugar
25g lard
25g fresh yeast **or** 1 × 15ml spoon
    dried yeast

500ml warm water
flour for kneading
fat for greasing
salted water

Mix together the flours, salt, and sugar in a large bowl. Rub in the lard. Blend the fresh yeast into the warm water or reconstitute the dried yeast. Add the yeast liquid to the flour mixture and mix to a soft dough. Turn on to a floured surface, and knead for about 4 minutes or until the dough is smooth and no longer sticky. Cut it into 2 equal portions and form each into a loaf shape. Place the dough in 2 greased 23 × 13 × 7cm loaf tins, and brush the surface with salted water. Place the tins in a large, lightly oiled polythene bag and leave in a warm place for about 50 minutes or until the dough has doubled in size. Bake in a very hot oven, 230°C, Gas 8, for 30–40 minutes until the loaves are golden-brown and crisp and sound hollow when tapped lightly on the bottom.

Granary Bread

Makes two 800g loaves

800g granary flour **or** meal
1 × 10ml spoon salt
1 × 10ml spoon molasses
500ml warm water
25g fresh yeast **or** 1 × 15ml spoon
   dried yeast

1 × 10ml spoon corn oil
flour for kneading
fat for greasing
salted water
1 × 15ml spoon cracked wheat

Mix together the flour and salt in a large bowl. Stir the molasses into the water, and when dissolved, blend in the fresh yeast, or reconstitute the dried yeast. Add the yeast liquid and the oil to the flour, and mix to a soft dough. Turn on to a floured surface and knead for about 4 minutes or until it is smooth, elastic, and no longer sticky. Place in a large, lightly oiled polythene bag and leave in a warm place for about 1¼ hours or until doubled in size. Knead the dough again until firm. Cut into 2 equal portions, and form each into a loaf shape. Place the dough in 2 greased 23 × 13 × 7cm loaf tins, brush the surface with salted water, and sprinkle with the cracked wheat. Place the tins in the polythene bag and leave in a warm place for about 45 minutes or until the dough has doubled in size. Bake in a very hot oven, 230°C, Gas 8, for 30–40 minutes until the loaves are browned and crisp and sound hollow when tapped on the bottom.

Rye Cobs

Makes 4 loaves

900g strong white flour
25g fresh yeast **or** 1 × 15ml spoon
   dried yeast
250ml warm water
450g coarse rye flour
500ml skimmed milk (from dried milk
   powder and water)

4 × 5ml spoons salt
4 × 15ml spoons molasses
4 × 15ml spoons cooking oil
flour for kneading
fat for greasing
warm water

Sift the white flour into a large bowl. Blend the fresh yeast into the warm water or reconstitute the dried yeast. Mix the rye flour into the white flour, then add the yeast liquid, skimmed milk, salt, molasses and oil, and knead to a soft dough. Place the mixing bowl inside a large, lightly oiled polythene bag and leave in a warm place for 1½–2 hours until the dough has doubled in size. (Rye bread is slow to rise.) When risen, shape into 4 round loaves. Place on a lightly greased baking sheet or press into 4 greased 15cm sandwich tins. Place again in the polythene bag and leave to rise for 30–45 minutes. Sprinkle with warm water, and bake in a fairly hot oven, 190°C, Gas 5, for about 40 minutes until the loaves sound hollow when tapped on the bottom.

Brioches

Makes 22 brioches

400g strong white flour
1 × 5ml spoon salt
1 × 10ml spoon sugar
50g butter
25g fresh yeast **or** 1 × 15ml spoon
   dried yeast

4 × 10ml spoons warm water
2 eggs
flour for kneading
fat for greasing
beaten egg for glazing

Sift the flour, salt, and sugar into a large bowl. Rub in the butter. Blend the fresh yeast into the warm water or reconstitute the dried yeast. Beat the eggs into the yeast liquid and stir into the flour to form a soft dough. Turn on to a floured surface and knead for about 5 minutes or until the dough is smooth and no longer sticky. Place in a large, lightly oiled polythene bag and leave in a warm place for about 45 minutes or until doubled in size. Grease twenty-two 7cm brioche or deep bun tins. Knead the dough again until firm and cut into 22 equal pieces. Cut off one-quarter of each piece used. Form the larger piece into a ball and place in a tin. Firmly press a hole in the centre and place the remaining quarter as a knob in the centre. Place the tins on a baking sheet and cover with the polythene bag. Leave in a warm place for about 30 minutes or until the dough is light and puffy. Brush with beaten egg and bake in a very hot oven, 230°C, Gas 8, for 15–20 minutes until golden-brown.

Bara Brith

Makes 12 slices

250ml milk
1 × 5ml spoon sugar
25g fresh yeast
75g lard **or** butter
450g strong plain flour
50g cut mixed peel
150g seedless raisins
50g currants

75g soft brown sugar
1 × 5ml spoon mixed spice
a pinch of salt
1 egg
flour for dusting
oil for greasing
honey for glazing

Warm the milk to tepid with the sugar. Blend the fresh yeast into the milk, and put to one side for 10–20 minutes until frothy. Rub the lard or butter into the flour. Stir in the peel, raisins, currants, brown sugar, mixed spice, and salt. Beat the egg until liquid. Make a well in the centre of the dry ingredients and add the yeast mixture and the beaten egg. Mix to a soft dough, place in a large, lightly oiled polythene bag, and leave in a warm place for about 2 hours until the dough has doubled in size.

Turn the dough out on to a floured board and knead well. Put it into a greased 19 × 13 × 8cm loaf tin, pressing it well into the corners. Return to the polythene bag, and leave to rise for a further 30 minutes. Remove from the bag and bake in a fairly hot oven, 200°C, Gas 6, for 15 minutes. Reduce the heat to warm, 160°C, Gas 3, and bake for about 1¼ hours. Turn out on to a wire rack, and brush the top with clear warm honey while still warm. Serve sliced, spread with butter.

Croissants
Makes 12

400g strong white flour
1 × 5ml spoon salt
100g lard
25g fresh yeast **or** 1 × 15ml spoon
  dried yeast
200ml warm water

1 egg
flour
75g unsalted butter
beaten egg for glazing
fat for greasing

Sift the flour and salt into a large bowl. Rub in 25g of the lard. Blend the fresh yeast into the warm water or reconstitute the dried yeast. Beat the egg until liquid. Stir the egg and yeast liquid into the flour and mix to a soft dough. Turn on to a lightly floured surface and knead for about 8 minutes or until the dough is smooth and no longer sticky. Place the dough in a large, lightly oiled polythene bag and leave at room temperature for 15 minutes.

Meanwhile, beat together the rest of the lard and the butter until well mixed; then chill. On a lightly floured surface, roll the dough carefully into an oblong 50 × 20cm. Divide the chilled fat into three. Use one-third to dot over the top two-thirds of the dough, leaving a small border clear. Fold the dough into three by bringing up the plain part of it first, then bringing the top, fat-covered third down over it. Seal the edges together by pressing with the rolling-pin. Give the dough a quarter turn and repeat the rolling and folding twice, using the other 2 portions of fat. Place the dough in the polythene bag and leave in a cool place for 15 minutes.

Repeat the rolling and folding 3 more times. Rest the dough in the polythene bag in a cool place for 15 minutes. Roll it into an oblong 24 × 36cm and then cut it into six 12cm squares. Cut each square into triangles. Brush the surface of the dough with beaten egg and roll each triangle loosely, towards the point, finishing with the tip underneath. Curve into a crescent shape. Place on a greased baking sheet and brush with beaten egg. Place the sheet in the polythene bag again and leave in a warm place for about 30 minutes or until the dough is light and puffy. Bake in a hot oven, 220°C, Gas 7, for 15–20 minutes until golden-brown and crisp.

Grant Loaf (unkneaded bread)
Makes three 400g loaves

800g wholemeal flour
1 × 10ml spoon sugar
1 × 15ml spoon salt
25g fresh yeast **or** 1 × 15ml spoon
  dried yeast

700ml warm water
fat for greasing

Mix together the flour, sugar, and salt in a large bowl. Blend the fresh yeast into the warm water or reconstitute the dried yeast. Pour the yeast liquid into the flour and stir until the flour is evenly wetted. The resulting dough should be wet and slippery. Spoon it into 3 greased 20 × 10 × 6cm loaf tins. Place the tins in a large, lighty oiled polythene bag and leave in a warm place until the dough has risen by a third. Bake in a fairly hot oven, 190°C, Gas 5, for 50–60 minutes until the loaves are golden-brown and crisp and sound hollow when tapped on the bottom.

Bath Buns
Makes 12

400g strong white flour
1 × 5ml spoon sugar
125ml milk
75ml warm water
25g fresh yeast **or** 1 × 15ml spoon
    dried yeast
1 × 5ml spoon salt
50g butter

50g caster sugar
150g sultanas
50g chopped mixed peel
2 eggs
fat for greasing
beaten egg for glazing
50g sugar nibs **or** lump sugar, coarsely
    crushed

Sift about 75g of the flour and the 5ml spoon sugar into a large bowl. Warm the milk until hand-hot. Add the water to the milk and blend in the fresh yeast or sprinkle on the dried yeast. Pour the yeast liquid into the flour and sugar and beat well. Leave the bowl in a warm place for 20 minutes. Sift the rest of the flour and the salt into a bowl. Rub in the butter. Add the caster sugar and dried fruit. Beat the eggs into the frothy yeast mixture and add the flour, fat, and fruit mixture. Mix to a very soft dough. Beat with a wooden spoon for 3 minutes. Cover the bowl with a large, lightly oiled poly-thene bag and leave in a warm place for about 45 minutes or until the dough has almost doubled in size. Beat the dough again for 1 minute. Place 15ml spoonfuls of the mixture on a greased baking sheet leaving plenty of space between them. Place the sheet in the polythene bag and leave in a warm place for about 20 minutes or until the buns have almost doubled in size. Brush the surface of each with beaten egg and sprinkle with the sugar nibs or lump sugar. Bake in a hot oven, 220°C, Gas 7, until golden-brown.

Cooking time 15–20 minutes
VARIATIONS

Hot Cross Buns
Make as for Bath Buns but substitute 100g currants for the sultanas and use only 1 egg. Add 3 × 2.5ml spoons mixed spice, 1 × 2.5ml spoon ground cinnamon, and 1 × 2.5ml spoon grated nutmeg to the flour. After mixing to a soft dough, knead for about 5 minutes on a lightly floured surface until the dough is smooth and no longer sticky. Place in a large, lightly oiled polythene bag and leave to rise for about 1 hour until the dough has almost doubled in size. Knead again until firm. Cut into 12 equal pieces and shape each into a round bun. Place on a floured baking sheet. With a sharp knife, slash a cross on the top of each bun, or make crosses with pastry trim-mings or a fairly stiff flour and water paste. Cover with polythene and leave for about 35 minutes until the dough has doubled in size. Bake as for Bath Buns.

Glaze the hot buns by boiling together 2 × 15ml spoons milk, 2 × 15ml spoons water, and 40g caster sugar for 6 minutes and brushing the surface of each with the glaze.

Bun Loaf
Makes one 800g loaf
Make as for Hot Cross Buns but bake the mixture in a greased 23 × 13 × 7cm loaf tin. Increase the cooking time to 30–40 minutes.

Chelsea Buns
Makes 16

400g strong white flour
1 × 5ml spoon sugar
200ml milk
25g fresh yeast **or** 1 × 15ml spoon
  dried yeast
1 × 5ml spoon salt
50g butter
1 egg

flour
1 × 15ml spoon butter
150g currants
50g chopped mixed peel
100g soft brown sugar
fat for greasing
honey for glazing

Sift about 75g of the flour and the 5ml spoon of sugar into a large bowl. Warm the milk until hand-hot and blend in the fresh yeast or sprinkle on the dried yeast. Pour the yeast liquid into the flour and sugar and beat well. Leave the bowl in a warm place for 20 minutes. Sift the remaining flour and the salt into a bowl. Rub in the 50g butter. Beat the egg into the frothy yeast mixture and add the flour and fat. Mix to a soft dough. Turn on to a lightly floured surface and knead for about 6 minutes or until smooth and no longer sticky. Place the dough in a large, lightly oiled polythene bag and leave in a warm place for about 1 hour or until the dough has doubled in size. On a floured surface, roll the dough into a 50cm square. Melt the 15ml spoon of butter and brush it all over the surface of the dough. Sprinkle with the dried fruit and sugar. Roll up the dough like a Swiss roll. Cut the roll into 16 equal pieces. Place the buns, about 3cm apart, on a greased baking sheet with the cut side uppermost. Place the baking sheet in the polythene bag and leave in a warm place for about 30 minutes or until the buns have joined together and are light and puffy. Bake in a hot oven, 220°C, Gas 7, for 20–25 minutes until golden-brown. While still hot, brush the buns with honey.

Cornish Splits
Makes 14

400g strong white flour
50g sugar
125ml milk
125ml water
15g fresh yeast **or** 1 × 10ml spoon
  dried yeast

1 × 5ml spoon salt
50g butter
flour for kneading
fat for greasing

Sift about 75g of the flour and 1 × 5ml spoon of the sugar into a large bowl. Warm the milk and water until hand-hot. Blend the fresh yeast into the liquid or sprinkle on the dried yeast. Pour the yeast liquid into the flour and sugar and beat until well mixed. Leave the bowl in a warm place for 20 minutes. Sift the rest of the flour and sugar and the salt together. Rub in the butter. Stir into the frothy yeast mixture and mix to form a soft dough. Turn on to a lightly floured surface and knead for about 6 minutes or until smooth and no longer sticky. Place the dough in a large, lightly oiled polythene bag and leave in a warm place for about 1 hour or until it has doubled in size. Knead the dough again until firm. Divide it into 50g pieces and form each into a round bun. Place the buns on a greased baking sheet. Place the sheet in the polythene bag and leave in a warm place for about 30 minutes or until the buns have doubled in size. Bake in a hot oven, 220°C, Gas 7, for 15–20 minutes until golden-brown.

Serve cold, split, and spread with cream and jam.

Crumpets
Makes 10–12

200g strong white flour	15g fresh yeast **or** 1 × 10ml spoon
1 × 2.5ml spoon salt	dried yeast
1 × 2.5ml spoon sugar	a pinch of bicarbonate of soda
100ml milk	1 × 15ml spoon warm water
125ml water	fat for frying

Sift together the flour, salt, and sugar into a large bowl. Warm the milk and water until hand-hot. Blend the fresh yeast into the liquid or reconstitute the dried yeast. Add the yeast liquid to the flour and beat to a smooth batter. Cover with a large, lightly oiled polythene bag and leave in a warm place for about 45 minutes or until the dough has doubled in size. Dissolve the bicarbonate of soda in the 15ml spoon warm water and beat into the batter mixture. Cover and leave to rise again for 20 minutes. Grease a griddle or thick frying pan and heat until a bread cube browns in $\frac{1}{4}$ minute. Grease metal rings, poaching rings or large plain biscuit cutters, about 8cm in diameter. Place the rings on the hot griddle. Pour about 1 × 15ml spoonful of batter into each ring so that the batter is about 3mm deep. Cook until the top is set and the bubbles have burst. Remove the ring and turn the crumpet over. Cook the other side for 2–3 minutes only until firm but barely coloured. Crumpets should be pale on top. Repeat until all the batter has been used up.

Serve toasted, hot, with butter.

VARIATIONS
Welsh Crumpets
These are cooked without rings on a buttered griddle or frying pan. Pour 3–4 × 15ml spoonfuls batter on to the hot surface, and cook the first side until small holes appear on the surface; turn and cook the second side until just golden.

Serve with bacon and chipolata sausages or butter and brown sugar or honey. These griddle cakes are more like small pancakes or thin pikelets.

Pikelets
Pikelets are cooked without rings like Welsh Crumpets. Some experts use double the amount of yeast and slightly more water (about 50ml) than in the basic crumpet batter, but no bicarbonate of soda.

Most pikelets are thinner than crumpets, cook more quickly, and are more like small pancakes. However, in some areas, they can be as thick as muffins. In Yorkshire, Lancashire, and parts of Derbyshire, pikelet is another name for crumpet.

Ring Doughnuts (1)
Makes 12

200g strong white flour
1 × 2.5ml spoon salt
150g caster sugar
2 eggs
50g butter
15g fresh yeast **or** 1 × 10ml spoon
    dried yeast

2 × 10ml spoons warm water
flour
oil for deep frying
1 × 2.5ml spoon ground cinnamon
    (optional)

Sift the flour, salt, and 50g of the sugar into a large bowl. Beat the eggs until liquid. Melt the butter and leave to cool slightly. Blend the fresh yeast into the warm water or reconstitute the dried yeast. Stir the eggs, butter and yeast liquid into the flour and mix to a soft dough. Turn on to a lightly floured surface and knead for about 5 minutes or until the dough is smooth and no longer sticky. Place the dough in a large, lightly oiled polythene bag and leave in a warm place for about 1 hour or until the dough has almost doubled in size. On a floured surface, roll out the dough to 1cm thickness. Cut into rings, using a 7cm plain cutter for the outside and a 4cm one for the inside. Place on a floured tray and cover with the polythene bag. Leave in a warm place for about 15 minutes or until the dough is light and puffy. Deep fry in hot oil (p11) until crisp and golden-brown, turning frequently. Drain on soft kitchen paper. Toss in the rest of the sugar or in the sugar and cinnamon mixed.

VARIATION

Jam Doughnuts
Cut the rolled-out dough into circles using a 7cm plain cutter. Place a little stiff jam in the centre of each circle and pinch up the edge of the dough to form a ball. Leave to rise, and fry as above.

Muffins
Makes 20

400g strong white flour
1 × 5ml spoon salt
25g butter **or** margarine
225ml milk
15g fresh yeast **or** 1 × 10ml spoon
    dried yeast

1 egg
flour
fat for frying

Sift together the flour and salt into a large bowl. Rub in the fat. Warm the milk until hand-hot. Blend the fresh yeast into the milk or reconstitute the dried yeast. Beat the egg into the yeast liquid. Stir the liquid into the flour to make a very soft dough. Beat the dough with your hand or a wooden spoon for about 5 minutes or until smooth and shiny. Put the bowl in a large, lightly oiled polythene bag and leave in a warm place for 1–2 hours, or until the dough has almost doubled in size. Beat again lightly. Roll out on a well floured surface to 1cm thickness. Using a plain 8cm cutter, cut the dough into rounds. Place the rounds on a floured tray, cover with polythene, and leave to rise at room temperature for about 45 minutes or until puffy. Lightly grease a griddle or heavy frying pan and heat until a bread cube browns in $\frac{1}{4}$ minute. Cook the muffins on both sides for about 8 minutes until golden-brown.

To serve, split open each muffin around the edges almost to the centre. Toast slowly on both outer sides so that the heat penetrates to the centre of the muffin. Pull apart, butter thickly, put together again, and serve hot.

Sally Lunn
Makes two 15cm Sally Lunns

400g strong white flour	15g fresh yeast **or** 1 × 10ml spoon
1 × 5ml spoon salt	dried yeast
1 × 5ml spoon sugar	1 egg
50g butter	fat for greasing
150ml milk	

Glaze

1 × 15ml spoon water	1 × 15ml spoon caster sugar

Sift together the flour, salt, and sugar into a large bowl. Rub in the butter. Warm the milk until hand-hot. Blend the fresh yeast into the milk or reconstitute the dried yeast. Beat the egg into the yeast liquid and stir into the flour mixture to form a very soft dough. Beat well. Pour the mixture into 2 greased 15cm round cake tins. Place the tins in a large, lightly oiled polythene bag and leave in a warm place for about $1\frac{1}{4}$ hours or until the dough has doubled in size. Bake in a hot oven, 220°C, Gas 7, for 20–25 minutes until golden-brown.

To make the glaze, boil together the water and sugar until syrupy. Brush the hot glaze over the top of the Sally Lunns.

To serve, split each Sally Lunn crossways into 3 rounds and toast each piece lightly on both sides. Butter thickly or fill with clotted cream, re-form the cake, and cut into slices or wedges.

Quick Breads

Basic Quick Bread
Makes 2 bun loaves

400g self-raising flour **or** a mixture
  of white and brown self-raising
  flours **or** 400g plain flour and
  2 × 10ml spoons baking powder
1 × 5ml spoon salt

50g margarine **or** lard
250ml milk **or** water **or** a mixture as
  preferred
flour for kneading
fat for greasing

Sift the flour, baking powder (if used), and salt into a large bowl. Rub in the fat. Mix in enough liquid to make a soft dough. Turn on to a floured surface, and knead lightly for 1 minute. Shape the dough into 2 rounds and place them on a greased baking sheet. Make a cross in the top of each with the back of a knife. Bake in a fairly hot oven, 200°C, Gas 6, for 30–40 minutes. Cool on a wire rack.

VARIATIONS

Wholemeal Quick Bread
Substitute 400g wholemeal flour for the plain flour in the basic recipe. Note that wholemeal flour will give a closer-textured loaf.

Nut Bread
Make Wholemeal Quick Bread; add 75g chopped nuts and 50g sugar to the dry ingredients, and add 1 beaten egg to the liquid.

Apricot and Walnut Loaf
Make the basic Quick Bread Mixture but use butter as the fat. Add 100g dried and soaked chopped apricots and 50g chopped walnuts to the dry ingredients, and add 1 beaten egg to the liquid.

Basic Soured Milk Quick Bread
Makes 2 loaves

400g plain flour
1 × 5ml spoon salt
1 × 10ml spoon bicarbonate of soda
1 × 10ml spoon cream of tartar

250ml soured milk **or** buttermilk
  (approx)
fat for greasing

Sift the flour, salt, bicarbonate of soda, and cream of tartar into a large bowl. Mix to a light spongy dough with the milk. Divide the dough into 2 equal pieces and form each into a round cake. Slash a cross on the top of each loaf with a sharp knife. Place on a greased baking sheet and bake in a hot oven, 220°C, Gas 7, for about 30 minutes until golden-brown. Cool on a wire rack.

Note The keeping quality of this bread is improved by rubbing 50g lard into the sifted flour.

Almond Bread
Makes 12 slices (approx)

75g almonds	6 × 15ml spoons oil
250g plain flour	a few drops almond **or** vanilla essence
2 × 10ml spoons baking powder	flour
a pinch of salt	fat for greasing
2 eggs	50g caster sugar
100g granulated sugar	

Blanch and skin the almonds and chop them coarsely. Sift the flour, baking powder, and salt. Beat the eggs and granulated sugar lightly together in a large bowl. Add the oil, flavouring, flour, and almonds, and mix to form a dough. With floured hands, form into a long roll about 8cm wide. Place on a greased and floured baking sheet and bake in a moderate oven, 180°C, Gas 4, for about 30–40 minutes or until lightly browned. Leave until nearly cold, then cut slantways into slices about 1cm thick. Sprinkle lightly with caster sugar and return to a cool oven, 150°C, Gas 2, for about 50–60 minutes, until dry and lightly browned.

American Coffee Bread
Makes 12 slices (approx)

200g plain flour	1 egg
100g light soft brown sugar	200ml milk
2 × 5ml spoons baking powder	75g chopped walnuts
1 × 5ml spoon salt	fat for greasing
2 × 15ml spoons butter	

Sift together the dry ingredients into a large bowl. Melt the butter, add it to the flour mixture with the egg, milk and walnuts, and beat thoroughly. Spread the mixture in a greased 23 × 13 × 7cm loaf tin, level the top, and bake for about 1 hour in a moderate oven, 180°C, Gas 4. Cool on a wire rack.

VARIATION
Banana Nut Coffee Bread
Reduce the milk to 100ml; add 3 ripe medium-sized bananas, well mashed.

Fatless Fruit Loaf
Makes 12 slices (approx)

300g mixed dried fruit	1 egg
150g dark Barbados sugar	300g self-raising flour
200ml strong hot tea	fat for greasing

Put the fruit and sugar in a large bowl. Pour the hot tea over them, cover, and leave overnight.

Next day, beat the egg until liquid and stir it into the tea mixture. Stir in the flour and mix well. Put the mixture into a lined and greased 19 × 13 × 8cm loaf tin and cook in a moderate oven, 180°C, Gas 4, for 1½ hours. Cool on a wire rack. When cold, wrap in foil and store in a tin.

Date and Walnut Loaf
Makes 20 slices (approx)

275g plain flour
50g cornflour
150g caster sugar
1 × 5ml spoon salt
50g walnuts
225g cooking dates

2 × 15ml spoons oil
1 large egg
2 × 5ml spoons bicarbonate of soda
250ml boiling water
fat for greasing

Sift the flour, cornflour, sugar, and salt into a bowl. Chop the walnuts and dates and add to the dry ingredients. Whisk together the oil and egg and add to the flour, fruit, and nuts. Dissolve the bicarbonate of soda in the boiling water, and stir into the other ingredients. Beat well to a soft consistency. Pour into a greased 23 × 13 × 7cm loaf tin and bake in a moderate oven, 180°C, Gas 4, for about 1 hour until firm to the touch. Leave to cool slightly before turning out of the tin.

Date or Raisin Bread
Makes 12 slices (approx)

200g plain flour
1 × 15ml spoon baking powder
1 × 5ml spoon salt
¼ × 2.5ml spoon bicarbonate of soda
100g dates **or** seedless raisins
50g walnuts **or** almonds, whole **or** chopped

25g lard
50g black treacle
50g dark Barbados sugar
150ml milk
fat for greasing

Sift the flour, baking powder, salt, and bicarbonate of soda into a large bowl. Chop the fruit and nuts finely if necessary, and add them to the dry ingredients. Warm the lard, treacle, sugar, and milk together. The sugar should dissolve, but do not overheat it. Add the liquid to the dry ingredients, and mix to a stiff batter. Pour into a lined and greased 19 × 13 × 8cm loaf tin and bake in a moderate oven, 180°C, Gas 4, for 1½ hours. Cool on a wire rack. When cold, wrap in foil, and store for 24 hours before cutting.

Malt Bread
Makes 12 slices (approx)

400g self-raising flour
1 × 10ml spoon bicarbonate of soda
100g sultanas **or** seedless raisins
250ml milk

4 × 15ml spoons golden syrup
4 × 15ml spoons malt extract
2 eggs
fat for greasing

Sift the flour and bicarbonate of soda into a large bowl. Add the dried fruit. Warm together the milk, syrup, and malt extract, in a saucepan. Beat in the eggs. Stir the mixture into the flour. Put it into a greased 23 × 13 × 7cm loaf tin and bake in a fairly hot oven, 190°C, Gas 5, for 40–50 minutes until a skewer pushed into the bread comes out clean. Cool on a wire rack.

Scones

Important points to remember when making scones:

1) Because the basic mixture has only a small proportion of fat to flour, it should be mixed to a soft, slightly sticky dough and handled quickly and lightly.

2) Scones are baked in a hot, preheated oven to ensure maximum rising; the top should be brown and the texture open.

3) Cool baked scones on a wire rack so that they are crisp outside. Griddle scones and dropped scones are best cooled in a clean tea-towel so that they keep their traditional softness.

4) Raising ingredients
   When plain flour is used, add either baking powder
   or
   bicarbonate of soda and cream of tartar
   or
   bicarbonate of soda, cream of tartar, and soured milk or buttermilk.
   The exact quantities of the raising ingredients required are given in the recipes.

5) Using a griddle
   Grease or flour the griddle lightly, according to the recipe used, and place over heat until a faint blue haze rises or until the griddle feels comfortably warm if the hand is held about 2cm above it. If the griddle is too hot, the scones brown on the outside before being cooked through to the centre.
   Most griddle scones take about 5 minutes to cook on each side.

Plain Scones (1) *Basic recipe using* plain *flour*
Makes 10–12

200g plain flour
½ × 2.5ml spoon salt
50g butter **or** margarine
and *one of the following raising agents:*
1 × 5ml spoon bicarbonate of soda
1 × 10ml spoon cream of tartar
125ml fresh milk
or
4 × 5ml spoons baking powder
125ml fresh milk

or
1 × 5ml spoon bicarbonate of soda
1 × 5ml spoon cream of tartar
125ml soured milk **or** buttermilk
and
flour for rolling out
fat for greasing
milk **or** beaten egg for glazing
   (optional)

Heat the oven to hot, 220°C, Gas 7. Sift together the flour and salt into a large bowl. Rub in the fat. Sift in the dry raising agents and mix well. Add the milk and mix lightly to form a soft spongy dough. Knead very lightly until smooth. Roll out on a floured surface to 1.5–2cm thickness and cut into rounds, using a 5cm cutter. Re-roll the trimmings, and re-cut. Place the scones on a greased baking sheet and brush the tops with milk or beaten egg, if liked. Bake for 7–10 minutes until well risen and golden-brown. Cool on a wire rack.

Note If preferred, the mixture can be divided into 2 equal portions, each half rolled into a round, 1.5–2cm thick, and each round marked into 6 wedges.

VARIATIONS
Cheese Scones
Add 75g grated cheese to the dry ingredients before mixing in the milk. Cut into finger shapes or squares.

Fruit Scones
Add 50g caster sugar and 50g currants, sultanas or other dried fruit to the basic recipe.

Griddle Scones
Add 50g sultanas to the basic dough. Roll out to 5mm–1cm thickness, then cut into 6cm rounds. Cook on a moderately hot, lightly floured griddle or heavy frying pan for 3 minutes or until the scones are golden-brown underneath and the edges are dry. Turn over and cook for about another 2 minutes until golden-brown on both sides. Cool in a linen tea-towel or other similar cloth.

Nut Scones
Add 50g chopped nuts to the basic recipe.

Potato Scones
Use 100g flour and 100g sieved cooked mashed potato. Reduce the milk to 60–65ml.

Syrup or Treacle Scones
Add 2 × 10ml spoons light soft brown sugar, 1 × 2.5ml spoon ground cinnamon or ginger, 1 × 2.5ml spoon mixed spice, and 1 × 15ml spoon warmed golden syrup or black treacle to the basic recipe. Add the syrup or treacle with the milk.

Wheatmeal Scones
Use half wholemeal flour and half plain white flour to make the dough.

Plain Scones (2) *Basic recipe using* self-raising *flour*
Makes 12

200g self-raising flour	flour for kneading
1 × 2.5ml spoon salt	fat for greasing
25–50g butter **or** margarine	milk **or** beaten egg for glazing
125ml milk	(optional)

Heat the oven to hot, 220°C, Gas 7. Sift together the flour and salt into a large bowl. Rub in the fat and mix to a soft dough with the milk, using a round-bladed knife. Knead very lightly on a floured surface until smooth. Roll out to about 1.5cm thickness and cut into rounds, using a 6cm cutter, or divide into 2 equal portions as described for Plain Scones (using plain flour) (p399). Re-roll the trimmings, and re-cut. Place the scones on a lightly greased baking sheet, and brush the tops with milk or beaten egg, if liked. Bake for 10–12 minutes. Cool on a wire rack.

Cream Scones
Makes 12 (approx)

200g plain flour
$\frac{1}{2}$ × 2.5ml spoon salt
1 × 5ml spoon bicarbonate of soda
1 × 10ml spoon cream of tartar
75g butter **or** margarine

65ml milk
4 × 15ml spoons single cream
flour for rolling out
fat for greasing

Heat the oven to hot, 220°C, Gas 7. Sift together the dry ingredients 3 times. Rub in the fat and mix to a soft dough with the milk and cream. Knead lightly and roll out on a floured surface to just over 1cm thick. Cut into rounds, using a 6cm cutter. Re-roll the trimmings, and re-cut. Place the scones on a greased baking sheet and bake for 10–12 minutes.

Serve warm or cold, buttered or filled with thick cream and jam.

Dropped Scones (Scotch Pancakes)
Makes 24 (approx)

200g plain flour
1 × 5ml spoon salt
25g caster sugar
1 × 10ml spoon cream of tartar

1 × 5ml spoon bicarbonate of soda
1 egg
175ml milk
fat for greasing

Sift together the dry ingredients 3 times. Add the egg and milk gradually and mix to a smooth thick batter. Heat a lightly greased griddle or a very thick frying pan. Drop 10ml spoonfuls of the mixture on to the griddle or pan. Tiny bubbles will appear and when these burst, turn the scones over, using a palette knife. Cook the underside until golden-brown; then cool the scones in a clean tea-towel on a rack. The scones will take about 3 minutes to cook on the first side and about 2 minutes after turning.

CAKES AND BISCUITS

Preparing Tins for Baking

The best fats to use for greasing are lard, cooking fat or oil. If butter or margarine is used, it must be clarified (p563) first to remove any salt and water which it may contain.

There are 4 principal ways of preparing the insides of cake and bun tins, and the surface of baking sheets for biscuits.

1) Bun and patty tins, and baking sheets for biscuits should be greased; for some biscuits, sheets should be dusted with flour after greasing.
2) For rubbed-in cakes, grease the tin and line the base with greased greaseproof paper or non-stick vegetable parchment.
3) For creamed mixtures, it is advisable to line both the sides and the base of the tins with greased greaseproof paper or vegetable parchment, particularly when the baking time is more than 1 hour. Cake tins for gingerbread should also be lined and greased.

4) For sponge cakes, brush the tin with fat, then coat it with equal quantities of flour and caster sugar, sifted together.

Note Where preparation differs from the above, this is indicated within the recipe in question.

Cake tins, bun tins, and baking sheets are available with special non-stick finishes which do not usually need greasing. Consult the manufacturer's instructions as to whether you need grease the tin or not.

Round and Square Tins

A square tin holds the same amount of mixture as a round tin about 2cm larger in diameter, eg a recipe calling for an 18cm square tin can equally well be baked in a round 20cm tin, provided the tins are the same depth.

The length of time needed for cooking any cake depends on the depth of the mixture. If a smaller tin than specified is used, increase the baking time, and vice versa for a larger tin.

To line a tin – round or square
1) Measure and cut a single or double piece of paper to fit the base of the tin; ensure that it is not bigger than the base or it will spoil the shape of the cake.
2) Measure and cut a strip, single or double, long enough to line the sides of the tin, allowing for a slight overwrap. Make the strip 5cm deeper than the height of the tin.
3) Make a 2cm fold along the bottom of the strip and snip diagonally at 1cm intervals up to the fold.
   Paper for a square tin need only be snipped at the corners.
4) Grease the tin and place the strip round the sides of the tin with the cut edge lying flat against the base. Fit in the round. Grease the lined tin.

To line a Swiss roll tin
1) Cut a piece of paper large enough to fit both the base and sides of the tin. Do not make it higher than the sides of the tin as this may prevent the heat from browning the top.
2) Place the tin on the paper and make a cut on each corner of the paper from the edge to the corner of the tin.
3) Place the paper in the greased tin, folding the corners to give a neat fit. Grease the lined tin.

Storing Cakes and Biscuits

Wrap very rich cakes and wedding cakes in greaseproof paper and a clean tea-towel. Store in a cool, dry place. Biscuits and other cakes may be stored in a tin but should be used as soon as possible. The prepared dough can be frozen for 2 months (see p585).

Measuring paper to fit the base of the tin

Measuring a strip to fit the sides of the tin

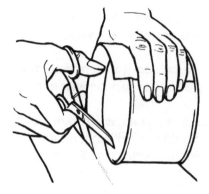

Cutting a strip of paper 5cm deeper than the rim

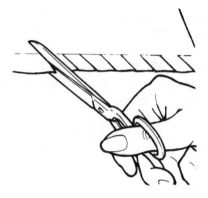

Snipping along the bottom edge of the strip towards the fold

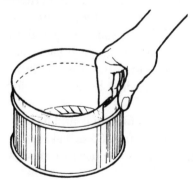

ABOVE *Placing the strip in the tin*
RIGHT *Lining a Swiss roll tin*

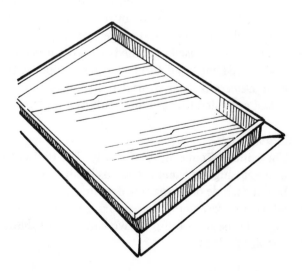

Main Ingredients for Making Cakes and Biscuits

Flour

General purpose household flour gives better results in most cases than strong flour, as used for breadmaking. Most flours are fine enough to make sifting unnecessary, unless it is used as a method of mixing several dry ingredients such as spices, cocoa, and salt with the flour.

Raising Ingredients

Baking powder is the raising agent most often used. Bicarbonate of soda and cream of tartar can be used instead of baking powder in the proportion of 1 part bicarbonate of soda to 2 parts cream of tartar. The most suitable raising agent to use is given in the individual recipes.

Fats

Butter gives the best flavour, particularly to rich fruit cakes and shortbread.

Margarine is excellent for general everyday use and is available in several different textures.

Lard which is 100% fat, contributes little colour or flavour; it is sometimes used with spices, treacle, and syrup for gingerbread but is seldom used otherwise in cake-making.

Dripping, being highly flavoured with meat juices, is not suitable for most cakes, but it is used for a few traditional regional ones. It should be clarified (p98) first.

Other special fats can be used if the manufacturers' instructions are followed.

Sugar

As a general rule, *granulated sugar* is used for rubbed-in and melted mixtures, and *caster sugar* is used for cakes prepared by the creaming method, whisking method, and all-in-one method. Generally, a recipe specifies the most suitable type of sugar to use when it is important for texture or flavour. *Soft dark brown sugar* gives a dark crumb, for instance, to some Christmas and wedding cakes, and to gingerbreads. If in doubt about the type of sugar to use, choose caster rather than granulated for light-coloured and delicately flavoured cakes, and light rather than dark brown sugar for spicy and fruit cakes, and gingerbreads.

Icing sugar is used in some biscuits, but is mainly employed for icings and fillings.

Crushed lump sugar can be used as a topping for some yeast buns. Some cakes may have *Demerara sugar* sprinkled on top before baking; it can also be used to make a baked or grilled topping after baking.

Eggs

These make a cake light and fluffy. The higher the proportion of eggs, the less of any other raising ingredient, such as baking powder, will be needed. Eggs may be added beaten, whole or separated, depending on the type of mixture. Separated egg whites, whisked before being added to a mixture, should be folded in lightly after the other ingredients. A spoonful or two can be stirred into the mixture to lighten it before the rest are folded in.

Dried Fruit

If fruit needs washing, do this well ahead of using it and dry thoroughly. If *glacé cherries* are very sticky or moist, wash and dry them before use, and toss in a little of the weighed flour.

Nuts

Almonds can be bought in their skins or already blanched. Blanched nuts can be bought whole, flaked, split, kibbled (lightly crushed) or as nibs (chopped).

Almonds bought in their skins need blanching for almost all cake recipes. Unless bought ready blanched, use the following procedure: place the almonds in a saucepan with plenty of cold water, bring just to boiling point, drain in a sieve under a running cold tap, pinch off the skins and dry on soft kitchen paper. If the almonds are required split, as for the top of a Dundee cake, do this with a small, sharp knife while the nuts are still warm from blanching.

Browned (or roasted) almonds are often used. They can be browned on a baking tray in a cool oven, or under the grill. If using the oven, almonds should be turned over once or twice during baking. If the grill pan is used, it should be shaken frequently to turn and move the nuts and to prevent dark scorch spots.

Desiccated coconut is used in many cakes, puddings, and biscuits. It can also be used as a decoration on top of jam or icing on a cake. It can be coloured or toasted (see p441).

Hazelnuts need skinning for most cakes. Place the nuts on a baking tray in the oven, and bake until the skins can be removed by rubbing in a cloth or in a paper bag. Rub off the skins. Alternatively, toast gently under the grill, shaking the pan to turn them over. Chop coarsely, or grind in a nut mill, coffee grinder or in an electric blender, or use whole as a decoration.

Peanuts: skin as for hazelnuts.

Pistachios: skin as for hazelnuts.

Walnuts do not need blanching. They can be bought whole or as roughly chopped pieces.

Brazils, pecans, and other nuts such as *unsalted peanuts* can be used for some cakes, buns, and cookies. Treat pecans like walnuts. *Chopped mixed nuts* are also available in packets. They are a useful substitute for chopped hazelnuts or walnuts.

How to Test when a Cake is Cooked

When fully baked a cake should be evenly browned and have come away from the sides of the tin slightly. If the top crust is pressed very lightly with the finger, the mixture should spring back or, in the case of fruit cakes, feel firm. If a fruit cake feels spongy, cover loosely with greaseproof paper and return to the oven for a short time. Re-test before taking the cake out of the oven.

Another way of testing rich cakes is to insert a thin, warmed poultry skewer or thin-bladed knife into the centre of the cake. If it comes out clean the cake is done; if there are crumbs or wet mixture sticking to it, return the cake to the oven for a short time. Re-test before taking the cake out of the oven.

How to Turn a Cake on to a Rack to Cool

If the cake tin has been lined, lift out the paper with the cake in it, place on a cooling rack and peel off the paper. Leave the cake to become quite cold. If the tin is unlined, place it on its side and gently ease out the cake. Turn it on to its base on the cooling rack.

Plain Cake *Basic recipe*

fat for greasing	50–100g margarine **or** other fat
200g self-raising flour **or**	75g sugar
200g plain flour and 1 × 10ml spoon	2 small eggs
baking powder	125ml milk (approx)
½ × 2.5ml spoon salt	

Grease a 15cm cake tin and line the base with greased paper. Mix the flour and salt together, cut the fat into small pieces in the flour, and rub in until the mixture resembles fine breadcrumbs. Add the baking powder, if used, and the sugar. Beat the egg with some of the milk and stir into the mixture. Add a little more milk if necessary, to give a consistency which just drops off the end of a wooden spoon. Put the mixture into the cake tin and smooth the top. Bake in a moderate oven, 180°C, Gas 4, for 1–1½ hours.

VARIATIONS

Cherry, Currant or Sultana Cake

Add 100g fruit, cut up if necessary, with the sugar.

Countess or Spice Cake

Use 100g flour, 100g cornflour, 1 × 2.5ml spoon ground ginger, 1½ × 2.5ml spoons ground nutmeg, and 1½ × 2.5ml spoons ground cinnamon. Add 50g currants and 50g seedless raisins after adding the milk.

Lemon or Orange Cake

Add the grated rind of 1 lemon or orange with the sugar. Replace some of the milk with the juice of the fruit.

Date and Walnut Cake

fat for greasing	75g dates
200g self-raising flour **or**	25g walnuts
200g plain flour and 1 × 10ml spoon	75g soft light brown sugar
baking powder	2 small eggs
a pinch of ground nutmeg	125ml milk (approx)
75g margarine	

Grease a 15cm tin and line the base with greased paper. Mix the flour and nutmeg together, and rub in the fat. Chop the dates and walnuts and add to the flour with the sugar and baking powder, if used. Beat the eggs and milk together and mix into the dry ingredients. Bake in a moderate oven, 180°C, Gas 4, for 1¼–1½ hours.

Dripping Cake

fat for greasing
200g self-raising flour
a pinch of salt
$\frac{1}{2} \times 2.5$ml spoon mixed spice
100g beef dripping (see **Note**)

75g granulated sugar
75g seedless raisins
50g currants
1 egg
100ml milk

Grease a 15cm round cake tin and line the base with greased paper. Mix the flour, salt, and spice together. Rub in the dripping, and add the sugar and dried fruit. Beat the egg with the milk and add to the dry ingredients; stir in, then beat until smooth. Put into the tin and smooth the top level. Bake in a moderate oven, 180°C, Gas 4, for 1 hour 10 minutes. Cover the top with greaseproof paper after 1 hour if the cake is already brown enough.

Note Use clarified dripping (p98) which does not have too strong a flavour. If it has been kept in the refrigerator, allow it to come to room temperature.

Plain Buns *Basic recipe*
Makes 12–14

200g self-raising flour **or**
   200g plain flour and 1×10ml spoon
   baking powder
$\frac{1}{2} \times 2.5$ml spoon salt
75g margarine

75g sugar
1 egg
milk
fat for greasing

Decoration (optional)
glacé icing (p431)

Heat the oven to fairly hot, 200°C, Gas 6. Sift or mix the flour and salt together. Cut the margarine into small pieces in the flour, and rub in until the mixture resembles fine breadcrumbs. Stir in the baking powder, if used, and the sugar. Beat the egg until liquid and add enough milk to make up to 125ml. Add the liquid to the dry ingredients and mix with a fork to a stiff consistency. This produces a sticky mixture which supports the fork. Divide the mixture into 12–14 portions and form into rocky heaps on a well-greased baking sheet, allowing about 2cm space between each. Bake above the centre of the oven for 15–20 minutes until firm to the touch on the underside.

Coat, if liked, with a spoonful of glacé icing when cool.

Note When small buns are baked in paper cases or greased patty tins, the consistency should be softer than when the buns are put on a baking sheet. Use 1 egg and 125ml milk, or enough to allow the mixture to drop off the spoon with a slight shake. The number of buns obtained will be 14–16, using the same quantity of flour.

VARIATIONS

Chocolate Buns
Add 50g cocoa to the flour and 1×5ml spoon vanilla essence with the milk.

For further **variations**, see over

Coconut Buns

Add 75g desiccated coconut with the flour and an extra 2 × 5ml spoons milk.

Lemon or Orange Buns

Add the grated rind of 1 lemon or orange with the flour.

Raspberry Buns

Form the mixture into 12–14 balls with lightly floured hands. Make a deep dent in the centre of each ball and drop 1 × 5ml spoon raspberry jam inside each. Close the mixture over the jam. Brush with egg or milk and sprinkle with sugar.

Rock Buns

Add ½ × 2.5ml spoon ground nutmeg to the flour and 75g mixed fruit (currants, peel, etc, according to taste) with the sugar.

Seed Buns

Add 1 × 15ml spoon caraway seeds with the sugar.

Spice Buns

Add an extra 1 × 5ml spoon mixed spice or 1 × 2.5ml spoon ground cinnamon and 1 × 2.5ml spoon ground nutmeg to the flour.

Ring Doughnuts (2)

Makes 12 (approx)

200g plain flour
½ × 2.5ml spoon salt
a pinch of ground cinnamon **or** nutmeg
3 × 2.5ml spoons baking powder
40g butter **or** margarine
3 × 15ml spoons sugar

1 egg
4 × 15ml spoons milk (approx)
flour for rolling out
fat **or** oil for deep frying
caster sugar

Sift the flour, salt, spice, and baking powder into a bowl. Rub in the fat. Stir in the sugar. Beat the egg lightly. Make a well in the centre of the dry ingredients and add the egg. Gradually work it into the dry ingredients, adding enough milk to make a soft dough. Roll out the dough 1cm thick on a floured board. Heat the fat (p11). Cut the dough into rings using a 6cm and a 3cm cutter. Re-roll and re-cut the trimmings. Fry 1 or 2 doughnuts in the hot fat until light brown underneath; turn and cook the second side. Lift the doughnuts out and drain well. Put some caster sugar in a large paper bag and put in the doughnuts while still hot. Toss them gently until coated. Leave on soft kitchen paper dusted with sugar. Continue until all the doughnuts are fried. Bring the fat back to the correct temperature between each batch.

Serve warm or cold the same day.

Gingerbread *Basic recipe*

fat for greasing
200g plain flour
$\frac{1}{2} \times 2.5$ml spoon salt
$2-3 \times 5$ml spoons ground ginger
1×2.5ml spoon bicarbonate of soda
50–100g lard

50g brown sugar
100g golden syrup **or** black treacle (**or** a mixture)
1 egg
milk

Grease a 15cm square tin and line with greased paper. Sift together the flour, salt, ginger, and bicarbonate of soda into a bowl. Warm the fat, sugar, and syrup in a saucepan until the fat has melted. Do not allow the mixture to become hot. Beat the egg until liquid and add enough milk to make up to 125ml. Add the melted mixture to the dry ingredients with the beaten egg and milk. Stir thoroughly; the mixture should run easily off the spoon. Pour into the tin and bake in a warm oven, 160°C, Gas 3, for $1\frac{1}{4}-1\frac{1}{2}$ hours until firm to the touch.

Rich Cake *Basic recipe*

fat for greasing
200g plain flour
$\frac{1}{2} \times 2.5$ml spoon salt
1×2.5ml spoon baking powder

4 eggs
150g butter **or** margarine
150g caster sugar
1×15ml spoon milk

Grease a 15cm round cake tin and line with greased paper. Sift together the flour, salt, and baking powder. Beat the eggs in a basin and stand it in tepid water (or make sure you use eggs at room temperature). Beat the fat until very soft, add the sugar, and cream well together until light and fluffy. Add the eggs gradually, beating well after each addition. If the mixture shows signs of curdling, add a little flour. Fold in the dry ingredients lightly but thoroughly. Add the milk if too stiff. Put into the tin, smooth the top and make a hollow in the centre. Bake in a moderate oven, 180°C, Gas 4, for 30 minutes, reduce the heat to warm, 160°C, Gas 3, and bake for a further 50 minutes or until firm to the touch.

VARIATIONS

Cherry Cake

Add 125g quartered glacé cherries with the flour.

Cornflour Cake

Use 100g cornflour and 100g plain flour.

Fruit Cake

Add 100g dried fruit (currants, seedless raisins, sultanas), 50g chopped glacé cherries, and 50g cut mixed peel. Bake in a 17cm tin.

Ginger Cake

Add 1×5ml spoon ground ginger with the flour and stir in 100g crystallized ginger.

For further **variations**, see over

Ground Rice Cake
Use 150g flour and 50g ground rice.

Lemon or Orange Cake
Add the grated rind of 2 lemons or oranges and use fruit juice instead of milk.

Seed Cake
Add 3 × 5ml spoons caraway seeds with the flour.

Birthday Cake

200g mixed dried fruit
65ml milk or brandy
fat for greasing
100g butter or margarine
100g soft light brown sugar
35g golden syrup
3 eggs
150g plain flour or 125g plain flour
   and 25g cocoa

1 × 2.5ml spoon salt
1 × 5ml spoon baking powder
1 × 5ml spoon mixed spice
50g cut mixed peel or coarse-cut
   marmalade
75g glacé cherries
milk

Coating and Icing (optional)
almond paste (p436)   royal icing (p439)

Soak the dried fruit in the brandy, if used, for 2 hours before making the cake. Grease and line a 16cm round cake tin. Cream the fat, sugar, and syrup together thoroughly. Beat the eggs lightly. Sift together the flour (or flour and cocoa), salt, baking powder, and spice. Mix 25–50g of the flour with the dried fruit and peel, if used. Chop the glacé cherries and marmalade, if used. Mix the eggs and the flour alternately into the creamed mixture, beating well between each addition. Mix in lightly the floured fruit, cherries, and peel or marmalade. Mix in just enough milk to make a soft dropping consistency. Turn the mixture into the cake tin and bake in a moderate oven, 180°C, Gas 4, for 25 minutes, reduce the heat to cool, 150°C, Gas 2, and bake for another 2–2½ hours. Coat with almond paste and decorate with royal icing, if liked.

Christmas Cake

fat for greasing
200g plain flour
$\frac{1}{2}$ × 2.5ml spoon salt
1–2 × 5ml spoons mixed spice
200g butter
200g caster sugar
6 eggs
2–4 × 15ml spoons brandy **or** sherry

100g glacé cherries
50g preserved ginger
50g walnuts
200g currants
200g sultanas
150g seedless raisins
75g cut mixed peel

Coating and Icing
almond paste (p436)   royal icing (p439)

Grease and line a 20cm cake tin with doubled greaseproof paper and tie a strip of brown paper round the outside.

Sift the flour, salt, and spice together. Cream the butter and sugar together until light and fluffy. Gradually beat in the eggs and the brandy or sherry. Cut up the cherries, chop the ginger and walnuts, and stir with the dried fruit, peel and the flour into the creamed mixture. Put into the tin and make a slight hollow in the centre. Bake in a warm oven, 160°C, Gas 3, for 45 minutes, reduce the heat to cool, 150°C, Gas 2, and bake for a further hour. Reduce the heat to very cool, 140°C, Gas 1, and continue cooking for 45 minutes–1 hour until firm to the touch. Cool in the tin. Cover with almond paste and decorate with royal icing.

Devil's Food Cake

fat for greasing
plain flour for dusting
100g butter
350g granulated sugar
1 × 5ml spoon vanilla essence
3 eggs

275ml cold water
250g plain flour
50g cocoa
3 × 2.5ml spoons bicarbonate of soda
1 × 5ml spoon salt

Filling and Decoration
Seafoam Frosting (p434)

Grease and lightly flour three 20cm sandwich tins. Cream the butter with 225g of the sugar until light, then add the vanilla essence. Separate the eggs, and add the yolks, one at a time, to the creamed mixture alternately with the water, beating well after each addition. Beat in the flour, cocoa, soda, and salt. Whisk the egg whites until soft peaks form; add the remaining sugar and continue whisking until stiff peaks form again. Fold the egg whites into the creamed mixture, lightly but thoroughly. Gently pour one-third of it into each sandwich tin. Bake in a moderate oven, 180°C, Gas 4, for 30–35 minutes or until the cakes are firm in the centre, and have shrunk from the sides of the tins. When cold, fill and frost with Seafoam Frosting.

Dundee Cake

fat for greasing
200g plain flour
1 × 2.5ml spoon baking powder
½ × 2.5ml spoon salt
150g butter
150g caster sugar
4 eggs
100g glacé cherries

150g currants
150g sultanas
100g seedless raisins
50g cut mixed peel
50g ground almonds
grated rind of 1 lemon
50g blanched split almonds

Grease and line an 18cm cake tin. Sift together the flour, baking powder, and salt. Cream the butter and sugar together well, and beat in the eggs. Cut the cherries into quarters. Fold the flour, dried fruit, peel, and ground almonds into the creamed mixture. Add the lemon rind and mix well. Put into the tin and make a slight hollow in the centre. Bake in a moderate oven, 180°C, Gas 4, for 20 minutes, when the hollow should have filled in. Arrange the split almonds on top. Return the cake to the oven, bake for a further 40–50 minutes, then reduce the heat to warm, 160°C, Gas 3, and bake for another hour.

Madeira Cake

fat for greasing
150g butter or margarine
150g caster sugar
4 eggs
200g plain flour

2 × 5ml spoons baking powder
a pinch of salt
grated rind of 1 lemon
caster sugar for dredging
2 thin slices candied or glacé citron peel

Grease and line a 15cm cake tin. Cream the fat and sugar together until light and fluffy. Beat the eggs until liquid and add gradually to the creamed mixture, beating well after each addition. Sift the flour, baking powder and salt together, and fold into the creamed mixture. Mix in the lemon rind. Mix well. Turn into the tin. Dredge the top with caster sugar. Bake in a moderate oven, 180°C, Gas 4, for 20 minutes, then lay the slices of peel on top. Bake for a further 45–50 minutes.

Mrs Beeton's Nice Useful Cake

fat for greasing
100g butter **or** margarine
100g caster sugar
300g plain flour
2 × 5ml spoons baking powder

3 eggs
200ml milk
1 × 2.5ml spoon almond essence
50g flaked almonds

Grease and line a 15cm cake tin. Cream the fat and sugar until light and fluffy. Sift together the flour and baking powder. Beat the eggs until liquid with the milk. Add the dry ingredients to the creamed mixture in 3 parts, alternately with the egg and milk. Beat well after each addition. Lightly mix in the almond essence and the flaked almonds. Turn lightly into the tin, and smooth the top level. Bake in a warm oven, 160°C, Gas 3, for $1\frac{1}{4}$–$1\frac{1}{2}$ hours.

Simnel Cake

Dundee Cake mixture (p412)

Decoration
750g almond paste (p436)
   or prepared marzipan
apricot jam
1 egg

white glacé icing (p431) using
   50g icing sugar
Easter decorations

Prepare the Dundee cake recipe. Put half the mixture into the lined 18cm tin. Cut off one-third of the almond paste and roll it into a 17cm round about 1cm thick. Place it on the cake mixture lightly, and put the remaining cake mixture on top. Bake in a moderate oven, 180°C, Gas 4, for 1 hour, reduce the heat to warm, 160°C, Gas 3, and bake for a further $1\frac{1}{2}$ hours. Cool in the tin, then turn on to a wire rack.

Warm, then sieve the apricot jam. When the cake is cold, divide the remaining almond paste into 2 equal portions. Roll one-half into a 17cm round. Brush the top of the cake with the apricot jam and press the almond paste lightly on to it. Trim the edge neatly. Beat the egg until liquid. Make small balls from the remaining paste (11 is the traditional number), and place them round the edge of the cake. Brush the balls with beaten egg and brown under the grill. Pour glacé icing into the centre of the cake and decorate with chickens and Easter eggs.

Three Tier Wedding Cake

If possible, prepare the 3 tiers together, using a very large bowl. Cream the butter and sugar, and mix in the other ingredients by hand. Few ovens are large enough to bake the 3 cakes at the same time; leave the cake(s) awaiting baking in a cool place, overnight if necessary.

Make the cakes at least 2 months before covering and icing them with almond paste and royal icing. For instructions on icing and decorating the cakes, see pp435–39.

If liked, the outside of each un-iced cake can be pricked with a skewer when cooled and sprinkled with a little extra brandy.

To store, wrap the cakes in clean greaseproof paper and a clean tea-towel, and keep in a cool, dry place.

If the top tier of a wedding cake is to be kept for some time (for instance to be used as christening cake), fresh almond paste and royal icing should be applied when it is used.

Small tier

fat for greasing	100g plain flour
125g currants	$\frac{1}{2}$ × 2.5ml spoon salt
100g sultanas	1 × 2.5ml spoon mixed spice
100g seedless raisins	1 × 2.5ml spoon ground nutmeg
50g glacé cherries	1 × 15ml spoon treacle
25g blanched whole almonds	100g butter
25g cut mixed peel	100g soft dark brown sugar
grated rind of 1 small orange	2 large eggs
25ml brandy	25g ground almonds

Grease and line a 15cm round or 13cm square cake tin with doubled greaseproof paper and tie a strip of doubled brown paper round the outside.

Pick over the dried fruit, removing any stalks. Chop the cherries and almonds coarsely. Put in a bowl with the peel, orange rind, and dried fruit, add the brandy, and stir well. Cover and put to one side while preparing the rest of the cake mixture.

Sift the flour, salt, and spices together in a mixing bowl. Put the opened treacle tin in a pan of hot water to make measuring easier. Cream the butter and sugar well together until pale and fluffy. Beat the eggs until liquid and add one-quarter at a time, together with a little flour, to the creamed mixture; beat well after each addition. Beat in the treacle. Add the rest of the flour, the ground almonds, and the fruit in brandy, and stir until evenly mixed. Put the mixture in the tin and make a slight hollow in the centre. Bake in a very cool oven, 140°C, Gas 1, for $2\frac{3}{4}$–3 hours, until firm to the touch. Cover with ungreased greaseproof paper after $1\frac{1}{2}$ hours. Cool in the tin. Leave for 24 hours before turning out.

Middle tier

250g currants	1 × 2.5ml spoon salt
200g sultanas	1 × 5ml spoon mixed spice
200g seedless raisins	1 × 5ml spoon ground nutmeg
100g glacé cherries	2 × 15ml spoons treacle
50g blanched whole almonds	200g butter
50g cut mixed peel	200g soft dark brown sugar
grated rind of 1 large orange	4 large eggs
50ml brandy	50g ground almonds
200g plain flour	

Make as for the small tier. Bake in a prepared 20cm round tin or 18cm square tin, in a very cool oven, 140°C, Gas 1, for 4–4½ hours. Cover the top with ungreased greaseproof paper when the cake is sufficiently brown. Cool as for the small tier.

Large tier

625g currants	1 × 5ml spoon salt
500g sultanas	1 × 10ml spoon mixed spice
500g seedless raisins	1 × 10ml spoon ground nutmeg
250g glacé cherries	75ml treacle
125g blanched whole almonds	500g butter
125g cut mixed peel	500g soft dark brown sugar
grated rind of 2 large oranges	10 large eggs
125ml brandy	125g ground almonds
500g plain flour	

Line a 28cm round or 25cm square cake tin with doubled greaseproof paper. Tie at least 3 bands of brown paper round the outside of the tin. Make the cake as for the small tier. Bake in a very cool oven, 140°C, Gas 1, for about 5½ hours. After 2 hours cover the top with doubled greaseproof paper, and give the tin a quarter turn, gently. Turn again after each 30 minutes to avoid overbrowning. Cool as for the small tier.

Small Rich Cakes (Fairy Cakes) *Basic recipe*
Makes 12–14

100g self-raising flour	100g caster sugar
a pinch of salt	2 eggs
100g butter **or** margarine	fat for greasing

Heat the oven to moderate, 180°C, Gas 4. Mix the flour and salt. Cream the fat and sugar together until light and fluffy. Beat the eggs until liquid, then beat into the mixture gradually. Stir in the flour and salt lightly. Divide the mixture evenly between 12–14 paper cases or greased bun tins, and bake for 15–20 minutes.

VARIATIONS

Cherry Cakes
Add 50g chopped glacé cherries with the flour.

Chocolate Cakes
Add 2 × 15ml spoons cocoa with the flour and add 1 × 15ml spoon milk.

Coconut Cakes
Add 50g desiccated coconut with the flour and 1–2 × 15ml spoons milk with the eggs.

Coffee Cakes
Add 2 × 5ml spoons instant coffee, dissolved in 1 × 5ml spoon water, with the eggs. Add cold.

Queen Cakes
Add 100g currants with the flour.

Apricot Baskets
Makes 12–14

basic Small Rich Cakes mixture

Decoration

1 × 425g can apricot halves	1 × 142ml carton double cream
¼ × 500ml pkt lemon jelly	1 × 5ml spoon caster sugar
1 × 15cm piece angelica	

Make and bake the cakes in bun tins as directed in the basic recipe, then cool.

Meanwhile, drain the apricots and heat 125ml of the syrup to boiling point. Pour it on to the jelly cubes and stir until dissolved. Leave to cool. Soak the angelica in a little hot water until pliable, drain, and pat dry on soft kitchen paper. Cut into strips 5mm wide. Whip the cream and sugar until stiff.

When the cakes are cold and the jelly is just starting to set, place half an apricot on the top of each cake, rounded side uppermost. Coat each apricot with jelly. Using a forcing bag with a small star nozzle, pipe stars of cream around the apricots. Arch the angelica over the cakes to form handles, pushing them into the sides of the cakes.

Butterfly Cakes
Makes 12–14

basic Small Rich Cakes mixture (p416)

Decoration

1 × 5ml spoon caster sugar

½ × 2.5ml spoon vanilla essence

1 × 142ml carton double cream

icing sugar for dusting

Make and bake the cakes in bun tins as directed on p416, then cool.

Meanwhile, add the caster sugar and the vanilla essence to the cream and whip until stiff. Transfer to a forcing bag with a large star nozzle.

When the cakes are cold, cut a round off the top of each and cut these in half. Pipe a star of cream on each cake. Place the two halves of each round upright, cut side down, in the cream to resemble wings. Dust lightly with icing sugar.

Brownies
Makes 9 (approx)

fat for greasing

150g margarine

150g caster sugar

2 eggs

50g plain flour

2 × 15ml spoons cocoa

100g chopped walnuts

Grease and line a shallow 15cm square tin. Cream the fat and sugar until light and fluffy. Beat in the eggs. Sift together the flour and cocoa, and fold in. Chop the walnuts finely, and add half of them to the mixture. Spread evenly in the tin and bake in a moderate oven, 180°C, Gas 4, for 10 minutes; then sprinkle the rest of the walnuts all over the surface. Bake for a further 15 minutes. Cool in the tin. When cold, cut into squares.

Note The texture of Brownies should be the same as that of a fruit cake. When cooked, the top crust should just be firm to the touch, the inside soft or moist.

Victoria Sandwich Cake

fat for greasing

150g butter **or** margarine

150g caster sugar

3 eggs

150g self-raising flour **or** plain flour

  and 1 × 5ml spoon baking powder

a pinch of salt

raspberry **or** other jam for filling

caster sugar for dredging

Grease and line two 18cm sandwich tins. Cream the fat and sugar together until light and fluffy. Beat the eggs until liquid, and add them gradually, beating well after each addition. Sift together the flour, salt, and baking powder, if used. Stir into the mixture, lightly but thoroughly, until evenly mixed. Divide between the tins and bake in a moderate oven, 180°C, Gas 4, for 25–30 minutes. When cold, sandwich together with jam, and sprinkle the top with caster sugar.

For **variations**, see over

VARIATIONS
The cake can be baked in a 20cm tin for 40 minutes, cooled, then split and filled. This gives a softer centred cake. All loose crumbs must be brushed off the cut sides before filling. Too moist a filling will seep into the cake.

Chocolate Sandwich Cake
Use 125g self-raising flour and 25g cocoa, and add a few drops of vanilla essence with the eggs. Fill with chocolate butter icing (p433).

Coffee Sandwich Cake
Add 1 × 15ml spoon instant coffee dissolved in 1 × 10ml spoon water. Fill with coffee butter icing (p433).

Orange or Lemon Sandwich Cake
Add the grated rind of 1 orange or lemon to the creamed fat and sugar. Fill with orange or lemon butter icing (p434).

Small Victoria Sandwich Cake
Make the cake in two 15cm sandwich tins. Use only 100g fat, 100g sugar, 2 eggs, 100g self-raising flour, and a pinch of salt.

Feather-Iced Sandwich Cake

1 × 20cm Victoria Sandwich Cake (p417)

Decoration

white butter icing (p433) using 50g butter	glacé icing (p431) using 150g icing sugar
browned cake crumbs	food colouring

Coat the sides of the cake with the butter icing and roll in the browned crumbs, pressing them into place. Decorate the cake with Feather Icing (p431).

Battenburg Cake

fat for greasing	2 eggs
100g self-raising flour	pink food colouring
a pinch of salt	apricot glaze (p449)
100g butter **or** margarine	200g almond paste (p436)
100g caster sugar	

Decoration (optional)

glacé cherries	angelica

Grease and line a Battenburg tin, 22 × 18cm, which has a metal divider down the centre; or use a 22 × 18cm tin and cut double greaseproof paper to separate the mixture into 2 parts. Mix the flour and salt together. Cream the fat and sugar together until light and fluffy. Add the eggs, one at a time with a little flour, stir in, then beat well. Stir in the remaining flour lightly but thoroughly. Place half the mixture in one half of the tin. Tint the remaining mixture pink, and place it in the other half of the tin. Smooth both mixtures away from the centre towards the outside of the tin. Bake in a fairly hot oven, 190°C, Gas 5, for 25–30 minutes. Leave the cakes in the tin for a few minutes, then transfer them to a wire rack and peel off the paper. Leave to cool completely.

To finish the cake, cut each slab of cake into 3 strips lengthways. Trim off any crisp edges and rounded surfaces so that all 6 strips are neat and the same size. Arrange 3 strips with 1 pink strip in the middle. Brush the touching sides with the glaze and press together lightly. Make up the other layer in the same way, using 2 pink with 1 plain strip in the middle. Brush glaze over the top of 1 layer and place the other on this.

Roll out the almond paste thinly into a rectangle the same length as the strips and wide enough to wrap round them. Brush it with glaze and place the cake in the centre. Wrap the paste round the cake and press the edges together lightly. Turn so that the join is underneath; trim the ends. Mark the top of the paste with the back of a knife to make a criss-cross pattern. Decorate with glacé cherries and angelica, if liked.

Sponge Cake *Basic recipe*

fat for greasing	75g caster sugar
flour for dusting	75g plain flour
caster sugar for dusting	a pinch of salt
3 eggs	a pinch of baking powder

Grease an 18cm round cake tin or two 15cm sandwich tins. Mix small equal quantities of sifted flour and caster sugar and use to dust the sides and base of the tins.

Whisk the eggs and sugar together in a bowl over a pan of hot water, taking care that the base of the bowl does not touch the water. Continue whisking for 10–15 minutes until thick and creamy. Remove the bowl from the pan. Whisk until cold. Sift and fold in the flour, salt, and baking powder, using a metal spoon. Do this lightly, so that the air incorporated during whisking is not lost. Pour the mixture into the prepared tins. Bake in a moderate oven, 180°C, Gas 4, for 40 minutes in an 18cm tin, or for 25 minutes in two 15cm tins. Leave the sponge in the tins for a few minutes, then turn on to a cooling rack and leave until cold.

Note If an electric mixer is used, there is no need to place the bowl over hot water. Whisk at high speed for about 5 minutes until thick. Fold in the flour by hand.

VARIATION

Mrs Beeton's Savoy Cakes or Sponge Fingers

Prepare a baking sheet by greasing and then dredging with caster sugar and flour. Make the sponge mixture and put it in a forcing bag with a 1.5cm plain nozzle. Pipe out about 14 fingers, 8–9cm long. Dredge with caster sugar and bake in a moderate oven, 180°C, Gas 4, for 7–10 minutes.

Note Special sponge finger tins can be used, prepared as above. Fill three-quarters full, dredge with sugar and bake for 10–12 minutes.

Swiss Roll

fat for greasing
3 eggs
75g caster sugar
1 × 2.5ml spoon baking powder

75g plain flour
a pinch of salt
jam **or** butter cream (p441)
caster sugar for dusting

Heat the oven to hot, 220°C, Gas 7. Grease and line a Swiss roll tin 20 × 30cm. Whisk the eggs and sugar together in a bowl over a pan of hot water, taking care that the base does not touch the water. Whisk for 10–15 minutes until thick and creamy. Remove from the pan and whisk until cold. Sift the baking powder with the flour and salt, and fold in lightly. Pour into the prepared tin and bake for 10 minutes. Meanwhile, warm the jam, if used.

When the cake is cooked, turn it on to a large sheet of greaseproof paper dusted with caster sugar. Peel off the lining paper. Trim off any crisp edges. Spread the cake with the warmed jam and roll up tightly. Dredge with caster sugar and place on a cooling rack with the cut edge underneath.

Note If the Swiss roll is to be filled with butter cream, cover with greaseproof paper and roll up tightly with the paper inside. Cool completely. When cold, unroll carefully, spread with the filling, and re-roll. Dust with caster sugar.

VARIATION

Chocolate Swiss Roll

Use the recipe for Swiss roll but substitute 1 × 15ml spoon cocoa for 1 × 15ml spoon of flour. When cooked, roll up with greaseproof paper inside. When cold, prepare chocolate butter icing (p433). Unroll carefully, spread with just over half the butter icing and roll up. Spread the remainder over the top and, if liked, mark with a fork to resemble a log.

For a Yule log, put a robin or sprig of holly on top of the roll.

Genoese Sponge or Pastry (1)

fat for greasing
100g plain flour
1 × 2.5ml spoon salt
75g clarified butter (p563) **or**
    margarine

4 eggs
100g caster sugar

Grease and line a 20 × 30cm Swiss roll tin. Sift together the flour and salt, and put in a warm place. Melt the fat without letting it get hot. Put to one side. Whisk the eggs lightly, add the sugar, and whisk over hot water for 10–15 minutes until thick. Remove from the heat; the fat should be as cool as the egg mixture. Remove from the heat and continue whisking until at blood-heat. Sift half the flour over the eggs, then pour in half the fat in a thin stream. Fold in gently. Repeat, using the remaining flour and fat. Turn gently into the tin, and bake in a moderate oven, 180°C, Gas 4, for 30–40 minutes.

Genoese Sponge or Pastry (2)

Make as for Genoese Sponge (1), using 75g flour, a pinch of salt, 50g clarified butter or margarine, 3 eggs, and 75g caster sugar. Bake in an 18cm square or 15 × 25cm oblong cake tin.

French Cakes or Iced Petits Fours

Makes 18–24

Genoese Sponge (1) **or** (2) baked in
   an oblong tin

Filling
jam, lemon curd **or** butter icing (p433)
   using 50g butter

Icing
glacé icing (p431)   food colouring

Decoration
crystallized violets, silver balls,
   glacé fruits, angelica, chopped nuts,
   etc

Cut the cold sponge through the centre crossways; spread with the chosen filling and sandwich together again. Cut the cake into small rounds, triangles or squares, and place these small cakes on a wire rack over a large dish. Brush off any loose crumbs. Make up the icing to a coating consistency which will flow easily. Tint some of it with different colourings. Using a small spoon, coat the top and sides of the cakes with the icing or, if preferred, pour it over the cakes, making sure that the sides are coated evenly all over. Place the decorations on the tops and leave to set. The cakes can be served in paper cases.

Rubbed-in Biscuits *Basic recipe*

Makes 24–26

200g plain flour
$\frac{1}{4}$ × 2.5ml spoon salt
75–100g butter **or** margarine
50g caster sugar

1 × 5ml spoon baking powder
1 egg yolk
flour for rolling out
fat for greasing

Heat the oven to moderate, 180°C, Gas 4. Mix the flour and salt together. Rub in the fat, stir in the sugar and baking powder. Bind to a stiff paste with the egg yolk. Knead well and roll out just under 1cm thick on a lightly floured surface. Cut into rounds with a 5cm cutter. Re-roll and re-cut any trimmings. Place on a greased baking sheet. Prick the top of each biscuit in 2 or 3 places. Bake for 15–20 minutes or until firm to the touch and pale golden-brown. Leave to stand for a few minutes, then cool on a wire rack.

For **variations**, see over

VARIATIONS
Plain Chocolate Biscuits
Add 50g powdered drinking chocolate and 2 × 5ml spoons instant coffee dissolved in 3 × 2.5ml spoons water.

Plain Cinnamon or Spice Biscuits
Add 1 × 5ml spoon ground cinnamon or mixed spice to the flour. When cold, sandwich 2 biscuits together with jam, and dredge with icing sugar.

Plain Coconut Biscuits
Use 150g flour and 50g desiccated coconut. As soon as the biscuits are cooked, brush with warm jam glaze (p440) and sprinkle with coconut.

Almond Fingers
Makes 14 (approx)

150g plain flour
50g ground almonds
¼ × 2.5ml spoon salt
75–100g butter **or** margarine
50g caster sugar

1 × 5ml spoon baking powder
1 egg yolk
flour for rolling out
fat for greasing

Topping
1 egg white
75g icing sugar

50g nibbed almonds
raspberry jam

Heat the oven to moderate, 180°C, Gas 4. Mix together the flour, ground almonds, and salt. Rub in the fat, stir in the sugar and baking powder. Bind to a stiff paste with the yolk. Knead well and roll into a strip 8cm wide. Prick the surface well. Transfer to a greased baking sheet and pinch the long edges to decorate. Bake for 15 minutes.

Meanwhile, make the topping. Whisk the egg white until it stands up in peaks, and fold in the sugar and almonds. Remove the baked base from the oven and spread with raspberry jam. Spread the topping over the jam, and bake for 7–10 minutes, until the meringue is set and lightly browned. Cut into fingers while still warm.

Catherine Wheel Biscuits
Makes 24 (approx)

150g plain flour
¼ × 2.5ml spoon salt
1 × 5ml spoon baking powder
75g butter
75g caster sugar

a few drops vanilla essence
25ml water
1 × 5ml spoon cocoa
flour for rolling out
fat for greasing

Sift together the flour, salt, and baking powder into a mixing bowl. Rub in the butter, and stir in the sugar. Make the mixture into a pliable paste with the essence and water. Divide the paste into 2 equal portions. Put 1 portion back in the mixing bowl. Sprinkle the cocoa over it and work it in evenly, using a fork.

Roll out the plain paste on a lightly floured surface into a rectangle 18 × 22cm. Put to one side. Roll out the chocolate paste to the same size and place it on top of the plain piece. Roll lightly with the rolling-pin to make them stick together. Roll up both pieces from the long side, like a Swiss roll, keeping the join underneath. Chill until firm.

Heat the oven to moderate, 180°C, Gas 4. Cut the paste into slices 1cm thick. Reshape into neat rounds with the hands and place on a greased baking sheet, spaced well apart. Bake for 15–20 minutes until the plain biscuit mixture is golden-brown.

Coffee Kisses
Makes 12 pairs (approx)

75g butter **or** margarine	1 egg yolk
150g self-raising flour	1 × 5ml spoon liquid coffee essence
50g caster sugar	fat for greasing

Filling

coffee butter icing (p433)	icing sugar for dusting (optional)

Heat the oven to fairly hot, 190°C, Gas 5. Rub the fat into the flour, then stir in the sugar. Mix the egg yolk with the coffee essence and use to bind the dry ingredients together to a stiff paste. Roll the mixture into balls about the size of a walnut and place on a greased baking sheet. Bake for 10 minutes. When cooked, leave to cool on a wire rack.

Use the coffee butter icing to sandwich the biscuits together in pairs. If liked, dust with icing sugar.

Digestive Biscuits
Makes 12 (approx)

75g wholemeal flour	1 × 15ml spoon soft light brown sugar
25g plain white flour	50g butter **or** margarine
25g fine **or** medium oatmeal	2 × 15ml spoons milk
1 × 2.5ml spoon baking powder	flour for rolling out
$\frac{1}{2}$ × 2.5ml spoon salt	fat for greasing

Heat the oven to moderate, 180°C, Gas 4. Mix all the dry ingredients, sifting the sugar if it is lumpy. Rub in the fat and mix to a pliable dough with the milk. Knead lightly on a floured board and roll out just under 5mm thick. Cut into rounds with a 6cm round cutter, place on a greased baking sheet and prick with a fork. Bake for 15 minutes.

Jumbles
Makes 20

50g plain flour
a pinch of salt
50g caster sugar
40g butter **or** margarine

1 × 10ml spoon beaten egg
flour for rolling out
fat for greasing

Heat the oven to warm, 160°C, Gas 3. Mix the flour, salt, and sugar together. Rub in the fat lightly. Stir in the egg and mix to a soft paste. Roll out with the hands on a floured surface to a long sausage shape about 2cm thick. Divide into 20 pieces, and roll each into an 8cm long sausage. Form into an S shape and place well apart on a greased baking sheet. Bake for 12–15 minutes. Allow the jumbles to cool for a few seconds, then slip a palette knife under each and place on a wire rack to finish cooling.

Oatmeal Biscuits
Makes 22–24

100g medium oatmeal
100g self-raising flour
1 × 2.5ml spoon salt
a pinch of sugar
100g butter **or** margarine

2 × 15ml spoons beaten egg
2 × 15ml spoons water
flour for rolling out
fat for greasing

Heat the oven to moderate, 180°C, Gas 4. Mix all the dry ingredients together and rub in the fat. Mix the egg with the water and use this to bind the dry ingredients together into a stiff paste. Roll out on a lightly floured surface to just under 1cm thick. Cut into rounds with a 5–6cm cutter. Prick the surface of the biscuits with a fork and place on a greased baking sheet. Bake for 15–20 minutes.

Shortbread
Makes 8 wedges

100g plain flour
½ × 2.5ml spoon salt
50g rice flour, ground rice **or** semolina

50g caster sugar
100g butter
fat for greasing

Mix all the dry ingredients together. Rub in the butter until the mixture binds together to a paste. Shape into a large round about 1cm thick. Pinch up the edges to decorate. Place on an upturned greased baking sheet, and prick with a fork. Bake in a moderate oven, 180°C, Gas 4, for 40–45 minutes. Cut into 8 wedges while still warm.
VARIATION
Shortbread Biscuits
Roll out the paste on a lightly floured surface to just under 1cm thick. Cut into rounds with a 5–6cm cutter. Prick the surface in several places with a fork. Bake for 15–20 minutes.

Mrs Beeton's Dessert Biscuits
Makes 30–36

100g butter
200g flour
100g caster sugar
3 eggs

1–2 × 2.5ml spoon of any of the
  following flavourings:
  ground ginger, ground cinnamon,
  grated lemon rind **or** a few drops
  lemon essence
fat for greasing

Heat the oven to warm, 160°C, Gas 3. Cream the butter and beat in the flour gradually, incorporating each addition thoroughly. Beat in the sugar, eggs, and flavouring. Place heaped dessertspoonfuls, well apart, on lightly greased baking sheets, flatten slightly, and bake for about 15 minutes. Cool on the baking sheets.

Creamed Biscuits *Basic recipe*
Makes 26–30

200g plain flour
$\frac{1}{2}$ × 2.5ml spoon salt
100–150g butter **or** margarine
100–150g caster sugar

1 egg yolk **or** $\frac{1}{2}$ beaten egg
flour for rolling out
fat for greasing
caster sugar for dredging (optional)

Heat the oven to moderate, 180°C, Gas 4. Mix the flour and salt together. Beat the fat until soft, add the sugar, and cream until light and fluffy. Beat the egg into the creamed mixture. Fold in the flour, using a knife and then the fingers. On a lightly floured surface, knead lightly and roll out to 5mm–1cm thick. Cut into rounds with a 6cm cutter. Re-roll and re-cut any trimmings. Prick the surface of the biscuits in 2 or 3 places with a fork. Place on a well-greased baking sheet. Bake for 15–20 minutes. Leave on the baking sheet for 5 minutes before transferring to a cooling rack. Dredge with caster sugar, if liked.

VARIATIONS

Almond Biscuits
Use 150g plain flour and 50g ground almonds instead of 200g flour. When cold, sandwich the biscuits together in pairs with jam and dredge with icing sugar.

Dover or Easter Biscuits
Mix 1 × 2.5ml spoon ground cinnamon with the flour and salt, and add 50g currants. Brush with beaten egg white, and sprinkle with caster sugar 5 minutes before removing from the oven.

Lemon or Orange Biscuits
Add the grated rind of 1 lemon or 1 orange to the flour.

Shrewsbury Biscuits
Use 200g self-raising flour or 200g plain flour and 1 × 5ml spoon baking powder. Omit the salt and use only 100g fat and 100g sugar. Add 1 × 5ml spoon grated lemon rind to the yolk. Bake in a warm oven, 160°C, Gas 3, for 30–40 minutes.

Bourbon Biscuits
Makes 14–16

50g butter **or** margarine
50g caster sugar
1 × 15ml spoon golden syrup
100g plain flour

15g cocoa
1 × 2.5ml spoon bicarbonate of soda
flour for rolling out
fat for greasing

Filling
75g icing sugar
50g butter **or** margarine
1 × 15ml spoon cocoa

1 × 5ml spoon coffee essence **or**
   1 × 2.5ml spoon instant coffee
dissolved in 1 × 5ml spoon water

Heat the oven to warm, 160°C, Gas 3. Cream the fat and sugar together very thoroughly; beat in the syrup. Sift the flour, cocoa, and soda together, and work into the creamed mixture to make a stiff paste. Knead well, and roll out on a lightly floured surface into an oblong strip about 5mm thick. Cut into two 6cm fingers. Place on a greased baking sheet covered with greased greaseproof paper. Bake for 15–20 minutes. Cut into equal-sized fingers while still warm. Cool on a wire rack.

    Prepare the filling. Sift the icing sugar. Beat the fat until soft, add the sugar, cocoa, and coffee. Beat until smooth. Sandwich the cooled fingers with a layer of filling.

Melting Moments
Makes 16–20

100g margarine **or** 50g margarine and
   50g white cooking fat
75g caster sugar
25ml beaten egg
125g self-raising flour

a pinch of salt
rolled oats for coating
fat for greasing
4–5 glacé cherries

Heat the oven to moderate, 180°C, Gas 4. Cream the fat and sugar until pale and fluffy. Add the egg, a little flour, and the salt, and beat again. Stir in the remaining flour and shape the mixture into 16–20 round balls with the hands. Place the rolled oats on a sheet of greaseproof paper and toss the balls in them to coat them evenly all over. Place on 2 greased baking sheets. Place a small piece of glacé cherry in the centre of each. Bake for about 20 minutes until pale golden-brown. Leave to cool for a few minutes on the trays, then cool on a wire rack.

Piped Almond Rings
Makes 24 (approx)

175g butter
125g caster sugar
1 egg
250g self-raising flour

50g ground almonds
1–2 drops vanilla essence
2 × 5ml spoons milk (approx)
fat for greasing

Cream the butter and sugar together until light and fluffy. Beat the egg until liquid and add it to the creamed mixture, beating thoroughly. Blend in the flour and ground almonds gradually. Add the vanilla essence and enough milk to give a piping consistency. Leave the mixture to stand for about 20 minutes in a cool place.

Heat the oven to fairly hot, 200°C, Gas 6. Put the mixture into a forcing bag with a medium-sized star nozzle, and pipe small rings on to a well-greased baking sheet. Bake for 10 minutes.

Note These biscuits can be served as petits fours.

Princess Cakes
Makes 10 pairs

100g butter **or** margarine
25g caster sugar
a pinch of salt

100g self-raising flour
grated rind of ½ orange
fat for greasing

Filling
orange butter icing (p434) using
    25g butter

Heat the oven to moderate, 180°C, Gas 4. Cream the fat and sugar well together. Work in the salt, flour, and orange rind. Place the mixture in a forcing bag with a large star nozzle, and pipe 9cm lengths on to a greased baking sheet, making 20 biscuits. Bake for 15 minutes. Cool on the sheet.

When cool, sandwich together in pairs with orange butter icing.

Brandy Snaps
Makes 14–18

50g plain flour
1 × 5ml spoon ground ginger
50g margarine
50g soft dark brown sugar

2 × 15ml spoons golden syrup
2 × 5ml spoons grated lemon rind
1 × 5ml spoon lemon juice
fat for greasing

Heat the oven to warm, 160°C, Gas 3. Sift the flour and ginger. Melt the margarine in a small saucepan. Add the sugar and syrup and warm gently but do not allow to become hot. Remove from the heat. Add the sifted ingredients, the lemon rind and juice, and mix well. Put small spoonfuls on to greased baking sheets, spaced well apart to allow the mixture to spread. Do not put more than 6 spoonfuls on a 20 × 25cm baking sheet. Bake for 8–10 minutes.

Remove from the oven and leave to cool for a few moments until the edges begin to firm. Lift with a palette knife and roll loosely round the handle of a greased wooden spoon. Leave to cool before removing the spoon handle. (Several spoon handles will be needed.)

Note If the brandy snaps are to be served at a party or as a dessert, fill at the last moment with fresh whipped cream, confectioners' custard (p442) or a similar filling. Use either a small spoon or a forcing bag with a large star or rose nozzle.

Ginger Snaps
Makes 56 (approx)

200g self-raising flour
a pinch of salt
1 × 5ml spoon ground ginger
100g soft light brown sugar

75g margarine
100g golden syrup
1 egg
fat for greasing

Heat the oven to warm, 160°C, Gas 3. Sift together the flour, salt, ginger, and sugar. Melt the margarine and syrup in a medium-sized saucepan. Beat the egg until liquid. When the fat has melted, add the dry ingredients and egg alternately and beat until smooth and thick. Using 2 teaspoons, place rounds of mixture on to well-greased baking sheets, spaced well apart to allow the mixture to spread. Bake for 15 minutes. Leave on the sheets for a few moments, and finish cooling on a wire rack.

Note The mixture will thicken as it cools. If necessary, wash the sheets for the second and later batches, regrease them and shape the mixture into small balls in the hands. Place on the sheets and bake as before. If the biscuits become too crisp to remove from the sheets easily, put back in the oven for a minute or two.

Flapjacks
Makes 20 (approx)

50g margarine
50g soft light brown sugar
2 × 15ml spoons golden syrup

100g rolled oats
fat for greasing

Melt the margarine, add the sugar and syrup, and warm gently. Do not boil. Remove from the heat and stir in the oats. Press into a greased 28 × 18cm tin. Bake in a warm oven, 160°C, Gas 3, for 25 minutes or until firm. Cut into fingers while still warm and leave in the tin to cool.

Oatcakes
Makes 16 (approx)

50g bacon fat **or** dripping
100g medium oatmeal
1 × 2.5ml spoon salt
$\frac{1}{2}$ × 2.5ml spoon bicarbonate of soda

boiling water
fine oatmeal for rolling out
fat for greasing

Melt the fat and stir in the dry ingredients. Add enough boiling water to make a stiff paste. Knead well. On a surface dusted with fine oatmeal, roll out into a round 5mm thick and cut into wedge-shaped pieces. Place on a greased baking sheet and bake in a warm oven, 160°C, Gas 3, for 20–30 minutes.

Canadian Crispies
Makes 12–14

100g plain block chocolate
50g crisp rice cereal

25g seedless raisins **or** sultanas

Break the chocolate into small pieces and put it in a basin over hot (not boiling) water until it melts and is liquid. Stir in the cereal and the dried fruit. Place in rough heaps in paper cases and leave to cool and set.

Florentines
Makes 20–24 (approx)

oil for greasing
25g glacé cherries
100g cut mixed peel
50g flaked almonds
100g chopped almonds

25g sultanas
100g butter **or** margarine
100g caster sugar
2 × 15ml spoons double cream
100g plain **or** couverture chocolate

Heat the oven to moderate, 180°C, Gas 4. Cover 3–4 baking sheets with oiled grease-proof paper. Cut up the glacé cherries and chop the mixed peel a little more finely if necessary. Mix with the flaked and chopped almonds and the sultanas. Melt the fat in a small saucepan, add the sugar, and boil for 1 minute. Remove from the heat and stir in the fruit and nuts. Whip the cream and fold it in. Place small spoonfuls of the mixture on to the baking sheets, leaving room for spreading. Bake for 8–10 minutes. After the biscuits have been in the oven for about 5 minutes, neaten the edges by drawing them together with a plain biscuit cutter. Leave the biscuits to firm up slightly before removing the paper, then cool completely on a wire rack.

To finish, melt the chocolate in a basin over hot water and use to coat the flat underside of the biscuits. Mark into wavy lines with a fork as the chocolate cools.

Mrs Beeton's Almond Macaroons
Makes 16–20

fat for greasing
2 egg whites
150g caster sugar

100g ground almonds
1 × 10ml spoon ground rice
split almonds **or** halved glacé cherries

Heat the oven to warm, 160°C, Gas 3. Grease a baking sheet and cover with rice paper. Whisk the egg whites until frothy but not stiff enough to form peaks. Stir in the sugar, ground almonds, and ground rice. Beat with a wooden spoon until thick and white. Place small spoonfuls of the mixture 5cm apart on the paper or pipe them on. Place a split almond or halved glacé cherry on each. Bake for 20 minutes or until pale fawn.
VARIATION

Ratafias
Make as above, but only 2cm in diameter. Omit the almond. Ratafias are used in trifles, to decorate desserts, and as petits fours.

Mrs Beeton's Coconut Pyramids
Makes 12

fat for greasing   150g caster sugar
2 egg whites   150g desiccated coconut

Grease a baking sheet and cover with rice paper. Whisk the egg whites until stiff, then fold in the sugar and coconut, using a metal spoon. Divide the mixture into 12 portions and place in heaps on the rice paper. Using a fork, form into pyramid shapes. Bake in a very cool oven, 140°C, Gas 1, for 45 minutes–1 hour until pale brown in colour.

ICINGS, FILLINGS AND DECORATIONS

Glacé Icing

Points for use: The correct consistency is stiff enough to coat the back of a wooden spoon thickly, otherwise it will run off the surface of the cake.

Glacé icing should be used immediately. If left to stand, even for a short while, it should be covered completely with damp greaseproof paper. Any crystallized icing on the surface should be scraped off before use.

Decorations: Decorations must be put on before the icing sets or it will crack. Do not use decorations liable to melt, run or be damaged by damp. Crystallized flower petals, chocolate decorations and some small sweets should not be used.

To Coat a Cake, Gâteau or Pastries with Glacé Icing

Top: If only the top of a cake or gâteau is to be iced, tie a band of doubled greaseproof paper round it which rises about 1 cm higher than the top. This will prevent the icing spilling over the sides.

Top and sides: If the sides as well as the top are to be iced, omit the band, and place the cake, gâteau or pastries on a revolving cake stand (a turntable), on an upturned plate, or on a wire cooling rack with greaseproof paper underneath. Brush any loose crumbs off the surface, using a soft pastry brush.

Pour the icing on to the top of the cake, gâteau or pastries from the centre outwards; spread it lightly if necessary with a hot, wetted palette knife. Tilt the cake or gâteau so that the icing runs down the sides. Spread extra icing over any bare patches.

Decorations: Quickly put on any decorations and leave, undisturbed, to set. Trim off any icing round the base with a sharp knife, and transfer to a serving plate, using a cake slice or fish servers.

A trickling technique called fricking is used mostly for decoration; a coloured coating, eg chocolate, is trickled over a cake on which a white or pale glacé icing coating has been applied to the top and sides and allowed to set. The trickled icing drips over the edges of the cake to contrast with the base coating. Use a thin glacé icing which will spread easily.

Other methods: Very small pieces of Genoese Sponge (or similar cake), when used for petits fours are stuck on skewers and dipped in icing. They should be put immediately on to a wire rack, decorated and left undisturbed to dry.

Glacé icing can also be trickled over pastry desserts such as filled choux. No attempt is made to cover them completely. Éclairs, cream buns, and other dessert pastries are also only partially covered with a single line or cap of icing.

Glacé icing can also be used as a second coat over a base coat of royal icing.

Feather Icing
Enough to coat the top of one 18cm cake
Make up some white glacé icing, using 150g icing sugar. Remove 2 × 15ml spoons and tint it with a few drops of food colouring. Brown is the colour usually chosen as it shows up well.

Coat the top of the cake with the white icing. Place the tinted icing in a piping bag fitted with a fine writing pipe, and pipe parallel lines over the white icing; do this quickly before the coating sets. Then run a cocktail stick or fine skewer lightly across the cake in parallel lines, backwards and forwards at right angles to the piping. Allow to set firmly before cutting.

Feather icing is used on sponge and sandwich cakes, and on some gâteaux.

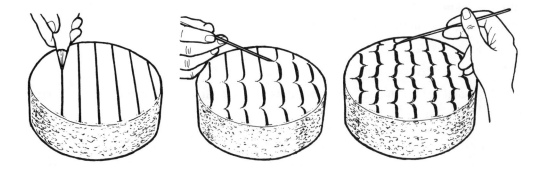

Glacé Icing
Enough to cover the top of one 18cm cake

100g icing sugar
2 × 10ml spoons water (approx)

1 × 2.5ml spoon strained lemon **or**
   orange juice (optional)
colouring (optional)

Sift the icing sugar. Put 1 × 15ml spoon water into a small non-stick or enamel saucepan with the icing sugar. If a mild lemon or orange flavour is required add the juice at this stage. Warm very gently, without making the pan too hot to touch on the underside. Beat well with a wooden spoon. The icing should coat the back of the spoon thickly. If it is too thick, add the extra 5ml water; if too thin add a very little extra sifted icing sugar. Add colouring, if liked. Use at once.

Note Icing sugars vary in the amount of liquid they will absorb.

For **variations**, see over

VARIATIONS
Coffee Glacé Icing
Dissolve 1 × 5ml spoon instant coffee in the water.

Lemon or Orange Glacé Icing
Substitute strained lemon or orange juice for the amount of water used.
Note Other fruit flavours can be achieved by using a small quantity of flavouring essence.

Liqueur-flavoured Glacé Icing
Substitute 1 × 10ml spoon liqueur for 1 × 10ml spoon of the water.

Chocolate Glacé Icing
Enough to coat the top of one 18cm cake

50g plain chocolate   2 × 5ml spoons butter
1 × 15ml spoon water   100g icing sugar

Grate the chocolate into a small, heavy-based pan. Add the water and butter. Warm very gently, stirring thoroughly until the mixture is smooth and creamy. Sift the icing sugar and stir it in a little at a time, adding a little extra water if necessary to make a coating consistency.
Note The icing will thicken as it cools.

Fondant Icing

To use fondant icing: Put the quantity required in a heatproof bowl with a little water or stock syrup (p433) and set the bowl over a pan of hot water. Using a wooden spoon, stir the fondant until it is of a creamy spreading consistency, adding more water or syrup if necessary, and any flavouring. Spread the fondant quickly over a large cake in the same way as royal icing (pp437–39). Let it dry undisturbed on a wire rack. Any fondant which drips off can be scraped up after the cake is dry, moulded into a ball and stored, provided it has no crumbs in it. Fondant icing stores well if kept in an airtight jar, covered with waxed paper and a lid.

Fondant Icing
Enough to cover one 18–20cm cake

450g caster **or** lump sugar   2 × 10ml spoons liquid glucose
150ml water

Put the sugar and water into a heavy-based saucepan which is absolutely free from grease. Heat gently until all the sugar has completely dissolved. Stir very occasionally. Wipe any crystals which form on the sides of the pan with a wet pastry brush. When the sugar has dissolved, add the glucose, and boil to 115°C without stirring. Keep the sides of the pan clean by brushing with the wet brush when necessary. Remove from the heat and allow the bubbles to subside.

Pour the mixture slowly into the middle of a wetted marble slab and allow to cool a little. Work the sides to the middle with a sugar scraper to make a smaller mass. Using a wooden spatula in one hand and the scraper in the other, make a figure-of-eight with the spatula, keeping the mixture together with the scraper. Work until the mass is completely white. Break off small amounts and knead well, then re-knead the small pieces together into one mass. Store in a jar, preferably of stoneware. Cover with waxed paper and a lid.

Stock Syrup (1) (for diluting fondant)

150g granulated sugar   125ml water

Dissolve the sugar in the water in a saucepan. When it has dissolved, boil without stirring for 3 minutes. Remove any scum as it rises, with a spoon. Allow to cool and strain into a jar with a lid. Store for future use if not required immediately.
Note This syrup can also be kneaded into commercially made almond paste to make the paste more pliable.

Butter Icing

Points for use: The icing must be soft in texture so that it spreads easily or it may drag off loose crumbs which will make the icing look speckled. The butter should be at room temperature and must be softened thoroughly before the sugar is added. If the final consistency is too stiff, place the bowl containing the icing over a pan of warm water and beat well.

Storage: Butter icing hardens as it sets. It can be stored in a refrigerator, but must be returned to room temperature and beaten well before it is used on a cake. Cakes filled or covered with butter icing can be frozen (see p586).

Butter Icing
Enough for 2 layers in one 18–20cm cake

250g icing sugar   1 × 15ml spoon liquid, eg milk, water
100g softened butter   **or** fruit juice

Sift the icing sugar and add gradually to the butter with the liquid, beating until the icing is smooth and of a soft spreading consistency.
VARIATIONS
Chocolate Butter Icing (1)
Grate 50g plain block chocolate. Put in a basin over hot water with 1 × 15ml spoon milk, stir until dissolved, then cool. Use instead of the liquid in the plain butter icing.

Chocolate Butter Icing (2)
Dissolve 1 × 15ml spoon cocoa in 1 × 15ml spoon hot water. Cool before use. Use instead of the liquid in the plain butter icing.

Coffee Butter Icing
Dissolve 1 × 5ml spoon instant coffee in 1 × 15ml spoon hot water. Cool before use. Use instead of the liquid in the plain butter icing.

Lemon or Orange Butter Icing
Use 1 × 15ml spoon juice and a little grated rind.

Vanilla Butter Icing
Add 1 × 2.5ml spoon vanilla essence with the milk.

Walnut Butter Icing
Add 25g finely chopped walnuts with the milk.

Frostings and Toppings

American Frosting
Enough to cover one 15–18cm cake

225g granulated sugar
4 × 15ml spoons water
a pinch of cream of tartar

1 × 2.5ml spoon vanilla essence **or**
    a few drops lemon juice (optional)
1 egg white

Have the cake standing ready to be iced, on a turntable, upturned plate, or wire cooling rack with paper spread underneath. Heat the sugar, water, and cream of tartar gently until the sugar dissolves. Add the flavouring if liked. Heat, without boiling, to 120°C, stirring all the time. Remove the syrup from the heat and leave to cool slightly until it stops swirling. Meanwhile, whisk the egg white until stiff. Pour the syrup on to the egg white in a thin stream, beating with a spoon all the time. Continue beating until the icing is of the required consistency. When thick enough, pour it over the cake and swirl with a round-bladed knife.

Seafoam Frosting
Enough to cover the top, sides, and fill one 20cm sandwich cake

2 egg whites
350g soft light brown sugar
$\frac{1}{2}$ × 2.5ml spoon cream of tartar

125ml cold water
a pinch of salt
1 × 5ml spoon vanilla essence

Put all the ingredients, apart from the essence, into the top of a double boiler or heatproof bowl. Beat until blended. Place over boiling water: do not allow the bottom of the top pan or bowl to touch the water. Cook, beating all the time, for about 7 minutes, until the frosting forms soft peaks. Do not overcook. Remove from the boiling water, add the vanilla essence, and beat the frosting for about 2 minutes until of spreading consistency.

Grilled Nut Topping
Enough to cover two 15cm square cakes

50g butter **or** margarine
100g soft light brown sugar

3 × 15ml spoons single cream
100g chopped mixed nuts

Cream the fat and sugar together, then beat in the cream. When fully blended, stir in the nuts. Spread the topping on the cake while still warm or just after cooling. Place under gentle grill heat, and grill for 2–3 minutes until the topping is light gold and bubbling. Remove from the heat at once. Leave to cool completely before cutting the cake.

Note Use on plain and light fruit cakes instead of icing.

VARIATION

100g finely chopped walnuts can be used instead of the mixed nuts.

Almond Paste and Marzipan

To Coat a Cake with Almond Paste or Marzipan

Always level the top of the cake first. If it has risen to a peak in the centre, do not cut it off. Cut out a thin strip of paste and put it round the edge to level the top. Roll it flat.

Brush the cake free of any loose crumbs, then brush it with warm apricot glaze (p440) or warmed apricot jam. Let it cool. If covering only the top of the cake with paste, do not coat the sides unless you want to cover them with crumbs or chopped nuts (p440).

To cover the top of a cake only: On a surface lightly dusted with icing sugar, roll out the almond paste or marzipan into a round or square of the required thickness, and 5mm larger than the top of the cake all round. Invert the cake on to the paste. Hold the cake down with one hand and, using a knife, mould and press the paste into the sides of the cake, to give a neat, sharp edge.

Turn the cake the right way up, and roll the top lightly with a rolling-pin dusted with icing sugar. If not level, make it so by rolling, then invert it again and press the excess paste into place on the sides.

To cover the top and sides of a round cake: Roll out the almond paste or marzipan into a circle of the required thickness, and 3–4cm larger than the top of the cake all around. On a cake of average height, this should give an almond paste coating for the sides about half as thick as on top. (If the cake is more than 8cm high, make the circle a little thicker or larger.)

Invert the cake on to the paste, placing it in the centre of the circle. Using the palms of both hands, mould and press the paste on to the sides of the cake, working it

upward to cover them. Press it on firmly and evenly. Press down on the cake to get a sharp edge between the top and sides. Then roll a straight-sided bottle or jar all round

Smoothing the sides of a cake coated with almond paste or marzipan

the cake to make the paste on the sides an even thickness. Turn the cake the right way up, and check that it is level.

To cover the top and sides of a square cake: Cover the sides first. Divide the paste into 2 parts and put 1 aside for the top. Cut the other part into 4 pieces, and roll each into a strip to fit one side of the cake. Lay them on a surface lightly dusted with icing sugar. Up-end the cake, and press each side in turn on to a strip of paste. Trim the edges of the paste with a knife if necessary.

Cover the top of the cake exactly as when covering the top only.

Leave any cake covered with almond paste or marzipan for at least 72 hours, or if possible, a full week, before icing it, to prevent any risk of almond oil from the paste seeping through the icing and staining it.

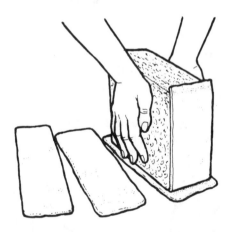

Almond Paste *Basic proportions*

100g ground almonds
100g icing sugar **or** 50g icing sugar
   and 50g caster sugar
1 egg yolk **or** 1 egg white **or** $\frac{1}{2}$ beaten
   standard egg

One of the following flavourings:
1 × 15ml spoon lemon juice **or**
   1 × 2.5ml spoon vanilla essence
or 1 × 2.5ml spoon almond essence
or 1 × 5ml spoon brandy

Work all the ingredients together to make a pliable paste. For a sweeter paste, in-crease the quantities of icing and caster sugar equally to give $1\frac{1}{2}$ times the weight of the almonds in sugar; eg when using 100g ground almonds as above, use 75g icing sugar and 75g caster sugar, giving 150g sugar in all.

Note When making almond paste, handle it as little as possible, as the warmth of the hands draws out the oil from the ground almonds.

Quantities to use

For the top only of an 18cm cake, use the basic proportions of ingredients as above.

For the top only of a 20 or 23cm cake, use 150g ground almonds, 150g sugar, enough egg (white, yolk or whole egg) to bind, and flavouring to taste.

For the top only of a 25cm cake, use 200g ground almonds, 200g sugar, $1\frac{1}{2}$–2 egg whites or yolks or 1 egg, and flavouring to taste.

For the top and sides of an 18cm cake, use 200g ground almonds, 200g sugar, $1\frac{1}{2}$–2 egg whites or yolks or 1 egg, and flavouring to taste.

For the top and sides of a 20 or 23cm cake, use 300g ground almonds, 300g sugar, 2 egg whites or yolks or $1\frac{1}{2}$ eggs, and flavouring to taste.

For the top and sides of a 25cm cake, use 400g ground almonds, 400g sugar, 3–4 egg whites or yolks or 2 eggs, and flavouring to taste.

Use the almond paste for covering cakes before applying icing, and for covering or filling some other cakes such as Simnel cake (p413). If the paste is not to be covered by icing, use egg yolk for binding; it is less brittle, and less likely to flake or crack when dry. The egg whites can be used for making royal icing if they can be stored on the bottom shelf of a refrigerator or a cool place in the larder for 2 days, or in a freezer until the almond paste has dried out.

Marzipan can be used, if preferred.

Marzipan *Basic proportions*

200g icing sugar

1 egg

1 egg white

200g ground almonds

flavourings as for almond paste (p436)

Sift the icing sugar. Whisk the egg, egg white, and sugar in a heatproof basin over hot water until thick and creamy. Add the ground almonds with the flavourings and mix well. Work in more flavourings if necessary. Knead until smooth.

Royal Icing

This classic icing cannot be applied directly to a cake, since it will drag crumbs off the surface. When it is spread on a cake coated with almond paste or marzipan, it should be the consistency of thick cream.

To Ice a Cake with Royal Icing

If an electric mixer is used for beating royal icing, leave the icing to stand for 2–3 hours afterwards, to let any air bubbles escape. Whenever it is left to stand, either during preparation or when fully prepared, cover it with a clean, damp cloth to prevent the surface drying out and forming a crust.

First coat: Put the cake, covered with well-dried almond paste or marzipan, on an upturned plate or on an icing turntable. Take just under half of the icing and put it in the middle of the cake top. Smooth it all over the top quickly with a spatula or palette knife. If necessary, dip the knife into a deep jug of very hot water, shake off surplus water and smooth the surface of the cake with the hot knife.

Smooth the rest of the icing over the sides, lifting a little at a time from the bowl, using a hot wetted knife. Have a fine skewer ready to prick any bubbles gently before the surface sets. See that the top edge is sharp and clean. Do not overwork the icing or it will lose its gloss. Allow the cake to dry, away from dust, for 24 hours.

Second coat: Once the first coating is completely dry, a second, thinner coat of icing can be poured over the cake if the first coat is not perfectly smooth. This second coat should be thick enough to need a little help with a knife to make it flow gently over the top and sides. Extra egg white can be added to make a coating with a very smooth finish. Alternatively, glacé icing (p431) can be used for this second coat.

Snow scene surface: For a 'snow scene', ie a coating with peaks and swirls, flick up the icing with a knife, making small peaks. If desired, sprinkle the icing, when dry, with sifted icing sugar to represent newly fallen snow.

To Decorate a Cake with Piped Royal Icing

The icing which coats the cake must be completely dry and hard before decorations are applied.

Decorative piping: Icing required for star or rose pipes (see diagram below) needs a little extra sifted icing sugar added so that it is slightly stiffer. When pulled up with a spoon, a 1cm point of icing should hold its shape; the stars will flatten if the icing is too thin. For writing pipes, the icing should be only slightly stiffer than icing for coating a cake, and should pull up into soft points. Beat it very thoroughly before use or it may break in the middle of a line or letter.

A design can be pricked out directly on the cake, using a long clean pin, eg a decorator's pin. However, if the design is to be geometrical or if writing is to be used, it is wise to draw the design on a piece of paper first. If this is done to scale, the paper can be placed on top of the cake and the design pricked through the paper on to the cake with a long clean pin.

To make a paper icing bag or cone: Use greaseproof paper or vegetable parchment. Cut a square about 25cm in diameter, and cut it into 2 triangles, following the diagrams below.

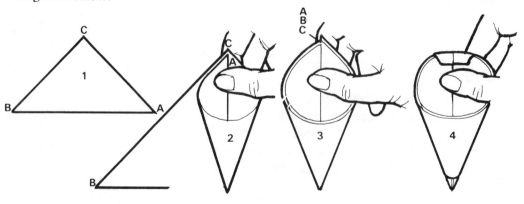

Take 1 triangle and fold A over C as shown. Wrap B round to A and C, and fold in the ends. Cut about 1cm off the point and insert the pipe to be used. Repeat the process, using the other triangle, if a second bag is required.

Greaseproof paper cones can only be used once, but vegetable parchment ones can be wiped and re-used. The same applies to bought nylon icing bags.

Note Metal or plastic syringes can be bought and used for icing.

To fill the bag: After inserting the pipe required, place the bag in a clean jar with the piping tube or nozzle resting on the base of the jar. This will prevent loss of some of the contents while filling. Half fill the bag with icing, using a dessertspoon. Fold over the broad end, and tuck in the sides of the bag. Do not fill the bag more than half full.

For easier filling, the top half of a nylon bag can be folded back before filling; it prevents smears of icing on the part of the bag to be folded over.

Icing pipes to use: Use pipes 1, 2, and 3 (fine, medium, and thick) for straight lines, dots, and writing. These are called writing pipes.

Star or rose pipes may have 5, 6, 8 or more points. They are used for scrolls, shell edgings etc, as well as for rosettes and stars. The size of the decoration will depend on the amount of icing forced through the pipe.

Petal and leaf pipes for flowers and leaves, ribbon pipes for basket work, and many other decorative pipes are also available.

General hints on piping: Practise first on an upturned plate. If the icing is scraped off before it hardens, it can be re-used.

If possible, place the cake to be decorated on a turntable; it makes turning the cake easier and safer. The end of the pipe should be free of icing before starting. Begin close to, but not touching, the surface to be decorated. Exert an even pressure while forcing icing through the pipe, and stop pressing before lifting the pipe.

Start decorating in the centre of a cake and work outwards. When writing, work from left to right.

Allow all piped-on decorations to dry thoroughly before adding other decorations.

Keep some icing aside for attaching decorations. Cover with a damp cloth to prevent a crust forming.

Royal Icing

450g icing sugar	1 × 5ml spoon lemon juice
2 egg whites	1 × 5ml spoon glycerine

Sift the icing sugar. Put the egg whites and lemon juice into a bowl and, using a wooden spoon, beat just enough to liquefy the whites slightly. Add half the sugar, a little at a time, and beat for 10 minutes. Add the rest of the sugar gradually, and beat for another 10 minutes until the icing is white and forms peaks when the spoon is drawn up from the mixture. Add the glycerine while mixing.

Quantities to use
The quantities above will cover the top and sides of a 20cm cake. Use half quantities for the top only.

For a 25cm cake, double the quantities above, to cover the top and sides.

Glazes, Coatings, Fillings and Decorations

Apricot Glaze
Enough to coat the top and sides of one 15–18cm cake

200g apricot jam   2 × 15ml spoons water

Heat the jam and the water gently in a saucepan until smooth. Sieve the mixture and return to the cleaned saucepan. Bring slowly to the boil and heat gently until thick. **Note** The glaze is used to cover a cake before applying marzipan, almond paste, or a coating of ground or chopped nuts or crumbs. It is slightly thinner than jam used on its own, spreads more easily over a cake, and is therefore less likely to drag crumbs off the surface. It can be stored in a refrigerator for at least 2 weeks.

Sweet Coating Glaze for Flans and Tartlets
Enough to cover one 18cm fruit flan or 12–16 tartlets

1 × 5ml spoon arrowroot   1–3 drops food colouring
125ml fruit syrup from canned **or**   lemon juice
   bottled fruit **or** 125ml water and
   15–25g sugar

Blend the arrowroot with a little of the cold fruit syrup or water. Heat the remaining fruit syrup, or water and sugar, to boiling point in a small pan. Pour on to the blended arrowroot, stirring gently. Return to the pan and heat just to boiling point, stirring very gently, to avoid air bubbles (which cloud the glaze). Remove from the heat, add the colouring and lemon juice to taste. Pour or spoon the hot glaze carefully over the flan or tart. Leave to cool and set before serving.

To Apply Coatings over Jam Glaze or Butter Cream
Make sure that any coatings, ie nuts, crumbs or praline are finely crushed or ground, and that the coconut shreds are separated, otherwise they will not stick on the cake. Scatter the coating evenly across a sheet of greaseproof paper. Have ready a fine pastry brush for putting loose crumbs in place.

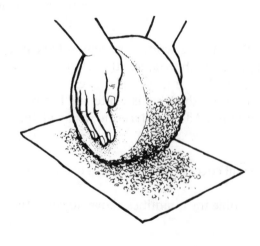

Using jam glaze: Brush any loose crumbs off the cake. Brush the sides with a warm apricot glaze (p440). Hold the cake on end between your palms, and roll the sides in the coating, pressing gently. Transfer the cake to a plate or wire rack and brush off any surplus crumbs. Brush the top with glaze and distribute the coating evenly over the surface. Use the fine brush to put loose crumbs, nuts, etc in place. Lay a piece of greaseproof paper over the top, and press lightly to make the coating stick.

Using butter cream: The butter cream should be soft enough to spread easily, and should be applied thinly. Proceed as when applying coatings to a jam glaze.

Glacé icing or whipped cream top: If the sides of a cake are to be coated with butter cream or jam glaze, and the top with glacé icing or whipped cream, ice and coat the sides first. Allow to set before applying the glacé icing. If using butter cream, mould it into a small ridge round the top of the cake to stop the icing spilling over the edge.

Coconut for Coating or Decoration

To colour: Place the coconut in a small bowl, and add a few drops of food colouring. Stir briskly until evenly coloured. Spread the coconut out on a baking tray, and leave to dry in a very cool oven, 120°C, Gas ½. Shake the pan and turn the coconut over to dry it evenly.

To toast: Spread the coconut on the grill pan under very low heat. Shake the pan and turn the coconut over to brown it evenly.

To Coat a Cake, Gâteau or Dessert with Whipped Cream

Flavour the cream and add food colouring, if liked. Whip the cream until very stiff. For a really firm coating, eg if the completed cake, gâteau or dessert must stand in a warm place for a time before being served, add a very little dissolved and cooled gelatine to the cream when whipping; about half the usual setting quantity is enough. Work quickly.

Place the cake on a turntable, an upturned plate or a wire rack. Smooth the whipped cream on the sides first, with a palette knife; then cover the top.

If liked, the cream can be flicked up with a knife, making a 'snow scene' surface like that used for Christmas cakes.

The cake, gâteau or dessert should be coated or decorated before the cream becomes too firm. Avoid decorations which may be spoiled by damp. If possible, chill the cake, gâteau or dessert until required for use.

Butter Cream
Enough for 2 layers in one 18cm cake

200g icing sugar	100g butter
2 egg whites	flavouring and colouring as required

Sift the icing sugar. Whisk the egg whites until stiff. Add the icing sugar, a third at a time, whisking between each addition until the mixture forms peaks. Cream the butter until fluffy and gradually beat in the meringue mixture. Flavour and colour as required.

For **variations**, see over

VARIATIONS
Chocolate Butter Cream (1)
Grate 50g plain block chocolate into a saucepan. Heat gently until the chocolate melts, then cool. Use to flavour the butter cream.

Chocolate Butter Cream (2)
Dissolve 1×15ml spoon cocoa in 1×15ml spoon hot water, then cool. Use to flavour the butter cream.

Coffee Butter Cream
Dissolve 1×5ml spoon instant coffee in 1×15ml spoon hot water, then cool. Use to flavour the butter cream.

Chantilly Cream
4 helpings

250ml double cream   vanilla essence
25g caster sugar

Chill the cream for several hours. Whip it lightly. Just before serving, whip in the sugar and a few drops of vanilla essence to taste.

Confectioners' Custard
Makes 250ml (approx)

1 egg	25g plain flour
1 egg yolk	250ml milk
50g caster sugar	a few drops vanilla essence

Put the egg, egg yolk, and sugar in a basin and beat with a wooden spoon until light and fluffy. Add the flour and stir in gently. Mix in the milk gradually, keeping the mixture smooth. Transfer to a saucepan, and bring the mixture to the boil, stirring all the time. Add the vanilla essence, pour into a basin, and cover with damp grease-proof paper to prevent a skin forming. Leave to cool.

When cold, use as a filling for cakes, small pastries, and tartlets.

VARIATIONS
Chocolate-flavoured Confectioners' Custard
Dissolve 25g grated chocolate in the milk.

Crème St Honoré
Whisk 4 egg whites until stiff with 1×15ml spoon caster sugar. Fold into the hot confectioners' custard. Use as a filling for choux puffs or as an alternative to whipped cream.

Crème Frangipane
Beat 40g melted butter into the hot confectioners' custard, then add 75g crushed almond macaroons or ground almonds and a few drops of almond essence. Use as a tartlet or pancake filling.

Coconut Filling
Enough to fill 1 layer in one 15–18cm cake

50g icing sugar
1 egg yolk

1 × 15ml spoon lemon juice
25g desiccated coconut

Sift the icing sugar into a heatproof bowl, add the egg yolk and lemon juice and mix to a smooth paste. Place the bowl over a saucepan of hot water over low heat. Cook for 5–7 minutes until thick, stirring all the time. Remove from the heat and stir in the coconut. Leave to cool before using.

Crème Fraîche
Enough to fill 2 layers, or to fill and coat one 20cm sponge cake

250ml double cream

2 × 5ml spoons buttermilk

Pour the cream into a small basin or glass jar. Gently stir in the buttermilk. Cover, and leave it to stand at 25°C for 6–8 hours. Stir, and chill until needed.

This French cream has a slightly sharp taste, and is delicious served with rich desserts or gâteaux.

Mock Cream
Enough to fill 2 layers in one 18cm cake or gâteau

2 × 5ml spoons cornflour
125ml milk
50g softened butter

50g icing **or** caster sugar
$\frac{1}{2}$ × 2.5ml spoon vanilla essence

Blend the cornflour with the milk, bring to the boil in a small saucepan, and cook for 4–5 minutes, stirring all the time, until thick. Cover with damp greaseproof paper, and cool until tepid.

Cream the butter and sugar until it is the same consistency as the cornflour sauce. Add the sauce, a spoonful at a time, beating well after each addition. Beat in the essence and use as required.

Mrs Beeton's Sherry or Liqueur-flavoured Whipped Cream
4 helpings

grated rind and juice of $\frac{1}{2}$ lemon
1–2 × 15ml spoons sweet sherry **or**
  brandy-based liqueur (see **Note**)

2 × 15ml spoons caster sugar
250ml double cream
1 egg white (optional)

Put the lemon rind, juice, sherry or liqueur, and sugar into a bowl. Stir until the sugar is dissolved. Add the cream and whip lightly, gradually increasing speed until the cream is firm but not very stiff. Whisk the egg white, if used, until it holds soft peaks, and fold it gently into the cream.
Note A fruit-flavoured liqueur should be used, eg apricot brandy or Grand Marnier. Alternatively, brandy or a strong sweet white wine give a good flavour.

To attach decorations

Scratch the surface of the cake very lightly with a pin in the spot where the decoration will be placed. Put a tiny blob of icing on the underside of the decoration or on the edge of a greeting card if it is to stand upright, and press it lightly into place.

Suggestions for decorating cakes iced with glacé icing are given on pp430–31. For piping with royal icing, see pp438–39.

Moulded Decorations

Flowers, leaves, fruit, etc can be moulded from small pieces of fondant icing (pp432–33), moulding icing (p445) or marzipan (p437). Marzipan is smoother and easier to use than almond paste. Before adding any moulded decorations to an iced cake or gâteau, let them dry thoroughly.

Knead the icing or marzipan until pliable, working in any flavouring or food colouring desired. Use concentrated confectioners' colours if possible, but do not colour heavily. If very bright decorations are wanted, eg Christmas holly berries, the decorations can be painted with undiluted food colouring when set and dry.

Break off small pieces of the moulding material, roll or pat flat if necessary, and model into the desired shapes.

To make one-piece flowers: Cut out flat circles of the moulding material and pinch up the centres. Make cuts radiating from the pinched-up centres to the outer edges, to make petals. Pinch and shape the end of each petal and place a mimosa or silver ball in the centre of each flower.

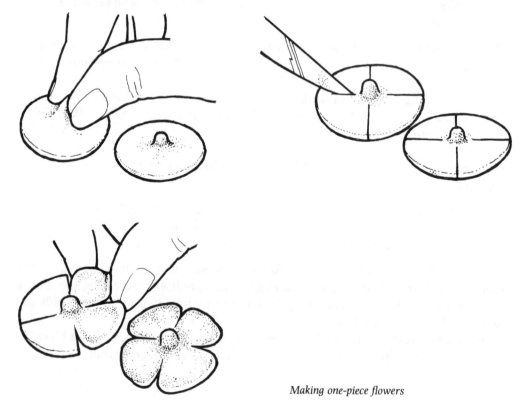

Making one-piece flowers

To make leaves: Cut small ovals or circles using a small pastry cutter. Pinch one side or end to form a stalk. For holly leaves, cut out flat diamonds of moulding material, and scallop the edges with a tiny curved cutter.

Other silhouette shapes: Cut shapes, eg a moon and stars, out of any of the moulding materials. Cut out the shape required in paper, using, for instance, an illustration in a magazine. Lay it on the moulding material and cut round it.

Note For moulded marzipan fruits and vegetables, see pp483–84.

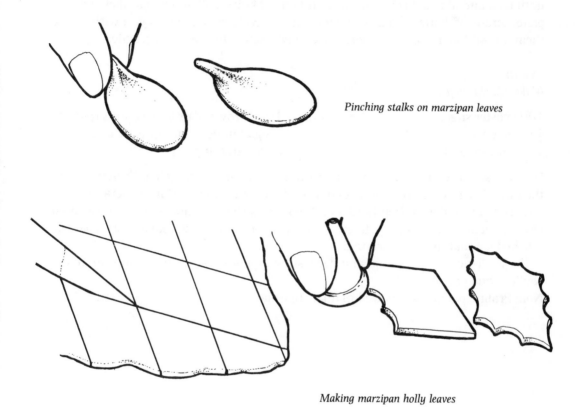

Pinching stalks on marzipan leaves

Making marzipan holly leaves

Moulding Icing for Decorations (made with gelatine)
Makes 225g (approx)

200g icing sugar
1 × 5ml spoon gelatine
1 × 10ml spoon hot water

1 × 5ml spoon glycerine (scant)
3 × 5ml spoons liquid glucose
food colouring

Sift the icing sugar. Dissolve the gelatine in the hot water, add the glycerine and glucose, and work in the icing sugar. Knead well and work in colouring as required.

Keep the mixture warm while working, and break off small pieces to make leaves, flowers, etc. Leave these to set on waxed paper.

Chocolate Curls or Scrolls
Makes enough scrolls to decorate one 20cm cake

200g plain chocolate   1 × 15ml spoon salad oil

Break up the chocolate and put it on a heatproof plate. Place the plate over a pan of simmering water. When the chocolate has melted, work in the salad oil. Remove from the heat and leave to cool slightly, then spread out thinly on the plate. Leave until cold and almost firm. With a round-ended knife held almost parallel with the plate, scrape off bands or curls of chocolate, as wide or narrow as you wish. Place them on soft kitchen paper as you make them, since they are very fragile.

Praline
Makes 200g (approx)

100g caster sugar   100g browned or toasted nuts (p405)
½ vanilla pod   eg almonds, hazelnuts, walnuts
1 × 15ml spoon water   oil for greasing

Heat the sugar, vanilla pod, and water until the sugar is light golden-brown. Stir in the nuts. Turn the mixture immediately on to an oiled marble slab or metal surface, and leave to harden. When hard, crush with a pestle in a mortar, or process in an electric blender. Crush very finely if wanted for flavouring; leave more coarsely crushed for coating or decorating.

   Use for flavouring, coating, and decorating cream desserts, ice creams, mousses, soufflés, and gâteaux.

Note Praline powder keeps well in an airtight jar.

PASTRY MAKING AND PASTRY GOODS

General Hints

1) Work in a cool place, if possible on a stone slab, and keep your hands cool.
2) Always sift the flour and salt after measuring, since this helps to lighten the pastry.
3) When rubbing the fat into the flour, use the finger-tips and lift the hands up from the bowl so that air is trapped as the flour falls back into the bowl.
4) Use cold water and a round-bladed knife for mixing. Flours vary in the amount of water which they absorb, so the quantities given in the recipes can only be approximate. It is important not to use too much water or the pastry will be hard.
5) Lemon juice strengthens the gluten or protein in flour and helps give a lighter and crisper result when making flaky, puff, or rough puff pastry.
6) Handle the pastry as little and as lightly as possible. Work quickly.
7) Chill the pastry, or leave in a cool place for 15–30 minutes after making and before rolling out.
8) Roll the pastry lightly, quickly, and evenly with short strokes, lifting the rolling-pin between each stroke. Do not roll off the edge of the pastry or the air will be pressed out.
9) Always roll away from yourself, never from side to side, and do not turn the pastry over.
10) Use very little flour for rolling out and remove any surplus flour with a pastry brush.
11) Use the rolled side of the pastry for the outside of a pie case, tart shell or crust.
12) Most pastries are baked in a fairly hot oven; the richer the pastry, the hotter the oven required for cooking. A high temperature is necessary to create steam within the dough and to make the pastry light. It also makes the starch grains burst; the starch then absorbs the fat. Unless the heat is high enough to act on the flour in this way, the melted fat runs out and leaves the pastry heavy and tough, and less rich.

Note Hot water crust and choux pastry are exceptions to these rules.

To Keep Pastry
Pastry which must be kept for several hours or overnight before baking should be wrapped closely in greaseproof paper and kept in a refrigerator or cool place.

Using Pastry

Open Tarts

Open tarts are usually baked on ovenproof glass or enamel plates. Sweet tarts can be filled with cooked or uncooked fruit, or with jam, syrup or treacle, mincemeat or a custard mixture. For an 18cm plate, pastry using 125g flour will be needed.

Shape the pastry into a ball or round bun shape. Then roll it out into a circle 2cm bigger than the plate all round, and about 2mm thick. Fold the pastry loosely over the rolling-pin and lift it on to the plate. Smooth it carefully with the fingers so that no air is trapped between the pastry and the plate. Take care not to stretch the pastry as it will shrink back during baking, leaving an uneven edge.

If the pastry shell is baked without a filling, prick the bottom well with a fork all over before baking, or bake blind (see p450).

Flans

A flan may be baked in a flan ring, which is a circular, often fluted, hoop of metal without a base. The ring is placed on a flat baking sheet during baking. After baking, the ring is lifted off the set pastry shell, which is then transferred to a serving plate.

Alternatively, a flan can be baked in an ovenproof ceramic or metal flan case, like a shallow sandwich tin but with fluted sides. In this case the flan is served from the dish.

To line a flan ring 18cm in diameter, pastry using 125g flour will be needed. Place the flan ring on a baking sheet. Roll the pastry into a round at least 5cm larger than the flan ring and 2mm thick. Lift the pastry with a rolling-pin to prevent it stretching, and lay it in the flan ring. Press the pastry gently down on the baking sheet so that no air bubbles are trapped. Working from the centre outward, press down lightly all over the base. Press the pastry right into the angle where the sides meet the base. Then work up the sides, making sure that the pastry fits into the flutes, and is of even thickness all round. Trim off any surplus pastry with a sharp knife, or roll across the top of the ring with the rolling-pin to cut off the pastry cleanly.

Line a ceramic flan case in the same way.

Double Crust Plate Pies or Tarts

Double crust pies or tarts can be made in ovenproof glass, enamel, metal or foil plates with a raised flat rim or border. A 20cm plate will need pastry made with 225g flour.

Divide the pastry into two portions, form each into a round shape, and roll one portion into a round 2cm larger than the plate and about 2mm thick. Fold it over the rolling-pin and lift on to the plate; smooth to fit the plate without stretching the pastry. Trim off any surplus pastry with a sharp knife. Put in a layer of filling, sprinkle with sugar if required, and cover with another layer of filling. Do not add any extra liquid or the pastry will become soggy.

Roll the remaining piece of pastry into a round slightly larger than the plate. Dampen the edge of the pastry lining the plate with cold water. Lift on the cover and ease it into position without stretching the pastry. Press the edges together firmly and knock up with the back of a knife. Make a small hole in the centre to allow steam to escape.

Cabinet Pudding (p.321)

Golden Syrup Pudding (p.333)

Plums with Port (p.341), Eve's Pudding (p.336) and Mrs Beeton's Bachelor's Pudding (p.334)

Jam Sponge Pudding (p.335)

Roly-poly Jam Pudding (p.330)

Deep Pies or Tarts

These can be made with a single top crust or with a double crust. A 750ml pie dish will need pastry made with 150g flour for the top crust. Allow slightly more than double this quantity if the dish is to be lined as well.

Either sweet or savoury fillings, eg stewed fruit, steak and kidney or vegetable, can be used. About 600g filling will be needed for a 750ml pie dish. If the filling is likely to shrink during cooking, or if there is not enough to fill the dish, place a pie funnel or inverted ceramic egg cup in the centre of the dish.

If using fruit, place half of it in the dish, sprinkle with sugar and any flavouring used, then add the remaining fruit, piling it high in the centre. Sugar should not be sprinkled on top of the fruit because it will dissolve and make the top crust soggy. Wet fruit can be dredged lightly with flour, if liked.

If making a double crust pie, line the pie dish in the same way as for a plate pie; then dredge the bottom crust lightly with flour or rolled oats before adding the filling if it is very moist.

For the top crust roll out the pastry 2mm thick and at least 2cm larger than the dish. If the dish has not been lined, cut off a strip of pastry the width and length of the rim of the dish. Dampen the rim of the dish with water, and place the strip of pastry on it. Join the cut ends by pressing them firmly together. Brush the strip of pastry with water.

Lift the pastry lid with the rolling-pin, and lay it over the dish, taking care not to stretch it. Press the two layers of pastry together firmly, trim off any overhanging pastry with a sharp knife, and knock up the edge with the back of the knife. Make a small hole in the centre to allow steam to escape.

Note To line a basin with suet crust pastry, see p329.

Guide to Shortcrust Pastry Quantities

1) To line a flan ring or make a top or bottom crust for a plate pie:

18cm – pastry made with		125g flour
20cm	,,	150g flour
23cm	,,	175g flour
25cm	,,	200g flour

2) To make a double crust plate pie:

18cm	,,	200g flour
20cm	,,	225g flour
23cm	,,	250g flour

3) To make a top crust for a deep oval pie dish:

500ml	,,	125g flour
750ml	,,	150g flour
1 litre	,,	200g flour

Use double these quantities to make a double crust deep pie.

4) Tartlets:

Pastry made with 100g flour will make approximately twelve 7cm tartlets.

Note To make a puff or flaky pastry cover for a 1 litre oval pie dish, use 100g flour.

Baking Blind

In many cases, a tart, flan or patty case must be cooked empty or 'blind' before the filling is added. A partially cooked case is used if the filling will need cooking at a low temperature or for a short time only; a fully baked case is used if the filling will need only brief re-heating or will not be cooked at all.

To bake a case empty or blind, prick the bottom of the case well with a fork. Cover the base with a piece of greaseproof paper, then fill the case with dried beans, bread crusts or rice. Bake the case at the usual temperature for the type of pastry used, for 8–12 minutes if a partially cooked case is needed, ie until the pastry is set, or for 20–30 minutes if a fully cooked case is required. In either case, remove the paper and dry filling, and return the case to the oven for 5–7 minutes to dry out the inside. The dry filling can be stored and re-used many times.

The times given above are based on an average cooking temperature of 190°–200°C, Gas 5–6, for shortcrust or similar pastry. The time will however vary with the size of the case and the depth of the dry filling used. Tartlet cases may cook in a shorter time, large tart or flan cases may take a little longer if the dry filling is dense. With partially baked cases, care must be taken that the walls or sides of the case are of uniform thickness all round and are adequately firm before the dry filling is removed, or they may collapse while drying out.

If the top rim of the pastry case is already browned when the dry filling is removed, the case should be dried out at a lower temperature than that used for setting or cooking the pastry.

Pastry Decorations for Flans, Tarts, etc, Baked Blind

Cut out the required shapes in pastry, glaze if liked, and bake beside the main pastry. Cover loosely with foil or remove from the oven if they are cooked and brown before the main pastry.

Greasing Containers

It is not necessary to grease tins, baking sheets, etc when making pastry, unless choux pastry, pâte sucrée or suet crust pastry are used.

If using a container (jam jar, etc) to mould a raised pie, this should be greased and floured.

Finishes and Decorations

For Deep Pies or Double Crust Tarts (using shortcrust, rough puff, flaky or puff pastry)

Edges

Line the edge of a pie dish with a pastry strip, cover, and trim with a sharp knife held at an angle away from the dish to allow for shrinkage during baking. Knock up the edges with the back of a knife.

To flute (scallop) edges: Pressing the top with the thumb, draw the edge towards the centre of the pie for about 1cm using the back of a knife. Repeat round the pie edge. For savoury pies, leave about 2cm between the cuts and for sweet pies about 5mm.

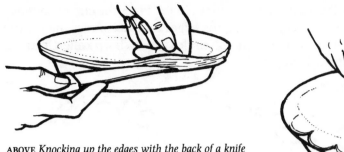

ABOVE *Knocking up the edges with the back of a knife*

RIGHT *Fluting the edges*

To fork edges: Press the back of a fork into the edge of the pie with the prongs pointed towards the centre. Repeat all round the pie edge.

To crimp edges: Pinch the edge between the thumb and first finger of both hands, then twist slightly in opposite directions.

Forking the edges

Crimping the edges

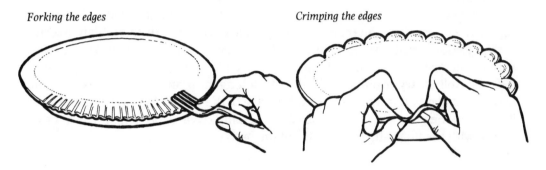

Tops

Make a small hole in the centre of any top pie crust to let the steam out. Decorate savoury pies with pastry leaves, a tassel or a rose. Dampen the shapes lightly before putting them in place.

To make leaves: Roll out a strip of pastry 2–3cm wide. Cut into diamond-shaped pieces. Mark veins on each leaf with the back of a knife. Pinch in one end for a stalk.

To make a tassel: Roll out a strip of pastry 2 × 15cm. Make 1–2cm cuts every 5mm along the strip. Roll up, place in the centre of the pie, and spread the ends into a fan shape.

LEFT *Making pastry leaves*

BELOW *Making a pastry tassel*

To make a rose: Make a ball of pastry and 2 pastry circles. Place the circles on top of each other and wrap round the ball, pressing the edges together under the ball, to seal. Cut a cross in the top of the ball through the circles with a sharp knife. Open out and turn back the segments to form petals.

For Open Tarts and Flans (using shortcrust pastry)

Edges
Use any of the finishes suggested for double crust tarts on pp450–51, or one of the following:

Twist: Roll pastry trimmings into a long thin strip. Trim to 2cm wide. Moisten the edge of the pastry. Press one end of the strip on to the edge of the tart or flan to secure it, then twist the strip with the right hand and press down gently between the twists with the index finger of the left hand.

Braid: Roll pastry trimmings thinly into a long strip and cut 2 pieces the same length and about 1cm wide. Moisten the edge of the tart or flan. Keeping the strips flat, secure the ends together on the edge, then interweave, pressing the plait down lightly with the finger-tip on the edge of the pastry.

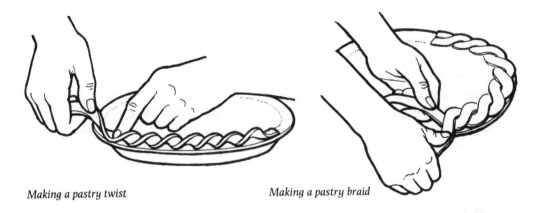

Making a pastry twist   *Making a pastry braid*

Pastry shapes: Roll out the pastry trimmings thinly and cut into 1cm circles, plain or fluted, or into small triangles or stars. Moisten the edge of the tart or flan, and arrange the shapes on it, overlapping them slightly.

Tops
Plain lattice: Cut thinly rolled pastry strips 5mm–1cm wide. Place in a lattice design on top of the filling, trimming the ends to fit the top neatly.

Making a plain lattice

Twisted lattice: Make as above but twist the strips before laying them on the filling.

Pastry shapes: Cut pastry trimmings into shapes as described on p452. Use to mark a tart or flan into serving portions or to make a lattice design.

To Glaze Pastry

Meat pies, patties, sausage rolls, etc are usually brushed with well beaten egg before or during baking. If a deeper glaze is desired, the yolk alone is used. If milk or water is beaten with the egg or egg yolk to increase the quantity, the glaze is called an *egg wash.* Salt or sugar in the proportion of 1×2.5ml spoon per egg should be added to make the egg easier to brush on evenly.

Fruit tarts, puffs, etc may be brushed with cold water and dredged with caster sugar before baking. If a thin coating of icing is required, the pastry may be brushed with well whisked egg white and dredged with caster sugar when almost baked.

Shortcrust Pastry (1) (for pies, tarts, etc)
Makes 350g (approx)

200g plain flour
1×2.5ml spoon salt
100g fat, eg 50g lard and 50g butter
  or margarine

3×15ml spoons cold water
flour for rolling out

Sift together the flour and salt into a bowl. Rub the fats into the flour until the mixture resembles fine breadcrumbs. Mix to a stiff dough with cold water. Roll out on a lightly floured surface, and use as required.

Bake in a fairly hot oven, 200°C, Gas 6, until set, then reduce the heat to cook the filling ingredients, if necessary.

Shortcrust Pastry (2) (for pies, tarts, etc)
Makes 350g (approx)

200g plain flour
1×2.5ml spoon salt
1×5ml spoon baking powder

75g lard **or** clarified fat (p563)
4×15ml spoons cold water
flour for rolling out

Sift together the flour, salt, and baking powder into a bowl. Rub in the fat until the mixture resembles fine breadcrumbs. Mix to a stiff paste with cold water. Roll out on a lightly floured surface, and use as required.

Bake in a very hot oven, 230°C, Gas 8, until set, then reduce the heat to cook the filling ingredients, if necessary.

Sweet Paste or Pâte Sucrée (for sweet flans, tarts, and tartlets)
Makes 400g (approx)

200g plain flour
½ × 2.5ml spoon salt
125g butter
50g caster sugar

1 egg yolk
1 × 15ml spoon cold water
flour for rolling out

Sift together the flour and salt into a bowl. Cut the butter into small pieces and rub into the flour until the mixture resembles fine breadcrumbs. Mix in the sugar, then the egg yolk, and enough cold water to make a stiff dough. Roll out on a lightly floured surface, and use as required.

Bake in a fairly hot oven, 200°C, Gas 6, until set, then reduce the heat to cook the filling ingredients, if necessary.

Note In warm weather very little water is required.

Suet Crust Pastry (for meat puddings, dumplings, fruit puddings, and roly-poly puddings)
Makes 400g (approx)

200g plain flour
1 × 2.5ml spoon salt
1 × 5ml spoon baking powder

75g shredded suet
125ml cold water

Sift together the flour, salt, and baking powder into a bowl and mix in the suet. Mix to a firm dough with cold water. Bake, boil or steam as directed in the recipe.

Rich Suet Crust Pastry (for meat and fruit puddings and roly-poly puddings)
Makes 600g (approx)

200g plain flour
1 × 2.5ml spoon salt
1 × 5ml spoon baking powder

75g soft white breadcrumbs
125g shredded suet
175ml cold water

Sift together the flour, salt, and baking powder into a bowl and mix in the breadcrumbs and suet. Mix with cold water to form a dough which is firm but soft enough to roll out easily. Bake, boil or steam as directed in the recipe.

Note This makes a very light, easily digested pudding, but the pastry is liable to break if turned out of the basin.

Choux Pastry (for cream buns, cream puffs, éclairs, etc)
Makes 450g (approx)

100g plain flour
250ml water
50g butter **or** margarine

a pinch of salt
1 egg yolk
2 eggs

Sift the flour. Put the water, fat and salt in a saucepan, and bring to the boil. Remove from the heat and add the flour all at once. Return to the heat and beat well with a wooden spoon until the mixture forms a smooth paste which leaves the sides of the pan clean. Remove from the heat, cool slightly, add the egg yolk, and beat well. Add the other eggs, one at a time, beating thoroughly between each addition. Use as required.

Bake in a fairly hot oven, 200°C, Gas 6.

Note This pastry rises better if used while still warm, but if this quantity is not all required at once, raw pastry or baked shells can be successfully frozen (see p586).

Potato Pastry (for covering meat or vegetable pies)
Makes 500g (approx)

200g freshly cooked potatoes (see **Note**)	½ × 2.5ml spoon salt
200g plain flour	1 × 5ml spoon baking powder
25g lard **or** dripping	2 × 5ml spoons beaten egg
25g butter	2 × 15ml spoons warm milk
	flour for rolling out

Mash the potatoes, or rub them through a fine metal sieve. Leave until cold.

Sift the flour. Rub the fats lightly into the flour and add the cold potatoes, salt, and baking powder. Add the beaten egg and enough milk to mix to a smooth dough; the amount of milk needed depends on the type of potato used. Roll out on a lightly floured surface and use as required.

Bake in a fairly hot oven, 200°C, Gas 6, until set, then reduce the heat to cook any filling ingredients, if necessary.

Note Freshly made-up instant potato can be used to make this pastry.

Cheese Pastry (for savoury pies and canapés)
Makes 450g (approx)

200g plain flour	100g finely grated cheese
a pinch of dry mustard	1 egg yolk
a pinch of salt	1–2 × 15ml spoons cold water
a pinch of Cayenne pepper	flour for rolling out
100–125g butter (see **Note**)	

Sift together the flour and seasonings into a bowl. Rub in the butter until the mixture resembles fine breadcrumbs. Add the cheese, egg yolk, and enough cold water to form a stiff dough. Roll out on a lightly floured surface and use as required.

Bake in a fairly hot oven, 200°C, Gas 6, until set, then reduce the heat to cook the filling ingredients, if necessary.

Note Use the smaller quantity of fat if the cheese is fatty and crumbly, the larger if it is fine and dry.

Rich Cheese Pastry (for savoury pies and canapés)

Makes 250g (approx)

100g plain flour
a pinch of dry mustard
a pinch of salt
a pinch of Cayenne pepper
75g butter

75g grated Parmesan cheese
1 egg yolk
1 × 10ml spoon cold water
flour for rolling out

Sift together the flour and seasonings into a bowl. Cream the butter until soft and white, and then add the flour, cheese, egg yolk, and enough cold water to form a stiff dough. Roll out on a lightly floured surface and use as required.

Bake in a fairly hot oven, 200°C, Gas 6, until set, then reduce the heat to cook the filling ingredients, if necessary.

Hot Water Crust Pastry (for pork, veal and ham, and raised game pies)
Makes 350g (approx)

200g plain flour
1 × 2.5ml spoon salt

75g lard
100ml milk **or** water

Sift the flour and salt into a warm bowl, make a well in the centre, and keep the bowl in a warm place. Meanwhile, heat the lard and milk or water together until boiling, then add them to the flour, mixing well with a wooden spoon until the pastry is cool enough to knead with the hands. Knead thoroughly and mould as required.

Bake in a hot oven, 220°C, Gas 7, until the pastry is set, then reduce the heat to moderate, 180°C, Gas 4, until fully baked.

Note Throughout the mixing, kneading, and moulding, keep the pastry warm, otherwise moulding will be very difficult. If the pastry is too warm, however, it will be so soft and pliable that it will not retain its shape or support its own weight.

To Mould a Raised Pie
Makes one 13cm diameter pie

hot water crust pastry using
    200g flour

fat for greasing
flour

The pastry must be raised or moulded while still warm (see **Note** above).

Reserve one-quarter of the pastry for the lid and leave in the bowl in a warm place, covered with a greased polythene bag. Roll out the remainder to about 5mm thick, in a round or oval shape. Shape the pie gently with the hands. If this proves too difficult, use a jar, round cake tin or similar container, as a mould: grease and flour the sides and base of the mould, invert it, lay the pastry over it, and mould the pastry round the sides, taking care not to pull the pastry and making sure that the sides and base are of an even thickness. Leave to cool. When cold, remove the pastry case from the mould and put in the filling. Roll out the pastry reserved for the lid, dampen the rim of the case, put on the lid, and press the edges firmly together. Tie 3 or 4 folds of greaseproof paper round the pie to hold it in shape during baking and to prevent it becoming too brown.

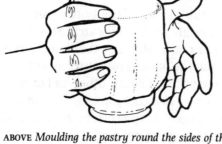

ABOVE *Moulding the pastry round the sides of the jar*
RIGHT *Using greaseproof paper to hold the pie in shape*

Note If the pie is raised without using a jar, moulding is made easier by firmly pressing some of the filling into the lower part of the pie when it has been raised to the required shape and thickness.

Alternatively, line a hinged raised pie mould with the pastry and bake in the container.

Rough Puff Pastry (for pie crusts, tarts, tartlets, sausage rolls)
Makes 500g (approx)

200g plain flour
$\frac{1}{2}$ × 2.5ml spoon salt
150g butter **or** 75g butter and 75g lard

1 × 2.5ml spoon lemon juice
cold water
flour for rolling out

Sift together the flour and salt into a bowl. If butter and lard are used, blend them together evenly with a round-bladed knife. Cut the fat into pieces the size of a walnut and add to the flour. Make a well in the centre of the flour, mix in the lemon juice, then gradually add enough cold water to make an elastic dough. On a lightly floured surface, roll into a long strip keeping the edges square. Fold the bottom third over the centre third, and fold the top third over it. With the rolling-pin, press to seal the edges. Turn the pastry so that the folded edges are on the left and right. Repeat the rolling and folding until the pastry has been folded 4 times. Allow it to rest in a cool place for 10 minutes between the second and third rollings. Use as required.

Bake in a hot oven, 220°C, Gas 7, until set, then reduce the heat to cook any filling ingredients, if necessary.

Puff Pastry (for pies, tarts, tartlets, bouchées, vol-au-vents, patties, etc)
Makes 500g (approx)

200g plain flour
$\frac{1}{2}$ × 2.5ml spoon salt
200g butter

1 × 2.5ml spoon lemon juice
100ml cold water (approx)
flour for rolling out

Sift together the flour and salt into a bowl and rub in 50g of the butter. Add the lemon juice to the flour and mix to a smooth dough with cold water. Shape the remaining butter into a rectangle on greaseproof paper. Roll out the dough on a lightly floured surface into a strip a little wider than the butter and rather more than twice its length. Place the butter on one half of the pastry, fold the other half over it, and press the edges together with the rolling-pin. Leave in a cool place for 15 minutes to allow the butter to harden. Roll out into a long strip. Fold the bottom third up and the top third down, press the edges together with the rolling-pin, and turn the pastry so that the folded edges are on the right and left. Roll and fold again, cover, and leave in a cool place for 15 minutes. Repeat this process until the pastry has been rolled out 6 times. Finally, roll out as required and leave in a cool place for 20 minutes before cooking.

Bake in a hot oven, 220°C, Gas 7. Do not open the oven door until the pastry has risen and become partially baked, since a current of cold air may make it collapse.

Flaky Pastry (for pies, tarts, and tartlets)
Makes 450g (approx)

200g plain flour
$\frac{1}{2}$ × 2.5ml spoon salt
125g butter **or** 75g butter and 50g lard

1 × 2.5ml spoon lemon juice
125ml cold water
flour for rolling out

Sift together the flour and salt into a bowl. If butter and lard are used, blend them together evenly with a round-bladed knife. Divide the fat into 4 equal portions. Rub one-quarter of the fat into the flour. Mix to a soft dough with lemon juice and cold water. On a lightly floured surface roll the pastry into an oblong strip, keeping the ends square. Divide another quarter of the fat into small knobs, and place them at intervals on the top two-thirds of the pastry. Fold the bottom third up on to the fat and fold the top third down over it. With the rolling-pin, press the edges lightly together to prevent the air escaping. Turn the pastry so that the folded edges are on the left and right. Press the rolling-pin on the pastry at intervals, to make ridges and to distribute the air evenly. Cover the pastry with greaseproof paper and leave to rest in a cool place for 10 minutes. Repeat the rolling and folding 3 more times; the last rolling will be without fat. Leave the pastry to rest between each rolling. Use as required.

Bake in a hot oven, 220°C, Gas 7, until set, then reduce the heat to cook any filling ingredients, if necessary.

To Make Vol-au-vent Cases

*Makes twenty-four 5cm or twelve 7cm bouchées or eight 9cm or
two 15cm vol-au-vent cases*

puff pastry (p458) using 200g flour   beaten egg for glazing
flour for rolling out

Heat the oven to hot, 220°C, Gas 7. Roll out the pastry about 2cm thick (1cm thick for bouchées) on a lightly floured surface and cut into round or oval shapes as liked. Place on a baking sheet and brush the top of the pastry with beaten egg. With a smaller, floured cutter, make a circular or oval cut in each case, to form an inner ring, cutting through about half the depth of the pastry. Bake until golden-brown and crisp. When baked, remove the inner circular or oval lid, and scoop out the soft inside while still warm.

Note For a better appearance a separate piece of pastry can be baked for the lid instead of using the centre portion of the case.

To Make Patty Cases

Makes twelve 7cm cases

puff **or** flaky pastry (p458) using   flour for rolling out
   200g flour   beaten egg **or** milk for glazing

Heat the oven to hot, 220°C, Gas 7. Roll out the puff or flaky pastry about 3mm thick on a lightly floured surface and cut into rounds with a 7cm cutter. Remove the centres from half these rounds with a 3cm or 4cm cutter to use as lids. Moisten the uncut rounds with water and place the rings neatly on top. Prick the centres. Place both cases and lids on a baking sheet and leave to stand for at least 10 minutes in a cool place. Brush the cases and the lids with beaten egg or milk, and bake for 10–15 minutes.

Crumb Crusts

Biscuit crumbs or similar fine dry crumbs can be used to make a plate pie, flan or tart shell. The method is quick and easy, and is popular for making cheesecakes.

The crumbs should be prepared by crushing the biscuits with a rolling-pin in a polythene bag. Care should be taken to see that the crumbs are fine and even. The fat is melted gently with the sugar if used, cooled slightly, and mixed thoroughly with the crumbs. The mixture is then pressed firmly into the plate, ring or tin. The rim should be levelled by running a sharp knife round it (or over its surface if thick) and any loose crumbs should be brushed off.

The crust can then either be chilled until firm and used as required for a cold filling; or it can be baked in a moderate oven, 180°C, Gas 4, for about 15 minutes until firm, then chilled before filling. A baked case can be rebaked if the filling requires it.

Rolled oats are sometimes used in the same way as biscuit crumbs, and crushed cornflakes can also be used, with a slightly higher proportion of fat and sugar.

Savoury Dishes using Pastry

Bacon Pasties
6 helpings

potato pastry (p455) using 100g flour
flour for rolling out
200g raw minced steak
150g streaky bacon, without rinds
100g lamb's kidney

1 large onion
salt and pepper
1 × 5ml spoon Worcestershire sauce
beaten egg for glazing

Roll out the pastry on a lightly floured surface and cut out six 18cm rounds. Put the steak into a bowl. Chop the bacon finely. Skin and core the kidney, and chop it finely. Skin and chop the onion. Mix all these ingredients with the steak, and season with salt, pepper, and Worcestershire sauce. Put a spoonful of mixture in the centre of each pastry round, dampen the edges, and fold up the pastry to form pasties. Crimp the tops with the thumb and forefinger and seal the edges firmly. Brush the pasties with the egg to glaze, place on a baking sheet and bake in a hot oven, 220°C, Gas 7, for 15 minutes. Reduce the temperature to moderate, 180°C, Gas 4, and bake for a further 45 minutes. Serve hot or cold.

Cheese Flan
4–6 helpings

cheese pastry (p455) using 150g flour
flour for rolling out
75g Cheddar cheese
2 eggs

200ml milk
a pinch of salt
Cayenne pepper

Roll out the pastry on a lightly floured surface and use it to line a 20cm flan ring about 2cm deep. Bake blind until set, then cool.

Meanwhile, grate the cheese for the filling. Whisk together with the eggs, milk, and seasonings. Pour into the flan shell, and bake in a fairly hot oven, 190°C, Gas 5, for 25–35 minutes or until firm in the centre and golden-brown.

Cheese and Onion Pie
6–8 helpings

3 small onions
shortcrust pastry (p453) using
    225g flour
flour for rolling out

2 × 10ml spoons plain flour
salt and pepper
100g Cheddar cheese
3 × 15ml spoons milk

Skin and parboil the onions. Roll out the pastry on a lightly floured surface and use half of it to line a 20cm pie plate. Season the flour with the salt and pepper. Slice the onions, toss them in the seasoned flour, and spread the slices over the base of the lined plate. Grate the cheese and sprinkle it over the onion. Sprinkle with 2 × 15ml spoons of the milk. Dampen the edges of the pastry, and use the remaining pastry to cover the dish, sealing the edges well. Knock up the edge and decorate, if liked. Brush the pastry lid with the remaining milk. Bake in a fairly hot oven, 200°C, Gas 6, for about 40 minutes.

Note If preferred, make the pie as an open tart, using pastry made with 150g flour. Reduce the cooking time to about 30 minutes.

Chicken Vol-au-vent (using cooked meat)
4 helpings

150g cooked chicken meat	a pinch of nutmeg
50g cooked ham **or** tongue	salt and pepper
50g button mushrooms	one 15cm vol-au-vent case (p459)
250ml Béchamel sauce (p245)	

Garnish
parsley sprigs **or** mustard and cress

Dice the chicken and the ham or tongue. Clean and slice the mushrooms thinly. Add to the Béchamel sauce, and heat thoroughly, stirring all the time. Add the nutmeg and seasoning.

Meanwhile, re-heat the vol-au-vent case in a warm oven, 160°C, Gas 3, for 10 minutes. Fill with the hot mixture, and serve at once, garnished with parsley or mustard and cress.

Note Small vol-au-vent or patty cases (p459) can be used instead of the large case. This quantity of filling is enough for twelve 7cm cases. Make as above, heating the baked cases for 6–9 minutes before filling.

Gougère (Choux Pastry with Cheese)
6 helpings

fat for greasing	salt and pepper
freshly prepared choux pastry (p454)	150g Gruyère cheese
using 150g flour	1 egg yolk

Lightly grease a shallow 18cm pie plate or sandwich tin. Season the pastry well with salt and pepper, and keep it in a warm bowl. Cut half the cheese into 5mm dice and grate the rest. Reserve about 25g of each, and put to one side. Mix the rest lightly into the pastry. Using a small round or oval spoon, place large spoonfuls of the mixture side by side in a circle all round the dish. Make a second circle just inside the first, and repeat until the dish is full. Make the last central choux rather bigger than the rest. Beat the egg yolk with a little water and brush the tops of the choux with it. Sprinkle with the reserved cheese. Bake in a fairly hot oven, 190°C, Gas 5, for 30–35 minutes, until risen and golden-brown. Serve hot or cold.

Note This is the traditional *gougère*. Quite often, the pastry is now used to line a soufflé dish, and is then filled with diced chicken or game in a savoury sauce.

Quiche Lorraine (Bacon and Cream Tart)
4–6 helpings

shortcrust pastry (p453) using
   125g flour
flour for rolling out
6 rashers streaky bacon, without rinds
3 eggs

300ml single cream
1 × 2.5ml spoon salt
a grinding of black pepper
a pinch of grated nutmeg
25g butter

Roll out the pastry on a lightly floured surface. Use it to line an 18cm flan ring placed on a baking sheet. Bake blind for 10 minutes until the rim of the pastry is slightly browned but the base still soft.

Cut the bacon rashers in strips 2cm × 5mm. Blanch in boiling water for 3 minutes. Drain well and scatter the strips over the pastry base. Press in lightly. Beat together the eggs, cream, seasoning, and nutmeg until fully mixed. Pour the mixture into the shell, and dot with flakes of butter. Bake in a fairly hot oven, 190°C, Gas 5, for 30 minutes. Serve at once.

Sausage Rolls
Makes 8

200g prepared puff (p458) **or** rough
   puff pastry (p457)
flour for rolling out

8 sausages **or** 200g sausage-meat
1 egg yolk

Roll out the pastry on a lightly floured surface and cut it into 8 equal-sized squares. Skin the sausages if required, or divide the meat into 8 equal portions. Form each portion into a roll the same length as a square of pastry. Place 1 roll of sausage-meat on each pastry square, dampen the edges of the pastry, and fold the pastry over so that they meet. Seal the joined edges and turn the rolls over so the joints are underneath. Leave the ends of the rolls open. Make 3 diagonal slits in the top of each roll. Brush the rolls with egg yolk. Bake in a very hot oven, 230°C, Gas 8, for 10 minutes or until the pastry is well risen and brown. Reduce to moderate, 180°C, Gas 4, and continue baking for 20–25 minutes. Cover loosely with greaseproof paper if the pastry browns too much.

Tomato and Mushroom Patties
Makes 6

300g tomatoes
200g mushrooms
1 small onion
25g butter **or** margarine
salt and pepper

1 × 5ml spoon chopped basil (optional)
shortcrust pastry (p453) using
   200g flour
flour for rolling out

Skin and slice the tomatoes. Clean and slice the mushrooms. Skin and chop the onion. Melt the fat in a frying pan and fry the onion gently for 5 minutes. Add the mushrooms and cook for a further 10 minutes, then add the tomatoes and cook for a further 5 minutes. Season to taste and add the basil, if liked. Leave to cool.

Roll out the pastry on a lightly floured surface and cut into six 18cm rounds. Drain the vegetable mixture and place in heaps covering half of each pastry round. Dampen the edges, fold the other half over, and pinch the edges together. Place on a baking tray and bake in a fairly hot oven, 190°C, Gas 5, for 20–30 minutes. Serve hot.

Desserts and Other Sweet Pastry Dishes

Apple Amber (2)
6 – 7 helpings

shortcrust pastry (p453) using
   150g flour
flour for rolling out
600g cooking apples
2 × 15ml spoons water

grated rind of 1 lemon
2 eggs
50g butter **or** margarine
75g brown sugar
50g caster sugar

Decoration (optional)
glacé cherries

angelica

Roll out the pastry on a lightly floured surface and use it to line a 750ml pie dish. Peel, core, and slice the apples. Put into a saucepan with the water and lemon rind, and stew until soft. Sieve, or process in an electric blender. Return the apple to the pan and re-heat slightly. Separate the eggs and add the yolks, fat, and brown sugar to the apple. Mix well. Put the mixture into the lined pie dish and bake in a moderate oven, 180°C, Gas 4 for about 30 minutes or until set. Whisk the egg whites until stiff and fold in the caster sugar. Pile on top of the apple mixture and decorate, if liked, with pieces of glacé cherry and angelica. Bake in a very cool oven, 140°C, Gas 1, for 30–40 minutes or until the meringue is golden-brown. Serve hot or cold.
Note For extra flavour, a good pinch of ground cinnamon and ground cloves can be added to the apples when stewing.

Apple Pie (basic deep fruit pie or tart)
6 helpings

shortcrust pastry (p453) using
   300g flour
flour for rolling out
600g cooking apples
100g sugar

6 cloves **or** 1 × 2.5ml spoon grated
   lemon rind
cold water for glazing
caster sugar for dredging

Roll out the pastry on a lightly floured surface and use just over half to line a 750ml pie dish. Peel, core, and slice the apples. Place half in the dish, add the sugar and flavouring, and pile the remaining fruit on top. Cover with the rest of the pastry and seal the edges. Brush the pastry with cold water and dredge with caster sugar. Bake in a fairly hot oven, 200°C, Gas 6, for 20 minutes, then reduce the temperature to moderate, 180°C, Gas 4, and bake for another 20 minutes or until the pastry is golden-brown. Dredge with caster sugar and serve hot or cold.
Note The pastry can be brushed with egg white and sprinkled with sugar before cooking, if liked.

Apricot Pudding
6 helpings

shortcrust pastry (p453) using
   150g flour
flour for rolling out
250ml milk
50g bread or plain cake crumbs

1 × 375g can apricots
25g sugar
grated rind of 1 lemon
2 eggs
75g caster sugar

Roll out the pastry on a lightly floured surface and use it to line a 750ml pie dish. Put the milk in a pan and bring to the boil. Pour it over the bread or cake crumbs. Drain the apricots and sieve, or process in an electric blender. Stir the apricot purée into the milk mixture with the sugar and lemon rind. Separate the eggs and beat the yolks into the milk mixture. Pour the mixture into the pie dish, and bake in a fairly hot oven, 200°C, Gas 6, for 25–30 minutes or until the pastry is golden-brown and the filling is set. Whisk the egg whites until stiff and fold in the caster sugar. Spread the mixture over the filling. Return to a very cool oven, 140°C, Gas 1, and bake for a further 30 minutes or until the meringue is crisp and golden.

VARIATIONS

Chester Pudding
Make as for Apricot Pudding, but increase the sugar to 100g and use 2 × 15ml spoons ground almonds instead of the apricots.

Gooseberry Pudding
Make as for Apricot Pudding, but use gooseberry purée instead of apricot purée.

Apple Strudel
8 helpings

Pastry
200g plain flour
½ × 2.5ml spoon salt
2 × 15ml spoons oil

1 egg
4 × 15ml spoons warm water
flour for rolling out

Filling
400g cooking apples
50g butter
50g soft brown sugar

1 × 5ml spoon ground cinnamon
50g sultanas

To make the pastry, sift the flour and salt into a bowl and add the oil, egg, and warm water. Mix to a firm dough. Cover with foil and leave in a warm place for about 1 hour.

Meanwhile, peel and core the apples, and chop them finely. Melt the butter in a saucepan.

On a floured tea-towel, roll out the dough very thinly to a rectangle 25 × 50cm. Brush with melted butter and sprinkle with the brown sugar, cinnamon, and sultanas. Top with the chopped apple, and roll up the strudel like a Swiss roll. Slide on to a baking sheet and brush the top with more melted butter. Bake in a fairly hot oven, 190°C, Gas 5, for 40 minutes or until golden-brown. Serve hot or cold.

Basic Fruit Flan
5–6 helpings

shortcrust pastry (p453) using
   125g flour
flour for rolling out
1 × 375g can fruit **or** 300g fresh fruit
   (strawberries, pears, pineapple, etc.)

25g sugar (optional)
1 × 5ml spoon lemon juice
1 × 5ml spoon arrowroot

Decoration (optional)
125ml whipped cream

Roll out the pastry on a lightly floured surface and use it to line an 18cm flan ring. Bake blind, then leave to cool. If fresh fruit is used, prepare it, put in a saucepan with 1 × 15ml spoon water, cover, and stew gently until tender. Make up the stewed fruit to 125ml with water. Canned fruit and some fresh fruit, eg strawberries, do not need cooking. Drain the fruit and arrange it in the cold pastry shell. Return most of the liquid to the saucepan, add the sugar, if used, and the lemon juice, and simmer for a few minutes. Blend the arrowroot with the remaining liquid and add it to the hot syrup, stirring all the time. Cook for 3 minutes, still stirring. Cool slightly, and spoon the liquid over the fruit. When cold, decorate with piped whipped cream, if liked.

Coconut Custard Pie
5–6 helpings

shortcrust pastry (p453) using
   175g flour
flour for rolling out
3 eggs

100g sugar
½ × 2.5ml spoon salt
75g desiccated coconut
375ml milk

Roll out the pastry on a lightly floured surface and use it to line a deep 23cm pie plate. Beat the eggs until liquid and add the rest of the ingredients. Pour into the pastry case and bake in a hot oven, 220°C, Gas 7, for 10 minutes, then reduce to moderate, 180°C, Gas 4, and bake for another 25–30 minutes or until set.

Jam Tart
6 helpings

shortcrust pastry (p453) using
   150g flour **or** puff pastry (p458)
   using 150g flour
flour for rolling out

4–6 × 15ml spoons any firm jam
   (see **Note**)
beaten egg **or** milk for glazing
   (optional)

Heat the oven to hot, 220°C, Gas 7. Roll out the pastry on a lightly floured surface and use it to line a 20cm pie plate. Decorate the edge with any trimmings. Fill with jam, and glaze the uncovered pastry with beaten egg or milk, if liked. Bake for about 15 minutes or until the pastry is cooked. Serve hot or cold.

Note the larger quantity of jam will be needed if a whole fruit jam is used. Lightly cover very firm jams with greaseproof paper while cooking to prevent scorching.

Hampshire Pudding
6–7 helpings

puff pastry (p458) using 150g flour
flour for rolling out
2 × 15ml spoons jam
2 eggs

1 egg yolk
75g butter
75g caster sugar

Roll out the pastry on a lightly floured surface and use it to line a deep 20cm pie plate. Spread the jam over the bottom. Beat the eggs and extra yolk together in a heatproof basin until frothy. Melt the butter in a saucepan. Gradually add the sugar and melted butter to the eggs. Place the basin over a pan of hot water and whisk the mixture until thick. Pour it over the jam and bake in a fairly hot oven, 200°C, Gas 6, for 30 minutes or until firm and golden-brown. If necessary, reduce the heat to moderate, 180°C, Gas 4, after 15–20 minutes to prevent the pastry browning too quickly. Serve hot.

Lemon Chiffon Pie
4 helpings

Pie Shell
100g digestive biscuits
50g butter

25g caster sugar

Filling
100g caster sugar
1 × 10ml spoon gelatine
3 eggs

50ml water
juice and grated rind of 2 lemons

To make the pie shell, crush the biscuits with a rolling-pin. Melt the butter and mix in the crumbs and sugar thoroughly. Line an 18cm shallow pie plate with the mixture; press it firmly in an even layer all over the base and sides. Put into a cool place to set.

To make the filling, mix 50g of the caster sugar with the gelatine. Separate the eggs. Blend the yolks, water, and lemon juice in a pan or basin over a pan of hot water, or in a double boiler. Stir in the gelatine and sugar mixture. Cook over very gentle heat for about 10 minutes, stirring all the time, until the custard thickens. Do not let it boil. Pour into a cold basin, cover with damp greaseproof paper, and chill until on the point of setting.

Stir the lemon rind into the cooled mixture. Whisk the egg whites until foamy, gradually whisk in the remaining sugar and continue whisking until stiff and glossy. Fold the lemon custard mixture into the meringue, pile into the pie shell and chill for at least 1 hour until set.

Lemon Meringue Pie

6 helpings

shortcrust pastry (p453) using
   175g flour
flour for rolling out
300g granulated sugar
3 × 15ml spoons cornflour
3 × 15ml spoons plain flour
a pinch of salt

300ml water
2 × 15ml spoons butter
1 × 5ml spoon grated lemon rind
75ml lemon juice
3 eggs
75g caster sugar

Roll out the pastry on a lightly floured surface and use it to line a 23cm pie plate. Bake blind until golden-brown, then cool.

Meanwhile, mix the sugar, cornflour, plain flour, and salt in the top of a double boiler. Boil the 300ml water separately, and add it slowly to the dry mixture, stirring all the time. Bring the mixture to the boil, stirring all the time; then place the top of the double boiler over hot water, cover, and cook gently for 20 minutes. Draw the pan off the heat. Add the butter, lemon rind, and lemon juice. Separate the eggs. Beat the yolks until just liquid, and add a little of the cooked mixture. Mix into the cooked ingredients. Replace over heat and cook, stirring all the time, until the mixture thickens. Remove from the heat and leave to cool. Whisk the egg whites until stiff and fold in the caster sugar. Pour the lemon custard into the baked pastry case and top with the meringue, making sure that it covers the top completely. Bake in a moderate oven, 180°C, Gas 4, for 12–15 minutes, until the meringue is lightly browned. Cool before cutting.

Mrs Beeton's Bakewell Pudding

4–5 helpings

shortcrust pastry (p453) using
   125g flour
flour for rolling out
jam
50g butter
50g caster sugar

1 egg
50g ground almonds
50g fine plain cake crumbs
a few drops almond essence
icing sugar for dusting

Roll out the pastry on a lightly floured surface and use it to line an 18cm flan ring. Spread over it a good layer of any kind of jam. Beat together the butter and sugar until pale and fluffy. Beat in the egg. Add the almonds, cake crumbs, and essence. Beat until well mixed, then pour the mixture into the flan shell, over the jam, and bake in a fairly hot oven, 200°C, Gas 6, for 30 minutes or until the centre of the pudding is firm. Sprinkle with icing sugar, and serve hot or cold.

VARIATION

Bakewell Tart

Make as for Bakewell Pudding, but use raspberry jam, and only 25g breadcrumbs or cake crumbs and 25g ground almonds. Bake for 25 minutes.

Mrs Beeton's Flan of Apples

6 – 7 helpings

6 dessert apples
4 cloves
3 × 15ml spoons medium-dry sherry
shortcrust pastry (p453) using
   175g flour

flour for rolling out
2 × 15ml spoons soft light brown sugar
3 egg whites
5 × 15ml spoons caster sugar

Peel and core each apple, and cut it into 8 sections. Place the sections in a heatproof bowl, add the cloves and sherry, cover closely and stand in a deep pan containing boiling water. Cook for about 20 minutes or until the apple sections are tender but not soft enough to break easily.

Meanwhile, roll out the pastry on a lightly floured surface and use it to line a 23cm flan case. Bake blind until the pastry is set. Fill the case with the apple sections arranged in a neat layer, strain 2 × 15ml spoons of the cooking juice over them, and sprinkle with the brown sugar. Whisk the egg whites until stiff with 2 × 5ml spoons of the caster sugar, and spread lightly over the apples. Sprinkle with the remaining caster sugar, and bake in a very cool–cool oven, 140°–150°C, Gas 1–2, for 1 hour. Serve either hot or cold.

Treacle Tart

6 helpings

shortcrust pastry (p453) using
   150g flour
flour for rolling out
3 × 15ml spoons golden syrup

50g soft white breadcrumbs
1 × 5ml spoon lemon juice **or** a good
   pinch of ground ginger

Roll out the pastry on a lightly floured surface and use most of it to line a 20cm pie plate, reserving a little for decoration. Warm the syrup in a saucepan until melted. Stir in the breadcrumbs and lemon juice or ground ginger, and pour the mixture into the pastry case. Roll out the remaining pastry into an oblong, and cut into 1cm strips. Arrange the strips in a lattice on top of the tart. Bake in a fairly hot oven, 200°C, Gas 6, for about 30 minutes.

Note If preferred, the tart may be baked as a double crust tart (p448). Use double the amount of pastry and bake for 50 minutes.

Crushed cornflakes can be substituted for the breadcrumbs, if liked.

Small Pastries and Tartlets

Banbury Cakes
Makes 14

rough puff (p457) **or** puff **or**
  flaky (p458) pastry using 200g flour
flour for rolling out
25g butter **or** margarine
3 × 10ml spoons plain flour
½ × 2.5ml spoon ground nutmeg **or**
  ground cinnamon

100g currants
2 × 10ml spoons cut mixed peel
50g brown sugar
2 × 15ml spoons rum
1 egg white
25g caster sugar

Heat the oven to hot, 220°C, Gas 7. Roll out the pastry 5mm thick on a lightly floured surface and cut into rounds using a 7cm pastry cutter.

To make the filling, melt the fat in a saucepan and stir in the flour and spice. Cook for 2 minutes. Remove from the heat, and add the fruit, sugar, and rum. Place a spoonful of filling in the centre of each pastry round. Dampen the edges with water and gather them up to form a ball; turn the ball over so the join is underneath. Roll or pat each ball into an oval shape, 10 × 6cm. With a sharp knife make 3 cuts in the top. Put on a baking sheet and bake for 15–20 minutes or until golden-brown.

Whisk the egg white lightly and brush over the hot cakes; dust immediately with caster sugar. Return to the oven for a few minutes to frost the glaze.

Cherry Tartlets
Makes 12

shortcrust pastry (p453) using
  100g flour
flour for rolling out
1 × 375g can red cherries in syrup
25g lump sugar

1 × 5ml spoon arrowroot
1 × 10ml spoon lemon juice
a drop of red food colouring (optional)
125ml double cream

Roll out the pastry on a lightly floured surface and use to line twelve 7cm patty tins or small boat-shaped moulds. Bake blind, then cool. Drain and stone the cherries, reserving the syrup. Place a layer of cherries in the pastry cases. Make up the syrup to 125ml with water. Heat the liquid and dissolve the sugar in it, bring to the boil, and boil for 5 minutes. Blend the arrowroot to a smooth paste with the lemon juice and add to the syrup, stirring all the time. Boil for 2 minutes until the syrup is clear and thick. Add the colouring, if liked. Cool slightly, then pour a little glaze over the cherries. Leave to set. Whip the cream until stiff, and pipe a large rosette on each tartlet.
VARIATIONS

Blackcurrant Tartlets
Replace the cherries with 400g blackcurrants stewed in 2 × 15ml spoons water and 4 × 15ml spoons sugar. Omit the food colouring.

Strawberry or Raspberry Tartlets
Fill the tartlets with fresh strawberries or raspberries. Make the glaze using 125ml water instead of fruit syrup.

Beatrice Tartlets
Makes 20

pâte sucrée (p454) using 150g flour
flour for rolling out
butter for greasing
3 bananas
juice of 1 lemon

1 × 15ml spoon caster sugar
50g chopped walnuts
125ml double cream
50g plain chocolate

Roll out the pastry on a lightly floured surface and use it to line 20 lightly greased 7cm patty tins. Bake blind, then cool. Chop the bananas and mix with the lemon juice and sugar. Stir the walnuts into the bananas. Pile the mixture into the pastry cases. Whip the cream until stiff, and pipe a large rosette on top of each tartlet. Grate the chocolate finely and sprinkle it over the cream.

Cream Eclairs
Makes 10–12

choux pastry (pp454–55) using 100g
    flour
fat for greasing
250ml whipping cream

25g caster sugar and icing sugar,
    mixed
3–4 drops vanilla essence
chocolate **or** coffee glacé icing (p432)

Make the pastry and use it while still warm. Put it in a forcing bag with a 2cm nozzle, and pipe the mixture in 10cm lengths on to a lightly greased baking sheet. Cut off each length with a knife or scissors dipped in hot water. Bake in a hot oven, 220°C, Gas 7, for 30 minutes. Do not open the oven door while baking. Reduce the heat to moderate, 180°C, Gas 4, and bake for a further 10 minutes. Remove the éclairs from the oven, split them, and remove any uncooked paste. Return to the oven for 5 minutes if still damp inside. Cool completely on a wire rack.

Meanwhile, whip the cream until it holds its shape, adding the mixed sugars gradually. Add the vanilla essence while whipping. Fill the éclairs with the cream, close neatly, and cover the tops with glacé icing.

VARIATION
Cream Buns
Pipe the pastry in 5cm balls, use any of the fillings described above, and sift icing sugar over the tops instead of glacé icing.

Mrs Beeton's Jam Tartlets

puff pastry (p458) trimmings
flour for rolling out

jam **or** marmalade

Heat the oven to fairly hot, 200°C, Gas 6. Roll out the pastry 5mm thick on a lightly floured surface and use it to line 7cm patty tins or foil tartlet cases. Bake blind for 7–10 minutes. Dry the empty cases in the oven for another 3–4 minutes. Cool, then fill with jam or marmalade.

Cream Horns
Makes 8

puff pastry (p458) using 100g flour
flour for rolling out
beaten egg and milk for glazing
3 × 15ml spoons sieved raspberry jam
4 × 15ml spoons liqueur-flavoured
   whipped cream (p443)

2 × 15ml spoons finely chopped nuts
(preferably pistachios) **or**
green-tinted desiccated coconut
(p441)

Heat the oven to hot, 220°C, Gas 7. Roll out the pastry 5mm thick on a lightly floured surface and cut into strips 35cm long and 2cm wide. Moisten the strips with cold water. Wind each strip round a cornet mould, working from the point upward, keeping the moistened surface on the outside. Lay the horns on a dampened baking tray, with the final overlap of the pastry strip underneath. Leave in a cool place for 1 hour. Brush with beaten egg and milk, and bake for 10–15 minutes or until golden-brown. Remove the moulds and return the horns to the oven for 5 minutes. Cool completely on a wire rack. When cold, put a very little jam in the bottom of each horn. Fill the horns with the cream. Sprinkle with the chopped nuts or desiccated coconut.

Note Chantilly Cream (p442) or 2 × 15ml spoons confectioners' custard (p442) and 2 × 15ml spoons stiffly whipped cream can also be used to fill Cream Horns.

Cream Slices
Makes 8

puff pastry (p458) using 100g flour
flour for rolling out
royal icing (p439) using 100g icing
   sugar

2 × 15ml spoons smooth seedless jam
125ml sweetened whipped cream
white glacé icing (p431) using
   100g icing sugar

Heat the oven to hot, 220°C, Gas 7. Roll out the pastry 1cm thick on a lightly floured surface into a neat rectangle. Cut it into 8 oblong pieces 10 × 2cm. Place on a baking sheet and spread the tops thinly with royal icing. Bake for 20 minutes or until the pastry is well risen and the icing is slightly browned. Leave to cool completely. When cold, split in half crossways. Spread the top of the bottom half with jam, and the bottom of the top half with cream; then sandwich the halves together again. Spread a little glacé icing on top of each slice, over the browned royal icing.

VARIATION

Vanilla Slices
Make as for Cream Slices but without the royal icing. When the slices are cold, fill with vanilla-flavoured confectioners' custard (p442) instead of cream. Ice the tops with white glacé icing.

Custard Tartlets
Makes 12

shortcrust pastry (p453) using 100g flour and 1 × 5ml spoon caster sugar	1 egg
	1 × 15ml spoon caster sugar
	125ml milk
flour for rolling out	a pinch of grated nutmeg

Roll out the pastry on a lightly floured surface and use to line twelve 7cm patty tins. Beat the egg lightly and add the sugar. Warm the milk and pour it on to the egg. Strain the custard into the pastry cases and sprinkle a little nutmeg on top. Bake in a moderate oven, 180°C, Gas 4, until firm and set. Cool before removing from the tins.

VARIATION

Custard Meringue Tartlets
Omit the nutmeg and bake for 15 minutes only. Whisk 2 egg whites until stiff and fold in 75g caster sugar. Pile on to the tartlets and bake in a very cool oven, 140°C, Gas 1, for 30 minutes or until the meringue is crisp and very slightly browned.

Eccles Cakes
Makes 12–14

flaky (p458) **or** rough puff (p457) pastry using 200g flour	75g currants
flour for rolling out	25g cut mixed peel
25g butter **or** margarine	½ × 2.5ml spoon mixed spice
1 × 15ml spoon sugar	½ × 2.5ml spoon ground nutmeg
	caster sugar for dusting

Heat the oven to hot, 220°C, Gas 7. Roll out the pastry 5mm thick on a lightly floured surface and cut into rounds using a 10cm pastry cutter. Cream together the fat and the sugar, add the currants, peel and spices, and place spoonfuls of the mixture in the centre of each pastry round. Gather the edges of each round together to form a ball. With the smooth side uppermost, form into a flat cake. Make 2 cuts in the top of each cake with a sharp knife. Brush with water and dust with caster sugar. Put on a baking sheet and bake for 20 minutes or until golden-brown.

Fruit or Jam Turnovers
Makes 8

shortcrust pastry (p453) using 150g flour **or** flaky **or** puff (p458) **or** rough puff (p457) pastry using 100g flour	flour for rolling out
	100g stewed fruit **or** 2 × 15ml spoons jam
	1 × 15ml spoon caster sugar

Heat the oven to fairly hot, 200°C, Gas 6. Roll out the pastry 3mm thick on a lightly floured surface and cut into rounds using a 10cm cutter. Place spoonfuls of fruit or jam in the centre of each pastry round. Moisten the edges with water and fold the pastry over the filling. Press the edges well together and crimp or decorate with a fork. Place the turnovers on a baking sheet, brush with water, and dredge with the caster sugar. Bake for about 20 minutes or until golden-brown.

Granville Tartlets
Makes 18

shortcrust pastry (p453) using 200g
  flour
flour for rolling out
50g butter
75g sugar
50g currants
25g ground rice
25g cut mixed peel

75g plain cake crumbs
1 × 15ml spoon single cream
  (optional)
4–5 drops lemon essence
2 egg whites
white glacé icing (p431)
25g desiccated coconut

Heat the oven to fairly hot, 200°C, Gas 6. Roll out the pastry on a lightly floured surface and use it to line 18 deep 7cm patty tins. Cream together the butter and sugar until pale and fluffy. Add the currants, ground rice, mixed peel, cake crumbs, cream, if used, and lemon essence. Whisk the egg whites until stiff and fold gently into the mixture. Place spoonfuls in the pastry cases and bake for 15–20 minutes until golden-brown. Cool, then coat with glacé icing and sprinkle with coconut.

Lemon Cheesecakes
Makes 12

shortcrust pastry (p453) using
  100g flour
flour for rolling out

3 × 15ml spoons lemon curd
25g whole candied peel

Heat the oven to fairly hot, 200°C, Gas 6. Roll out the pastry on a lightly floured surface and use it to line twelve 7cm patty tins. Half fill each pastry case with the lemon curd. Cut the candied peel into fine strips and use to decorate. Bake for about 20 minutes or until the pastry is golden-brown.

Maids of Honour
Makes 20

puff pastry (p458) using 200g flour
flour for rolling out
200g ground almonds
100g caster sugar

2 eggs
25g flour
4 × 15ml spoons single cream
2 × 15ml spoons orange flower water

Heat the oven to fairly hot, 200°C, Gas 6. Roll out the pastry on a lightly floured surface and use it to line twenty 7cm patty tins. Mix together the ground almonds and sugar. Add the eggs, and mix in the flour, cream, and orange flower water. Put the mixture into the pastry cases and bake for about 15 minutes or until the filling is firm and golden-brown.

Mince Pies
Makes 12

shortcrust pastry (p453) using
   300g flour **or** flaky **or**
   puff (p458) **or** rough puff
   (p457) pastry using 200g flour

flour for rolling out
250g mincemeat
25g caster **or** icing sugar for dredging

Heat the oven to very hot, 230°C, Gas 8. Roll out the pastry 2mm thick on a lightly floured surface, and use just over half to line twelve 7cm patty tins. Cut out 12 lids from the rest of the pastry. Place a spoonful of mincemeat in each pastry case. Dampen the edges of the cases and cover with the pastry lids. Seal the edges well, brush the tops with water, and dredge with the sugar. Make 2 small cuts in the top of each pie. Bake for 15–20 minutes or until golden-brown.

Palmiers

puff pastry (p458) trimmings
flour for rolling out

caster sugar

Heat the oven to hot, 220°C, Gas 7. Roll out the pastry on a lightly floured surface into a long strip about 30cm wide for large palmiers, 10–12cm wide for petits fours. Sprinkle well with caster sugar. Roll up the pastry from one long side to the centre of the strip. Then roll up, from the other long side so that the two rolls meet in the centre. Chill until firm, then cut the roll in slices; for petits fours, cut thin slices. Sprinkle the slices with more sugar, and place them, sugared side up, on a dampened baking sheet. Bake for 10–12 minutes, depending on the thickness of the slices. Lift off the sheet with a palette knife, and cool on a wire rack.

   Serve large palmiers as afternoon tea biscuits, very small ones as petits fours.

Sly Cakes
Makes 16–20

rough puff pastry (p457) using
   200g flour
flour for rolling out
25g butter **or** margarine
1 apple
200g currants

25g cut mixed peel
50g sugar
1 × 10ml spoon mixed spice
beaten egg **or** milk for glazing
caster sugar for dusting

Heat the oven to hot, 220°C, Gas 7. Divide the pastry in half, and roll out each piece on a lightly floured surface into a 15cm square about 2mm thick. Melt the fat. Peel, core, and chop the apple and mix it with the currants, peel, sugar, spice, and melted fat. Spread the mixture on one piece of pastry, lay the other piece on top and seal the edges well. Mark the top into squares or oblongs with the back of a knife, without cutting through the pastry. Glaze with beaten egg or milk. Put on a baking sheet and bake for 20–30 minutes until golden-brown. Cut into squares or oblongs and dust with caster sugar.

HOME-MADE SWEETS AND CHOCOLATES

Equipment for Sweet-making

Sugar boiling thermometer: The markings should be clear and register up to 200°C. The thermometer is usually mounted on a metal frame with a handle at the top, and a movable clip that fits on the side of the saucepan. After buying one put it in a saucepan of cold water, heat slowly to boiling point and check that it reads 100°C. Leave to cool in the water. When using the thermometer, place it in a jug of warm water while the sugar is dissolving. When placing it in the saucepan, make sure the bulb is wholly covered by the mixture. For an accurate reading, hold the thermometer at eye level. Once the correct temperature is reached, return it to the jug of warm water. Always wash it well after use to dissolve any syrup on it.

Saucepan: Choose a strong, thick-based saucepan to prevent sticking and burning. Make sure it is large enough because sugar tends to rise very quickly during cooking. Some older enamel pans are not suitable, as the high temperature of the sugar syrup may damage the surface.

Scraper: This makes the turning of fondant much easier. It is a piece of metal about 10 × 7cm, with either a wooden handle or a piece of the metal turned over in a curve to form a handle.

Marble slab: This is expensive, and large china or earthenware dishes can be used instead. An enamel tray can be used for cooling fondant syrup, but plastic surfaces should be avoided as they can only withstand a temperature of about 140°C.

Fondant mat: This is a sheet of rubber about 2cm deep, with fancy shapes inset, into which the liquid fondant, jelly or chocolate is poured and then allowed to set. When the sweets are set, they can be removed by bending back the rubber.

Dipping forks: These are metal with 2–3 prongs or a loop at the end. Useful for lifting sweets out of a coating mixture and for decorating the tops of chocolates.

Metal rings: A ring of metal about 1.5cm in diameter and 2cm deep. These rings are used mostly for shaping peppermint creams and setting jelly sweets.

Rules for Sugar Boiling

1) Always put the liquid into the pan first, before the sugar.
2) Always allow the sugar to dissolve completely before bringing the syrup to the boil; one or two grains of undissolved sugar can wholly spoil the texture of a sweet. To speed up the process, tap the bottom of the saucepan with a wooden spoon and draw the spoon through the sugar. Take great care, or the syrup will swirl up, splash on the sides of the saucepan and crystallize.

3) If crystals do form on the sides of the saucepan, brush the sides with a clean pastry brush dipped in cold water. If this is not done, sweets which should be clear and smooth may be sugary and rough when finished.
4) When boiling to a particular temperature, do not stir unless the recipe says so. Where milk or treacle is used, it may need stirring gently to prevent burning. In fudge and caramel mixtures, you will often need to stir near the end of the cooking time to get a grainy conistency.
5) Once the sugar is dissolved and the syrup is brought to the boil, heat very rapidly to the required temperature. As soon as this temperature is reached, remove the pan from the heat and stand the bottom of the saucepan in cold water for a few seconds. This will prevent the temperature rising any further.

Degrees for Sugar Boiling

The different degrees to which sugar is boiled are:

Thread	102°–103°C	Hard ball	120°C
Pearl	104°–105°C (seldom used)	Small crack	140°C
Blow	110°–112°C (seldom used)	Large crack	155°C
Soft ball	115°C	Caramel	177°C

Simple Tests

A sugar boiling thermometer gives exact temperatures, but sugar can be boiled and the degree gauged approximately by using the following tests:

Thread: Dip the handles of two wooden spoons into oil, then into the boiling syrup, then into cold water. If, on immediately separating the handles, the syrup is drawn into a fine thread, the sugar is boiled to the required temperature.

Pearl: Proceed as above but boil the syrup for 2–3 minutes longer before testing. The thread will be pulled a little longer without breaking.

Blow: Dip the top of a metal skewer in the syrup, drain over the saucepan, and blow through the hole. A small bubble should form which floats in the air for a second.

Soft ball: Pour a little of the syrup in a cup of cold water. If it can be rolled into a soft ball with the fingers, the correct temperature has been reached. The temperature can be tested as for the blow but instead of a bubble, the syrup will be blown into small irregular 'feathers'. This is sometimes called the 'feather' stage.

Hard ball: Proceed as above but boil for 2–3 minutes longer. A larger, harder ball will be formed on testing.

Small crack: A few drops of syrup in cold water will soon become brittle and a thin piece will snap.

Large crack: Proceed as above but boil for 2–3 minutes longer. The syrup will be very brittle and will not stick to the teeth when bitten.

Caramel: The syrup changes colour to become 'caramel'; the longer it boils, the darker it becomes. Remove the pan from the heat as soon as the syrup begins to darken, since it can then overcook in seconds. It cannot be used for sweets if it reaches a temperature above 177°C, as it will taste burnt. (Burnt caramel or Black Jack is used as food colouring; see p478.)

How to 'Pull' Sugar

In some sweet recipes, the boiled sugar mixture is 'pulled' while still warm and pliable to give it a satiny, shiny look.

When the syrup has reached the correct temperature, pour the mixture on to an oiled, heat-resisting surface. Allow the syrup to settle for a few minutes until a skin has formed, then turn the mixture sides to the centre using two oiled palette knives, until it cools enough to handle. Working quickly, pull the syrup between the hands into a sausage shape, fold in the ends, twist and pull again. Repeat the pulling until the candy has a shiny surface. When it is beginning to harden, shape it into a long rope as thick as needed, and cut quickly into small pieces with oiled scissors. If all the mixture cannot be pulled at once, leave it on an oiled tin in a warm place to keep soft. Several colours can be introduced by dividing the hot sugar mixture into different portions to cool and adding a few drops of colouring to each portion. Pull these separately, then lay them together for the final pulling and shaping. One portion may be left unpulled and clear and added at the final stage of shaping.

Note When working with pulled sugar, it is necessary to oil one's hands well to prevent burning.

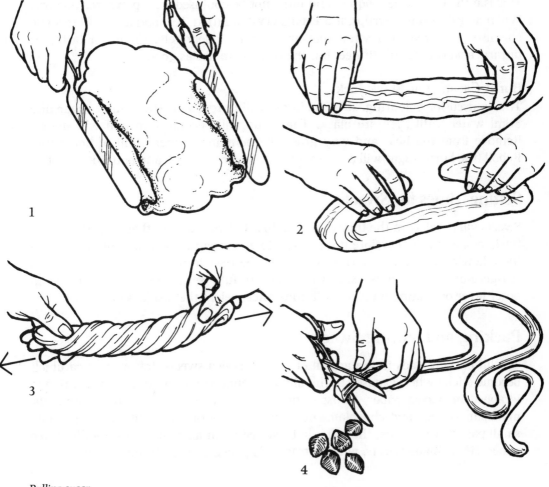

Pulling sugar

Ingredients

Apart from sugar, the following are also used:

Gum Arabic

This is used for mock crystallizing, for giving a bright finish to marzipan sweets and in some jelly-type sweet centres. It can be bought from a specialist supplier, and is very expensive. To use, dissolve 25g gum arabic in 50ml warm water. Stir, then strain through wet muslin into a screw-top jar. Keep covered. The solution will keep for months, but a harmless mould may appear on the surface.

Stock Syrup (2)

Stock syrup is added to fondant, when melting, to obtain the correct consistency. It is made by dissolving 400g of granulated sugar in 250ml water. Bring to the boil, and boil to 104°C. Strain through wet muslin or a jelly bag into a wide-mouthed jar with a stopper or screw-top.

Glucose

This is a thick colourless liquid, and must not be confused with powdered glucose. When added to sugar syrups, it prevents crystallization. It is obtainable from some chemists. If stored in a screw-top jar, it keeps indefinitely. Cream of tartar or tartaric acid can be substituted, but the results are not as good.

Burnt Caramel or Black Jack

This is used for colouring. It is made by boiling together 100g lump sugar and 50ml water until they are black. The syrup will become thin and will smoke. Remove from the heat and very gradually pour in another 50ml of hot water. Reboil (the burnt sugar will dissolve into a thin syrup). Cool, and pour into a bottle.

Setting Times for Sweets

Sweets vary widely in the time they take to set, depending on their size, shape and thickness, and it is therefore not possible to give accurate setting times in most of the following recipes. As a rule, sweets are best set in a cool place, but not in a refrigerator. Always make sure that they are fully set before packing them; an outer layer or coating may be set, for instance, before the inside is firm.

Packing and Storing Sweets

Careful packing adds to the appeal of sweets. Boiled sweets, toffees, and caramels become sticky when exposed to the air, so should be put in an airtight container, wrapped in waxed paper, transparent cellulose paper or foil. Fudges, fondants, marzipan sweets, and chocolates need no special wrapping, but can be put into small paper sweet cases; they should be stored in an airtight tin lined with waxed paper. Home-made sweets, when attractively packed, make delightful gifts.

Toffees, Caramels, Fudges and Candy

Simplest Ever Toffee
Makes 400g (approx)

oil for greasing
125ml water

400g lump sugar
a pinch of cream of tartar

Grease a 15cm square tin. Put the water and sugar into a saucepan and dissolve the sugar, gently stirring occasionally. Bring to the boil, add the cream of tartar, and boil to the small crack stage (140°C). Pour into the prepared tin, leave to cool, then score the surface deeply with a knife, marking into squares. When set, break into squares as marked, wrap in waxed paper, and store in an airtight tin.

Cooking time 20 minutes (approx)

Everton Toffee
Makes 325g (approx)

oil for greasing
175ml water
200g granulated sugar
75g soft light brown sugar

a pinch of cream of tartar
1 × 10ml spoon lemon juice
50g butter

Grease a 20cm square tin. Put the water and sugars into a saucepan and dissolve the sugar gently. Add the cream of tartar, bring to the boil, and boil to the small crack stage (140°C). Stir in the lemon juice and the butter, and continue boiling (without stirring) to the large crack stage (155°C). Pour at once into the prepared tin, and when beginning to set, score the surface, marking into squares. When set, break into squares as marked, wrap in waxed paper, and store in an airtight tin.

Cooking time 25 minutes (approx)

Treacle Toffee
Makes 300g (approx)

oil for greasing
100g butter
100g black treacle

150g soft dark brown sugar
2 × 15ml spoons water
a pinch of cream of tartar

Grease a 15cm square tin. Put the butter, treacle, sugar, and water into a saucepan, and dissolve the sugar over low heat. Add the cream of tartar, bring to the boil, and boil to the hard ball stage (120°C). Pour into the prepared tin, and when beginning to set, score the surface deeply, marking into squares. When set, cut or break into squares as marked, wrap in waxed paper, and store in an airtight tin.

Cooking time 20 minutes (approx)

Toffee Apples
Makes 12

12 ripe eating apples
400g granulated sugar
100g butter

2 × 15ml spoons water
oil for greasing

Wash and dry the apples and push a large wooden skewer into the centre of each. Put the sugar, butter, and water into a saucepan and dissolve the sugar very slowly. Bring to the boil, and boil to the small crack stage (140°C). Dip the apples, one at a time, into the hot toffee. Put on a well-greased plate and leave to set.

Cooking time 20–30 minutes

Peanut Brittle
Makes 1kg (approx)

oil for greasing
300g unsalted peanuts
125ml water
350g granulated sugar

150g soft brown sugar
150g golden syrup
50g butter
$\frac{1}{2}$ × 2.5ml spoon bicarbonate of soda

Grease a 20cm square tin. Warm the nuts very gently in the oven. Put the water, sugars and golden syrup into a strong saucepan and dissolve over low heat, stirring all the time. Add the butter, bring to the boil and boil gently to the large crack stage (155°C). Add the bicarbonate of soda and the warmed nuts. Pour into the prepared tin and, when almost set, score the surface, marking into bars.

Cooking time 20–25 minutes

Butterscotch
Makes 225g (approx)

oil for greasing
100g caster sugar
100g butter

75ml liquid glucose
125ml single cream

Grease a 17cm square tin. Put all the ingredients into a large saucepan and dissolve the sugar very slowly over low heat, stirring all the time. If possible, put a metal trivet under the pan as the mixture tends to burn easily. When the sugar has dissolved, bring to the boil, and boil to the small crack stage (140°C). Pour at once into the prepared tin, and, when beginning to set, score the surface into squares. When set, cut or break into squares as marked, wrap in waxed paper, and store in an airtight tin.

Cooking time 30 minutes (approx)

Candied Popcorn
Makes 75g (approx)

3 × 15ml spoons oil
75g popping corn
3 × 15ml spoons water

200g caster sugar
25g butter

Put the oil and popping corn into a large saucepan and heat quickly until one corn 'pops'. Immediately remove the pan from the heat for 1 minute, cover, and return to the heat. When the corn starts popping again, shake the pan constantly until the popping stops. Put the water, sugar and butter into a clean saucepan and heat gently until the sugar has dissolved. Bring to the boil and boil to the soft ball stage (115°C). Add the prepared corn and stir briskly until the corn is completely coated. Remove from the heat and continue stirring until cool to prevent the corn from sticking together.

Note It is particularly important to keep the pan covered when the corn is popping.
Cooking time 20 minutes (approx)

Cream Caramels
Makes 400g (approx)

oil for greasing
200g granulated sugar
200g golden syrup

125ml evaporated milk
1 × 2.5ml spoon vanilla essence

Grease a 20cm square tin. Put all the ingredients, except the vanilla essence, into a heavy-bottomed saucepan, and dissolve the sugar gently. Bring to the boil, and boil to the hard ball stage (120°C). Stir in the essence and pour the mixture into the prepared tin. When the caramel is cold, score the surface deeply, marking into squares. When set, cut into squares as marked, wrap in waxed paper, and store in an airtight tin.

Cooking time 20 minutes (approx)

Nut Caramels
Makes 400g (approx)

oil for greasing
50g walnuts
125ml milk
400g granulated sugar

50g golden syrup
25g butter
1 × 5ml spoon vanilla essence

Grease a 20cm square tin. Chop the walnuts. Put the milk, sugar, syrup, and butter in a saucepan and dissolve the sugar gently, stirring occasionally. Bring to the boil, and boil to the hard ball stage (120°C). Remove the pan from the heat, and stir in the walnuts and essence. Pour into the prepared tin and, when beginning to set, score deeply, marking into squares. When set, cut into squares as marked, wrap in waxed paper, and store in an airtight tin.

Cooking time 20 minutes (approx)

Chocolate Caramels
Makes 300g (approx)

oil for greasing
150g caster sugar
1 × 15ml spoon drinking chocolate
5 × 15ml spoons milk

1 × 15ml spoon liquid glucose
100g butter
75ml single cream
1 × 2.5ml spoon vanilla essence

Grease a 17cm square tin. Put the sugar, chocolate powder, milk, glucose, and one-third of the butter in a saucepan and dissolve the sugar slowly. Bring to the boil quickly, stirring to prevent burning, and boil to the blow stage (110°C). Stir in half the remaining butter. Continue boiling to the 'large' blow stage (112°C). Remove the saucepan from the heat and quickly stir in the rest of the butter, cream, and vanilla essence. Return the pan to the heat and boil quickly to the soft ball stage (115°C), stirring all the time. Pour into the prepared tin and, when beginning to set, score deeply, marking into squares. When set, cut in squares as marked, wrap in waxed paper, and store in an airtight tin.

Cooking time 20 minutes (approx)

Simple Fudge
Makes 500g (approx)

oil for greasing
400g granulated sugar
125ml milk

50g butter
1 × 2.5ml spoon vanilla essence

Grease an 18cm square tin. Put all the ingredients into a large saucepan and dissolve the sugar gently. Bring to the boil and boil to the soft ball stage (115°C), stirring all the time. Remove the pan from the heat and stir in the essence. Cool for 2 minutes, then beat the mixture until it becomes thick and creamy. Pour into the prepared tin and, when nearly set, score deeply, marking into squares. When set, cut into squares as marked, and store in an airtight tin lined with waxed paper.

Cooking time 15–20 minutes

Chocolate Fudge
Makes 500g (approx)

oil for greasing
400g granulated sugar
50g golden syrup
50g butter

25g cocoa powder
75ml milk
50ml single cream

Grease a 15cm square tin. Make as for Simple Fudge until the soft ball stage is reached. Cool for 5 minutes, then beat until creamy and matt in appearance. Pour the mixture into the prepared tin. Leave until cold before cutting into squares. Pack as for Simple Fudge.

Cooking time 15–25 minutes

Candy Twist
Makes 350g (approx)

125ml water
375g Demerara sugar
a few drops caramel food colouring
  (gravy browning)

a few drops almond essence
oil for greasing

Put the water and sugar into a saucepan and dissolve the sugar over low heat. Bring to the boil, and boil to the small crack stage (140°C). Add colouring and flavouring to taste. Pour the syrup on to an oiled, heat-resistant surface and, as the edges cool, fold them over to the centre. When the syrup is cool enough to handle, 'pull' it as described on p477. Cut into 15cm pieces and twist each into a spiral. Leave until set. Pack and store between layers of waxed paper in an airtight tin.

Cooking time 30–35 minutes

Marzipan, Nuts and Fruit

Boiled Marzipan
Makes 350g (approx)

6 × 15ml spoons water
200g granulated sugar
1 × 5ml spoon liquid glucose
150g ground almonds

1 egg white
1 × 5ml spoon lemon juice
1 × 5ml spoon almond essence
icing sugar for dusting

Put the water and sugar in a saucepan and dissolve the sugar gently. Add the glucose, bring the syrup to the boil, and boil to the soft ball stage (115°C). Remove the saucepan from the heat and dip the bottom of the saucepan in a bowl of cold water for a few seconds, to prevent a further rise in temperature. Stir in the ground almonds, then the unbeaten egg white. Return the pan to low heat and cook for 3 minutes, stirring occasionally. Add the lemon juice and almond essence. Turn the mixture on to a board and stir with a wooden spoon in a figure of eight movement, until the mixture is stiff and cool enough to be kneaded with the hands. Knead the marzipan with a little icing sugar until quite smooth. Wrap in waxed paper and store in a polythene bag, in a container, until required.

Note This marzipan is almost white and colours well for cake decorating and sweet-making. It is very pliable for moulding and will keep for months in a cool, dry place, although the outside may get a little dry. If so, knead lightly with a little egg white.

Cooking time 20 minutes (approx)
VARIATIONS
Marzipan Apples
Add green food colouring to the marzipan. Divide it into small pieces and shape each piece into a ball. Paint a little red food colouring on each apple for rosiness. Make a leaf from green marzipan, and use a clove as a stalk.
For more **variations** see over

Marzipan Bananas

Add a little yellow food colouring to the marzipan. Divide it into small pieces and shape each piece into a roll, curving it to the shape of a banana. Brush cocoa powder on for shading and stick a clove into one end.

Marzipan Carrots

Add orange food colouring to the marzipan and shape small pieces into rolls, tapered at one end. Make uneven indentations with the point of a knife and put a small piece of angelica at the top as a stalk. Dust with drinking chocolate powder.

Marzipan Lemons

Add yellow food colouring to the marzipan. Divide it into small pieces and shape each piece into an oval with points at each end. Roll lightly on a grater to make indentations.

Marzipan Logs

Add 75–100g melted chocolate to 350g marzipan and roll out into a rectangle 2mm thick. Make a roll of plain marzipan about 1cm in diameter and the same length as the chocolate rectangle. Wrap the chocolate marzipan round the plain roll, and press lightly. Mark the roll lengthways with the back of a knife to represent the bark. Cut into straight or diagonal pieces.

Marzipan Oranges

Add orange food colouring to the marzipan. Divide into small pieces and shape each piece into a ball. Roll on a grater to make indentations and toss in caster sugar. Press a clove into the top of each orange.

Marzipan Strawberries

Add red food colouring to the marzipan. Divide into small pieces and shape each piece into a strawberry shape. Roll each strawberry lightly on a grater to make indentations. Top with a stalk made from a strip of angelica.

Uncooked Marzipan or Almond Paste

Makes 400g (approx)

200g ground almonds	1 × 2.5ml spoon almond essence
200g icing sugar	2 × 5ml spoons lemon juice
1 egg white	

Mix the ground almonds and icing sugar together. Beat the egg white lightly and add to the mixture with the almond essence and lemon juice. Work to a firm paste.

Use this marzipan for sweets, fondant, and chocolate centres, or for covering cakes before icing.

Note This marzipan can be kept for 1–2 months. Store wrapped in foil and in a polythene bag in a refrigerator.

Buttered Almonds, Walnuts or Brazils
Makes (approx) 50 almonds, 20 walnuts, 15 Brazils

50g blanched almonds **or** halved
   walnuts **or** whole Brazil nuts
oil for greasing
6 × 15ml spoons water

200g Demerara sugar
1 × 10ml spoon liquid glucose
a pinch of cream of tartar
50g butter

Warm the nuts and space them out on an oiled tray. Put the water and sugar into a saucepan and dissolve the sugar, then bring to the boil. Add the glucose, cream of tartar, and butter. Let the butter melt. Boil the syrup to the small crack stage (140°C). Using a teaspoon, pour a little toffee over each nut; it should set very quickly. When cold, remove the nuts from the tray, wrap separately in waxed paper, and store in an airtight container.

Cooking time 25–30 minutes

Almond Rock
Makes 500g (approx)

250ml water
400g lump sugar
75ml liquid glucose

100g blanched almonds
a few drops almond essence
oil for greasing

Put the water and sugar into a saucepan and dissolve the sugar gently. Add the glucose, bring to the boil, and boil to the small crack stage (140°C). Draw the pan off the heat, add the almonds and essence to taste. Return the pan to the heat and boil for 2–3 minutes until golden-brown. Pour on to an oiled tray and leave to set. Break into pieces, wrap in waxed paper, and store in an airtight tin.

Cooking time 30–35 minutes

Stuffed Dates
Makes 24

200g dessert dates
100g whole blanched almonds

25g desiccated coconut

Stone the dates and place an almond in each hollow date. Roll them in coconut and put in paper sweet cases.
VARIATION
Stuff the dates with marzipan and roll in caster sugar.

Glazed Fruits

Makes 200g (approx)

200g fresh **or** candied fruit (see
  Method)
50ml water

200g lump sugar
a few drops lemon juice
oil for greasing

Grapes, mandarins or cherries can be used. Remove the pips but do not peel grapes or cherries; peel mandarins and break into segments. Dry fresh fruit thoroughly; wash candied fruit free from sugar and dry it.

Put the water and sugar into a saucepan and dissolve the sugar gently. Add the lemon juice, bring to the boil, and boil to the small crack stage (140°C). Remove the pan from the heat and place the bottom of the pan in cold water for a minute to prevent further cooking. Dip the prepared fruit in the syrup as when dipping chocolates (p493). Only dip one piece at a time. Place the glazed fruits on an oiled tray and leave to set. Serve with after-dinner coffee.

Cooking time 15 minutes (approx)

Soft and Hard Sugar Sweets

Snowballs

Makes 30–35

25g gelatine
300ml water
400g granulated sugar

1 × 5ml spoon vanilla essence
plain chocolate for coating
desiccated coconut for coating

Soften the gelatine in 125ml of the water in a small heatproof container. Stand the container in a pan of hot water and stir until dissolved. Dissolve the sugar in the remaining water and boil for 5 minutes. Add the gelatine and boil for another 10 minutes. Remove from the heat, add the essence, and whisk until the mixture is stiff enough to roll into balls. Form into 30–35 small balls. Melt the chocolate in a heatproof bowl over a pan of water and dip the balls as described on p493. Drain well. Toss in the coconut. Leave to set for 1 hour, then place in paper sweet cases.

Cooking time 25 minutes (approx)

Peppermint Creams

Makes 48 (approx)

400g icing sugar
2 egg whites

2 × 5ml spoons peppermint essence
icing sugar for dusting

Sift the icing sugar into a bowl, and work in the egg white and peppermint essence. Mix well to a moderately firm paste. Knead well and roll out, on a board dusted with a little icing sugar, to about 5mm thick. Cut into small rounds and put on greaseproof paper. Leave to dry for 12 hours, turning each sweet once. Pack in an airtight container lined with waxed paper.

Note These creams are suitable for coating with chocolate; see pp492–93.

Raspberry Jellies
Makes 400g (approx)

125ml water
400g lump sugar
25g gelatine

a few drops raspberry essence
a few drops red food colouring
caster sugar for coating

Put 100ml water and the sugar into a saucepan and dissolve the sugar gently. Soften the gelatine in the remaining 25ml water in a small heatproof container. Stand the container in a pan of hot water and stir until the gelatine dissolves. Pour the dissolved gelatine into the saucepan. Stir in the essence and colouring. Strain the liquid through muslin into a wetted 15cm square tin and leave it to set. Cut into shapes such as cubes or crescents, and coat with caster sugar.

Cooking time 10 minutes (approx)

Lemon Quarters
Makes 100g (approx)

125ml lemon juice
100g granulated sugar
25g gelatine

6 × 15ml spoons liquid glucose
caster sugar for coating

Put the lemon juice and sugar in a saucepan and dissolve the sugar gently. Stir the gelatine into the glucose. Add the glucose and gelatine to the pan and heat until the gelatine dissolves. Wet a 15cm square tin and pour in the mixture. Leave to set. When firm, turn out on to a board and cut into crescent shapes. Roll the sweets in caster sugar.

Cooking time 10 minutes (approx)

Coconut Ice
Makes 400g (approx)

oil for greasing
125ml water
300g granulated sugar

1 × 2.5ml spoon liquid glucose
100g desiccated coconut
a few drops pink food colouring

Grease a 15cm square tin well. Put the water and sugar into a saucepan and dissolve the sugar gently. Add the glucose, bring to the boil, and boil to the soft ball stage (115°C). Remove the saucepan from the heat and add the coconut. Stir as little as possible, but shake the pan to mix the syrup and coconut together. Pour the mixture quickly into the prepared tin and leave to set. Do not scrape any mixture left in the saucepan into the tin as it will be sugary.

Make a second quantity of mixture, adding a few drops of pink food colouring just before 115°C is reached. Pour on top of the set white mixture and leave to set, then cut into squares.

Cooking time 20 minutes (approx)
Note Make 2 separate quantities of ice rather than adding colouring to half the first mixture, as the extra stirring will make the mixture 'grain'.

Turkish Delight
Makes 400g (approx)

50g nuts, pistachios, almonds **or**
   walnuts (optional)
250ml water
25g gelatine
400g granulated sugar
$\frac{1}{2}$ × 2.5ml spoon citric acid
1 × 2.5ml spoon vanilla essence

2 × 5ml spoons triple-strength rose-
   water
a few drips pink food colouring
   (optional)
50g icing sugar
25g cornflour

If using nuts, skin them and chop coarsely. Put the water into a large saucepan, sprinkle in the gelatine and allow to soften. Add the sugar and citric acid. Heat slowly, stirring all the time, until the sugar has dissolved. Bring to the boil, and boil steadily for 20 minutes without stirring. Remove from the heat and leave to stand for 10 minutes. Stir in the vanilla essence, rose-water, and colouring, if used. (Half the mixture can be coloured and half left white, if liked.) Stir the nuts into the mixture. Pour into a wetted 15cm square tin and leave uncovered in a cool place for 24 hours.

Sift the icing sugar and cornflour together and sprinkle on a sheet of grease-proof paper. Turn the Turkish Delight on to the paper and cut into squares, using a sharp knife. Toss well in the mixture, so that all sides are well coated. Pack in airtight containers lined with waxed paper and dusted with extra icing sugar and cornflour.

Cooking time 30 minutes (approx)

Nougat
Makes 200g (approx)

50g blanched almonds
25g glacé cherries
75g icing sugar

1 × 5ml spoon liquid glucose
50g honey
1 egg white

Line the sides and bottom of a 15 × 10cm tin with rice paper. Chop the almonds and brown them lightly under the grill. Chop the cherries. Put the sugar, glucose, honey, and egg white into a saucepan. Whisk over very low heat for about 20 minutes or until thick and white. Use a metal trivet, if possible, under the pan to prevent browning. Remove the pan from the heat, and stir in the almonds and cherries. Turn the mixture into the prepared tin, and press it down well. Cover with a single layer of rice paper. Place a light, even weight on top and leave until quite cold. Cut into oblong pieces or squares and wrap in waxed paper.

Cooking time 30 minutes (approx)

Marshmallows
Makes 40–44

oil for greasing
250ml water
400g granulated sugar
1 × 15ml spoon golden syrup
2 × 15ml spoons gelatine
2 egg whites

1 × 2.5ml spoon vanilla **or** lemon
    essence
a few drops pink food colouring
    (optional)
50g icing sugar
25g cornflour

Line a 20cm square tin with oiled greaseproof paper. Put 125ml water, the sugar, and golden syrup into a saucepan and dissolve the sugar gently. Bring to the boil, and boil to the hard ball stage (120°C). Meanwhile, soften the gelatine in the rest of the water in a small heatproof container. Stand the container in a pan of water and stir until the gelatine dissolves. When the syrup is ready, remove the pan from the heat, and stir in the gelatine. Whisk the egg whites until stiff, then pour the hot syrup gradually on to the whites, whisking all the time. Add the flavouring and colouring. Continue to whisk the mixture until it is thick and foamy. Pour into the prepared tin and leave at room temperature for 24 hours.

Remove from the tin and cut into squares. Mix the icing sugar and cornflour together and roll each piece of marshmallow thoroughly in the mixture. Leave on a dry tray, in a single layer, at room temperature for 24 hours, then pack and store in boxes lined with waxed paper.

Note All or only part of the mixture may be coloured pink.

Cooking time 25 minutes (approx)

Mint Humbugs
Makes 375g (approx)

250ml water
400g granulated sugar
75ml liquid glucose
1 × 2.5ml spoon cream of tartar

1 × 2.5ml spoon oil of peppermint **or**
    to taste
oil for greasing
a few drops green food colouring

Put the water, sugar, and glucose into a saucepan and dissolve the sugar over low heat. Add the cream of tartar, bring to the boil, and boil to the small crack stage (140°C). Remove the pan from the heat and add oil of peppermint to taste. Pour on to an oiled surface and divide into 2 portions. Add green colouring to 1 portion. Allow the syrup to cool until workable, then 'pull' each portion separately as described on p477. When on the point of setting, lay the 2 portions together and 'pull' into a thick rope. Using oiled scissors, cut into 1cm pieces, turning the rope at each cut. When cold and hard, wrap the humbugs individually and store in an airtight tin.

Cooking time 25–30 minutes

Barley Sugar

Makes 350g (approx)

250ml water
400g lump sugar
1 × 2.5ml spoon lemon juice

a pinch of cream of tartar
oil for greasing

Put the water and sugar into a saucepan and dissolve the sugar gently. Bring to the boil, and boil to the small ball stage (115°C). Add the lemon juice. Continue boiling to the large crack stage (155°C) and add the cream of tartar. Pour the mixture on to a lightly oiled slab or large flat plate. Allow the mixture to cool for a few minutes, then fold the sides to the centre using an oiled palette knife. Cut into strips with oiled scissors, and twist each strip. When cold and set, store in an airtight jar.

Cooking time 20–25 minutes

Fruit Drops

Makes 200g (approx)

fat for greasing
200g granulated sugar
1 × 10ml spoon liquid glucose
50ml water

a pinch of cream of tartar
flavouring (see **Note**)
food colouring (see **Note**)

Grease metal sweet rings and a tray to put them on, or a shallow 15cm square baking tin. Put the sugar, glucose, and water in a saucepan and dissolve the sugar gently. Add the cream of tartar, bring to the boil, and boil to the hard ball stage (120°C). Remove the pan from the heat and cool for 5 minutes. Add the flavouring and colouring. Stir the syrup with a wooden spoon, pressing a little syrup against the sides of the saucepan to 'grain' it. Pour the syrup at once into the rings or into the tin in a 1cm layer. If the syrup is poured into a tin, mark at once into squares and break into pieces when cold. Wrap in waxed paper and store in an airtight container.

Cooking time 25–30 minutes
Note Flavourings and colourings: Lemon flavour – colour pale yellow; Raspberry or Strawberry flavour – colour pink; Pineapple flavour – colour yellow; Orange or Tangerine flavour – colour orange.

Lemon Acid Drops

Makes 250g (approx)

125ml water
300g lump sugar
½ × 2.5ml spoon cream of tartar
oil for greasing

1 × 2.5ml spoon lemon essence
1 × 5ml spoon tartaric acid
icing sugar for coating

Put the water and sugar into a large saucepan and dissolve the sugar gently. Add the cream of tartar, bring to the boil, and boil to the small crack stage (140°C), when the syrup should be pale yellow in colour. Add the essence. Quickly pour the syrup on to an oiled slab or dish. Sprinkle the tartaric acid over it and work it in well, using a wooden spoon. As soon as the mixture is cool enough to handle, form into a long roll. Using oiled scissors, cut off pieces about 1cm long, and shape with oiled hands into balls. Coat with sifted icing sugar. Allow to dry thoroughly before storing in an airtight container.

Cooking time 20–25 minutes

Fondant Sweets

Fondant is a solution of sugar and water boiled to the soft ball stage (115°C). It makes soft creamy sweets, forms the basis for other sweets or can be used for chocolate centres. It can be coloured and flavoured to choice. Any fondant left unused can be stored in an airtight jar.

When required, it may be necessary to thin down the fondant using stock syrup (p478). When adding the syrup to the fondant, work it in well, and place the basin containing the mixture over a pan of hot water. Avoid over-heating the fondant however; it should only be lukewarm. The colder the fondant syrup is before being worked, the smoother the fondant will be. If worked too hot, the grain will be too large and the fondant will feel and taste gritty.

Basic Fondant for Sweets
Makes 300g (approx)

125ml water
300g granulated sugar

1 × 5ml spoon liquid glucose

Put the water and sugar into a large saucepan and dissolve the sugar slowly over low heat. Tap the bottom of the saucepan with a wooden spoon to make sure every grain of sugar is dissolved. Add the glucose, bring to the boil, and boil rapidly to the soft ball stage (115°C). It is very important to brush down the sides of the saucepan with cold water during this process to prevent crystals forming.

Rinse a slab or large meat dish with cold water. Pour the fondant syrup on to it and lightly sprinkle the surface of the syrup with cold water. Do not scrape any syrup from the pan on to the fondant in the dish. Leave the syrup to cool for 20–25 minutes, then work it with a wooden spoon, palette knife or scraper, turning the mixture with a figure of eight movement. With working, the fondant will become dry and white. Gather into a ball and cover with a damp cloth. Leave to rest for about 30 minutes until the fondant softens. Knead into a ball and continue kneading until quite smooth. Store in a jar, covered with waxed paper and an airtight lid or polythene cover.

Cooking time 30 minutes (approx)

Fondant Fruits or Nuts
Any firm fruit can be used except those that discolour, eg apple or banana. Clean and dry the fruit, and remove any stones or pips. Divide oranges or mandarins into segments.

Put the fondant in a small basin over a saucepan of hot water, and stir until it has the appearance of thick cream. If necessary, add some stock syrup (p478). Dip any fruits or nuts, one by one, into the fondant, coating thoroughly. Cherries and grapes can be held by the stem, but other fruits and nuts must be immersed and lifted out with a fork like chocolates (p493). Place on a plate to dry.

Use about 200g fondant to coat 18–20 small fruits such as grapes, or 36–40 nuts.

Note These sweets will not keep long.

Chocolates

To Make and Coat Simple Chocolates

A good many of the recipes above are suitable for coating with chocolate, but the process requires time and patience. Couverture chocolate, which is the type used commercially, is not easy to use at home because success depends upon having exact temperatures and controlled atmospheric conditions. Couverture contains a high proportion of cocoa butter and needs to be 'tempered' properly before use (see below). It can be bought in small quantities from a supermarket or delicatessen.

The home chocolate-maker can get quite good results by using a super-fatted commercial dipping chocolate or coating chocolate.

Tempering Couverture Chocolate

Break the chocolate into pieces and put it in the top of a double boiler, or in a basin over a pan of hot water. Do not allow steam or condensation to get on to the chocolate, as the slightest drop of moisture will thicken it and make it useless for coating or dipping sweets. The chocolate must be heated over the hot water to a temperature higher than that at which it will be used for coating, usually about 50°C. It should be cooled until it thickens (at about 28°C), then heated again to between 30°–32°C, when it should be just thin enough to use but thick enough to set quickly. If milk couverture is needed, the best temperature for using is between 28°–30°C. Frequent stirring and an even temperature is necessary in either case, to keep the cocoa particles well distributed throughout the cocoa butter.

If chocolate other than couverture is used, break it into pieces, put in a basin over a saucepan of hot water and stir frequently until melted and of a coating consistency, but which will not run into pools when the chocolate is setting.

Centres to Use for Coating

1) Marzipan (p484), coloured, flavoured, and cut into attractive shapes.
2) Fondant (p491), coloured, flavoured, shaped, and allowed to dry before coating.
3) Preserved ginger or glacé pineapple cut into small pieces.
4) Blanched almonds, Brazil nuts or walnuts.
5) Caramels, toffee (pp479–82) or nougat (p488) cut into squares or rectangles.
6) Coconut ice (p487); dip completely in the chocolate or just half dip each piece.
7) Maraschino cherries, well drained, and coated with fondant (p491).
8) Chopped nuts or cornflakes can be mixed with the chocolate in a basin, and spoonfuls of the mixture put into paper cases and allowed to set. These are suitable with after-dinner coffee.

Chocolate Dipping and Marking

Arrange the centres to be coated on a tray, and also any decorations to be used, eg flaked almonds, toasted or nibbed almonds, chopped nuts, crystallized roses or violets. Place a sheet of foil or waxed paper on a flat tray to hold the finished chocolates. Place the bowl of melted chocolate between the centres and the tray for the finished sweets. Beside it place a dipping fork or an ordinary 3–4 pronged table fork for holding and dipping the centres.

When the chocolate is ready, drop in a centre, make sure it is completely covered with the chocolate, then lift it out, right side up, using the fork. Tap the fork on the side of the basin to remove any surplus chocolate. Place the sweet on the tray and gently pull the fork from underneath. Any decoration must be put on each chocolate before another one is dipped. The prongs of the fork can be used for marking the top of the chocolate for a simple decoration. The finished chocolates should be left to dry for several hours before putting them carefully into paper sweet cases.

Simple Truffles

Apricot Truffles
Makes 20 (approx)

100g stale plain cake	apricot jam
100g caster sugar	2 × 15ml spoons rum
100g ground almonds	chocolate vermicelli for coating

Rub the cake through a coarse sieve or process briefly in an electric blender to obtain even crumbs. Add the caster sugar and ground almonds. Warm and sieve the apricot jam. Add the rum to the dry ingredients with enough jam to make a stiff paste. Shape the mixture into small balls and leave to dry for 1 hour. Dip each ball in warmed jam and coat with vermicelli. Leave to dry overnight. These can be stored for 1–2 weeks in an airtight container.

Nut Truffles
Makes 20 (approx)

100g stale sponge cake	1 egg yolk
100g plain chocolate	2 × 15ml spoons rum
50g butter	100g walnuts
100g icing sugar	

Rub the cake through a coarse sieve or process briefly in an electric blender to obtain even crumbs. Break the chocolate into small pieces and put in a basin over a pan of hot water. Add the butter and allow to melt. Remove the basin from the pan, add the sugar, crumbs, yolk, and rum. Mix together well. If the mixture is soft, leave for 10 minutes in a cool place. Chop the walnuts finely. Shape the cooled mixture into small balls and coat with the nuts. Leave to harden for 1–2 hours.

Chocolate Truffles
Makes 24 (approx)

50g nibbed almonds
100g plain chocolate
100g ground almonds
2 × 15ml spoons double cream

75g caster sugar
a few drops vanilla essence
grated chocolate **or** vermicelli for
    coating

Brown the nibbed almonds lightly under the grill. Break the chocolate into small pieces and melt it in a basin over a pan of hot water. Remove the basin from the pan. Add all the other ingredients except the coating chocolate and mix to a stiff paste. Roll into small balls, and toss at once in grated chocolate or chocolate vermicelli. Put into paper sweet cases to serve.

Rich Rum Truffles
Makes 15 (approx)

75g plain chocolate
1 egg yolk
15g butter

1 × 5ml spoon rum
1 × 5ml spoon evaporated milk
drinking chocolate powder for coating

Break the chocolate into small pieces and melt in a basin over a pan of hot water. Add the egg yolk, butter, rum and evaporated milk. Leave the basin over the hot water and beat the mixture until it is thick. Remove from the heat and beat for a further 2–3 minutes. Put the mixture on a board and shape into a roll. Cut off pieces and shape them into balls. Roll in drinking chocolate powder, and leave to harden for 1 hour. Put into paper sweet cases to serve.

Marzipan Truffles
Makes 12 (approx)

25g plain chocolate
100g uncooked marzipan (p484)
25g walnuts

2–3 drops vanilla essence
1 × 15ml spoon sweet sherry
chocolate vermicelli for coating

Break the chocolate into small pieces and melt in a basin over a pan of hot water. Work the melted chocolate into the marzipan. Chop the walnuts finely and add to the marzipan. Mix in the vanilla essence and sherry. Shape into balls and roll in the vermicelli, pressing well to make the coating stick. Leave for 1–2 hours to harden.

CREAM OR GANACHE TRUFFLES

In the following more elaborate truffles, a Ganache Paste is used. This is a mixture of melted chocolate and warm cream, cooled until it hardens. The texture of the paste depends upon the type of cream and chocolate used. Plain chocolate is harder than milk chocolate, so more cream can be used. If any other liquid is used in the recipe, the amount of cream must be reduced accordingly. When the paste is made, it can be moulded and then coated with chocolate (pp492–93) to help keep it moist. This centre mixture does not keep for more than 2 weeks and the truffles should be kept in a refrigerator.

Basic Vanilla Cream Truffles
Makes 15 (approx)

200g milk chocolate	4 × 15ml spoons cocoa powder
75ml whipping cream	1 × 15ml spoon icing sugar
a few drops vanilla essence	chocolate for coating

Break the chocolate into small pieces and put in a basin over a saucepan of hot water. The water should not be more than 50°C. Stir the chocolate until melted. Put the cream into a small saucepan and bring to the boil, then leave to cool until it is hand-hot. Add the vanilla essence. Pour the cream into the chocolate and stir until well mixed. Leave the mixture to cool, stirring occasionally. The paste should be quite thick but not hard. Beat the mixture with a wooden spoon or an electric hand mixer until pale and light. Leave to cool in a refrigerator until the mixture hardens.

Sift the cocoa and icing sugar together on to a board. Put teaspoonfuls of the cream mixture on the board, coat with the cocoa and sugar, and roll into balls. Do not use more cocoa and sugar than necessary. Return the truffles to the refrigerator to harden again.

Have ready a bowl of melted dipping chocolate (p492). Spear a truffle centre on a fine skewer and pour a teaspoonful of melted chocolate over it, turning until well coated. Toss each truffle in a little of the cocoa and sugar mixture. Leave for 1–2 hours to set, then put the truffles into paper sweet cases to serve.

VARIATIONS

Orange Cream Truffles
Make as for Vanilla Truffles, substituting plain chocolate, and adding 115ml spoon concentrated orange juice when the chocolate and cream are stirred together. Use 100ml double cream instead of the whipping cream. Coat the finished truffles with 50g nibbed almonds instead of the sweetened cocoa.

Coffee Cream Truffles
Make as for Vanilla Truffles using 125g milk chocolate and 125g plain chocolate. Substitute 125ml double cream for the whipping cream, and stir in 1 × 15ml spoon instant coffee with the cream. Coat the finished truffles with chocolate vermicelli.

JAMS, JELLIES, MARMALADES, AND OTHER SWEET PRESERVES

Jams

Choose firm, ripe fruit or a mixture of just ripe and slightly under-ripe fruits. Over-ripe fruit will not give a set and should be used for some other preserve such as syrup or pulp. To retain the natural green colour of gooseberries, really young, under-ripe fruit must be used. Ripe red gooseberries make a fragrant jam, but the skins, like those of blackcurrants, can be tough unless softened by long gentle cooking before the sugar is added.

Choice of Preserving Pan
Money is well spent on a good quality preserving pan which will give good service without constant fear of burning the jam. Aluminium, stainless steel, and unchipped enamel are good choices. Iron and zinc pans are not suitable as the fruit will react with the metal and spoil the colour and flavour of the preserve. This can also occur with exposed iron in a chipped enamel pan. Copper and brass pans are not recommended. They enhance the colour of jam, especially green gooseberries, but a considerable proportion of the vitamin C in the fruit is destroyed. If copper and brass pans are used for cooking, they must be cleaned with salt and lemon juice and not with metal polish.

It is important to have a large enough pan so that the jam can boil rapidly without it overflowing. A 6 litre capacity is recommended for yields of 2–3kg.

The inside of the pan can be rubbed with unsalted margarine or butter before use to prevent the jam from sticking. But this is usually unnecessary if a good quality, heavy preserving pan is used.

Pectin Stock (to add to fruit deficient in pectin)
Prepare cooking apples, gooseberries or redcurrants, and cook with enough water to cover until thoroughly pulped. Crush with a wooden spoon and pour through a scalded jelly bag or double tea-towel. The resulting stock can be added to fruit weak in pectin. The usual allowance is 125ml of stock to 2kg of fruit, but more is required in vegetable jams, such as marrow where there is little natural pectin. For storing, pectin can be bottled in the same way as Fruit Syrups (pp526–27).

General Method for Making Jam

First, the fruit must be softened and broken down before the sugar is added. For this, water is added to firm fruit to prevent burning. If acid or lemon juice is used, it is also added to the fruit before simmering. The usual quantity of water required is indicated in the recipes but there is no hard and fast rule. A wide shallow pan will need more water than a deep narrow one. The fruit and water should be simmered until the fruit is soft and the bulk is reduced by one-third.

Testing for Pectin

If the setting quality of the fruit is in doubt, a pectin test can be carried out when the fruit is sufficiently softened and reduced, and before any sugar is added.

Take 1 × 5ml spoon of juice from the cooked-down fruit and put it into a small glass or jar. Leave it to cool and then add 1 × 15ml spoon methylated spirit. Do not stir but shake gently and leave for 1 minute. Tip the glass and pour off the liquid carefully. If there is plenty of pectin present there will be a single firm clot of jelly; for medium pectin there will be a soft clot or 2 or 3 smaller ones. If there is a feathery clot or no clot at all, pectin stock or some pectin-rich fruit must be added. Alternatively, commercial pectin may be added; this, however, is done after skimming the cooked fruit which is only boiled for a short time. (See Apricot Jam (2) p499.)

Adding Sugar

Either granulated or preserving sugar can be used for jam-making and it should generally be stirred into the fruit over low heat until thoroughly dissolved. Preserving sugar tends to cause less foaming. Warmed sugar dissolves more quickly than cold sugar. Once the sugar has dissolved, the heat can be increased to give a good rolling boil. When a good quality pan is used, an occasional stir will be enough to prevent burning. Constant stirring tends to produce an excess of foam.

Testing for Setting Point

Start to test for set when the frothing subsides and the jam boils noisily with distinctive heavy plopping bubbles. There is a short period when the jam has a good jellied set. If it is allowed to boil past this point its consistency will become sticky. The 2 usual tests for set are:

Cold plate test: Draw the pan off the heat (to prevent overcooking while testing). Put a small spoonful of the jam on a cold plate or saucer and leave it to cool. Push a fingertip through the cooled jam and if it has reached setting point the surface will wrinkle. If it does not wrinkle, reboil the jam for 3 minutes and test again. With a little experience, it is not difficult to decide if it has reached setting point.

Flake test: Draw the pan off the heat. Dip a clean wooden spoon into the jam, remove it and hold it above the pan for a minute to cool the jam on it. Then hold the spoon at an angle to allow the jam to run off. If setting point has been reached, the cooled jam will hang from the spoon in a curtain and then break off sharply and cleanly in a flake. If setting point has not yet been reached, the cooled jam will run off in a series of drops.

Note The temperature and volume tests on page 498 are also recommended.

Testing for Soluble Solids

If home-made jam is to be sold, it must comply with statutory requirements regarding soluble solids content. One of the 2 following tests should be used as well as a setting test. These can also be used at home as a guarantee of quality.

Temperature test: For this an accurate thermometer marked in degrees up to at least 120°C is required. A sugar boiling thermometer can be used. Its accuracy should be checked occasionally by standing it in a saucepan of cold water. When the water is heated to boiling point the thermometer should register 100°C. If it registers slightly below or above this, then a similar correction must be made when reading the jam temperature. Stand the thermometer in hot water before and after use. Stir the jam to give an even temperature throughout. Hold the thermometer in the jam, ensuring that about 5cm of the stem is immersed and that the bulb is not resting on the base of the pan. Normally a temperature of 104°–105°C indicates that the jam is acceptable for sale.

Volume test: For most jams the final yield is $1\frac{2}{3}$ times the weight of sugar used, ie sugar is 60% of the total yield. The following recipes are based on 1.5kg of sugar which gives a yield of 2.5kg of jam, sufficient to fill 5×450g jars and a small sampling jar. If the volume of jam is measured on a dip-stick principle, the yield can be checked before potting. Fill a 450g jar with water 5 times, pour the water into the preserving pan, and then add water from 1×225g jam jar. Make sure that the pan is standing level. Hold the handle of a wooden spoon carefully upright in the centre of the pan and mark on it the level of the water. Empty the pan and make the jam. Draw the pan off the heat and test for set. When bubbling has subsided, test the level by holding the handle of the wooden spoon upright in the centre of the jam. If the mark is submerged, reboil for a few minutes and test again. **Note** If one preserving pan is used consistently, time can be saved if one spoon handle is marked off for different yields or, for jelly making, for different quantities of liquid (a 450g jar holds approximately 300ml of fluid).

Potting and Finishing Jam

When the jam reaches setting point, remove the pan from the heat and remove the scum. This is done most economically with a warm perforated spoon or slice. The scum on jam made from fibrous fruits, eg strawberries or apricots, may be difficult to remove, but for the appearance of the jam it is worth doing well. Where there is very little scum, eg on blackcurrant jam, it can be gently stirred in with the addition of a little butter or margarine. The scum removed can be used to sweeten stewed fruit, or can be served over a steamed pudding. It comprises largely air bubbles, so its flavour, although fruity, is rather weak.

Using a small jar or cup pour the jam while really hot into warm, clean, dry jars, filling them right to the brim (since jam shrinks considerably on cooling). The modern jam jar with a twist-top is ideal for keeping jam in good condition especially in centrally heated homes. The twist-top *must* be put on the preserve as soon as it is potted as it acts as a seal.

Alternatively, with plain-necked jars, a transparent cellulose or waxed disc to fit the surface of the jam should be pressed on the hot preserve. The top cellulose cover can be put on at once while the jam is still very hot, but it is usually easier to wait until the preserve is quite cold. Never put it on *warm* jam as this encourages the growth of mould. Slightly dampen one side of the cover and place that side uppermost over the jam before securing with a rubber band or string.

Label the jars with the type of preserve, the date, and any other details about the fruit or the recipe which will be of interest later. Store preserves in a cool, dry place, preferably dark. The store for jams that are not sealed with twist-tops should have some ventilation.

Because of variations in utensils and ingredients, even a well-tried jam recipe may differ from household to household. The following recipes have been thoroughly tested but yields may vary slightly according to the equipment used.

Apricot Jam (1) (fresh fruit)
Yield 2.5kg (approx)

1.5kg apricots   1.5kg sugar
300ml water

Wash, halve, and stone the fruit and put it into a preserving pan with the water. If desired, crack a few of the stones, remove and halve the kernels and blanch them by dipping in boiling water. Add the halved kernels to the pan. Simmer until tender and reduced by one-third. Add the sugar and stir over low heat until dissolved. Bring to the boil and boil rapidly until setting point is reached. Remove from the heat, skim, pot, cover, and label.

Cooking time 50 minutes (approx)

Apricot Jam (2) (with added pectin)
Yield 2.5kg (approx)

1kg ripe apricots   1.5kg sugar
200ml water $\frac{1}{2} \times 227$ml bottle pectin (generously
3 × 15ml spoons lemon juice   measured)

Wash, stone, and slice the apricots. Put the fruit in a preserving pan with the water and lemon juice. Simmer gently for 20 minutes until the fruit is tender. Add the sugar and stir over low heat until dissolved. Bring to the boil and boil rapidly for 1 minute, stirring occasionally. Remove from the heat, skim if required, and stir in the pectin thoroughly. Cool for 5 minutes, then pot and cover immediately before labelling.

Cooking time 30 minutes (approx)

Apricot or Peach Jam (dried fruit)

Yield 2.5kg (approx)

500g dried apricots **or** peaches
1.5 litres water (apricots) **or** 1 litre
  (peaches)

50g blanched almonds (optional)
1.5kg sugar
2 × 15ml spoons lemon juice

Wash the fruit and cut it up, apricots into 2 or 3 pieces, peaches into 5 or 6 pieces. Put the fruit into a basin with the water and leave to soak for 24–48 hours. Shred the almonds, if used. Transfer the fruit and water to a preserving pan and simmer for about 30 minutes or until tender, stirring occasionally. Add the sugar, lemon juice, and shredded almonds, if used. Stir over low heat until the sugar is dissolved. Bring to the boil and boil rapidly until setting point is reached. Remove from the heat, skim, pot, cover, and label.
Note This can be made in the winter when fresh fruit is scarce.

Cooking time 1 hour (approx)

Apple and Ginger Jam

Yield 2.5kg (approx)

1.5kg apples
25g ginger root
600ml water
juice of 1 lemon (2 × 15ml spoons
  approx)

100g crystallized ginger
1.5kg sugar

Peel, core, and cut up the apples. Bruise the ginger root. Tie the peel, cores, and bruised ginger loosely in muslin. Put the apples, water, and bag of peel in a preserving pan with the lemon juice and cook slowly until tender. Remove the bag of peel after squeezing it into the preserving pan. Cut the crystallized ginger into neat pieces. Add to the pan with the sugar. Stir over low heat until the sugar has dissolved, then bring to the boil and boil rapidly until setting point is reached. Remove from the heat, skim, pot, cover, and label.

Cooking time 45 minutes (approx)

Blackberry Jam

Yield 2.5kg (approx)

1.5kg blackberries
2 × 15ml spoons lemon juice

1.5kg sugar

Pick over the blackberries and wash gently but thoroughly. Put in a preserving pan with the lemon juice and simmer gently until the fruit is cooked and well softened. Add the sugar and stir over low heat until dissolved. Bring to the boil and boil rapidly until setting point is reached. Remove from the heat, skim, pot, cover, and label.

Cooking time 30–40 minutes (approx)

Blackberry and Apple Jam
Yield 2.5kg (approx)

350g sour apples (peeled and cored)   1kg blackberries
300ml water   1.5kg sugar

Slice the prepared apples and cook them in half the water until pulped. Pick over the blackberries and wash them gently but thoroughly. Put in another pan with the rest of the water and cook until tender. (If the 2 fruits are cooked together, the apple will not cook to a pulp.) Mix the cooked fruits in a preserving pan and add the sugar. Stir over low heat until the sugar is dissolved, then bring to the boil and boil rapidly until setting point is reached. Remove from the heat, skim, pot, cover, and label.

Cooking time 1 hour (approx)

Blackcurrant Jam
Yield 2.5kg (approx)

1kg blackcurrants   1.5kg sugar
1 litre water

Remove the currants from the stalks. If the fruit is dirty, wash and drain it thoroughly. Put into a preserving pan with the water, and cook slowly until the skins are soft. This will take at least 30 minutes, probably more. As the pulp thickens, stir frequently to prevent burning. Add the sugar, stir over low heat until dissolved, then bring to the boil and boil rapidly until setting point is reached. (Test for set at intervals after about 10 minutes of rapid boiling.) Remove from the heat, skim, pot, cover, and label.

Cooking time 50 minutes (approx)

Cherry (Morello) Jam (1) (with redcurrant juice)
Yield 2.5kg (approx)

300ml redcurrant juice (see recipe)   1.5kg sugar
1.5kg Morello cherries

To obtain the redcurrant juice, prepare 700g currants and cook in enough water barely to cover until tender. This will take about 1 hour. Strain through a jelly bag or fine nylon sieve, without squeezing. Return the juice to the pan and boil down to 300ml.

Meanwhile, wash the cherries, remove the stones and tie them in a loose muslin bag. Put the cherries and the bag into the redcurrant juice in a preserving pan, and simmer gently until the cherries are very tender. Remove the bag of stones. Add the sugar and stir off the heat until dissolved. Return to the heat, bring to the boil and boil rapidly until setting point is reached. Cool for 7–10 minutes to prevent the fruit from rising in the jars. Skim if required, stir gently, pot, cover, and label.

Cooking time for jam 45 minutes (approx)

Cherry (Morello) Jam (2) (with added pectin)
Yield 2.5kg (approx)

1kg Morello cherries (stoned)
200ml water
3 × 15ml spoons lemon juice

1.5kg sugar (scant)
1 × 227ml bottle pectin

Wash the cherries and put them in a preserving pan with the water and lemon juice. Cover, and simmer for 15 minutes. Remove the lid, add the sugar and stir over low heat until dissolved. Bring to the boil and boil rapidly for 3 minutes. Remove from the heat, skim if required, and stir in the pectin thoroughly. Cool for 15 minutes, pot, and cover with discs. Tie down and label when cold. Do not use twist-tops.

Cooking time 30 minutes (approx)

Damson Jam
Yield 2.5kg (approx)

1.25kg damsons
500ml water

1.5kg sugar

Remove the stalks, wash the damsons, and put into a preserving pan with the water. Cook slowly until the damsons are well broken down. Add the sugar, stir over low heat until dissolved, then bring to the boil and boil rapidly. Remove the stones as they rise to the surface (a stone basket clipped to the side of the pan is useful for holding the stones, and allows any liquid to drip back into the pan). Continue boiling rapidly until setting point is reached. (Test for set after about 10 minutes of rapid boiling.) Remove from the heat, skim, pot, cover, and label.

Cooking time 45 minutes (approx)

Gooseberry Jam
Yield 2.5kg (approx)

1–1.25kg gooseberries
500ml water

1.5kg sugar

Use gooseberries which are still green, before they have ripened or turned colour. Top and tail and wash them and put in a preserving pan with the water. Simmer gently until the fruit is soft (this may take 30 minutes or longer). Add the sugar and stir over low heat until dissolved. Bring to the boil and boil rapidly until setting point is reached. (Test for set after about 10 minutes of rapid boiling.) Remove from the heat, skim, pot, cover, and label.
Note This is a good jam for beginners, because it sets very easily. It is especially good served on scones with whipped cream.

Cooking time 50 minutes (approx)

Peach Jam
Yield 2.5kg (approx)

1.8kg peaches
300ml water

1×5ml spoon tartaric acid
1.5kg sugar

Use small, firm peaches. Dip the fruit into boiling water for 30 seconds, then into cold water, and peel off the skin. Cut up the fruit and put it in a preserving pan with the water and acid. Simmer until the fruit is tender. Add the sugar and stir over low heat until it is dissolved. Bring to the boil and boil rapidly, removing the stones as they rise (a stone basket clipped to the side of the pan is useful for holding the stones, and allows any liquid to drip back into the pan). Test for set after about 10 minutes of rapid boiling. Remove from the heat, skim, pot, cover, and label.

Cooking time $1\frac{1}{4}$ hours (approx)

Raspberry Jam (quick method)
Yield 2.5kg (approx)

1.25kg raspberries

1.5kg sugar

Do not wash the raspberries unless absolutely necessary; if they have to be washed, drain very thoroughly. Bring the fruit gently to the boil without any added water, then boil rapidly for 5 minutes. Warm the sugar. Draw the pan off the heat, add the warmed sugar, then stir well over low heat until all the sugar has dissolved. Bring to the boil and boil rapidly for 1 minute. Remove from the heat, skim quickly, pot at once, cover, and label.
Note This jam does not set firmly, but it has a delicious fresh flavour.

Cooking time 10 minutes (maximum)

Strawberry Jam
Yield 2.5kg (approx)

1.5kg strawberries (hulled)
juice of 1 lemon

1.5kg sugar

Put the strawberries and lemon juice in a preserving pan. Heat gently for 10 minutes, stirring all the time, to reduce the volume. Add the sugar, stir over low heat until dissolved, then bring to the boil and boil rapidly until setting point is reached. Remove from the heat and skim. Leave the jam undisturbed to cool for about 20 minutes until a skin forms on the surface and the fruit sinks. Stir gently to distribute the strawberries. Pot and cover with discs. Tie down and label when cold. This jam will have cooled too much for the use of a twist-top.

Cooking time 20 minutes (approx)

Whole Strawberry Jam (with added pectin)
Yield 2.5kg (approx)

1kg small strawberries
1.5kg sugar
3 × 15ml spoons lemon juice

a little butter **or** margarine
$\frac{1}{2}$ × 227ml bottle pectin

Hull the strawberries and put them in a preserving pan with the sugar and the lemon juice. Leave to stand for 1 hour, stirring occasionally. Place over low heat and, when the sugar has dissolved, add a small piece of butter or margarine to reduce the foam. Bring to the boil and boil rapidly for 4 minutes. Remove from the heat and stir in the pectin thoroughly. Leave to cool for 20 minutes to prevent the fruit rising. Stir gently, then pot and cover with discs. Tie down and label when the jam is cold. Do not use twist-tops.

Cooking time $1\frac{1}{2}$ **hours (approx)**

JELLIES

General Method for Making Jelly

Choose fruit which is firm and ripe or slightly under-ripe. Remove any leaves, large stalks or diseased parts before use. Wash the fruit briefly if necessary; do not leave it soaking to become water-logged. If the quantity of fruit is small, it is better to use a saucepan rather than a large preserving pan. Either must be bright and clean inside. Put in the required amount of water, add the prepared fruit and any lemon juice or other acid, if required. Simmer until the fruit is tender and well broken down (usually 45 minutes–1 hour).

Testing for Pectin
A thick, sticky juice indicates good setting quality but it is advisable to take a pectin test (p497) to check the pectin clot. A firm clot is essential; it is a waste of effort to continue making the jelly without one. To correct a weak clot which may occur from poor quality fruit, either simmer the fruit for a further 20 minutes and then retest, or add a proportion of fruit of good-setting quality, such as apple, and simmer until it is well broken down before retesting.

Straining
While the fruit is cooking, fix a jelly bag or cloth on a stand, or from the legs of an upturned chair or stool. A felt or flannel cloth will give a much clearer jelly than thinner material. Place a bowl under the bag and pour boiling water through the cloth to scald it. Empty the bowl and replace it before pouring the juice from the preserving pan into the cloth. Leave the juice to drip for 45 minutes–1 hour. Do not squeeze or press the bag as this may make the jelly cloudy. Very little dripping occurs after 1 hour, so there is no advantage in leaving it longer.

Sometimes, with pectin-rich fruit, a second extraction can be made. To do this, return the contents of the bag to the pan after 20 minutes, add about half the original quantity of water, stir and then simmer for 30 minutes before straining.

Straining jelly

Mix the 2 extracts together, or make 2 grades of jelly, a richer and fruitier one from the first extraction and a milder blend from the second.

Adding the Sugar

The amount of sugar required has to be worked out from the strength of the clot and the yield of juice. For an average clot, allow 800g sugar per litre of juice; reduce the sugar to 650g per litre for a less firm clot; increase to 900g for a very firm one. The yield of jelly will be approximately $1\frac{2}{3}$ times the weight of the sugar.

Measure the extract, put it in the cleaned pan and let it simmer. Weigh out the required sugar and stir it into the extract. When dissolved, bring to a steady boil. Very rapid boiling may spoil the clarity of the jelly. After 10 minutes, test for set by either of the methods recommended for jam, and for volume or temperature. The flake test and temperature test are recommended (see pp497–98).

Potting and Finishing Jelly

Skim very carefully. The last traces of scum can be removed from the surface with the torn edge of a piece of soft kitchen paper. Transfer the jelly gently to clean, warm jars, preferably 225g in size. At first, pour down the side of the tilted jar to avoid including air bubbles. Work quickly to finish potting before the jelly begins to set. Seal or cover at once. Leave the pots of jelly undisturbed, preferably in a warm place, for 24 hours before labelling. Store in a cool, dark cupboard (with some ventilation if the jars are not sealed). Traditionally, jelly is potted into straight-sided jars and turned out for serving. Small jars are recommended because the set begins to 'weep' as soon as a pot of jelly is broken into, so the sooner it is used up the better.

An exact yield of jelly from a particular recipe cannot be given because losses in straining the juice vary. However, the method for calculating an approximate yield from the sugar used is given above. Cooking times in the recipes which follow refer to the time needed to bring the jelly to setting point after straining.

Apple Jelly

2kg well-flavoured crab-apples,
  cooking apples or windfalls
1.5–2 litres water

25g ginger root or thinly pared rind
  of 1 lemon
sugar (see recipe)

Wash and cut up the apples without peeling or coring. If windfalls are used, weigh after removing the damaged parts. Use just enough water to cover, bruise the ginger, if used, add the chosen flavouring and simmer for about 1 hour until tender and well mashed. If the apples do not break down, press them after 30 minutes with a potato masher. Test for pectin (p497), and if the clot is satisfactory, strain the juice through a scalded jelly bag. Leave to drip for 1 hour, then measure the extract, return it to the cleaned pan, and heat gently. Weigh and add the required sugar (usually 800g for every litre of extract). Stir over low heat until dissolved. Bring the jelly to a steady boil and test for set after 10 minutes. Remove from the heat, skim carefully, pot, cover, and label.

Cooking time 30 minutes (approx)

Blackberry and Apple Jelly

1.5kg cooking apples
1.5kg blackberries

1 litre water
sugar (see recipe)

Wash and cut up the apples without peeling or coring. If windfalls are used, weigh after removing the damaged parts. Pick over and rinse the blackberries if necessary. Simmer the fruits separately, giving the larger share of water to the apples. When the fruits are tender, after about 1 hour, mash them and pour both into a scalded jelly bag. Leave to drip for 1 hour, then measure the extract, return it to the clean pan, and heat gently. Add 800g sugar for each litre of extract. Stir over low heat until dissolved. Boil steadily until setting point is reached. Remove from the heat, skim, pot, cover, and label.

Cooking time 30 minutes (approx)

Cranberry and Apple Jelly

1kg apples
700g cranberries

sugar (see recipe)

Wash the fruit. Slice the apples without peeling or coring, and place in a pan with the cranberries and enough water to cover. Simmer gently until thoroughly mashed. Test for pectin (p497). Strain through a scalded jelly bag. Leave to drip for 1 hour, then measure the extract, return it to the cleaned pan and heat gently. Weigh and add the required sugar (usually about 800g for each litre of extract). Stir over low heat until dissolved, then boil steadily until setting point is reached. Remove from the heat, skim, pot, cover, and label.

Cooking time 25 minutes (approx)

Blackcurrant Jelly

2kg blackcurrants
2 litres water

sugar (see recipe)

Remove the leaves and the larger stems, and wash the blackcurrants if necessary. Place in the preserving pan, add 1 litre of the water, and simmer gently until thoroughly tender. Mash well, then strain through a scalded jelly bag, leaving it to drip for at least 15 minutes. Return the pulp left in the jelly bag to the pan, add the rest of the water and simmer for 30 minutes. Strain this pulp through the bag and leave to drip for 1 hour. Mix the 2 extracts together. Measure the extract, return it to the cleaned pan, and bring to the boil. Add 800g sugar for each litre of extract and stir until dissolved. Boil steadily, without stirring, until setting point is reached. Remove from the heat, skim, pot, cover, and label.

Cooking time 20 minutes (approx)

Mint Jelly

1kg green apples
500ml water
a small bunch of fresh mint
500ml vinegar

sugar (see recipe)
5 × 10ml spoons chopped mint
a few drops green colouring (optional)

Wash the apples, cut in quarters and put in a preserving pan with the water and the bunch of mint. Simmer until the apples are soft and pulpy, then add the vinegar and boil for 5 minutes. Strain through a scalded jelly bag and leave to drip for 1–2 hours. Measure the juice and return it to the cleaned pan. Add 800g sugar for each litre of juice, and bring to the boil, stirring until the sugar is dissolved. Boil rapidly until setting point is nearly reached, add the chopped mint and colouring, if used, then boil steadily until setting point is reached. Remove from the heat, pot, and cover immediately. When cold, label and store.

Cooking time 30 minutes (approx)

Redcurrant Jelly

2kg large, juicy redcurrants **or**
  redcurrants and white currants
  mixed

sugar (see recipe)

Remove the leaves and the larger stems, and wash the fruit if necessary. Put in a preserving pan, without any water, and heat very gently for about 45 minutes or until the currants are softened and well cooked. Mash, then strain the pulp through a scalded jelly bag. Leave to drip for 1 hour. Measure the extract, and return to the cleaned pan. Add 1kg sugar for each litre of extract. Bring to the boil, stirring all the time, then boil, without stirring, for 1 minute. Skim quickly, and immediately pour into warmed jars before the jelly has a chance to set in the pan. Cover and label.

Cooking time 10 minutes (approx)

MARMALADES

Marmalade-making is similar to jam-making and nearly all the same rules apply. As in jam-making, the fruit is first simmered gently, usually in an uncovered pan, until it is thoroughly softened. It is this long, slow cooking which releases the setting agent pectin. After this, the sugar is added and stirred over gentle heat until dissolved. The marmalade is then boiled rapidly, with a full, rolling boil, until setting point is reached. The tests for setting point are the same as for jam-making (p497).

These are the essential differences: the peel of citrus fruit takes longer to soften than the fruit used for jams. Because most of the pectin is in the pips and the pith, rather than in the fruit pulp or fruit juice, these are important ingredients in marmalade recipes. The pips and pith should not be discarded (unless they are being replaced by pectin stock) but should be tied loosely in muslin and cooked with the fruit until the pectin has been extracted. If the muslin bag is tied to the handle of the pan, it can easily be removed before adding the sugar. When the bag is removed, squeeze it thoroughly between 2 plates and pour the resulting liquid into the preserving pan.

Because citrus fruit is rich in pectin it requires ample acid and sugar to produce a good result. Many jam recipes use an equal weight of fruit and sugar, whereas with thick marmalades twice as much sugar as fruit can be used.

Points to Note

1) All citrus fruits should be only just ripe, and must be used as soon as possible.
2) It is not usually easy for the inexperienced to distinguish between the true Seville orange and other imported bitter oranges. Seville have a superior flavour, but ordinary bitter oranges can replace them in the recipes.
3) To peel citrus fruit easily, soak in boiling water for 1–2 minutes to loosen the skin.
4) To cut the peel into shreds, use a very sharp stainless knife and resharpen it from time to time. Drop the shreds into a bowl of water as soon as they are cut, to prevent them drying out. The peel will swell slightly during cooking. For shredding large quantities, it is worthwhile using a special machine which cuts the peel quickly and easily, although not as evenly as when done by hand.

   If a course cut marmalade is preferred, use the method on p509 (Dark Coarse-cut Marmalade). Alternatively, with some other methods, the uncooked fruit can be put through a coarse mincer, but this looks less attractive and gives a paste-like texture.
5) Many recipes used to recommend soaking the peel, etc for 24–48 hours to soften it before cooking. This is no longer considered necessary, but it may be convenient to do so, if, for instance, the fruit cannot be prepared and cooked on the same day, or if particularly tough skins such as grapefruit are being used. The softening effect of long soaking on the peel is minimal but some pectin is extracted, so setting point is reached more rapidly.

6) The sugar should not be added until the peel will disintegrate when a piece is pressed between thumb and forefinger, and the quantity in the pan has reduced considerably. Stir until the sugar is dissolved, then boil the marmalade briskly until setting point is reached. This should be after 15–20 minutes boiling, but depends to some extent on the quantity and recipe.

Potting and Covering Marmalade

Skim as for jams (p498) immediately setting point is reached. If the scum is not removed immediately, it subsides on the peel and is very difficult to skim off.

To prevent the peel rising to the top of the pots, leave the skimmed marmalade to cool undisturbed in the pan until a thin skin begins to form on the surface. Then stir gently to distribute the peel. Do *not* stir clear jelly marmalades.

Pour into warm, clean, dry jars, fill to the brim, and continue as for jams (pp498–99).

Dark Coarse-cut Marmalade
Yield 5kg (approx)

1.5kg Seville oranges	3kg sugar
2 lemons	1 × 15ml spoon black treacle
4 litres water	

Wash the fruit and cut it in half. Squeeze out and strain the juice. Tie the pips and pulp loosely in a muslin bag. Slice the peel into medium-thick shreds, and put into a preserving pan with the juice, muslin bag, and water. Simmer for about 1½–2 hours, or until the peel is tender and the liquid reduced by at least one-third. Remove the bag of pips and squeeze the juice out gently. Remove the pan from the heat, add the sugar and treacle, then stir over low heat until the sugar is dissolved. Bring to the boil and boil rapidly until setting point is reached. Remove from the heat, skim, cool until a skin forms, then stir, pot, cover, and label.

Cooking time 2–2½ hours (approx)

Seville Orange Marmalade
Yield 3kg (approx)

1kg Seville oranges	3 litres water
3 × 15ml spoons lemon juice	sugar (see recipe)

Wash the fruit and cut in half. Squeeze out the juice and the pips. Cut the peel into shreds. Tie the pips in a muslin bag and put into a basin with the orange and lemon juice, water, and peel. Soak for 24–48 hours. Transfer to a preserving pan and cook gently for about 1½ hours or until the peel is soft. Remove the bag and squeeze out the juice. Draw the pan off the heat, add 800g sugar for each litre (see volume test p498) and stir until dissolved. Return to the heat, bring to the boil and boil rapidly until setting point is reached. Remove from the heat, skim, cool, then stir, pot, cover, and label.

Cooking time 2½ hours (approx)

Clear Shred Orange Marmalade

Yield 4kg (approx)

1.5kg Seville **or** bitter oranges
2 lemons
1 sweet orange

4 litres water
sugar (see recipe)

Wash the fruit and cut it in half. Squeeze out and strain the juice, keeping the pulp and pips. Scrape all the white pith from the peel, and put pips, pulp, and pith into a basin with 2 litres of the water. Shred the peel finely and put this into another basin with the remaining water and the juice. Leave both to soak for 24 hours, if liked.

Strain the pips, etc through a muslin bag and tie loosely. Put the bag and strained liquor, the peel and juice into a preserving pan and bring to simmering point. Simmer for $1\frac{1}{2}$ hours or until the peel is tender. Remove from the heat and squeeze out the muslin bag gently. For a very clear jelly, allow to drip only. Add 800g sugar for each litre of juice and dissolve the sugar completely over low heat. Bring to the boil and boil rapidly for 20–25 minutes or until setting point is reached. Remove from the heat, skim, and cool until a skin forms on the surface. Pot and cover immediately, then label.

Cooking time 2 hours (approx)

Five Fruit Marmalade

Yield 2.5kg (approx)

1 kg fruit: 1 orange, 1 grapefruit,
  1 lemon, 1 large apple, 1 pear

2 litres water
1.5kg sugar

Wash the citrus fruit, peel it, and shred the peel finely. Scrape off the pith, and chop the flesh coarsely. Put the pips and pith in a basin with 500ml water. Put the peel and chopped flesh in another basin with the remaining water. Soak for 24 hours, if liked. Strain the pips and pith through a muslin bag and tie loosely. Put into a preserving pan with the fruit, peel, and all the liquid. Peel and dice the apple and pear and add to the other fruit. Bring to the boil, reduce the heat and simmer for $1\frac{1}{4}$ hours until the volume is reduced by one-third. Remove the bag and squeeze out the juice. Add the sugar, and stir over low heat until dissolved. Bring to the boil and boil rapidly for about 30 minutes, or until setting point is reached. Remove from the heat, skim, cool slightly, then stir, pot, cover, and label.

Cooking time 2 hours (approx)

OTHER SWEET PRESERVES

These should be potted and covered in the same way as jams (pp498–99) unless otherwise indicated.

Mincemeat
Yield 1.8kg (approx)

200g cut mixed peel
200g seedless raisins
25g preserved stem ginger
200g cooking apples
200g shredded suet
200g sultanas
200g currants

200g soft brown sugar
50g blanched chopped almonds
a generous pinch each of mixed spice,
   ground ginger, ground cinnamon
grated rind and juice of 2 lemons and
   1 orange
150ml sherry, brandy or rum

Mince or chop finely the peel, raisins, and ginger. Peel, core, and grate the apples. Combine all the ingredients thoroughly in a large basin. Leave, covered, for 2 days, in a cool place, stirring occasionally. (This prevents fermentation later.) Pot, cover, and label. Store in a cool dry place.

Mrs Beeton's Very Nice Preserve of Damsons
Yield 1kg (approx)

700g firm, ripe damsons

250g granulated or caster sugar

Remove the stalks from the damsons and discard any that are blemished. Damp the sound fruit slightly with water and put into a large jar; mix with the sugar. Cover loosely and stand in a heavy saucepan with a false bottom (p522). Cover completely with cold water. Bring the water gradually to the boil, reduce the heat and simmer for about 30 minutes until the fruit is tender. Leave until cold. Pour off the liquid, boil to reduce it by about one-quarter, strain through a scalded jelly bag and pour it over the fruit. Seal securely, label, and keep in a cool place.
Note This very fruity preserve does not set as a jam but is delicious served with cream or used in a fruit tart. It contains many stones.

Apricot Conserve
Yield 800g (approx)

300ml water
juice of 1 lemon

500g sugar
500g stoned, under-ripe apricots

Boil the water, lemon juice, and sugar together for 10 minutes. Skim, then add the fruit. Crack half the stones, skin the kernels, and add them to the syrup. Boil gently for about 45 minutes. Test the syrup on a plate for set and when ready put the conserve into dry, warm pots, cover at once, and label.
Note If the apricots are large, they may be halved or even quartered.

Cooking time 1 hour (approx)

Lemon Curd
Yield 300g (approx)

2 lemons	75g butter
225g lump **or** granulated sugar	3 eggs

Wash and dry the lemons. Grate the rind or pare it into strips; squeeze out the juice. Put the rind, juice, and sugar into the top of a double boiler or basin over boiling water. Stir occasionally until the sugar dissolves. Remove from the heat and stir in the butter. Leave to cool. Beat the eggs lightly and pour the cooled mixture over them. Strain it back into the pan or basin and place over gentle heat. Stir frequently with a wooden spoon until the mixture begins to thicken. When it coats the back of the spoon lightly, pour into small jars, taking care to fill to the brim. Cover and label.

Cooking time 30 minutes (approx)
VARIATIONS
Grapefruit Curd
Substitute 2 grapefruit, and use 250g granulated sugar and 100g butter.

Orange Curd
Substitute 2 oranges, and add the juice of 1 lemon. Use only 50g butter and melt it in the double boiler or basin before adding the rind, juices, and sugar.

Apple Butter
Yield 3.25kg (approx)

3kg crab-apples **or** windfalls	granulated sugar (see recipe)
2 litres water **or** 1 litre water and 1	1 × 5ml spoon ground cloves
litre cider	1 × 5ml spoon ground cinnamon

Wash the fruit and cut it up roughly, discarding any damaged parts. Simmer the fruit in the water, or water and cider, until well softened, and then sieve. Weigh the pulp, return it to the pan, and simmer until it thickens. Add three-quarters of the pulp weight in sugar, and the ground spices. Stir until the sugar dissolves, then boil steadily, stirring frequently, until no free liquid runs out when a small sample is cooled on a plate. Pot, cover at once, and label.
Note Apple can be used to extend more expensive fruits.

Cooking time 1–1½ hours

Damson Cheese
Makes 3.2kg (approx)

2.75kg ripe damsons	sugar (see recipe)
250ml water	glycerine for jars

Remove the stalks and wash the fruit. Put into a heavy-bottomed saucepan, flameproof casserole or (traditionally) an ovenproof earthenware jar. Add the

Bananas in Rum (p.543)

Steak Diane (p.541)

Mixed Pickle (p.531)

Mrs Beeton's Charlotte Russe (p.362)

Bottled Fruit (p.519-24)

Jam Omelettes (p.326)

Meringue Shells (p.370)

water, cover closely, and either simmer or bake for several hours until the fruit is very tender. (Bake in a very cool oven at 110°–120°C, Gas $\frac{1}{4}$–$\frac{1}{2}$.) Drain, reserving the juice. Sieve the fruit, and weigh the pulp (there should be about 2.3kg). Put into an uncovered pan with a little of the drained juice, and boil gently until very thick. Add 350–450g sugar per 450g pulped fruit and continue cooking, stirring all the time, until the cheese leaves the sides of the pan clean, and a spoon drawn across the bottom of the pan leaves a clean line. Turn at once into small heated jars without shoulders, smeared with glycerine inside; tap the jars on the table-top two or three times while filling to knock out air-holes. Cover while still hot, cool, then label.

Store for several weeks, then use like jam. For a traditional stiff cheese, store for at least a year, then turn out, slice and serve with plain gingerbread, butter, and Cheshire or Lancashire cheese.

Cooking time 1 hour (approx)

Apricots in Brandy

400g sugar	1kg firm ripe apricots
300ml water	brandy (see recipe)

Put 200g of the sugar and the water in a pan, and cook, without stirring, for about 5 minutes until a syrup is formed.

Wash and drain the apricots, prick them with a darning needle, and put them in the boiling syrup. Bring the syrup back to the boil, and remove the riper fruit at once. Firmer fruit should be boiled for 2 minutes, but do not let it become too tender. Pack the fruit into clean, tested bottling jars. Remove the syrup from the heat, and stir in the remaining sugar. When the sugar has dissolved, boil the syrup steadily to 102°C (approx). Leave the syrup to cool, and drain off any syrup which has accumulated in the packed jars. Add 100ml brandy to each 100ml syrup, mix together, and pour into the jars to cover the fruit. Cover the jars and continue as for the Quick Deep Pan method of bottling (pp521–22), leaving the jars in the pan for 2 minutes after they have simmered at 90°C, and before sealing.

Candied and Crystallized Fruit

Shop-bought candied fruit is a succulent and expensive luxury, but it can be made at home to a professional standard without great skill or special equipment. The main requirement is patience, the process taking about 15 minutes a day for 10–14 days.

To obtain a good result, the water in the fruit must diffuse out slowly to be replaced by syrup. This is achieved by cooking the fruit gently in water, then steeping it in progressively sweeter syrup until it is preserved, plump, and tender. Any attempt to increase the strength of the syrup too quickly will result in tough, hardened, and shrivelled fruit. Sugar alone can be used for syrup making but the fruit's texture is better if part of the sugar is replaced by glucose. Powdered glucose weighs the same as sugar, but if using liquid glucose, increase the weight by one-fifth.

Well-flavoured fruits, fresh or canned, are used, eg apricots, pineapple or large, juicy plums. Very soft fruits, such as raspberries, tend to disintegrate. Fresh fruit should be firm yet ripe. Good quality canned fruit can be used; it lacks some of the full fresh flavour, but the canning process gives a good texture for candying.

The method is given in detail below. Once the details are understood, it should be enough to refer to the charts on p517.

To Candy Fresh Fruit

Note For angelica, orange, grapefruit, and lemon peel, see the special recipes on p516.

Day 1:

Peaches: Peel and stone.

Pears: Peel, core, and cut into quarters.

Cherries: Stone.

Pineapples: Peel and slice, then cut into wedge-shaped pieces.

Small crab-apples, apricots, fleshy plums, greengages: Prick several times to the centre with a stainless fork.

Cover the prepared fruit with boiling water and simmer gently until just tender when tested with a fine skewer, 10–15 minutes for firm fruits, only 3–4 minutes for tender fruit. Test often because overcooking at this stage makes the fruit squashy, while undercoooking makes it dark and tough.

For each 500g of fruit, make a syrup from 250ml of the water in which the fruit was cooked, plus 50g sugar and 125g glucose. Alternatively, use 250ml of the water and 150g granulated or preserving sugar. Stir until the sugar is dissolved, then bring to the boil.

Drain the fruit and place it in a small bowl, then pour the boiling syrup over it. If there is not enough syrup to cover it, make up some more, using the same proportions. Leave the fruit in the syrup for 24 hours, keeping it below the surface under a plate or saucer.

Day 2: Drain off the syrup into a saucepan, add 50g sugar for each original 250ml (ie add 100g if you originally made up 500ml syrup), bring to the boil and pour the syrup over the fruit in the bowl.

Day 3: Repeat Day 2.

Day 4: Repeat Day 2.

Day 5: Repeat Day 2.

Day 6: Repeat Day 2.

Day 7: Repeat Day 2.

Day 8: Add 75g sugar for every original 250ml syrup, heat and stir until dissolved. Add the drained fruit and boil for 3–4 minutes, then pour it all back into the bowl. (Boiling the fruit in the syrup in these final stages helps to make it plump.) Leave for 48 hours.

Day 10: Repeat Day 8. When the resulting syrup cools, it should then be of the consistency of fairly thick honey. Leave for 4 days. If the syrup is still thin when it cools on Day 10, repeat Day 8 again before leaving to soak for the 4 days.

Day 14: The process is now nearly complete. The fruit may be left at this stage, if liked, as it will keep in this heavy syrup for 2–3 weeks, or for 2 months in a covered jar in the refrigerator. To complete the process, remove the fruit from the syrup, using a fork to lift out. *Do not pierce the fruit.* Place it on a wire cake rack with a plate beneath to catch the drips. Allow the syrup to drain for a few minutes.

Put the rack into a very cool oven (not higher than 50°C). With an electric cooker, use residual heat after cooking. With gas, turn to the lowest glimmer. On some cookers there is a very cool control which can be used. Take care that the rack does not touch the walls of the oven. Candied fruit caramelizes easily and the flavour is then spoilt. Drying should take 3–6 hours if the heat is continuous; it may take 2–3 days if residual heat on several occasions is used. Turn the fruit gently with a fork, until it is no longer sticky to handle. In summer, the fruit can be dried by putting it in the sunshine for a few hours, turning it over at least once.

Pack in cardboard boxes lined with waxed paper separating the layers. Store in a dry, cool place. Do not keep long as the succulence will be lost.

Candied fruit should have a dry surface. If it remains sticky, the final sugar concentration in the fruit is probably too low. Avoid humid storage conditions.

Note Only 1 variety of fruit should be candied in the syrup; if you are candying several fruits at the same time, use separate syrups. Do not waste any surplus syrup; use it for fruit salads or stewed fruit, or for sweetening puddings. Alternatively, use it instead of sugar in fruit chutneys.

To Candy Canned Fruit

Pineapple rings or cubes, plums, peaches sliced or halved, and halved apricots are all recommended. Keep the sizes as uniform as possible. The quantities below are for about 500g drained fruit.

Day 1: Drain off the syrup and put the fruit into a large bowl. Measure the syrup into a pan and make it up to 250ml by adding water if necessary. Add 200g sugar or, better, 100g sugar and 100g glucose. Heat gently and stir until the sugar has dissolved, bring to boiling point, and pour the syrup over the fruit. If there is not enough syrup to cover the fruit, prepare some more by using 225g sugar to 200ml water. The quantity of syrup increases as the process continues, so avoid making extra if possible. Keep the fruit under the syrup with a plate. Leave for 24 hours.

Day 2: Drain the fruit, dissolve 50g sugar in the syrup, bring to the boil and pour over the fruit. Leave for 24 hours.

Day 3: Repeat Day 2.

Day 4: Repeat Day 2.

Day 5: Pour the syrup into a saucepan, add 75g sugar, warm the syrup to dissolve the sugar, and then add the fruit; bring to the boil and boil for 3–4 minutes. Return the fruit and syrup to the bowl. Leave for 48 hours.

Day 7: Repeat Day 5 and let the fruit boil until a little syrup cooled on a plate has the consistency of thick honey. Leave to soak for 3 or 4 days. If the syrup seems thin, add a further 75g sugar, dissolve it and boil the syrup with the fruit for a further few minutes. Leave to soak for 3 or 4 days. These final boilings help to make the fruit plump.

Day 11: Finish the fruit as when candying fresh fruit (Day 14).

Crystallizing Candied Fruit

The simplest method is to have ready some fine granulated sugar on a sheet of polythene, greaseproof paper or foil. Lift a piece of fruit on a fork, dip it quickly into *boiling* water, allow a moment to drain, and then roll it in the sugar until it is evenly, but not too thickly coated. Pack as for candied fruit.

Making a Glacé Finish

This is used for cherries and some other fruits and gives a smooth, shiny finish.

Dissolve, over gentle heat, 500g granulated sugar in 150ml water, then bring to the boil. Dip each fruit into boiling water for 20 seconds, then drain. Pour a little of the boiling syrup into a warm cup, quickly dip the fruit and place it on a rack. When all the fruit has been dipped, place the rack in a temperature not exceeding 50°C, and turn the fruit often to ensure even drying. Pack as for candied fruit.

The main difficulty in preparing glacé fruits is to prevent the syrup from crystallizing or becoming too diluted. When the syrup in the small cup becomes cloudy, it must be discarded and replaced from the saucepan, which must be kept hot (but not boiling) and closely covered while processing.

Note For those specializing in candying or glacé finishes, it is worthwhile buying a suitable hydrometer to ensure the correct density of syrup.

Candied Angelica

Pick the stalks in April, when they are tender and brightly coloured. Cut off the root ends and leaves. Make a brine with 15g salt in 2 litres water, bring it to the boil and cover the stalks with it. Leave to soak for 10 minutes. Rinse in cold water. Put in a pan of fresh boiling water and boil for 5–7 minutes. Drain. Scrape to remove the outer skin. Continue as for candying fresh fruit, pp514–15, beginning with the instructions for making the syrup, Day 1.

Note Add edible green colouring to the syrup if the stalks lose colour.

Candied Peel

Use oranges, lemons or grapefruit, and wash the fruit thoroughly, scrubbing with a clean brush if necessary. Cut in halves, remove the pulp carefully to avoid damaging the peel. Boil the peel for 1 hour. Give grapefruit peel, which is bitter, several changes of water. Drain, and continue as for candying fresh fruit pp514–15, beginning with the instructions for making the syrup, Day 1. It is customary to pour some glacé syrup into half peels to set.

Candied Peel (quick method)

Use oranges, grapefruit or lemons, but soak peel from grapefruit or lemons overnight to extract some of the bitterness. Cut the peel into long strips 5mm wide. Put in a saucepan, cover with cold water and bring slowly to the boil. Drain, add fresh water and bring to the boil again. Drain, and repeat 3 more times. Weigh the cooled peel and place with an equal quantity of sugar in a pan. Just cover with boiling water, and boil gently until the peel is tender and clear. Cool, strain from the syrup, and toss the peel in fine granulated sugar on greaseproof paper. Spread out on a wire rack to dry for several hours. Roll again in sugar if at all sticky. When quite dry, store in covered jars. Use within 3–4 months.

Candied Fresh Fruit Chart

Day	Amount of sweetening per 250ml	Method	Leave soaking for
1	50 sugar + 100g glucose *or* 150g sugar	Dissolve sugar. Bring syrup to boiling point. Pour over the drained cooked fruit.	24 hours
2	50g sugar	,,　　　　,,　　　　,,	24 hours
3	50g sugar	,,　　　　,,　　　　,,	24 hours
4	50g sugar	,,　　　　,,　　　　,,	24 hours
5	50g sugar	,,　　　　,,　　　　,,	24 hours
6	50g sugar	,,　　　　,,　　　　,,	24 hours
7	50g sugar	,,　　　　,,　　　　,,	24 hours
8	75g sugar	Dissolve sugar, add fruit, boil in the syrup for 3–4 minutes. Then return all to the bowl.	48 hours
10	75g sugar	As above. Repeat, if necessary, so that the syrup, when cold, is the consistency of a fairly thick honey.	4 days
14	nil	Dry in a very cool oven, not exceeding 50°C, or in the sunshine.	

Candied Canned Fruit Chart

Day	Amount of sweetening per 250ml	Method	Leave soaking for
1	100g sugar + 100g glucose *or* 200g sugar	Dissolve sugar. Bring syrup to boiling point and pour over.	24 hours
2	50g	,,　　　　,,　　　　,,	24 hours
3	50g	,,　　　　,,　　　　,,	24 hours
4	50g	,,　　　　,,　　　　,,	24 hours
5	75g	Dissolve sugar, add fruit, boil in the syrup for 3–4 minutes. Return to bowl.	48 hours
7	75g	As above, and boil until cooled syrup has thick honey consistency.	4 days
11	nil	If syrup thin, repeat Day 7. Otherwise, dry fruit in very cool oven, not exceeding 50°C, or in the sunshine.	

BOTTLED PRESERVES

FRUIT BOTTLING

Types of Bottling Jars

To ensure a seal, a jar must have (1) a gasket, such as a rubber or plastic band or washer, which may be built into the lid or separate, and (2) a sealing device such as a screwband or bail-type clip (on continental jars).

Purpose-made bottling jars with glass lids and separate screwbands are recommended, especially for light-coloured, less acid fruits, but more homely substitutes can be used. The twist-top type of jam jar lid makes a suitable seal if in good condition. This type of lid has an in-built gasket and four lugs which engage in the ridges at the neck of the jar. Twist-top lids can be bought separately to convert the older type of jam jar and some instant coffee jars.

Synthetic skin is sold at some chemists, hardware and stationery stores, and this can be used for sealing jars for which no lids are available. Paraffin wax is also sold by chemists and makes a satisfactory seal for jars sealed after processing; it can either be melted and poured direct on the bottled fruit or brushed on a clean piece of linen tied over the jar. It is easy and cheap to use.

To Prepare the Jars

It is important to test that the jars are sound and are not chipped at the neck or on the lid as this can affect the seal. Rubber bands must still be elastic and soaked in warm water before use. They are comparatively cheap and should only be used once. Metal lids should also be discarded after use, and should certainly never be re-used if scratched or bent.

Corks for syrup, squash, and other bottled liquids should be new if possible. All corks should be boiled for 15 minutes before use.

Jars must be thoroughly clean. Wash them, then rinse in clean water and turn them upside down until required. The fruit will pack more easily if there is a film of water in the jar.

Preparing the Liquid

Any fruit can be bottled in water alone, but the addition of sugar improves the flavour and colour. If sugar must be avoided, bottle the fruit in water and add any permitted sweetening just before use. Many people like to use honey or brown sugar instead of granulated sugar; when first trying this, substitute only half the quantity to test the result, since both honey and brown sugar add their own flavour to that of the fruit.

There is no rule about the quantity of sugar to use when making syrup for fruit bottling, but heavy syrups tend to make the fruit rise in the bottle. This does not matter for everyday use, but will lose points for exhibitors at shows.

Making Syrup

	sugar per litre of water	suitable for
light syrup	200g	apple slices
medium syrup	400–600g	all fruit
heavy syrup	800g	peaches

Heat the water in a saucepan which is light-coloured inside. Stir in the sugar and allow it to boil for 2 minutes only. Place a lid on the pan and remove from the heat. If the syrup is left on the boil longer it evaporates quickly, darkens, and is extravagant to use. A well-made syrup looks bright.

If cold syrup is required quickly, make it up with half the required quantity of water and add the rest cold.

Brine

Brine is used for some tomato preserves. It is very simply prepared by adding 15g salt to 1 litre of water and boiling for 1 minute.

Choice and Packing of Fruit

Select fruit which is fresh, free from blemishes, and just ripe (except for gooseberries, which should be firm and green). Dirty fruit must be washed but good quality fruit is usually clean. Prepare the fruit as described below, grade it by size, and pack it evenly and firmly in the preserving jars.

Solid packs save storage space. To pack the fruit closely but without squashing it, push it into place with a 15cm long stick about 1cm square with a pointed end, or with the handle of a wooden spoon.

Preparing the Fruit

Apples: Peel, core, and cut into slices or rings 5mm thick. To prevent discoloration drop them into brine and keep them under the surface with a plate until ready to use. Drain, rinse, and pack immediately.

Apples – solid pack: After draining from brine, dip the fruit in boiling water for 2 minutes. This shrinks the fruit so that the jar can be tightly filled, with no airspaces and little or no added liquid.

Apricots: Choose fully ripe fruit, not too soft. Remove stalks, and rinse. Pack whole, or halve by slitting and twisting the fruit; remove stones and pack halves quickly to prevent them browning. Crack some of the stones and add a few kernels to each jar.

Blackberries: Choose large, juicy, fully ripe berries. Remove stalks and leaves and discard any unsound fruit.

Cherries: Use Morello cherries for choice. Any cherries used should have small stones and plump flesh. Remove stalks, and rinse. They can be stoned, but take care not to lose the juice.

Currants (black, red, white): Choose large, firm, juicy, and well-flavoured currants. They should be evenly ripened and unbroken. Remove stalks; rinse if necessary. Red and white currants have large seeds and are best mixed with raspberries.

Damsons: Choose ripe, firm, purple fruit. Remove stalks, and wipe to remove bloom.

Gooseberries: Choose green, hard, and unripe berries. Top and tail and, if preserving in syrup, cut off a *small* slice at either end with a stainless steel knife to prevent the skins shrivelling and toughening.

Greengages: Choose firm, ripe fruit. Remove stalks and wipe to remove bloom. After processing, the fruit will turn greenish-brown and the syrup may become cloudy.

Loganberries: Choose firm, deep red fruit. Handle as little as possible. Remove stalks and leaves, and discard any fruit attacked by maggots.

Mulberries: Choose ripe and really freshly picked fruit. Handle as little as possible. Remove over-ripe and mis-shapen fruit.

Peaches: Choose a free-stone variety (eg Hale) just fully ripe. Dip in a pan of boiling water for 1 minute, then put into cold water; the skin should peel off easily. Halve and stone by slitting and twisting the fruit. Pack quickly.

Pears – dessert: Choose one of the best varieties, eg William's, Bon Chrétien, Conference, Doyenne du Comice, just fully ripe. Peel, halve, and scoop out cores and fibres with a sharp-pointed teaspoon. Place in an acid brine (1 litre water, 1×15ml spoon salt, and 1×5ml spoon citric acid), and keep below the surface with a plate. Rinse when ready for packing. Pack quickly.

Pears – cooking: Prepare as for dessert pears; then stew until tender in sugar syrup (400–600g sugar to 1 litre water). Drain, pack, and cover with the syrup in which they were cooked. Process as for dessert pears. Cooking pears will be darker in colour than dessert fruit.

Pineapples: Remove both ends, the peel, eyes, and centre core. Cut the fruit into rings or cubes. Process in heavy syrup.

Plums: If using Victoria plums, choose them when they are fully grown but firm and just turning pink. Choose purple varieties before the colour has developed, when they are still bright red. Choose yellow varieties when they are firm and lemon-yellow. Remove stalks, and wipe to remove the bloom. Free-stone varieties can be halved; others must be packed whole.

Raspberries: Choose large, firm, bright red, and fully flavoured berries. Pick carefully, putting the fruit gently in shallow baskets to prevent squashing. Remove plugs and damaged fruit. Preserve as soon as possible – it is not usually necessary to rinse the fruit first.

Rhubarb: Bottle rhubarb in the spring when it is tender and needs no peeling. Wipe the stalks and cut into short lengths. Pack immediately (in water or syrup) or after soaking. To soak, pour a hot syrup (400g sugar to 1 litre water) over the prepared rhubarb. Leave to soak and shrink for 8–12 hours; then pack, and cover with syrup.

To avoid a white deposit (unsightly but harmless) use previously boiled or softened water.

Strawberries: Hull the berries and if necessary rinse in cold water. The strawberries should be preshrunk, like rhubarb.

Tomatoes – in their own juice: Dip into boiling water for up to 30 seconds (according to ripeness), then into cold water; the skins should peel off easily. Leave them whole, or pack in halves or quarters if large. Press tightly into the jars, sprinkling the layers with sugar and salt (use 1 × 5ml spoon sugar, 1 × 10ml spoon salt, and a pinch of citric acid to each 1kg of tomatoes). No additional liquid is required.

Tomatoes – whole, unskinned: These are best oven-bottled (see page 523). Remove stalks, rinse tomatoes, and pack into jars. Use a brine (1 × 15ml spoon salt to 1 litre water and a pinch of citric acid) instead of water or syrup.

See p525 for recipes for Tomato Purée and Tomato Juice.

Whortleberries: Prepare as for blackcurrants.

Solid pack: For small soft fruit, such as elderberries, blackberries, raspberries, strawberries, and mulberries: roll the fruit in caster sugar, then pack into the jars tightly, without any added liquid. This gives an excellent flavour although the fruit will have shrunk.

Methods of Bottling

If bottling mixed fruits, the timing and temperature must be based on the fruit which needs the highest temperature.

Quick Deep Pan Method

1) Have ready a pan deep enough to submerge the bottles. It must have a false bottom, or wooden slats; alternatively, layers of newspaper will do. Half fill it with water and heat it to 40°C.
2) Pack the prepared fruit tightly into tested jars. Put rubber rings, if used, to soak in warm water.
3) Fill jars to overflowing with *hot* (about 60°C) syrup or water. For tomatoes use hot brine.
4) Dip the rubber rings in boiling water and put them on the jars, with the lids. Fasten with screwbands, clips or other grips.
5) If using screwbands, tighten them, *then unscrew one-quarter turn to allow for expansion.* Clips are self-adjusting.
6) Stand jars in the pan on the false bottom. See that they do not touch each other or the side of the pan. They should be completely covered with the warm water. Put the lid on the pan.
7) Bring up to *simmering point* (90°C) in 25–30 minutes. Simmer for the time indicated on p522, then remove the jars one at a time on to a wooden surface.

Wooden slats are a useful way of providing a false bottom when bottling fruit

Use tongs to lift out the jars or, using a cup, empty out sufficient water to enable the jars to be lifted with a cloth.

8) Tighten screwbands. Clips should hold properly without attention. Leave for 24 hours.

9) Next day, remove screwbands or clips. Hold each jar in turn over a basin, and lift it by its lid. If properly sealed, the lid will stay on securely. Label with the date and other details, and store in a cool, dark, dry place. Wash, dry, and grease the screwbands or clips and keep to use again.

If one jar has not sealed, put it in the refrigerator and use the contents within 4–5 days. If a number of jars are unsealed, they must be reprocessed. Check the neck of each jar for chips, use new rubber bands and screwbands, and repeat the whole process.

Processing Times for Quick Deep Pan Method

The following times are for jars up to 1 litre maximum capacity.

Simmer for –

2 minutes: apple rings, blackberries, currants (black, red, white), gooseberries (for pies), loganberries, mulberries, raspberries, rhubarb (for pies), strawberries, whortleberries

10 minutes: apricots, cherries, damsons, gooseberries (for dessert), greengages, plums (whole), rhubarb (for dessert), solid pack of soft fruit (except strawberries)

20 minutes: apples (solid pack), nectarines, peaches, pineapples, plums (halved), solid pack of strawberries

40 minutes: pears, tomatoes (whole)

50 minutes: tomatoes (in own juice).

Slow Deep Pan Method

This is the same as the quick deep pan method, except that:

At step 1), do not heat the water in the pan.

At step 3), fill the jars with *cold* syrup, water or brine.

At step 7), raise the water gradually (ie in 90 minutes) to the temperature indicated below, and maintain it at that temperature for the time stated below.

Processing Times for Slow Deep Pan Method

Raise to 74°C and maintain at that temperature for 10 minutes: apple rings, blackberries, currants (black, red, white), gooseberries (for pies), loganberries, mulberries, raspberries, rhubarb (for pies), strawberries, whortleberries

Raise to 82°C and maintain at that temperature for 15 minutes: apples (solid pack), apricots, cherries, damsons, gooseberries (for dessert), greengages, nectarines, peaches, pineapples, plums (whole or halved), rhubarb (for dessert), solid pack of soft fruit

Raise to 90°C and maintain at that temperature for 30 minutes: pears, tomatoes (whole)

Raise to 90°C and maintain at that temperature for 40 minutes: tomatoes (in own juice).

Oven Method

In the traditional oven method, the fruit is packed into the jars, processed in the oven, then removed and boiling liquid added. However, the dry heat of the oven makes the fruit shrink.

The newer moderate oven method given below is more successful.

1) Fill the warmed jars tightly with the prepared fruit.
2) Fill to within 2cm of the top with boiling syrup or water.
3) Put on the rubber rings and lids (both first dipped in boiling water). Clips and screwbands should not be put on until after processing.
4) Line a baking tray with 3 or 4 layers of newspaper to catch any liquid that boils over during heating. Stand the jars, 5cm apart, on the paper.
5) Heat the oven for 15 minutes to cool, 150°C, Gas 2. Put the jars in the centre of the oven, then process for the times given below. To ensure that the jars are in the centre of the oven, the rack on which they stand should be about one-third of the way up.
6) Remove the jars to a wooden surface. Immediately check that the necks of the jars are free from boiled-out fruit, then fasten clips and screwbands. Leave for 24 hours. Next day, test for fit (see step 9, Quick Deep Pan Method p522), label, and store.

Processing Times Using a Moderate Oven

Note 4 × 350ml jars require the same processing time as 2 × 700ml jars.

30–40 minutes (up to 2kg) or 50–60 minutes (2–4.5kg): apple rings, blackberries, currants (black, red, white), gooseberries (for pies), loganberries, mulberries, raspberries, rhubarb (for pies), whortleberries

40–50 minutes (up to 2kg) or 55–70 minutes (2–4.5kg): apricots, cherries, damsons, gooseberries (for dessert), greengages, plums (whole), rhubarb (for dessert)

50–60 minutes (up to 2kg) or 65–80 minutes (2–4.5kg): apples (solid pack), nectarines, peaches, pineapples, plums (halved)

60–70 minutes (up to 2kg) or 75–90 minutes (2–4.5kg): pears, tomatoes (whole)

70–80 minutes (up to 2kg) or 85–100 minutes (2–4.5kg): tomatoes (in own juice).

Note Campden tablets, obtainable from home winemaking shops, can be used for bottling fruit. They are useful when quick processing is necessary, eg for a glut crop, or when heating facilities are limited. Use as when processing fruit syrups (p526). Ensure that any metal lids and screw caps are protected from the preservative fumes by a layer of wax or oil between the fruit and cover.

Bottling Fruit Pulp

This is an economical process, as the sound parts of damaged fruits can be used, and fewer bottling jars are required for pulp than for the same weight of bottled whole fruit. Any fruit can be pulped but apples, particularly windfalls, are the most useful and popular. Prepare the fruit as for cooking, removing any stalks or leaves and discarding blemished or damaged parts. As soon as the apples are prepared, immerse them in salted water (1 × 15ml spoon salt to 1 litre water) to prevent browning. Large plums should be stoned, but it is easy to sieve out the stones of small plums or damsons after cooking. Put into an aluminium, stainless steel or unchipped enamel saucepan with just enough water to prevent burning. Sugar, if required, should be added to taste at this stage. Heat very gently until the fruit begins to soften; increase the heat slightly, and cook until the fruit is of an even, firm, pulped consistency. Have ready a supply of dry, clean, and warm bottling jars and seals on a dry wooden board or on layers of newspaper. Quickly pour the boiling pulp into the jars; then seal them, but not too tightly. Place the filled jars on a false bottom in a pan of water at 90°C (fast simmer). The water must cover the jars. Heat the water to boiling point (100°C) and maintain for 5 minutes. Remove the jars to a dry wooden board or sheets of newspaper, and secure the seals. The following day test the seal, and clean, label, and store the jars as described on p522.

If fruit is pulped without sweetening and its weight is recorded on the label, it can be converted into jam by heating (with acid if necessary) in a saucepan of suitable size, adding the appropriate amount of sugar, as for making jam.

Tomato Pulp

Choose well-coloured tomatoes; the size and shape are immaterial. It is usual to remove the skins of tomatoes (p521) before pulping. Cut up the fruit roughly, removing hard cores for really smooth pulp. To each 2kg of prepared tomatoes add 1 × 5ml spoon sugar, 1 × 10ml spoon salt, and $\frac{1}{4}$ × 2.5ml spoon citric acid. Only a very small quantity of water, if any, is needed. Proceed as for fruit pulp but boil the filled bottles for 10 minutes.

When processing tomatoes it is important to carry through the whole job without delay, to achieve a good consistency.

Bottling Fruit Purée

Whereas pulp contains fruit skins and seeds, a purée is completely smooth; it is in fact a sieved pulp.

Prepare the fruit by removing leaves, stalks, and blemished parts, but do not bother to peel it or remove stones. However, for a good white apple purée, peel and core the apples, and add a little lemon juice to brighten the colour and enhance the flavour.

Cook the fruit gently with just enough water to prevent burning. When thoroughly softened, press the pulp through a stainless sieve, stir in sugar to taste if liked, re-heat in a clean saucepan, then bottle and finish as for fruit pulp (p524).

Bottled Tomato Purée

tomatoes

for each 2kg prepared tomatoes:

1 × 5ml spoon sugar
1 × 10ml spoon salt

$\frac{1}{4}$ × 2.5ml spoon citric acid **or**
4 × 15ml spoons vinegar

Choose well-coloured fruit, cut it up roughly and put in a saucepan with the sugar, salt, and citric acid or vinegar. Add a few spoons of water to prevent the tomatoes burning until the juice begins to run. Heat gently and cook until the fruit is well pulped; press the pulp through a stainless sieve, re-heat in a clean saucepan, then bottle and finish as for Tomato Pulp (p524).

Bottled Tomato Juice

tomatoes

for each litre of prepared juice:
250ml water
25g granulated sugar

1 × 5ml spoon salt
a pinch of pepper

Choose firm, ripe, red tomatoes, cut them roughly into quarters and heat them in a covered saucepan until they are soft. Rub through a stainless sieve and measure the juice. Add the water, sugar, salt and pepper in the proportions given above. Stir to mix, re-heat, and bottle, leaving 1cm headspace under the screw cap. Process and finish as for Tomato Pulp (p524).

FRUIT SYRUPS

Modern Method for Making Fruit Syrups

The aim is to extract the fruit juice with as little loss of its fresh fruit flavour as possible, then to sweeten and preserve it. Soft fruits are most often used and blackcurrant syrup, correctly made, has a high vitamin C content.

Fruit syrups can be stored in any bottles which have screw-on caps or tight corks; these should be painted with paraffin wax to seal the join. Either kind should be boiled for 15 minutes before use.

Extracting the Juice

Cold Method
The best method is to place the fruit in a china or earthenware bowl, crush it with a wooden spoon, and leave it, covered with a plate, for 4–8 days, repeating the crushing daily. During this period the natural pectin loses its quality and the juice is released. The process can be hastened by using a pectin-decomposing enzyme; this is particularly useful for firmer fruits such as blackcurrants. The enzyme can be bought in small quantities from any shop which sells home winemaking equipment.

If the fruit is very ripe there is a chance that mould may develop; in this case use the following method:

Hot Method
Place the fruit in a bowl over gently boiling water. Crush the fruit and add 600ml water per kg for blackcurrants and 100ml water per kg for blackberries. Other soft fruits do not need any water. Heat the fruit until the juice flows freely, which will take about 1 hour for 3kg of fruit. Take care not to let the saucepan boil dry.

Straining the Juice

With either method, the fruit has to be strained. For a very clear syrup, a scalded felt or flannel bag or cloth should be used and the juice allowed to drip through. Where clarity is less important, scalded muslin or a fine nylon strainer can be used.

Processing Syrup

Cold Method Using Campden Tablets
Measure the juice and steadily stir in 800g sugar per litre, until dissolved. Re-measure the syrup. For strawberry juice, add 10g citric acid per litre. It is not necessary to acidify other fruit juices. For each litre of syrup, crush and dissolve 2 Campden tablets in 2×15ml spoons warm water and stir into the syrup with a wooden or plastic spoon. Bottle at once leaving 1cm headspace under the screw caps, which should be tightened. Label and store.
Note The sulphur in the tablets will bleach the syrup, but most of the colour will return when the syrup is exposed to air. If you wish, add a few drops of food colouring.

Cold Method Using Extra Sugar

One continental method of making syrup is to add 1.6kg sugar to each litre of juice, and to stir until dissolved. Some heating is almost essential to dissolve the sugar, but the syrup can then be bottled and will keep without further processing. It is, however, excessively sweet.

Hot Method – Recommended for Home Use

Measure the juice and stir in 600g granulated sugar per litre; use a little heat if necessary to make sure the sugar is dissolved. This quantity of sugar reinforces the fruit flavours so that the syrup can be considerably diluted for use. If less sugar is used the syrup will be less economical in use. Pour the syrup into bottles, leaving 2cm headspace under the screw caps, which should be slightly loosened. Stand the bottles on a false bottom or on layers of newspapers in a deep pan of water. The water should come to the top of the bottles and it will be necessary to wedge them upright with cardboard. Heat the water to 76°C, and maintain for 30 minutes; or heat to simmering point (88°C), and maintain for 20 minutes.

Remove the bottles from the water, then leave to cool. Polish the bottles, label, and store in a dry, preferably cool and dark place.

Uses for Fruit Syrups

Syrups can be diluted with about 4 parts of water, soda water, or other aerated beverage for plain cold drinks. For milk shakes, add the syrup to the milk slowly; stir or whisk briskly to prevent curdling.

Undiluted syrup is delicious on ice cream, natural yoghurt, puddings, batter puddings, and many other desserts. It can be used to make sweet jellies, sauces, and glazes for fruit flans, and is excellent in fruit salads and in sweet-sour savoury dishes.

Traditional Method of Making Fruit Syrups

In this method the fruit juice is boiled before bottling, and so the final product is somewhat different from that made by the more modern process, which strives to retain the fresh flavour of the fruit. For all the recipes which follow on pages 528–29, a little olive oil may be poured on the top of the syrup in the bottle as a seal. The oil must be carefully removed with a clean piece of cotton-wool before use. Alternatively, to ensure better keeping quality, all the recipes, except those containing brandy, could be heat-processed as above.

Note The leftover fruit pulp from the recipes which follow could be used to make fruit cheeses (pp512–13), although they will not have full food value or flavour.

Apricot Syrup

sound ripe apricots

olive oil (optional)

800g crushed lump sugar for each
   litre of juice

Stone and halve the apricots. Three-quarters fill a large jar, or jars, with apricots. Crack half the stones and add the kernels to the jar(s). Stand the jar(s) in a pan of boiling water and simmer until the fruit is quite soft and the juice flows freely. Strain off the liquid through a fine sieve or jelly bag. Measure it carefully and add sugar in the proportion given above. Boil again for 10 minutes, then skim, and pour the hot syrup into clean dry bottles. If screw caps are used, leave at least 2cm headspace; if corks are used, allow for a 2cm space below the cork. As soon as any bubbling ceases, seal securely as described in the general method (p526).
VARIATIONS
Substitute cherries, greengages, peaches, plums or rhubarb for apricots.

Blackberry or Blackcurrant Syrup

blackberries or blackcurrants

100ml brandy for each litre of syrup

1kg crushed or preserving sugar and
   1 × 15ml spoon water for each kg
   of fruit

Put the fruit, sugar, and water in a large jar with a close-fitting cover. Stand the jar in a saucepan of boiling water, and cook gently until the juice flows freely. Strain the juice, measure it, put it into a preserving pan or stewpan (preferably enamelled), and boil gently for 20 minutes. Skim, and when the syrup has cooled, add the brandy; then bottle, leaving a headspace, and seal securely as described in the general method (p526).

Cranberry Syrup

sound, ripe cranberries

800g crushed lump sugar for each
      litre of juice

Crush the fruit in a jar. Stand the jar in a pan of boiling water. Cook gently for 2 hours. Strain off the liquid through a fine sieve, measure carefully, and add sugar in the proportion given above. Bring to the boil again and cook for 15 minutes. Skim when boiling is finished. Leave until quite cold, then pour into bottles, leaving a headspace. Seal securely as described in the general method (p526).
VARIATIONS
Use gooseberries, raspberries or strawberries instead of cranberries.

Elderette

sound, ripe elderberries
800g crushed lump sugar, 7 cloves,
   and 1 × 2cm piece bruised
   cinnamon stick for each litre of
   liquid

100ml brandy for each litre of syrup

Crush the elderberries and strain the juice. Mix the juice with an equal quantity of cold water. Add the sugar, cloves, and cinnamon in the proportions given above and boil together for 10 minutes. Strain and measure the syrup. When cool, stir in the brandy. When quite cold, bottle and seal securely as described in the general method (p526).

Rose-hip Syrup

3 litres water
1kg ripe, wild rose-hips

650g preserving sugar

Boil 2 litres of the water. Mince the hips coarsely and put immediately into the boiling water. Bring the water back to the boil, then cool for about 15 minutes. Strain the pulp twice through fine linen or muslin to make sure that all the hairs are removed. Put the liquid obtained to one side. Boil the pulp again with the remaining water, cool for 15 minutes, and strain twice again. Return both extracted liquids to the pan, and boil until the juice is reduced to less than 2 litres. Add the sugar, stirring well. Pour into warmed bottles, leaving a headspace, and seal securely as described in the general method (p526). Store in a dark cupboard.

Vanilla Syrup

3 vanilla pods **or** 3 × 5ml spoons
   vanilla essence
800g crushed lump sugar

1 litre water
250ml brandy

Crush the vanilla pods, if used, and break them into small pieces. Put the pods or essence into an enamel pan with the sugar and water. Bring slowly to the boil. Simmer for 20 minutes, skimming from time to time as necessary. Leave to cool. When cold, strain, and add the brandy. Bottle, leaving a headspace, and seal securely as described in the general method (p526).

   Dilute with plain or aerated water when required for use, or use as a concentrated sweet flavouring in cocktails, ice creams, custards, etc.

PICKLES, CHUTNEYS, SAUCES AND KETCHUPS

All these preserves depend on vinegar for their keeping quality, although some pickles also need salting first. Both vinegar and salt flavour the food, but there is scope for varying the final taste.

General Method

1) Vegetables and fruit must be fresh and not over-ripe. Mis-shapen produce of good quality can be used for chutney or sauces.
2) For pickling, most vegetables are treated in salt water to reduce moisture content and to improve texture. They are soaked in brine or dry salt is scattered on them. It is important to allow a good proportion of vinegar when packing them; there should be a depth of 1.5cm above the pickle in the jar, to prevent evaporation.
3) For chutney, the main ingredients should be chopped or finely minced before gentle, thorough cooking with vinegar and spices. The cooking time depends on the quantity made and the toughness of the vegetables but, as a rule, a chutney using more than 1kg of the main ingredient should be cooked gently for at least 2 hours for a mellow flavour and a smooth consistency. Sugar is not added until the chutney has cooked down well if a light-coloured preserve is wanted; long cooking with sugar darkens the colour. The chutney is ready when no free liquid runs out of a teaspoonful cooled on a plate. Pour into clean jars, then seal or cover with vinegar-proof covers (see 6) below). When making an unfamiliar recipe, try it out by making a small quantity first, so that the spicing can be adjusted. Remember that freshly made chutney is more spicy than matured chutney.
4) For making sauce, the ingredients should be roughly cut up and cooked in the vinegar with the spices, until soft. They are then sieved and returned to the saucepan to cook with the sugar until they are of a creamy, pouring consistency. Pour into clean bottles and cover securely.
5) Use aluminium, unchipped enamel or stainless steel pans, stainless knives, and stainless or nylon sieves. A special wooden spoon should be kept for stirring vinegar preserves if possible. If not, the spoon must be very thoroughly cleaned and aired before it is returned to general use.
6) Vinegar preserves, especially chutneys, must have acid-proof covers which will prevent evaporation and wasteful drying out. Suitable covers are:
   a) the type of twist-top or screw-on plastic-coated lids used commercially
   b) press-on plastic covers
   c) synthetic skin
   d) a circle of clean card or paper, cut to fit the top of the jar, covered with a piece of linen dipped in melted paraffin wax and tied on
   e) a circle of clean greaseproof paper, cut to fit the surface of the chutney and covered with 2cm of melted paraffin wax. A jam cover should be tied over to keep the wax clean.

f) a boiled cork to fit the bottle and either waxed or covered with greaseproof paper tied securely over (for ketchups and sauces).

Note A chutney will shrink, evaporate, and lose quality quickly if a cellulose tissue jam cover is used.

Vinegar for Preserving

As vinegar is the main preservative, it is important to buy a good quality product containing at least 5% acetic acid. Malt vinegar has a flavour that blends well with pickles, but distilled or white vinegar is often preferred when colour is important, eg for ripe tomato chutney or sauce.

Wine vinegar is esteemed for its delicate flavour but as refinement is rarely a feature of pickles, it is wasteful to use it. Cider vinegar gives a good flavour to fruit chutneys and pickled fruits.

Spicing vinegar improves the flavour of pickles. Whole spices are used so that they can be strained out to leave a clear vinegar. If no special spicing is given in a recipe, a good result can be obtained by adding to 1 litre of vinegar, 5–10g of each of the following whole spices: cloves, allspice, cinnamon, white peppercorns, ginger. The smaller quantity will be enough for a mild pickle but for strongly flavoured ones such as onion, the full quantity may be used. Put the spices in a folded cloth and beat them lightly with a rolling-pin to release their flavour. Put the bruised spices into the vinegar and seal the bottle. It may be more convenient to add a double or treble quantity of spices and dilute later with more vinegar, but label the container accordingly if this is done. If time allows, leave the spices in the well-sealed bottle of vinegar for 2 months, shaking daily for the first month. Strain out the spices carefully and re-bottle the vinegar.

For quick use, put the spices and vinegar in a heatproof bowl and cover with a plate. Stand the bowl in a saucepan of cold water, bring the water gently to the boil and draw the pan off the heat. Leave for 2 hours, taking care not to move the plate or flavour will be lost. Strain the vinegar and, if not required immediately, return to the bottle and seal.

Mixed Pickle

mixed vegetables (see Method)   spiced vinegar
60g cooking salt for each kg of
   vegetables

Make a selection of available vegetables. Any of the following are suitable: small cucumbers, cauliflower, small onions, French beans. Prepare the vegetables; only the onions need be peeled, the rest should merely be cut into suitably sized pieces. Weigh the prepared vegetables.

Put all into a large bowl, sprinkle with the required amount of salt, and leave for 24 hours. Rinse, drain thoroughly, and pack into prepared jars. Cover with cold spiced vinegar, and seal with vinegar-proof covers. Leave for at least a month before using.

Piccalilli

1kg mixed vegetables (see Method)
60g cooking salt
700ml vinegar
12 chillies

225g granulated sugar
25g mustard powder
15g turmeric
2 × 15ml spoons cornflour

Cut a variety of vegetables such as cauliflower, cucumber, shallots, and young broad beans into small pieces. They should weigh about 1kg in all when prepared. Put in a large earthenware bowl and sprinkle with the cooking salt. Leave to stand for 24 hours, then rinse, and drain well.

Boil the vinegar and chillies for 2 minutes, leave to stand for 30 minutes, and then strain the vinegar. Mix together the sugar, mustard, turmeric, and cornflour. Blend with a little of the cooled vinegar. Bring the rest of the vinegar back to the boil, pour it over the blended mixture, return to the saucepan and boil for 3 minutes. Remove from the heat and fold in the drained vegetables. Pack into prepared jars and cover at once with vinegar-proof covers.

Pickled Apples and Onions

equal quantities of onions and sour
  apples
spiced vinegar (p531)

10g salt for each litre of spiced
  vinegar

Skin the onions and peel and core the apples. Slice them. Mix well together and pack into prepared jars. Measure out and heat as much vinegar as you think you will need to cover the pickles, taking into account the size of the jars and the closeness of the packing. Salt the vinegar. Cover the onions and apples with the hot vinegar. Put on vinegar-proof covers.

This pickle is ready to use as soon as it is cool.

Pickled Beetroot

beetroot
unspiced or spiced vinegar (p531)

25g salt for each litre of vinegar

Wash off any soil still clinging to the roots of the beetroot, taking care not to break the skin, since beetroot bleeds easily.

If pickling for immediate use, simmer for 1½–2 hours. When cold, skin and cut into cubes or slices, and cover with unspiced or spiced vinegar.

If pickling for storage, bake in a moderate oven, 180°C, Gas 4, until tender. Cool, then skin and cut into cubes; beetroot packs better that way for keeping. Measure out enough spiced vinegar to cover the beetroot, and add the salt. Bring to the boil. Pack the beetroot into prepared, wide-mouthed jars. Cover with the boiling vinegar. Put on vinegar-proof covers.

Beetroot contains a good deal of sugar, and fermentation is more likely than with other vegetables, so seal carefully to exclude all air.

Pickled Gherkins

small dill cucumbers
brine, using 225g salt to every 2 litres
   water

spiced vinegar (p531)

The small immature cucumbers that are known as dills or gherkins require longer processing than most vegetables, especially if their deep green colour is to be fixed; they also need partial cooking.

Select gherkins of the same size, put in a saucepan, and cover with the brine. Bring nearly to boiling point. Do not actually boil, but simmer for 10 minutes. Drain and leave until cold, then pack into prepared jars, and cover with spiced vinegar, preferably aromatic. Put on vinegar-proof covers.

VARIATION

Cocktail Gherkins

These are quite easy to prepare from the ordinary pickled vegetable. Simply add a spoonful of sugar to taste to the jar, shake it up, and then leave to stand for 24 hours. It is not advisable to do this too long in advance, as sugar added to a cold pickle in this way may easily start to ferment.

Alternatively, turn the gherkins out on to a shallow dish in which they will be served, and sprinkle with sugar. This can be done a few hours before use.

Pickled Cucumber

cucumbers
salt

spiced vinegar (p531)

The easiest way to pickle cucumbers is to quarter them lengthways, cut into smaller pieces, and brine with dry salt for 24 hours. Rinse, pack into prepared jars, and cover with cold spiced vinegar. Put on vinegar-proof covers. Like most vegetables, they are best mixed with others.

Pickled Lemons

lemons
salt
vinegar
whole peppercorns

ginger root
25–50g mustard seed for each jar
   used
2 cloves garlic for each 6 lemons used

Select small lemons with thick peel. Slit them lengthways in quarters, but do not cut right through. Rub dry salt sparingly into these cuts and leave the lemons for 5 days, or until all the salt has melted, turning them in the liquor which forms. Drain off this liquor and reserve it. Pack the lemons into prepared jars. Add enough vinegar to the liquor to cover the lemons completely. Boil the liquid with a few whole peppercorns and a small piece of ginger root. Skim well while boiling. Allow the mixture to cool and pour it over the fruit. Add the mustard seed to each jar. Cut up the garlic and divide between the jars. Put on vinegar-proof covers.

Note This pickle goes well with fish. It is also very hot, so a little goes a long way.

Pickled Onions

pickling onions
water to cover
1 × 5ml spoon salt (approx) for each
    500ml water

spiced vinegar (p531)

Use small even-sized pickling onions. Skin with a stainless knife and drop them into a basin of salted water until all are skinned. Remove from the water, and drain thoroughly before packing into prepared jars or bottles. Cover with cold spiced vinegar and put on vinegar-proof covers. Keep for at least a month before using.
VARIATION
Put the unskinned onions into a brine made from 225g salt to each 2 litres of water. Leave for 24 hours. Drain and skin the onions, and put them in fresh brine for a further 24 hours. Drain, rinse, and pack into jars as above.

Pickled Red Cabbage

1 medium-sized red cabbage
salt
onions

soft brown sugar (light or dark)
spiced vinegar (p531)

Choose a firm, fresh cabbage. Remove any discoloured outer leaves. Cut the cabbage into quarters and then into shreds. Put layers of the shreds into a large basin or dish, sprinkling each layer with salt. Leave overnight. Next day, drain very thoroughly in a colander, pressing out all the surplus liquid.

Pack a layer of cabbage, about 7cm, into large jars. Cover with a layer of very thinly sliced onion, and sprinkle with 1 × 5ml spoon brown sugar. Then add another 7cm of cabbage, another layer of onion, and another spoon of sugar. Continue until the jars are filled, ending with the onion and sugar. Cover with cold spiced vinegar, put on vinegar-proof covers and leave for at least 5 days to a week before opening.
Note Do not make too much at one time as the cabbage quickly loses its crispness.

Pickled Walnuts

soft green walnuts
brine, using 100g salt for each litre of
    water

spiced vinegar (p531)

Use walnuts whose shells have not begun to form. Prick well with a stainless fork; if the shell can be felt do not use the walnut. The shell begins to form opposite the stalk, about 5mm from the end.

Cover with the brine and leave to soak for about 6 days. Drain, make fresh brine, and leave to soak for a further 7 days. Drain, and spread on a single layer of clean newspaper leaving them exposed to the air, preferably in sunshine, until they blacken (1–2 days). Pack into prepared jars and cover with hot spiced vinegar. Put on vinegar-proof covers when cold. Leave for at least a month before using.
Note To prevent stained hands, always wear gloves when handling walnuts.

Apple Chutney
Yield 5kg (approx)

3kg apples
1kg sultanas
300–400g preserved ginger **or** 30g
   ground ginger

2 litres vinegar
1.5kg sugar
30g salt
1 × 5ml spoon ground allspice

Peel, core, and chop the apples into small pieces; chop up the sultanas and preserved ginger. Mix together the vinegar, sugar, salt and spice, and bring to the boil; then add the apples and simmer for 10 minutes before adding the ginger and sultanas. Simmer until fairly thick. Meanwhile, heat enough jars to hold the chutney. Stand them on a newspaper, to catch any drips. Pour in the chutney and cover as described on pp530–31. Cool, wipe the jars, label, and store.

Red Tomato Chutney
Yield 3kg (approx)

3kg ripe red tomatoes
500g white sugar
20g salt

a pinch of paprika
a pinch of Cayenne pepper
300ml spiced white vinegar (p531)

Blanch the tomatoes for 30 seconds in fast boiling water. Put into cold water, then skin. Cut up the tomatoes and remove the hard cores. Put into a saucepan with a very little water, bring gently to the boil, then reduce the heat and simmer until thick. Add all the other ingredients, stirring in well. Continue cooking until the whole mixture is thick. Put a spoonful on a cold plate to test its consistency. When ready, pour into hot jars or bottles, and cover at once as described on pp530–31. **Note** The final colour of this chutney depends largely on the redness of the tomatoes and the use of white sugar and vinegar. To give it a good texture, it should be processed without a pause once the tomatoes are blanched.

Green Tomato Chutney
Yield 3kg (approx)

450g cooking apples
450g onions
2kg green tomatoes
1 × 15ml spoon mustard seed
1 × 1cm piece ginger root (optional)

450g sultanas
15g salt
$\frac{1}{2}$ × 2.5ml spoon Cayenne pepper
700ml malt vinegar
450g Demerara sugar

Peel, core, and chop the apples. Skin and chop the onions. Cut up the tomatoes roughly. Tie the mustard seed and ginger root, if used, in a piece of muslin or thin cotton. Put these ingredients with the sultanas, salt, and Cayenne pepper into a large pan, and add just enough vinegar to cover. Bring to simmering point and simmer for 20 minutes. Meanwhile, dissolve the sugar by warming it in the remaining vinegar. Add the mixture to the pan, and boil steadily until the chutney is a good consistency. Pot and cover as described on pp530–31.

Banana Chutney
Yield 3kg (approx)

30 bananas
60g onions
25–50g fresh chillies
1.5 litres white vinegar

250g seedless raisins
50g salt
50g ground ginger
500g brown sugar

Slice the bananas and onions, and chop the chillies finely. Put all the ingredients into a saucepan and boil gently for 2 hours, stirring occasionally. When the chutney is of a good consistency, pot and cover as described on pp530–31.

Worcestershire Sauce
Yield 1.25 litres (approx)

4 shallots
1 litre good malt vinegar
6 × 15ml spoons walnut ketchup
  (p537)

75ml anchovy essence
4 × 15ml spoons soy sauce
1 × 2.5ml spoon Cayenne pepper
salt

Skin and chop the shallots very finely. Put with all the other ingredients into a large bottle, and cork it tightly. Shake well 3 or 4 times daily for about 14 days, then strain the sauce into small, prepared bottles, leaving a headspace. Cork tightly (pp530–31), label, and store in a cool, dry place.

Store Sauce
Yield 2 litres (approx)

1.5 kg tomatoes
100g onions
250g brown sugar
250g raisins
100g salt (approx)

25g ground ginger
½ × 2.5ml spoon Cayenne pepper
1 litre vinegar

Cut up the tomatoes, skin and slice the onions, and put all the ingredients into a saucepan. Simmer until soft. Rub through a nylon or stainless sieve, re-heat and continue cooking until the texture is as thick as required. Bottle, leaving a headspace, and seal at once (pp530–31). Label when cold.
Note Red tomatoes give a better colour to this brown sauce than green ones, but either can be used.

Tomato Ketchup
Yield 1.5 litres (approx)

3kg ripe tomatoes
2 × 15ml spoons salt
600ml white vinegar
250g white sugar

1 × 2.5ml spoon each of ground
  cloves, cinnamon, allspice, and
  Cayenne pepper

Quarter the tomatoes, place them in a preserving pan with the salt and vinegar, and simmer until they are soft and quite broken up. Rub the mixture through coarse muslin or a fine nylon sieve; then return it to the pan and add the sugar. Simmer until the ketchup starts to thicken, and then add the spices to taste, a little at a time, stirring thoroughly.

Meanwhile, heat enough bottles to hold the ketchup, and prepare seals (pp530–31). When the ketchup is thick enough, fill the hot bottles, leaving a headspace. Seal immediately, or allow the ketchup to cool slightly; then fill up the bottles, leaving a headspace, and sterilize at 88°C for 30 minutes. Seal immediately. Label when cold.

Note Remember that the ketchup will be thicker when cold, so do not reduce it too much.

Walnut Ketchup
Yield 1.5 litres (approx)

100 green walnuts (approx)
400g onions
2 litres vinegar
200g salt

25g whole peppercorns
15g whole allspice berries
1 × 2.5ml spoon whole cloves
1 × 2.5ml spoon ground nutmeg

Walnuts must be picked before the shell has hardened. The first week in July is usually the latest time to gather them for pickling.

Skin and chop the onions. Boil all the ingredients together, except the walnuts. Wearing gloves to prevent staining your hands, cut up the walnuts, crush them, and put into a large pan or basin. Pour the boiling vinegar over them, and leave for 14 days, stirring daily. Strain off the liquid and simmer it in a pan for about an hour. Pour it into prepared bottles, leaving a headspace, and seal at once (pp530–31). Label when cold. Discard the crushed walnuts.

Herb and Other Savoury Vinegars

The general method of making these is to boil the vinegar with perhaps a little salt and spice, and then to pour it hot over the freshly picked and prepared herb or vegetable, packed in a wide-necked bottle. The bottle is sealed with a vinegar-proof cork or cover, and is then shaken daily for about 10 days. It can then be left for another 10–14 days before the flavoured vinegar is gently poured off and re-bottled for use as required.

Fruit Vinegars

These traditional preserves are an excellent way of using up over-ripe soft fruit. Discard stalks and any leaves and put the fruit in a china or glass bowl. Crush with a wooden spoon or vegetable presser and pour the vinegar over it, allowing 500ml vinegar for each 400g of fruit. To obtain a clear, bright colour in fruit such as raspberries, use white vinegar; but malt vinegar is quite suitable for blackcurrants and blackberries.

Cover the bowl with a cloth and leave for 3–5 days, stirring once or twice daily. Strain off the liquid into a pan, using a scalded felt or flannel bag if you want a very clear vinegar; a nylon or stainless strainer will give a less clear vinegar.

Measure the liquid and return it to the pan. Add 800g sugar to each litre of liquid. Granulated sugar gives a better colour, but if you prefer the characteristic flavour of brown sugar, use that instead. Stir the vinegar over gentle heat until the sugar has dissolved, then boil it steadily for 10 minutes. Test a spoonful by pouring it on to a plate. Boil until the vinegar is syrupy. Bottle and seal at once.

If you wish you can use less sugar or none at all at the boiling stage, but it does enhance the fruit flavour and gives a more rounded taste than if sugar is only added just before use.

Raspberries are most often used, but loganberries, blackberries, blackcurrants, mulberries, and strawberries all make pleasant vinegars. These fruit vinegars formerly had their place in the medicine cupboard as gargles and cough cures, but nowadays they are more likely to be used in sweet-sour recipes, or as a sauce to add zest to a plain dessert. It is unusual to use firmer fruit to make vinegar, but the following recipe gives the method.

Stone Fruit Vinegar

fruit with stones (see Method)
1 litre white vinegar for every 3 litres of fruit

800g sugar for each litre of liquid
200ml brandy for each litre of syrup (optional)

Suitable fruits are apricots, cherries, damsons, greengages, peaches, and plums.

Choose good quality, well-ripened fruit, and measure its volume. Halve the fruit (but do not remove the stones) and put into a bowl. Add the vinegar. Cover the bowl with a clean cloth and leave to stand for 6 days, stirring and pressing down the fruit with a wooden spoon once a day. Finally press the fruit again and pour off the liquid through a fine sieve or jelly bag.

Measure the liquid into a pan and stir in the sugar. Boil steadily for 15 minutes or until the vinegar is syrupy when a small quantity is cooled on a plate. Skim, bottle, and seal at once. Label when cold.

If liked, leave the mixture in the pan until cold, then add the brandy. Stir, bottle, and seal securely.

TABLE COOKERY

Table-cooked dishes can be divided into two main categories; those cooked, usually at a side table, for the other diners as they wait, and those cooked in a pot, placed on the dining table, from which the guests are served or serve themselves. Most dishes cooked at the table are particularly suitable for a small, informal dinner party.

Never attempt to cook more than one dish per meal at the table; the process will seem laborious the second time; and since many table-cooked dishes are rich, one in the meal is usually enough.

SIDE TABLE COOKERY

Equipment

It is best to place all the necessary ingredients and equipment on a trolley or side table rather than on the dining table. The cook can then work unimpeded and there is less risk of fire or spillage. A portable electric hotplate can be used for the cooking, though a spirit lamp or butane-type gas burner fitted with a trivet allows the cook to regulate the heat most easily.

All the dishes in this section can be cooked in an ordinary heavy metal frying pan, though traditionally a special chafing-dish is used, which consists of two parts, with a lid. The top pan is called the 'blazer', and it can be used over direct heat for quick cooking and frying. It can also be placed on top of the lower pan, which is filled with simmering water, to make a kind of double saucepan in which food can be heated gently without boiling. For stir frying, a *wok* or similar round-bottomed pan can be used over a spirit lamp or burner with a trivet. An electric frying pan is also suitable for shallow frying and simmering. This is usually a fairly large pan, deeper than a normal frying pan, with an enclosed heating element in the bottom. It is thermostatically controlled, which makes the cooking easier.

Plates and dishes which will be served with the one cooked at the table, can be kept hot on a heated trolley or candle-warmed hotplate. Cooking utensils will be the same as those used in the kitchen. A small stainless steel jug or sauce-boat, or a large ladle is extremely useful for heating alcohol, or for holding small quantities of liqueurs or other ingredients.

Lobster Newburg
4 helpings

1 cooked lobster (1kg approx) **or** 2 small cooked lobsters (500g each approx)
50g butter
2 egg yolks

125ml single cream
salt and pepper
Cayenne pepper
125ml Madeira **or** sweet sherry

In the kitchen, split the lobster in half lengthways and remove the head cavity, gills, and intestinal tract. Crack the claws and remove the meat from the shell, keeping the pieces as large as possible. Separate any coral and beat it to a smooth paste with 25g of the butter. Beat the egg yolks lightly, add the cream, and season with salt, pepper, and Cayenne pepper.

At the table, melt the remaining butter in a frying pan or chafing-dish. Add the lobster pieces and heat gently, without browning, for 5 minutes. Pour in the Madeira or sherry and continue cooking for another 5 minutes or until the liquid is reduced by half. Reduce the heat and stir in the egg yolks and cream. Stir very gently and cook until the sauce thickens and coats the back of the spoon. Do not let the sauce boil or it will curdle. Stir in any coral butter.

Serve with boiled rice or hot buttered toast.

Cooking time at table 15 minutes (approx)
VARIATION
The lobster can be flamed with 2×15ml spoons brandy after it has been heated with the butter. Reduce the Madeira or sherry to 100ml.

Beef Stroganoff
4 helpings

250g onions
250g mushrooms
750g thinly sliced rump steak
3×15ml spoons flour

salt and pepper
50g butter
250ml soured cream

In the kitchen, prepare and slice the onions and mushrooms thinly. Wipe the steak and trim off any excess fat. Beat the slices with a cutlet bat or rolling-pin, trim, and cut into strips. Season the flour with salt and pepper and toss the meat in it.

At the table, melt 25g of the butter in a pan and fry the onions for about 5 minutes until golden. Add the mushrooms and continue cooking for a further 2–3 minutes. Remove the vegetables from the pan and add the rest of the butter. When the butter has melted, add the meat and fry rapidly for 2–3 minutes, turning frequently. Return the onions and mushrooms to the pan and re-heat for 1 minute. Pour in the soured cream, stir once or twice, and heat for about 1 minute, until warmed through. Do not let the sauce boil once the cream has been added or it will curdle.

Serve with boiled rice or potatoes, and green salad.

Cooking time at table 15 minutes (approx)

Stir-fried Chicken and Mushrooms
4 helpings

1 whole chicken breast
1 thin slice ginger root
½ green pepper
50g button mushrooms
a pinch of salt

3 × 15ml spoons cornflour
1 × 10ml spoon oil
2 × 15ml spoons chicken stock

In the kitchen, skin and bone the chicken breast and cut it into 1cm cubes. Mince the ginger. Remove the membranes and seeds from the pepper and cut into 4cm strips. Clean the mushrooms. Mix together the salt, pepper, and 2 × 15ml spoons of the cornflour. Toss the chicken in it until well coated. Carry the ingredients to the table.

At the table, heat the oil in a deep frying pan or *wok* until very hot. Add the ginger root and stir fry for 30 seconds. Add the chicken and stir fry until all traces of pink have disappeared. Remove the chicken from the pan, and keep hot. Add the mushrooms and green pepper and stir fry for 1½ minutes. Mix the remaining cornflour to a smooth paste with the chicken stock. Return the chicken to the pan, add the cornflour mixture, and stir until thickened.

Serve immediately, with rice or noodles.

Cooking time at table 7 minutes (approx)

Steak Diane
4 helpings

4 minute, fillet **or** rump steaks
    (150–200g each)
1 small onion (50g approx)
75g unsalted butter
grated rind and juice of 1 lemon

1 × 5ml spoon caster sugar
Worcestershire sauce
1 × 15ml spoon chopped parsley
2 × 15ml spoons brandy

In the kitchen, wipe the steaks and trim off any excess fat. Beat them flat with a cutlet bat or rolling-pin until they are no more than 6mm thick. Skin the onion and chop it finely. Take all the ingredients to the table.

At the table, melt 50g of the butter in a large, heavy-based frying pan and fry the onion for about 5 minutes until soft. Remove the onion from the pan and keep warm on a plate. Raise the heat under the pan. Using the remaining butter, fry 2 steaks at a time over high heat for 1 minute on each side. Remove from the pan and keep warm. Return the onions to the pan, and add the lemon rind and juice, the sugar, and a few drops of Worcestershire sauce. Stir in the parsley and cook lightly. Warm the brandy. Put the steaks into the pan and flame with the warmed brandy. Serve immediately, with the sauce spooned over them, and with chipped potatoes, grilled mushrooms and/or tomatoes.

Cooking time at table 15–18 minutes

Sautéed Kidneys (2)
4 helpings

12 lamb's kidneys	3 × 15ml spoons brandy
100g mushrooms	salt and pepper
75g onion	1 × 5ml spoon made English mustard
2 × 5ml spoons cornflour	150ml double cream
1 × 15ml spoon water	
25g butter	

In the kitchen, cut the kidneys in half, and remove the skin and cores. Clean and slice the mushrooms. Skin and chop the onion. Blend the cornflour and water. Take all the ingredients to the table.

At the table, melt the butter in a blazer or frying pan, and add the kidneys, mushrooms, and onion. Fry over high heat, stirring all the time for 2–3 minutes, until the kidneys are browned all over. Reduce the heat and cook for a further 3–4 minutes, until the kidneys no longer exude any blood. Care must be taken not to overcook the kidneys, or the flesh shrinks, becomes tough, and exudes a lot of juice. Warm the brandy, add to the pan and light it. When the flame burns out, add the blended cornflour and water, and the salt, pepper, and mustard. Bring to the boil, stirring all the time, and boil for 1 minute. Remove from the heat and stir in the cream. Serve immediately, with boiled rice.

Cooking time at table 10–12 minutes

Haddock and Fennel Flambé
4 helpings

1kg thin fillets of haddock **or** hake	fresh **or** dried fennel leaves
salt and pepper	4 × 15ml spoons brandy
200g butter	dried fennel stalks

Garnish
lemon wedges

In the kitchen, wash and dry the fish. Place it on the grid of the grill pan, skin side up. Grill under moderate heat for 5 minutes. Remove the skin carefully. Turn the fillet over, using a fish slice. Season with salt and pepper and dot with 2 × 15ml spoons of butter. Chop a few fennel leaves and sprinkle over the fish. Grill under moderate heat for a further 10 minutes. Melt the remaining butter, and keep it warm. Carry the ingredients to the table.

At the table, warm the brandy. Pile dried fennel stalks on a metal serving dish to a depth of 5cm. Place the cooked fish, still on the grid from the grill pan, over the fennel. Pour the warm brandy over the fish, then light the brandy and dried fennel, using a long match or taper. When the flame has burned out, garnish with lemon wedges and serve with the melted butter and boiled potatoes.

Cooking time at table 5 minutes (approx)

Bananas in Rum
4 helpings

4 large bananas
3 × 15ml spoons soft brown sugar
1 × 2.5ml spoon ground cinnamon

25g butter
3–4 × 15ml spoons rum

In the kitchen, cut the bananas in half lengthways, and put them flat on a plate. If this is done some time before the dish is cooked, sprinkle the bananas with a little lemon juice to prevent the fruit turning brown. Mix together the soft brown sugar and the cinnamon. Take all the ingredients to the table.

At the table, sprinkle the bananas with the sugar and cinnamon mixture. Melt the butter in a blazer or frying pan, and fry the bananas flat side down for 1–2 minutes until lightly browned underneath. Turn them over carefully, sprinkle with any remaining sugar and cinnamon, and continue frying. When the bananas are soft but not mushy, pour the rum over them. Tilt and baste, then light the rum; baste again. Scrape any caramelized sugar from the base of the pan and stir it into the rum. Shake the pan gently until the flames die down.

Arrange the bananas on warmed serving plates, pour the rum sauce over them and serve with double cream.

Cooking time at table 8–10 minutes

Cherries Jubilée
4 helpings

50g sugar
250ml water
500g dark red fresh cherries

2 × 5ml spoons arrowroot
4 × 15ml spoons Kirsch

In the kitchen, make a sugar syrup with the sugar and water. Stone the cherries. Poach them in the syrup until just tender, then drain and cool. Reserve the syrup. Blend the arrowroot with a very little of the syrup, then stir it into the remainder. Pour into a saucepan and bring to the boil, stirring all the time. Boil for 3–5 minutes until thickened and syrupy. Arrange the cherries in individual heatproof serving bowls and pour the thickened syrup over them. Take the bowls and the Kirsch to the table.

At the table, warm the Kirsch in a small jug or ladle. Pour 1 × 15ml spoon of it over each helping, light it, and serve while still alight if possible.

Cooking time at table 5 minutes (approx)
Note This famous dish was originally created for Queen Victoria's Diamond Jubilee.

Crêpes Suzette

4 helpings

12 small, thin pancakes, using 350ml
  cream pancake batter (p226)

Sauce

8 lumps sugar	2 × 15ml spoons strained orange juice
2 large coarse-skinned oranges	2 × 15ml spoons Cointreau
75g clarified butter (p563) for frying	2 × 15ml spoons brandy

In the kitchen, rub the lumps of sugar over the oranges until the sugar is soaked with the oil and coloured with the zest. Crush the lumps in a basin with the end of a rolling-pin, or process briefly in an electric blender. Take all the ingredients to the table.

At the table, melt the clarified butter in a metal pan over gentle heat. Add the orange sugar, orange juice and the Cointreau. Stir until the sugar dissolves. Put a pancake into the pan, turn it over, and baste with the sauce. When hot, fold it in half and then in half again, to form a triangle. Push it to one side of the pan. Repeat the process with each of the other pancakes. When all are folded, arrange them in the centre of the pan, spoon the sauce over them once more and turn up the heat. When the pan is hot, tilt it to one side, pour in the brandy and light it. Make sure all the pancakes are coated evenly with the sauce. Quickly put the pancakes on warm plates, stir the remaining sauce to make sure that any caramelized sugar is removed from the bottom of the pan, and spoon it over the pancakes. Serve immediately.

Cooking time at table 10 minutes (approx)

Note To re-heat all the pancakes at once needs a very large pan. If using a suzette pan, make up only half the quantity of sauce at first, and re-heat 6 pancakes; then repeat the process.

VARIATIONS

1) Instead of rubbing the lumps of sugar on the oranges to absorb the flavour, 50g caster sugar and the finely grated rind of 1 large orange can be added to the melted butter. This means that the rind remains in the sauce.

2) The original French recipe did not include orange juice or brandy, and used instead a mixture of 2 × 15ml spoons maraschino, 2 × 15ml spoons Kirsch and 2 × 15ml spoons curaçao. Half this was added to the pan to make the sauce and the other half added at the end and flamed.

CENTRE-PIECE COOKERY

Fondue Bourguignonne

Equipment

Special Fondue Bourguignonne sets can be bought at most good stores. A set usually consists of a copper, stainless steel or iron pot which fits over a spirit lamp or burner, and a set of long-handled forks. Since the point of this dish is to cook the meat quickly in very hot oil, the pot must be made of heavy metal to withstand the strong heat and must be deep enough to prevent dangerous splashes from the hot oil. A heatproof or cast iron casserole can be used over a spirit lamp or burner in place of a fondue pot, and it is also possible to keep the oil hot in a thermostatically controlled electric table cooker, but these are sometimes large and not sufficiently attractive for the dining table.

Several small dishes are also needed to hold uncooked food, side dishes, and sauces.

Fondue Bourguignonne

150g good quality fillet **or** rump steak per person
garlic (optional)

salt and freshly ground black pepper
oil for deep frying

Sauces

Agro-dolce sauce (p251)
Béarnaise sauce (p252)
Curry mayonnaise (p262)
Hollandaise sauce (p257)

Cold Horseradish cream (p52)
Tartare sauce (p264)
Tomato mayonnaise (p263)

In the kitchen, wipe the meat and remove any excess fat. Cut the meat into 2cm cubes. Grate or mince a little garlic, if used, and season the meat with the garlic and with salt and pepper. Choose and prepare 4–5 of the sauces. Fill the fondue pot one-third full of oil, and heat it to 190°C. If possible, have a second pot of oil heating so that the first pot, in use on the dining table, can be replaced when it cools. Carry the first pot carefully to the table.

At the table, light the spirit lamp or burner and put the pot on the trivet. If using an electric table cooker, fill it one-third full of oil, set the thermostat, and heat it up at the table itself. Bring the meat and the sauces to the table, arrange the sauces round the fondue pot in the centre, and place a dish of meat and two long-handled forks in front of each diner. The diner spears a piece of meat on a fork, dips it into the hot oil and holds it there until cooked. After cooking, he transfers the meat to the second, cold fork and dips it into one or other of the sauces before eating.

This dish is given much of its character by the side dishes served with it. Choose accompaniments from among the following: beetroot sliced in vinegar, chopped celery, chopped nuts, cocktail onions, cucumber in soured cream or thick yoghurt sprinkled with dill, green salad with French dressing, sliced gherkins, sliced potato in French dressing, sliced tomato with chives and French dressing. French bread and butter should also be served.

Swiss Cheese Fondue

Equipment

To make and serve a cheese fondue properly requires a *caquelon*, which is an open ceramic or earthenware pan about 8cm deep. The pan is set on a spirit lamp or burner which can be regulated to keep the cheese mixture at an even, very low heat; if the fondue gets too hot it becomes stringy and inedible. To serve a fondue without a proper *caquelon*, use a shallow casserole or pan set on a burner or hotplate on the dining table. Make the fondue in the casserole in the kitchen, and transfer it to the burner or hotplate for serving.

Swiss Cheese Fondue

4–6 helpings

300–450g white bread
250–350g Emmental cheese
500–750g Gruyère cheese
1 clove of garlic
350ml light dry white wine
2 × 5ml spoons fresh lemon juice
   (approx)

1 × 10ml spoon cornflour **or** potato
   flour
1 × 15ml spoon Kirsch
white pepper and grated nutmeg

In the kitchen, cut the bread into 2cm cubes, providing about 75g per person. Put into a basket.

To make the fondue, grate the cheeses. Cut the garlic clove in half, and rub the cut sides over the inside of the *caquelon* or casserole. Warm the wine in the casserole and add lemon juice to taste. Add the cheese in 15ml spoonfuls and bring slowly to the boil, stirring all the time with a whisk. Blend the cornflour or potato flour with the Kirsch to make a smooth paste. Add in 5ml spoonfuls to the cheese mixture, stirring with a figure of eight movement, until the mixture is smooth, thick, and creamy. Season to taste with the pepper and nutmeg. Transfer to the dining table with the basket of bread.

At the table, place the *caquelon* or casserole on the lit burner or hotplate, and eat immediately. Each diner serves himself from the *caquelon* or casserole by spearing bread cubes on a long-handled fork, and dipping them into the fondue mixture.

Plain green salad and Kirsch are the only accompaniments traditionally served with a fondue, although wine can be served instead of Kirsch.

Cooking time in kitchen 30 minutes (approx)

Table Beignets

Equipment

Table Beignets need a pot similar to that used for a Fondue Bourguignonne (p545), set on a trivet over a spirit lamp or burner.

Table Beignets

4–6 helpings

350–400g prepared choux pastry   oil for deep frying
   (pp454–55)

In the kitchen, make the choux paste. This can be made in advance and rewarmed just before use, if necessary, although it will not puff up as much as when it is freshly made. Fill the fondue pot or heavy casserole one-third full of unflavoured oil.

At the table, place the pot of oil in the centre, over the spirit lamp or burner. When ready to fry, heat the oil until just before smoking point, and bring the warmed choux paste to the table. Lower small spoonfuls of the paste into the hot fat, a few at a time, and fry until puffed and golden-brown. Allow the oil time to regain its original heat before adding another batch. Lift out with a perforated spoon, drain over the pot and serve on to the diners' plates.

Bowls of chocolate sauce (p265), whipped cream, and icing sugar should be arranged around the pot so that diners may help themselves.

CANAPÉS, SAVOURIES, SANDWICHES, AND FLAVOURED BUTTERS

CANAPÉS AND SAVOURIES

Anchovy Croûtes
12 savouries

1 hard-boiled egg
$\frac{1}{2}$ × 2.5ml spoon curry paste **or**
   1 × 2.5ml spoon curry powder
50g butter

4 slices toast
12 anchovy fillets
paprika
a few drops lemon juice

Garnish
chopped parsley

Heat the oven to hot, 220°C, Gas 7. Separate the egg yolk from the white and chop the white finely. Rub the yolk through a fine sieve and combine with the curry paste or curry powder, and butter. Mix to a soft paste. Cut the toast into rounds or triangles and spread with the mixture. Arrange an anchovy fillet on each piece of toast and season with paprika. Add 2–3 drops of lemon juice. Place in the oven for 3–4 minutes. Decorate with chopped egg white and parsley just before serving.

Angels on Horseback
8 savouries

8 large shelled oysters
8 rashers streaky bacon, without
   rinds

2–3 slices hot toast
butter

Garnish
watercress leaves

Heat the oven (if used) to fairly hot, 200°C, Gas 6. Wrap each oyster in a bacon rasher. Fasten the rolls with small poultry skewers, and grill for 4–6 minutes, or bake for 10 minutes in the oven. Butter the toast and cut into small fingers. Remove the skewers from the 'angels' when cooked, and serve on the fingers of toast. Garnish with watercress.

Bacon Olives
8 savouries

125g cooked ham **or** tongue
7 × 10ml spoons breadcrumbs
1 × 2.5ml spoon finely chopped onion
1 × 2.5ml spoon finely chopped parsley
a pinch of dried mixed herbs
a pinch of grated nutmeg

salt and pepper
1 egg
8 thin rashers streaky bacon, without rinds
8 small rounds toast **or** pastry canapés

Chop the ham or tongue finely. Mix together with the breadcrumbs, onion, parsley, and herbs, add a pinch of nutmeg, and season to taste with salt and pepper. Beat the egg until liquid, and stir in gradually as much as is needed to bind the mixture. Leave to stand for 30 minutes. Divide the mixture into 8 portions. Form each portion into a cork shape, roll in a rasher of bacon, and secure with string or small skewers. Bake in a fairly hot oven, 190°C, Gas 5, for about 30 minutes. Serve on toast or pastry canapés.

Cocktail Sausages

Cooked whole or halved small sausages are popular with most people. If you cannot buy cocktail sausages, use chipolatas instead. Make each into 2 small sausages, squeeze the middle, push the meat to each end, give the casing a good twist, and cut through the twisted casing.

Sausages can be served speared on to cocktail sticks. They are particularly good eaten hot, accompanied by a spicy sauce.

They can also be served on croûtes. Cut the sausages in half lengthways and set each, cut side down, on a small toasted finger-shaped croûte. Put a pat of any savoury butter on top, and garnish with a maraschino cherry, pickled cocktail onion, a tiny cube of cheese or a small chunk of canned pineapple.

Frankfurter sausages can be treated in the same way. Alternatively, split them lengthways, leaving 1 long edge joined. Spread the cut side generously with full-fat soft cheese; then re-form the sausages for serving.

Devilled Smoked Salmon Croûtes
9–12 savouries

3–4 slices toast
butter
salt and pepper

150g smoked salmon trimmings
curry butter (p564)

Garnish
parsley sprigs

Heat the oven to fairly hot, 200°C, Gas 6. Cut off the crusts, butter the toast, and sprinkle with pepper and a little salt. Chop the salmon finely, and pound thoroughly to make a fairly smooth mixture which can be spread evenly. Spread the mixture on the toast, and coat with curry butter. Cut each slice into 3 fingers. Heat in the oven for 4–5 minutes. Garnish with sprigs of parsley and serve hot.

Devils on Horseback

8 savouries

butter for shallow frying
1–2 chicken livers **or** 100g calf's liver
salt and pepper
a pinch of Cayenne pepper

8 cooked prunes
8 short thin rashers streaky bacon,
 without rinds
8 small fried bread squares

Garnish
4 olives stuffed with pimento

Heat the oven to very hot, 230°C, Gas 8. Melt the butter and cook the liver gently, then cut into 8 pieces. Season well and dust with Cayenne pepper. Stone the prunes and stuff with the liver. Stretch the bacon to double its size. Wrap each prune in a piece of bacon. Place in a baking tin with the bacon edges underneath. Bake for 8 minutes. Place one 'devil' on each square of fried bread and garnish with olives.

Haddock Croustades

12 savouries

1 small smoked haddock
2 eggs
2 × 15ml spoons milk
a good pinch of pepper

25g butter
a pinch of grated nutmeg
croustades of bread

Garnish
Cayenne pepper

Cook the fish in boiling water until just tender. Skin and bone, and flake the flesh. Beat the eggs until liquid with the milk and pepper. Heat the butter in a pan, and add the eggs, milk, pepper, fish, and nutmeg. Cook very gently until lightly set. Fill the croustades with the mixture. Garnish with Cayenne pepper.

Cooking time 12 minutes (approx)

Ham Fingers

8–10 savouries

100g lean cooked ham
1 onion
25g butter
2 eggs
salt and pepper

mixed mustard
1 × 5ml spoon chopped parsley
fingers of baked cheese pastry (p455)
 or toast

Chop the ham finely. Skin and chop the onion finely. Melt the butter and fry the onion without browning. Beat the eggs until liquid. Add with the ham to the pan. Stir over gentle heat until the eggs begin to thicken. Add the seasoning, mustard to taste, and half the parsley. Cover the pastry or toast fingers thickly with the mixture, sprinkle with the remaining parsley, and serve very hot or quite cold.

Cooking time 10 minutes (approx)

Sardine and Cheese Fingers

12 savouries

100g Cheddar cheese
4 slices toast
2 × 10ml spoons tomato ketchup

2 × 125g cans sardines in tomato
  sauce

Garnish
parsley sprigs

Grate the cheese. Cut off the crusts, spread the toast with tomato ketchup, and lay the sardines evenly on the toast. Sprinkle with the cheese and cut into fingers. Grill under a slow heat for about 5 minutes or until the cheese melts. Serve hot, garnished with parsley.

Scotch Woodcock

8–16 savouries

4 slices toast
75g butter
6 eggs
3 × 15ml spoons milk

salt and pepper
1 × 50g can anchovy fillets
capers

Cut the crusts off the toast. Butter each slice, using half of the butter, and cut each slice in half or quarters. Melt the remaining butter in a pan. Beat the eggs, milk, salt and pepper together lightly. Pour into the pan, reduce the heat, and cook gently, stirring all the time, until just set and creamy. Divide between the pieces of buttered toast and garnish with small pieces of anchovy fillet and the capers.

Cooking time 15 minutes (approx)

VARIATION

Instead of using anchovy fillets, the toast can be spread with anchovy paste or essence.

Asparagus Rolls

8–10 savouries

thin slices of fresh brown bread
butter
1 small bundle cooked or 1 × 300g
  can asparagus tips

mayonnaise or Hollandaise sauce
  (p257)
salt and pepper

Cut off the crusts and butter the bread. Drain the asparagus and put 1 tip on each piece of bread and butter; add a little mayonnaise or Hollandaise Sauce, and season to taste. Roll up the bread, enclosing the asparagus tip. If the bread is difficult to roll up, flatten it first with a rolling-pin. Keep the rolls under a damp cloth, or cover with foil or clingfilm until required.

VARIATION

The bread and butter can be spread with any full-fat soft cheese.

Stuffed Cucumber Croûtes

12 savouries

6 slices fried bread
200g cold meat, eg ham, veal, beef,
   chicken
2 large cucumbers
50g butter
4 × 15ml spoons soft white
   breadcrumbs

1 × 15ml spoon chopped parsley
½ × 2.5ml spoon chopped mixed herbs
1 egg
chicken stock
salt and pepper
Worcestershire sauce (optional)

Garnish
parsley sprigs

Cut each slice of bread in half. Mince the meat. Peel the cucumbers and cut into 5cm lengths. Scoop out the seeds with an apple corer or knife. Steam for about 5 minutes until soft. Meanwhile, melt the butter in a saucepan. Stir in the meat, crumbs, parsley, and herbs, and heat thoroughly. Beat the egg lightly, and add with enough stock to moisten the stuffing. Season well, and if necessary add Worcestershire sauce for extra flavour. Drain the cucumber and put each piece on a slice of bread. Fill with the stuffing, piled up high. Garnish with parsley sprigs.

Cooking time 10 minutes (approx)

Aspic Fingers

slices of toast
butter (optional)
anchovy butter **or** creamed savoury
   butter (p563) **or** tomato butter
   (p566)

250ml aspic jelly for every 6 slices
   toast

Garnishes
sardines
anchovies
small pieces of smoked salmon
prawns

shrimps
sliced hard-boiled egg
asparagus tips
ham

Aspic fingers are small strips of toast covered with a spread and garnish which are kept in place with a coating of aspic.

    Butter the toast or spread it with a flavoured butter. Arrange the garnish on the toast. Pipe a flavoured butter either on the topping before coating with aspic, or later on top of the set aspic. Make the aspic jelly and allow it to cool. When it begins to thicken, spread it over the topping with a knife dipped in hot water or with a pastry brush. It is better to cover the topping with several thin coatings, allowing each layer to set before adding the next, than to try and use too much aspic at one time. Stand the slices on a tray or pastry board when coating with jelly, so that any jelly that drips off can be picked up and used again.

    When the jelly is quite set, cut the slices of toast into small fingers with a sharp knife dipped in hot water.

Celery Stem Savouries

crisp, white celery stalks (enough to
produce 20–25 × 4cm pieces)

filling (see Method)

Fill the celery stalks with one of the following mixtures before cutting them into
4cm pieces:

Egg Filling: To 3 chopped hard-boiled eggs, add 75ml mayonnaise. Season with
salt and pepper and a little finely chopped onion to taste. Fill the celery stalks and
sprinkle with chopped parsley.

Low-fat Egg Filling: Chop the whites of 4 hard-boiled eggs finely and rub the
yolks through a coarse sieve. Add a few drops of oil and vinegar to the egg yolks,
season with salt and pepper, and stir in the egg white. Fill the celery stalks, and
garnish with a little chopped parsley or shredded lettuce.

Roquefort Filling: To 100g Roquefort or Danish Blue cheese, add 1 × 15ml spoon
Worcestershire sauce, 1 × 15ml spoon mayonnaise, salt and pepper. Blend all the
ingredients well together and fill the celery stalks. Sprinkle with paprika.

Cucumber Bonnes-Bouches
10 savouries (approx)

1 large **or** 2 small cucumbers
75g cooked chicken, veal **or** rabbit
6 small cooked mushrooms
25g cooked ham
salt and pepper
a pinch of grated nutmeg

4 × 15ml spoons aspic jelly
4 × 15ml spoons thick foundation
   white sauce (p236)
4 × 15ml spoons whipped cream
brown **or** white bread
lemon juice

Garnish
parsley butter (p565)

Peel the cucumber, cut into slices 2cm thick, and remove the seeds with an apple
corer, potato peeler or knife. Blanch the pieces in salted water for 30 seconds and
drain on a cloth. Keep aside. Rub the meat, mushrooms, and ham together
through a fine sieve, mince and pound them, or process in an electric blender to
make into a fine paste. Season with salt and pepper and a pinch of grated nutmeg.

Blend the aspic jelly with the white sauce while both are still warm. Leave to
cool. When the mixture is cool and beginning to thicken, add the whipped cream.
Blend in the minced meat and mushroom mixture.

Cut out rounds of bread slightly larger than the cucumber shapes, spread with a
little of the purée; then place a round of cucumber on each piece of bread and fill
the centre with the purée piled up high. Season with lemon juice, salt and pepper,
and garnish with the parsley butter.

Ham Rolls
12 savouries

4 thin slices cooked ham
50ml double cream **or** cottage cheese
   or curd cheese

2–4 × 10ml spoons apricot chutney
small rounds of toast **or** pumpernickel

Lay each slice of ham on a board, and trim off the fat. Whip the cream lightly, if used; sieve the cottage cheese or mash the curd cheese. Mix together the cream or cheese and the chutney. Spread over the ham and roll up like small Swiss rolls. Slice into 2cm lengths, and place on small rounds of crisp toast or pumpernickel.

Liver Pâté Croûtes
12 savouries

100g liver pâté
double cream **or** foundation white
   sauce (p236)

salt and pepper
12 rounds fried bread **or** toast

Garnish
chopped parsley **or** paprika

Pound the liver pâté until very smooth, and blend in enough cream or white sauce to make it the consistency of thick whipped cream. Taste, and season if necessary Spread or pipe the liver mixture on the bread or toast. Garnish with a little finely chopped parsley or sprinkle with paprika.

Sardine Cassolettes
8–10 savouries

3 large slices stale bread (2cm thick
   approx)
fat for shallow frying
1 × 65g can sardines
1 × 15ml spoon foundation white
   (p236) **or** Fresh Tomato sauce (p255)

anchovy essence (optional)
salt and pepper
a few drops lemon juice
2 × 5ml spoons grated Parmesan
   cheese **or** 1 × 15ml spoon grated
   Cheddar cheese

Garnish
watercress leaves

Heat the oven to moderate, 180°C, Gas 4. Stamp out 8–10 round shapes of bread with a 5cm biscuit cutter. Using a smaller cutter, about 3cm, make an inner circle, but do not cut right through the bread.

Heat the fat and fry the bread until lightly browned, then drain. With the point of a knife, lift out the inner ring from each shape, to form a hollow case. Put the cases in the oven for a few minutes to crisp the insides. Cool before using.

Mash the sardines thoroughly, and mix with the white or tomato sauce; if using white sauce, add a few drops of anchovy essence. Season, then blend in a few drops of lemon juice and the cheese. Put into the crisp cases and garnish with watercress.

Princess Mushrooms
12 savouries

12 button mushrooms
50g butter
75g full-fat soft cheese
a few drops cochineal (optional)

paprika
12 rounds buttered toast **or** fried
 bread

Remove the stalks from the mushrooms. Melt the butter in a pan and cook the mushrooms and stalks gently for about 10 minutes. Drain thoroughly, and cool. Meanwhile, colour the cheese with a few drops of cochineal, if liked. Pipe a rosette of cheese in the centre of each mushroom. Dust with paprika and put the stalk back in place. Serve on the toast or fried bread.

Note If preferred, the mushrooms can be simmered in water and vinegar for about 10 minutes. Use in the proportion of 2 × 15ml spoons vinegar to 250ml water.

Pastry Cases
Vol-au-vents, patty cases, or cornet-shaped cases filled with savoury mixtures are very useful for buffet and cocktail parties. For the latter they should be small enough to eat in one mouthful. They can be served hot or cold. If the filling is put into cold pastry cases, make sure it is quite cold. If, on the other hand, the filling is put into hot pastry cases, heat the filling and the pastry separately, and fill the cases at the last minute so that the filling does not make the pastry soft. If soft cheese is used as the basis of a filling, use it cold, mix it with any hot ingredients and fill into hot cases; the heat of the case and the other ingredients should warm it through.

Directions for making vol-au-vent and patty cases, and cornet shapes are given on p459 and p471.

Note Small vol-au-vent cases suitable for cocktail parties can be bought frozen; so can the larger ones for serving at a buffet.

Cocktail Vol-au-vent Fillings
1) To 250ml foundation white sauce (p236) made with 175ml milk and 75ml single cream, add one of the following mixtures:
   a)   100g cooked flaked haddock, 100g prawns, 1 × 15ml spoon sherry, 1 × 5ml spoon very finely chopped onion, salt and pepper to taste
   b)   100g chopped cooked mushrooms, 100g chopped cooked chicken, 1 × 5ml spoon lemon juice, salt and pepper to taste.

2) Divide 75g full-fat soft cheese into 2 equal portions, and arrange the following mixtures in 2 layers in vol-au-vent cases or in toasted sandwiches:
   a)   Mix half the cheese with 100g cooked, chopped streaky bacon rashers; mix the other half with 100g finely chopped cooked mushrooms and a little freshly ground pepper.
   b)   Mix half the cheese with a small onion, finely chopped and gently fried; mix the other half with 100g chopped cooked chicken, adding paprika to taste.

Rutland Anchovies

12 savouries

cheese pastry (p455) using 75g flour
flour for rolling out
1 hard-boiled egg
1 × 50g can anchovy fillets **or** 4
   whole anchovies (boned and
   filleted)

1 × 15ml spoon double cream **or**
   foundation white sauce (p236)
a pinch of Cayenne pepper
anchovy essence
cochineal

Garnish
watercress leaves

Heat the oven to fairly hot, 200°C, Gas 6. Roll out the pastry thinly on a lightly floured surface, cut into 3–4cm squares, and bake until crisp. Cool before using.

Separate the egg yolk and white. Sieve the yolk finely and cut the white into thin strips. Chop the anchovies, and mix with the cream or white sauce, and the sieved yolk. Season lightly with Cayenne pepper, and add a few drops of anchovy essence and cochineal, drop by drop, until a pale pink colour is obtained. Pile the mixture on the pastry biscuits, and garnish with the strips of egg white and the watercress.

Cheese Straws

48–60 straws

rich cheese pastry (p456) using
   100g flour

flour for rolling out

Heat the oven to fairly hot, 200°C, Gas 6. Roll out the pastry about 5mm thick on a lightly floured surface and cut into fingers, about 10 × 1cm. From the pastry trimmings make several rings about 4cm in diameter. With a palette knife, lift both rings and straws on to a baking sheet. Bake for 8–10 minutes, or until lightly browned and crisp. Cool on the baking sheet.

To serve, fit a few straws through each ring and lay the bundles in the centre of a plate with any remaining straws criss-crossed around them.

Mrs Beeton's Cayenne Cheeses

24–30 savouries

200g butter
200g plain flour
200g Cheshire **or** Lancashire cheese

$\frac{1}{2}$ × 2.5ml spoon Cayenne pepper
$\frac{1}{2}$ × 2.5ml spoon salt
flour for rolling out

Rub the butter into the flour. Grate and add the cheese with the Cayenne pepper and salt. Work thoroughly by hand, to make a smooth dough. Use a few drops of water if necessary, but the cheeses will be shorter and richer without it. When blended, chill for 30 minutes.

Heat the oven to moderate, 180°C, Gas 4. Roll out the dough 5mm thick on a lightly floured surface, and cut into fingers about 10 × 1cm. Bake for 15–17 minutes. Cool.

Note Do not serve while still warm as the fingers crumble and break easily.

SANDWICHES

Plain Sandwiches

Use a firm tin loaf rather than a round loaf shape which makes it difficult to remove crusts. If cutting the sandwiches from an unsliced loaf, butter each slice thinly before cutting to avoid crumbling or breaking the bread. Cut each slice not thicker than 5mm and cover the buttered side with the relevant filling which should be prepared in advance. Press an uncovered slice lightly on top, buttered side down, and continue in this way until the required number of sandwiches have been made. Stack 3–4 sandwiches together, remove the crusts, if liked, and cut into triangles, squares or fingers, as required. Bread for fancy sandwiches can also be prepared in this way.

Double or Triple Decker Sandwiches

Use 3 or 4 slices white or brown bread and 2 or 3 different fillings.

Striped Deckers: Alternate slices of brown and white bread, or use different coloured fillings.

Toasted Deckers: Make ordinary decker sandwiches with bread, press the slices firmly together, brush the outsides with melted butter and grill both sides, using moderate heat. Turn each sandwich over to grill the second side as soon as the first is golden-brown. Toasted deckers have a soft untoasted slice of bread in the centre, unlike club sandwiches (see below). Serve with a knife and fork.

Club sandwiches

Stack 3 slices of hot toast and 2 non-melting fillings. Be generous with the fillings. Cut the sandwiches in large triangles, and spear with cocktail sticks to hold them together. Top each sandwich with a small salad garnish if possible, and serve hot. These are good for using stale bread, as the filling moistens the toast.

Super Club Sandwiches: Cover club sandwiches with a good cheese sauce, and brown gently under a low grill before serving. Serve club or super club sandwiches with a knife and fork.

Open Sandwiches

Use a single large slice of wholemeal, wheatmeal or rye bread with a decorative topping. The attraction of these lies in the arrangement and colour of the ingredients which must be trimmed neatly to form a balanced pattern of colour contrasts.

For party open sandwiches, use 1cm thick slices of white or brown bread or slices of pumpernickel. Cut into fancy shapes, such as triangles, rounds, diamonds or hearts. Spread with creamed butter and suitable sandwich topping. Garnish with stuffed olives, small radishes cut into water lilies (p62), slices of hard-boiled egg, small pieces of tomato, slices of cucumber, gherkins, shredded lettuce, watercress, piped cream cheese, finely sprinkled paprika, etc. Be careful not to overdo the topping or garnish especially if the sandwiches are to be eaten as finger food, eg at an informal buffet, as they will then be unstable or top-heavy, awkward to handle, and may fall off.

Toppings

1) Cover brown bread with a lettuce leaf, with piped rosettes of cream cheese, and chips of apple dipped in lemon juice piled on top. Decorate with thin radish slices.

2) Cover brown bread with mustard-flavoured butter, then with a lettuce leaf. Top with sliced liver sausage, and decorate with crumbled hard-boiled egg yolk.

3) Cover brown bread with cream cheese. Decorate with skinned orange segments and halved cucumber slices (unpeeled). Sprinkle with chopped parsley.

4) Cover brown bread with thin slices of gammon or ham, then lay 2 asparagus spears diagonally across each bread slice, and hold in place with piped rosettes of a savoury butter.

5) Cover brown bread with Brie cheese instead of butter, and decorate with alternate stripes of crumbled hard-boiled egg yolk and finely chopped parsley.

Fancy or Party Sandwiches

Bread for party sandwiches must be cut very thin, and the crusts removed; amusing and unusual shapes can be cut with pastry or biscuit cutters. For occasions such as cocktail parties and weddings it is usual to serve very small sandwiches, by cutting 6 rather than 4 sandwiches from each round of bread, for instance. Some attractive party sandwiches are given below.

Rolled sandwiches: Use 1 thin white or 1 thin brown slice of bread, cut lengthways from a loaf. Cut off the crusts. Spread thinly with filling, and roll up like a Swiss roll; if necessary secure with a cocktail stick. Wrap in foil, and chill. To serve, cut thin rounds from the roll.

Pinwheel sandwiches: Make as for rolled sandwiches but use 1 thin slice of white and 1 thin slice of brown bread. Spread the white slice very thinly with filling, place the brown slice on top, spread it, and roll up. Chill and serve like the rolled sandwiches.

Making rolled sandwiches

Pyramid sandwiches: Cut out 5 different sized bread rounds from 2–10cm. Butter, spread with gaily coloured fillings, and stack with the smallest round on top. Vary the colours and flavour of the spreads.

Cornucopia or horn shape sandwiches: Cut thin slices of bread into squares. Spread with butter and filling. Treating one corner of the bread slice as the pointed end of the shell, and the opposite corner as the open end, roll one of the remaining corners over to the centre. Wrap the fourth corner over it, thus forming a cornucopia or horn shape. Add more filling if required.

Ribbon sandwiches: Use a white and a brown loaf. Cut off all crusts and cut thin slices lengthways from the loaf. Butter the white loaf first, and spread with filling. Repeat the process using the brown loaf. Put white and brown slices together in alternate layers, to build up a new striped loaf. Press the slices together firmly, wrap in clingfilm, and chill. To serve, cut the bread through the layers.

Chequerboard sandwiches: Prepare a ribbon sandwich loaf, cutting all the bread slices 1cm thick. Cut only 4 layers of each bread, and spread the filling evenly. Make up the slices into a loaf. Cut this ribbon loaf into 1cm slices and spread each slice with butter and filling. Pile 4 slices one above the other with the strips of bread all running in the same direction, and with brown strips over white strips and vice versa, making a design of squares when seen from the side. Place the top slice buttered side down. Press the stack firmly together, wrap in clingfilm, and chill well. Repeat this process with all the remaining slices. To serve, cut each stack in slices with a chequerboard design.

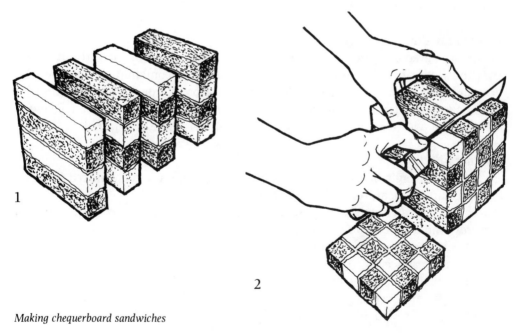

1

2

Making chequerboard sandwiches

Mosaic sandwiches: Prepare equal numbers of thinly cut white and brown sandwiches, with a smooth filling. Using a small fancy-shaped biscuit cutter, cut out the centres. Exchange these small centre pieces so that all the white sandwiches have brown centres and vice versa.

Sandwich kebabs: Make equal numbers of white and brown sandwiches, using 3 different fillings. Chill for at least 2 hours. Remove the crusts from all the sandwiches, and cut each into 8 or 16 × 1cm squares. Thread 3 mini-sandwiches (2 white and 1 brown or vice versa), each with a different filling, on to thin skewers or cocktail sticks.

Savoury Sandwich Loaf

Trim the crusts off an oblong loaf, and cut the top flat. Cut into slices horizontally, and butter each slice. Then reassemble the loaf, with 2 or 3 different coloured fillings used alternately (see below). Put on the top slice, buttered side down. Press the slices together, wrap closely in clingfilm, and chill. To serve, unwrap, cover with curd or cottage cheese, and decorate with small pieces of gaily coloured salad ingredients.

Fillings

Yellow filling: Blend 75g softened butter with 4 crumbled hard-boiled egg yolks, 25g finely grated Cheddar cheese, and salt and pepper to taste. Add a few drops of yellow food colouring, and work to a smooth paste.

Green filling: Blend 75g softened butter with 100g finely chopped frozen, thawed spinach, well drained, 25g cottage cheese, 2–3 finely chopped spring onions, and salt and pepper to taste. Work together until smooth.

Red filling: Blend 75g softened butter with 1 × 212g can herrings in tomato sauce. Work until smooth.

Fillings for Plain Sandwiches

The main ingredients should be chopped into very small bits or sliced thinly so that the sandwich can be bitten through cleanly; the filling combination must be fairly firm and dry so that the sandwich does not sag or break apart when picked up.

Some combinations for main and flavouring ingredients are given below as a guide. Use with a relevant savoury or sweet binder if one is required.

Savoury Fillings

Use red and strongly flavoured meats such as beef, lamb, tongue, smoked sausage, venison, hare or meat from game birds, with:
1) a chopped, grated or sliced salad vegetable with a cool flavour (eg cucumber, carrot) and a little strong mustard
2) finely chopped gherkin or capers with lemon juice
3) horseradish sauce
4) chopped herbs with a strong flavour, eg rosemary, sage or thyme
5) a freshly ground, strong spice such as juniper, black pepper or allspice
6) sherry, port or Madeira (mixed with the binder).

Use ham, bacon or pickled pork with any of the above, or with:
1) chopped green or red pepper and onion salt
2) finely chopped dried apricots or other dried fruit with freshly ground black pepper
3) chutney or sweet pickles.

Use white meats such as chicken or pork, with:

1) Russian salad (p23)
2) a chopped or sliced well-flavoured salad vegetable such as green pepper, flavoured with lemon juice
3) chopped pineapple or soaked dried fruit with ground black pepper
4) chopped fresh herbs in season
5) a little curry paste or powder, chilli sauce or powder, or paprika mixed into the binder.

Note If a pâté or potted meat is used, any clarified fat from the top should be removed before use. Neither are suitable for toasted or fried sandwiches. Bought liver sausage can also be used if any outside skin is removed.

Use cooked white fish with:

1) finely chopped canned salmon, or shellfish such as prawns or shrimps
2) canned pimento, capers or dill pickles
3) chopped anchovy fillets or anchovy essence.

Use canned fish, anchovy fillets or smoked fish (cooked if required) with:

1) a chopped, sliced or grated salad vegetable such as cucumber, shallot or chives
2) a coarsely grated fruit such as apple, sprinkled with lemon or orange juice
3) chopped gherkins, capers, fennel or dill stem or seeds
4) hard-boiled egg and ground black pepper.

Note Any fish filling is improved by a few drops of lemon juice among its flavourings.

Use cheese (hard or soft) with:

1) chopped or sliced salad vegetables such as cucumber or celery with ground black pepper
2) chopped olives, gherkin or chives
3) chutney or sweet pickles
4) chopped nuts such as walnuts, peanuts
5) crisply cooked, crumbled bacon
6) sherry, port or Madeira (with hard or blue cheese)
7) concentrated tomato purée, Worcestershire sauce or anchovy essence.

Use eggs (chopped hard-boiled or scrambled) with:

1) finely chopped ham or frankfurters
2) flaked kipper, mashed sardine or lumpfish roe
3) sauerkraut and a few dill or caraway seeds
4) chopped or sliced fresh salad vegetables and soured cream
5) chopped fresh herbs such as spring onion green, mint, chives, parsley.

Use nuts (chopped) with:

1) finely chopped or grated salad vegetables, flavoured with lemon juice
2) mashed avocado pear, flavoured with lemon juice to prevent discoloration
3) chopped oranges in a French dressing.

Use cooked or salad vegetables on their own, or mixed with another vegetable and a spicy seasoning, together with a well-flavoured binder.

Sweet Fillings
Use fresh fruit (chopped, mashed or grated), with:
1) chopped dried fruit
2) chopped nuts
3) a well-flavoured jam, eg apricot or plum, or honey.

Always include a few drops of lemon juice to prevent discoloration and to vitalize the flavour. Full-fat cheese or cream make interesting binders.

Fillings for Packed Meal Sandwiches and Rolls
1) sliced Gruyère cheese spread with French mustard, mustard and cress
2) minced cooked chicken and ham or tongue moistened with melted butter and bound with mayonnaise
3) good pâté with thin cucumber slices
4) sliced Cheddar or Cheshire cheese topped with thin slices of tomato and chopped fresh mint
5) sliced boiled ham spread with tomato sauce or chutney
6) sliced cold roast beef topped with slices of tomato and cucumber, with a little horseradish sauce
7) minced turkey or chicken with peanut butter and ordinary butter mixed together
8) cooked skinned sausages split lengthways and spread with apple sauce
9) rasher(s) of fried bacon covered with sautéed mushrooms
10) cooked skinned sausages split lengthways, spread with scrambled egg, and a few drops of anchovy essence.

Fillings for Decker Sandwiches
Choose two of the fillings for plain or packed meal sandwiches, using one salad filling and one meat, fish or cheese filling. As a typical example, use:
   1st layer: Sliced cold roast beef, spread with horseradish sauce
   2nd layer: Drained, sliced beetroot with vinegar and chopped watercress
or
   1st layer: Sliced Cheddar cheese spread with mango chutney
   2nd layer: Grated apple mixed with mayonnaise.

FLAVOURED BUTTERS

Anchovy Butter

50g softened unsalted butter

6 anchovy fillets **or** anchovy essence

lemon juice

pepper

Cream the butter until light. Pound the anchovy fillets, if used, to a paste or process in an electric blender with a little of the butter. Beat the anchovy and seasonings into the butter gradually. Do not over-flavour; the butter becomes stronger as it matures. Leave to stand at room temperature for at least 30 minutes before use. Press into small pots or cartons, tapping while filling to knock out all the air; alternatively, form into pats. Use at once, or cover and chill in a refrigerator. Do not freeze.

Creamed Savoury Butter (for sandwiches)

100g unsalted butter

2 × 15ml spoons double cream

made English mustard

salt and pepper

Cayenne pepper

Beat the butter until soft and creamy. Whip the cream until stiff, and blend it into the butter gradually, using a metal spoon. Season to taste with mustard, salt, pepper, and Cayenne pepper. Use at room temperature.

Note This butter is used mainly for spreading savoury sandwiches as an alternative to plain butter or margarine. It is useful when a bland filling or a mild-flavoured cheese filling is used. If not used at once, it stores well in the refrigerator. Bring to room temperature before use.

Clarified Butter

This is used when a clear butter, free from any milk solids, salt or water is required. It is used to fry white fish, chicken and veal, as it gives a light golden colour; to moisten the surface of food to be grilled; to seal potted meats; to oil moulds or baking tins; and to add to Genoese sponge mixtures.

Hot clarified butter, or as it is sometimes called, oiled or melted butter, is often served instead of sauce with fish, meat or vegetables.

To clarify butter, put the butter in a saucepan, heat it gently until it melts, then continue to heat slowly without browning, until all bubbling ceases (this shows the water has been driven off). Remove from the heat and skim off any scum that has risen to the top. Let it stand for a few minutes for any sediment to settle, then gently pour off the clear butter into a basin or jar, leaving the sediment behind. If there is a lot of sediment, it may be necessary to strain the fat through a fine sieve or muslin.

Curry Butter

100g softened butter
1 × 5ml spoon curry powder (approx)
1 × 2.5ml spoon lemon juice

salt
a pinch of ground black pepper

Beat the butter until light. Beat in the curry powder, lemon juice, salt, and pepper. Leave to stand at room temperature for at least 10 minutes, then taste and add extra curry powder if required. Chill to firm up. Use at once, or pot and chill as for Anchovy Butter (p563).

Devilling Butter

100g softened butter
a good pinch of Cayenne pepper
a good pinch of white pepper

$\frac{1}{2}$ × 2.5ml spoon curry powder
$\frac{1}{2}$ × 2.5ml spoon ground ginger

Blend all the ingredients together thoroughly, using the back of a spoon, then re-season if required. Shape into pats and chill until firm for use at once, or pot and chill as for Anchovy Butter (p563).

Garlic Butter

1 clove of garlic

50–75g softened butter

Skin and chop the garlic. Either pound it, grate it, or squeeze it through a garlic press. Mix well with the butter, adjusting the quantity of butter to give the flavour you prefer. Use at once, or pot and chill as for Anchovy Butter (p563). Use within 2 days.

Herb Butter

a good pinch of dried parsley
a good pinch of dried thyme

50g softened butter
$\frac{1}{2}$ × 2.5ml spoon salt

Work the herbs into the butter lightly. Season to taste. Use at once, or pot and chill as for Anchovy Butter (p563).

Maître d'Hôtel Butter

2–4 large sprigs parsley
50g softened butter
salt

a small pinch of pepper
a few drops lemon juice

Blanch the parsley, and chop it finely. Work it into the butter with the seasonings and lemon juice. Use at once, or pot and chill as for Anchovy Butter (p563).

Montpelier Butter

2 × 15ml spoons mixed fresh spinach
   leaves plus parsley, chervil, cress,
   tarragon, chives
1 small clove of garlic
1 small cocktail gherkin

a few capers
a few drops anchovy essence
1 hard-boiled egg yolk
50g butter

Blanch the vegetables apart from the chervil, dry them well, and chop finely. Squeeze the garlic through a garlic press and add it to the herbs. Chop and add the gherkin and capers, with the anchovy essence and hard-boiled egg yolk. Pound all these ingredients together, adding the butter gradually until a smooth green butter is obtained. Sieve. Use at once, or pot and chill as for Anchovy Butter (p563).

Mustard Butter

25g softened butter
1 × 2.5ml spoon dry mustard

a few drops lemon juice
salt

Beat the butter until light. Beat in the mustard, lemon juice, and salt. If very soft, chill until almost firm but still workable. Form into 2 small pats, and chill until really firm for use at once, or pot and chill as for Anchovy Butter (p563). Bring to room temperature and form into pats for use when required.

Parsley Butter

50g softened butter
1 × 10ml spoon chopped parsley

a few drops lemon juice
salt and pepper

Cream the butter with the parsley. Leave to stand at room temperature for 10 minutes, then add the lemon juice, and season to taste. Use at once, or pot and chill as for Anchovy Butter (p563).

Peanut Butter

100g freshly shelled and roasted
   peanuts, salted **or** unsalted

2 × 5ml spoons groundnut oil
salt

Grind the nuts very finely in a nut mill. Put into a bowl, and beat in the oil, drop by drop, using a balloon whisk or wooden spoon. Beat until fully blended and smooth; season to taste.

If using an electric blender, feed the nuts into the goblet slowly, with the motor running. Add the oil in two separate spoonfuls while blending. Blend at high speed for 15 seconds or until smooth. Put into a bowl and season to taste.

Pack into a sterilized dry jar with a screw-topped lid. Store in a cool place, away from strong sunlight.

Ravigote Butter

2 × 15ml spoons mixed fresh herbs
(parsley, chervil, shallot, tarragon,
chives)

1 small clove of garlic
25g softened butter
salt and pepper

Chop the herbs finely. If chervil is used it should be chopped separately and not blanched. Crush the garlic clove. Tie the herbs and garlic in a small piece of muslin. Blanch in a little boiling water, then drain and squeeze dry. Work the herbs into the butter with the back of a spoon, and season to taste. Sieve. Use at once, or pot and chill as for Anchovy Butter (p563). Use within 2 days.

Tomato Butter

1 × 5ml spoon concentrated tomato
purée **or** tomato ketchup

50g softened butter
a few drops lemon juice **or** vinegar

Work all the ingredients together until smooth. Use at once, or pot and chill as for Anchovy Butter (p563).

Almond Butter

100g ground almonds
100g softened butter
4 × 10ml spoons caster sugar (approx)

1 × 5ml spoon lemon juice (approx)
a few drops almond essence

Work the ground almonds into the butter thoroughly, adding the sugar and flavourings gradually. Use at once, or pot and chill as for Anchovy Butter (p563).

Brandy Butter

50g butter
100g caster sugar

1–2 × 15ml spoons brandy

Cream the butter until soft. Beat the sugar gradually into the butter until it is pale and light. Work in the brandy, a little at a time, taking care not to allow the mixture to curdle. Chill before using. If the mixture has separated slightly after standing, beat well before serving.

This sauce is traditionally served with Christmas pudding and mince pies.

Note An egg white whisked until stiff can be stirred into the butter and sugar mixture to give a softer texture.

VARIATIONS

Sherry Butter

Make as for Brandy Butter but substitute sherry for the brandy.

Vanilla Butter

Make as for Brandy Butter but substitute 1 × 5ml spoon vanilla essence for the brandy.

Orange Butter

Cream the grated rind of an orange with the butter and sugar, and then gradually beat in 1 × 15ml spoon orange juice. Omit the brandy.

Lemon Butter

Make as for Orange Butter but substitute the grated rind of half a lemon and 1 × 5ml spoon lemon juice for the orange.

Cumberland Rum Butter

100g unsalted butter
100g light soft brown sugar
2 × 15ml spoons rum (approx)

1 × 2.5ml spoon grated orange peel
grated nutmeg

Squeeze and cream the butter with your hand until very soft and light-coloured. Crush any lumps in the sugar. Work it into the butter with your hand until completely blended in. Work in the rum, a few drops at a time, taking care not to let the mixture separate. Mix in the orange peel. Taste, and add extra rum if liked, and a little grated nutmeg. Pile into a dish, and leave to firm up before serving; or turn lightly into a screw-topped jar without leaving air holes, and store in a cool place until required. Use within 4 days, or refrigerate for longer storage. Bring to room temperature before serving.

Mrs Beeton's Fairy Butter

1 × 10ml spoon orange juice
25g icing sugar
2 hard-boiled egg yolks

1 × 10ml spoon orange flower water
100g softened butter

Decoration (optional)
1 × 10ml spoon grated orange rind

Strain the orange juice, and sift the sugar. Sieve the egg yolks. Using a rotary beater, beat in the juice, orange flower water, sugar, and butter alternately until all the ingredients are blended to a smooth paste.

To use, press the fairy butter through a sieve on to a decorative serving plate, in a pile of thin strands. Do not press them down; flick any stray strands into place with a fork. Sprinkle with grated orange rind, if liked. Serve as a rich sweet with small crisp biscuits, or on a trifle or gâteau instead of whipped cream.

Rum Butter

50g butter
100g light soft brown sugar

2 × 15ml spoons rum

Cream the butter until soft, beating in the sugar gradually. When light and creamy, work in the rum, a little at a time. Chill before using.

PUNCHES, CUPS AND COCKTAILS

PUNCHES

Bishop
Fills 12 sherry glasses

12 cloves
1 large orange

1 bottle port (70–75cl)
white sugar

Press the cloves into the orange, put it into an ovenproof bowl, cover tightly, and roast it in a moderate oven, 180°C, Gas 4, until lightly browned. Cut the orange into 8 pieces and remove the pips. Pour the port into a clean saucepan, add the pieces of orange, and heat gently to simmering point. Sweeten to taste with sugar and simmer for 20 minutes, taking care not to let the liquor boil. Strain the liquid through a fine sieve and serve at once, very hot.

Mulled Wine
Fills 12 wine glasses

500ml water
6 cloves
10g piece of bruised cinnamon stick
a pinch of grated nutmeg

finely pared rind of $\frac{1}{2}$ lemon
1 bottle claret (70–75cl)
white sugar

Put the water in an enamel saucepan and heat gently; then stir in the cloves, cinnamon stick, nutmeg, and lemon rind. Heat to boiling point and simmer for 10 minutes. Strain the liquid into a basin and add the wine. Sweeten to taste with sugar. Return the liquid to the pan and heat without boiling it.

   Serve at once with fingers of dry toast.

Negus
Fills 10 wine glasses

100g lump sugar
1 lemon
1 bottle port (70–75cl)

500ml boiling water
$\frac{1}{4}$ small nutmeg
2–3 drops vanilla essence

Rub the sugar on the rind of the lemon until all the zest is extracted. Crush it in a basin and pour the port and boiling water over it. Add the nutmeg and the vanilla essence. Serve hot.

Whisky Punch
Fills 15 wine glasses

juice and finely pared rind of
   3 lemons
1 litre boiling water

1 bottle whisky (75cl)
200g lump sugar

Strain the lemon juice and put it into a basin with the lemon rind. Pour boiling water over them; then add the whisky, and stir in the sugar. When the sugar has dissolved, strain the liquid and serve at once.

Hot Rum Toddy
Fills 2 mugs

2 × 5ml spoons Demerara sugar **or** to
   taste
juice of 1 lemon

50ml rum
2 lemon slices
boiling water

Mix the sugar with the lemon juice and rum. Put 1 lemon slice into each of 2 heated mugs, and pour half the rum mixture into each mug. Add boiling water to give the desired strength of toddy. Taste, and add extra sugar if needed. Serve at once, as hot as possible.

CUPS

Champagne Cup
Fills 12 Champagne glasses

1 bottle Champagne (70–75cl)
400ml soda water
a few strips lemon rind

1 × 2.5ml spoon maraschino
1 liqueur glass brandy (65ml)
1 × 5ml spoon caster sugar (optional)

Chill the Champagne and soda water for 1 hour. When ready to serve, put the lemon rind into a large glass jug, and stir in the maraschino, brandy, Champagne, and soda water. Serve at once. If sugar is added, it should be stirred in gradually.

Cider Cup
Fills 12 wine glasses

1 litre cider
500ml soda water
1 liqueur glass brandy (65ml)
a few thin strips cucumber rind

a few thin strips lemon rind
1 × 10ml spoon lemon juice
1 × 10ml spoon caster sugar (approx)

Chill the cider and soda water for 30 minutes. Put the rest of the ingredients into a large jug, and stir in the chilled cider and soda water. Serve at once.

Sauternes Cup
Fills 12 wine glasses

1 litre Sauternes
cracked ice
1 liqueur glass maraschino (65ml)
1 liqueur glass curaçao (65ml)
1 liqueur glass (65ml) Cognac **or**
  peach brandy

12 large **or** 24 small slices fresh
  peaches
a few strips lemon rind
a few drops lemon juice (optional)
250ml soda water (approx)

Decoration
2–3 sprigs fresh mint

Chill the wine for 1 hour. Put the ice in a 2 litre (approx) jug and pour the wine over it. Add the liqueurs, brandy, peach slices, and lemon rind. Add lemon juice if either the wine or fruit is very sweet. Just before serving, pour in the soda water as required, and decorate with the mint.

Fruit Claret Cup
Fills 12 wine glasses

cracked ice
7 × 5ml spoons brandy
7 × 5ml spoons caster sugar
7 × 5ml spoons maraschino
6 maraschino cherries
2 × 15ml spoons lemon juice

1 sliced lemon
1 sliced orange
6 thin slices fresh pineapple
1 litre claret (approx)
175ml soda water (approx)

Put some cracked ice into a large jug. Add the brandy, sugar, maraschino, and cherries. Strain the lemon juice and add it. Cut the lemon, orange, and pineapple slices into quarters, and add them. Stir in the claret. Just before serving, add the soda water, and stir once.
Note You can add extra claret or vary the proportions of claret and soda water, if liked.

Sangria
Fills 8 wine glasses

50g sugar
50ml water
1 sliced orange

1 sliced lime **or** lemon
1 bottle red **or** white wine (70–75cl)
12 ice cubes

Put the sugar and water in a saucepan and stir over gentle heat until the sugar has dissolved. Pour the syrup over the sliced fruit and leave to cool.

Pour the fruit and the syrup into a jug, and add the wine and ice cubes. Stir well, and serve at once. Put 2–3 slices of fruit in each glass.

Fruit Punch
Fills 50 wine glasses

300g caster sugar (approx)
3.5 litres water
150ml strong tea, without milk
juice of 13 lemons
juice of 14 oranges

1 litre grape juice
1 × 227g can crushed pineapple
2 litres ginger ale (approx)
ice cubes

Decoration
slices of lemon
slices of orange

1 × 170g bottle maraschino cherries

Boil the sugar and water together for 6 minutes. Add the tea, leave to cool, then chill. When cold, add the fruit juices and pineapple. Chill for about 2 hours. Just before serving, pour in the ginger ale to taste. Add ice cubes and decorate with the sliced fruit and cherries.

Iced Tea Punch
Fills 6 tumblers

750ml cold tea (see **Note**)
100g caster sugar
juice of 2 lemons

juice of 3 oranges
cracked ice
375ml ginger ale

Decoration
6 slices lemon

6 sprigs mint

Strain the tea liquor into a deep jug. Stir in the sugar until dissolved, then add the lemon and orange juices. Stir and chill thoroughly. Put the cracked ice into 6 tumblers, divide the tea between them, and fill up with the ginger ale. Decorate each glass with a slice of lemon and a sprig of mint before serving.
Note Use strong Indian tea without milk or sugar. Strain while hot, and leave to cool in a covered container.
　　For a perfectly clear liquid, put 25g dry tea into a bowl with 500ml cold water. Leave to soak overnight, then strain off the liquid.

Honey Fruit Cup
Fills 12 wine glasses

2 large oranges
250ml clear honey (approx)
2 bananas
4–6 slices fresh pineapple

2 litres grape juice (approx)
250ml soda water (approx)
1 × 15ml spoon lemon juice

Peel the oranges, removing the pith, and crush the flesh to a pulp, discarding the pips. Mix with the honey in a large jug. Peel the bananas and pineapple and chop finely. Add to the jug and slowly pour in the grape juice and soda water to taste. Add the lemon juice. Leave for 20 minutes, then stir well and serve.

COCKTAILS AND OTHER DRINKS

Besides spirits, wines, liqueurs, bitters, and soft drinks such as quinine tonic, it is necessary to have a source of soda water which can be quickly replenished, and a supply of clean, clear ice. Snowy ice melts quickly.

For serving cocktails and similar 'short' drinks, it is helpful to have the following equipment:

1) *Cocktail shaker:* There are various types, but the most usual consists of a deep container with a perforated screw-on top and an outer lid. The drink and ice are shaken in the deep container with both caps screwed on. The outer cap is then removed, and the drink is poured through the holes of the inner cap. This holds the ice back and prevents it from splashing into the glass. Never fill a cocktail shaker more than four-fifths full, and never shake an effervescent drink. If serving a variety of drinks, keep one shaker for drinks with highly flavoured ingredients and another for milder ones.

2) *Mixing glass and spoon:* This is needed for mixing clear drinks such as dry Martinis.

3) *Ice:* Make ice cubes in the ice making trays in a refrigerator or freezer. Different shaped trays are available to make ice balls, wedges, squares or oblongs. For a party, ice can be made several days in advance and stored in the freezing compartment of a refrigerator, or in a freezer. Tip the ice into a large polythene bag and squirt with soda water to keep the pieces separate, before storing them. Ice cubes are also obtainable from specialist suppliers, or sometimes from fishmongers. To make cracked ice for cocktails, use an ice hammer with a pointed head or a special ice cracker. For crushed ice, put the cubes into a polythene bag and hammer them hard with a rolling-pin, mallet or rubber-headed hammer. For shaved ice, use a special shaver, which is not unlike a plane.

Decorative ice is attractive in many drinks, especially soft drinks and fruit cups. Fill a 'ball' ice tray with cocktail cherries, inserting cocktail sticks if you wish; top up with water, and freeze. Slices of lemon or orange, sprigs of mint or lemon balm also look attractive set in ice. Edible food dyes (red, green or yellow) can be used to colour ice shapes; a few drops of yellow dye, a little lemon juice and thin slices of lemon cut to size, make ice cubes both look and taste delicious.

4) *Measures:* Tots and similar measures for cocktails are widely available, and most are marked at the $\frac{1}{4}$, $\frac{1}{2}$ and $\frac{3}{4}$ tot levels. Some measures give 5 tots to 125ml, some give 6 tots.

Cocktail glasses generally hold 50ml, 75ml or 125ml.

Americano

$\frac{2}{3}$ sweet vermouth
$\frac{1}{3}$ Campari
1 ice cube

soda water
a twist of lemon rind

Stir the vermouth and Campari together in a mixing glass, and strain into an 'old fashioned' glass. Add the ice. Top up with soda water. Decorate with the lemon rind.

Black Velvet

½ chilled Guinness   ½ chilled dry Champagne

Pour the Guinness and Champagne simultaneously. Do not add ice. Serve in a tumbler or a tankard.

Bloody Mary

ice cubes   a few drops Worcestershire sauce
⅓ vodka   a few drops fresh lemon juice
⅔ chilled tomato juice   salt and pepper (optional)

Put the ice cubes into a medium-sized glass. Stir or shake all the ingredients together.

Bronx

½ gin   ⅙ sweet vermouth
⅙ dry vermouth   ⅙ fresh orange juice

Shake all the ingredients together in a cocktail shaker; then strain into a cocktail glass.

Bucks Fizz

juice of 1 orange   chilled dry Champagne

Strain the orange juice and chill it. Pour into a Champagne glass and top up with the Champagne. Do not add ice.

Champagne Cocktail

1 lump of sugar   chilled Champagne
a few drops Angostura bitters   ½ slice orange
1 × 5ml spoon brandy

Put a lump of sugar in a Champagne glass and soak it in the Angostura bitters. Add the brandy and top up with chilled Champagne. Place the orange slice on top.
VARIATION
Add 1 × 5ml spoon Dubonnet.

Daiquiri

¾ white rum   ½ × 2.5ml spoon caster sugar
¼ fresh lime or lemon juice

Shake all the ingredients together in a cocktail shaker; then strain into a wine or cocktail glass.
VARIATION
Frozen Daiquiri
Shake the ingredients briskly in a cocktail shaker; then pour the liquid over plenty of shaved or crushed ice in a Champagne glass. Do not strain. Drink with a short straw.

Dry Martini

$\frac{2}{3}$ dry gin
$\frac{1}{3}$ dry vermouth

cracked ice
a twist of lemon rind

Stir the gin and vermouth together in a mixing glass, and strain into a wine or cocktail glass. Stir in the ice and serve with the lemon rind.

Horse's Neck

1 lemon
ice cubes
4 × 10ml spoons brandy

dry ginger ale
a few drops Angostura bitters
  (optional)

Pare the rind of the lemon in one piece in a spiral. Place one end of the rind over the edge of a tumbler, allowing the remainder to curl inside. Anchor it with 2 cubes of ice at the bottom of the glass. Add the brandy and fill with dry ginger ale. Add a few drops of Angostura bitters, if liked.

Manhattan

$\frac{2}{3}$ bourbon whisky
$\frac{1}{3}$ sweet vermouth
a few drops Angostura bitters

cracked ice
1 maraschino cherry

Stir the liquid ingredients together in a mixing glass, and strain into a cocktail glass. Add the ice, and decorate with a cherry.

Negroni

2–3 ice cubes
$\frac{1}{3}$ dry gin
$\frac{1}{3}$ sweet vermouth

$\frac{1}{3}$ Campari
soda water (optional)
1 slice of orange

Put the ice cubes in a tall glass. Pour the spirits over them and top up with soda water, if liked. Decorate with the slice of orange.

Old Fashioned

1 lump of sugar
a few drops Angostura bitters
2 × 5ml spoons water (approx)
1 measure bourbon whisky

ice cubes
1 maraschino cherry
$\frac{1}{2}$ slice orange

Put a lump of sugar in an 'old fashioned' glass and soak it in the Angostura bitters. Add enough water to dissolve the sugar. Add the whisky and ice cubes, and decorate with a cherry and an orange slice.

Rum Nog

double measure of dark rum
1 egg
250ml cold milk

a little sugar
a pinch of grated nutmeg

Mix all the ingredients together thoroughly. Serve in a tumbler.

Screwdriver

$\frac{1}{3}$ vodka
$\frac{2}{3}$ fresh orange juice

ice cubes
1 slice of orange

Stir the liquid ingredients with the ice cubes, in a wine or cocktail glass. Decorate with a slice of orange.

Sidecar

$\frac{1}{2}$ brandy
$\frac{1}{4}$ Cointreau

$\frac{1}{4}$ fresh lemon juice
cracked ice

Shake all the ingredients together in a cocktail shaker; then strain into a wine or cocktail glass.

Vodkatini

$\frac{2}{3}$ vodka
$\frac{1}{3}$ dry vermouth

cracked ice
a twist of lemon rind

Stir the vodka and vermouth together in a mixing glass, and strain into a wine or cocktail glass. Stir in the ice and serve with the lemon rind.

Whisky Sour

4 × 15ml spoons whisky
juice of $\frac{1}{2}$ lemon
1 × 5ml spoon beaten egg white

white sugar
cracked ice
soda water

Shake the whisky, lemon juice, egg white, sugar, and ice together in a cocktail shaker; then strain into a wine or cocktail glass. Top up with soda water.

White Lady

$\frac{1}{2}$ dry gin
$\frac{1}{4}$ Cointreau
$\frac{1}{4}$ fresh lemon juice

ice cubes
$\frac{1}{2}$ × 2.5ml spoon egg white

Shake all the ingredients together in a cocktail shaker; then strain into a wine or cocktail glass.

WINE AND FOOD

While it is important not to be tied rigidly to rules concerning suitable wines for particular foods, the following can be used as general guide-lines:

1) With most first course, cold, and fish dishes and white meat dishes in a white sauce, serve a dry or medium white wine or rosé.

2) With red meat dishes, casseroles and stews, roasts and grills, serve red wine.

3) The richer, the fuller, and the spicier the food, the richer and fuller the wine must be. Do not let the delicacy of a light wine be killed by an over-assertive food flavour, or vice versa.

Suggested wines for certain dishes:

1) Cold fish dishes eg oysters, fish mousse: Muscadet, Pouilly Blanc Fumé, Chablis.

2) Hot fish dishes: as 1) but also Bourgogne Aligote, Pouilly Fuissé, Sylvaner, Alsace Riesling, and other light, dry wines.

3) Crustaceans – lobster, crab, etc generally in richer sauces: serve one of the better white Burgundies or Alsace wines, although the four mentioned above will not be out of place, especially if the dish is cold.

4) Cold meat dishes, pâtés and pies, and smoked fish: as 2) or 3), according to taste. The more flavoured and spicy the dish, the more assertive the wine should be; the fruity Alsace wines are generally very good. With ordinary cold meat and salad, German wine is suitable.

5) White meat in white sauces: as 2) or 3), also dry white Bordeaux. Many people prefer German wines. When veal or chicken is served in a brown sauce or one containing Madeira or sherry, one has the choice of white or red wines, of which the best would be a light, young claret or a Beaujolais.

6) Roasts and grills: all red wines, except the very richest and heaviest.

7) Casseroles and stews: red wines, of a weight and richness approximating to the dish.

It is usual to allow at least half at 70cl bottle (three glasses) of wine per head at a main meal. This gives one the chance to serve a glass of white wine with the first course, and two glasses of red with the main course. However, one may well find that more is needed, so it is wise to have a bottle or two in reserve, if possible.

If serving more than one wine, it is wise to abide by the following rules:

1) White wine before red

2) A light wine before a heavy one

3) A young wine before an old one

4) Dry wine before sweet.

Once a bottle has been broached, it will keep quite well for a few days in a cool place (for red wines), or in a refrigerator (for whites). Alternatively, use for cooking.

HOME FREEZING

Nearly all fresh foods, and many cooked foods, freeze well, but there are a few items to avoid entirely, or to freeze only with great care. There are also a few foods which cannot be frozen and then eaten raw, although they can be used for cooking.

Foods Not to Freeze
1) hard-boiled eggs (including Scotch eggs, eggs in pies and in sandwiches)
2) soured cream, single cream (less than 40% butterfat), and half-cream which separate
3) yoghurt
4) cottage cheese; this becomes watery
5) custards (including tarts); the custard mixture of eggs and milk can be frozen uncooked, but there is little point in this
6) soft meringue toppings
7) mayonnaise and salad dressings
8) milk puddings
9) royal icing and other icings and frostings without fat; they crumble and chip in the freezer
10) salad vegetables with a high water content, eg lettuce, watercress, radishes
11) old boiled potatoes (potatoes can be frozen mashed, roast, baked or as chips)
12) stuffed poultry
13) food with a high proportion of gelatine
14) whole eggs in shells which will crack

Foods to Freeze with Care
1) Cooked onions, garlic, spices, and herbs. They sometimes get a musty flavour in cooked dishes in the freezer, and recipe quantities should be reduced in such dishes as casseroles; they can be adjusted during re-heating. Careful packing will help to prevent these strong flavours spreading to other foods, but a short time in storage is recommended.
2) Rice, spaghetti, and potatoes should only be frozen without liquid. They become mushy in liquid and should not be frozen in soups or stews.
3) Sauces and gravy are best thickened by reduction, or with a vegetable purée. If flour is used, the sauce or gravy must be re-heated with great care, preferably in a double boiler, to avoid separation. Cornflour can be used but gives a glutinous quality. Egg and cream thickening should only be added after freezing.

4) Apples, pears, avocados, melons, and bananas cannot be successfully frozen whole to eat raw. They can be prepared and frozen for use in various other ways (although pears are never very satisfactory). Bananas are not worth freezing as they are in season at a reasonable price throughout the year.

5) Cabbage cannot be frozen successfully to eat raw, and is not really worth freezing since it occupies a lot of freezer space. Red cabbage may be worth freezing, as it has a short season and is never very plentiful.

6) Celery and chicory cannot be frozen to eat raw. They are useful frozen in liquid to serve as vegetables. Celery can be used in stews or soups.

7) Tomatoes cannot be frozen to eat raw, but are invaluable frozen as purée or juice or to use in soups, stews, and sauces.

8) Milk must be homogenized and packed in waxed cartons. However, it is hardly worth freezing since several types of milk can be stored without refrigeration.

Labelling and Recording

All items should be labelled carefully with the contents, weight, date of freezing, and any special instructions for thawing or re-heating. All packs should be recorded on a board or in a book, and a note made when items are used.

Thawing

Thawing speeds up the chemical reactions which have been halted by freezing. It therefore encourages rapid deterioration, so that food is best thawed in a cold atmosphere such as a refrigerator. It must be eaten or cooked immediately after thawing.

Remove food from its wrappings before thawing if possible, unless otherwise directed.

Frozen cooked food must never be thawed and then refrozen. Raw materials should not be thawed and refrozen, but can be made into cooked dishes and then frozen.

Freezing Methods

Meat, Poultry, and Game

If buying a whole carcass, it is best to ask the butcher to freeze this quantity of meat, because it will take 3 or 4 days in a home freezer. Smaller quantities of meat, poultry, and game can be frozen successfully at home. Meat must be frozen quickly and the fast-freeze switch should be turned on well ahead of freezing time so that the cabinet is at the lowest setting.

It is best to freeze meat in the way in which it will be used, such as cubed or minced, as this will save many hours' thawing and preparation time. Poultry should be plucked, drawn, and jointed if necessary. Most game must be hung for the required time, then plucked or skinned, and drawn. Surplus fat should be removed, and the meat will take up less space if boned and rolled. Any bones should be padded with a twist of foil or paper before the meat is packed in polythene. Pack chops, steaks, and sausages in small quantities, separated by clingfilm. Remember that salted meats have a limited storage life since fat and salt react together in the freezer to cause rancidity.

Type of meat, poultry, and game	Preparation for freezing	High quality storage life	Thawing instructions
Cubed meat	Pack in small quantities in polythene, pressing together tightly	2 months	Thaw in refrigerator for 3 hours
Ham and bacon	Vacuum packed ham or bacon should be frozen sliced or in joints	1 month (sliced) 3 months (joints)	Thaw in wrappings in refrigerator
Offal	Wash and dry well, remove blood vessels and cores. Wrap in polythene, separating pieces with clingfilm	2 months	Thaw in wrappings in refrigerator for 3 hours
Joints	Trim, bone, and roll, if possible. Pack in polythene	12 months (beef) 9 months (lamb and veal) 6 months (pork)	Thaw in refrigerator allowing 4 hours per 500g
Minced meat	Use lean mince and pack in small quantities. Wrap in polythene	2 months	Thaw in refrigerator for 3 hours. If cooked while still frozen, mince may be tough
Sausages and sausage-meat	Pack in small quantities in polythene	1 month	Thaw in refrigerator for 2 hours
Steaks, chops or sliced meat	Pack in small quantities, separating pieces with clingfilm. Wrap in polythene	6–12 months (according to meat)	Cook slowly from frozen, or thaw in refrigerator
Chicken, guinea-fowl or turkey	Hang, pluck, and draw, if neccessary. Truss or cut in joints. Chill for 12 hours, pack in polythene bags, excluding giblets. Do not stuff	12 months	Thaw in wrappings in refrigerator. Must be totally thawed before cooking
Giblets	Clean, wash, dry, and chill. Pack in polythene bags	2 months	Thaw in refrigerator for 2 hours
Duck and goose	Hang, pluck, and draw, if necessary. Chill for 12 hours and pack in polythene bags, excluding giblets	6 months	Thaw in wrappings in refrigerator. Must be completely thawed before cooking
Grouse, partridge, pheasant, pigeon	Hang as liked after removing shot and cleaning wounds. Pluck, draw, and truss, and pad bones. Pack in polythene bags	6 months	Thaw in wrappings in refrigerator
Plover, quail, snipe, woodcock	Prepare as other game but do not draw	6 months	Thaw in wrappings in refrigerator
Hares	Clean shot wounds and hang, bleeding the animal and collecting the blood. Paunch, skin, clean, and cut into joints. Separate joints with clingfilm and pack in polythene bags. Pack blood separately	6 months	Thaw in wrappings in refrigerator
Rabbits	Paunch, skin, clean, and prepare as for hare	6 months	Thaw in wrappings in refrigerator
Venison	Clean, and hang before jointing. Skin, then pack in polythene bags	12 months	Thaw in a marinade in refrigerator

Fish

Only freshly caught fish should be frozen, and this should be done very quickly. Fish bought from a shop is not suitable for freezing. Clean and prepare fish completely and pack in polythene. Separate steaks or fillets with clingfilm, but avoid making packs deeper than 5cm so that fish is frozen quickly. To keep the flavour and colour of white fish, add the juice of a lemon to the water in which it is washed.

Plainly frozen fillets and whole fish (ie uncoated), should be thawed before cooking. Do not place the fish in water or hold it under a tap as this will wash away the natural moisture.

Commercially frozen breaded fish or fish in batter can be fried straight from the freezer, bearing in mind that the temperature of the fat will be reduced by the frozen fish, and this must be allowed for in the overall timing.

Type of fish	Preparation for freezing	High quality storage life	Thawing instructions
Crab, crayfish, and lobster	Cook and cool. Remove flesh and pack in polythene bags or rigid containers	1 month	Thaw in container in refrigerator and serve cold, or add to cooked dishes
Mussels	Scrub and clean thoroughly. Put in a large pan over medium heat for 3 minutes to open. Cool, remove from shells, and pack in rigid containers with juices	1 month	Thaw in container in refrigerator before adding to dishes
Oily fish (eg herring, mackerel, salmon)	Clean well, fillet, cut in steaks or leave whole. Separate pieces of fish with clingfilm. Wrap in polythene, excluding air carefully	2 months	Thaw large fish in refrigerator, but cook small fish from frozen
Oysters	Open and reserve liquid. Wash fish in brine (1 × 5ml spoon salt to 500ml water). Pack in rigid containers in own liquid	1 month	Thaw in container in refrigerator and serve cold, or add to cooked dishes
Prawns and shrimps	Cook and cool in cooking liquid. Remove shells and pack in polythene bags or rigid containers. Shrimps may be covered in melted spiced butter	1 month	Thaw in container in refrigerator and serve cold, or add to cooked dishes
Smoked fish	Pack in polythene bags, wrapping individual fish in clingfilm	2 months	Thaw in refrigerator to eat cold, or cook haddock and kippers from frozen
White fish (eg cod, sole)	Clean, fillet or cut in steaks, or leave whole. Separate pieces of fish with clingfilm. Wrap in polythene, excluding air carefully	3 months	Thaw large fish in refrigerator, but cook small fish from frozen

Vegetables

All vegetables for freezing should be young, fresh, and clean, and they should be frozen as soon as possible after picking. Grade vegetables for size and prepare in small quantities (ie 500g is the largest quantity which should be blanched at one time). All vegetables must be blanched by being cooked briefly in boiling water to retard enzymic action and retain colour, flavour, and nutritive value. Use a wire blanching basket in a large saucepan which will hold 4 litres water and has a lid. Vegetables should be put into the boiling water, and the water returned to boiling point as quickly as possible. Timing must be accurate, as under-blanching results in colour change and loss of nutritive value while over-blanching causes loss of flavour and crispness.

After blanching, vegetables must be cooled rapidly in water chilled with ice cubes, not under running tap water which is not cold enough. It should take as long to cool as to blanch each vegetable, and then the vegetables must be well-drained. They may be spread out on open freezing trays and frozen before packing, or packed directly into polythene bags or rigid containers. Vegetables with strong smells, eg onions and garlic, may need overwrapping.

After freezing, vegetables need little cooking. Most vegetables should be put straight into a small quantity of boiling water and cooked until just tender. Vegetables can also be cooked in butter, without any water, in a covered casserole or heavy saucepan, either in the oven or over heat.

Type of vegetable	Preparation for freezing	Blanching time	High quality storage life	Cooking instructions
Artichokes (globe)	Remove outer leaves, stalks, and chokes. Add lemon juice to blanching water	7 minutes	12 months	Cook in boiling water for 10 minutes
Artichokes (Jerusalem)	Peel and slice. Cook in chicken stock and purée	—	3 months	Heat purée and add milk or cream
Asparagus	Clean and grade. Cut in 15cm lengths	2 minutes (thin) 3 minutes (medium) 4 minutes (large)	9 months	Cook in boiling water for 5 minutes
Aubergines	1) Peel and cut into 2cm slices	4 minutes	1) 12 months	1) Place in boiling water for 5 mins
	2) Coat in batter and deep fry	—	2) 2 months	2) Heat in warm oven or fry
Avocado pears	Mash pulp with lemon juice (1 × 15ml spoon juice to each pear)	—	2 months	Thaw for 3 hours in refrigerator
Beans (broad)	Shell small young beans	1½ minutes	12 months	Cook in boiling water for 8 minutes
Beans (French)	Top and tail young beans. Leave whole or cut into 2cm chunks	3 minutes (whole) 2 minutes (cut)	12 months	Cook in boiling water for 7 minutes (whole) 5 minutes (cut)
Beans (runner)	Cut in chunks; do not shred	2 minutes	12 months	Cook in boiling water for 7 minutes
Beetroot	Cook very young beet, under 3cm diameter. Peel and leave whole or dice	—	6 months	Thaw for 2 hours, and add dressing

Chart continues over

Type of vegetable	Preparation for freezing	Blanching time	High quality storage life	Cooking instructions
Broccoli	Trim stalks and soak in brine for 30 minutes (1 × 15ml spoon salt to 4 litres water). Wash before blanching	3 minutes (thin) 4 minutes (medium) 5 minutes (thick)	12 months	Cook in boiling water for 8 minutes
Brussels sprouts	Grade and wash well	3 minutes (small) 4 minutes (medium)	12 months	Cook in boiling water for 8 minutes
Cabbage	Shred crisp young cabbage	1½ minutes	6 months	Cook in boiling water for 8 minutes (do not use raw)
Carrots	Use very young carrots. Wash and scrape. Leave whole, dice or slice	3 minutes	12 months	Cook in boiling water for 8 minutes
Cauliflower	Wash and break into florets. Add lemon juice to blanching water	3 minutes	6 months	Cook in boiling water for 10 minutes
Celery	Scrub crisp young stalks and cut into 2cm slices	2 minutes	6 months	Cook in stock, or add to soups and stews (do not use raw)
Corn on the cob	Use fresh tender corn and grade for size. Remove husks and silks	4 minutes (small) 6 minutes (medium) 8 minutes (large)	12 months	Thaw in wrappings. Cook in boiling water for 10 minutes
Herbs	Wash and pack whole sprigs or chop into ice cube trays, freeze, and wrap frozen cubes	—	6 months	Thaw and drain, or add herb cubes to dishes
Leeks	Clean and cut into rings	2 minutes	12 months	Cook in boiling water for 8 minutes or add to soups and stews
Marrows and courgettes	1) Cook and mash marrows and freeze purée 2) Cut courgettes into 1cm slices without peeling	3 minutes	2 months	1) Re-heat from frozen in double boiler 2) Fry in oil and season well
Mushrooms	Wipe but do not peel. Pack into bags without blanching	—	3 months	Thaw and cook as fresh
Onions	Skin and chop or slice. Wrap well	2 minutes	2 months	Add to dishes while frozen
Parsnips, turnips, and swedes	Peel and dice	2 minutes	12 months	Cook in boiling water for 15 minutes
Peas	Shell young sweet peas	1 minute	12 months	Cook in boiling water for 5 minutes
Peppers	Remove seeds and membranes	3 minutes (halves) 2 minutes (slices)	12 months	Thaw for 1 hour (halves) or add frozen slices to dishes
Potatoes	Cook and mash, or make into croquettes. Jacket, baked and roast potatoes can be frozen. Slightly under-cook new potatoes, and freeze in bags which can be boiled for re-heating. Fry chips for 4 minutes but do not brown	—	3 months	Re-heat mashed or croquette, roast or jacket potatoes. New potatoes should be kept in bag and heated in boiling water for 10 minutes. Fry chips while frozen

Type of vegetable	Preparation for freezing	Blanching time	High quality storage life	Cooking instructions
Spinach	Remove any thick stalks and wash leaves very well. Press out moisture after blanching	2 minutes	12 months	Re-heat gently in butter
Tomatoes	Wipe, grade and pack in bags	—	12 months	Thaw for 2 hours (skins will drop off). Do not use raw

Cooked and Other Prepared Dishes

Make dishes to standard recipes, observing one or two special details. Thicken sauce or gravy by reducing, or by adding vegetable purée or cornflour; this is to prevent curdling during re-heating. Add rice, pasta or potatoes to liquid dishes only when re-heating, since they become too soft during freezing. Use onions, garlic, herbs, and spices with care, as flavours can deteriorate during freezing.

Pack cooked foods in freezer containers, or in ordinary dishes which will withstand freezing and heating. Label carefully if additional ingredients have to be included during re-heating. Use cooked foods within 2 months to retain high quality.

Type of dish	Preparation for freezing	High quality storage life	Thawing/re-heating instructions
Casseroles and stews	Slightly undercook vegetables. Do not add rice, pasta or potatoes. Remove surplus fat	2 months	Heat in double boiler, or thaw and bake in casserole in a moderate oven, 180°C, Gas 4 for 1 hour
Flans (sweet and savoury)	Prepare and bake. Open freeze and wrap in foil or polythene	2 months	Thaw at room temperature for 3 hours. Re-heat if required
Ices – fresh fruit purée	Fully prepare	3 months	Serve straight from freezer
– ice cream	Fully prepare	3 months	Allow to soften slightly in refrigerator before serving
– sorbets and water ices	Fully prepare	3 months	Serve straight from freezer
– bombes and other moulded desserts	Wrap in foil	3 months	Unmould on to chilled plate, using cloth wrung out in hot water to release ice cream. Wrap in foil and return to freezer for one hour before serving
– ice cream gâteaux	Pack in rigid containers or wrap in foil	3 months	Place on plate and serve at once. Slice with knife dipped in boiling water

Chart continues over

Type of dish	Preparation for freezing	High quality storage life	Thawing/re-heating instructions
Meat	Do not freeze cooked joints or grilled meats which can become tough, rancid, and dry 1) Slice cooked meat thinly and separate with clingfilm. Pack tightly in rigid or foil containers 2) Slice meat and pack in gravy or sauce in rigid or foil containers	2 months	Thaw in wrappings in refrigerator for 3 hours. Bake in a moderate oven, 180°C, Gas 4, for 40 minutes
Meat pies	1) Bake and cool. Wrap in foil or polythene	1) 2 months	1) Thaw in refrigerator for 6 hours to eat cold, or bake in a fairly hot oven, 190°C, Gas 5, for 1 hour
	2) Cook meat filling. Cool and cover with pastry. Wrap in foil or polythene	2) 2 months	2) Bake from frozen in a fairly hot oven, 200°C, Gas 6, for 1 hour
Mousses	Prepare in freezer-tested serving dishes	1 month	Thaw in refrigerator for 8 hours
Pancakes	Cool and pack in layers with clingfilm. Wrap in greaseproof paper, foil or polythene	2 months	Thaw at room temperature and separate. Heat in cool oven, 150°C, Gas 2, or on a plate over steam, covered with a cloth
Pasta	Slightly undercook, drain well, cool, and pack in polythene bags	1 month	Put into boiling water, bring back to the boil, and cook for 2–3 minutes until tender
Pasta dishes	Pack pasta and sauce in foil dish with lid	1 month	Remove lid and bake in a fairly hot oven, 200°C, Gas 6, for 45 minutes
Pâté	Cool completely and wrap in foil or polythene. Pâté may also be prepared in freezer-tested dishes	1 month	Thaw in refrigerator for 6 hours
Pizza	Prepare, using fresh herbs, not dried. Do not add anchovies. Bake. Cool and wrap in polythene	1 month	Unwrap and thaw at room temperature for 1 hour. Top with anchovies and bake in a fairly hot oven, 190°C, Gas 5, for 20 minutes
Rice	Slightly undercook, drain well, cool, and pack in polythene bags	1 month	Put into boiling water, bring back to boil, and cook for 2–3 minutes until tender
Rice dishes	Cook completely, but avoid adding hard-boiled eggs. Pack into bags or rigid containers	1 month	Heat in double boiler, stirring well and adding additional ingredients

Type of dish	Preparation for freezing	High quality storage life	Thawing/re-heating instructions
Sauces (savoury)	Prepare completely, but season sparingly. Pack in rigid containers, leaving headspace. Do not freeze sauces thickened with eggs or cream	1 month	Heat in double boiler and re-season if required
Sauces (sweet)	1) Fresh or cooked fruit sauces should be packed in rigid containers, leaving headspace	1) 12 months	1) Thaw in refrigerator for 3 hours to serve cold, or heat in double boiler
	2) Thicken pudding sauces with cornflour and pack in rigid containers, leaving headspace	2) 1 month	2) Heat in double boiler
Soup	Use standard recipes but avoid flour for thickening. Do not include rice, pasta, barley, potatoes, milk or cream. Pack in rigid containers, leaving headspace	2 months	Heat in double boiler, adding additional ingredients
Steamed and baked puddings	Steam or bake puddings in foil containers. Cool and cover with lid, or pack in polythene bag	2 months	Thaw at room temperature for 2 hours, and steam for 45 minutes, or bake from frozen in a fairly hot oven, 190°C, Gas 5, for 45 minutes

Cakes, Pastry and Breads

Use very fresh ingredients when baking for the freezer. Use butter for good flavour, but margarine for a light texture. Margarine is especially suitable for strongly flavoured cakes such as chocolate and coffee.

Icings and fillings made from fat and sugar can be frozen separately or on cakes. But do not attempt to freeze icings made without fat. Fruit or jam fillings in cakes become soggy after thawing, and are better added just before serving. Decorations are also better added then, since they absorb moisture during thawing and may stain the cake. Sweetened whipped cream can be frozen like a cake filling. Pack cakes carefully to avoid crushing during storage. It is better to open freeze iced cakes before packing to avoid smudging the surfaces.

Type of cake, pastry or bread	Preparation for freezing	High quality storage life	Thawing/baking instructions
Biscuits	Form dough into 2cm diameter roll. Wrap in foil or polythene. **Note** Baked biscuits are best stored in tins without freezing	2 months	Thaw in refrigerator for 45 minutes. Cut in slices and bake in a fairly hot oven, 190°C, Gas 5, for 10 minutes
Bread	Pack in polythene bags. Crusty bread quickly loses its crispness in the freezer	1 month	Thaw at room temperature for 4 hours
Breadcrumbs (plain)	Pack in polythene bags	3 months	Thaw in wrappings at room temperature, or sprinkle directly on food to be cooked

Type of cake, pastry or bread	Preparation for freezing	High quality storage life	Thawing/baking instructions
Bread dough	Knead dough and put in greased polythene bag without proving	2 months	Unseal bag and tie loosely to allow space for rising. Thaw at room temperature for 6 hours. Knock back, shape, prove, and bake
Brioches and croissants	Pack in rigid containers to prevent crushing, immediately after baking and cooling	1 month	Thaw at room temperature for 30 minutes and heat in oven or under grill
Cakes (uniced)	Cool completely and wrap in foil or polythene	4 months	Thaw at room temperature for 2–3 hours
Cakes (iced)	Fill and ice cake but do not add decorations. Open freeze on tray, and pack in a rigid container	4 months	Thaw at room temperature for 3 hours
Cheesecakes	Make baked or refrigerated variety in cake tin with removable base. Open freeze and pack in rigid container	1 month	Thaw for 8 hours in refrigerator
Choux pastry	Bake but do not fill or ice. Pack in polythene bags or boxes	1 month	Thaw in wrappings at room temperature for 2 hours. Fill and ice
Crumpets and muffins	Pack in polythene bags	1 month	Thaw in wrappings at room temperature for 30 minutes before toasting
Danish pastries	Bake but do not ice. Pack in foil trays with lids, or in rigid containers	2 months	Thaw at room temperature for 1 hour. Heat if liked
Fruit pies	Brush bottom crust with egg white to prevent sogginess. 1) Bake, cool, and pack 2) Use uncooked fruit and pastry, open freeze, and pack	1) 4 months 2) 2 months	1) Thaw to serve cold, or reheat 2) Bake from frozen in a fairly hot oven, 200°C, Gas 6, for 1 hour
Pastry cases	Freeze baked or unbaked, using foil containers	4 months	Bake frozen cases at recommended temperatures for type of pastry. Re-heat baked cases, or fill with hot filling
Sandwiches	Do not remove crusts. Spread thickly with butter or margarine. Do not use salad fillings, mayonnaise or hard-boiled eggs. Separate sandwiches with clingfilm and pack in foil or polythene	1 month	Thaw at room temperature and remove crusts, or toast under grill while still frozen
Scones and drop scones	Pack in small quantities in polythene bags	2 months	Thaw in wrappings at room temperature for 1 hour. Alternatively, bake frozen scones in a moderate oven, 180°C, Gas 4, for 10 minutes

Dairy Produce

Most cheeses can be frozen successfully but tend to crumble after being frozen. They should be frozen in small pieces, and cut when still slightly hard. Cream cheese tends to separate on thawing. It is best blended with heavy cream before freezing and used as a dip. Cottage cheese tends to separate and should not be frozen. Only homogenized milk in waxed cartons should be frozen, and then only in small quantities which can be used quickly. The texture of frozen cream can be heavy and grainy, but light beating will improve it. If used in hot coffee, the oil will rise to the surface. Only really good thick cream responds well to freezing. Eggs should be very fresh. They should be washed and then broken into a dish to check for quality. They should be frozen already beaten or separated, in rigid containers, and sugar or salt added in the proportions below to prevent coagulation.

Dairy produce	Preparation for freezing	High quality storage life	Thawing instructions
Butter and margarine	Overwrap in foil or polythene	6 months (unsalted) 3 months (salted)	Thaw enough for 1 week's use in refrigerator
Cheese – hard	Cut in 200g pieces and wrap in foil or polythene. Pack grated cheese in polythene bags. Pack blue cheeses in polythene and overwrap well	3 months	Thaw in open wrappings at room temperature for 3 hours. Cut while slightly frozen to avoid crumbling
– cream	Blend with heavy cream	3 months	Thaw in container in refrigerator overnight. Blend with fork to restore smoothness
Cream	Freeze all creams in cartons. Do not freeze single, soured or half-cream	6 months	Thaw in carton at room temperature and stir with a fork to restore smoothness
Whipped cream	Sweeten with 2 × 10ml spoons sugar to 500ml cream. Freeze in containers, or open freeze piped rosettes	6 months	Thaw in container at room temperature. Rosettes thaw in 15 minutes at room temperature
Eggs	Do not freeze in shell. 1) Mix yolks and whites, adding 1 × 5ml spoon salt or 1 × 10ml spoon sugar to 5 eggs 2) Mix yolks, adding 1 × 5ml spoon salt or 1 × 10ml sugar to 5 yolks 3) Put whites in containers with no addition	12 months	Thaw in refrigerator but bring to room temperature before use
Milk	Only homogenized milk can be frozen. Leave 2cm headspace	1 month	Thaw at room temperature and use quickly

Fruit

Freeze only fresh, top-quality fruit. Fruit can be frozen dry and unsweetened, with sugar, in syrup, or as purée, and in cooked dishes.

Note As in bottling, white sugar is normally used because it does not colour or flavour the fruit. Other sugar can be used, but Barbados sugar or molasses may develop an unpleasant flavour in storage, and colour the fruit.

Dry Unsweetened Pack

This is best for fruit to be used in pies, puddings, and jams, and for berries and currants to be eaten raw. Do not use it for fruit which discolours badly, since sugar helps to retard the action of the enzymes which cause darkening. Clean any fruit well and open freeze on trays, or pack into bags or rigid containers.

Dry Sugar Pack

Use 1 part sugar to 4 parts fruit, mixing lightly before packing. Sugar draws out juices, and some fruit, eg berries, can become over-soft during thawing.

Sugar Syrup Pack

Use this for non-juicy fruits and those which discolour easily. Make a syrup with white sugar and water, dissolving the sugar completely in boiling water and chilling before use. Three syrup strengths are generally used:

> *Light syrup*　　175g sugar to 500ml water
> *Medium syrup*　275g sugar to 500ml water
> *Heavy syrup*　　400g sugar to 500ml water

Vitamin C helps to retard discoloration of fruit, and the juice of 1 lemon should be added to each litre of syrup for fruit such as apricots and peaches.

Cover the fruit completely in syrup and crumble a piece of greaseproof paper or clingfilm in the headspace to prevent the fruit rising above the syrup and discolouring.

Fruit Purée

Prepare purée from raw raspberries or strawberries, but cook other fruit in a little water first. Sweeten to taste before freezing and pack with 1.5cm headspace to allow for expansion.

Fruit Juices

Prepare fruit juice and freeze in trays. Wrap frozen cubes individually in foil and store in polythene bags. Apple juice will ferment quickly and should only be stored for a month. Other fruit juices will be at their best for 9 months.

Type of fruit	Preparation for freezing	Method of freezing	High quality storage life	Thawing/cooking instructions
Apples	Peel, core, and slice	1) Dry sugar 2) Medium syrup 3) Cooked purée	12 months 4 months	Cook in puddings or pies, or re-heat purée
Apricots	Skin and cut in halves or slices. Add lemon juice to pack	1) Dry sugar 2) Medium syrup 3) Raw purée	12 months 4 months	Thaw for 4 hours in covered pack in refrigerator

Type of fruit	Preparation for freezing	Method of freezing	High quality storage life	Thawing/cooking instructions
Blackberries and raspberries	Clean and hull	1) Unsweetened 2) Dry sugar 3) Raw or cooked purée	12 months 4 months	Thaw for 3 hours at room temperature
Blueberries	Wash and drain. Crush slightly to soften skins	1) Unsweetened 2) Dry sugar 3) Heavy syrup	12 months	Cook in puddings, pies or jam
Cherries	Chill in water for 1 hour and stone	1) Dry sugar 2) Medium syrup for sweet fruit 3) Heavy syrup for sour fruit	12 months	Thaw for 3 hours at room temperature. Use cold or cook
Cranberries	Wash and drain	1) Unsweetened 2) Cooked whole or purée	12 months 4 months	Cook while frozen, or thaw purée or cooked fruit for 3½ hours at room temperature
Currants (red, white, and black)	Strip fruit from stems	1) Unsweetened 2) Dry sugar 3) Medium syrup 4) Cooked purée	12 months 4 months	Thaw for 2 hours at room temperature
Damsons	Wash, drain, and stone	1) Heavy syrup 2) Cooked purée	12 months 4 months	Thaw for 3 hours at room temperature or cook while frozen
Dried fruit (dates, figs, raisins, currants, sultanas)	Pack in polythene bags	—	12 months	Thaw for 2 hours at room temperature and use in recipes
Figs	Wash ripe figs and remove stems. Do not bruise	1) Unsweetened 2) Light syrup if peeled	12 months	Thaw for 3 hours at room temperature. Eat raw or cooked in syrup
Gooseberries	Clean, top, and tail	1) Unsweetened 2) Medium syrup 3) Cooked purée	12 months 4 months	Thaw for 3 hours at room temperature, or cook while frozen
Grapefruit	Peel, remove pith, and divide into segments	1) Dry sugar 2) Heavy syrup	12 months	Thaw for 3 hours at room temperature
Grapes	Pack seedless grapes whole. Skin, de-seed, and halve large ones	Light syrup	12 months	Thaw for 3 hours at room temperature
Greengages and plums	Cut in half and stone	Medium syrup	12 months	Thaw for 3 hours at room temperature
Lemons and limes	Peel and slice, or slice without peeling and pack for drinks	Light syrup	12 months	Thaw for 1 hour at room temperature, or put in drinks while frozen
Melons	Peel and cut in cubes or shape into balls. Toss in lemon juice	Light syrup	12 months	Thaw for 3 hours in covered pack in refrigerator
Oranges	Peel, remove pith, and divide into segments, or slice	1) Dry sugar 2) Light syrup	12 months	Thaw for 3 hours at room temperature
Peaches and nectarines	Skin, cut in halves or slices, and brush with lemon juice. Alternatively, make a raw purée with 1 × 15ml spoon lemon juice to 500g fruit	1) Medium syrup 2) Raw purée	12 months 4 months	Thaw for 3 hours in covered pack in refrigerator

Type of fruit	Preparation for freezing	Method of freezing	High quality storage life	Thawing/cooking instructions
Pears	Peel, quarter, and remove cores. Dip pieces in lemon juice. Poach in medium syrup for 1½ minutes, drain, and cool before packing in syrup	Medium syrup	12 months	Thaw for 3 hours at room temperature
Pineapple	Peel and cut in slices or chunks	1) Dry sugar 2) Light syrup	12 months	Thaw for 3 hours at, room temperature
Rhubarb	Wash in cold water and trim sticks	1) Unsweetened 2) Medium syrup 3) Cooked purée	12 months 4 months	Thaw purée at room temperature. Cook raw fruit while frozen
Strawberries	Clean and grade for size	1) Unsweetened 2) Dry sugar 3) Medium syrup 4) Raw purée	12 months 4 months	Thaw for 2 hours at room temperature

INDEX

Note All recipe entries are in italic, eg *Bakewell tart 421*